THE NAVAL HISTORY OF GREAT BRITAIN

Acknowledgements

The introduction and collection of papers began life as part of a study of three British pioneers of naval history, for the 1999 Symposium at the United States Naval Academy, Annapolis. Pressure of time on an excellent panel led me to restrict my presentation to a discussion of William James, the one name that was guaranteed some degree of recognition in the audience. The lively discussion that followed persuaded me that there was a pressing need to re-examine this most misunderstood of naval historians. In 2001, I presented another paper dealing with James to the Anglo–American Historians Conference at the Institute of Historical Research in London. I am indebted to the organizers of both events for the opportunity to present my findings, to the convenors, fellow contributors and audience at the two papers for their advice, argument and ideas. Finally, I must record my thanks to Martin Robson at Conway Maritime Press, who persuaded many people that William James had something to say to the twenty-first century.
Crown Copyright material in the Public Record Office is reproduced by permission of the Controller of Her Majesty's Stationery Office, that from the British Library by kind permission of the British Library Board.

Andrew Lambert, Kew, August 2001

Conway Maritime Press would like to express their immense gratitude to Peter Goodwin (Keeper and Curator) and Lieutenant Commander Frank Nowosielski RN (Commanding Officer) of HMS *Victory*, who kindly loaned the set of *The Naval History of Great Britain* from the library onboard *Victory* from which this edition has been reprinted.

This edition first published in Great Britain by Conway Maritime Press,
a division of Chrysalis Books Plc
64 Brewery Road
London N7 9NT

A member of Chrysalis Books plc

www.conwaymaritime.com

ISBN 0 85177 906 9

British Library Cataloguing in Publication Data
A CIP catalogue record for this book is available from the British Library

Conway Editorial: Martin Robson
New index compiled by: Christian Tripodi

Printed and bound in the UK

THE NAVAL HISTORY OF GREAT BRITAIN

DURING THE FRENCH REVOLUTIONARY
AND NAPOLEONIC WARS

W. M. JAMES

NEW INTRODUCTIONS BY
ANDREW LAMBERT

VOLUME 2 — 1797-1799

CONWAY MARITIME PRESS

CONTENTS

Volume 2: 1797-1799

Illustrations

1797

1798

1799

Diagrams

General Introduction

It might be asked why, at the beginning of the twenty-first century, when the study of naval history is in better health than it has ever been, there should be any need to re-examine a text written 180 years ago? In fact the need is real and pressing, for William James's six-volume masterpiece *The Naval History of Great Britain* remains the most comprehensive history of the operations of the Royal Navy between 1793 and 1815. Exhaustively researched, utilizing despatches, logs, gazettes, foreign reports and eye-witness accounts, this narrative chronological history charts all the fleet battles, minor engagements and single ship actions.

James created and defined the study of naval warfare introducing analytical rigour and critical comparison of sources. *The Naval History of Great Britain*, first published between 1822 and 1824, marked an essential stage in the development of naval history and is one of those rare great works that retains the power to inform, enlighten and encourage, as well as to annoy and confound, decades after their first publication. This book can still provide insight to any who read it, evidence of the nature of naval warfare in an age long past, and first hand testimony from a host of great commanders, while enraging patriotic Americans and admonishing contemporary historians to reflect carefully on their methods. Naval history needs such texts, and it needs to understand how they came to be written, if it is to profit from the example. The following introductory essay and correspondence, divided across the volumes, will consider why James wrote, the audience he was addressing, his methods of obtaining and analyzing information, and the immediate impact of his work.

William James worked in the Prize Court at Jamaica between 1803 and 1812 before heading for Canada via the United States. After being detained as an enemy alien in Philadelphia during the War of 1812 and reacting to the 'vaporizing' and suspect accounts of the 'famous' victories of the US Navy over Royal Navy ships, in particular the USS *Constitution's* victory over HMS *Guerriere*, propagated by the US press, James decided to investigate. His 'research' methods included going on board American warships to measure them and even discussing the actions with their officers and men. James later returned to London convinced that the truth about these events needed to be told to a British public misled by the American falsehoods. He concluded that, despite American opinion, no British ship was ever captured by an American vessel of equal force. His work was even more controversial when criticizing American heroes such as Stephen Decatur, John Rodgers and Isaac Hull, although it must be noted that he also criticized Royal Navy officers, driving one to suicide and another to seek satisfaction by striking the historian over the head with a heavy oak stick. The contemporary American press, unable to criticize his methodology, reacted not with informed debate but with personal abuse trying to defame his character: he was called a common criminal, horse thief, a convicted forger and even an incompetent veterinary surgeon! In Britain his work attracted praise from the Admiralty, who ordered twenty sets of *The Naval History*, naval officers, such as William Hoste, Thomas Hardy and Pulteney Malcolm, and politicians such as the then Prime Minister Lord Liverpool, the Duke of Wellington and Robert Peel. This success convinced James to commence work on a full and detailed history of the operations of the Royal Navy up to 1793, but the project was prematurely ended by his death in 1827. However, he had, thanks to *The Naval History of Great Britain*, made his point.

In examining the Wars of the French Revolution and Empire, and the War of 1812, later historians such as Theodore Roosevelt, who only utilized American official sources, William Laird Clowes, who relied heavily on James's work, and Alfred Thayer Mahan who concentrated on the 1793–1805 period, failed to match the sheer depth and quality contained in these six volumes. Their twentieth-century successors have greatly enhanced the quality of research in naval history, but for all the effort devoted to understanding the naval dimension of our past, naval historians have thus far failed to create an informed appreciation of the origins and purposes of this specialist branch of the discipline. In consequence they lack a vital point of contact with other historians, among whom a well-defined historiographical literature is the critical point of departure. Although the failure to build a critical mass of scholarly literature was realized as early as 1874 by Sir John Knox Laughton in his seminal study 'The Scientific Study of Naval History', it is only now that the study of naval history is ceasing to be a niche subject through increased academic recognition by drawing upon, and making itself relevant to, the full range of historical scholarship. While the lack of a serious historiography may not be the only reason why naval history receives so little attention from the wider profession, it is not insignificant. It is therefore worth revisiting the birth of the subject and the career of the most important British naval historian of the early nineteenth century.

It is too easy to read William James's groundbreaking study out of context, and to mistake the carefully crafted text for a rather dull catalogue of events. In fact James was a thoughtful, calculating writer who introduced new methods, higher standards and an overt recognition of the purpose of naval history. He was a careful historian, who weighed his evidence and made judgements and he was not afraid to utilize the evidence to criticize naval officers or to censure other historians who failed to meet his standards. Over the past 170 years the contemporary objects and background to his effort have faded, leaving a core text to stand alone, and entirely out of context, as a narrative reference. This contextual isolation has led many to complain about a xenophobic Tory bias, particularly in the sections dealing with the United States. In truth, whatever his personal views, James was anxious that his fellow countrymen recognize the insidious threat contained in American propaganda, gave all due honour to their own fleet, and above all hold their heads high among the nations of the world. In the process he provided the Royal Navy with a record of unparalleled achievement, and a constant source of inspiration.

From an analysis of *The Naval History of Great Britain* and James's important correspondence, much of which is published here (in volumes 4 and 5) for the first time, it becomes clear that he saw himself meeting a vital national need. In completing this task he set out much of the analytical framework deployed by naval historians today, as well as the didactic objectives that many of his successors have adopted. In essence his work can only be understood through a study of the man, his methods and his objectives. Once the origins and development of his thinking, and the environment in which he operated, are understood *The Naval History of Great Britain* can be read in context. Armed with this insight it becomes a work of far greater significance, accessible at many more levels. This is hardly surprising, for James was an educated, intelligent and passionate man, who saw his work as a vital contribution to the self image of post-1815 Britain. The man, his books and his letters remain essential to any understanding of the origins of naval history, and of the events of the age in which he lived.

Introduction

William James, The War of 1812 and the Origins of *The Naval History of Great Britain*

Part 2

'The most perfect and comprehensive naval history ever published.'[1]

Although he claimed to have suffered financially in producing his two studies of the War of 1812, which he attributed to the failure to find a publisher, James was unable, or unwilling, to abandon his new line of work. He still lived well enough. The praize of senior officers, and the commendation of the press, had convinced him that he should persevere with naval history. In late 1818 or early 1819 James began a new and larger project, to write detailed naval narrative of the French wars since 1793. The subject was attractive, as many of the leading figures of the period were still active. When Lord Liverpool received an advance notice he immediately subscribed, while the Admiralty ordered twenty copies, as it had of the *Military Occurrences*.[2] By this stage the Admiralty was rather better disposed towards James' he was now given copies of log entries to meet specific enquiries.[3] However, the Board drew the line at paying in advance for their copies.[4]

Introducing his new book James reported that while working on the War of 1812 he had realized that existing accounts of the European wars were equally faulty. There were, as he characteristically observed, 'gross mistakes' that he, as a legally trained professional, had the skills to correct through a thorough analysis of the evidence. The object was to produce something better than the usual run of naval histories, mere lists of ships, men and events. He took encouragement from the work of two great British historians of the previous century.[5]

By 1819 James had so far mastered his art, and established

his method, as to quote the eighteenth-century philosopher/historian David Hume[6] on the difficulty of describing a naval battle, and the blatantly propagandistic nature of national naval histories. Hume declared:

> There is a natural confusion attending sea-fights, even beyond other military transactions, derived from the precarious operations of wind and tides, as well as from the smoke and darkness in which everything is there involved: no wonder, therefore, that relations of these battles are apt to contain uncertainties and contradictions, especially when compared by writers of the hostile nations, who take a pleasure in exalting their own advantages, and suppressing those of the enemy.[7]

Nor was the link with Hume without intellectual significance. Hume's great historical work, *The History of England from the Invasion of Julius Caesar to the Revolution of 1688*, had been published between 1754 and 1762, and in many subsequent editions. It was the most ambitious, intellectually coherent, and durable work of the day, and still the standard when James was writing. The critical approach Hume adopted towards older accounts and the essentially contemporary purpose of his work may have influenced James's intellectual development, and inspired the more ambitious project he began in early 1819. Because such accounts as Hume censured were of little value, James strove for impartiality by stressing the materiel side of combat.[8] He devoted considerable attention to an accurate record of the armament fitted to the ships, their crews and the size of the ships. While his battle narratives tend to be more catalogue than analysis, they established a basic method that has been followed, and developed, ever since. Hume's smokescreen of obfuscation had been replaced by number crunching. As James observed:

> Henceforth no naval historian will dare to describe a battle without shewing the exact force in weight of metal, men, and size, of the contending ships, and without submitting to his reader, the enemy's as well as his own, account of the transaction.[9]

This approach was consistent with his purpose. If combat could be assessed, and relative merit determined without hyperbole then British superiority would rest not on myth and common understanding, but on an objective standard. Both the United States Navy and the French academician Charles Dupin had adopted his method of computing the real force of ships, broadside weight of metal. The only critic was General Sir Howard Douglas. Despite his rank Douglas was the pioneer of modern gunnery training.[10] To support his case Douglas needed to establish that the key to success in war lay in precision of fire, not weight of metal. Consequently the first edition of his key text,

A Treatize on Naval Gunnery, explicitly rejected James's argument.[11] But James was content to stand his ground.[12]

In the new book James moved on to a larger field of study, the Wars of the French Revolution and Empire. For this altogether greater task, his well-developed methodology, extensive contacts and growing recognition by the profession enabled him to master a mass of detail and provide full coverage. It was critical to his method that he should travel to Paris and research the French side of the story.[13] The results of his effort are obvious. The new work cited 15 French books, and while the majority of citations were of an essentially factual nature, conforming to his previous practice, there were some more ambitious attempts to understand the French side of the story. Two works *Victoires et Conquêtes* and *Précis des Evènements Militaires &c* were the key sources for the French version of the numerous actions to be covered. They provided the numbers of men, size of ships, and weight of metal, so familiar from the War of 1812 studies.[14]

The value of his critical, questioning methodology was immediately apparent. Where previous accounts had been content to repeat the assumptions and assertions made inevitable by the exigencies of writing contemporary history while the war was still in progress, James checked the newly accessible French materials. One of the first such cases was the partial engagement of the frigate HMS *Iris* with a French ship of the same class in mid-1793. As the ships parted without conclusion the identity of the French ship was unknown, but it was assumed, on the basis of plausible interpretation, to have been *La Medée*. Isaac Schomberg had accepted this version in his three-volume *Naval Chronology* of 1812, the most detailed account of recent naval operations in print when James started work. Having satisfied himself, from the French archives, that this was incorrect James went back to the Admiralty to inspect the *Iris's* log. By this time the Admiralty was prepared to assist and he was able to extract information on the location, weather and casualties to improve his account.[15] By now he knew that the French ship was the *Citoyenne-Française*. When he wrote up this incident James included a discussion of his methodology, showing the value of his in-depth research; in effect this was a quality check for the rest of the book.[16] With his credibility thus established on page 91 the remaining 3,000 pages could, unless the events were particularly controversial, be filled with shorter, more matter-of-fact accounts. Nor did he have any time for pictures, finding those already painted were generally inaccurate, and therefore gave a misleading impression of the actions he was describing.[17]

With careful reading the French sources also helped James to understand that the French did not use their naval forces in the same way as the British, or the Americans. French strategic objectives invariably took precedence over tactical considerations, and battle did not have the central place that it was accorded by the British. Other works offered insight into the naval architectural aspects of the conflict. Perhaps the most interesting source consulted was Charles Dupin's *Voyages dans la Grande-Bretagne*. An official French Government study, written by a leading academician, this work was an attempt to comprehend the basis of British success. The second part of this work, published in 1821, was devoted to the Royal Navy. James took great pleasure in the discovery that the eminent Frenchman had adopted his standard method of calculating force. He also extracted critical evidence of French methods, and a priceless insight into the greatness of Nelson. Dupin recognized the vital role of 'mission-analysis' at the heart of Nelson's tactical system, and stressed that he:

> ought to be held up as a pattern for admirals, by the extreme pains he took to impress upon his flag-officers and captains, the spirit of the enterprizes which he resolved to undertake. He unfolded to them his general plan of operations, and the modifications with which the weather, or the manoeuvres of the enemy, might force him to qualify his original design. When once he had explained his system to the flag and superior officers of his fleet, he confided to them the charge of acting according to circumstances, so as to lead, in the most favourable manner, to the consummation of the enterprize thus planned. And Nelson, who was allowed to choose the companions of his glory, possessed the talent and the happiness to find men worthy of his instruction and confidence; they learnt, in action, to supply what had escaped his forethought, and in success, to surpass even his hopes.[18]

There is no better appreciation of Nelson's genius in the contemporary literature, nor one so close to the modern understanding of 'mission-analysis' as the basis of tactical excellence. While James did not write it, he had the merit to find and reproduce it. In view of his purpose he deliberately left the remarks to a Frenchman, thereby according them a greater degree of objectivity.

In the new work James moved on from the literal, catalogue style of the War of 1812 studies to create a wider, more truly historical method. The first two volumes of *The Naval History of Great Britain* were published in 1822, carrying the narrative conveniently up to the Peace of Amiens, but the second pair outgrew their design, appearing in 1824 as a trio of full-sized texts. Even then they had to sacrifice much of the coverage of the War of 1812, for want of room. Instead he provided coverage of the bombardment of Algiers, and a section on Polar exploration to bring the story up to the closing date of 1820. The extra cost of the fifth volume was largely, though not entirely, borne by James.[19] The reduced coverage of the American War was also in part explained by the continued availability of the 1817 and 1818 works, which were advertized among the end-papers of the new book.[20]

As ever the financial side of the project required James to lay out large sums on printing and materials. Fortunately James's reputation secured him a long list of subscribers, the East India Company alone taking 40 copies. In addition he found prominent backers willing to accord him long credit, but still had to find over £1,000 to pay for the 1,000 copies of the books. As the Admiralty refused to pay in advance, he sent the first advance sheets in June 1821, to demonstrate that the book existed, in the hope he could secure an advance. He was rebuffed again.[21] Only in January 1824, when the final set of volumes was delivered, could he demand payment.[22] While he recognized that the freedom to write without official control was critical to the success of his work[23], the resultant financial uncertainty was a constant problem. Although the edition of 1,000 copies had required the usual financial juggling, it was immediately recognized as by far the best account of its type.

The Naval History would remain the standard for a century. As the French wars were more extensive and generally less controversial than the War of 1812, there being little doubt about the relative naval merits of the British and French navies on either side of the Channel[24], James modified his approach. In *The Naval History* the conclusions are presented largely shorn of the analytical discussion that had been such a feature of the War of 1812 studies. As the French literature on the war, while substantial, was not as dangerous as that produced in America the matter could be set out as a relatively straightforward narrative. From the thin, and rather slanted, treatment they were accorded it is clear that the events of the French wars from 1812 were used as a backdrop to the American War.

In the event the new book proved no less controversial than its predecessors. In establishing that the triumphs of the American frigates were by no means unique, or especially the province of American sailors, he examined the action between the frigates HMS *Eurotas* and the French *Clorinde* which occurred on 25 February 1814.[25] The British ship was armed with Congreve pattern light 24pdr guns, the French ship regular 18pdrs. Both ships were crippled, but the arrival of fresh British units secured the prize. James's description of the action required four pages; the next five were given over to explaining why the results were not more decisive, given the disparity of broadside weight of metal. This was an essential elaboration, for broadside weight of metal had been the basic analytical tool of his works to date, not only the War of 1812 series, but the preceding four volumes of the new work as well, for James wrote and published volume by volume. If this action demonstrated that weight of metal was an insignificant factor, then all of the publications, where it had been heavily used, were irrelevant. James argued, on the evidence of the damage done, that the *Eurotas*'s crew had not been adequately trained to use their guns. He did, however, praize the seamanship evident in the quick refitting of the ship after she had been dismasted.

This criticism enraged the Captain of the *Eurotas,* John Phillimore, who took leave from his current command at Portsmouth and came up to London. On 2 April 1824 he visited the Admiralty before taking his coach to Lambeth. Here, with a companion, he entered James's house and barged into his study. Phillimore, apparently foaming at the mouth with rage, insulted the historian, 'said something about his guns having been put on board for an experiment' and hit James over the head with a heavy oak stick. The following scuffle, which pitted the two officers against James and his sickly, diminutive wife, ended when Mrs James sent the servant to call a constable.[26] Phillimore and his companion fled. The affair reached the pages of *The Times*[27], and the angry Captain was taken to court for assault, where he was fined £100. Phillimore paid his fine, having 'had his satisfaction' for the insult. Nor did his hasty and violent action appear to harm his career.

On reflection James could see nothing with which to reproach himself, having based himself on an Admiralty Order and the *Naval Chronicle.* By 1826 he had examined the log of the *Eurotas* and noted that Phillimore had made no complaints about the guns at the time, or even subsequent to the action: indeed he had praized them, and this action had played a major part in persuading the Admiralty to adopt them more widely.[28] In the second edition James confidently maintained his opinion. He also suggested that any officers who had a complaint should address it to him in writing, 'because none but a written statement can serve his purpose or mine, and not because I fear him or any other man, or have the least expectation of a renewal of the disgraceful business that once occurred'.[29]

The first edition of *The Naval History* generated another controversy for James, this time with Captain Edward Pelham Brenton RN.[30] The first part of Brenton's five-volume *The Naval History of Great Britain from the year 1783 to 1822*, appeared in 1823, between the first and second sections of James's *Naval History.* Brenton stressed that his object was 'the great work of improving the naval profession'.[31] However, his methodology was too weak to bear the weight of his ambition. Brenton conceived of the past as a great repository of experience, on which present and future generations could draw, but his work was vitiated by inaccuracies and overt bias, notably his opposition to impressment and his support for the controversial ship designs of Sir William Symonds. More significant was his membership of the Whig naval 'family' of Admiral Sir John Jervis, Earl St. Vincent, who allowed him access to his papers. Brenton's agenda was to advance contemporary Whig causes and elevate the record of his patron, and other Whig officers above their Tory contemporaries. His list of subscribers was longer than James's, but less 'official'. It contained more officers, but like the politicians, they were a distinctly Whig collection.[32] In addition he was, according to Sir John Laughton, 'constitutionally incapable of sifting such evidence as came before him, and to have been guided more frequently by prejudice than by judgement'. Indeed, his credibility as a recorder of fact was slight.[33] As was often the case Laughton was being unduly harsh. Brenton had the merit of insight, and recognized the contemporary value of a sound naval history, notably for the strategy of any future American War.[34]

Like James, Brenton soon found that contemporary history was a minefield of personal vanity and muddled recollection. In volume III he apologized to Admiral Montagu, for inferring that he should have tried harder to find the French fleet after the Glorious 1st of June.[35] He claims to have been widely ostracized by fellow officers over this issue. By the time he compiled the second edition, in 1837, he was apologising to the family and friends of Lord Howe for his Whiggish reflections on a great Tory officer.[36] These problems reflected the fact that while many of his aims were laudable, Brenton was a political partisan, rather than a patriot, and did not share James's thorough approach to his subject. Finding a powerful and well-received rival already on the field he sought to cover his inadequacies by discrediting James, both as a mere landsman who had no business writing about the Navy, and by accusing him of plagiarism:

> I still deny that a landsman is capable of writing a naval history. He may give the letter, but he cannot give the spirit; he can neither instruct nor reprove without the charge of folly or presumption.[37]

Neither charge had any validity, but the 'spirit' had to serve as a counter to the catalogue of errors of fact that James took such delight in pointing out in Brenton's own work. This quarrel outlived James, being continued in subsequent editions by Brenton and Chamier.[38] James mocked Brenton for relying on the *Annual Register* to fill out his text, and for wasting the opportunities that a 'professional', that is naval, author had to obtain more reliable evidence.[39]

The Naval History of Great Britain sold quickly and by late 1825 a new edition was needed. This time James revized the main text and added more details of the War of 1812. The new material was closely based on his earlier publications, the account of the battle of Lake Champlain, for instance, being almost entirely taken from *Military Occurrences*.[40] These sections, omitted from the first edition 'for want of room' retain the acerbic character of the earlier versions, for James recognized this was the subject on which his countrymen would need to be well informed in the near future. In 1826, as he was preparing the second edition of the *Naval History*, Anglo–American relations had reached a post-war low point. Recognizing that he would be charged with 'national prejudice' James reflected that his accusers had not had the same opportunities that he had to form an opinion of 'the American character'. However, this was one point on which American-born Brenton, whose loyalist family had been driven into exile during the War of Independence, agreed.[41] Relying on his earlier studies he now argued: 'My analysis of the American accounts has already ... sufficiently shown that, in the art of boasting and misrepresenting, the French could never compete with the Americans.'[42]

Just as the new edition appeared, in July 1826, American attempts to secure access to British inter-colonial trade had finally provoked the British to issue an Order in Council closing the British West Indies ports to American shipping. Tension remained high until the following August, when the British Prime Minister George Canning died.[43] At the same time the United States abandoned the post-war naval programme that had been used to bolster their diplomacy.[44] James would not live to see the political defeat of his American critics.

The crisis of 1826 provided a market for the book, and a rationale for the new edition. James recognized that this form of history required updating. It has to be stressed, at this remove, that James was a 'contemporary' historian. Unfortunately the importance of the subject was not matched by any enthusiasm on the part of publishers. Once again James published at his own expense, but this time he entered into a complex contract with Joseph Harding and John Lepard, booksellers of Pall Mall, and on the second part Augustus Applegarth, printer of Duke Street. In January 1826 James, described as a 'gentleman', contracted to sell Applegarth the copyright of the book that he was now printing, along with 1,000 abstracts and the wood blocks for the diagrams for £1,400. James undertook to deliver the rest of the manuscript within three months. The contract included the copyright of any future editions. Harding and Lepard bought exclusive rights to sell and 900 copies of the book from Applegarth, for £1,800, leaving James with 100 copies to dispose of on his own account. No new edition was to be printed until the 900 sets had been sold. James had the right to repurchase the copyright for £500, which he did on 1 December 1826. In essence the copyright was sold as part of a complex financial package that paid the printer £400, and provided the booksellers with 900 sets, for which they had paid £1,300. James saw his book in print, recovered his intellectual property, and had 100 copies to sell, to add to his profit of £900.[45]

Despite the Admiralty only taking one set, the new edition garnered further praize and a new crop of naval endorsements, which James used to renew his approach to the Government. This time he presented Robert Peel, the Home Secretary, with the new volumes, and again requested a post. Among his references were two of the finest frigate captains of the age. Sir Philip Broke, to whom the 1817 book had been dedicated, declared:

> Your work will remain in my opinion, the best naval history that has ever been written, and you will always be feeling an increased satisfaction in having been the author of such a standard national work ... a useful national instruction on that naval power which is so important to our country.

Sir William Hoste, protégé of Nelson and victor at Lissa in 1811, agreed. 'I can not help admiring the second edition of your naval history: it is highly instructive as well as interesting, and no naval officer should be without it.'[46] There could be no more explicit acknowledgement that he had succeeded in his purpose. With such testimonials to the national value of his work, Peel could not fail to be impressed; but he could only advize James to apply to the Prime Minister, or the First Lord of the Admiralty for his reward.[47]

However, James took a different line. Recent events would have drawn his attention to the dominant role played by one man in British American policy, and he presented the second edition to George Canning, the Foreign Secretary, in January 1827. James linked his book to the menacing tone recently adopted by President Adams, which drew support from fresh bluster about the War of 1812 and the power of the United States Navy. James was anxious to dispel the myth then current in Britain, based on widely circulated American claims, that the Americans had won the War of 1812. His books had begun to counter 'Yankee' propaganda, a task for which factual narrative was the most effective weapon. James now sought a wider audience for his ideas. As a skilled strategist and a calculating player of the diplomatic game, Canning appreciated the work, and the potential diplomatic value of the material. In his covering letter James went beyond his narrative text, providing Canning with the 'lessons of history', beginning with an appreciation of the reasons for the early British defeats. He lamented the premature termination of a conflict, which by 1814 was already won. He advized Canning to rebut American bluster in Parliament, and provided a resumé of American strategic geography and political prospects to inform any future conflict.[48] In this letter James made explicit the higher function of his work. He wanted to create an accurate record that could inform contemporary officers and decision-makers about the experience of the past, in a form that could assist their planning and preparation.

The point takes on a greater significance when the consequences of mistaken historical understanding are considered. In 1914 American President Woodrow Wilson, an academic historian by profession, responded to the outbreak of the First World

War by reflecting on the fate of his predecessor James Madison. He believed that Madison had been forced into a war with Britain by problems over the rights of American shipping, trying to carry on neutral trade while all Europe was at war. Wilson was anxious to avoid this problem, because Britain, in 1812 and 1914, represented civilization and democracy, while Napoleon and the Kaizer stood for tyranny. To avoid being dragged into a war he did not want, Wilson made only a feeble protest when Britain imposed a blockade of questionable legality.[49] In reality Madison had not been dragged into the war by maritime issues, but by a desire to conquer Canada, Indian lands and Spanish Florida. He merely used the maritime issues to cloak naked, opportunistic aggression. As this assessment did not feature in American histories Wilson's error is easily understood.

While Canning sent an appreciative reply to James's letter, it was not accompanied by a more tangible reward. If James had failed to secure an official post, he had accepted the calling of a naval writer. He remained anxious to 'perfect' the *Naval History* in another edition, and had invited subscriptions for a new history, initially covering the events of the American War of Independence, which was planned in the later volumes of the 1826 edition. But in February 1827 he issued a new prospectus for a three-volume study going back 'to the utmost limits of English naval history'. The 'long hidden source of manuscript information' which had recently become accessible to him, containing the details he needed, remains a mystery. On receipt of the circular, Robert Peel subscribed 'with pleasure'.[50] The Admiralty was less enthusiastic, and refused to subscribe for 20 copies.[51] Perhaps the truly 'historical' past held little interest for a service that had more than enough recent experience of war on which to base policy decisions.[52]

James also planned 'a history of signal making in the British and French navies, as exemplified in the different general actions fought between them'.[53] The Signal Book was revized in 1816, but the Committee had been composed of practical seamen, and dominated by Lord Keith, so the results were sound, rather than brilliant.[54] It is possible that James's naval friends suggested the subject, binding him ever closer to the service in whose interests he worked. In the event James did not live to complete the new projects. He died suddenly at his home, 12 Chapel Field, South Lambeth on 28 May 1827. His health had been poor since his years in Jamaica and his subsequent stressful existence had not helped. His merits were immediately, if belatedly, acknowledged. The *Annual Register* noted his passing, while the *Gentleman's Magazine* observed that 'the name of his excellent work is a sufficient eulogium', while a subscription to support his widow had been launched with a donation of £50 from the Literary Fund Society.[55] It would have been a comfort to James to know that his wife, for whom he had always expressed concern, was also awarded a state pension of £100.[56] The *Naval and Military Magazine* was moved to hyperbole:

> that intelligent patriot, and fearless, and indefatigable writer, who, emerging from an attorney's office instead of the cockpit, and without ever acting the part of a seaman, qualified himself, through the sole force of genius, for the most scientific, as well as the most minute detail of naval affairs; - it was Mr. James who, beginning with the moment of the first naval actions of the late war with the United States, and ceasing only at his death, first laboured to undeceive his countrymen as to the real character of our naval defeats.[57]

Allowing for the shared agenda of the historian and his panegyrist, this rings true. James had made his point.

[This introductory essay is continued in volume 3.]

NOTES

1 C S M Phillipps review in the *Edinburgh Review* April 1840 vol. LXXI p.121. Although only 25, Phillipps, the son of a prominent lawyer and regular reviewer, would go on to write a number of notices for the *Edinburgh*, the most prestigious of contemporary reviews.
2 James to Liverpool, 14.7.1820, Add. 38,574 f.202-3 & endorsements; 1818, unpaginated list of Subscribers preceding the Preface; James to Admiralty, 11.7.1820 and endorsement, ADM 1/4787 Pro. J82.
3 James to Admiralty, 18.5.1820 and endorsement, ADM 1/4787 Pro. J 52.
4 James to Admiralty, 31.10.1820 and endorsement, ADM 1/4787 Pro. J121.
5 W James *The Naval History of Great Britain, from the Declaration of War by France in 1793 to the Accession of George IV*, 5 vols, (London: 1822-24 [henceforth 1822 or 1824]) vol 1, pp. xii-xxiii.
6 N Phillipson, *Hume*, (London: Weidenfeld & Nicolson, 1989), pp.3-4; D Hume (1711-1776) *The History of England from the Invasion of Julius Caesar to the Revolution of 1688.* (Published 1754-1762), and in many subsequent editions. Cited in 1822, vol 1 at p. xxiii. It is not clear when James first encountered Hume's work, although 1818 would be consistent with the letter to Melville of 4.1.1819, below, and the enhanced ambition of his new project. He also cited the equally present-minded work of Edward Gibbon (1737-1794).
7 Hume *History of England*, (London: 1778), vol 7. p.507.
8 James to Melville, 4.1.1819, Add. 38,276 f.186.
9 *Ibid.*
10 S Fullom, *Life of Sir Howard Douglas,* (London: John Murray, 1862).
11 H Douglas, *A Treatize on Naval Gunnery,* (London: John Murray, 1820). p.5 & 244.
12 1822 p.xxvi.
13 James to Admiralty, 31.10.1820, ADM 1/4787 Pro. J121.
14 For James's list of works cited see 1822, vol 2 p.397.
15 James to Admiralty, 18.5.1820, ADM 1/4787 Pro.J52; I Schomberg, *Naval Chronology*, 3 vols, (London: 1812).
16 1837 vol 1, pp.91-3.
17 1822 Preface pp.xxxiii-v. This problem persists. For a recent example of the integration of imperfect pictures with a carefully researched text see: S W

H Duffy, *Captain Blakeley and the Wasp: The Cruise of 1814,* (Annapolis: NIP, 2001) captions to the four prints of the *Wasp-Reindeer* action following p.150.

18 1837 vol 4 p.86; C Dupin, *Voyages dans la Grand-Bretagne, entrepris relativement aux services publics de la Guerre de la Marine, et des Ponts et Chaussées, de la 1816 à 1821*, (Paris: 1821), vol 4, p.66.
19 1824, vol 3, Preface pp.vii-xii.
20 1822 & 1824, Sir John Knox Laughton, 'Historians' 1913, pp.19-20.
21 James to Admiralty, 23.6.1821 & endorsement, ADM 1/4788 Pro. J98.
22 James to Admiralty, 8.1.1824, ADM 1/479 Pro. J8.
23 James to Melville, 4.1.1819, Add 38,276 f.186.
24 The work of Charles Dupin demonstrates the extent to which the French were prepared to learn from the British.
25 1837 vol 6, pp.268-77.
26 James to Admiralty, 3 & 6.4.1824, ADM Pro. J45.
27 *The Times* 6.4.1824 p.4.
28 R Gardiner, *Frigates of the Napoleonic Wars*, (London: Chatham, 2000) esp. pp.119-20.
29 1826 Preface xviii.
30 E P Brenton (1774-1839) like so many of James's critics, was born in America, he also served as commander of the frigate HMS *Spartan* on the North American station for much of the War of 1812.
31 Brenton, *The Naval History of Great Britain from the year 1783 to 1822*, (London: Colburn, 1837 2nd ed), Preface p.vii.
32 Brenton, 1825, vol 3, list of subscribers.
33 Laughton, DNB 1886, p.264.
34 Brenton, 1825 vol 5, pp.199-200, 205.
35 Brenton, 1824 vol 3, Preface.
36 Brenton, 1837, vol 1, p.viii.
37 Brenton, 1837, vol 1, p.xii.
38 Chamier in 1837, Brenton in 1837.
39 1826 p.viii, xv.
40 Compare, 1837 vol 6, pp.338-48 with 1818 vol 2, pp.205-228.
41 Brenton, 1825 vol 3, p.205.
42 1826, Preface pp.xii-xiii.
43 K Bourne, *Britain and the Balance of Power in North America, 1815-1908*, (London: Longman, 1967) p.28.
44 Symonds, pp.232-5.
45 Contract of 3.1.1826, Add. 46,612 f.210-12.
46 James to Peel 19.9.1826, Add. 40,389 f.73-5.
47 Peel to James, 2.11.1826, *ibid*, f.77.
48 James to Canning, 8.1.1827 and reply of 10.1.1827, in E J Stapleton, *Some Official Correspondence of George Canning; 1820-1827*, (London: Longman, 1887) vol 2, pp.340-6.
49 J W Coogan, *The End of Neutrality: The United States, Britain and Maritime Rights, 1899-1915*, (Cornell: Cornell University Press, 1981), pp.216-19.
50 James to Peel, 17.2.1827, Add. 40,392 f.28-30 & encl.
51 James to Admiralty, 19.2.1827 & endorsement, ADM 1/4791 Pro.J27.
52 A D Lambert, *The Last Sailing Battlefleet: Maintaining Naval Mastery, 1815-1850*, (London, Conway Maritime, 1991).
53 1837 vol 1, p.xviii.
54 Sir John Laughton took up the subject, and provided inspiration and evidence for Julian Corbett who produced two standard texts on the subject in the early twentieth century. *Fighting Instructions, 1530-1816* (London, Navy Records Society 1905) offers extended treatment reproducing the documentary evidence. Corbett's relationship with the Royal Navy was similar to James's. He worked tirelessly to tell them what they needed to know, often with limited thanks, and was only saved from following his predecessor's fate by his personal wealth.
55 Vol. 97/2, p.281.
56 Sir John Laughton's entry on James in the DNB.
57 *The Naval and Military Magazine Vol. II* (London: 1827) p.205.

XVI

Mr. WILLIAM JAMES

ENGRAVED BY W. READ, FROM A PAINTING BY W. McCALL.

London. Richard Bentley, 1836.

THE

NAVAL HISTORY

OF

GREAT BRITAIN,

FROM THE

DECLARATION OF WAR BY FRANCE IN 1793,

TO THE ACCESSION OF GEORGE IV.

BY WILLIAM JAMES.

A NEW EDITION, WITH ADDITIONS AND NOTES,

AND

AN ACCOUNT OF THE BURMESE WAR AND THE BATTLE OF NAVARINO,

BY CAPTAIN CHAMIER, R.N.

VERITE SANS PEUR.

IN SIX VOLUMES.

VOL. II.

LONDON:

RICHARD BENTLEY, NEW BURLINGTON STREET.

Publisher in Ordinary to His Majesty.

1837.

XVIII

ADMIRAL VISCOUNT EXMOUTH.

FROM A PICTURE BY SIR WILLᴹ BEECHEY, R.A.

London. Richard Bentley, 1836.

ADMIRAL SIR THOMAS DUCKWORTH.

FROM A PICTURE BY SIR Wm BEECHEY, R.A.

London, Richard Bentley, 1836.

XX

W. Greatbach, sc.

ADMIRAL, LORD COLLINGWOOD.

FROM AN ORIGINAL PICTURE IN THE POSSESSION OF LADY COLLINGWOOD.

London. Richard Bentley. 1836.

XXI

ADMIRAL, LORD BRIDPORT.

FROM A PICTURE BY L. F. ABBOT.

London. Richard Bentley, 1836.

XXII

CAPT^N. SIR WILLIAM HOSTE, BAR^T.

FROM AN ORIGINAL PICTURE IN THE POSSESSION OF LADY HOSTE.

London, Richard Bentley, 1836.

NAVAL HISTORY OF GREAT BRITAIN

BRITISH AND FRENCH FLEETS

In the number of line-of-battle cruisers, the abstract of the British navy for this year agrees precisely with that of the last; but, in commissioned ships of the line, the former shows a trifling superiority.* There is also, in the whole number of vessels, an increase of 51; but the total of commissioned cruisers, the best criterion of improvement, is not proportionably affected. The number of ships and vessels, the result of captures from the French, Dutch, and Spaniards, appears considerable.† On the other hand, the loss sustained by the British navy during the year 1796, and which, with the exception of one vessel, and that of a very small class, captured, and three accidentally burnt, happened through bad weather, far exceeds the loss of any similar period since that memorable year for hurricanes, 1780. The loss of life too, as will appear by the proper list,‡ was afflictingly severe. Among the acquired line-of-battle ships, are four that were purchased, while building, of the East India company; and the whole of the seven new frigates, two of which averaged 1000 tons each, were built of fir.

By an admiralty order, dated on the 20th of June, 1796, the complements of the different classes of frigates in the British navy were fixed on a new scale as follows:

Class in Abstracts			Men and boys. Establ.	Net§
Z and *A*	38 gun-frigate		284	281
B and *C*	36 gun-frigate	18-pdr	264	261
D	36 gun-frigate	12-pdr	240	237
E and *F*	32 gun-frigate	18-pdr	254	251
G	32 gun-frigate	12-pdr. large	240	237
H	32 gun-frigate	12-pdr. small	215	212
I	28 gun-frigate		195	193
K	24 gun-frigate		155	153

* See Appendix, Annual Abstract No. 5.

† See Appendix, Nos. 1, 2, 3.

‡ See Appendix, No. 4.

§ Deducting the widows' men.

The number of commissioned officers and masters, belonging to the British navy at the commencement of the year, was

Admirals		24
Vice-admirals		38
Rear-admirals		35
Rear-admirals	superannuated	27
Post-captains		483
Post-captains	superannuated	23
Commanders, or sloop-captains		282
Lieutenants		2038
Lieutenants	superannuated	26
Masters		451

and the number of seamen and marines, voted for the service of the year, was 120,000.*

As soon as the royalists in La Vendée were subdued, and Spain was on the eve of becoming an ally in the war, France bent her serious thoughts upon the invasion of England; in which attempt she was to be assisted by the fleets of Holland and Spain. A close intimacy subsisted between Vice-admiral Truguet, the French minister of marine, and General Hoche, who was to command the army destined to be employed in the expedition; and, as is not invariably the case in combined operations, both the admiral and the general entered alike heartily into the cause, and concurred in all the principal details of the gigantic plan which their united labours had prepared.

Before, however, the plan was finally settled, a secret committee was summoned to meet at the house of the Director Carnot. Here it was discovered, that the state of the treasury would not admit of the plan's being adopted to its full extent. It was therefore resolved to confine the expedition, "for the present," to a descent upon Ireland; a country whose disaffected inhabitants would, it was known, greet the invaders with joy, and yet whose capture by France would be inflicting a blow upon England, of which she might never recover.

In the summer of 1796 two agents, from the secret Executive Directory of the Society of United Irishmen, repaired to Paris, and held several conferences with the members of the French Directory; from whom the former received renewed assurances of the most prompt succour in men, arms, and munitions of war. The republican government offered to send 25,000 men; but the Irish directory expressed themselves satisfied with 15,000. As soon as matters were nearly ripe, Lord Edward Fitzgerald and Mr. Arthur O'Connor feigned a journey to Germany, and, having traversed that country, had an interview, by appointment, with General Hoche, at Bâle in Switzerland. Here the traitors and the French general finally arranged their plan of proceedings.

According to Vice-admiral Truguet's plan, the Brest fleet was

* See Appendix, *No. 5.*

to have a double destination. The 15 two-deckers, of which with the Océan (late Peuple) and Invincible three-deckers, and two others repairing in the harbour, it was then composed, were first to escort to the coast of Ireland a strong division of Hoche's troops, distributed on board the fleet, consisting, besides those 15 line-of-battle ships, of 12 frigates and several transports.

The debarkation effected, Vice-admiral Villaret Joyeuse, to whom the naval command of the expedition had been intrusted, was to detach himself, without loss of time, with the eight best sailing line-of-battle ships of the fleet, and hasten to the Isles of France and Bourbon. There he was to embark the black troops, which the agents of the Directory, who had gone out in Rear-admiral Sercey's frigate-squadron, had, after enfranchising all the slaves in the colony, been directed to organize. These troops Admiral Villaret was to carry to the succour of Tippoo-Saib; and, having landed the men, was to co-operate with Rear-admiral Sercey in doing all possible mischief to the British factories and commerce on the coasts of Malabar and Coromandel. After this M. Villaret and his eight sail of the line and five or six frigates would probably pass to the aid of the Dutch, who had already paid over to the hands of the French minister of marine the sum of 1,200,000 francs, as the estimated cost of equipping the squadron which France had promised should, in conjunction with a Dutch squadron, attempt the recapture of their late eastern possessions.

The seven sail of the line expected at Brest under Richery, and the five which M. Villeneuve was bringing from Toulon, would amply replace the eight carried off by M. Villaret, and were to transport to Ireland the remainder of the troops attached to the expedition. As, however, M. Villaret saw nothing but India, and General Hoche nothing but Ireland, there was a want of harmony between the two chiefs; and Hoche, as possessing the greatest interest with the government, got M. Villaret removed from the naval command, and Vice-admiral Morard-de-Galles appointed in his stead.

It was the intention of M. Truguet, that the expedition should leave Brest before the end of October, or the beginning of November at the latest; but General Hoche, being desirous to transport the whole of his troops in one trip, preferred waiting the arrival of the two daily-expected squadrons.

On the 5th of November M. Richery, having gained intelligence that a British squadron, whose force, if he had been informed of it, he would have found to consist of only seven sail of the line (one a three-decker) and two frigates, was cruising about 90 miles to the south-west of Belle-Isle, considered it too hazardous to attempt entering Brest: he therefore, with his seven two-deckers and three frigates, put into Rochefort. Here the French admiral remained until information reached him, that Sir Roger Curtis had returned into port with his squadron. Thus left at liberty to proceed, M. Richery, on the 8th of December, got under way with five of the best conditioned of his line-of-battle ships and his three frigates; and, on the morning of the 11th, passing barely in sight of Sir John Colpoys's fleet, and chasing away his frigates stationed off the mouth of the harbour, the French admiral anchored in Brest.

Two only of M. Richery's five ships, the Pégase (late Barras) and Révolution, were in a state soon to put to sea again: and these were ordered to be refitted, and have their troops (600 each) and stores embarked within 24 hours, it being the determination of General Hoche not to wait any longer for the arrival of M. Villeneuve.

The chief point of debarkation was to be Bantry bay; in which three different anchorages were chosen, to be used according to the state of the weather. If the wind blew from the eastward, which was out of the bay, the fleet was to anchor in Bear haven, situated between Great-Bear island and the main. If the wind blew from the westward, the fleet was to descend the bay to its bottom, and anchor, one division between the eastern extent of Whiddy island and the main, and the other directly athwart the entrance of Glengary harbour. If, in addition to a favourable wind, the weather should be moderate, the whole fleet was to anchor at the entrance of the river Cumbola. Should any unforeseen circumstances prevent the fleet from entering Bantry bay, it was to proceed to the mouth of the river Shannon, and there effect the debarkation. Every captain in the fleet was provided with a large chart of the intended scene of operations, on which the different anchorages, as well in Bantry bay as at the mouth of the Shannon, were clearly marked out. In short, every precaution had been taken, by the able officer who then presided over the French marine, to prevent any failure in the naval part of the expedition.

On the 15th of December, the day on which the Pégase and Révolution were to have been ready, the fleet got under way from the road of Brest, and anchored in front of the goulet, between Camaret and Bertheaume bays. Here Vice-admiral Morard-de-Galles awaited the arrival of two ships; and, while he is doing so, we will give a description of the whole of the force placed under his command. It consisted of the

Gun-ship		
80	Indomptable	Vice-admiral Morard-de-Galles. Commodore Jacques Bedout.
74	Droits-de-l'Homme	Rear-admiral François-Joseph Bouvet. Commodore Jean Raimond La Crosse.
	Constitution	Rear-admiral Joseph Marie Nielly. Commodore Louis L'Héritier.
	Pégase	Rear-admiral ——— Richery. Captain Clement Laronier.
	Nestor	Commodore Chas.-Alex.-Léon Durand-Linois.
	Révolution	Commodore P.-René-M.-Et.Dumanoir-le-Pelley.

Gun-ship		
74	Fougueux	Commodore Esprit-Tranquille Maistral.
	Trajan	Commodore Julien Le Ray.
	Mucius	Commodore Pierre-Maul. Jul. Querangal.
	Tourville	Captain Jean-Baptiste Henry.
	Pluton	Captain Jean-Marie Lebrun.
	Eole	Captain Joseph-Pierre-André Malin.
	Wattigny	Captain Henri-Alexandre Thévenard.
	Cassard	Captain —— Dufay.
	Redoutable	Captain —— Moncousu.
	Patriote	Captain —— La Fargue.
	Séduisant	Captain —— Dufossey.

Frigates, Scévola (rasé), Impatiente, Romaine, Immortalité, Tortue, Bellone, Bravoure, Charente, Cocarde, Fraternité, Résolue, Sirène, and Surveillante.

Brig-corvettes, Affronteur, Atalante, Mutine, Renard, Vautour, and Voltigeur.

Transports, Nicodème, Fille-Unique, Ville-de-Lorient, Suffren, Justine, Allegro, Expériment; and

Powder-vessel Fidéle, a frigate armed en flûte.

So that the expedition was composed of 17 ships of the line, 13 frigates, six corvettes, seven transports, and a powder-ship, in all 44 sail of vessels. On board of each line-of-battle ship were 600 troops. The Scévola carried 400; each of the frigates 250; the six corvettes 300 between them; three of the transports 450 each; three others 300 each, and one (a horse transport) 50; making a total of 16,200 men, that is, rank and file, or, including officers of all ranks, at least 18,000. But some of the English accounts represent the number at 20,000 and others as high as 25,000. In addition to the troops, which consisted of both cavalry and infantry, the fleet carried a quantity of field-artillery, besides ammunition and stores of every description. The commander-in-chief of the land forces, as already mentioned, was General Hoche, having under him, among other general officers of note, Generals Grouchy, Borin, and Humbert.

On the 16th, in the afternoon, just as the Pégase and Révolution were descried coming through the goulet, the French fleet at anchor in Camaret bay began getting under way, with the wind from the eastward, and consequently as fair as it could blow. At 4 P.M., which at this season of the year is nearly dark, all ships were under sail, and steering for the passage du Raz, the route which had been selected by M. Morard-de-Galles, in spite of the dangers it presented, the better to conceal his movements from the British admiral cruising off Ushant; and whose fleet had that morning been counted from the look-outs at 30 sail great and small; so the French accounts state, but the number appears to have been greatly overrated.

Contrary, as it would appear, to the directions of the minister of marine, all the French admirals, except Richery, embarked on board frigates: the two commanders-in-chief were in the Fraternité; Rear-admiral Bouvet, with the second in command of the troops in the Immortalité; and Rear-admiral Nielly in the Résolue. Finding the darkness coming rapidly on and the wind growing variable, M. Morard-de-Galles resolved not to attempt the passage du Raz, and accordingly signalled his fleet to steer for the passage d'Iroise, or that directly in front of the port. Owing to the darkness, few of the ships saw the signal, or the alteration which the Fraternité, the better to mark the admiral's intention, had made in her course. The consequence was, that the greater part of the fleet entered the narrow passage du Raz; while the remainder followed the admiral through the wide opening of l'Iroise, hoping to rejoin their companions soon after rounding the Saintes.

Several circumstances, besides the darkness and the partial change in the course, conspired to disorganize the fleet at its departure from port; a fleet of ships, by the composition of their crews and the lumbered state of their decks, ill prepared at best to encounter difficulties of any kind. Besides the guns fired and lights shown by the Fraternité, to denote the change in her course, the corvette Atalante was directed to stand into the middle of the fleet, and there fire guns to enforce the signal of the commander-in-chief. While this was doing, guns were heard, and rockets and blue lights seen, in various directions. Part of the guns proceeded from the Séduisant 74, which had struck on the Grand-Stevenet rock, near the entrance of the passage du Raz; and which ship in the course of the night, was entirely lost, with her captain, several other officers, and about 680 out of her 1300 in crew and passengers. Other guns, with some rockets, proceeded from a British frigate, and contributed in no small degree, to add to the confusion which prevailed in the French fleet.

This was the 44-gun frigate Indefatigable, Captain Sir Edward Pellew; who, having under his orders the 38-gun frigate Révolutionnaire, Captain Francis Cole, 36-gun frigates Amazon and Phœbe, Captains Robert Carthew Reynolds and Robert Barlow, and hired armed lugger Duke-of-York, commanded by Mr. Benjamin Sparrow, had been directed to watch the Brest fleet, and communicate every movement to Vice-admiral Colpoys, at his rendezvous about eight leagues to the westward of Ushant. On the 11th, when Sir Edward descried, as already related, the squadron of M. Richery entering the road, he despatched the Amazon to England and the Phœbe to the admiral. On the 15th, at 3 h. 30 m. P.M., although he had been chased several times by a line-of-battle ship and five frigates stationed in Bertheaume bay, Sir Edward was close enough in to discover the French fleet coming through the goulet, and immediately sent the Phœbe, who had since rejoined, to Vice-admiral Colpoys.

On the 16th, at daylight, having stood off and on during the night, the Indefatigable and Révolutionnaire made sail on a wind towards Brest; and at noon, when Saint-Mathias point bore from the Indefatigable east by north and Ushant north by east, the two frigates again got a sight of the French fleet, which had now anchored between Camaret and Bertheaume bays. At 3 h. 30 m P.M., on seeing the fleet get under way, Sir Edward despatched the Révolutionnaire to the admiral, and, with the Indefatigable alone, continued at his post. Having, at 4 h. 15 m. P.M., the Bec du Raz bearing south by east half-east. The Indefatigable now managed to keep just ahead of the French fleet on its way out, and was sometimes within half-gun shot only of the leading ship. At 7 P.M. she began firing guns and sending up rockets; at 7 h. 30 m. hove to, and at 8 h. 30 m., having observed several of the French ships haul close round the Saintes, filled and made all sail to the north-west.

On losing sight of the enemy a few minutes afterwards, the Indefatigable fired half and quarter minute guns, burnt blue lights, and hoisted a light at each mast-head. At midnight she hauled by the wind to the southward; and, at 6 h. 30 m. A.M. on the 17th, Sir Edward sent the lugger with despatches to Falmouth, and shortly afterwards proceeded thither himself. The Brest fleet and its memorable proceedings on this occasion now claim our exclusive attention.

On the 17th, at daybreak, Rear-admiral Bouvet, having cleared the passage du Raz, found himself in company with only nine sail of the line, six frigates, including his own, and one transport. He therefore opened his despatches, as directed in the case of separation, and by them learnt, that he was to make Mizen Head on the coast of Ireland, and cruise off there during five days, when a frigate would join him with fresh instructions. Making sail, about noon, with this destination in view, the rear-admiral did not proceed straight to Cape Clear, lest he should encounter the British fleet, but steered to the westward, and continued sailing in that direction until daylight on the 19th, when he altered his course to north. Shortly afterwards his advanced frigate signalled 16 vessels; which proved to be part of the expedition, and at noon joined company. Rear-admiral Bouvet now had under his command 15 sail of the line, 10 frigates including the Scévola, three corvettes, and five transports. The missing line-of-battle ship was the Nestor, and the missing frigates, the Fraternité, Cocarde, and Romaine.

On the 20th the weather was extremely foggy. On the 21st, at 7 h. 30 m A.M., the advanced frigates gained a sight of Dursey island, and shortly afterwards of Mizen Head. Having arrived off the entrance of Bantry bay, the rear-admiral made the signal to prepare to anchor. By this time several pilot-boats, mistaking the fleet for British, had got among the leading frigates, and were detained by the orders of the admiral, who thus found himself provided with pilots for almost every ship in his fleet. M. Bouvet now learnt that, for three days, no ship had appeared off the coast, and that the only force at anchor in Cork harbour consisted of six frigates.

During the whole of the 21st, and a part of the 22d, the fleet beat against a fresh easterly wind, and made very little way. Finding this to be the case, the rear-admiral, at 4 P.M., anchored his frigate a little to windward of the eastern extremity of Great-Bear island, and was soon joined by eight ships of the line, a second frigate, four corvettes, and one transport. The remainder of the ships, their captains having been signalled to act according to their own discretion, kept under way, and at daylight on the 23d were not to be seen by the ships at anchor.

During the whole of this day and night it blew hard from the eastward, and there was a heavy sea in the bay; but on the next day, the 24th, the wind moderated, not sufficiently, however, in rear-admiral Bouvet's opinion, for the ships to weigh: they therefore continued at their anchors. A council of war, held this day on board the Immortalité, decided that the 6000 troops on board the ships present should be disembarked; and General Grouchy, now the commanding officer of the land-forces, made a formal requisition to that effect to Rear-admiral Bouvet.

Although he had received no instruction on that head, to guide him in case of separation, the rear-admiral immediately despatched a corvette to reconnoitre the coast; and, on learning that there was a creek near at hand, where several boats might land together, he got under way with his ships. This was at 4 P.M., and consequently too late to effect much at this season of the year. Moreover the wind and sea began to get up, and the pilots pronounced that a storm was brewing. The ships thereupon reanchored; and at night the gale came on so violently from the eastward, that the frigates pitched forecastle under.

On the 25th the gale increased. Several of the line-of-battle ships drove from their anchors and stood out to sea. One of them, the Indomptable, ran foul of the Résolue, and carried away all the frigate's masts. In the evening the Immortalité, having parted one cable, was obliged to cut the other, to save herself from going on shore. On clearing the bay, the frigate could do nothing but scud, and continued, for three days, running before the wind.

On the 29th the wind moderated, and became fair for returning to Bantry bay, from which the Immortalité then bore south-west distant about 20 leagues. Apprehensive, however, that he should find none of his ships there, and having only a few days' provisions on board, Rear-admiral Bouvet steered for Brest, and on the 1st of January at 1 A.M. entered the road; where he was joined the same day by the Indomptable 80, and the Fougueux, Mucius, Redoutable, and Patriote 74s.

We have already mentioned that, on the 20th of December, the Nestor 74, and Fraternité, Romaine, and Cocarde frigates were sailing in company. At this time, as appears by their journals, they were very near to the division of Rear-admiral Bouvet; but each admiral was concealed from the other's view by the thick fog that prevailed. The violent wind, which dispersed that fog, separated those four ships in spite of all their endeavours to keep together; and on the next day, the 21st, when nearly in sight of the coast of Ireland, the Fraternité found herself almost under the guns of an English frigate (described as "un vaisseau rasé"), which she at first took for the Romaine. As soon as the mistake was discovered, the Fraternité made all sail, closely pursued by the frigate; and from whom her escape appeared doubtful, until darkness enabled her to alter her course.

This chase had carried the Fraternité to a great distance from the Irish coast; and, now that the admiral wished to return, the wind blew violently from the eastward. After beating about until the morning of the 29th, the Fraternité obtained a shift of wind in her favour, and stood towards Bantry bay. In her way thither, the frigate met the Révolution, in company with the Scévola rasé; whose crew and passengers the 74 was occupied in removing, to save them from perishing in the vessel, which, unable from age and weakness to withstand the violence of the gale, was then in a sinking state. The two mortified commanders-in-chief now learnt that not a ship of their fleet remained in the bay: they persevered, however, in steering towards it, until, on the second day, Captain Dumanoir sent to inform the admiral that, with so many hands as he now had on board (upwards of 1600), his provisions would not hold out much longer. This determined the two chiefs, on board of whose frigate a part of the Scévola's crew had also been received, to return home.

On the 8th of January, at 7 A.M., in latitude 51° north, longitude 13° 11' west from Greenwich, the wind at north-east, the Fraternité and her consort fell in with, and immediately tacked away from, the British 32-gun frigate Unicorn, Captain Sir Thomas Williams, and 36-gun frigate Doris, Captain the Honourable Charles Jones; from whom the 32-gun frigate Druid, Captain Richard King, had just parted company, along with the French transport Ville-de-Lorient, captured the preceding evening. This precipitate flight of the French 74 and frigate brought with it an evil little suspected by the two commanders-in-chief on board the latter. Eleven ships belonging to their fleet were at that very time to windward, chasing the Unicorn and Doris; and which ships the Révolution and Fraternité might also have discovered, had the latter continued a short time longer upon the course they had been steering.

On the next morning, the 9th, the Unicorn and Doris again fell in with the two French ships, who again tacked to the westward; at which time the Unicorn was within two miles of them. Having escaped this imaginary danger, the French 74 and frigate, on the morning of the 10th, had a real cause for their fears, finding themselves chased by Lord Bridport's fleet; and from which they owed their escape to the hazy and tempestuous state of the weather. Considering it no longer safe to persist in steering to the eastward, the Révolution and Fraternité altered their course to south. On the morning of the 14th they made the Isle of Ré, and entered Rochefort the same afternoon.

If the ships, which did not reach or were driven out of Bantry bay, suffered so much by stress of weather, several of those that remained in it met a still worse fate. On the 30th of December the Justine transport was captured, and the Impatiente frigate cast away, on the coast near Crookhaven, with the loss of all the latter's crew and passengers, except seven. Early in January the Surveillante went on shore in Bantry bay, and a portion of her crew fell into the hands of the British: the remainder got on board some of the ships in company. On the 7th the Ville-de-Lorient transport was taken as already mentioned; as on the 5th had been the Tortue frigate by the Polyphemus 64. On that, or the following day, the Fille-Unique transport foundered in the bay; and two or three of the men of war which eventually escaped, were, on more than one occasion, very critically circumstanced.

Eight or nine of the ships made their appearance off the river Shannon; but all at length quitted the coast of Ireland, and steered towards that of France. On their way thither, the Suffren and Allegro transports were taken; also the Atalante brig-corvette. The loss of one, and the return to port of six of the line-of-battle ships, we have already noticed. On the 11th of January the Constitution, Trajan, Pluton, Wattigny, and Pégase, arrived at Brest, the latter having in tow the dismasted Résolue; and on the 13th the Nestor, Tourville, Eole, and Cassard, reached the same port. This leaves but one line-of-battle ship unaccounted for, and to her we shall attend presently. With respect to the frigates not already mentioned as captured or lost, the whole of them arrived at Brest, either on the 1st, 11th, or 13th of January, except the Bravoure and Fraternité, one of which put into Lorient, and the other, as already stated, into Rochefort.

Among the ships which, after the failure at Bantry bay, proceeded to the mouth of the river Shannon, the second point of debarkation intended to be attempted, was the Droits-de-l'Homme, the flag-ship of Rear-admiral Bouvet, but now commanded, during his absence in the Immortalité, by Commodore la Crosse, a very able and experienced officer; and on board of which ship, as commanding officer of one division of the troops, was the famous General Humbert. On the 5th of January, when about four leagues from the mouth of the Shannon, the Droits-de-l'Homme was fortunate enough to fall in with the Cumberland, Captain Peter Inglis, a deeply-laden ship letter-of-marque, from Barbadoes bound to Liverpool. Having removed all the crew and passengers except the chief mate and cook, consisting of three infantry-officers, two masters of merchantmen, two women, and 48 seamen and soldiers, the French commodore sent on board a prize-master and ten men, and ordered the ship for France. On the 7th, having cruised eight days off Loup Head, the Droits-de-l'Homme looked a second time into Bantry bay, and, seeing there no signs of the fleet, steered for the French coast, intending to make her first landfall at Belle-Isle.

On the 9th the commodore lost sight of the coast of Ireland, and on the 13th considered himself to be about 25 leagues from the coast of France, in the latitude of Penmarck point. Thick weather coming on, M. la Crosse determined, for the present, to approach no nearer to the land. The Droits-de-l'Homme, accordingly, stood to the southward under easy sail, with the wind fresh on her starboard beam.

At 1 P.M. a ship was seen to windward which loomed very large in the fog, and appeared to be chasing the Droits-de-l'Homme, from whom she was distant very little more than a league. Shortly afterwards a second ship was seen astern of the first. Judging them to be enemies, the French 74 immediately made sail to escape, or, at all events, to allow time for preparation. The wind, which still blew from the westward, had now increased considerably, and the sea was becoming very turbulent. At 3 h. 30 m. P.M., having run some distance to the south-east, two other ships were seen on the lee bow, manœuvring, apparently, to cut off the Droits-de-l'Homme from the land.

These were the British 44-gun frigate Indefatigable, Captain Sir Edward Pellew, and 36-gun frigate Amazon, Captain Robert Carthew Reynolds; and who, it appears, when by their account in latitude 47° 30' north, Ushant bearing north-east distant 50 leagues, had discovered the Droits-de-l'Homme, bearing from them north-west, about the same time that the latter descried the two ships to windward. These seem to have been considered by M. la Crosse as a part of Sir Edward's squadron; but we rather think they were the French 74 Révolution and frigate Fraternité, on their way to the Isle of Ré. At all events, we have ascertained from the best authority, the Indefatigable's log, that no other vessel than the Amazon was cruising with her; nor had been, except the Duke-of-York lugger, and she had parted company a fortnight previous.

At 4 h. 15 m., which was shortly after the Indefatigable had discovered the stranger to be an enemy's two-decker without a poop, and with her lowerdeck ports shut, the Droits-de-l'Homme, in a squall, carried away the maintopsail braces, and, almost at the same instant, her fore and main topmasts. This important circumstance, although omitted in Sir Edward Pellew's letter, is mentioned in the Indefatigable's log. The utmost despatch was now used in clearing the wreck from the lee-guns, lest the enemy, profiting by the circumstance, should commence his attack on that side. In the course of a quarter of an hour or 20 minutes, this necessary duty was performed, and the Droits-de-l'Homme, under her courses and mizen topsail, was going at the rate of five knots an hour.

As the two British ships, having lost none of their masts, were probably running a third faster, the leading ships, the Indefatigable, then between seven and eight miles of her consort, arrived, at about 5 h. 30 m. P.M., within hail of the Droits-de-l'Homme astern, and shortening sail to close-reefed topsails, did not run to leeward, as the French think she ought,* but hauled up to pour in a raking fire. The two-decker, however, managed to haul up also, and a broadside was exchanged, accompanied on the part of the French ship by an immense discharge of musketry. The Indefatigable now tried to pass ahead of her antagonist, and rake her in that direction; but the Droits-de-l'Homme defeated that manœuvre likewise, and attempted to run the frigate on board. This the latter, very naturally, did her best to evade, and succeeded; not, however, without receiving into her stern a close, but, owing in a great degree, no doubt, to the violent motion of the sea, comparatively harmless broadside.

Another cause may, and indeed must, have contributed to the diminution of effect produced by the two-decker's fire: her lower-deck ports, being nearer to the water's edge by 14 inches† than those of the generality of French 74s, were obliged to be shut almost as soon as opened, to keep out the quantity of water that was rushing through them, and which actually poured down upon the prisoners in the cable-tier.‡ It was not merely the roughness of the sea, but the heavy rolling of the ship for the want of sails to steady her, that thus rendered her lower battery useless to her: a disadvantage of so serious a nature, as to give quite a new feature to the combat she was engaged in.

That combat continued between the Indefatigable and Droits-de-l'Homme until about 6 h. 45 m. P.M.; when the Amazon, having come up under a press of sail, poured a broadside, within pistol-shot distance, into the French ship's quarter. The Amazon then tried to pass astern of her antagonist; but, as in the

* "Alors le bâtiment ennemi le plus proche (c'était celui du commodore), qui se trouvait à petite portée de canon dans les eaux du vaisseau les Droits-de-l'Homme, serra toutes les voiles qu'il avait mises dehors pour chasser, et s'établit sous une voilure commode pour le combat. Il perdit par-là un temps précieux. En effet, s'il eût sur-le-champ prolongé le vaisseau français par dessous le vent, il eût pu le canonner sans qu'il eût été possible à celui-ci de lui riposter d'un seul coup, à cause du danger qu'il eût couru de mettre le feu aux voiles, qui couvraient une grande partie de ses canons, et dont il lui fût devenu bien difficile de se débarrasser sous le feu de l'artillerie ennemie." — *Victoires et Conquêtes*, tome vii., p. 293.

† A British army officer, who was a prisoner on board, and whose "Narrative, &c." is given at p. 465, vol. vii. of the "Naval Chronicle," says, "two feet and a half lower than usual;" but the above account, as taken from the French themselves, is probably the more correct.

‡ Lieutenant Pipon's Narrative. See last note.

Indefatigable's case, the Droits-de-l'Homme appears to have so manœuvred as to avoid the raking fire, and bring both her antagonists on one side. Between them and her the cannonade was maintained, with mutual spirit, until about 7 h. 30 m. P.M.; when both British ships shot ahead, the Amazon, chiefly on account of the quantity of sail she carried, and the Indefatigable, in order to repair her damaged rigging. The Droits-de-l'Homme profited by this interval of non-action, to put herself a little to rights; and her crew found time to recover from the confusion caused by the recent bursting of one of the 18-pounders. The ship, meanwhile, continued running to the east-south-east; partly because, in her disabled state, and especially since the wind had drawn more to the southward, she could lie no higher, and partly as it would appear, because the haziness of the weather of late had prevented her commander from knowing exactly where he was.

At 8 h. 30 m. P.M. the two British ships, the one having reduced her sails, and the other refitted as well as the time would allow, reapproached, and recommenced the action with great judgment as well as spirit. They stationed themselves one on each bow of the French ship; and, by regulating their speed, and yawing to starboard and port alternately, raked her by turns. In the mean while the Droits-de-l'Homme, by yawing first on one tack and then on the other, managed to get her two opponents occasionally under her guns. With such disadvantages on her side in the cannonade, the 74, numerously manned as she was, naturally had recourse to boarding whenever an opportunity offered; but neither frigate was so imprudent, or so inattentive, as to suffer her to come in contact, although, in manœuvring to get out of the way of their huge antagonist (in reference to the Amazon at least), both ships received an occasional raking fire, not much more effectual, however, than that first received by the Indefatigable.

At 10 h. 30 m. P.M., the mizenmast of the Droits-de-l'Homme, being in a tottering state from the wounds it had received, was cut away to enable it to fall clear of the deck. After this, the two British ships changed their positions, and attacked their opponent on the quarter. Having expended all her round shot but 50, the Droits-de-l'Homme began firing shells; and if even, as the French state, these kept the British ships at a greater distance, they did not, as far as we can learn, produce any very serious effect either upon their hulls or their crews. Many of the French crew had by this time been killed or disabled at their quarters; but the ship's fire did not slacken on that account, as fresh hands, out of the numerous party on board, were constantly sent from below to supply the loss.*

At 1 A.M. on the 14th no officer belonging to the Droits-de-l'Homme had been badly hurt: one of her lieutenants, however,

* Victoires et Conquêtes, tome vii., p. 297.

then received a grape-shot in the arm, and several other officers, in succession, were wounded. With the exception of a second interval from its commencement, of three quarters of an hour or so (but which we are unable precisely to fix), occasioned by the British ships retiring to secure their wounded masts, the action continued to be furiously maintained on both sides until, by the Indefatigable's time, about 4 h. 20 m. A.M.; when the sudden appearance of land, close on board of all three ships, caused the Indefatigable and Amazon to haul off from the threatened danger, and the far more disabled Droits-de-l'Homme to make a similar effort. Thus terminated an engagement, which had lasted, including the two intervals of suspension, for which an hour and a half may be allowed, about ten hours and a half: the French, indeed, fixing the time of its commencement at 5 h. 15 m. P.M., and of its close at 6 h. 15 m A.M., make the duration of the action 13 hours.

During the whole of this long engagement, the sea ran so high, that the people on the main decks of the frigates were up to their middles in water. So violent, too, was the motion of the ships, that some of the Indefatigable's guns broke their breechings four times; some drew their ring-bolts from the side, and many of the guns, owing to the water having beaten into them, were obliged to be drawn immediately after loading. A scene nearly similar was acting on board the Amazon; and, when the firing ceased, the crews of both ships, notwithstanding the increased demand for their exertions owing to the new perils that assailed them, were almost worn out with fatigue.

The Indefatigable had four feet water in the hold, and all her masts were in a wounded state. The main topmast was completely unrigged, and was saved only by uncommon alacrity. The Amazon had nearly three feet water in her hold. Her mizen topmast, gaff, spanker-boom, and maintopsail yard, were entirely shot away; her four and main masts and four and main yards, cut through by shots, and her sails and rigging of every sort, more or less injured. As an augmentation to her loss of rigging, the Amazon had expended, in reeving new braces and other purposes, every inch of spare cordage.

For so much injury in matériel, that which the two British ships suffered in personnel bore, in comparison with other cases, a somewhat inadequate proportion. The Indefatigable, out of her crew (admitting all to have been on board) of 330 men and boys, had her first lieutenant (John Thompson) and 18 men wounded; 12 of these not in a serious manner, and chiefly with splinter-contusions. The Amazon's loss, out of a crew of about 260, amounted to three men killed, and 15 badly wounded. The casualties on board this frigate being thus at least equal to those of the Indefatigable,* a ship so much more large and

* Sir Edward, when he said, in reference to the Amazon, "Her condition, I think, was better than ours," could only have judged from appearances, having had no communication with his consort.

powerful, no doubt can remain, that the Amazon most nobly sustained her part in the engagement.

The loss on board the Droits-de-l'Homme, out of a crew, including her army-passengers, of at least 1350 men,* amounted to three army-officers and 100 sailors and soldiers killed, and seven officers of the ship, about an equal number of army-officers and 100 sailors and soldiers, placed "hors de combat," or badly wounded. Therefore, including the slightly wounded, we may fairly state the total at 103 killed and 150 wounded. The severity of this loss reduces that on board the two frigates to little or nothing. That no more than three men should have been killed and 34 wounded by the fire of a two-decker (nominally so, at least), continued for eight or nine hours, the chief of the time at close quarters, can indeed only be accounted for by the violent motion of the sea, felt the more by the Droits-de-l'Homme on account of the loss of her masts, the height of the line of fire to which the 74 was restricted, especially as against antagonists so comparatively low in the water, and the excellent bow and quarter positions, which those antagonists, by their superior activity, were enabled to maintain.

The powerless state of the Droits-de-l'Homme's principal battery, during the greater part, if not the whole, of the engagement, would render unfair any statement that did not, upon the face of it, make allowance for so very important a circumstance. Hence, we have omitted the usual statement of comparative force. We need only remark that, in broadside weight of metal, the two frigates, chiefly on account of the powerful battery of the Indefatigable, who carried long 24s below and 42-pounder carronades above, would have had rather the advantage, even against the French ship with the whole of her guns in a condition to act. The action undoubtedly did credit to all that were concerned in it; yet, had the combatants possessed sea-room, the 74 not lost her topmasts and been eased of her superfluous hands, and the state of the weather been such as to have admitted the constant use of her long 36-pounders, who is there that can say which party would have ultimately prevailed?

Having gone through all that relates to this extraordinary

* This is less by 200 than the number for which head-money was paid; but, in this instance, the customary vouchers, the certificates of the three principal French officers, were necessarily obliged to be dispensed with. In lieu of them, there were depositions, first by the master of the Cumberland, that he believed the number of men on board the Droits-de-l'Homme to have been between 1500 and 1600; and then, by the first and second captains of the captured French frigate Tortue, that they believed the crew of the Droits-de-l'Homme to have been 700, and the soldiers on board about 800. In opposition to this, a French semi-official account of the action states the crew at 650 (in which number Lieutenant Pipon agrees), and the troops, exclusive of several staff-officers, at 600. The amount in the text admits the troops to have been 700.

action, we shall now endeavour to describe the awful but interesting occurrences that so closely followed its sudden termination. At about 4 h. 20 m. A.M. the moon, opening rather brighter than it had done, showed to Lieutenant George Bell, who was watchfully looking out on the Indefatigable's forecastle, a glimpse of the land, bearing north-east, or right ahead, distant about two miles; and, scarcely had the lieutenant reached his captain with the intelligence, ere the breakers were visible to all. The Indefatigable was then close to the Droits-de-l'Homme's starboard bow, and the Amazon was near to her on the larboard one. The Indefatigable's crew, with that calm self-possession which characterizes British seamen, instantly hauled on board the tacks, and the ship made sail to the southward.

The land could not then be ascertained, but it was supposed to be Ushant; and, in that case, no particular fears were entertained. But, just before day, breakers were seen upon the lee bow. The ship was instantly wore to the northward, and the lingering approach of daylight was by all anxiously expected. It came at about 6 h. 30 m.; and, the land appearing very close ahead and on the weather bow, and breakers to leeward, the ship was again wore to the southward, in 20 fathoms' water. In the direction of the land was seen, at 7 h. 10 m. A.M., the French 74, broadside uppermost, with a tremendous surf beating over her. The Indefatigable, the wind blowing dead on the shore now known to be that of Audierne bay, passed, at the distance of about a mile, the wreck of her late opponent, without the possibility, unfortunately, of affording her any succour. Her own safety, indeed, depended on her weathering the much dreaded Penmarcks. This, at about 11 A.M., the Indefatigable accomplished, passing to windward of the rocks about half, or, as the log says, three quarters of a mile.

At the time that the Indefatigable, on first discovering her danger, had wore to the southward, the Amazon, to whom her consort had promptly made the night-signal of danger, had wore to the northward. In about half an hour afterwards, every effort of her officers and crew to work their crippled ship off the shore having proved unavailing, the Amazon struck the ground. The ship's company, with the exception of six men that stole the cutter and were drowned, preserved themselves by making rafts. These conveyed the people in safety to the shore, but it was only to be made prisoners. Every officer and man of the Amazon's crew that survived the action, with the exception of the above six, were by 9 A.M. safely landed. A party of French soldiers immediately marched them off to Audierne, a town situated about a league from the wreck; thence to Duarnez, and subsequently to Quimper. Here the prisoners remained, and were well treated.

It is almost superfluous to state that, when Captain Reynolds and his officers, of the 29th of the succeeding September (having just before been exchanged), were put to trial for the loss of the Amazon, they were "most honourably and fully acquitted of all blame, and with every sentiment of the court's highest approbation." Both first lieutenants, Mr. John Thompson, of the Indefatigable, and Mr. Bendall Robert Littlehales, late of the Amazon, were most deservedly promoted to the rank of commanders.

In describing the Amazon's loss by the fire of the Droits-de-l'Homme, we omitted to state, that Lieutenant Littlehales, while standing by the side of his captain, was knocked down by the wind of a 36-pound shot. Captain Reynolds lifted him from the deck, and ordered some of the men to take him below. By the time, however, that the men had reached the foot of the quarterdeck ladder, Lieutenant Littlehales recovered his senses, and forthwith returned to his post; but his chest and the upper part of his arms were for several weeks afterwards black and blue.*

The details we are about to give of the melancholy fate that attended the Droits-de-l'Homme and her numerous crew, we shall extract partly from a French account, and partly from the narrative of Lieutenant Pipon, to which we have already alluded. The proximity of the land was discovered at about the same time on board the Indefatigable and Droits-de-l'Homme; but the latter, partly perhaps owing to accident, makes the time 6 h. 15 m. instead of 4 h. 20 m. A.M. Very soon after the fatal discovery had been made, and just as she had altered her course to avoid the danger, the foremast and bowsprit of the 74 fell over her bows. This checked the way which the ragged mainsail had given to the ship, and hastened the catastrophe.

The French commodore now resolved to bring up; but all the anchors, except two, had been lost in Bantry bay, and the cables of these had been rendered useless by the enemy's shot. However, a stout hawser was bent to one of the anchors, ready for letting go. Meanwhile, the remains of the mainsail having blown from the yard, the ship scarcely moved ahead. The anchor was now dropped in 12 fathoms; but it did not hold an instant, and the ship presently struck (according to the French account, at 7 A.M.) on a bank of sand, directly opposite to the town of Plouzenec in the bay of Audierne. The second shock carried away the mainmast by the board. Four or five guns of alarm were fired; and, to ease the ship and endeavour to keep her upright, several of the guns were thrown overboard.

The instant the danger had become evident to the French crew, the exclamation, "Pauvres Anglais! pauvres Anglais! montez bien vite, nous sommes tous perdus!" resounded through the ship. The English prisoners, whose station during the battle had been the cable-tier, rushed on deck. Here was an awful sight:

* Marshall, vol. ii., p. 287.

the decks slippery with human gore, the ship without a mast standing, and the breakers all around. The Indefatigable was seen on the starboard quarter, standing off, in a most tremendous sea, from the Penmarck rocks, which threatened her with instant destruction. On the larboard side, at the distance of about two miles, was seen the Amazon, whose fate had just been sealed. That of the Droits-de-l'Homme drew near. She struck. Shrieks issued from every quarter of the ship, and all was horror and dismay. Many early victims were swept from the wreck by the merciless waves, which kept incessantly breaking over the ship. Daylight appeared, and the shore was seen lined with people; but who, in the stormy state of the weather, could not render the least assistance.

As soon as it was low water some of the boats were launched. The first two were carried away by the waves before a person could embark in them, and were dashed to pieces against the rocks that lined the beach. A pass-rope, or *vat-et-vient*, was next tried; and a raft, constructed of spare yards, was made fast to the end of a rope, which was slackened by degrees from the ship, to allow it to drift on shore; but, the weight of the rope retarding the raft in its progress, and a sea washing off some of the men that were upon it, the remainder cut themselves clear and gained the shore. The attempt to get a rope on shore by this means was again tried, and again failed. At length the ship's master-sailmaker, Lamandé by name, offered to swim on shore with a cord, to which a suitable pass-rope might afterwards be attached; but, by the time he had reached about half way to the shore, he became exhausted with fatigue, and was dragged on board again by his own cord, without the aid of which he would certainly have perished. The day closed, and an awful night ensued.

The dawn of the second day, the 15th, brought with it but an increase of misery. Owing to the sea having stove in the stern, and filled the hold with water, the people had now been nearly 30 hours without any food, and the wants of nature could by many scarcely be endured. At low water this day a small boat was hoisted out, and an English captain and eight seamen, part of the prisoners, succeeded in reaching the store. Elated at the success of these daring fellows, all thought their deliverance at hand, and many of the Frenchmen launched out on their rafts; but alas! Death soon put an end to their hopes. Another night was lingered through. On the third day, the 16th, larger rafts were constructed, and the largest boat was got over the side. The intention was, to place in this boat the surviving wounded, the two women and six children, and the helpless men; but the notion of equality, prevailing over every other consideration, destroyed all subordination, and nearly 120 men, in defiance of their officers, jumped into the boat and sank it. A wave of an enormous magnitude came at the same instant; and, for nearly a quarter of an hour, neither the boat nor its contents were visible. Too soon, however, were seen the bodies of the wretched victims floating in all directions. Touched with the melancholy fate of so many of his brave comrades, a French adjutant-general, named Renier, resolved to gain succour from the shore, or perish in the attempt. He plunged into the sea, and was drowned.

Already nearly 900 souls (according to Lieutenant Pipon, but we think the number is overrated) had perished, when the fourth night came with renewed horrors. "Weak, distracted, and wanting every thing," says the lieutenant in his narrative, "we envied the fate of those whose lifeless corpses no longer needed sustenance. The sense of hunger was already lost, but a parching thirst consumed our vitals. Recourse was had to wine and salt water, which only increased the want. Half a hogshead of vinegar floated up, and each had half a wineglass full. This gave a momentary relief yet soon left us again in the same state of dreadful thirst. Almost at the last gasp, every one was dying with misery, the ship, which was now one third shattered away from the stern, scarcely afforded a grasp to hold by, to the exhausted and helpless survivors. The fourth day (the 17th) brought with it a more serene sky, and the sea seemed to subside; but to behold, from fore and aft, the dying in all directions, was a sight too shocking for the feeling mind to endure. Almost lost to a sense of humanity, we no longer looked with pity on those who were the speedy forerunners of our own fate, and a consultation took place to sacrifice some one to be food to the remainder. The die was going to be cast, when the welcome sight of a man-of-war brig renewed our hopes. A cutter speedily followed, and both anchored at a short distance from the wreck. They then sent their boats to us, and, by means of large rafts, about 150, of near 400 who attempted it, were saved by the brig that evening: 380 were left to endure another night's misery, when, dreadful to relate, above one half were found dead next morning."

The man-of-war brig was the Arrogante, commanded by Enseigne de Vaisseau Provost, and the cutter the Aïguille. Mr. Pipon thus concludes his interesting narrative: "I was saved at about 10 o'clock on the morning of the 18th, with my two brother officers, the captain of the ship, and General Humbert. They treated us with great humanity on board the cutter, by giving us a little weak brandy-and-water every five or six minutes, after which a basin of good soup. I fell on the locker in a kind of trance for nearly 30 hours; and was swelled to that degree as to require medical aid to restore my decayed faculties. We were taken to Brest almost naked, having lost all our baggage. There they gave us a rough shift of clothes, and, in consequences of our sufferings, and the help we afforded in saving many lives, a cartel was fitted out by order of the French government, to send us home without ransom or exchange. We arrived at Plymouth on the 7th of March following."

Thus had this mighty fleet, from which so much had been anticipated, utterly failed in its object: some of the ships belonging to it had perished on the rocks or in the waves, others had been captured by the enemy, and the remainder, jaded and weather-beaten, had returned into port. The following little table will show, at one view, how the 44 sail, of which that fleet at its departure consisted, were ultimately disposed of:

	Captured	Wrecked	Foundered	Total lost	Port arrived at in Janry.				Total that arrived safe	Total that had sailed from Brest
					Brest			Roch. & Lor		
					1st	11th	13th	14th		
Ships of the line	—	2	—	2	5	5	4	1	15	17
Frigates	1	2	1	4	1	1	5	2	9	13
Brig-corvettes	2	—	—	2	1	1	2	—	4	6
Transports and powder-ships	4	—	1	5	—	—	3	—	3	8
Total	7	4	2	13	7	7	14	3	31	44

That a succession of storms, such as those with which the British Channel was visited in the winter of 1796–7, should disperse and drive back an encumbered and (nautically, if not numerically considered) ill-manned French fleet, ought not to create surprise. But that, during the three or four weeks that the ships of this fleet were traversing, in every direction, the English and Irish Channels, neither of the two British fleets appointed to look after them should have succeeded in capturing a single ship, may certainly be noted down as an extraordinary circumstance. How it happened we will endeavour in part to explain.

On the 17th of December, at noon, when Rear-admiral Bouvet, having run through the passage du Raz, made sail to the westward with his nine ships of the line, Vice-admiral Colpoys, with 13 sail, was in latitude 48° 17' north, longtitude 6° 7' west, or just 15 leagues to the westward of Ushant; towards which he was working against a fresh east-south-east wind. On the 19th, at 9 h. 30 m. A.M., when the Phœbe joined with the news of the French fleet's having quitted Brest for Camaret, the vice-admiral was in latitude 48° 51' north, longitude 5° 43' west, or about 12 leagues north-west by west of Ushant, where a strong south-westerly wind had driven him.

The wind, however, subsequently changed to north-west by

west, and, blowing strong, carried the British fleet, by noon on the 20th, to latitude 48° 7' north, longitude 5° 49' west, or to a spot at about equal distances (13 to 14 leagues) from Ushant and the Saintes. In the morning of this day the squadron of Rear-admiral Villeneuve from Toulon made its appearance to windward and was chased, in almost a gale of wind, by the Impêtueux, Minotaur, Bellerophon, Marlborough, and some of the frigates; but, owing in a great degree to the haziness of the weather, the French admiral, with his five sail of the line and two (having parted company with one) frigates, effected his escape, and on the 23d entered Lorient. On the day previous the Révolutionnaire had joined Vice-admiral Colpoys; but several of his ships having suffered in the gale and been obliged to part company, the admiral soon afterwards bore away for Spithead; where he arrived on the 31st with only six sail of the line under his command.

It was on the 20th of December, late in the evening, that Sir Edward Pellew, in the Indefatigable, anchored in Carrig road, Falmouth; and from him, or from the Duke-of-York lugger, which may have arrived a few hours earlier, the British government became apprized of the escape of the French fleet from Brest. As a proof that no time was lost in forwarding orders to Spithead, Lord Bridport, on the 25th, got under way with his fleet; but a series of accidents prevented him from sailing, and became, as we shall see, the principal cause of his missing a strong division of the fleet, whose capture or destruction was the sole object of his putting to sea. The Prince 98, as was no uncommon thing with her, missed stays, and, paying round off, ran foul of the Sans-Pareil abreast of the starboard gangway, thereby doing herself so much injury, that she was obliged to remain behind to be docked. The Formidable got on board the Ville-de-Paris, by which a mutual injury was sustained; and the Atlas grounded. Having at length succeeded with eight line-of-battle ships in reaching St.-Helen's, the admiral was prevented from sailing by a sudden change of wind; which although favourable for his getting to sea, was directly on the bows of the ships coming to join him from Spithead. This made it the morning of the 3d of January before the fleet, consisting of 14 sail of the line, six frigates, a fireship, and a cutter, got away from the anchorage.

Lord Bridport, pursuant to his instructions, proceeded straight for Ushant, and in two days arrived off the island. Thence he stretched across to Cape Clear, and on the 9th looked into Bantry bay, but of course saw nothing of the enemy; although, had the fleet sailed on Christmas-day, or even the day after, the British admiral would probably have given the French admiral something else to complain of than bad weather. On the 10th the British fleet, as already mentioned, chased unsuccessfully the Révolution and Fraternité. On the 11th, in the morning,

Lord Bridport steered to the southward; and at noon, which was about the time that the second division of the French fleet entered Brest, the Channel fleet was in latitude 40° 29' north, and longitude 12° 6' west. On the same afternoon the Unicorn and Doris frigates joined, with information of their having been chased on the 8th by a division of the French fleet. On the 13th, at noon, about the time that the same division reached Brest, the British admiral was in latitude 48° 29' north, and longitude 6° 25' west, or about 19 leagues to the westward of Ushant.

On the 19th, having ascertained that the last of the Brest ships had returned into port, Lord Bridport, then being in latitude 47° 31' north, and longitude 6° 47' west, detached, as he had been ordered, Rear-admiral Parker, with the Prince-George, Namur, Irresistible, Orion, Colossus, and Thalia frigate, to Gibraltar, and continued, with his fleet by successive reinforcements now numbering 12 sail of the line, to cruise for a few days longer in the vicinity of Ushant. The admiral then, having had several of his ships damaged by the severity of the weather, steered for Torbay. After remaining a few hours only at that anchorage, Lord Bridport sailed on the 31st for Spithead, and arrived there on the 3d of February.

Having thus shown in what way the fleets of Vice-admiral Colpoys and Admiral Lord Bridport had missed the French fleet, we shall merely add, that the principal losses which the latter sustained by capture, arose from the diligence and activity of a 64-gun ship and four or five frigates, part of which, on the 29th of December, were lying in the harbour of Cork.

It had almost escaped us that, in the latter end of the year 1796, France and England, at the invitation of the latter, had, what the Indians call, a *talk* on the subject of peace. Lord Malmesbury, the commissioner on the part of England, arrived at Paris on the 22d of October; and on the 24th the negotiations were opened between his lordship and M. de Lacroix; but the parties split upon the first proposal, a reciprocal restoration of what had been lost and taken by the respective belligerents. Had each party been sincere in the wish for peace, it is probable that this and other difficulties would have been got over; but, that not being the case, Lord Malmesbury quitted the French capital on the 22d of December, and the French territory in a day or two afterwards.

On the 3d of March, Lord Howe still continuing indisposed, Lord Bridport with 15 sail of the line, again quitted Spithead, on a cruise off Brest. Having ascertained that all was quiet in the port, and that there was no probability of the fleet's sailing for some weeks, the British admiral, on the 30th, returned to Spithead. A squadron of observation was now deemed sufficient to send off Brest; and accordingly, on the 6th of April, Rear-admiral Sir Roger Curtis, with nine sail of the line, proceeded upon that service.

On the 15th of April Lord Bridport, to whom Lord Howe had just resigned the command of the Channel fleet, and who was then with the fleet at Spithead, threw out the signal to prepare for sea; when, instead of weighing the anchor, the seamen of the Royal-George ran up the shrouds and gave three cheers: a proceeding which, from the awful responses it produced through the fleet, at once betrayed it as the signal of disaffection. The captains and officers of the different ships were astonished, nay, almost astounded, at this sudden act of disobedience, and, as may be supposed, did their utmost to persuade the men to return to their duty; but all their efforts were vain. The spirit of mutiny had taken deep root in the breasts of the seamen, and, from the apparent organization of the plan, seemed to be the result of far more reflection than for which the wayward mind of a jack-tar is usually given credit. The subject is a melancholy one, and one which we would fain pass over; but historical impartiality forbids any such fastidiousness. At the same time, the subject not being an international one, nor one of which the details have acquired any permanent interest, we may, consistently with our plan, abridge the account.

It appears that, in the latter end of February, Lord Howe, while on shore indisposed, received sundry petitions, as from the seamen at Portsmouth, all praying for an advance of wages; but that, none of the petitions being signed, and all dated and, with the exception of four or five, written by one hand, no notice was taken of them. Lord Howe subsequently directed Rear-admiral Lord Hugh Seymour to ascertain whether or not any discontent did really exist in the fleet. The reply was so favourable, that his lordship considered the whole plot as the work of some incendiary, and, towards the end of March, sent the different petitions to the first lord of the admiralty, Earl Spencer. The seamen, not aware that the papers they had transmitted were looked upon as forgeries, could only attribute the silence of Lord Howe to a disregard of their complaints. In this state were matters, on the fleet's refusal to obey Lord Bridgport's signal to prepare for sea.

On the next day, April 16, the respective ships' companies appointed two of their number to act as delegates; and the place selected for their deliberations was the state, or flag-officer's cabin of the Queen-Charlotte. On the 17th every man in the fleet was sworn to support the cause in which he had embarked. Ropes were then reeved, *in terrorem*, at the fore yard-arms of each ship: and the seamen ordered on shore such of the officers as, in their opinion, had been guilty of oppression. On the same day the delegates, 32 in number, drew up and signed two petitions, one to the parliament, the other to the admiralty. Both petitions were couched in respectful language. That to the admiralty, which was the fullest, prayed, that the wages of the seamen should be increased; that their provisions should be raised to the weight of 16 ounces to the pound,* and be of a better quality; that their measures should be the same as those used in the commercial trade; that vegetables, instead of flour, should be served with fresh beef; that the sick should be better attended to, and their necessaries not be embezzled; and that the men might have, on returning from sea, a short leave to visit their families.

On the 18th a committee of the board of admiralty, consisting of Lord Spencer and Lord Arden, Rear-admiral Young, and Mr. Marsden, the second secretary, arrived at Portsmouth; and in answer to the petition of the seamen, declared, that the board would recommend the king to propose to parliament an increase of their wages in the following proportions: four shillings per month, in addition, to the wages of petty-officers and seamen, three, to the wages of ordinary seamen, and two, to the wages of landmen; and that the board had resolved, that seamen, wounded in action, should be continued in pay until their wounds were healed, or, until, being declared unserviceable, they should be pensioned, or received into Greenwich hospital.

To this, on the following day, the seamen, through their delegates, transmitted a reply, urging, that there never existed more than two orders of men in the navy, able and ordinary, and that, therefore, the distinction between ordinary and landmen was new: and humbly proposing, that the old regulations should be adhered to, that the wages of able seamen should be raised to one shilling a day, and the wages of petty-officers and ordinary seamen in the same proportion, and that the marines, while serving on board, should have their pay augmented in the same proportion as that of ordinary seamen; and further, that the Greenwich pension should be raised to ten pounds per annum; that, to maintain the additional fund, every merchant-seaman should thereafter pay one shilling instead of sixpence a month, and that the regulation should extend to the seamen of the East India company. The seamen then repeated their former demands, for an increased weight and measure, and an improved quality, of provisions, and for a supply of vegetables, instead of flour, with fresh beef; concluding with a declaration that, until their grievances, including those of particular ships, should be redressed, and an act of indemnity passed, they were determined not to lift an anchor.

On the next day, the 20th, the admiralty-committee sent, through Lord Bridport, a letter to the seamen, agreeing to the increase of wages demanded, and to the full weight and measure

* The seaman's pound, according to a government regulation, was not more than 14 ounces, the remaining two being retained by the purser, to allow for waste, leakage, &c. A similar reduction occurred in the measures; and the purser received no other pay than the difference, if any, between the real and the assumed loss by waste, leakage, &c.

of provisions, and promising pardon, but taking no notice of any increase in the Greenwich pensions, or any additional allowance of vegetables when in port. On the same, or the following day, the seamen returned a reply, expressing, in very grateful terms, their thanks for what had been granted them, but persisting to declare that, until the flour in port should be removed, the vegetables and pensions augmented, the grievances of private ships redressed, an act of parliament passed, and the king's pardon to the whole fleet granted, the men would not lift an anchor; unless, indeed, as had been always excepted, the enemy's fleet should put to sea.

On the 21st, in the hope to remove these remaining impediments in the way of a reconciliation, Vice-admirals Sir Alan Gardner and Colpoys, and Rear-admiral Pole, went on board the Queen-Charlotte, and had a conference with the delegates. The latter, however, assured the admirals that no arrangement would be considered as final, until sanctioned by the king and parliament, and guaranteed by a proclamation of pardon. This bold avowal so incensed Admiral Gardner, that he seized one of the delegates by the collar, and swore he would have them all hanged, together with every fifth man in the fleet.

On the return of the offended delegates to their respective ships, those of the Royal-George resolved to summon a meeting on board of their ship, and immediately hoisted the preconcerted signal of the red or bloody flag; a signal which, owing to its usual sanguinary report, alarmed all the well-disposed in the fleet. Instantly, on the display of that signal, the officers of the Royal George, ashamed to see it flying with Lord Bridport's flag, hauled down the latter. The seamen of the fleet now proceeded to load all their guns; ordered watches to be kept, the same as at sea, and put their ships in a complete state of defence. They also prevented their officers from going on shore; but, beyond that, neither offered any violence, nor put any constraint upon them.

On the 22d, having become somewhat pacified, the seamen caused two letters to be written; one to the lords of the admiralty, in which they stated the cause of their conduct on the two preceding days; the other to Lord Bridport, in which they styled him their father and friend, and disclaimed offering him any intentional offence. This induced Lord Bridport on the following day, the 23d, to go on board the Royal-George, the crew of which immediately rehoisted his flag. The admiral, then at the close of an energetic address, informed the men that he had brought with him a redress of all their grievances, and the king's pardon for the offenders. After a short deliberation, these offers were accepted, and every man returned with cheerfulness to his duty.

All disputes were now considered as settled, and the fleet dropped down to St.-Helen's, except the London, Minotaur, and Marlborough. The crews of the two latter refused to go to sea under their present officers, and the London had been directed to remain in company with them, to afford to Vice-admiral Colpoys an opportunity of exerting his influence in restoring the disobedient ships' companies to a sense of their duty. We omitted to state, that on the second day of the mutiny, when the boats of the Royal-George and Queen-Charlotte were visiting the different ships, Vice-admiral Colpoys refused to allow the delegates to come on board the London, telling them it was their duty to wait until the board of admiralty had decided upon their complaints. In the mean while the crew of the London were encouraging the delegates to enter the ship; but, as the marines had not yet been seduced from their duty, that could have been successfully opposed, if an officer had not just then arrived from Lord Bridport, directing the vice-admiral to permit the boats' crews to come on board.

A foul wind unfortunately detained the ships at St.-Helen's until the morning of the 7th of May; when, having just received intelligence that the French fleet had dropped into the other harbour of Brest preparatory to sailing, Lord Bridport made the signal to weigh and put to sea; but which signal every ship in the fleet, as on the 15th of the preceding month, refused to obey. As a reason for this second act of disobedience, the seamen alleged the silence that government had observed respecting their complaints; by which they were led to suspect that the promised redress of grievances would be withheld. This idea was forcibly impressed on the minds of the seamen, by the contents of some seditious hand-bills, which had been extensively circulated throughout the fleet.

At about 1 P.M. it was discovered on board the London at Spithead, that boats were pulling to and fro among the ships at St.-Helen's, and that yard-ropes were reeved in the same manner as on the 17th of the preceding month. Convinced that a renewal of the mutiny had taken place, Vice-admiral Colpoys addressed the crew of the London, and asked them if they had any grievances remaining. They replied, they had not. He then, as a measure of security, ordered the seamen below, and the officers and marines to arm themselves. On observing the boats of the delegates from the fleet at St.-Helen's approaching the Marlborough, the London's people below began to unlash the second-deck guns, and to point them aft and up the hatchways. The officers were immediately ordered by the vice-admiral to fire on those that were forcing their way on deck. This was done; and five men were mortally, and six others badly wounded. The marines throwing down their arms, the seamen now rushed in crowds up the hatchways; and the vice-admiral, unwilling to spill more blood where no good could arise, ordered the officers to cease firing.

The seamen now called for and seized the first lieutenant, Mr. Peter Turner Bover, and were proceeding to hang him, when

Vice-admiral Colpoys, interfering, told them that Lieutenant Bover had acted in conformity to his, the Vice-admiral's, orders, grounded upon instructions received from the admiralty. These instructions the seamen, whom the delegates from the fleet had now joined, demanded and obtained. They then ordered Vice-admiral Colpoys, Captain Edward Griffith, and the whole of the officers, to their respective cabins. Matters remained in this unhappy state until the 11th, when the crew of the London expressed a wish that their admiral and captain should go on shore. Vice-admiral Colpoys and Captain Griffith accordingly did so, accompanied by the Reverend Samuel Cole, the ship's chaplain.

During these four days of renewed discontent, many captains and other officers, whose general conduct on board their ships was of an oppressive nature, or deemed so, were unceremoniously turned on shore. At length, on the 14th, Lord Howe arrived from London, with plenary powers to settle all matters in dispute; bringing with him an act of parliament, which had been passed on the 9th, agreeably to the wishes of the seamen; also a proclamation, granting the king's pardon to all who should immediately return on their duty.

On the 15th the delegates from the several ships landed at Portsmouth, and proceeded to the governor's house; whence, after partaking of some refreshment, they marched in processions to the sally-port, and there, accompanied by Lord and Lady Howe, and several officers and persons of distinction, embarked on board the men-of-war's barges. Having visited the ships at St.-Helen's, the party proceeded to Spithead, where the squadron under Rear-admiral Sir Roger Curtis had just anchored from a cruise. The seamen of the latter had manifested symptoms of disaffection; but, on a representation of what had taken place, they became reconciled to their officers. At 7 P.M. the boats returned to Portsmouth, and the delegates carried Lord Howe on their shoulders to the governor's house.

Of the officers that had been turned on shore by the seamen, some were recalled, and nearly the whole of the remainder tacitly received back. A few of the captains, however, refused to resume the command of their ships, and were, in consequence, superseded by others. Affairs being amicably adjusted, the flag of disaffection was struck; and on the succeeding day, the 16th, at 10 A.M., Lord Bridport, with his fleet amounting to 15 sail of the line, got under way, but, the wind suddenly veering to the southward, again came to an anchor. On the morning of the 17th the fleet again weighed; and, although the wind was extremely scant, got round the ledge before noon, and finally to sea.

On arriving off Brest, the admiral found the French fleet in port, and likely to remain there. In consequence of this, the Channel fleet, now augmented to 21 sail of the line, continued its cruise to the westward, Sir Edward Pellew, with the Indefatigable, and two or three other frigates, being left cruising off the harbour. By way of preventing Sir Edward from repeating his reconnoitring visits to the port, the admiral in Brest had ordered Commodore Ganteaume, with the Mont-Blanc 74, Brave rasé, 40-gun frigates Romaine and Immortalité, 36-gun frigates, Précieuse and Coquille, corvette Lévrette, and three armed luggers, to quit the harbour and lay at single anchor in Bertheaume bay. By this French squadron the Indefatigable and her consorts were frequently chased, but not to any distance; nor can we find that any shots were ever exchanged. The French accounts tell us, however, that M. Ganteaume got praised by the directory for having had several engagements with the enemy's light squadrons, commanded by Sir John Borlase Warren and Sir Edward Pellew; whom he is represented to have chased from the coast, and thereby to have favoured the arrival of several convoys.*

Lord Bridport had been ordered, very properly in the present posture of affairs, to keep as much at sea as possible. Hence, during the summer months, the fleet returned to port, only to refit or revictual, and then was presently out again. The seamen of the fleet, with very few exceptions, obeyed officers, and conducted themselves with propriety. But, at Plymouth, the men belonging to most of the ships evinced a mutinous disposition, and, in some instances, proceeded to a great length. Finally, however, the seamen at this port became satisfied with the terms that had been accepted by their brethren at Portsmouth, and tranquillity was restored. The inactive state of the Brest fleet, during the remainder of this year, afforded to the seamen belonging to the Channel fleet no opportunity of evincing, how little their loyalty and courage had been affected by the recent unhappy events.

The fact that, in the latter end of June, owing to the junction of the ships from Lorient and Rochefort, and the great exertions of the French minister of marine, Truguet, there were at anchor in the road of Brest 19 full-armed sail of the line, besides a great many others armed en flûte for the reception of troops, renders it extraordinary that no effort should have been made to get the Brest fleet to sea; especially, when it was the intention of the French government, by the aid of the Dutch fleet, and more than treble the quantity of troops they had previously employed, to attempt, a second time, the invasion of Ireland. General Hoche, who was again to be the commander-in-chief, had gone to Holland to inspect Admiral De Winter's fleet lying in the Texel, as well as the troops under General Daendels, that were to embark on board of it. He had also obtained from the chiefs of the Batavian republic funds, sufficient not only to pay the troops,

* Victoires et Conquêtes, tome viii., p. 255.

but to enable him to transmit a considerable sum of money to M. Truguet, to be applied as an advance to the seamen of the Brest fleet. Nothing more, in short, was required, than to embark the troops and set sail, each fleet from its respective port; when a convulsion at Paris marred all.

Without going into particulars, we need only state, that the executive directory and legislative body quarrelled; and that the latter, gaining the ascendancy, felt itself bound, regardless of consequences, to undo all that had been done by the former. On the 16th of July the able minister of marine, Vice-admiral Truguet, was removed, and his place filled by M. Pléville-le-Peley, a man who at least had the modesty to own, that he was ignorant of the duties of his office. By the directions of his masters, the new minister disarmed the Brest fleet, discharged the seamen, and actually sold by public auction several frigates and corvettes belonging to the republic. This blight upon the French marine lasted until the directory, on the 4th of September, regained their influence in the state. An order now issued to re-arm all the ships; but, as Fresh seamen were to be raised, and the ships sold to private individuals purchased back, much time elapsed, and an enormous expense was incurred, before the Brest fleet could be restored to the state in which it was on the 1st of July. Ere the utmost exertions of the French government could accomplish that object, the year 1797 had run itself out.

The year, however, had not passed away without a second effort on the part of Great Britain to obtain for Europe the blessings of peace. On the 30th of May Lord Malmesbury proceeded for that purpose to Lisle, but, after a negotiation purposely protracted by the French directory, returned home on the 20th of September without having succeeded in his mission.

At the close of the preceding year, we left the Spanish fleet in Carthagena, and Admiral Sir John Jervis at anchor in the Tagus with 11 sail of the line, exclusive of one 80-gun ship, the Gibraltar, bound to Plymouth for repairs, one 74, the Zealous, undergoing a repair at Lisbon, and one 64, the St.-Albans, waiting to proceed to England with convoy.

On the 18th of January the British admiral stood for the mouth of the river with his 11 line-of-battle ships, having, for his first object, the escort of some Brazil merchantmen and Portuguese men-of-war to a safe latitude, and, for his next, a junction with the long-expected reinforcement from England at the appointed rendezvous off Cape St.-Vincent.

Comparatively small as Sir John's force was, a new, or rather the repetition of an old, disaster reduced it still more. At 7 h. 30 m. P.M. the 98-gun ship St.-George, Captain Shuldham Peard, having previously run foul of a Portuguese frigate and carried away the latter's jib-boom and fore topgallantmast, got aground upon the South Cachop. At 9 P.M., the ship striking very hard, the tiller was broken and the rudder unshipped. The St.-George's fore and mizen masts were now cut away to ease her; but, notwithstanding every exertion on the part of her officers and crew, the St.-George remained aground until the evening of the 20th; when, chiefly by the aid of the St.-Albans, she again got afloat, and was obliged, of course, to return to Lisbon to repair. With his remaining 10 sail, the British admiral proceeded to sea, accompanied by the Portuguese convoy.

On the 6th of February, while Sir John, having parted from the Portuguese ships, was on his return to his station off Cape St.-Vincent, the five sail of the line* and one frigate, which had been detached to him from the Channel fleet, effected their junction. Thus reinforced, the admiral had under his command the

Gun-ship		
100	Victory	Admiral (b.) Sir John Jervis, K.B. Captain Robert Calder. Captain George Grey.
	Britannia	Vice-adm. (b.) Charles Thompson. Captain Thomas Foley.
98	Barfleur	Vice-adm. (b.) the Hon. Wm. Waldegrave. Captain James Richard Dacres.
	Prince-George	Rear-adm. (r.) William Parker. Captain John Irwin.
	Blenheim	Captain Thomas Lenox Frederick.
90	Namur	Captain James Hawkins Whitshed.
74	Captain	Commodore Horatio Nelson.† Captain Ralph Willett Miller.
	Goliath	Captain Sir Charles H. Knowles, Bart.
	Excellent	Captain Cuthbert Collingwood.
	Orion	Captain Sir James Saumarez.
	Colossus	Captain George Murray.
	Egmont	Captain John Sutton.
	Culloden	Captain Thomas Troubridge.
	Irresistible	Captain George Martin.
64	Diadem	Captain George Henry Towry.

The frigates, by the time some had joined and others parted company, remained as follows:

Gun-frig.		
38	Minerve	Captain George Cockburn.
32	Lively	Captain Lord Garlies.
	Niger	Captain Edward James Foote.
	Southampton	Captain James Macnamara.
Slps	Bonne-Citoyenne	Captain Charles Lindsay.
	Raven	Captain William Prowse.
Cut.	Fox	Lieutenant John Gibson.

It so happened, that the accession of these five ships did no more than make up the number which the admiral had with him,

* See p. 22. Captain Brenton (vol. ii., p. 150) by mistake says six.

† Did not come on board until after the Minerve joined company.

when he sent home requesting an addition to his force; and a sixth, in the list of serious accidents that befell this fleet, very nearly deprived him of the use of another of his ships. Early on the morning of the 12th, when quite dark, as the ships were tacking in succession, the Colossus, keeping her wind a little too long, compelled the Culloden to bear up to clear her. The former then suddenly bore up also, and the two ships ran foul of each other. To the Colossus the concussion did but slight injury; merely staving some of her upper works, and carrying away her fore topgallantmast. But the Culloden fared differently. The knee and cheeks of her head, the head-rails, larboard cat-head, bowsprit-cap, bumpkins, jib-boom, and fore topgallantmast were entirely carried away, and the bowsprit itself was badly sprung.

This was so serious an injury, that, under any other circumstances, the Culloden might with propriety have steered for the nearest port. But Captain Troubridge prized too highly the chance of distinction likely soon to be afforded him; and the Culloden, after the partial repairs which the utmost exertions of her active crew could give her, was, to the surprise of all who had witnessed her appearance at daylight, reported, in the afternoon, again ready for service.

Sir John Jervis, with his fifteen sail of the line, persevered in working up, against a strong south-east wind, to the neighbourhood of his rendezvous; not doubting that he should there gain a sight, or at least hear tidings, of the Spanish fleet; whose force, he knew, could not well be less than 19, and might amount to 30, sail of the line. On the 13th, in the morning, the British frigate Minerve, Captain George Cockburn, bearing the broad pendant of Commodore Nelson, and having on board Sir Gilbert Elliot, late Viceroy of Corsica, Lieutenant-colonel Drinkwater, and others of the viceroy's suite, came into the fleet with the intelligence, that on the 11th, soon after quitting Gibraltar, she had been chased by two Spanish line-of-battle ships, and that afterwards, when in the mouth of the Straits, she got sight of the Spanish fleet; of whose strength and probable destination Commodore Nelson communicated some important information.

Before sunset the signals were made for the British fleet to prepare for battle, and to keep in close order during the night; at intervals of which the signal-guns of the Spaniards were distinctly heard. At 2 h. 30 m. A.M. the Portuguese frigate Carlotta, commanded by Captain Campbell (a native of Scotland, we believe), spoke the Victory, and gave information that the Spanish fleet was only five leagues to windward. While the night-glasses of the British fleet are handing about, and every eye is straining for a glimpse of the enemy, we will endeavour to trace his route, from the day of his departure from port.

The grand fleet of Spain, under the command of Admiral

Don Josef de Cordova (by whom Admiral Langara, had been recently superseded), in the Santisima Trinidad four-decker, had sailed from Carthagena on the 1st of the month. It was composed of the

Gun-ship		Gun-ship		Gun-ship	
130	Santisima-Trinidad,	74	Atalante,	74	San-Firmin,
112	Concepcion,	74	Bahama,	74	San-Fsco.-de-Paula,
112	Conde-de-Regla,	74	Conquistador	74	San-Genaro,
112	Mexicano,	74	Firme,	74	San-Ildefonso,
112	Principe-de-Asturias,	74	Glorioso,	74	San-Ju.-Nepomuceno,
112	Salvador-del-Mundo,	74	Oriente,	74	San-Pablo,
112	San-Josef,	74	Pelayo,	74	San-Ysidro,
80	Neptuno,	74	San-Antonio,	74	Soberano,
80	San-Nicholas,	74	San-Domingo,	74	Terrible,

exclusive of twelve 34-gun frigates and one brig-corvette, but in the names of which scarcely two accounts agree.

Some gun-boats, and about 70 transports having on board two battalions of guards and a Swiss regiment, besides a great quantity of ammunition and other military stores, all of which they had brought from Barcelona and were conveying to the camp of San-Roque, had quitted port along with the fleet.

On the 5th, at daylight, this numerically powerful fleet passed Gibraltar, and, on the afternoon of the same day the Neptuno, Bahama, Terrible, and the Guadalupa frigate, escorted the gun-boats and transports into Algesiras, where the troops and stores were disembarked. One of the two-deckers immediately rejoined the fleet; and, in a day or two afterwards, the two other line-of-battle ships stood out for the same purpose, but the fleet had made sail. While in search of the latter, these two ships fell in with and chased the Minerve, as already related.

The primary destination of the Spanish admiral was Cadiz; but the strong easterly gale, which had quickened his passage through the Straits, soon blew right in his teeth, and drove his ships considerably to the westward of their port. The rumour was, that this fleet, if not blockaded in Cadiz, as it no doubt would have been, intended afterwards, if not stopped by the way, to proceed to Brest, there to join the French and (if another stubborn *if* could be got over) Dutch fleets; and that then, with this assembled force, England was to be invaded.

On the evening of the 13th, while still buffeting with adverse winds, the look-out frigates of the Spanish fleet, now consisting of 25 sail of the line, 11 frigates, and one brig, got sight of some of the British ships; but the latter, being taken for part of a convoy, excited very little attention. As the night advanced, the Spaniards busied themselves in making the most of a sudden favourable change of wind, and, without much regard to order, were crowding sail to get near the land.

The morning of the 14th, that disastrous day to the Spaniards, broke dark and hazy upon the two fleets. The fleet of the British was formed in two compact divisions, standing on the starboard tack with the wind at west by south, Cape St.-Vincent bearing east by north, distant eight leagues. At about 6 h. 30 m. A.M. the Culloden made the signal for five sail in the south-west by south; and the frigates Lively and Niger (the latter of which had joined at 5 A.M., after having kept company with the Spanish fleet for some days) presently confirmed the same; adding, that the strangers were by the wind, on the starboard tack. The Bonne-Citoyenne sloop was now directed to reconnoitre. At 8 h. 15 m. A.M. the admiral made the signal for the fleet to form in close order, and in a few minutes afterwards, repeated that of the preceding evening, to prepare for battle.

At 9 h. 30 m. A.M. the Culloden, Blenheim, and Prince-George proceeded by signal to chase in the south by west quarter; and, upon the Bonne-Citoyenne's signalling, at 9 h. 55 m. that she saw eight sail in that direction, the Irresistible, Colossus, and Orion were directed to add themselves to the former. At about 10 A.M. the chasing ships had advanced so far ahead, as to be seen, and, as we learn from the Spanish accounts, made out to be ships of the line, by the Spanish reconnoitring frigates Santa-Catalina and Preciosa.

It was then, and not till then, that the Spaniards recovered from their delusion, as to the ships in sight being part of a convoy. But they fell into another. An American, who had passed through the British fleet on the 4th, previously to Rear-admiral Parker's junction, and while the Culloden was absent in chase, afterwards spoke the Spanish admiral, and informed him, that Sir John Jervis had with him, as was true enough, but nine sail of the line. The partial view obtained of the British fleet through the intervening fog, especially before the ships had extended themselves into a single line, tended to confirm the statement; and the Spaniards were in high glee at the thought of the triumphant entry they should make into the harbour of Cadiz.

Since 9 A.M. 20 sail of the line, and 31 sail together, had been counted from the Victory's mast-head. At 10 A.M. the Minerve made a signal to nearly the same effect. At 10 h. 15m. A.M. the Bonne-Citoyenne announced by signal, that 20 of the strange ships in the south-west by south were of the line. At 10 h. 40 m. A.M., owing to the weather becoming more hazy, Captain Lindsay could discover but 16 to be of the line; but at 11 A.M. he made the signal for 25.*

By this time the fog having cleared away, had left the two fleets at liberty to form an estimate, as far as counting numbers could afford it, of their relative strength. What was the surprise of the Spaniards, at seeing 15, instead of nine sail of the line; and those 15 ships, formed in two close lines, which steadily

* So stated in the Bonne-Citoyenne's log, and except in the substitution of the Victory's for the Bonne-Citoyenne's time, in the Victory's log, and in Sir John Jervis's letter; at least in that published in the London Gazette; but stated to be twenty-seven sail of the line, both in what purports to be a copy of that letter, inserted at p. 157, vol. ii. Of "Brenton's Naval History," and in the author's account of the action, as given at p. 151 of the same volume.

advanced to cut off the ships that, owing either to mismanagement, or a blind confidence in their numerical strength, had been allowed to separate from the main body. The ships of the latter, grouped together in what may be called a square, were running under all sail, with the wind on the starboard quarter; while the leewardmost ships were close hauled on the same tack, striving hard to effect a junction with their companions, in time to frustrate, if possible, the evident design off the British admiral.

As, besides the object of cutting of the six detached sail of the line, it was now an equally important one, to be ready to receive the 19 (one with her fore topmast gone), bearing down from to-windward, and the advanced ships of which, at a few minutes before 11 A.M., began wearing and trimming in succession on the larboard tack, the British admiral, at 11 A.M., ordered his fleet to form in line of battle ahead and astern of the Victory, as most convenient, and to steer south-south-west; a course that kept the enemy's lee or detached division, consisting of one three-decker with a vice-admiral's flag, five two-deckers, and a few frigates, upon the lee or larboard bow.

The advanced position of the Culloden in the morning's chase conferred upon her the honour of being the leading ship in the line about to be formed; which line, when the whole had fallen into their stations, was composed of the following ships, standing close hauled on the starboard tack, in the order in which they are named: Culloden, Blenheim (rather to windward), Prince-George, Orion, Colossus (to windward), Irresistible, Victory, Egmont, Goliath, Barfleur, Britannia, Namur, Captain, Diadem, Excellent.

Thus formed, the British fleet steered straight for the opening, still wide, but gradually narrowing, between the two divisions of the Spanish fleet: the leedwardmost of which divisions, as if to avoid the British line in its approach, had just bore away to nearly south-east by south; while the weather division, or the advanced portion of it, in very irregular order (several of the ships doubling upon each other, and some lying three abreast), was steering about north-north-east, with the apparent intention, after having passed the British line on the contrary tack, to round its rear, and thereby effect the wished-for junction.

At 12 h. 28 m. A.M. the Victory and the other ships of the fleet hoisted their colours; and in the next minute the signal No. 40 was made, to pass through the enemy's line, the British ships still steering about south-south-west, with the wind, as before, at west by south. About this time five out of the six line-of-battle ships, in the Spanish lee division, observing that the British admiral by keeping his wind had no immediate design upon them, hauled sharp up on the starboard tack, as if intending to weather the whole British fleet. The sixth Spanish ship, a two-decker, continued under a crowd of sail steering to the south-east, and soon disappeared.

At 11 h. 31 m. A.M., having arrived abreast of the van-ships of the Spanish weather division, the Culloden, by signal (No. 5) from the admiral, commenced a cannonade with her starboard guns, and received a fire in return from such ships of the Spanish weather division, as could open their batteries without firing into a friend. This engagement between the two vans, we have endeavoured to illustrate by the following diagram:

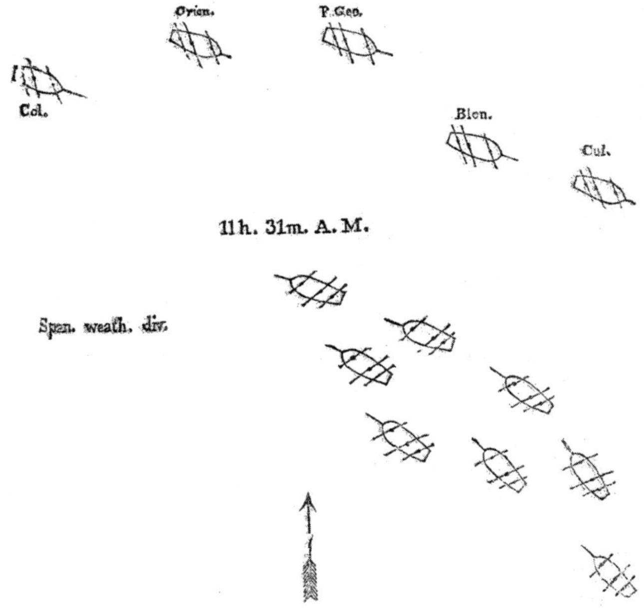

About the time that the British van-ship opened her fire in the manner above stated, two Spanish three-deckers and a two-decker, from the weather division, stood across the head of the British line, and joined the one three, and four two deckers on the starboard tack; thus augmenting the Spanish lee division (excluding the fugitive ship) to eight, and reducing the weather division to 16 sail of the line.

At 8 m. past noon, having passed the sternmost of the Spanish weather ships, the Culloden, by signal No. 80, tacked, and in six minutes was followed by the Blenheim, who, like her leader, had been distantly engaged on the starboard side. In ten minutes afterwards the Prince-George tacked, but had fallen so much to leeward as to point nearly towards the centre of the remainder of the fleet, as it kept advancing on the starboard tack. A little before the Prince-George tacked, the Spanish lee division, as if it had received some directions from the two three, and one two decker that were then joining it from to-windward, and which we take to have been the Principe-de-Asturias, Conde-de-Regla, and

Oriente, put about on the larboard tack, and stood after the Prince-George, or rather, towards the head of that part of the British line still on the starboard tack.

The Orion tacked, next in succession to the Prince-George; and the Colossus, as soon as she had arrived in the wake of the former, prepared to do the same, but, while in stays, had her fore yard and foretopsail yard shot away in the slings, and her fore topmast shot away a little above the cap. Thus disabled from tacking, the Colossus was obliged to wear, and, just as she had got her head to the eastward, was menaced with a raking broadside from the leading three-decker of the Spanish lee division. This manifestation of an attack upon her disabled companion, induced the Orion, in a very gallant manner, to back her main topsail and lay by to cover her. The Spanish ship, however, made no such attack, and the Orion pressed on to the assistance of the van; the ships of which had been directed, by signal No. 34, to alter course a point to starboard, and directly afterwards, by No. 40, to pass through the enemy's line.

The four next British ships, coming up in line on the starboard tack, were the Irresistible, Victory, Egmont, and Goliath. The first of these, having fired her starboard guns at the enemy's weather division, became exposed to the successive fire of the two leading three-deckers of the lee division. After discharging three or four broadsides in return, the Irresistible stood on a little, and then tacked to support the van.

Meditating, now, a bold manœuvre, the Spanish vice-admiral steered to cut the British line ahead of the commander-in-chief; but the Victory was too rapid in her advance, and forced the Spanish three-decker to tack close under her lee; raking her, while in stays, with destructive effect. This three-decker, which was, we believe, the Principe-de-Asturias, now bore up, in utter confusion; as, after exchanging a few broadsides with the Egmont and Goliath in passing, did the second three-decker, followed by all the six remaining ships of the lee division, except the Oriente: which ship gallantly kept on upon the larboard tack, and, passing to leeward of the British line unobserved in the smoke, succeeded, after the exchange of a few shot with the Lively and one or two of the other British frigates in the rear, in joining her van. This interesting period of the action, we have endeavoured to render more intelligible by the following diagram:

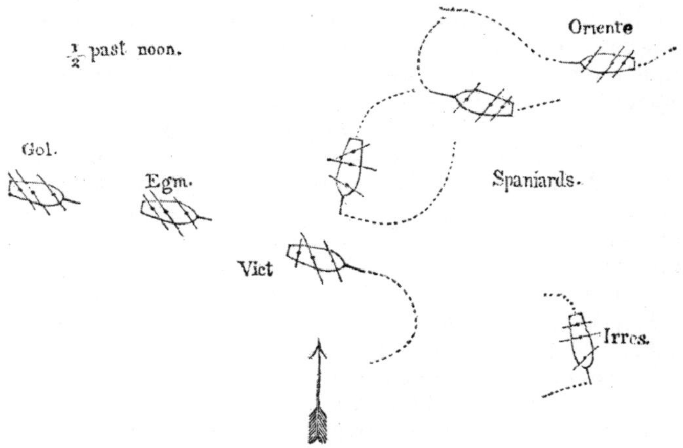

At about 1 h. P.M., just as the rearmost ship of that part of the British line, which was still on the starboard tack, had advanced so far ahead, as to leave an open sea to leeward of the Spanish weather division, then passing in the contrary direction, the advanced ships of the latter, as the last effort to join their lee division, bore up together. Scarcely was the movement made, ere it caught the attention of one, who was as quick in foreseeing the consequences of its success, as he was ready, in obedience to the spirit, if not the letter, of a signal just made, in devising the means for its failure. That signal (No. 41) had been hoisted on board the Victory at 51 m. past noon, and directed the ships of the fleet "to take suitable stations for mutual support, and engage the enemy, as coming up in succession."*

Commodore Nelson, accordingly, directed Captain Miller to wear the Captain. The latter was soon round; and, passing between the Diadem and Excellent, ran athwart the bows of the Spanish ships as far as the sixth from the rear, reckoning the outside or leewardmost ships. The sixth or most advanced ship was known, from her four tiers of ports, to be the Santisima-Trinidad; and four of the remaining five ships were the San-Josef, Salvador-del-Mundo, (three-deckers), San-Nicolas, and San-Ysidro. The fifth ship was a three-decker, and, we believe, the Mexicano; but the exact stations of any of these

* That the Captain wore out of the line in compliance with any signal is, we know, contrary to received opinion; but the following stands as an entry in the log-book of a flag-ship then at no great distance from her. "At 1, Sir John Jervis made the signal for the English fleet to form line as most convenient. On this, the Captain pressed all sail from her station of sailing, and stood on and fell into our van ahead of us." Although the signal here specified was No. 31 instead of 41, there is every reason to suppose that the latter, the first signal not having been made since 11 A.M., was the signal to which the entry had reference.

ships we are unable to state. Indeed, all the Spanish ships were huddled together in a very irregular manner, in some cases three or four deep, and must have suffered greatly, as their disabled appearance soon testified, not only from the fire of their opponents, but from the fire of each other.

At about 1 h. 30 m. the Captain opened her fire upon the Santisima-Trinidad and the ships near her; with the rearmost of which the Culloden, about ten minutes before, had recommenced firing. Frustrated thus by the spirited conduct of the Captain and Culloden, and seeing the near approach of the Blenheim, Prince-George, and other ships, the Spanish admiral gave up the design of running to leeward of the British fleet, and, making the signal to that effect, hauled up on the larboard tack.

At about 2 P.M. the Culloden had stretched so far ahead, as to cover the Captain from the heavy fire poured upon her by the Spanish four-decker and her companion, as they hauled up and brought their broadsides to bear. Of the respite thus afforded to her, the Captain took immediate advantage; replenishing her lockers with shot, and splicing and repairing her running rigging. Shortly afterwards the Blenheim, passing also to windward of the Captain, afforded her a second respite, which was taken advantage of as before. The two more immediate opponents of the Captain and Culloden had been the San-Ysidro and Salvador-del-Mundo: these, having already lost some of their topmasts, and being otherwise in a crippled state, the Blenheim, by a few of her heavy broadsides, sent staggering astern, to be cannonaded afresh by the Prince-George, Orion, and other advancing ships.

The Victory, soon after her heavy fire upon the Spanish three-decker whom she had caught so opportunely in stays under her lee, put about on the larboard tack, and, followed by the Barfleur, Namur, Egmont, and Goliath (the two latter partially disabled and dropping astern), pointed to windward of the Spanish fleet. At 1 h. 5 m. P.M. Sir John directed the Minerve, by signal, to take the disabled Colossus in tow; and at 1 h. 19 m. P.M., arriving abreast of the Excellent, who was in the rear of, what may now be called, the lee division of the British fleet, the Victory made the signal (No. 85), to come to the wind on the larboard tack.

In immediate compliance with this signal, the Excellent hauled sharp up, and at 2 h. 15 m., having reached a station ahead of the weather division, was ordered by the Victory, to pass through the enemy's line. Such was the expression of the signal (No. 40), but line there was none. The Spanish fleet, indeed, from its increased disorder, now evinced, more clearly than ever, that *sauve qui peut* was the only directing principle.

At 2 h. 26 m. the Excellent, having been directed by signal (No. 91) to bear up, edged away, and at 2 h. 35 m., arriving abreast of the disabled Spanish three-decker Salvador-del-Mundo, engaged the latter upon her weather bow for a few minutes; then passed on to the next Spanish ship in succession, the San-Ysidro, and whose three topmasts had already been shot away. This ship Captain Collingwood engaged closely on the lee beam until about 2 h. 53 m. P.M.; when, after a gallant defence in her crippled state from the fire of former opponent, the San-Ysidro hauled down the Spanish, and hoisted the English flag. The Excellent, then, in obedience to the signal (No. 66) just made by the Prince-George and repeated by the Victory, filled and stood on, first apprizing the admiral, by signal No. 26, that the San-Ysidro was not secured.

Very soon after the Excellent had quitted the Salvador-del-Mundo for the San-Ysidro, the Irresistible and Diadem commenced an attack upon the former; the 74 stationing herself upon the weather bow, and the 64 upon the lee quarter, of the Spanish three-decker, then with her fore and main topmasts gone, and otherwise much disabled. At 2 h. 35 m. P.M., finding the shot of the Irresistible and Diadem, particularly of the latter, falling near and over her as she advanced to rake the Salvador, the Victory directed her two friends to discontinue the engagement; but ships are very apt to misunderstand, or not to see, this signal, and, in the present instance, No. 52 required to be repeated three times before it was complied with. Observing the Victory about to pass under her stern, and that the Barfleur was following close, the Salvador-del-Mundo, whose mizen topmast had since shared the fate of the fore and main, very judiciously hauled down her flag as soon as some of the Victory's bow guns began to bear upon her.*

This was just at 3 P.M., and the Diadem and Lively were immediately directed by signal to take charge of the prizes; the frigate, of the San-Ysidro, and the 64, of the Salvador; but which latter the Diadem, by signal, afterwards resigned to the Bonne-Citoyenne, in order to attend upon the disabled Captain.

At about 3 h. 15 m. P.M. the Excellent, whom we left standing on from her prize, the San-Ysidro, to seek a fresh opponent among the flying Spaniards ahead, came to close action with the 80-gun ship San-Nicolas, then with her fore topmast gone, and who, until the Excellent arrived abreast of her to leeward, had been in hot action with the Captain. Passing within ten feet of the San-Nicolas's starboard side, the Excellent poured in a destructive fire, and, in compliance with the signal then flying,

* Relying upon the published accounts, we formerly stated, that the Victory poured in a destructive fire; but not a word appears in the Victory's log of her having fired at all at the Salvador-del-Mundo, and many persons present in the action are still of opinion that she did not. Yet the fact has been very differently represented. See Colonel Drinkwater's Narrative, p. 17; Marshall, vol. i, p. 26; and Brenton, vol. ii., p. 154.

to fill and stand on, made sail ahead. In luffing up to avoid Captain Collingwood's salute, the San-Nicolas ran foul of the San-Josef, whose mizenmast had already been shot away, and who had received considerable other damage, by the well directed fire in succession of the Captain, Culloden, Blenheim, and Prince-George, of the latter in particular.

As soon as the Excellent was sufficiently advanced to be clear of her, the Captain luffed up as close to the wind as her shattered condition would admit; when her fore topmast, which had already been severely shot through, fell over the side. In this unmanageable state, with her wheel shot away, and all her sails, shrouds, and running rigging, more or less cut; with the Blenheim ahead, and the Culloden crippled astern, no alternative remained but to board the Spanish two-decker. As a well-judged preparative, the Captain reopened, within less than 20 yards, her larboard broadside, the heavy fire from which the San-Nicolas returned with spirit for several minutes; when the Captain suddenly put her helm a-starboard, and, on coming to, hooked with her larboard cat-head the starboard quarter-gallery of the San-Nicolas, and with her spritsail quarter-gallery of the San-Nicolas, and with her spritsail yard the latter's mizen rigging. We prefer giving what immediately ensued in the words of Commodore Nelson himself. "The soldiers of the 69th," he says, "with an alacrity which will ever do them credit, and Lieutenant Pearson, of the same regiment, were almost the foremost on this service. The first man who jumped into the enemy's mizen chains, was Captain Berry, late my first lieutenant: (Captain Miller was in the very act of going also, but I directed him to remain;) he was supported from our spritsail yard, which hooked in the mizen-rigging. A soldier of the 69th regiment having broke the upper quarter-gallery window, I jumped in myself, and was followed by others as fast as possible. I found the cabin-doors fastened: and some Spanish officers fired their pistols: but, having broke open the doors, the soldiers fired; and the Spanish brigadier (commodore with a distinguishing pendant) fell, as retreating to the quarterdeck. I pushed immediately onwards for the quarterdeck; where I found Captain Berry in possession of the poop, and the Spanish ensign hauling down. I passed with my people and Lieutenant Pearson, on the larboard gangway, to the forecastle; where I met two or three Spanish officers, prisoners to my seamen: they delivered me their swords. A fire of pistols, or muskets, opening from the admiral's stern-gallery, of the San-Josef, I directed the soldiers to fire into her stern; and calling to Captain Miller, ordered him to send more men into the San-Nicolas; and directed my people to board the first-rate, which was done in an instant, Captain Berry assisting me into the main chains. At this moment, a Spanish officer looked over the quarter-deck rail, and said they surrendered. From this most welcome intelligence, it was not long before I was on the quarterdeck;

where the Spanish captain, with a bow, presented me his sword, and said the admiral was dying of his wounds. I asked him, on his honour, if the ship was surrendered. He declared she was: on which I gave him my hand, and desired him to call on his officers and ship's company, and tell them of it; which he did: – and, on the quarterdeck of a Spanish first-rate, extravagant as the story may seem, did I receive the swords of vanquished Spaniards; which, as I received, I gave to William Fearney, one of my bargemen; who put them, with the greatest *sang-froid*, under his arm. I was surrounded by Captain Berry, Lieutenant Pearson, of the 69th regiment, John Sykes, John Thompson, Francis Cooke, all old Agamemnons; and several other brave men, seamen and soldiers. Thus fell these ships."*

There is, it appears, a doubt whether the San-Josef got foul of the San-Nicolas just before, or during, Commodore Nelson's possession of the latter: at all events, it seems certain, that the San-Josef fell on board by the stern, and afterwards dropped broadside-to; in which position she was boarded from the San-Nicolas, as already described. But a more serious doubt attaches to the statement of the San-Josef's surrender having been the consequence of that boarding. As far as our researches have gone, it appears to be clearly established, that the Prince-George was engaging the San-Josef at the moment she got foul; and that the former ship only suspended her fire until, having edged away to leeward of the Captain and San-Nicolas, she was able to resume it ahead and clear of the Captain; that the San-Nicolas at this moment fired into the Prince-George, who accordingly bestowed part of her return fire upon the San-Nicolas, and continued her fire upon both Spanish ships until, at the end of some minutes, hailed from the Captain, to announce that they had struck.

Soon after quitting the San-Nicolas, the Excellent succeeded in getting close under the lee of the Santisima-Trinidad, then in hot action with the Blenheim, Orion, and Irresistible. At the end of an hour this four-decked ship, whose fore and mizen masts had been shot away, and whose damages, in sails, rigging, and hull, were conspicuous to all her antagonists, dropped, we will not say hauled down her colours. One might conjecture that they merely disappeared when the mizenmast fell; but, according to an entry in the Orion's log, the ship actually hoisted English colours in lieu of them. The Santisima-Trinidad had undoubtedly suffered enough, especially from the Blenheim, who had engaged her closely for some time, to render such a step no way discreditable to her.

At this crisis in the fate of Admiral Cordova's ship,† two of the van-ships, having wore, were advancing to her support; two

* Naval Chronicle, vol. ii. p. 500.

† It appears, however, that, like the French admirals, he had embarked on board a frigate.

fresh ships, under a crowd of sail (two of the three which had previously been detached to Algesiras*), were coming down from the west-south-west; and the lee division of seven sail of the line,† well formed, and including among them three three-deckers, having made a good stretch to windward on the starboard tack, were approaching on the opposite or larboard one, from the southward. These 11 ships, fast-closing round the yielding, if not already surrendered four-decker, saved her from further molestation.

It was about 3 h. 52 m. when the Victory, then on the starboard tack, observing the approach of those fresh ships, made the signal for the fleet to prepare to bring to, in order to be ready to cover the prizes and disabled British ships. At 4 h. 15 m. a signal was made for the frigates to take the prizes in tow, and at 4 h. 39 m. for the ships of the fleet to form in close line ahead in the wake of the Victory. At about 4 h. 50 m. P.M. the Britannia, who, from her slow sailing, had hitherto possessed no chance of getting into action, happening to lie in the way of the Spanish lee division in its approach to succour the Santisima-Trinidad, became exposed to a few comparatively harmless broadsides; which the Britainnia herself, assisted by the Orion, and one or two other ships, returned. This was the last of the battle of Valentine's day; and at 5 P.M., the British advanced ships having previously, in compliance with the signal to that effect, desisted from pursuit, the firing on both sides ceased.

The damages of the British ships, in a general point of view, were of very trifling amount. The only slip dismasted was the Captain; whose fore topmast, as already related, had been carried away: her hull was also much hit. With respect to the Colossus, when at 1 h. 30 m P.M., the Minerve approached to take her in tow, her assistance was declined, and, the former having, by 3 P.M., with creditable zeal and alacrity, got up a topsail yard for a fore yard, and set upon it a treble-reefed fore topsail, Captain Murray felt little inclined to have the Colossus considered as a disabled ship. The Egmont had received one shot through the main, and another through the mizen mast; and the Goliath, a shot through her foremast: in both cases from the two three-deckers belonging to the enemy's lee division.

The Culloden had her fore and main masts, main topmast, several other spars, and the chief of her rigging and sails shot through. Her boats had been cut to pieces; her hull was also pierced with shot, both above and below water, and the ship, in consequence, was very leaky. She had likewise one carronade, and two lower and two seconddeck guns dismounted. If we add to all this the damage she had previously sustained by running foul of the Colossus, the Culloden's state after the action may be pronounced to have been the worst in the fleet.

* See p. 32. The Guadalupa frigate had joined about an hour before.

† Log of Southampton; thus confirming our account.

The Blenheim also was much cut up. All her masts, yards, and bowsprit were more or less wounded. She had received 105 round shot in the hull, many of them near the water's edge; and her two foremost ports on the larboard side were knocked into one. Nor will this account of her damage be considered extraordinary, when it is known that, at one time during the action, she had five Spanish ships upon her at once, a three-decker on her larboard bow, two two-deckers astern, the four decker close on her larboard beam, and a second three-decker on her larboard quarter.

The loss sustained by the British was comparatively of no great amount, and fell, except in the cases of the Egmont and Colossus, where the damages were the heaviest. The Egmont had not a man hurt. The Britannia had one seaman, the Diadem, one seaman and one soldier, the Colossus, four seamen and one marine, the Barfleur, seven seamen, the Goliath, four seamen and four marines, and the Orion, one midshipman (Thomas Mansel), six seamen, and two marines wounded. The Victory had one seaman killed, and two seamen and three marines wounded; the Namur, two seamen killed and five wounded; and the Prince-George, seven seamen and one marine killed, and seven seamen wounded. The Irresistible (on board of which ship at 5 P.M. Commodore Nelson shifted his broad pendant), had one sergeant of marines and four seamen killed, one lieutenant (Andrew Thompson), one midshipman (William Balfour), one master's mate (Hugh M'Kinnon), 10 seamen, and one marine wounded. The Excellent, her boatswain (Peter Peffers), eight seamen, and two marines killed, one master's mate (Edward Augustus Down), nine seamen, and two marines wounded. The Culloden, one lieutenant of marines (George A. Livingstone), seven seamen, and two marines killed, 39 seamen and eight marines wounded. The Blenheim, 10 seamen and two soldiers killed, one lieutenant (Edward Libby), one master's mate Joseph Wixon, since dead), her boatswain (James Peacock), 39 seamen and seven soldiers wounded. The Captain, one major of marines (William Norris), one midshipman (James Goodench), 19 seamen, and three soldiers killed, the commodore (by a bruise), her boatswain (Mr. Carrington), one midshipman (Thomas Lund), 49 seamen, and four soldiers wounded; making a total of 73 killed, and 227 wounded.

The latter number, however, comprised only the badly wounded; a great number of whom died. In this case, contrary to what is customary, the slightly wounded, or those deemed so at the date of the despatches, were not allowed to be included in the returns. One consequence of this was, that amputations, arising from mortification and other unexpected changes, were actually undergone by several, who had not been returned as wounded. In comparing, therefore, the loss in this general action with that in any other, it will be fair to consider the total of killed and wounded to have amounted, not to 300, but, at the least, to 400 men.

According to the Spanish accounts, ten of their ships, exclusive of those captured, suffered materially in the action; but, at its close, not above half the number presented any appearance of being crippled. The chief of these was the Santisima-Trinidad. Another, probably, was the Soberano; and the Conde-de-Regla, Principe-de-Asturias, and Mexicano, three-deckers, having been the nearest ships to the English line, were doubtless more or less damaged by the latter's unremitting fire.

Of the prizes, we are enabled to give a somewhat more particular account. The Salvador-del-Mundo and San-Ysidro had each lost all three topmasts; the San-Josef, her mizenmast and main topmast; and the San-Nicolas, her fore topmast. All four ships had received innumerable shots in their hulls, and were very leaky in consequence. The San-Nicolas caught fire twice after possession had been taken of her; but the Captain's firemen, under the direction of Lieutenant Peter Spicer, the prize-master, extinguished the flames before they had spread to any injurious extent.

The loss sustained by the Santisima-Trinidad, according to the Spanish accounts, amounted to upwards of 200, in killed and wounded together. The Salvador-del-Mundo lost five officers, and 37 artillerists, seamen, and soldiers killed, three officers, and 121 artillerists, seamen, and soldiers wounded; the San-Ysidro, 29, including four officers, killed, and 63, including eight officers, wounded; the San-Josef, 46, including two officers, killed, and 96, including five officers, wounded; and the San-Nicolas, 144, including four officers, killed, and 59, including eight officers, wounded: making a total, on board the four prizes alone, of 261 killed, and 342 wounded.

Highly to the discredit of the Spanish government, the medical and chirurgical chests of the surgeons were deficient of almost every necessary article. It was fortunate for the poor wounded men, that the British surgeons were as able, as they were willing, to remedy the evil.

The addition of the loss alleged to have been sustained by the Santisima-Trinidad, makes a total of 803, in killed and wounded together. Some loss must undoubtedly have been sustained by three or four others of Admiral Cordova's ships; and, could the whole be computed, the amount would probably fall little short of 1000 men. Even this loss is barely adequate to the immense quantity of powder and shot reported to have been expended by the principally engaged British ships.

The Captain expended 146, the Culloden, 170, the Blenheim, 180, and the Prince George, 197, barrels of powder. The Captain, it is further stated, expended more shot than the quantity usually supplied to a ship of her class; and, when round shot or grape were wanted for her 32-pounder carronades, her seamen used seven 9-pound shot as a substitute: a discharge that, at a short distance, must have caused great slaughter.

The detached and confused state of the Spanish fleet at the beginning of the attack, and the consequent partial and irregular manner in which the ships came into action, would render unfair any statement of comparative force drawn up in the usual manner; that is, by confronting the totals on each side. We shall simply state that, as the British line consisted of 15, so the Spanish line (if line it could ever be called) consisted, at first, of 25, and afterwards of 27 sail, or rather of 26, one ship having, as already stated, fled just before the commencement of the engagement. Those, however, who wish to see the real force of the opponent fleets, may ascertain, with sufficient accuracy, the guns and men of every British ship, by referring to her class in the first annual abstract. The force of the Spanish ships of the three classes, 112s, 80s, and 74s, respectively, may be taken, upon an average, to have been the same as that of the captured ships; of which, as already has appeared, there were two belonging to the first, and one to each of the other classes.

As to the 130-gun ship, of four decks, we shall have no difficulty in showing, as near as will be necessary, what her force was. The Santisima-Trinidad was built at Havana in the year 1769, as a 112-gun ship, similar to the San-Josef or Salvador-del-Mundo, except probably in possessing rather more breadth of beam. It appears that, some time between the commencement of 1793 and the end of 1796, her quarterdeck and forecastle were formed into a whole deck, barricades built up along her gangways, and ports cut through them, so as to make the total number of 8-pounders on that deck, equal in amount to the 12s on the deck next below it. This accounts for 126 guns: the remaining four, we may suppose, were mounted on the poop. The Santisima-Trinidad was therefore a flush four-decker, that exceeded the three-decked 112s in force, only fourteen 8-pounders, and four pieces of a still smaller caliber.

The following short table contains the exact force, in guns and men, of the four prizes at the time of their capture:

	SAN-JOSEF.			SALVADOR-DEL-MUNDO			SAN-NICOLAS			SAN-YSIDRO		
	No.		Pdrs	No.		Pdrs.	No.		Pdrs.	No.		Pdrs.
First or lower deck.	30	long	36*	30	long	36	30	long	36	28	long	24
Second deck	32	"	18	32	"	18	32	"	18	30	"	18
Third deck	32	"	12	30	"	12						
Q.-deck& forecastle	18	"	8	20	"	8	18	"	8	16	"	8
Carriage-guns	112			112			80			74		
Men and boys† ...	917			850			630			525		

* Spanish caliber; see vol. i., p. 43.

† As enumerated in the head-money warrants. It is rather singular that, in

The most striking feature in this highly important victory is the boldness that prompted the attack. Another commander might have paused ere, with 15 sail of the line, he ran into the midst of 25; and then the separated ships would have closed, and the enemy's line been too compact to be attempted with any hope of success. But Sir John Jervis, relying upon the firmness of his band, and viewing with the eye of a practised seaman the loose and disordered state of the foe, resolved at once to profit by it: he rushed on and conquered. That, as usually asserted, he broke the enemy's line, cannot be said; for there was no line to be broken. An acknowledgement, which the gallant admiral himself was more ready to make than any of his commentators; for, in one of his letters relative to some charge that had been made against a Spanish rear-admiral engaged in the fleet, Sir John says, "I am ignorant in what part of the Spanish line, if it can be called one, Moralez served."* Sir John, in fact, chose the proper moment for advancing: he had a leader who knew not what it was to flinch or hang back; and he had all about him emulous to follow the example set them by Captain Troubridge.

On the other hand, the very front put on by the British was enough to sink the hearts of the Spaniards; for it is one of the characteristics of true valour, to daunt by its intrepidity, and to begin to subdue, ere it begins to combat. If the Spaniards were in confusion at the commencement, they were still more so during the progress, of the action. Their ships were so huddled together, that, if a shot did not strike one, it was almost sure to strike another; and many of the ships were unable to fire at all, without firing, as they frequently did, into their comrades. All this disorder infused additional confidence into the British; and they "rattled through" the business, more as if it were a game of harmless sport, than one in which the hazard thrown was for life or death. At length the separated divisions got together, and the Spanish admiral formed his ships in line. Instantly the British admiral assembled his scattered ships, and soon formed them in equal, if not better order. Each party then drew off, the one to lament, the other to exalt, over the occurrences of the day.

The acknowledged crippled state of the Santisima-Trinidad, and of one or two other ships of the Spanish fleet, at the close of the action, renders it doubtful whether more might not have been done, had the British fleet continued in pursuit. Night, it is true, was coming on; but it was that very night which would have brought the two fleets nearer to an equality. The greater were the difficulties of manœuvring, the greater were the chances in

an action about which so much has been said and written, no account of the complements of the captured ships should have been published; not even in the official letter, where the account ought to have appeared.

* Clarke and M 'Arthur's Life of Nelson, vol. ii., p. 15.

favour of the British; and, with 12 ships formed as British ships usually are formed, it is a question whether, when the darkness of a February night added its horrors to the destructive broadsides of a gallant and well-disciplined, though numerically inferior enemy, the Spaniard admiral would not have abandoned the whole of his crippled ships to the conquerors.

Before we take our final leave of this action, impartiality demands from us some inquiry into the more immediate causes which led to the defeat, such as it was, of an enemy, whose character for courage has ever been so justly extolled. One fact is certain, that the crews of the Spanish ships were the most worthless that can be conceived: they were composed of pressed landmen and soldiers of the new levies, with about 60, or at most 80, seamen to each ship. Is it necessary to go farther? Can it be surprising that "the poor panic-struck wretches," in the words of an intelligent writer,* "when called upon to go aloft to repair the injured rigging, fell immediately on their knees, and in that posture cried out, that they preferred being sacrificed on the spot, to performing a duty in the execution of which they considered death as inevitable?"

As a proof, too, of what little use their numerical superiority of guns was to the Spaniards, four or five of the San-Josef's quarterdeck guns on the starboard side, which was that chiefly engaged, were found with their tompions in. Innumerable other instances might be adduced, to show that their numbers were a detriment to them rather than an advantage.

Had eight of the 25 ships, present in the morning of the action, been left at Carthagena, and the 500 seamen they probably contained been substituted for twice the number of raw hands taken from the remaining 17 ships, the Spaniards would, at least, have made a better stand; and the victory have been achieved, for achieved it still would have been, at a far greater expense of lives. British lives are here meant: of Spanish lives, indeed, many were sacrificed, as the returns of the four captured ships fully testify. Nor must it be forgotten, how resolutely those ships were defended. Whatever may have been the quality of the crews, the courage of the officers was of the true Castilian stamp. It is with these that the act of surrender chiefly rests. The disaffected part of the crew may aim badly, fire slowly, and even skulk from their quarters; but the seamen cannot, without open mutiny, come aft and strike the colours. Upon the whole, the victory off Cape St. Vincent, although, from its consequences as a political event, pre-eminently great, from its merits as a naval combat, cannot be considered, especially when the quantum of effective resistance is taken into the account, in an equal degree glorious.

* Lieutenant-colonel Drinkwater. See his "Narrative of the proceedings of the British fleet, commanded by Admiral Sir John Jervis, K.B.," p. 25.

The English accounts, official and otherwise, demand from us a few words. Sir John Jervis's public letter has been complained of for its brevity. It is, indeed, both brief and obscure, and, for that reason, of very little use to the historian. Therefore, we must not bear too hard upon the accounts drawn up and published by private individuals. Against Admiral Ekins, however, we have a complaint to make, that applies to nearly all the cases he records. He suffers his reader to pore over half a dozen quarto pages of dry tactical matter, and to inspect an equal number of numerously figured plates (none of which are to be understood at a glance), merely to tell him, that all he has read, and all he has looked at, is erroneous: another account, and another set of plates, are then given, entirely altering the features of the battle of which he is desirous to give an account.

If any one was capable of doing justice to the St. Vincent victory, one might suppose it would be the writer who had been intrusted by the gallant chief with all his memoranda respecting it. But we do not hesitate to say, and we appeal to facts for the truth of our assertion, that Captain Brenton's account of his patron's action is the most imperfect of any that has been published. Its brevity may explain its incompleteness, but only renders the more extraordinary its many inaccuracies. That this writer should be contented with giving a superficial account is, indeed, most singular, for he actually begins by saying, "The particular details of this memorable day deserve our serious attention."* However, there is no deficiency of declaration, as the following passage will demonstrate: "From this day the old fashion of counting the ships of an enemy's fleet, and calculating the disparity of force, was entirely laid aside, and a new era may be said to have commenced in the art of war at sea." The opponents of Sir John Jervis, it is admitted, were Spaniards every man of them; and yet it is of Spaniards that Captain Brenton elsewhere says, "There is little credit to be gained in conquering such antagonists."† When an admiral and a post-captain have failed, a colonel of infantry has in a great measure succeeded; and this, strange to say, in drawing up an account of a battle at sea. For our part we cannot but acknowledge that, although we have discovered some errors in it, our difficulties have been greatly smoothed by a reference to Colonel Drinkwater's pamphlet.

During the night succeeding the action both fleets lay to repairing their damages; and daybreak on the 15th discovered them on opposite tacks, each formed in line of battle ahead. Although possessing the weathergage, the Spaniards made no serious attempt to renew the action. We say, no serious attempt, because, at about 2 h. 3 m. P.M., the Spanish fleet did bear down,

* Brenton, vol. ii., p. 152.

† Ibid. p. 142.

formed in order of battle, to the number, including the crippled ships, of 21 sail of the line, besides the Santisima-Trinidad, at a great distance off, in tow by a frigate. No sooner, however, did the British fleet, with the Captain in tow, and the Colossus and Culloden scarcely in a state to keep the line, haul its wind, than the Spaniards, very complaisantly, did the same. Had the latter persevered in their advance, it was the intention of Sir John Jervis, as given out in orders, to destroy the captured ships. Fortunately for the credit of the victory, this alternative was not resorted to, and the four prizes were preserved.

On the 16th, at about 3 P.M., the British fleet and prizes anchored in Lagos bay, Portugal. Shortly afterwards Sir John detached Captain Velterers Cornewall Berkeley, with the 18-pounder frigates Emerald and Minerve, 12-pounder frigate Niger, and sloops Bonne-Citoyenne and Raven, to look after the Santisima-Trinidad, which, it was known, had separated from her fleet in tow of a frigate.

On the 20th, at 3 P.M., Cape St.-Vincent bearing about north-north-west distant 27 leagues, and the wind blowing strong from the east-south-east, these three frigates and two sloops were fortunate enough to descry the object of their pursuit in the east by north, under her mainsail, with a jury mizenmast, being towed by a frigate. A brig was also seen in company. The British squadron, by signal from the commodore, made sail in chase. Immediately on observing this, the Spanish frigate cast off the four decker, set all sail, and stood to the westward. At 5 h. 30 m., by the Emerald's log, the signal was made to prepare for battle; and at 6 P.M., by the log of the Minerve, the Spanish ship was distant from her three miles. At this time – but, let us take the words from the log of the commodore's ship. "Made the signal to keep sight of the enemy, or make known their motions by day or night; only being answered by the Minerve, wore ship to the northward."

Soon after this extraordinary step was taken, the British 12-pounder 32-gun frigate Terpsichore, Captain Richard Bowen, joined company. Still the heads of the British frigates were kept to the northward, and the Santisima-Trinidad was soon out of sight. Even the Spanish frigate effected her escape; but not so the brig: the latter, at 6 A.M. on the 21st, was brought to by the Minerve, and proved to be a deep-laden Danish brig from Barcelona to Cadiz; a prize of course, and, we believe, a valuable one.

Let us see how a contemporary handles this affair. "Captain Berkeley did not think it right to attack her (the four-decker), and recalled Cockburn in the Minerve and Foote of the Niger, just as the former of these officers was about to bring her to close action. Captain Berkeley was much censured for his apparent want of resolution, but Cockburn gave the commander-in-chief so fair and impartial an account of the whole transaction, as to convince him that Captain Berkeley had acted with no more than becoming prudence. We may however be permitted to regret that the circumstance ever happened."*

Coupling this apologetical account with the entry in the Emerald's log, as to the omission of a part of the squadron to answer the signal to keep sight of the enemy, we are bound to consider that some such reason did induce Captain Berkeley to discontinue the chase. Why, then, did he not bring the captains of the Niger, Bonne-Citoyenne, and Raven, to a court-martial for their disobedience? We are persuaded, however, that the Niger was as ready to attack as the Minerve; and we believe that the Raven brig had just before parted company: hence, in this view of the case, the Bonne-Citoyenne was the only ship whose commander evinced a reluctance to unite with three frigates in keeping sight of an enemy's crippled first-rate. Had the Bonne-Citoyenne been a frigate like the Emerald or the Minerve, her defection might have been worth counting upon; but she was a ship of only 20 guns. Upon the whole, this was a sad business. Let us therefore hasten to relate a fact, that will operate as a far better comment upon Captain Berkeley's behaviour than any thing we, or any one else, can say.

We mentioned that, towards the close of this discreditable rencontre, a frigate joined company. Here, even upon Captain Berkeley's own showing, was a frigate of equal force to the one complained of; and yet no effort, that we can discover, was made to renew the pursuit of the retreating enemy. The Terpsichore soon afterwards parted company, and was cruising alone; whether with the intention, single-handed, of seeking an enemy's ship, which three frigates, two of them heavier than herself, had declined to follow, we cannot say; but we will say that, if there were any officer in the British navy who would undertake so bold and perilous an enterprise, it was Captain Richard Bowen.

On the 28th, at 7 P.M., Cape Spartel bearing east-north-east distant 23 leagues, by accident we must suppose, the very Santisima-Trinidad, so avoided, as she was striving to regain the coast, from which she had been driven by a gale, was fallen in with by the Terpsichore. On the 1st of March, daylight, the strange ship was descried in the east-south-east, at the distance of about three miles. Instantly the British frigate cleared for action, and at 9 A.M. bore down towards the enemy; whose four decks and dismasted state made her known at once to Captain Bowen, as the ship from which his friends had retreated.

At 10 A.M. the Terpsichore brought to and began engaging the Spanish first-rate, and so manœuvred as to keep tolerably clear of the broadside of the latter; who had therefore no guns but her chasers, wherewith to requite the temerity of her pigmy foe. At half-past midnight the Terpsichore ceased firing, and

* Brenton, vol. ii., p. 155.

commenced making new wads and filling powder, as well as repairing her running rigging and sails, which had been much cut by the four-decker's shot. The frigate sustained no loss; but it was afterwards reported, that the Santisima-Trinidad had nine men killed and several wounded by the Terpsichore.

On the 2d., at 8 A.M., the Santisima-Trinidad bore from the frigate south-west-half-south distant about six miles, the wind then at north-north-east. Captain Bowen continued to keep company with his opponent until noon; when, Cape Spartel bearing south-east-half-south distant eight or nine leagues, 12 sail of Spanish men of war, part of Admiral Cordova's fleet, hove in sight to the northward. On this Terpsichore made sail in an opposite direction, and anchored on the 4th in Tangier bay. The Santisima-Trinidad afterwards put into Algesiras; whence, on being partially refitted, she set sail for Cadiz, and, towards the end of the month, reached that port in safety. Of this spirited skirmish between a British 12-pounder frigate and a Spanish first-rate, we shall say no more than that, whether or not Captain Berkeley's conduct deserved a court-martial, Captain Bowen's conduct deserved the public thanks of the commander-in-chief.

While the British fleet lay at Lagos bay, the Spanish prisoners received from the four prizes, numbering about 3000, were landed; and, a receipt being first given for them by the proper officer, were allowed to remain on shore. On the 23d, after experiencing the tail of a gale of wind which, had it blown home, would probably have forced several of the ships on shore, Sir John departed; and, in five days afterwards, arrived in safety at Lisbon. Here it was remarked, that the four prizes, under their jury-masts, and poor manned as they necessarily were, beat all the English ships in working into the Tagus.

If the inhabitants of Lisbon were unbounded, and they had reason to be sincere, in their congratulations at the victory, the state of general feeling, on the first promulgation of the news in England, the land of the conquerors, may be readily conceived. Our business is merely to relate, that Sir John Jervis was created a peer of Great Britain, by the titles of Baron Jervis of Meaford, and Earl of St.-Vincent, with a pension of 3000*l.* per annum. Vice-admiral Thompson and Rear-admiral William Parker were created baronets; and the remaining vice-admiral was appointed to a lucrative post abroad. Commodore Nelson, he who in his own person had proved (and how often had he proved?) that the danger of a bold enterprise required only to be met to be overcome, received the insignia of the Bath, and, from the city of London, its freedom, suitably presented. The thanks of both houses of parliament were voted to the fleet; and gold emblematic medals, as on similar occasions, were distributed to all the flag-officers and captains. When the medal was offered to Captain Collingwood, he refused it until he should receive one for the 1st of June, in which action he declared he had equally done his duty: the medal was accordingly sent to him, with an apology for its having been delayed.*

Of the first lieutenants of the different line-of-battle ships present in this action, the following, we believe, is a correct list: William Selby, Victory; Valentine Collard, Britannia; John Bligh, Barfleur; Robert Campbell, Blenheim; Robert Williams, Prince-George; James Nash, Namur; Edward Berry, Captain; William Collis, Goliath; John Mortimer, Excellent; James Barker, Orion; Richard Prater, Colossus; Anselm John Griffiths, Culloden; William Bevians, Irresistible; George Burdett, Egmont; and Henry Edward Reginald Baker, Diadem. The whole of these, we believe, were promoted to the rank of commanders. If we speak doubtfully in this case, it is to be attributed to the strange custom, prevalent in those days, of omitting to make public the promotion of any naval officer unless it be to the rank of admiral; while an ensign, belonging to the most insignificant militia regiment or volunteer association in the kingdom, had the satisfaction of seeing his name recorded in the first London Gazette after the date of his commission.

The four Spanish prizes were commissioned and retained in service on the Lisbon station, and did not arrive at Plymouth until October. Only one of them, the San-Josef, became of any value as a cruising ship. She was built in 1783; the Salvador-del-Mundo, in 1787; the San-Nicolas, in 1769; and the San-Ysidro, in the year previous. The following are the principal dimensions of the two three-deckers; to which are subjoined those of the Ville-de-Paris, as the largest English-built ship of the period, and those of the Victory, as the largest English ship present in the action:

	Length of gun deck.		Breadth extreme.		Depth of hold.		Tons.
	ft.	in.	ft.	in.	ft.	in.	
San-Josef	194	3	54	3	24	5½	2457
Salvador-del-Mundo	190	0	54	3½	23	3	2398
Ville-de-Paris	190	2	53	2	22	2	2352
Victory	186	0	52	0	21	6	2162

Having given a summary of the honours bestowed upon the conquerors for their victory, we will here briefly relate in what manner a weak government, notwithstanding it was their own fault in sending a fleet so badly manned to sea, punished the vanquished for their defeat. Don Josef de Cordova was deprived of all his offices, declared incapable of ever serving in any rank, and prohibited from appearing at court, or in any of the chief towns of the maritime coasts. The second in command, Count Morales de los Rios, was deprived of his rank. The

* Brenton, vol. ii., p. 155.

Captains, Don Gonzales Vallego, Don Juan de Agairre, Don Josef de Torres, and Don Augustine Villavicencio, were deprived of their rank; and the latter declared incapable in future of holding any other. Several captains and officers were deprived of their offices for a limited time of six, four, and two years, according to the degree of their alleged criminality; and several captains, lieutenants, and ensigns were sentenced to be publicly reprimanded.

A reinforcement from England having joined the British admiral, and the ships that had suffered in the action having repaired their damages, Earl St.-Vincent, on the afternoon of the 31st of March, quitted Lisbon in the 110-gun ship Ville-de-Paris, and, with 21 sail of the line, proceeded direct for Cadiz; where lay the Spanish fleet, now all assembled, and numbering, with the ships previously in port, 26 sail of the line.

The British admiral continued cruising off Cadiz from the 4th of April to the 19th of May; on which day Sir John anchored the fleet in such a position as effectually to block up the port. On the 29th of June the number of Spanish ships of the line, reported ready for sea in the harbour, was 28; all of which, as far as soldiers could supply the deficiency of seamen, were fully manned.

With the view of provoking Admiral Massaredo to attempt putting to sea, and also perhaps, as a contemporary observes, "to employ the minds of the seamen and divert them from following the mischievous example of the ships in England,"* Earl St.-Vincent resolved to bombard the town of Cadiz. On the night of the 3d of July, every thing being in readiness, the Thunder bomb-vessel, Lieutenant John Gourly, covered by the gun-boats, launches, and barges of the fleet, under the orders of Rear-admiral Sir Horatio Nelson, who commanded the advanced or in-shore squadron, took her station near the tower of San-Sebastian, and within 2500 yards of the walls of the town; then containing a garrison of upwards of 4000 men, and protected on the bay side of 70 pieces of cannon and eight large mortars. The Thunder commenced throwing her shells, with great precision; but the large or 13½ inch mortar was soon discovered to have been materially injured by its former services. The safety of the bomb-vessel requiring that she should be immediately withdrawn out of gun-shot, the Goliath 74, Captain Thomas Foley, Terpsichore frigate, Captain Richard Bowen, and Fox cutter, Lieutenant John Gibson, kept under sail, to afford her the necessary protection.

The retreat of the Thunder was the signal for a number of Spanish gun-boats and armed launches to sally forth, in hopes to capture her. These were met by a similar description of force, led by Rear-admiral Nelson. The Spanish commandant,

* Brenton, vol. ii., p. 231.

Don Miguel Tyrason, attempted in his barge, with a crew of 26 men, to carry the comparatively small boat in which the Rear-admiral, with 15 hands besides himself, was pushing into the thickest of the fire. A hand-to-hand scuffle ensued, in which both commanders took a conspicuous personal part. At length Don Miguel Tyrason, having had 18 of his men killed, and himself and all the remainder wounded, was compelled to surrender. After this, the Spaniards were driven and pursued to the walls of Cadiz; leaving in the possession of the British two mortar-boats and the commandant's launch, with several prisoners.

The loss of the British, in this smart affair, amounted to one killed and 20 wounded; including, among the latter, Captain Thomas Francis Fremantle, who had accompanied Rear-admiral Nelson in his barge, slightly, three lieutenants (William Selby, Ville-de-Paris, Henry Nathaniel Rowe, Diadem, and Gregory Grant, Prince-George), one master's mate (Hugh Pearson, Barfleur), one midshipman (Robert Tooley, Prince-George), and John Sykes, a seaman, severely, in the act of defending the person of the Rear-admiral, to whom he was cockswain. When the brave meets the brave, the conquered party is sure to find a eulogist. Hence, Sir Horatio Nelson, in his official despatch, begs to be permitted to express his admiration of Don Miguel Tyrason, and declares that the latter's resistance was such as to honour a brave officer.

The night of the 5th was chosen by Rear-admiral Nelson for a second bombardment of Cadiz. On this occasion three bomb-vessels, the Thunder, Terror, and Strombolo, were most judiciously placed by the master of the Ville-de-Paris, Mr. Bartholomew Jackson; the covering ships being the Theseus 74, Captain Ralph Willett Miller, and the frigates Terpsichore, and Emerald, the latter, upon the very judicious retirement of Captain Berkeley, now commanded by Captain John Waller. The bombardment produced considerable effect, both in the town and among the shipping: so much so, that early on the following morning, to avoid a repetition of it, ten sail of the line, including the flag-ships of Admirals Massaredo and Gravina, warped with much precipitation out of shell-range. The British and Spanish gun-boats encountered each other, as on the first night. The loss sustained by the British, did not, however, exceed three seamen killed, and one captain of marines (Thomas Oldfield, Theseus), two lieutenants (John Collins, Victory, and John Hornsey, Seahorse, who greatly distinguished himself), two midshipmen (John Collier, Theseus, and John Stephenson, Audacious), and 11 seamen and marines wounded. The loss on the part of the Spaniards was probably much greater, but could not be ascertained.

On the night of the 8th Rear-admiral Nelson meditated a third bombardment of the town, under his own immediate direction; but, fortunately for the Spaniards, the wind blew so strong down the bay, that the bomb-vessels could not be got in time to the intended point of attack. The second bombardment was represented to have levelled several houses; a circumstance to be regretted, and yet not well to be avoided, considering that the legitimate object of the bombardment, the shipping, lay so close to the town.

The rumoured arrival at Santa-Cruz, in the island of Teneriffe, of a richly freighted Manilla ship, and the represented vulnerability of the town and shipping to a well-conducted sea-attack, induced Earl St.-Vincent to detach a force in order to attempt bringing out the galleon. Before, however, we enter upon the details of this cutting-out service, another in the same quarter is, by priority of date, entitled to our attention.

On the 28th of May, in the afternoon, the British frigates Lively, Captain Benjamin Hallowell, and Minerve, Captain George Cockburn, standing into the bay of Santa-Cruz, discovered at anchor in the road an armed brig, which, as the frigate approached, hoisted French colours. The two captains deeming it practicable to cut the vessel out, the boats of the frigates, on the following day, the 29th, were manned, and placed under the orders of Lieutenant Thomas Masterton Hardy of the Minerve, as the senior lieutenant. At about 2 h. 30 m. P.M. Lieutenant Hardy, supported by Lieutenants Loftus Otway Bland, Harry Hopkins, and John Bushby, and Lieutenant Robert Bulkley of the marines, belonging to the Lively, and by Lieutenants William Hall Gage and Thomas James Maling, of the Minerve, and their respective boats' crews, made a most resolute attack upon the brig, as she lay at anchor; and in the face of a smart fire of musketry, boarded, and almost immediately carried her. This alarmed the town, and a heavy fire of artillery and musketry was opened upon the brig, as well from every part of the garrison, as from a large ship that lay in the road. The lightness of the wind retarded the weighing of the anchor, and then made it necessary for the boats to take the brig in tow.

During the space of nearly an hour, an unremitting fire was kept up from the shore and ship. At length, at a little before 4 P.M., Lieutenant Hardy and his gallant comrades brought safe out of gun-shot, the French brig-corvette Mutine, mounting 14 guns, 12 of them long 6-pounders, and the remaining two brass 36-pounder carronades. Her complement was 135; but the Mutine, when the attack commenced, had on board only 113 men, the remainder, with their commander, capitaine de frégate Zavier Pommier, being on shore. In effecting this enterprise, 15 of Lieutenant Hardy's party, including himself and midshipman John Edgar, were wounded, but none killed. Being a remarkably fine brig of 349 tons, the Mutine was immediately put in commission by Earl St.-Vincent, and the command of her given, very properly, to the officer who led the party that so gallantly cut her out.

Now for the expedition to capture the galleon. If the following description of the place, in which she was supposed to be, is accurately given, there was certainly in some quarter, a great misconception of the probable difficulties of the enterprise. "Of all places which ever came under our inspection," says Captain Brenton, "none we conceive is more invulnerable to attack, or more easily defended, than Teneriffe. The island, like most of its neighbours, is a volcanic production, consisting of mountains, ravines, rocks, and precipices. The bay of Santa-Cruz affords no shelter for shipping; the shore is nearly a right line, and the bank so steep that no anchorage can be found beyond the distance of half a mile, and that in 45 fathoms' water; the beach, from north to south, is one continued series of broken masses of loose rock, and round, smooth stones, either rendered so by friction, or slippery from sea-weeds; on this a perpetual surf breaks, rendering the landing at all times difficult, except at the mole or pier of Santa Cruz. To these obstacles there is another, which Nelson experienced in its fullest force: Teneriffe, like all other mountainous countries, is liable to calms, sudden squalls, and violent gusts of wind, which, rushing down the ravines, frequently take a ship's topmasts over the side without a moment's warning."*

On the 15th of July, the following ships, one of which, the Terpsichore, did not join till the next day, and another, the Leander, not until several days afterwards, were placed under the orders of Rear-admiral Nelson:

Gun-ship		
74	Theseus	Rear-admiral (b.) Sir Horatio Nelson, K.B. / Captain Ralph Willett Miller.
	Culloden	Captain Thomas Troubridge.
	Zealous	Captain Samuel Hood.
50	Leander	Captain Thomas Boulden Thompson.
Gun-frigate		
38	Seahorse	Captain Thomas Francis Fremantle.
36	Emerald	Captain John Waller.
32	Terpsichore	Captain Richard Bowen.
Cut.	Fox	Lieutenant John Gibson.
	Mortar-boat.	

In about five days the squadron arrived off the island of Teneriffe. Every arrangement that sound judgment could devise having been completed, 200 seamen and marines from each of the three line-of-battle ships, and half of the number from each of the three frigates, exclusive of commissioned officers and servants, and a small detachment of royal artillery, the whole together amounting to about 1000 or 1050 men, were placed under the orders of Captain Troubridge; each captain, under his direction, commanding the detachment of seamen from his own ship, and Captain Thomas Oldfield of the marines, as the senior marine-

* Brenton, vol. ii., p. 234.

officer, the entire detachment from that corps. On the night of the 20th the three frigates, accompanied by the cutter and mortar-boat, and most of the boats of the squadron, stood close in, to land the men, and try to gain possession of a fort at the north-east side of the bay, and within gun-shot of the town; whence a summons was to be sent to the governor. But a strong gale of wind in the offing, and a strong current against them near the shore, prevented the boats from reaching the intended point of debarkation. On the 22d, at about 3 h. 30 m. A.M., the three line-of-battle ships bore up for Santa-Cruz, and, soon after daylight, were joined by the frigates and small-craft; whose unavoidable appearance off the coast had given to the islanders the very warning it was so desirous they should not have.

A consultation of the principal officers now decided that an attack should be made on the heights immediately over the fort already mentioned, and that, from that commanding position, the British seamen and marines should storm and endeavour to carry the fort itself. At 9 P.M. the frigates anchored in shore, off the east end of the town, and landed their men; but the latter, finding the heights too strongly guarded to be attempted, re-embarked in the course of the night, without loss. The three line-of-battle ships, meanwhile, had kept under way, to batter the fort, by way of causing a diversion, but, owing to calms and contrary currents, were unable to approach nearer than three miles.

Not being one to abandon an enterprise until after a stout struggle to accomplish it, Nelson resolved yet to bring his band of hardy fellows in contact with the Santa-Cruz garrison. On the 24th the Leander, Captain Thompson, who had only arrived at Cadiz from Lisbon on the 18th, joined the squadron. The local experience of her captain, and the accession of force in her marines, gave additional hopes to the rear-admiral, and those engaged with him in the perilous, and, at present, not very auspicious undertaking.

At 5 P.M., every thing being in readiness, the squadron anchored to the north-eastward of the town; the line-of-battle ships within six or eight miles, the frigates within two, as if intending to disembark their men in that direction. But this was only a feint; the mole head was to be the rendezvous of the boats. At 11 P.M. about 700 seamen and marines embarked in the boats of the squadron, 180 more on board the Fox cutter, and about 75 on board a large provision-boat that had just been captured; numbering, with a small detachment of royal artillery, about 1100 men. The different detachments of seamen, under the immediate command of their respective captains, the marines under Captain Oldfield, the artillery under Lieutenant Baynes, and the whole force, commanded by the rear-admiral in person, pushed off from the squadron. Every precaution had been taken to keep the boats together, in order that the attack might be simultaneous; but the rough state of the weather, and the extreme darkness of the night, rendered a close union next to impossible.

At about 1 h. 30 m. A.M. on the 25th the Fox cutter, attended by the rear-admiral's boat and three or four others, including the two in which Captains Fremantle and Bowen had embarked, reached, undiscovered, within half-gun shot of the mole head: when, suddenly, the alarm bells began to ring, and a fire opened from 30 or 40 pieces of cannon and a strong body of troops stationed along the shore. Two shots raked the Fox, and a third struck her between wind and water; whereby she instantly sank, and unfortunately 97 of the brave fellows that were on board met a watery grave. Among the number was her commander, Lieutenant Gibson. Another shot struck the rear-admiral on the elbow, just as he was drawing his sword and stepping out of the boat. It completely disabled him, and he was carried back to his ship. A third shot went through and sank the boat in which Captain Bowen had embarked; whereby seven or eight seamen perished. In spite of all this opposition, the British effected a landing; and stormed and carried the mole head, notwithstanding it was defended by 300 or 400 men, and six 24-pounders. Having spiked these, the men were about to advance, when a heavy fire of musketry and grape-shot, from the citadel and the houses near the mole head, mowed them down by scores. Here the gallant Captain Richard Bowen and his first lieutenant met each a glorious death; and here, indeed, fell nearly the whole of the party, by death or wounds.

Meanwhile, the boat of Captain Troubridge, being unable to hit the mole, had pushed on shore, under a battery close to the southward of the citadel. Captain Waller's and a few other boats landed at the same time; but the surf was so high, that many of the boats put back, and all that did not, were full of water in an instant, the very ammunition in the men's pouches being wetted and spoiled. Captain Troubridge, as soon as he had collected a few men, advanced with Captain Waller to the prado, or great square of the town, the appointed place of rendezvous on shore, in the hope of there meeting Rear-admiral Nelson, and Captains Thompson, Fremantle, Bowen, and their men; but who, as already related, had been already killed. Captain Troubridge now sent a sergeant, with two gentlemen of the town, to summon the citadel; but, although the sergeant (since supposed to have been shot in his way thither) did not return, and, the non-receipt of an answer implied a negative, yet the loss of the scaling ladders in the surf rendered impracticable any attempt to put in force the threatened alternative. After waiting an hour, Captain Troubridge marched to join Captains Hood and Miller; who, with a small body of men, had made good their landing to the south-west of the spot at which he had landed. By daybreak the survivors of Captain Troubridge's party amounted to about 340; consisting of about 80 marines, 80 pikemen, and 180 seamen with small-arms. Having procured some ammunition from the Spanish prisoners, this little band resolved to try what could be done with the citadel without ladders; but they soon found the whole of the streets commanded by field-pieces, and "upwards of 8000 Spaniards," with 100 Frenchmen, under arms, approaching by every avenue. The boats being all stove, no possibility existed of receiving a reinforcement. The ammunition, too, except the little taken from the persons of the prisoners, was wet; and the provisions had shared the fate of the boats. Under these circumstances, Captain Troubridge thought it best to send Captain Hood with a flag of truce to the governor, expressing his determination to burn the town, much as it would be to his regret, if the Spanish forces approached one inch farther, and enclosing terms of capitulation, to the following effect: That the British troops should be allowed to re-embark, with their arms, and take their boats, if saved, or be provided with others; and Captain Troubridge engaged, in case of compliance, that the ships then before the town should not further molest it, nor attack any one of the Canary islands.

Captain Hood waited upon the Spanish governor, Don Juan-Antonio Gutteri, with the message. The governor was astonished to receive such a proposal from men whom he had already considered as in his power; but nevertheless, he acceded to the terms. Captain Troubridge, accordingly, marched to the mole head; and then, with his men, embarked on board boats furnished by the Spaniards. The governor, being determined to end the thing as he had begun it supplied each of the retreating invaders with a ration of biscuit and wine; and directed that those of the British who were wounded should be received into the hospital. Moreover, he caused to be intimated to Rear-admiral Nelson, that he was at liberty to send on shore for, and purchase, whatever refreshments the squadron, during its stay off the island, might require.

Thus ended an expedition, of which the only advantages were the proofs it afforded of, what few had previously been inclined to dispute, the valour and intrepidity of British seamen; while, in addition to the dishonour of a defeat, there was the melancholy loss which it entailed upon the country. That loss amounted to, one captain (Richard Bowen), four lieutenants (John Weatherhead, Theseus, George Thorpe, Terpsichore, William Earnshaw, Leander, and John Gibson, Fox), two lieutenants of marines (Raby Robinson, Leander, and William Basham, Emerald), 23 seamen, and 14 marines killed; Rear-admiral Nelson (right arm amputated), two captains (Thomas Francis Fremantle and Thomas Boulden Thompson), one lieutenant (John Douglas), one midshipman (Robert Watts), 85 seamen, and 15 marines wounded; 97 seamen and marines drowned, and five missing; total, 141 killed and drowned, 105 wounded, and five missing: a loss which did not fall very far short of in the total number, and much exceeded in officers of rank and value, that which had won the battle of Cape St.-Vincent.

In noticing the loss of Captain Richard Bowen, the rear-admiral, in his despatch, emphatically adds, "than whom a more enterprising, able, and gallant officer does not grace his majesty's naval service." This eulogy from Nelson did more to ennoble the object, than the mere act of conferring an order of knighthood; and yet Captain Bowen had undoubtedly merited one, long before he met his death under the walls of Santa-Cruz.* Both Earl St.-Vincent and Rear-admiral Nelson strongly importuned Earl Spencer, then at the head of the admiralty, on the subject of a monument to Captain Bowen's memory. Nelson, in his usual energetic manner, writes Earl St.-Vincent's thus: "Why is not a monument voted in St. Paul's, to perpetuate the memory of the gallant Bowen? I put it strongly to Earl Spencer. If you have an opportunity, pray express my surprise, that no mention has been made of him in either house of parliament." But, on the plea, that the affair in which Captain Bowen had perished was a failure, this customary tribute of a nation's gratitude to her heroes was withheld; a plea, however, that, in the case of Captain James Cornwall of the Marlborough, who fell in February, 1744, was not allowed to interfere.

Not all the efforts of the British admiral off Cadiz could prevent the seeds of mutiny from spreading among his ships. The crews of two or three became extremely turbulent; but at length, by active measures the ringleaders were seized. On their trial by court-martial, three were sentenced to suffer death, and the sentence was ordered to be executed on board the St.-George, where the disaffection had first shown itself. The crew, on the arrival of the prisoners on board, drew up a remonstrance in their favour, and begged of Captain Shuldham Peard to intercede in their behalf with the commander-in-chief. The captain asserted, and laid their remonstrance before Earl St.-Vincent. The admiral's answer was, that he considered the sentence of the court-martial, convicting the prisoners, to be founded upon solid justice and imperious necessity; and consequently, that he could not think of retracting the sanction which he had given to it.

On learning the ill-success of their remonstrance, the crew of the St.-George manifested strong symptoms of disaffection. Their conduct was not unobserved by Captain Peard, who took the precaution to watch their movements. One of the seamen, who was well acquainted with their designs, informed his captain, that the men had entered into a resolution to seize the ship,

* See vol. i., p. 364.

depose the officers, and liberate their condemned companions; and that the evening previous to the day appointed for carrying the sentence into execution, was the time fixed for putting their plan in force. Captain Peard, observing the crew assembled in the waist, approached and addressed them to the following effect: "I am perfectly aware of your intentions, and shall oppose them at the risk of my life. You have determined to oppose the authority of your officers. I am resolved to do my duty, and to enforce strict obedience to my orders. I am sensible that you are, for the most part, the victims of delusion. I know the ringleaders, and do not hesitate to avow my intention of bringing them to justice. I command you to disperse, and to return to your duty."

Finding that this address did not produce the desired effect, Captain Peard and the first lieutenant, John Hatley, rushed amidst the crowd, resolutely seized two of the people, whom he knew to be the promoters of the conspiracy, dragged them out by main force and put them in irons, without experiencing any opposition from the crew. The determined courage of Captain Peard on this occasion produced such an effect upon the crew generally, that order was immediately restored and the men returned to their duty.

On the next morning, the 7th, the three mutineers, already mentioned as condemned, were hanged at the fore yard-arm of the St.-George; and on the 9th the two belonging to that ship, having on the preceding day been tried and convicted, were executed in a similar manner. For his very spirited and exemplary conduct, Lieutenant Hatley was soon afterwards promoted to the rank of commander.

Except for a few weeks at the commencement of the present year, when Commodore Nelson was on his passage from the isle of Elba, and again at its close, when a small squadron, as we shall presently see, was sent to Algiers, scarcely a British cruiser was to be met with to the eastward of Gibraltar. Previously to any mention of the advantages which France derived from the undisturbed egress and regress of her Toulon fleet, we will briefly advert to her recent territorial and other acquisitions along the shores of the Mediterranean.

The numerous and brilliant successes of the extraordinary man, who was at the head of her armies, had compelled, first the Pope, and then Austria, to sue for peace; and the treaty with the latter, which was begun at Leoben on the 18th of July, 1797, and concluded at Campo-Formio on the 17th of October following, gave to France, among other territories and advantages, the whole of the Austrian Netherlands; also Corfu, Zante, Cephalonia, and the remaining Venetian islands in that part of the Adriatic: while Austria was allowed to possess in return Istria, Dalmatia, with all the Venetian islands in the Adriatic, lying to the north-west of the gulf of Lodrino; also the city of Venice, which the troops of France had entered and seized on the 16th of May, with a large portion of the dominion of that celebrated republic, whose existence thus terminated after a lapse of 14 centuries. On the 6th of June the republic of Genoa also ceased to exist, and, under the name of Liguria, became a sovereignity of France.

Early in the month of June, which was some weeks before the order to disarm the French ships issued from the then dominant faction at Paris, Rear-admiral Brueys, by the orders of General Bonaparte, sailed from Toulon, with a squadron of six sail of the line and several frigates, bound to Corfu. Here the admiral found and took possession of six Venetian 64-gun ships, and six frigates. These were exclusive of three 64s and three frigates building at Venice, and exclusive also of 10 or 12 corvettes and eighteen galleys lying in that harbour.* On the 13th of June, which was a few days after the departure of Admiral Brueys, several transports laden with troops and provisions, and escorted by some frigates under the command of Captain Guillaume-François-Joseph Bourdé, also quitted Toulon, and on the 28th arrived at Corfu; where, soon afterwards, with the assistance of General Gentili and his army, the whole of the Seven Islands (subsequently known by the name of the Ionian Islands) were taken possession of and garrisoned. The names of the islands were retained; but the names of the ships General Buonaparte, by an assumption of power to which the directory subsequently gave their sanction, changed to those of the principal generals killed, and battles fought, in his campaign against Italy.

On the 16th of November, which was about the time that Rear-admiral Brueys returned to Toulon from his Mediterranean cruise, Earl St.-Vincent detached from the British fleet, then lying in the Tagus, the 50-gun ship Leander, Captain Thomas Boulden Thompson, the Harmadryad frigate, and a sloop of war, to Algiers, to settle some dispute with the dey; a service which Captain Thompson executed to the approbation of the admiral. About this time a small British squadron, associated with five Portuguese sail of the line, cruised off Cadiz and in the neighbourhood of the Straits, to prevent the French ships at Toulon, or the few Spanish ones at Carthagena, from effecting a junction, if such was their object, with the fleet of Admiral Massaredo at Cadiz.

The concessions made by government to the seamen of the Channel fleet necessarily comprehending the whole British navy, it was justly considered, that any lurking disaffection, that might exist in detached quarters of it, would disappear, the instant the benefits, of which all were to partake, became generally known. Hence a mutiny that had broken out at Sheer-

* Victoires et Conquêtes, tome viii., pp. 185, 274.

ness on the 10th of May was expected to subside of itself, when the accounts of what had occurred at Portsmouth on the 15th should have reached the malecontents. Unfortunately the news seemed to fan, rather than extinguish the flame; and, by the 20th of the month, many of the ships lying at the Nore, and soon afterwards, nearly the whole of those belonging to the North-sea fleet, hoisted the flag of defence. The complaints of the Portsmouth mutineers having been, for the most part, founded on justice, the sympathy of the nation went with them: and very few persons throughout the kingdom did or could grudge the additional allowances, (many of them a mere exchange of the real for the nominal,) which the British sailor, after a hard struggle, got permanently secured to him. On the other hand, the mutineers at Sheerness and Yarmouth had no solid, nor even plausible ground of complaint. They appear to have been actuated by a mere mischief-making spirit, with scarcely a knowledge of the object they had in view. The nation, therefore, although it naturally felt some alarm at the magnitude and growing extent of this second eruption, came at once to the resolution of making a firm stand against it; a resolution that instantly rid the evil of more than half the terrors which its first appearance had inspired.

The same motives, that actuated us in abridging the details of the Portsmouth mutiny, operate, in full force, on the present occasion. And if we decline, any more than we can avoid, to mention by name the individual ship whose crews were disaffected, it is because the mere naming of a ship, as connected with so disgraceful a proceeding, may tend to cast an undeserved stigma on a future ship of the same name, or even on the same ship, with a new and very differently disposed ship's company.

The mutineers at Sheerness, in imitation of those at Spithead, chose two delegates from every ship, but went further, by appointing, as a president over them, a man of the name of Richard Parker. On board each ship was also a committee, consisting of 12 men, who decided, as well upon all affairs relative to the internal management of the ship, as upon the merits of the respective delegates. On the 20th of May the seamen prepared a statement, which they required Vice-admiral Charles Buckner, whose flag was on board the 90-gun ship Sandwich, to transmit without delay to the admiralty. With the terms of it, they peremptorily demanded compliance, as the only condition on which they would return to obedience. The statement contained as many as eight articles, of which the first betrayed greater ignorance than one could suppose existed among men capable of discussing and drawing up such a document. It demanded, "that every indulgence granted to the fleet at Portsmouth should be granted to his majesty's subjects serving in the fleet at the Nore and places adjacent." Had this been the only item of the statement, the obvious answer that followed would have settled the affair to every one's satisfaction. But scarcely any one of the remaining seven articles was admissible, and most of them were frivolous and unnecessary.

On the 22d the admiralty replied to the seamen, pointing out how far the legislature had already complied with their wishes, refusing to accede to any further demands, and promising forgiveness if they would return to their duty. This answer served but to exasperate the delegates, who declared that nothing could be settled until three of the board of admiralty came down to Sheerness. On the following day the mutineers struck Vice-admiral Buckner's flag, hoisting, in its stead, that dreadful emblem of mutiny, the red or bloody flag; and, in order to concentrate the scene of their operations, compelled all the ships which lay near Sheerness to drop down to the Great Nore. On the 24th the offer of pardon was repeated, and again rejected. The delegates frequently went on shore, and, headed by Parker, marched in procession, to the great dismay of the inhabitants: they also sent deputations up the river and elsewhere, inviting the crews of other ships to join them. Many did so, including a part of the North-sea fleet under Admiral Duncan.

In this alarming state of affairs, a committee from the admiralty, on the 29th, went to Sheerness. The delegates were sent for, and every conciliatory measure tried, but in vain. The mutineers moored their ships in a line across the river, and detained every merchant vessel bound up or down. The seamen, at length, began to perceive their desperate situation; and, after adopting various expedients and committing several enormities, became deterred by the active measures that were pursuing on shore to reduce them to obedience. They deputed captain the Earl of Northesk, of the Monmouth 64, to endeavour to effect a reconciliation with government. The government, however, was firm: and just as force was about to be applied, symptoms of disunion among the mutineers raised hopes that the confederacy was working its own dissolution.

It is a singular fact that on the 4th of June, the late king's birthday, the whole fleet evinced its loyalty, by firing a royal salute and displaying the colours usual upon such occasions, the red flag being struck, during the ceremony, on board every ship except the Sandwich. In a day or two afterwards several of the ships deserted the rebels, and went for protection either up the Thames, or under the guns of the fort at Sheerness. By the 13th the red flag had disappeared from every ship's mast-head: and the crews in general, intimated a wish to surrender, provided a pardon was granted. At length, on the following morning, the crew of the Sandwich carried the ship under the guns at Sheerness, and quietly allowed Mr. Parker to accompany on shore a guard of soldiers which Vice-admiral Buckner had sent to arrest him. To make short of the business this man was tried, convicted, and executed; as were many of the ringleaders. Some were flogged through the fleet, and others sent to prison.

Thus was an end put to the Nore mutiny; a mutiny that, unlike the former, was as futile in its origin, as it happily proved unsuccessful in its issue; a mutiny that, in the opinion of many, entailed on the British navy more disgrace than could be washed away by the most brilliant triumph. It is notorious, that a custom had long prevailed for the London police, when a culprit possessed wit enough for his roguery just to elude the letter of the law, rather than discharge him that he might commit, with increased confidence, fresh depredations upon society, to send him on board a ship of war. He was generally a plausible fellow, with a smattering of learning and a knowledge of the world; two qualities which ranked him very high in the estimation of the unsophisticated sailor. He sang a good song, or at all events, he told a good story, and became, in time, the oracle of the forecastle. He knew his business (that which had brought him on ship-board) too well to practise on so circumscribed a spot; and therefore, as no one witnessed, no one believed, any harm of him. He was perhaps a dabbler in politics, and certainly, from the nature of his profession, a "bit of a lawyer." He therefore could expound acts of parliament to the sailors. In doing this, he read what he pleased, and explained how he pleased; told them where they were wronged, and pointed out how they might get redressed. In short, such a character (and how many such have been scattered over the British navy!) was capable of infecting a whole ship's company; and many of the mutinous crews could, no doubt, trace their disorganization to the first appearance among them of one of these pests of society.

A word respecting "private" grievances, or the grievances of particular ships, and we quit the subject of mutiny, we hope for ever. What a lamentable thing it is, that power and cruelty should be so often united. No monarch is more despotic, as far as respects the power of inflicting corporal punishment short of death, than the captain of a ship of war. If a man speaks or even looks to offend, he is ordered to the gangway; and the bloody furrows on his shoulders soon increase, in number and depth, beneath the vigorous arm that lays on the cat-o'-nine-tails. Captains there have been, and captains there are, who seemingly delight in such work; and who, were the cruise long enough, would not leave a sailor belonging to the ship with an unscarred back.

Such men, however, are but exceptions. Moreover, they are, for the most part, cowards at heart; and, what is worse, they frequently make cowards of those they command. Hence, officers of this stamp are commonly the cause, mediately, if not immediately, of dishonourable defeats. The brave officer punishes one man that he may not have to punish 20, and shares with the delinquent the pain which, for example sake, he is obliged to inflict. When he goes into battle, his men fight like lions; and, should they at any time be drawn aside from their duty, they, looking up to him as father, listen attentively to his admonitions, and, knowing both his benignity and his firmness, can neither controvert the justice, nor doubt the fulfilment, of his threats.

The British North-sea fleet had been so thinned by the secession of the disaffected ships, that Admiral Duncan, towards the end of May, found himself at sea with only the Venerable 74, and the Adamant 50. He nevertheless proceeded to his station off the Texel; in which harbour lay at anchor the Dutch fleet of 15 sail of the line (56s included), under the command of Vice-admiral de Winter. In order to detain the latter in port until a reinforcement should arrive, Admiral Duncan caused repeated signals to be made, as if to the main body of his fleet in the offing. This stratagem, it was supposed, had the desired effect. At length, about the middle of June, several line-of-battle ships, in detached portions, joined the British admiral, and the two fleets were again placed on an equal footing.

The Venerable, having been upwards of 18 weeks at sea, and during a part of the time exposed to very boisterous weather, was in want of almost every description of stores. Others of the ships had also suffered by the recent gales of wind, and were short of provisions. Thus circumstanced, the admiral, on the 3d of October, put into Yarmouth roads, to refit and revictual; leaving off the Dutch coast a small squadron of observation, under the orders of Captain Trollope, consisting of his own ship the Russel, the Adamant 50, Beaulieu and Circe frigates, and Martin sloop.

On the 9th, early in the morning, the Black-Joke hired armed lugger showed herself at the back of Yarmouth sands, with the signal flying, for an enemy. Immediately all was bustle and preparation; and, by a little before noon, Admiral Duncan, with 11 sail of the line, weighed and put to sea, directing his course, with a fair wind, straight across to his old station. His fleet, including the ships that joined him in the course of the next two days, consisted of the

Gun-ship		
74	Venerable	Admiral (b.) Adam Duncan. Captain William George Fairfax.
	Monarch	Vice-admiral (r.) Richard Onslow. Captain Edward O'Brien.
	Russel	Captain Henry Trollope.
	Montagu	Captain John Knight.
	Bedford	Captain Sir Thomas Byard.
	Powerful	Captain William O'Brien Drury.
	Triumph	Captain William Essington.

Gun-ship		
64	Belliqueux	Captain John Inglis.
	Agincourt	Captain John Williamson.
	Lancaster	Captain John Wells.
	Ardent	Captain Richard Rundell Burgess.
	Veteran	Captain George Gregory.
	Director	Captain William Bligh.
	Monmouth	Captain James Walker.
50	Isis	Captain William Mitchell.
	Adamant	Captain William Hotham.
Gun-frigate		
40	Beaulieu	Captain Francis Fayerman.
28	Circe	Captain Peter Halkett.
Slp.	Martin	Captain Hon. Charles Paget.

Cutters, Rose, King-George, Active and Diligent, and
Lugger, Speculator.

On the same day the Powerful, Agincourt, and Isis joined company; and on the afternoon of the 10th the advanced ships were near enough to count 22 sail of square-rigged vessels, chiefly merchantmen, at anchor in the Texel. Having received from Captain Trollope information of the course which the enemy's fleet was steering, the British admiral stood along shore to the southward. On the 11th, at 7 A.M., the Russel, Adamant, and Beaulieu were descried in the south-west, bearing at their mast-heads the joyful signal of an enemy in sight to leeward; and at 8 h. 30 m. A.M. the Dutch fleet made its appearance in the quarter pointed out by the signal, consisting of 21 ships and four brigs, named as follows:

Gun-ship		
74	Vryheid	Vice-admiral (b. at main) de Winter. Captain Van Rossem.
	Jupiter	Vice-admiral (b.) Reyntjes. Rear-admiral Menses.
	Brutus	Rear-admiral (b.) Bloys. Captain Van Treslong.
	States-General	Rear-admiral (w.) Storey. Captain ————
64	Cerberus	Captain Jacobson.
	Devries	Captain Zegers.
	Gelykheid	Captain Ruysen,
	Haerlem	Captain Wiggerts.
	Hercules	Captain Van Rysoort.
	Leyden	Captain Musquetier.
	Wassenaer	Captain Holland.
50	Alkmaar	Captain Kraft.
	Batavier	Captain Souters.
	Beschermer	Captain Hinxt.
	Delft	Captain Verdoorn.
Gun-frigate		
44	Mars	Captain Kolff.
40	Monnikendam	Captain Lancaster.
32	Ambuscade	Capt.-lieut. Huys.
	Heldin	Capt.-lieut Dumisuilde L'Estrille.

Ship-corvettes, Minerva and Waakzaamheid.
Brig-corvettes, Ajaz, Atalanta, Daphne, and Galatea.
Two advice-boats.

The Dutch fleet, thus composed, had quitted the Texel at 10 A.M. on the 8th, with a light breeze at east by north. The report at the time was, that it had been ordered to try to effect a junction with the French fleet in Brest road; but if we are to credit the French accounts, Admiral de Winter sailed with no other object in view than to seek and engage the fleet of Admiral Duncan.* On the night of the same day on which the Dutch fleet, for whatever purpose, put to sea, Captain Trollope's squadron, the wind then blowing from the south-west, was discovered to windward, and immediately chased; but the Dutch ships, being very indifferent sailers, were soon left without a chance in their favour. The fleet then stretched out towards the flat of the Meuse, where Admiral de Winter expected to be joined by a 64-gun ship. Not meeting her, he stood on to the westward, followed, or rather, as the wind was, preceded, by the squadron of Captain Trollope.

The wind, continuing westerly during the two succeeding days, prevented the Dutch fleet from getting abreast of Lowestoffe on the Suffolk coast until the evening of the 10th. The extreme darkness of that night induced Admiral De Winter to detach a few of his best-sailing ships, in the hope that they would be enabled, by daybreak, to get to windward of, and capture or chase away, the prying intruders; but, just as the chasers had crowded sail for the purpose, some friendly merchant ships came into the fleet and informed the admiral, that the English fleet was within 11 leagues of him, in the north-north-east, steering east by south. Instantly the detached ships were recalled; and the Dutch fleet, as soon as it was in compact order, edged away, with the wind at north-west, towards Camperdown, the appointed place of rendezvous.

On the 11th, at daylight, the Dutch fleet was about nine leagues off the village of Schevenningen, in loose order, speaking a friendly convoy, from whom some additional information was obtained. Shortly afterwards the persevering observers to windward were seen with numerous signals flying, which convinced Admiral De Winter that the British fleet was in sight. He accordingly ordered his captains to their respective stations, and, to facilitate the junction of the leewardmost ships, stood towards the land. On the Wykerdens bearing east distant about four leagues, the Dutch fleet hauled to the wind on the starboard tack, and shortly afterwards discovered Admiral Duncan's fleet in the north-north-west. Admiral De Winter then put about on the larboard tack; and, as soon as a close line was formed in the direction of north-east and south-west, the

* "La faction dominante obligea l'Amiral Dewinter à débarquer ses troupes et à sortir du Texel, sans autre but que de joindre la flotte Anglaise et de lui livrer bataille; elle espérait affermir sa domination par le prestige de gloire dont l'environnerait un succès naval." – *Victoires et Conquêtes*, tome viii., p. 271.

Dutch ships, squaring their main yards, resolutely awaited the approach of the British.

Owing chiefly to the inequality in point of sailing among the British ships, Admiral Duncan's fleet, when that of the Dutch appeared in sight, was in very loose order. To enable the dull sailors to take their allotted stations, the admiral, at about 11 h. 10 m. A.M., having previously made the signal for the van-ships to shorten sail, brought to on the starboard tack; but observing soon afterwards that the Dutch ships, by keeping their main topsails shivering and sometimes full, were drawing fast in-shore, he successively made the signals, for each ship to engage her opponent in the enemy's line, to bear up and sail large, and for the van to attack the enemy's rear. At 11 h. 30 m. A.M., the centre of the Dutch line then bearing about south-east distant four or five miles, the British fleet bore down, but, owing to the still disunited state of the ships, in no regular order of battle: some were stretching across to get into their proper stations; others seemed in doubt where they were to place themselves; and others, again, were pushing, at all hazards, for the thickest of the foe. At 11 h. 53 m. A.M., Admiral Duncan signalled that he should pass through the enemy's line and engage him to leeward. Unfortunately the prevailing thick weather rendered this signal, for the short time it was up, not generally understood. It was replaced, in less than a quarter of an hour, by the signal for close action; which was kept flying for an hour and a half, until, indeed, it was shot away by the enemy.

At about half past noon Vice-admiral Onslow, whose ship, the Monarch, was leading the larboard division of the British fleet, cut through the Dutch line, formed thus: Beschermer, Gelykheid, Hercules, Devries, Vryheid, States-General, Wassenaer, Batavier, Brutus, Leyden, Mars, Cerberus, Jupiter, Haerlem, Alkmaar, and Delft (with the nine frigates and corvettes stationed as an inner line, for the most part facing the intervals in the outer one), between the Jupiter and Haerlem, pouring into each of those ships, in passing, a well-directed broadside.

Then, leaving the Haerlem to the Powerful, the Monarch luffed up close alongside of the Jupiter; and the two latter of these ships became warmly engaged. The rounding to of the Monarch afforded to the Monnikendam frigate and Atalanta brig, in the rear, the opportunity of pouring some raking broadsides into the former; and the Atalanta, in particular, did not retire until considerably damaged by the Monarch's shot. The remaining ships of the larboard division, more especially the Monmouth and Russel, were soon in action with the Dutch rear-ships; among the last of which to surrender was the first that had been attacked, the Jupiter.

It was a quarter of an hour or 20 minutes after the Monarch

had broken the Dutch line, that the Venerable, frustrated in her attempt to pass astern of the Vryheid, by the promptitude of the States-General in closing the interval, put her helm a-port, and ran under the stern of the latter, pouring into the Dutch ship a broadside which soon compelled her to bear up; and the Triumph, the Venerable's second astern, found immediate employment for the Wassenaer, the second astern of the States-General. Meanwhile the Venerable had ranged up close on the lee side of her first intended antagonist, the Vryheid; with whom, on the opposite side, the Arden was also warmly engaged, and, in front, the Bedford, as the latter cut through the line astern of the Vryheid's second ahead.

The Brutus, Leyden, and Mars, not being pressed upon by opponents, advanced to the succour of their admiral, and did considerable damage to the Venerable, as well as to the Arden and others of the British van-ships. About this time the Hercules, having caught fire on the poop, bore up out of the line, and soon afterwards drifted close past the Venerable to leeward. The Dutch crew contrived, in a surprisingly quick manner, to extinguish the flames; but, having thrown overboard all their powder, they had no further means of defence, and therefore surrendered their ship, whose mizenmast had already been shot away, to the nearest opponent.

The serious damage which the Venerable had sustained obliged her to haul off, and wear round on the starboard tack. Seeing this, the Triumph, who had compelled the Wassenaer to strike, approached to give the coup de grâce to the Vryheid. That gallant ship, however, still persisted in defending herself. At length, from the united fire of the Venerable, Triumph, Arden, and Director, her three masts fell over the side and disabled her starboard guns: the Vryheid then dropped out of the line, an ungovernable hulk, and struck her colours.

With the surrender of Admiral De Winter's ship the action ceased; and the British found themselves in possession of the Vryheid and Jupiter 74s, Devries, Gelykheid, Haerlem, Hercules, and Wassenaer 64s, Alkmaar and Delft 50s, and the frigates Monnikendam and Ambuscade. The Wassenaer, although she had struck to the Triumph, was fired at by a Dutch brig, that followed her out of the line; and which brig actually compelled the 64 to rehoist her colours. The Russel soon afterwards coming up, the Wassenaer again struck them, and surrendered to her antagonist. The Monnikendam had been engaged by the Monmouth, and was finally taken possession of by the Beaulieu.

The Dutch van-ship the Beschermer, anticipating, naturally enough, too strong an opponent in the Lancaster, had very early wore out of the line. Her example was followed, with much less reason, by several of the other Dutch ships; who, although seen making off, could not be pursued, the land being only five miles distant, and the fleet in nine fathoms' water. Thus circumstanced, the British hastened to secure their prizes, in order that, before nightfall, they might get clear of the shore, which was that between Camperdown and the village of Egmont.

The appearance of the British ships at the close of the action was very unlike what it generally is, when the French or Spaniards have been the opponent of the former. Not a single lower mast, not even a topmast was shot away; nor were the rigging and sails of the ships in their usual tattered state. It was at the hulls of their adversaries that the Dutchmen had directed their shot; and this, not until the former were so near, that no aim could well miss. Scarcely a ship in the fleet but had several shot sticking in her sides. Many were pierced by shot in all directions; and a few of the ships had received some dangerous ones between wind and water, which kept their pumps in constant employment. The Arden had received no fewer than 98 round shot in her hull. The Belliqueux, Bedford, Venerable, and Monarch had likewise their share. As to the last-named ship, such was the entire state of her masts, rigging, and sails, that, were the topsail sheets which had been shot away hauled home, no one, viewing her from a little distance, would have believed that she had been in action.

With hulls so shattered, the loss of men could not be otherwise than severe. The Venerable had 13 seamen and two marines killed; two lieutenants (Edward Sneyd Clay and William Henry Douglas), one lieutenant of marines, (George Chambers, both feet shot off*), one midshipman (Mr. Stewart), two petty-officers 52 seamen, and four marines wounded; the Monarch two midshipmen (J. P. Tinlay and Moyle Finlay) and 34 seamen killed, one lieutenant (James Retalick), one lieutenant of marines (James J. Smith), four midshipmen (George Massey, Benjamin Clement, Daniel Sherwin, and Charles Slade), one master's mate (John Chimley), two petty-officers, 79 seamen, and 12 marines wounded; the Bedford, two midshipmen, 26 seamen, and three marines wounded; the Powerful, eight seaman and two marines killed, one lieutenant (Ulick Jennings), one lieutenant of marines (R. G. W. Walker), one midshipman (Daniel Rogers), the boatswain, and 74 seamen and marines wounded; the Isis, one seaman and one marine killed, one lieutenant of marines (Charles Rea), two midshipmen, and 18 seaman wounded; the Ardent, her captain, master, (Michael Dun), 33 seamen, and six marines killed, two lieutenants (James Rose and John Sobriel), one captain of marines (Richard Cuthbert), two master's mates (John Tracey and John Airey), two midshipmen (Thomas Leopard and John M 'Killier), one captain's clerk, 85 seamen, 11 marines and three boys wounded; the Belliqueux, one lieutenant (Robert Webster), one master's mate (James Milne), 20 seamen,

* The committee at Lloyd's, besides making this officer a present of a handsome gratuity in money, settled upon him 40*l*. per annum.

and three marines killed, one lieutenant (Robert England), one captain of marines (James Cassel), one midshipman (James Scott), 63 seamen, and 12 marines wounded; the Lancaster, three seamen killed, one lieutenant (Benjamin Morgan), one lieutenant of marines (John Sandys), 13 seamen, and three marines wounded; the Triumph, 25 seamen, three marines, and one boy killed, her captain, first and third lieutenants (Patrick Chapman and George Trollope), master (James Read), one midshipman (Mr. Jones), and 50 seamen and marines wounded; the Monmouth, one petty-officer, one seaman, two marines, and one boy killed, 16 seamen, two marines, and four boys wounded; the Director, six seamen and one marine wounded; the Montague, three seamen killed, one lieutenant (Ralph Sneyd), one midshipman (James Forbishly), two seamen, and one marine wounded; the Veteran, one lieutenant (Francis Ferrett), and three seamen killed, and 21 seamen wounded; and the Russel, one lieutenant (David Johnson), her master (Thomas Troughton), one master's mate (George Taylor), her boatswain, (John Brooks), two pilots (Thomas Abbot and Thomas Sherrard), and one sergeant of marines wounded: making a total of 203 killed, and 622 wounded.* So say the returns in the London Gazette; but, according to the report of "the committee appointed to manage subscriptions raised for the relief of the wounded, and the families or relations of those who were killed,"† the loss in this action amounted to 228 killed, and 812 (including 16 mortally) wounded: total 1040.

The captured ships were all, either dismasted outright, or so injured in their masts that most of the latter fell, as soon as the wind and sea, in the passage home, began to act powerfully upon them. As to their hulls, the ships were like sieves, and only worth bringing into port to be exhibited as trophies. The loss on board was proportionably severe. The Dutch vice-admiral and the two rear-admirals were all wounded, more or less; and Admiral De Winter died in London, shortly after his arrival there, not, however, of his wound, but of a chronic disease. Captain Holland, of the Wassenaer, was mortally wounded early in the action; and Admiral De Winter's captain, Van-Rossem, had his thigh shot off, of which wound he afterwards died. Many other officers suffered; and the total of killed and wounded in the Dutch fleet, including the loss on board the Monnikendam frigate, amounted, according to the Dutch returns, to 540 killed, and 620 wounded.‡

Our next business is to show the force of the rival fleets, in this their sanguinary engagement. The long-gun force, as established upon British ships in general, has already been so often adverted to, that we have only to point out any exceptions

* See Appendix, No. 6.

† This noble subscription, so characteristic of British feeling on such occasions, amounted to 52, 609*l*. 10*s*. 10*d*.

‡ See Appendix, No. 7.

that may exist in reference to the particular individuals composing Admiral Duncan's fleet.

Although early in the present year an order had issued establishing carronades very extensively upon line-of-battle ships, yet, as it was restricted to ships coming forward to be fitted, the order of November 1794,* must still be our guide. The only ships out of the 16, that appear to have been armed differently from the November establishment, are the Venerable and Ardent. The latter had been ordered, in July 1795, four instead of two 24-pounder carronades for her forecastle; and the former, in June, 1794, two 68-pounder carronades for her forecastle, and two 32-pounder ones in lieu of two of her quarter deck 9s. We have reason to think that the two 50-gun ships did not mount any poop-carronades, and shall therefore assign them none. To allow, also, for such of the other ships as may have taken on board less than their established number, or, as was often the case, had not been supplied with any carronades at all for their poop, we will fix the total amount of 18-pounders at half what it otherwise would be, that is, at 42 instead of 84.

In stating the crew of each British ship at her net establishment, we are satisfied that the amount will be rather over than under rated. We know, for instance, that the Ardent was 70, and the Lancaster 72, men short of their proper number; and it is probable, from circumstances to which we need not recur, that few if any of the ships in Admiral Duncan's fleet had their complement on board.

The gun-force of the Dutch ships may be stated without much difficulty. Of the seven that escaped from the British this time, five were subsequently captured: hence, there remain but two of the 16, the States-General and Brutus, whose armaments have not been obtained by actual inspection.

The Vryheid and Jupiter respectively mounted, on their first and second decks, the same nominal nature of guns as an English small-class 18-pounder 74, as O, for instance, in the first annual abstract. On the quarterdeck and forecastle the Vryheid mounted, when brought into port, sixteen 12-pounders; making, in the whole, two guns short (perhaps disabled and thrown overboard), of the number assigned to her, as well as to the Jupiter, by the Dutch admiral himself. The Jupiter arrived with ten 12, and four 8 pounders, instead, probably of six of the latter, and 12 of the former, as afterwards found on board the Washington, of the same nominal force. The Wassenaer, Devries, and Hercules appear to have each mounted twenty-six 32-pounders, and each of the four remaining 64s, the same number of 24-pounders, on the first deck, with twenty-six 18s on the second. On the quarterdeck and forecastle, the three first-named ships carried, of 8-pounders, 14, making a total of

* See Appendix, Annual Abstract No. 3.

66, and the four remaining ships, 16, making a total of 68 guns. The four 50s mounted 56 guns each: twenty-four 18, twenty-four 12, and eight 8 pounders; and the Mars, formerly a 60-gun ship, mounted, on her main deck, twenty-six 32, and on her quarter-deck and forecastle, eighteen 18 pounders. So that, although nominally a 44-gun frigate, the Mars, in broadside weight of metal, rather exceeded a British 64. With these explanations, the following will be the account of the number and nature of guns mounted by the two fleets:

BRITISH.			DUTCH.		
Long guns	No.	No.	Long guns	No.	No.
32 pounders	196		32 pounders	216	
24 pounders	226		24 pounders	104	
18 pounders	380		18 pounders	408	
12 pounders	44		12 pounders	168	
9 pounders	206		8 pounders	138	
6 pounders	12				
		1064			
Carronades			Carronades		
68 pounders	2				
32 pounders	14				
24 pounders	28				
18 pounders	42		None apparently.		
		86			
	Total	1150		Total	1034

The complements of the Dutch ships may be stated as they were returned by their own officers. From being expressed in round numbers, they were probably the full establishment of each ship; but any deficiency in that respect is more than counterbalanced by the liberal allowance made on the other side. Having thus analyzed the armaments of the different ships engaged, we can, with more confidence, proceed to our next task, that of exhibiting, in one view, the

COMPARATIVE FORCE OF THE TWO FLEETS.

		BRITISH,	DUTCH.
Ships	No.	16	16
Broadside-guns	No.	575	517
	lbs	11501	9857
Crews	Agg. No.	8221	7157
Size	Agg. tons.	23601	20937

When it is considered, that the Dutch had placed their frigates and ship and brig corvettes (even the latter carrying long 12, and some of them long 18 pounders), abreast of the intervals in their line, and that many of the British ships, in the van, centre, and rear, were much annoyed, as they luffed up to leeward of their opponents, by the raking fire of those vessels, the above statement, which excludes the whole of them, must appear, if favouring either party, to favour the Dutch. We might perhaps, fairly enough, owing to their active interference, having included in our comparative statement the three remaining Dutch frigates; and then, in all the items except the first, that statement would have shown an exact quality of force. But, if even there was a slight superiority on the part of Admiral Duncan, the battle of Camperdown, as a fleet-action, possessed the merit of being (to use the emphatic language of the Broughtonian school) the second *stand-up* fight of the war.

Admiral de Winter, it will be recollected, in the account he transmitted to the Batavian government, and a copy of which appeared in all the London journals, attributed his failure to four causes: first, the numerical superiority of the British as to ships of the line; secondly, their having been at sea together for 19 weeks, and hence become known to each other; thirdly, the advantage of the attack; and fourthly, the early retreat of six of his ships, and the bad sailing of four of those that remained. And he concludes with expressing a belief that, had his signals been obeyed and executed, with the same promptitude that Admiral Duncan's were, some of the British fleet would have reached the Texel, "as a memento of Batavian prowess, and a monument to the memory of the 11th of October, 1797."

Had the Dutch admiral wished to afford an additional cause of triumph to his adversary, he could not have succeeded better, than by inviting a discussion on the very points, on which he seems so confidently to rely for producing an opposite result. If Admiral De Winter withdraws the Mars from his line, because she passed for a frigate, why may not Admiral Duncan leave out the Adamant and Isis, which also were not strictly line-of-battle ships; and neither of which equalled by a third, the Mars in force? The numbers then would be, 14 English and 15 Dutch. So far from the British ships having been "nineteen weeks together," many of them had but recently joined; and some, as appeared on Captain Williamson's court-martial, were actually unknown to others of them in the fleet. Was it an "advantage," while bearing down to the attack, to be exposed to the raking fire of the Dutch line? Is it true that the Dutch ships bravely withheld their fire, until their adversaries were quite near; but the British ships had no right to calculate on such forbearance. Was it an "advantage" to be unexpectedly assailed by a second line, formed of nine frigates, heavy corvettes, and brigs, drawn up in the rear? Unexpectedly, we say, because it is not customary for frigates to fire; or, while they remain neuter, to be fired at.

Although none of the British ships "retreated," some of them, without doubt, were backward in advancing; otherwise, a part, if not the whole of those six ships, of whose misbehaviour Admiral De Winter complains, might have been stopped in their flight. It was owing chiefly to the "bad sailing" of several of Admiral Duncan's ships, that the onset was so irregular; and that any of the British ships, as was the case with several, had to doubt who were their proper opponents in the Dutch line. In point of signal-making, too, there was, as proved on the trial of the Agincourt's captain, about an equal share of misunderstanding: the hazy state of the weather, indeed, made this a common cause of complaint to both fleets. Upon the whole, the shattered hulls and blood-besmeared decks of the prizes, and the almost equally damaged state of the principally engaged ships among those that had taken them, gave decided proofs that, although it had lain by so long, "Batavian prowess" still claimed the respect of an enemy and the applause of the world.

Scarcely had the British admiral turned the heads of his ships in a homeward direction, ere a gale ensued, that scattered and endangered the whole of them. Most of the masts that had been tottering fell on the decks; and the rolling of the vessels occasioned the water to rush through shot-holes, that, in common weather, would not have taken in a drop. On the 13th the Delft, while in tow of the Veteran, exhibited a board with the words chalked on it, "The ship is sinking." As quickly as possible the British boats of all the nearest ships were hoisted out; and the greater part of the Delft's crew were fortunately saved.

The following particulars of the loss of the Delft, we extract from a Steel's list of March, 1803. "When Lieutenant Charles Bullen, first of the Monmouth, came on board to take possession of the ship, he found her much damaged, having many shot through her hull and rigging, and her mainmast and yard shot away, two officers and forty-one of her men killed, and one officer and seventy-five men wounded. He sent the captain, two officers, and ninety men on board his own ship, and requested the Delft's late first lieutenant, Mr. Heilberg, and who was not wounded, to assist him, with the men under his command, in preventing the ship from sinking; in which they succeeded until the 14th of the same month, when a storm came on and put the vessel in a very dangerous situation. She filled ten feet with water, so that all hope of saving her was soon at an end. Lieutenant Bullen represented this to Mr. Heilberg, telling him, at a certain signal, he should throw himself, with his men, into the longboat, and inviting him to avail himself of the opportunity of effecting his escape. 'But how can I leave these unfortunate men?' replied he, pointing to the wounded sailors, whom it had been necessary to bring on deck, as the hold was already full of water. Lieutenant Bullen, struck with the answer, exclaimed, 'God bless you, my brave fellow! Here is my hand; I give you my word I will stay here with you!' He then caused his own men to leave the ship, and remained behind himself to assist the Dutch. The Russel soon sent out her boats to their succour, and brought off as many as could be put on board them, and lost no time in making a second voyage with equal success: but few of the wounded could be got off, although the two officers had united their efforts for that purpose, and still remained with them in the vessel, with three subaltern officers and about thirty seamen. They were sill cherishing the hope that the boats would, a third time, come to their relief; but the fatal moment was now arrived, and on a sudden the Delft went down. Lieutenant Bullen sprang into the sea and reached his own ship; but the unfortunate Heilberg perished, the victim of his courage and humanity."

The Monnikendam frigate, in the custody of the Beaulieu, was wrecked on the Ressen sand, near West-Capel; but the whole of the people fortunately got safe on shore. The Ambuscade frigate, being driven on the Dutch coast, was recaptured. The remainder of the prizes, one by one, ultimately reached a British port. As trophies, their appearance was gratifying; but, as ships of war, they were not the slightest acquisition to the navy of England.

Of the seven Dutch line-of-battle ships that had quitted the action to return home, one only, the Brutus, met any obstruction in her way thither. On the afternoon of the 13th, while, in company with the Atalanta and another armed brig, this ship lay at anchor, in six fathoms, off the heights of Hinder, the British 40-gun (24-pounder) frigate Endymion, Captain Sir Thomas Williams, made her appearance in the north-east. As the frigate bore down, the two brigs weighed and stood further in shore; and the Brutus, hoisting her ensign and a rear-admiral's flag, waited the former's approach. At about 4 h. 3 m. P.M. the line-of-battle ship commenced firing, but Sir Thomas Williams reserved his fire until he came athwart the Dutch ship's bows; when the Endymion opened her larboard broadside, receiving a fire in return from her opponent's bow-chasers. Putting about presently, the frigate repeated the fire from her starboard guns, at a closer distance than before, and was again fired at in return from the bow-guns of the Brutus. No sooner had the Endymion passed ahead of her opponent, than the strength of the tide drifted her within range of the 74's broadside. This the frigate, as she stood on, answered with her stern-guns, until about 5 h. 30 m. P.M.; when the Endymion having passed out of gun-shot, the firing ceased.

Since the first discovery of the enemy, the Endymion had made signals and fired guns to windward, in the hope that some ship of Amdrial Duncan's fleet, from which she had parted only a few hours before, might be near enough to understand them. While stretching on in the direction of the fleet, the frigate continued to make signals for an enemy, adding to them, after dark, several rockets and blue lights. At length, at about 10 h. 30 m. P.M., the Beaulieu joined company; and the two frigates stood back to the spot on which the Brutus had been left at anchor. On the 14th, at 5 A.M., the Brutus was seen, but not in the same place: the ship had weighed, and was now at anchor, with Goree Gatt open astern of her. At 6 A.M., not considering herself safe with two British frigates for her opponents, the Brutus reweighed, and ran over the flats into the Maese. At 7 A.M. the Endymion and Beaulieu, being thus frustrated in their object, hauled their wind and stood off. The Endymion's casualties were confined to the loss of her foretopgallant yard, and some trifling injury to her sails and rigging.

On the 17th, the day of his arrival at the Nore, Admiral Duncan was created a baron and a viscount of Great Britain, by the titles of Baron Duncan of Lundie, and Viscount Duncan of Camperdown. At the same time Vice-admiral Onslow was created a baronet, and Captains Trollope and Fairfax were made knights-bannerets. Gold medals were also struck, to commemorate the victory, and presented to the admirals and captains, to be worn in the same manner as those given on Earl Howe's and Sir John Jervis's victories. The thanks of both houses of parliament were unanimously voted to the fleet; and the city of London presented Lord Duncan with its freedom and a sword of 200 guineas value, and the same, with a sword of 100 guineas value, to Sir Richard Onslow.

As on all similar occasions, the first lieutenant of every ship present in this battle received a step in his rank. The names of those serving on board the line-of-battle ships were, according to the best of our researches,* as follows: William Renton, Venerable; John Winne, Monarch; Charles Burroughs, Russel; Thomas Linthorne, Montagu; John Smith, Bedford; Ulick Jennings, Powerful; Richard Power, Triumph; Robert England, Belliqueux; William Lane, Agincourt; Christopher Watson, Lancaster; George Morris, Ardent; Thomas Halton, Veteran; John M 'Taggart, Director; Charles Bullen, Monmouth; William Lamb, Isis; and Christopher John Williams Nesham, Adamant.

Unfortunately, justice required that at least one captain should be tried by a court-martial, for his delinquency in the glorious battle for the successful result of which the above rewards had been so justly bestowed. Captain Williamson, of the Agincourt, was the officer so tried. The court sat from December 4th to January 1st, on board the Circe at Sheerness, upon two charges: one for disobedience of signals and not going into action; the other for cowardice or disaffection. The court considered the first charge as proved, but not the second, and sentenced Captain Williamson to be placed at the bottom of the list of post-captains, and to be rendered incapable thenceforward of serving in the navy.

* See p. 52.

LIGHT SQUADRONS AND SINGLE SHIPS.

In October of the last year we left the French Rear-admiral Sercey, with his six frigates, the Forte, Seine, Vertu, Cybèle, Régénérée, and Prudente, on his way to Batavia. He arrived there, and besides getting his ships thoroughly repaired and victualled, obtained a treaty from the Regency of Batavia, to supply the Isle of France with rice, as well as with cordage and canvass, to the amount of 300,000 rix-dollars. After a stay of two months, Rear-admiral Sercey put to sea on his return to the Isle of France. On the 28th of January, 1797, just as he had cleared the straits of Bali, and was off the east end of Java, M. Sercey met with, what he considered at the time, a fortunate escape from very superior force, but which, he was afterwards fain to confess, was the most unlucky occurrence that had befallen him during his long, and by no means inactive professional life.

Five (if not six) homeward-bound, richly-laden Indiamen, the Woodford, Captain Charles Lennox, Ocean, Captain Andrew Patton, Taunton-Castle, Captain Edward Studd, Canton, Captain Abel Vyvyan, and Boddam, Captain George Palmer, under the charge of the first-named officer, found themselves on the morning of the day mentioned, in sight of Rear-admiral Sercey's frigate-squadron. Knowing that, besides the inutility of running as a means of escape from men of war, the very act of doing so would expose the weakness of his force, Captain Lennox, with as much judgment as presence of mind, hoisted the flag of Rear-admiral Rainier, blue at the mizen, and made his other ships hoist pendants and ensigns to correspond. He even did more. He detached two of his ships to chase and reconnoitre the enemy. As these advanced towards the French reconnoitring frigate, the Cybèle, Captain Thréouart, the latter crowded sail to join her consorts, with the signal at her mast-head, "The enemy is superior in force to the French."*

On this the French admiral also made sail; and although, on the Forte's carrying away her main topmast, M. Sercey thought it extraordinary that the English did not continue the chase, the assurance by Captain Thréouart, on his passing within hail of the Forte, that he had clearly made out the enemy's force to consist of two line-of-battle ships and four frigates, and four frigates, induced the admiral to continue his retreat. In about four weeks after this well-managed ruse on the part of Captain Lennox, Rear-admiral Sercey arrived with his squadron at the Isle of France. There, to his mortification, he learnt, that Admiral Rainer had not been near the Bali straits, and consequently that the fears of one of his captains, coupled with a little

* L'ennemi est supérieur aux forces Françaises." – *Victoires et Conquêtes*, tome viii. P. 295.

remissness on his own part, had lost him at least five valuable Indiamen.

On the 31st of January, as a small frigate-squadron, under the orders of Lord Garlies, in the Lively 32, was crushing about nine leagues north-west of the Monsheque mountains, with the wind at east-north-east, a strange ship hove in sight to the northward. Chase was then given; and, by an hour after sunset, the 12-pounder 32-gun frigate Andromache, Captain Charles John Moore Mansfield, having run far ahead of her companions, came up with the stranger. After hailing and being answered in Spanish, the Andromache opened her fire; and the two ships continued closely engaged for upwards of 40 minutes, when the Andromache's opponent, having failed in an attempt to board, hauled down her colours.

It now appeared that the ship, which the British frigate had been engaging, was an Algerine, of much the same force as the Andromache, and who had taken the latter for a Portuguese frigate. This mutual mistake cost the British three men killed and six wounded, and the Algerine as many as 66 killed, and 50 badly, besides several slightly wounded. By far the greater number of the Algerine ship's killed consisted of those who had been rash enough to throw themselves upon the British frigate's deck, in the vain hope to carry her by boarding. After the action had terminated, the Lively and the rest of the squadron joined company.

On the 22d of February, in the evening, the French 40-gun frigates Résistance and Vengeance, 22-gun ship-corvette Constance, and lugger Vautour, anchored in Fisgard bay on the coast of Wales. During the night they landed 1200 galley-slaves, dressed and accoutred as soldiers, but without any cannon or camp-equipage. The alarm soon spread, and it was not long before a strong body of militia, under the command of Lord Cawdor, assembled near the spot. The Frenchmen, whose intentions were rather predatory than warlike, immediately surrendered, and were marched as prisoners to Haversfordwest. Meanwhile the vessels that had brought them weighed, and soon disappeared from the coast. What was the object of this silly expedition, no one, not even among the French, seems rightly to have understood.

On the 9th of March, early in the morning, the British 18-pounder 36-gun frigate San Fiorenzo, Captain Sir Harry Neale, and 12-pounder 36-frigate Nymphe, Captain John Cooke, while on their return to Admiral Lord Bridport's fleet off Ushant, after having reconnoitred the road to Brest, then bearing from them east by north distant three or four leagues, saw to the westward, standing in towards the port, two of the three ships which had been so creditably employed; one the 40-gun frigate Résistance, Captain (de vais) Jean-Baptiste Montagniés Laroque, the other the 22-gun corvette Constance, Captain

Desauney. The San-Fiorenzo and Nymphe immediately tacked and hauled close to the wind, until, having gained the weather-gage, they bore down for the two strangers, who had by this time hoisted French colours, and the headmost of whom now fired at the British ships. The distance from Pointe Saint-Mathieu being less than three leagues, the French fleet of 14 sail of the line and six frigates in sight from the tops, and the wind a leading one out of Brest, that which was likely to be the most decisive, was deemed the best, mode of attack.

Accordingly, the two British frigates stood for, and, at the distance of about 40 yards, soon engaged, the headmost ship, the Résistance; which, after a slight defence, struck her colours. By the time this ship was taken possession of, the other had arrived up, and, being attacked by both British frigates as warmly as her consort had been, in 10 minutes surrendered also. The action, which was a running fight, did not last longer than half an hour; but it is due to Captain Desauney to state, that, although commanding by far the weaker ship, he made a much more creditable defence than his commodore: the Constance, indeed, soon after being taken possession of, lost her mainmast and fore topmast, owing to the fire she had withstood. Just at the close of the action, the British 74-gun ship Robust, Captain George Countess, and 28-gun frigate Triton, Captain John Gore, hove in sight; a circumstance that, doubtless, had its effect in facilitating the capture.

Neither of the British ships suffered the slightest damage or loss. The Résistance, on the other hand, had 10 men killed, her first lieutenant and eight men wounded; the Constance, eight men killed and six wounded: total 18 killed and 15 wounded.

There is little doubt that, had the odds in this case been reversed, the British would have made an honourable, if not a successful defence. Taking into the account, however, that a British 74 and frigate were present at the close, and must have been in sight during the continuance, of the action, all that can be said is, that the British gained, without the occurrence on their part of a single casualty, two remarkably fine ships. The Résistance mounted 48 guns, or four more long 8s than No. 5 in the table at p. 54 of vol. i., (but not as a contemporary states, "24-pounders on the main deck,"*) and measured 1182 tons. The Vengeance was her sister-ship. The larger prize, under the name, in allusion to the spot at which the Résistance and her consorts had disembarked their convict freight, of Fisgard, continued for a long while at the head of the 38-gun frigate-class, and the smaller one retained her French name as a 22-gun post-ship.

On the 13th of March the British 14-gun cutter Viper, Lieu-

* Brenton, vol. i., p. 408.

tenant John Pengelly, being about seven leagues north-west from Alboran, on her return to Gibraltar from Algiers, descried in the north-west quarter, and gave chase to, a Spanish 10-gun brig-privateer, named "Piteous Virgin-Maria." At 1 P.M. the Viper fired a gun at the chase; who then hoisted Spanish colours, fired a shotted gun, and hove to. In half an hour the cutter got close alongside the brig, and a smart action ensued, which continued until 3 h. 10 m. P.M., when the latter hauled down her colours.

During the action, the Virgin-Maria attempted several times to set fire to her heretic opponent, by throwing on board flasks filled with powder and sulphur; but the Viper's people were too active to suffer the scheme to succeed. The cutter received 40 shots in her hull, and a 4-pound shot in her lower mast. Her rigging also was very much cut; but she fortunately sustained no loss. The brig was a good deal damaged, and lost one man killed, one mortally, and six dangerously wounded. The Viper's guns were 4-pounders, and her complement was about 48 men and boys. Of the brig's guns, six were Spanish 4, and four 6 pounders: she also mounted eight swivels, and had a complement of 42 men. Upon the whole, this little victory on the part of the cutter did great credit to her officers and crew.

On the 1st of April the 18-gun ship-sloop Hazard (eighteen 6-pounders and six 12 or 18 pounder carronades, with 121 men and boys), Captain Alexander Ruddach, while cruising close off the Skellocks on the coast of Ireland, fell in with the French brig-privateer Hardi, of 18 long 8-pounders and 130 men and boys, and after seven hours' chase, at the end of which the Hardi lost both her topmasts, captured the privateer without resistance. On the 2d of the preceding December the Hazard, under the same commander, captured, after the discharge of one or two broadsides, the French ship-privateer Musette, of 22 guns and 150 men and boys. Shortly after his capture of the second privateer, Captain Ruddach was, very deservedly, promoted to post-rank.

On the 26th of April at 6 A.M., the British 74-gun ship Irresistible, Captain George Martin, and 36-gun frigate Emerald, Captain Velterers Cornewall Berkeley, being on a cruise off the coast of Spain, fell in with and chased two Spanish frigates, the Ninfa and Santa-Elena, of 34 guns, 12 and 6 pounders, and 320 men each, from Havana, bound to Cadiz. On discovering by what superior force they were pursued, the two frigates ran for and anchored in Conil bay, near Trafalgar. Thither, at 2 h. 30 m. P.M., the Irresistible and Emerald, skilfully rounding the Laja de Cape Rocha, a dangerous ledge of rocks, a little to the northward of Conil, followed them, and a smart action ensued; which, at 4 P.M., terminated in the capture of the two frigates. The Santa-Elena, after she had struck, cut her cable and drove on shore; her crew effecting their escape. This frigate was subsequently got off, but in too damaged a state to be kept afloat: she accordingly went down. Part of the Ninfa's crew also escaped to the shore. The loss sustained by the two frigates was represented to have been 18 men killed and 30 wounded. The Irresistible had one man killed and one wounded. The Emerald escaped without a casualty. The Ninfa, under the name of Hamadryad, was taken into the British service as a 12-pounder 36.

The following anecdote we extract from the work of a contemporary, as believing the Ninfa and Santa-Elena to be the frigates alluded to. "While our fleet lay before Cadiz (the in-shore squadron* almost within gun-shot of the lighthouse, the main body of the fleet about five miles off, at anchor), two frigates came upon them in the night, and were reported to the captain of the flag-ship, by the officer of the watch. They were supposed to be either friends or neutrals; and the Spanish captains were not sensible of their danger, until, standing nearer to Cadiz, they learned from the fishing-boats, that the British fleet was without them, and the advanced squadron within them. Not a moment was to be lost, and the time was well employed. They were loaded with treasure, which was instantly got on deck, put into the fishing-boats, and landed safely at Cadiz without suspicion. Daylight discovered the fortunate Spaniards, after all their treasure was in safety; they were chased, and one taken, and the other destroyed, in a bay not far from the scene of their achievement."†

The Spaniards usually sent their frigates for treasure in pairs; and, at the very time that the Ninfa and Santa-Elena were thus lost to their country, another pair of Spanish frigates were either on their passage out to, or on their return from, South-America, two such frigates having been fallen in with, on the 20th of May, in latitude 34° 36' south, longitude 53° 14' west, which is a little to the northward of the mouth of the Rio de la Plata, by the British 12-pounder 36-gun frigate Oiseau (late Cléopâtre) captain Charles Brisbane.

At daylight on the day mentioned the Oiseau, standing on the starboard tack, with the wind at about south by west, discovered and immediately chased a strange sail bearing south-west by west, distant three or four leagues. At 7 h. 30 m. A.M. a second sail made her appearance astern of the first. At 9 h. 30 m. A.M. the leading ship, now seen to be a frigate, hauled up her mainsail and took in her topgallantsails, and in another quarter of an hour fired a gun to leeward and hoisted Spanish colours. The Oiseau, who had now approached without gun-shot, hoisted

* Of which Captain Sir James Saumarez, of the Orion, was, we believe the commanding officer.

† Brenton, vol iii., p. 4.

English colours and discharged her broadside in return. Perceiving, however, that the other ship, a frigate also, was coming up fast, under a press of canvass, the Oiseau made all sail from two opponents, either of which had the appearance of being at least equal to herself. At 2 h. 45 m. P.M., the headmost of the two Spanish frigates, finding that a longer chase would separate her from her consort, shortened sail and hauled to the wind; thus destroying the hope entertained by the Oiseau, of bringing one of the frigates to action without interruption by the other.

These details, or the principal part of them, are extracted from the Oiseau's log, which we were induced to search on reading the following paragraph in a work of naval biography recently published: "Whilst thus employed," cruising off the Rio de la Plata, "Captain Brisbane fell in with two large Spanish frigates, one of them bearing a commodore's broad pendant. A severe engagement ensued; but, notwithstanding the disparity of force, the l'Oiseau had the good fortune to beat off her opponents."*

Had this statement regarded an officer, whose professional fame was less firmly established than that of Captain Charles Brisbane, we should, as we have done in some similar cases in Mr. Marshall's book, have let it pass without notice, for fear of exciting an undue prejudice against the officer who has thus the misfortune to be the subject of biographical exaggeration. A writer should, indeed, be very cautious about introducing such loose, undated accounts; especially, as the same means of ascertaining their validity, and, if the main facts be true, of supplying any deficient particulars, are alike open to him and to us.

On the 16th of July, in the night, a British squadron, composed of the 40-gun frigate Anson, Captain Philip Charles Durham, 38-gun frigate Artois, Captain Sir Edmund Nagle, and 18-gun brig-sloop Sylph, Capt. John Chambers White, and Dolly, hired armed cutter, being on a cruise off Ushant, discovered and gave chase to a convoy of fourteen French vessels, in charge of the 28-gun frigate Calliope (mounting, like others of her class, 32 or 34 guns), and one ship, and one brig corvette, standing in for Audierne bay. The two corvettes hauled their wind to the southward and escaped round the Penmarcks; but the frigate, not being able to follow them, at about 2 h. 20 m. A.M., on the 17th, cut away her mast and ran on shore, and a brig, laden with ordnance stores, anchored close to her.

At 7 A.M. the Anson anchored with a spring on her cable, and opened a fire upon the frigate and brig, but at rather too great a distance to do much execution. At 9 h. 30 m A.M., the Sylph

* Marshall, vol. i., p. 734.

gallantly ran in and anchored between the Anson and the French frigate, and within 150 yards of the latter. As soon as she had got a spring upon her cable, the Sylph opened upon the Calliope a well-directed fire, which the frigate, at intervals, returned. At 11 h. 30 m. A.M. the Anson weighed and made sail, to join the Pomone and Artois; but the brig remained, and continued the cannonade with such spirit and effect, until recalled by signal at 6 P.M., that the French crew were ultimately prevented by it from using any means to save the ship or stores, and on the next day the Calliope went to pieces.

The fire from the French frigate had occasioned a loss to the Sylph of five seamen and one marine wounded; but the Calliope's loss by the brig's fire, it was impossible to ascertain. Of the convoy in charge of the Calliope and corvettes, one transport ship, three brigs, and four chasse-marées were taken, and one timber-ship and one brig were run on shore and burnt; the remainder effected their escape.

On the 11th of August, early in the morning, Sir John Warren, cruising off the coast of La Vendée, with, besides the Pomone, the 38-gun frigate Jason, Captain Charles Stirling, 12-pounder 32-gun frigate Triton, Captain John Gore, and 18-gun brig-sloop Sylph, Captain John Chambers White, discovered a French convoy of brigs and chasse-marées, under the escort of a ship-corvette and three or four gun-vessels, standing to sea out of the Pertuis-d'Antioche; and which, to avoid the danger that threatened them, ran for the river of Sable-d'Olonne.

Perceiving that the corvette and a brig gun-vessel had anchored at the entrance of the river under the protection of a fort, Captain White gallantly asked permission to stand in and cannonade them. Leave having been obtained, the Sylph, at 11 h. 30 m. A.M., anchored in seven fathoms, about a mile to the westward of Sable-d'Olonne, and opened her fire, which was presently returned by the fort and vessels. At noon the Pomone and Jason (the Triton was then in chase in the offing), keeping under way, joined in the cannonade; and soon afterwards the gun-vessel cut her cables, and endeavoured to rejoin her convoy at anchor in the river, and sank at its entrance. At about a quarter past noon, finding it impracticable to do more, the Sylph cut her cable and stood out, with the loss of one master's mate (Henry Wrickson) and two seamen killed, and three wounded. The Pomone, also, had one seaman killed, and one seaman and one marine wounded. The result of this attack was, that a French gun-vessel was destroyed, and a French ship-corvette, which was seen in the harbour of Olonne, by the Pomone, on the 16th, considerably damaged.

On the 27th, in the evening, Sir John, with the same squadron, cruising to the southward of the entrance of the river Gironde, discovered and chased in the south-west another French convoy. The chase continued all night, and the Jason and Triton, being far to windward and ahead, captured five of the vessels. On the 28th, at 2 A.M., the Pomone, being near the shore, discovered a cutter, and sent a boat to take possession of her; but the cutter, which was the Petit-Diable, of 12 or 14 guns, and 70 or 80 men, ordered the boat to keep off. On this the Pomone herself stood in, and, firing a few shots, cut away the Petit-Diable's mast, and compelled her to run on shore among the breakers upon the coast of Arcasson; where it is supposed she was lost.

This is a plain account of what was effected by Sir John Warren's squadron on the 11th and 28th of August; but the following is the result, as it stands in the London Gazette at the foot of Sir John Warren's letter: "A ship-corvette, 22 guns and 200 men, captured August 11, 1797, at Sable-d'Olonne; on shore, and bilged. A brig gun-vessel, 12 guns and 70 men, sunk. Le Petit-Diable, cutter, 18 guns and 180 men, captured August 29, 1797, on the coast of the Arcasson; on shore, bilged, and fell over," besides a long list of merchant vessels. We cannot say, at this moment, whether the head-money for the crews of these three vessels of war, which would amount to 1150*l*., was paid by the British government; but we may hereafter have to show, that an evil of incalculably greater magnitude arose from these, to say the least of them, highly-coloured gazette-letters of Sir John Borlase Warren.

On the 1st of August, while the British transport, Lady Shore, with 119 convicts on board, was on her way to Botany Bay, a number of French emigrants and deserters, very unwisely sent on board to guard the prisoners, having gained over the majority of the crew, revolted and took possession of the ship. A spirited opposition by the passengers, and the loyal part of the soldiers and seamen, might yet have saved the ship, had not a traitorous scoundrel, one "Adjutant Minchin," delivered up the arms and ammunition to the mutineers. On the 15th, when about 100 leagues from the land, in the latitude of Cape Sta.-Maria on the coast of Brazil, the mutineers sent away in the long boat 29 persons, men, women, and children, the youngest child not five weeks old! After great suffering from bad weather, the boat reached the port of San-Pedros, and the people, among whom was the notorious Major Semple, were hospitably received.

This occurrence we should scarcely have thought worth recording in these pages, but for a highly exaggerated account that has found its way into a respectable French historical work. The article, which is epitomized, "Enlèvement d'un vaisseau anglais de la compagnie des Indes, par huit prisonniers de guerre français," represents the two principal actors to be Sélis, one of the chief quartermasters, and Thierry, the pilot, late belonging to the French corvette, Bonne-Citoyenne, captured in March of the preceding year.

These men, it appears, after a confinement of seven months in the prison at Petersfield, contrived to effect their escape, but were arrested by the coast-fencibles, near Portsmouth, and reconfined in one of the prisons there. Thence they were removed, the account states, along with several other prisoners, to the hulks, preparatory to being transported to Botany Bay. From the hulks, Sélis and Thierry, with six other Frenchmen, effected their escape; but they were all retaken, and were finally embarked on board the Lady-Shore. These eight Frenchmen, with no other assistance than that afforded by three Germans and a Spaniard, are represented to have surprised and captured the convict-ship; which they afterwards carried to Monte-Video and sold.*

Accustomed as we are to the French manner of relating an occurrence of this kind, the chief surprise it excites in us is, that prisoners of war should have been sent to Botany Bay for having, as, by a law of nature almost as strong as that of self-preservation, they were justified in doing, attempted to escape from confinement. We think there must be a mistatement as to the cause that led to the banishment of MM. Sélis and Thierry; in short, that these French prisoners had committed some act of turpitude, the divulgement of which would have shown, not only that their punishment had been justly inflicted, but that their veracity was not to be relied upon.

On the 10th of August, at daylight, the British 38-gun frigate Arethusa, Captain Thomas Wolley, being in latitude 30° 49' north, longitude 55° 50' west, and having a detained Prussian ship in tow, discovered to windward three strange sail; one of which, at about 7 h. 30 m. A.M., bore down, under French colours, to within half gun-shot, and then opened her fire. This the Arethusa was not slow in returning; and the French ship, which, extraordinary to say, was only a corvette of 20 long 8-pounders, made no attempt to escape, until she had fought a British 18-pounder frigate, mounting 44 guns, for half an hour, and sustained, beside considerable damage in her sails and rigging, a loss of two seamen killed and eight wounded. The Gaieté's fire was not wholly ineffectual; for the Arethusa lost one seaman killed, the captain's clerk (leg amputated), and two seamen wounded.

The Gaieté had 186 men on board at the commencement of the action, and was commanded by Enseigne de Vaisseau Jean-François Guignier. One of the vessels in her company was the brig-corvette Espoir, of 14 guns. The latter kept to windward until the action was over, and then stood away. What the third vessel was, does not appear; but, unless she was a corvette nearly equal in force to the Gaieté, the temerity of M. Guignier in provoking the attack was highly censurable. At all events, his two consorts were not ambitious to take a share in an enterprise of such hardihood and danger as that in which the French

* Victoires et Conquêtes, tome viii., p. 265.

enseigne de vaisseau lost his ship. The Gaieté was quite a new vessel, measuring 514 tons, and became a great acquisition to the class of British 20-gun ships.

On the 15th of August the Alexandrian schooner, of six guns, 4-pounders, and 40 men and boys, commanded by Lieutenant William Wood Senhouse, and acting as tender to the Prince of Wales 98, Rear-admiral Harvey's flag-ship at Martinique, being on a cruise off the island, in quest of French privateers, fell in with, and, after a spirited action of 45 minutes, captured, the French privateer schooner Coq, of six guns, 4 or 6 pounders French, and 34 men; of whom two were killed and five wounded. On the same evening Lieutenant Senhouse attacked, another privateer schooner, of apparently greater force: but which, after a running action of some length, escaped, owing to the darkness of the night.

On the 21st of August, in latitude 48° 3' north, longitude 8° west, the British 16-gun brig-sloop Penguin, Captain John King Pulling, being on the larboard tack, with the wind blowing hard from the eastward, discovered, right ahead, two armed brigs, evidently cruisers, standing towards her. At 9 h. 30 m. A.M., the strangers, having weathered the Penguin by about a mile, bore down, the headmost brig under English colours. No doubt, however, existing as to their character, the Penguin opened her fire, and soon compelled them to haul up again on the starboard tack. The Penguin then wore, and, coming to on the same tack as they were, kept under their lee, pouring a steady fire into both of them. At 9 h. 45 m. A.M. the sternmost brig struck her colours and hove to; but the sea was running too high to allow the Penguin to take immediate possession of her. Moreover the remaining brig, which, both in appearance and reality, was by far the more formidable of the two, was endeavouring to escape. The Penguin lost no time in pursuing this vessel; and, after a running fight of an hour and 40 minutes, during which the British crew, owing to the high sea and press of sail necessary, had worked the guns knee-deep in water, compelled the French brig privateer Oiseau, of 18 guns, to surrender.

At noon the Penguin took possession of the prize, and in half an hour made sail after the Oiseau's consort; who, by this time, was nearly out of sight to leeward, using every effort to escape. At 4 P.M. the Penguin overtook and brought to the fugitive; which proved to be the Express, of Dartmouth, prize to the Oiseau, and formerly the French privateer, Appocrate, of 14 guns.

The Penguin came off with very little damage and no loss. The Oiseau, besides losing her main topmast a few minutes before she struck, suffered greatly in hull masts, and rigging, and had one man killed, and five wounded. The guns of the Penguin, formerly the Dutch brig Comet, as ordered for her when fitted were 14 long 9-pounders and two 18-pounder carronades, with a complement of 124 men and boys. The guns mounted by the Oiseau were 16 French 8 and two 12 pounders, all long guns, with a complement, on board, of 119 men and boys.

Even had the Oiseau been alone, the capture of her by the Penguin would have been a creditable affair. As it was, Captain Pulling evinced a commendable promptitude in following up his first advantage; and the Penguin's officers and crew, in general, gave a decided proof of their judgment and bravery in effecting the capture of two such opponents.

On the 17th September, at 7 h. 30 m A.M., Cape Nicholas-Mole in the island of St. Domingo bearing south by west half-west, the British 18-gun brig-sloop Pelican, Lieutenant Thomas White, acting commander, in absence of Captain John Gascoyne, who was ill on shore, saw in the north-north-west standing towards her on the larboard tack, with the wind at east, a strange brig, evidently of force; and which was the French privateer Trompeur, of 12 long French 6-pounders, and 78 men and boys. The Pelican immediately made sail in chase. At 8 h. 45 m. A.M. the Trompeur hoisted her colours; and the Pelican who had already hoisted hers, while crossing the Trompeur on the contrary track, opened her broadside. The Pelican then wore round her opponent's stern, and kept up a continued and well-directed fire, until 9 h. 20 m. A.M.; when the Trompeur, hauling on board her larboard tacks, made all sail to get away.

The Pelican, as soon as she had repaired her running rigging which had been very much cut, crowded sail to get again alongside of her opponent. This, at 45 minutes past noon, the Pelican accomplished; and opening her fire a second time, continued it with so much spirit and effect, the yard-arms of the two brigs being locked during the greater part of the time, that at 1 h. 10 m. P.M. the Trompeur blew up abaft, and in five minutes more went down by the head. The Pelican's boats were immediately hoisted out, and 60 of the drowning crew, including the captain, were happily rescued. No officer could have fought his ship more bravely than this captain had: he was seen, in the hottest of the fire, standing on the quarterdeck, exhorting his men to do their duty; and do their duty they did in the most valiant manner.

The loss on board the Trompeur by the Pelican's shot does not appear; but, from the effect of those shot upon the brig's hull, it must have been very severe. The loss sustained by the Pelican amounted to one killed, and five wounded.

The Pelican is the same "frigate with her mizenmast out,"* which, a twelvemonth previous, caused such great consternation on board the French frigate Médée. The effectual manner in which the crew plied their guns, in action with the Trompeur,

* See vol. i., p. 511.

incontestably shows that they had not fallen off in their discipline.*

On the 4th of October, at daybreak, the island of Barbadoes bearing west four or five leagues, the British 6-gun schooner Alexandrian, still commanded by lieutenant William Wood Senhouse, descried a schooner on her quarter, in chase of an American brig to leeward. No sooner did the strange schooner discover the Alexandrian to be an armed vessel, than she hauled her wind to the northward, and was immediately pursued by the latter. At 9 A.M. the Alexandrian overtook the schooner, and, after a close action of 50 minutes, compelled her to haul down her colours. The prize proved to be the French privateer Epicharis, mounting eight carriage-guns (probably 4-pounders), with a complement, as counted, of 74 men. The Alexandrian, in this contest, lost one seaman killed and four wounded; the Epicharis, four killed and 12 severely wounded.

On the 25th of October, near the island of Teneriffe, the French ship-privateer Hyène, of 24 long 8-pounders and 230 men from Bayonne, mistaking the British 44-gun frigate Indefatigable, Captain Sir Edward Pellew, for a Portuguese Indiaman, bore down to capture her. As soon as she was undeceived, the Hyène made all sail to escape, and would have succeeded, had she not carried away her fore topmast. Even with this accident, the Hyène led the Indefatigable, who was herself a good sailer, a chase of eight hours before she brought to and surrendered.

The account of the capture, in May, 1793, of the British 24-gun ship Hyaena, by the French 40-gun frigate Concorde, has already appeared. Thinking to improve the Hyaena's sailing, a quality in which she was remarkably deficient, the Frenchman, who purchased the vessel of the captors, cut away her quarter-deck and forecastle, and thus made her a flush ship. The plan completely succeeded, as was manifest, both during the chase by the Indefatigable, and on her restoration to the British service; in which, armed with twenty 32-pounder carronades and two long 9-pounders, the Hyaena, although built as long ago as 1778, continued for some years to be a useful cruiser.

On the 12th of November, latitude 49° 48' north, and longitude

* It appears that an omission not at all attributable to Mr. James, but to Captain White, has occurred in the relation of the action between the Pelican and the Trompeur. It is this: The Trompeur was joined in the early part of the day, during the time she was engaged with the Pelican, by a schooner. This vessel had sixty men on board, trained and intended to board the Drake, a vessel which had greatly annoyed the enemy's small-craft along the Island of St. Domingo. She might now have turned the scale against the Pelican, had not Captain White to avoid their united attack, kept to windward of the Trompeur, and thus prevented being boarded, which seemed the object of his opponents. As the Trompeur and schooner were a little distant from each other, Captain White depressed his guns, ran alongside the Trompeur, and, after three broadsides, she sank. The humanity of Captain White in rescuing the crew, afforded time for the schooner to effect her escape by running into Jean Rabet.——*Editor*.

22° 18' west, the British 18-pounder 32-gun frigate Cerberus, Captain John Drew, captured the French ship-privateer Epervier, of sixteen 4-pounders and 145 men; on the 13th recaptured a ship, her prize; and on the 14th captured another ship-privateer, the Renard, carrying eighteen 6-pounders and 189 men. The Cerberus also chased the ship-privateer Buonaparte, mounting, as represented, 32 guns, with a crew of 250 men, and would have captured her, had not the frigate's studding-sails and main topgallantmast been carried away. As it was, the Cerberus pressed the Buonaparte so closely, and annoyed her so much with her bow-guns, as to compel her to throw overboard the greater part of her guns and stores, and, as was understood, to return to Bordeaux.

On the 13th of November, early in the morning, while the British 16-gun ship-sloop Fairy, Captain Joshua Sydney Horton, and hired armed cutter Fox, having just weighed from off Calais, were cruising, with light winds, about nine miles to the westward of Seater cliff, the cutter, which was about seven miles ahead of her consort, made the signal for an enemy. The haze clearing discovered to the Fairy a lugger, about three miles to the westward of the Fox.

Captain Horton, hoisting out his boats, proceeded in them to the assistance of the cutter. During the chase, the Fairy's launch separated from the other boats, and went in chase of a second lugger, which Mr. James Middleton, the purser of the Fairy and the launch's commanding officer, discovered running along shore to the westward. At about 2 P.M. the breeze freshened, when, having no longer any prospect of overtaking the lugger in the offing, Captain Horton, with the Fox and boats, tacked in shore to the support of his launch; which, with a crew of only an officer and seven men, had already brought to action the French lugger privateer Epervier, mounting two 2-pound carriage guns and four swivels, besides musketoons and small arms, with a crew of 25 men, and lying at anchor within musket-shot of the westernmost of two batteries in Whitesand bay. In the face of this comparatively overwhelming force, Mr. Middleton carried the lugger just before captain Horton got up to his assistance.

Mr. Middleton was the only man of his little party hurt on this gallant occasion: a grape-shot had badly grazed his stomach, causing a very painful and rather a dangerous wound. The privateer was commanded by an Irishman named George Hammond; who, together with the lugger's crew, three of whom were badly wounded, effected his escape. Captain Horton concludes his letter to Admiral Peyton, transmitting an account of the Epervier's capture, with the following encomium upon the merit of Mr. Middleton: "His gallantry on this occasion speaks for itself, nor is it the first time I have witnessed it. I beg leave to recommend him strongly to your attention."

On the 20th of December at 10 A.M., the British 18-pounder 36-gun frigate Phœbe, Captain Robert Barlow, being in latitude 48° 58' north, longitude 8° 4' west, observed a strange ship standing towards her. At 11 h. 30 m. A.M. the stranger, which eventually proved to be the French 36-gun frigate Néréide, Captain Antoine Canon, hoisted a Dutch jack, and hauled to the wind. The Phœbe immediately tacked and stood after the Néréide, which ship was then on her weather bow. The chase continued during the day, with very little advantage on either side. At 4 P.M. the Néréide bore west-south-west, distant about five miles. At 6 P.M. both ships being taken aback, bore up. At 8 P.M. the Phœbe was drawing up fast with the enemy; who, at 9 P.M., burnt two blue lights, and commenced firing her stern-chasers, which did considerable damage to the Phœbe's masts, sails, and rigging.

At 9 h. 10 m. P.M., just as the Phœbe was in a situation to commence the attack, the Néréide hove in stays; and, owing to the crowd of sail carried by the Phœbe, and the extreme darkness of the night, the preparations for tacking on board the Néréide were unperceived by Captain Barlow, so as to enable him to make the necessary dispositions for adopting, with promptitude, his adversary's manœuvre. The delay this occasioned exposed the sails and rigging of the Phœbe to additional injury from the Néréide's fire; but, in a few minutes, the Phœbe came round, and the two frigates, in passing on opposite tacks, exchanged broadsides.

At 10 P.M. the Phœbe got fairly alongside her opponent; when both ships backed their main topsails, and commenced the action in earnest, the Néréide placing herself at about four ships' length to windward of the Phœbe. In a short time the Néréide, having received considerable injury in her masts, rigging, and sails, fell on board the Phœbe a little ahead of the main chains. The latter immediately bore up, and got clear of her; then hauled to the wind, and again approached; when, at 10 h. 45 m. P.M., just as the Phœbe was preparing to renew the attack, the Néréide hauled down the light which she had been carrying, and hailed that she surrendered. Neither ship appears to have had any mast shot away, but both had suffered much, particularly the Néréide, in their rigging and sails. The hull of the latter was also a good deal shattered, and her stern windows were entirely beaten in.

The Phœbe, whose force in guns was exactly that of the Phoenix,* sustained, out of a crew of 261 men and boys, a loss of three men killed and 10 wounded. The loss of the Néréide, whose force was less, by two 6-pounders and two 36-pounder carronades (taken from her forecastle), than that of the frigate of her class in the table at p. 54, vol. i., with a complement, as

* See vol. i., p. 327.

sworn to by her officers, of 330 men and boys, was much greater; she having had 20 killed and 55 wounded.

COMPARATIVE FORCE OF THE COMBATANTS.

		PHŒBE	NEREIDE
Broadside-guns	No.	22	18
	lbs.	407	268
Crew	No.	261	330
Size	tons.	926	892

Here, as in many other cases we have recorded, is a nominally equal match shown to have been decidedly otherwise. A third of superiority in weight of metal is far from counterpoised by a fifth of inferiority in number of men. The relative proportion of loss proves, however, that, had more been required of, more could have been performed by, Captain Barlow, his officers and ship's company. Captain Canon, on the other hand, as soon as an action became unavoidable, made a creditable defence.

The Néréide was purchased for the British navy, and under the same name registered as a 12-pounder 36. Captain Barlow, in his official letter, speaks thus of his first lieutenant: "From my first lieutenant, (Michael) Halliday, I experienced all the support which I with confidence expected from so gallant and skilful an officer, which, amidst the difficulties to be contended with in a night action, was an incalculable advantage." In July of the following year Lieutenant Halliday was promoted to the rank of commander.

On the 20th of December, in the middle of a dark night, close off Dungeness, the British gun-brig Growler, of ten 18-pounder carronades and two long guns, and 50 men and boys, commanded by Lieutenant John Hollingsworth, escorting, in company with some other ships of war, a coasting convoy, was surprised, boarded, and, after the loss of her commander, second officer (both mortally wounded), and several of her crew, carried, by the two French lugger-privateers Espiègle, of ten French 4-pounders and at least 80 men, commanded by Captain Duchesne, and Rusé, of eight 4-pounders and at least 70 men, Captain Denis Fourmentin; and both of whom mistook the Growler, in the first instance, for a merchant vessel. Having, at a very trifling loss, possessed themselves of the British gun-brig, the two privateers succeeded, the next morning, in reaching Boulogne with their prize; and, as might naturally be expected, Captains Duchesne and Fourmentin experienced from the inhabitants the most joyous reception. This was not all. The French minister of marine wrote the two captains a very flattering letter; which, indeed, was no less than they deserved.

Bad as the case was, it is not, now that, for the first time, the facts are made known to the English public, by any means so discreditable an affair as Steel, in his "Naval Chronologist," by the following incautiously admitted entry, has made it appear: "Growler, gun-vessel, taken off Dungeness by two French row-boats." Nor, singularly enough, have we ever been able to discover, until a French account met our eye, a contradiction to so humiliating a statement.

On the night of the 29th of December, off the coast of France, the British 44-gun frigate Anson, Captain Philip Charles Durham, having a few hours before parted in chase form the 38-gun frigate Phaëton, Captain the Honourable Robert Stopford, fell in with, and after the exchange of a few shot captured, the French ship-corvette Daphne, late the British 20-gun ship of the same name;* or, as Captain Durham, imitating the French, describes a ship of only 429 tons, "late his majesty's *frigate* Daphne, mounting 30 guns."

Out of a crew, as represented, of 276, including 30 passengers of various descriptions, the Daphne, before she could be induced to surrender, lost five men killed and several wounded. The Anson had no one hurt. Two of the French passengers were the civil commissioners Jacquelin and Lacaize, charged with despatches (thrown overboard) for Guadeloupe; whither the Daphne was bound.

COLONIAL EXPEDITIONS. – NORTH AMERICA.

The melancholy loss on this station of the British 12-pounder 36-gun frigate Tribune, Captain Scory Barker, is of too interesting a nature to be passed summarily over. The ship had quitted England in September, with a convoy for Quebec and Newfoundland; from which convoy, early in November, bad weather had compelled her to part company. On the 16th, at about 8 A.M., the harbour of Halifax, Nova-Scotia, was discovered; and as, owing to a strong wind from east-south-east, the ship fast approached the land, Captain Barker proposed to the master, Mr. James Clubb, to lie to until a pilot came on board. The master has been represented to have replied, that he had beat a 44-gun ship into the harbour, and had frequently been there; and that there was no necessity for a pilot, as the wind was favourable. Confiding in these assurances, Captain Barker went below, and busied himself in arranging some papers that he wished to take on shore. The master, in the mean time, had undertaken the pilotage of the ship, placing great confidence in the judgment of a negro-man on board, who had formerly belonged to Halifax. At about noon the ship had approached so near to the Thrum-cap shoals, that Mr. Clubb became alarmed, and sent for Mr. Galvin, one of the master's mates, who was sick below. Just as the latter stepped upon the deck, the man in the chains, with the lead, sang out, "By the mark five." At the same instant the black man forward called out "Steady." Mr. Galvin then got upon one of the carronades, to observe the situation of

* See vol. i., p. 236.

the ship: whereupon the master, in much agitation, ran to the man at the wheel; and took it from him, with the intention of wearing the ship; but, before this could be effected, the Tribune struck.

Signals of distress were immediately made, and were as promptly answered by the military posts and ships in the harbour. Some military boats, and one from the dock-yard, with Mr. Rackum, the boatswain of the ordinary on board, reached the ship; but none of the other boats were able to pull against the heavy wind and sea. By lightening the ship, the Tribune, at about 8 h. 30 m P.M., began to heave, and at 9 P.M. swang off from the shore; but without her rudder, and with seven feet water in the hold. By active exertions at the chain-pumps, the leak appeared to decrease, and the best bower-anchor was let go; but it failed to bring the ship up. The cable was then cut, and the jib and foretopmast staysail set. The south-east gale had by this time greatly increased, and was fast driving the ship to the western shore. To prevent that, if possible, the small bower was let go, in 13 fathoms, and the mizenmast cut away.

It was now about 10 P.M.; and, as the water continued to gain upon the ship, little hope remained of saving the Tribune or the lives of her unhappy crew. About this time two officers of the Fusileers, who had come from Halifax, quitted the sinking ship: which continued to drive before the storm towards the shore; the tremendous noise of the billows, as they dashed against the precipices that lined it, presenting to those, who might escape perishing with the vessel, nothing but the expectation of a more painful death. After making two dreadful lurches, the Tribune went down, and left, struggling for their existence, upwards of 240 men of her complement, besides other persons from the shore, and, what so augmented the horrors of the scene, several women and children. Mr. Galvin, who, when the ship sank, was below, directing the men at the chain-pumps, was washed up the hatchway and thrown into the waist, and thence into the sea. As he plunged, his feet struck a rock; but, presently ascending, he swam to gain the main shrouds. In his way thither, he was suddenly caught hold of by three poor wretches. To disengage himself from these, he dived into the water, and, on again rising, swam to the shrouds. Upon reaching the main top, he seated himself, with others, on an arm-chest that was lashed to the mast. The fore top was at this time occupied by about 10 persons; and there were upwards of 100 clinging to the shrouds and other parts of the wreck. Owing to the severity of the storm, however, and the length of a November night, nature became exhausted, and the persons on the shrouds, one by one, dropped and disappeared. The falling of the mainmast, soon after midnight, had plunged more than 40 persons into the waves, and only nine, besides Mr. Galvin, succeeded in regaining the top; which now rested on the mainyard, that being fortunately held to the ship by a portion of the rigging. Of the 10 who had regained the main top, four only, including Mr. Galvin, were alive by morning: of the 10 also in the fore top, three, being too much exhausted to help themselves, had been washed away; and three others had died as they lay, leaving, by daylight on the 17th, four men only in the fore top.

We will here relate an anecdote, strongly illustrative of that thoughtlessness of danger for which the British tar has been so famed. Among the survivors in the fore top were two seamen, named Robert Dunlap and Daniel Munroe. The latter, in the night, had disappeared; and it was concluded he had been washed away along with several others. However, after a lapse of more than two hours, Munroe, to the surprise of Dunlap, suddenly thrust his head through the lubber's hole, or the vacant space between the head of the lower mast and the edge of the top. His answer to his messmate's inquiry was, that he had been cruising for a better birth; that, after swimming about the wreck for a considerable time, he had returned to the fore shrouds, and crawling in on the catharpings (small ropes serving to brace in the shrouds of the lower masts behind their respective yards), had been sleeping there more than an hour.

The first exertion that was made from the shore for the relief of the sufferers was, at about 11 A.M. by a boy, 13 years old, from Herring cove, who pushed off, by himself, in a small skiff. With great exertions, and at extreme personal risk, this noble lad reached the wreck; and backing his little boat close to the fore top, was waiting to take off two of the men, all his skiff could safely carry, when occurred a trait of unparalleled, magnanimity. Dunlap and Munroe, who, throughout the night, had, in a wonderful manner preserved their strength and spirits, and who, of the four survivors in the fore top, were now the only persons in full possession of the faculties of mind and body, might have stepped into the boat, and saved themselves at least. But, no; they chose to save their two half-dying and unconscious companions. These they lifted up, and, with great difficulty, on account of the still raging sea, placed in the skiff; and the "manly boy" rowed them triumphantly to the cove. After having deposited his freight at the nearest cottage, the joyous lad, to the shame of many older persons who had larger boats, again put off with his skiff. His efforts to reach the wreck were, however, this time unavailing, and he returned to the shore, wrung with disappointment. Shortly afterwards two or three other boats, including the Tribune's jollyboat, which, with four men, had quitted the ship just before she sank, ventured out, and succeeded in bringing from the wreck the six survivors; making, with the four that had taken to the jollyboat and the two that had been saved by the boy, 12 only out of 240 or 250 souls; including, as already noticed, several women and children, and also, many of those humane persons, who had come on board from Halifax to lend their assistance. Among the number was an amiable young man, Lieutenant James,* of the Nova-Scotia regiment, to the unspeakable distress of the worthy parents, and the sincere regret of an extended circle of friends.

The loss of the Tribune should operate as a lesson upon all who are avariciously inclined. Had the master not been anxious to grasp the money allowed by government to the pilot who conducts the ship into port, the Tribune, and the many poor souls that perished in her, might have been saved.

A war with Spain necessarily rendered Spain's colonies an immediate object of attack to her powerful maritime opponent. Accordingly, on the 12th of February, an expedition, composed of four sail of the line, two sloops and a bomb-vessel, under the command of rear-admiral Harvey, in the Prince-of-Wales, having on board his ship Lieutenant-general Sir Ralph Abercromby, as the commanding officer of the troops to be employed, quitted Port-Royal, Martinique. On the 14th the rear-admiral arrived at the port of rendezvous, the island of Carinacou; and was there joined by another sail of the line (the Invincible), two frigates, three sloops, and several transports, containing the troops destined for the attack. On the junction of this reinforcement, the admiral's force consisted of the

Gun-ship		
98	Prince-of-Wales	Rear-admiral (r.) Henry Harvey. Captain John Harvey.
74	Bellona	Captain George Wilson.
	Vengeance	Captain Thomas Macnamara Russell.
	Invincible	Captain William Cayley.
64	Scipio	Captain Sydney Davers.
	Frigates, Arethusa, and Alarm.	
	Sloops, Favourite, Zebra, Zephyr, Thorn, and Victorieuse.	
	Bomb, Terror.	

On the 15th the squadron and transports again set sail, running between the islands of Carinacou and Grenada. On the morning of the 16th the whole arrived off Trinidad, and steered for the gulf of Paria; when at about 3 h. 30 m. P.M., just as the British squadron had passed through the Great Bocas channel, a Spanish squadron was discovered at anchor in Shaggaramus bay, consisting of the following four sail of the line and one frigate:

Gun-ship		
80	San-Vincente	Rear-admiral Don Sebastian Ruiz de Apodaca. Captain Don Geronimo Mendoza.
74	Gallardo	Captain Don Gabriel Sorondo.
	Arrogante	Captain Don Raphael Bonasa.
	San-Damaso	Captain Don Josef Jordan.
Gun-frig.		
34	Santa-Cecilia	Captain Don Manual Urtesabel.

* Neither related, nor personally known, to the author.

The advanced hour of the day, and the apparent strength of Gaspargrande island, which, mounting 20 pieces of cannon and two mortars, commanded, and might have disputed, the entrance to the enemy's anchorage, determined the rear-admiral to order the transports, under the protection of the Arethusa, Thorn, and Zebra, to anchor a little further up the gulf, at the distance of about five miles from the town of Port-d'Espagne; while the Alarm, Favourite, and Victorieuse kept under sail between the transports and Port-d'Espagne, to prevent the escape of any vessels from the latter. In the mean time, the rear-admiral, with his four sail of the line, anchored, in order of battle, within random-shot of the Spanish batteries and line-of-battle ships, to be prepared in case the ships, having all their sails bent and appearing to be ready for sea, should attempt, during the night, to effect their escape.

The British, while keeping a sharp look-out, were surprised, at about 2 A.M. on the 17th, to observe flames bursting out from one of the Spanish ships. In a short time three others were on fire, and all four continued to burn, with great fury, until daylight. The fifth ship, the San-Damaso, escaped the conflagration, and, without any resistance, was brought off by the boats of the British squadron. The Spaniards, meanwhile, had abandoned Gaspargrande island; and it was occupied, soon after daylight, by a detachment of the Queen's regiment. In the course of the day the remainder of the troops were landed, about three miles from Port-d'Espagne, without the slightest opposition; and, on the same evening, the town itself was quietly entered. This led to an offer of capitulation on the part of the Spanish governor; and, on the following day, the island of Trinidad surrendered to the British arms, without an effort at defence, and happily without a casualty, beyond one officer, Lieutenant Villeneuve of the eighth regiment, mortally wounded, but in what manner the official account omits to notice.

Even should one be disposed to excuse a garrison which, including the detachment on Gaspargrande island, numbered, even with 50 sick in the hospital, but 632 men, for so readily yielding, it seems, at first sight, unaccountable, that Rear-admiral Apodaca, with four sail of the line and a frigate, should not have made some show of resistance. The fact is, that not one of his ships had her complement on board; as is proved by the official returns numbering but 1704, for the total of his officers, seamen, and marines: whereas 2704 men would have barely exceeded the proper amount.

The island of Porto-Rico, as a Spanish colony, came the next in order of attack; but, before we go into the details of the expedition for the reduction of that island, we will describe a gallant little boat-exploit performed upon its coasts.

On the 22d of March the British 12-pounder 32-gun frigate

Hermione, Captain Hugh Pigot, standing in between the island of Zacheo and the west end of Porto-Rico, discovered a brig and several smaller vessels at anchor close in shore. The Hermione soon dropped her anchor within half a mile of the vessels, and abreast of a small battery, which immediately opened a fire upon the ship, but was very shortly silenced.

Captain Pigot then sent his boats, under the command of Lieutenants Samuel Reid and Archibald Douglas to take possession of the vessels. Although the latter, consisting of three small French privateers and their 12 prizes, including the brig, were aground, and a fire of musketry was kept up by the enemy, Lieutenant Reid and his party, without the loss of a man, brought them all out but two; and these they burnt. On the next day, the 23d, Lieutenant Reid landed, and spiked and dismounted the guns upon the battery, and returned to his ship with the same good fortune as before. Finding that the privateersmen had taken on shore the sails of their vessels, Captain Pigot was constrained to burn them all except the brig, which was a deep-laden and valuable vessel.

On the 8th of April, having made every necessary arrangement for the security of Trinidad, Rear-admiral Harvey, and Lieutenant-general Sir Ralph Abercromby, with the Prince-of-Wales, Bellona, Vengeance, and Alfred, Captain Thomas Totty (who with the 38-gun frigate Tamer, Captain Thomas Byam Martin, had just joined), and a few frigates and sloops, and with as many of the troops as could be spared, set sail from Martinique. On the 10th the squadron arrived at St.-Kitt's and, having there been joined by the 38-gun frigate Arethusa, Captain Thomas Wolley, with pilots and guides from Tortola and St.-Thomas's, steered direct for Porto-Rico.

On the 17th the squadron came to an anchor off Congrejos point. The whole of the north side of the island is bounded by a reef, and it was with much difficulty that a narrow channel was discovered about three leagues to the eastward of the town. Through this channel the ship-sloops Fury and Beaver, Captains Henry Evans and Richard Browne, with the lighter vessels, passed into a small bay; in which, on the following morning, the 18th, the troops were disembarked, after meeting a slight opposition from about 100 of the enemy. On approaching the town, however, the British troops found it too strongly fortified, and too actively defended by gun-boats and other armed craft, to be attacked with any hopes of success. After a bombardment of some days' continuance, and an ineffectual attempt to destroy a large magazine situated near the town, Lieutenant-general Abercromby, on the 30th, abandoned the enterprise; and the troops re-embarked, with the loss of one captain of the army and 30 rank and file killed, one lieutenant-colonel, one captain, and 68 rank and file wounded, and one captain, two lieutenants, and 121 rank and file missing, supposed to be taken prisoners, making a total of 225 killed, wounded, and missing.

On the 15th of April, early in the morning, while Vice-admiral Sir Hyde Parker, the British commander-in-chief on the Jamaica station, was lying at anchor in Cape Nicolas-Mole, St. Domingo, with the 98-gun ship Queen, Captain Man Dobson, and 74-gun ships Thunderer and Valiant, Captain William Ogilvy and Edmund Crawley, the 32-gun frigate Janus, Captain Janues Bissett, arrived with the intelligence of her having, the preceding evening, chased into the port of Marégot the French 36-gun frigate Hermione, or Harmonie, as named (we consider by mistake) in the British official account.

Sir Hyde Parker immediately despatched the Thunderer to the bay of Marégot, with orders, in case the French frigate should not be there, to proceed close alongshore between the island of Tortuga and Port-au-Paix; while, with the Queen and Valiant, the vice-admiral kept more in the offing. Captain Ogilvy discovered the French frigate, and chased her into Mostique inlet; and, having apprized Sir Hyde of the circumstance, was directed to take the Valiant under his orders, and endeavour to effect the Hermione's capture or destruction.

At 4 h. 15 m. P.M. the Thunderer and Valiant, in close order, bore up to examine the entrance of the inlet, keeping so close to the shore as to be, when abreast of the frigate, in four fathoms' water; but the wind blew so hard, that it was found impracticable to anchor without a certainty of driving upon the rocks. At a few minutes before 5 P.M. the Thunderer opened her fire upon the Hermione, and soon afterwards the Valiant did the same; but, the force of the wind not allowing the ships to remain long in their station, Captain Ogilvy, was obliged to haul off for the night.

On the 16th, early in the morning, the two 74s renewed their fire upon the frigate with such effect, that at 7 A.M. the Hermione was run on shore and set fire to by her crew, and at 8 h. 47 m. A.M. blew up. The remains of the wreck lay close to the shore, about four miles to windward of Jean-Rabel. The destruction of the Hermione was effected without the slightest loss or damage on the part of the two British ships. It appears that the frigate had been ordered to sea from Cape-François, by the French deputies resident there, contrary to the opinion of her officers, in order to convoy to that port a number of captured American vessels, laden with provisions, and which had been captured and carried into Port-au-Paix and Jean-Rabel by French privateers.

An expedition to the latter port was immediately concerted; and on the 20th Captain Pigot, of the British frigate Hermione, having under his orders the Quebec and Mermaid of the same force, Captain John Cooke and Robert Waller Otway, brig-sloop Drake, Captain John Perkins, and cutter Penelope, Lieutenant

Daniel Burdwood, proceeded towards the spot. The wind being very light, and the current setting strong to the eastward, the squadron stood to the north-west until 3 P.M.; keeping far enough from the land to avoid being seen, it being the commodore's intention to surprise the vessels with the boats under cover of the night.

Having stood in, so as to be close to the eastward of Jean-Rabel before the land wind came off, the frigates ran along to the westward until within two miles of the vessels; when the boats of the squadron were sent in, with directions to row close alongshore until they discovered the objects of their attack, which, owing to the extreme darkness, were not then visible from the frigates. The latter, in the mean while, kept running under easy sail, about a mile from the shore, in order to draw off the enemy's attention from the boats.

At about 1 A.M. on the 21st, a fire of musketry announced that the action between the boats and the French vessels had commenced. At this time the British were in possession of many of the vessels, and had got one of them under way. The batteries now opened a fire upon the ships, which they occasionally returned. At 4 A.M. nine vessels, consisting of one ship, three brigs, three schooners, and two sloops, being all in the port except two small row-boats, were in possession of the British, and standing out to the squadron with the land breeze. This dashing and not unimportant service was performed without the loss of a man; and we regret that Captain Pigot, by omitting them in his official letter, has prevented us from giving the names of the lieutenants and others who were present on the occasion.

On the 6th of April, in the night, the boats of the 32-gun frigate Magicienne, Captain William Henry Ricketts, and 44-gun ship (armed en flûte) Regulus, Captain William Carthew, placed under the orders of Lieutenants John Maples and Alexander M'Beath, first of their respective ships, assisted by Charles Cheshire and James Reid the masters of each, Philip Luscombe Perry, lieutenant of marines, Abraham Adams, purser, and John Jordain, surgeon, belonging to the Magicienne, and George Frazer, lieutenant of marines belonging to the Regulus, entered the harbour of Cape-Roxo, in the island of St.-Domingo, the grand receptacle for French privateers and their prizes.

Here the British boats captured, sank, and burnt 13 sail of square-rigged vessels and schooners, being the whole in the port, except one Danish ship. They also destroyed two batteries of two guns each, 6 and 4 pounders, at the entrance and head of the harbour. To add to the value of this gallant enterprise, it was performed without the loss of a man on the British side. We acknowledge ourselves indebted to Captain Ricketts for having subjoined to his official letter the surnames of the officers employed in this expedition, and should have been still more so, had the Christian names been added; the omission of which, coupled with the mispelling in the Gazette, has occasioned us no slight trouble.

On the 22d the Magicienne, Regulus, and Fortune schooner, upon doubling Cape Tiberon, discovered a privateer-sloop and four schooners at anchor in Carcasse bay. The presence of these vessels, and the firing of an alarm gun, convinced Captain Ricketts that the neighbouring post of Irois and its dependencies were about to be attacked by the French. To frustrate the designs of the latter, the Magicienne and Regulus stood in, and, after anchoring, commenced so heavy and well-directed a cannonade upon a battery near the shore, that, in a little while, the enemy abandoned it, and fled to the mountains; leaving in possession of the British his field-pieces, ammunition, and provisions, as well as the merchant vessels at anchor, which were laden with necessaries for carrying on the siege. The fire from the shore-battery occasioned a loss to the British of four seamen killed, one master's mate (Mr. Morgan), and ten seamen wounded, while in the Magicienne's boat, endeavouring to tow out the privateer. The spirited attack, made by Captain Ricketts with his little squadron, is acknowledged by Brigadier-general Church, in his public despatch, to have completely saved the fort of Irois, and the country to which it was the key.

Although our plan has been to be sparing of details in cases of mutiny, especially where restricted to individual ships, yet there was one case of the latter description in the West Indies, too flagrant in its proceedings, and too fatal in its immediate consequences, not to be made an exception. On the night of the 22d of September, while the 32-gun frigate Hermione, Captain Hugh Pigot, was cruising off the west end of Porto-Rico, a most daring and unexampled mutiny broke out on board of her. It appears that, on the preceding day, while the crew were reefing the topsails, the captain called aloud that he would flog the last man off the mizentopsail yard. "The poor fellows, well knowing that he would keep his word (and though the lot would naturally fall on the outermost, and consequently the most active), each resolved at any rate to escape from punishment: two of them, who from their position could not reach the topmast rigging, made a spring to get over their comrades within them; they missed their hold, fell on the quarterdeck, and were both killed. This being reported to the captain, he is said to have made answer, 'Throw the lubbers overboard.'"* It appears, also, that all the other men, on coming down, were severely reprimanded, and threatened with punishment.

This most tyrannical conduct on the part of Captain Pigot, operating upon a very motley and, from a succession of similar acts of oppression, ill-disposed ship's company, produced dis-

* Brenton, vol. ii., p. 436.

content; which kept increasing until the next evening, when it fatally burst forth. The men in addition to the loud murmurs they uttered, now began throwing double-headed shot about the deck; and on the first lieutenant's advancing to inquire into the cause of the disturbance, they wounded him in the arm with a tomahawk. He retired, for a while, and then returned; when the wretches knocked him down with a tomahawk, cut his throat, and threw him overboard. "The captain, hearing a noise, ran on deck, but was driven back with repeated wounds: seated in his cabin he was stabbed by his cockswain and three other mutineers, and forced out of the cabin windows, was heard to speak as he went astern."* In a similar manner did the mutineers proceed with eight other officers; cutting and mangling their victims in the most cruel and barbarous manner. The only officers that escaped destruction were, the master, Edward Southcott, the gunner, Richard Searle, the carpenter, Richard Price, one midshipman, David O'Brien Casey, and the cook, William Moncrief: those murdered were, the captain, three lieutenants, purser, surgeon, captain's clerk, one midshipman, the boatswain, and the lieutenant of marines.

Having thus rid themselves of every possible opponent, the mutineers carried the ship into La Guayra, a port of the Spanish Main; representing to the Spanish governor that they had turned their officers adrift in the jollyboat. The governor, soon afterwards, in spite of the remonstrances of Rear-admiral Henry Harvey, the British commander-in-chief on the Leeward-island station, who fully explained the horrid circumstances under which the ship had been taken possession of, fitted the Hermione for sea as a Spanish national frigate.

Could we descant upon the humanity or general kind behaviour of the Hermione's late captain, it might serve to heighten, if any thing could heighten, the guilt of his murderers; but a regard to truth compels us to state, that Captain Hugh Pigot bore a character very opposite to a mild one: in short, he has been described to us by those who knew him well, as one of the most cruel and oppressive captains belonging to the British navy.

Many of the Hermione's mutineers were afterwards taken, and suffered for their crimes; crimes that, had they each a dozen lives, merited the sacrifice of the whole. If the Ali Pacha of the ship had been the sole victim of their rage, the public indignation might have been appeased, the instant the daily practices of the tyrant become known; but the indiscriminate slaughter of their officers, even to the young clerk and midshipman, gave a shock to public feeling, which vibrates even yet when the subject is touched upon. That the mutineers of the Hermione should turn traitors to their offended country, was the natural

* Brenton, vol. ii., p. 436.

consequence of the enormity of their guilt. Of those subsequently taken and brought to punishment, some, from repentance, others, from hardened shamelessness, confessed their guilt, and gave minute details of the horrid transaction.

EAST INDIES.

Although no event of a strictly warlike character happened in the eastern quarter of the globe during the year 1797, an occurrence equally within the province of the naval annalist forces itself upon our attention. Sometime in the month of October that baneful spirit of mutiny and insubordination, which had caused such a sensation in England, burst forth among the few British ships of war stationed at the Cape of Good Hope. It began in the form of a complaint against the captain of a particular ship, and then spread over the whole squadron. Nothing but the most prompt measures on the part of the governor, Lord Macartney, and of Rear-admiral Pringle and General Dundas, put a stop to the violence of the mutineers. At length, the latter delivered up their delegates. Many of these were executed, and others severely flogged; and, after a short time, good order and discipline again prevailed in the squadron.

BRITISH AND FRENCH FLEETS.

DIRECTING our attention, as usual, to the abstract of the British navy, drawn up for the commencement of the present year,* we find an increase, though small, in the total of the line-of-battle cruisers, but a decrease, of equal amount, in those in commission. The whole number of cruisers, line and underline, has increased considerably since the last abstract; and so, as a necessary consequence, has the grand total of the navy. The vessels, captured from the French, Dutch, and Spaniards, amount to less than half those in the preceding abstract; but, among the latter, were only three sail of the line, while the line-of-battle ships in the former amount to 12: of these, however, one only, the San-Josef, was of any value as a cruiser.† The continuance of the stormy weather of 1796, through the winter months of the following year, filled the casualty-list of the latter with several melancholy cases of shipwreck. In other respects, the loss sustained by the British navy during the year 1797 was of trifling amount.‡

The "launched" columns of this abstract present nothing worthy of remark; except that we may notice the foundation of a new frigate class, the 40, carrying 24-pounders on the main deck. The new individual was the Endymion, a ship built as nearly as possible after the Pomone, captured from the French in April, 1794;§ but measuring 38 tons more, owing to an error in the mode of taking the dimensions of the Pomone. Had that been rectified, the two ships would have measured nearly alike.

* See Appendix, Annual Abstract No. 6.

† See Appendix, Nos. 8, 9, and 10.

‡ See Appendix, No. 11.

§ See vol. i., p. 291.

We formerly stated that the reign of the Pomone was a short one. In the year 1796, through the ignorance of a French pilot, the ship was run ashore in the night, on the Boeufs off Nantz, and was with difficulty got off by daylight. The Pomone's leaky state sent her home; nor could Sir John Borlase Warren, the commander of the squadron of which she formed a part, spare a ship to accompany her. At one time the leak, which was under the step of the foremast, had so depressed the ship, that no water could be got to the pumps; but finally, by great exertions on the part of her officers and crew, the Pomone reached Plymouth. Captain Eyles, her commander, ran her at once into the harbour, without asking the usual leave; and he and his officers and crew, received the thanks of the admiralty for their promptitude. After being docked, the Pomone was refitted for sea, but received on board 18, instead of 24 pounders for her main deck, on account of the weakness of her frame from the shock she had received. Subsequently the Pomone was again run on shore, at the island of Jersey. The ship again got off and returned to port; but was found to be so shaken in her frame, that she never afterwards went to sea.

There were two reasons why so few ships among the larger classes were ordered in the year 1797; one was, the great number, particularly of line-of-battle ships, already on the stocks, or about to be placed there; the other, the great number of fine frigates that, since the commencement of the war, had been captured from the French, among which were nine of one class, that averaged nearly 1100 tons.

In the early part of the preceding year, several applications had been made by captains of 74-gun ships to have their ships fitted with carronades, similar to the Minotaur; for which ship, since November, 1793, carronades had been ordered, in lieu of her 9s, at the request of Rear-admiral Macbride.

This induced the board of admiralty, on the 17th of March, to order that every line-of-battle ship, coming forward to be fitted, should be prepared to receive carronades all along her quarterdeck and forecastle, except in the wake of the shrouds. These carronades, except in special cases, were to be 32-pounders, and usually amounted to within four, or at most six, of the whole number of long guns originally established upon those decks. As an example of one special case, the carronades, 18 in number, of the Gibraltar, then refitting at Plymouth, were ordered to be 24-pounders; thus making all her guns, except the two forecastle 9s, of the same caliber: see notes § and K* to the first Annual abstract. As another exception, the Neptune, a small-class 98, was at a subsequent day, May 6th, 1800, also ordered 24-pounder carronades for her quarterdeck and forecastle.

Although no general order had as yet issued to arm frigates with 32-pounder carronades on the quarterdeck and forecastle, yet most of the captains, especially of the 38s and 36s, managed to get the greater part of their long 9s exchanged for carronades of that highly effective caliber. Six of the eight bomb-vessels, that had been purchased in the year 1797, were each ordered to be fitted with eight 24-pounder carronades, instead of eight long 6-pounders as formerly; and the 42 launched and purchased vessels of the gun-brig class (see the Annual Abstract for the year 1798) were armed wholly with 18-pounder carronades, except for chasers.

The number of commissioned officers and masters, belonging to the British navy at the commencement of the year, was,

Admirals	24
Vice-admirals	36
Rear-admirals	44
Rear-admirals superannuated	26
Post-captains	518
Post-captains superannuated	20
Commanders, or sloop-captains	338
Lieutenants	2030
Masters	492

and the number of seamen and marines, voted for the service of the years 1798, was 120,000.*

The Channel fleet, at the commencement of the present year, was still commanded by Admiral Lord Bridport. On the 25th of January a detachment from it, consisting of 12 ships of the line and three frigates, under the orders Vice-admiral Sir Charles Thompson in the Formidable 98, sailed on a cruise in the Bay of Biscay. On the 9th of April a second detachment of six ships of the line and three frigates, under Rear-admiral Sir Roger Curtis, in the Prince 98, sailed from Cawsand bay, to cruise off Ireland; and on the 12th Lord Bridport himself, with the remainder of the Channel fleet, consisting of 10 sail of the line, put to sea from St.-Helen's bound off Brest.

On the 21st, at 11 A.M., while Lord Bridport, with the fleet, was standing across the Iroise passage on the larboard tack, with the wind from the north-east by east, the 74-gun ships Mars, Captain Alexander Hood, and Ramillies, Captain Henry Inman, which, with two or three frigates were on the look-out to windward, discovered and gave chase to two strange sail, distant about four leagues to the eastward. At 2 P.M., as the British advanced ships were getting abreast of the two strangers, then ascertained to be enemy's ships, a third, and a much larger sail, made her appearance about five leagues off, in the east-south-east, working up alongshore towards Brest. The latter became the preferable object of pursuit, and was therefore at 5 h. 45 m. P.M., chased under all sail by the Mars, Ramillies, and

* See Appendix, No. 12.

38-gun frigate Jason, Captain Charles Stirling, the only three ships of Lord Bridport's fleet, that were near enough to obtain a sight of the stranger. At 6 h. 20 m. P.M. the Ramillies, carrying away her fore topmast, dropped astern; and the chase was continued by the Mars and Jason, the body of the British fleet then bearing from the former west, distant 10 or 11 miles, and the Penmarcks east-south-east, distant about nine miles.

Every effort was used to accelerate the sailing of the Mars; and she evidently gained, as well upon the Jason, as upon the enemy, now plainly seen to be a ship of the line. At 7 h. 30 m. P.M., the Penmarcks bearing south-east half-east distant seven or eight miles, the stranger evinced an intention to escape through the passage du Raz. Soon afterwards the Mars put about on the starboard tack; and at 8 h. 30 m. P.M., Bec du Raz bearing north by east two or three miles, the French 74-gun ship Hercule, Captain Louis l'Hèritier, finding herself unable to work up against a strong current, dropped anchor and furled her sails. This was just at the mouth of the passage, and at a distance from Brest, the port she was endeavouring to reach, of about seven leagues. The Hercule then carried a spring out abaft, and put herself in the best possible state to give a warm reception to the Mars, now fast coming up.

At 8 h. 45 m. P.M., the latter, who had by this time run the Jason nearly out of sight, hauled up her courses. At 9 h. 15 m. P.M. the Hercule opened her starboard broadside upon the Mars, and received an almost immediate return. Finding, however, that the strength of the current would not allow him, while under way, to take up a proper fighting position, Captain Hood resolved to anchor. Accordingly, at 9 h. 25m. P.M., the Mars ranged ahead of the Hercule, and, having passed on to a short distance, let go her anchor. As the Mars dropped astern, the anchor on her larboard bow caught the anchor on the starboard bow of the Hercule; and, thus entangled, with their sides rubbing together, did the two ships engage, until 10 h. 30 m. P.M.; at which time the Hercule having failed in two attempts to board, and being dreadfully shattered in her hull, particularly on the starboard side, hailed that she struck.

So close had the ships fought, that the guns on the lower deck of each could not, as usual, be run out, but were obliged to be fired within board. With the exception of the jib-boom of the Mars, neither ship lost a spar. During the first ten minutes of the action, however, while the latter was obstructed in her manœuvres by the wind and tide, her bowsprit, foremast and foreyard received several of the Hercule's shot. In other respects, the damage to both ships was confined to the hulls. The Mars had her hammocks, boats, and spars shot through, and three or four of her first-deck ports unhinged in the collision of the ships: her hull also, was hit in several places. The Hercule's starboard side was riddled from end to end. Several of the ports were unhinged; and, in some instances, the spaces between the ports entirely laid open. The contrast between the two sides of the ship was, indeed, most remarkable: the larboard side, which had been very slightly injured, was of a bright yellow; while the starboard side, or what remained of it, was burnt as black as a cinder. The five aftermost starboard lowerdeck guns of the Hercule were dismounted, and several of the others much damaged.

The loss sustained by the Mars, in this long and close fought action, was necessarily severe. Out of a crew of 634 men and boys, she had her commander, captain of marines (Joseph White) one midshipman (James Blythe), 15 seamen, and four private marines killed, three seamen and five private marines missing (but in what way neither the official letter, nor the log, gives any account), and her third and fifth lieutenants (George Argles, badly, but who would not quit the deck, and George Arnold Ford), one midshipman (Thomas Southey), 36 seamen, two sergeants of marines, and one drummer wounded; total, 30 killed and missing, and 60 wounded.

No accurate account has been given of the loss on board the French ship; whose crew, as deposed to by her principal surviving officers, consisted of 680, being 20 short of her established number according to the latest regulation, and which would probably have been filled up on her arrival at Brest. Some accounts reckoned the killed and wounded of the French ship at 400; but the Hercule's officers, who were the best judges, did not consider the number to exceed 290, an amount greater, as it was, than two-fifths of her complement.

The Mars was a 24-pounder 74; that is, she mounted that caliber of gun, 30 in number, upon her second deck, with, as it appears, 16 long 9s and two 32-pounder carronades on the quarterdeck and forecastle, and six 24-pounder carronades on the poop, total 82 guns. The guns of the Hercule, as found on board of her, were 78 in number, precisely of the nature established upon her class, as particularized at No. 4 in the small table at p. 54 of the first volume.

COMPARATIVE FORCE OF THE COMBATANTS.

		MARS.	HERCULE.
Broadside-guns	No.	41	39
	lbs.	984	985
Crew	No.	634	680
Size	tons	1853	1876*

* Principal dimensions of the two ships:

	ft.	in.		ft.	in.
Mars, length of gun-deck,	176	0	extreme breadth,	49	2
Hercule, length of gun-deck	181	3	extreme breadth,	48	6½

A fairer match one seldom sees on paper. But there were some qualifying circumstances, the absence of which, in the estimation of those who view the affair as a mere struggle for glory, would have rendered the prize a yet more honourable trophy. The Hercule had been out of port but 24 hours, and that for the first time since she had been launched; while the Mars, in the words of Earl St.-Vincent, was "an old-commissioned, well-practised ship."* Moreover an English 18-pounder frigate was not far off; and even Lord Bridport's fleet could see the flashes of the guns. Upon the whole, therefore, the action of the Mars and Hercule was one that, in the conduct of it throughout, reflected about an equal shore of credit upon both the contending parties.

Captain Hood was nephew to Lords Bridport and Hood, and received a musket-ball in the femoral artery, about 20 minutes after the action commenced; of which wound he died just as it terminated. Captain L'Héritier was the same officer who so gallantly fought the America in the action with Lord Howe. On his return to France after the loss of the Hercule, Captain L'Héritier was not only acquitted by a court-martial, but received, and no one can say he did not merit, a flattering letter from the minister of marine, Rear-admiral Bruix.

The Jason, who was about two miles off at the time of the Hercule's surrender, arrived on the spot in about 20 minutes afterwards, and was then of great service in exchanging the prisoners, and getting the prize out of the intricate passage in which she had anchored. The Hercule had been launched at Lorient about ten months, and, when fallen in with, was on her way to join the Brest fleet. She had on board a complete set of rigging for a 74-gun ship at the latter port; and which, as we conjecture, had been intended for the new 74-gun ship Quatorze-Juillet, set on fire and destroyed in the harbour of Lorient, a few weeks previous to the Hercule's departure, by, according to the French accounts, an incendiary. Fortunately, only three persons were in the ship at the time, and, it is believed, they escaped.

The holes in the Hercule's starboard side were so large and numerous, particularly under the counter and just above the water-line that, had the weather been at all boisterous, her arrival in a British port would have been very doubtful. With good management, however, the Hercule reached Plymouth in safety on the morning of the 27th, and was added to the British navy under her French name. The cost of simply making good the damages which the Hercule had sustained by the shot of the Mars, was computed at 12,5000*l*. Lieutenant William Butterfield, upon whom the command of the Mars devolved after Captain Hood had received his mortal wound, was of course promoted.

Although, during the greater part of the present year, there

* Clarke and McArthur's Life of Nelson, vol. ii., p. 57.

were from 13 to 15 sail of the line in Brest water, the French commander-in-chief, who was still, we believe, M. Morard-de-Galles, made no attempt to put to sea. The principal cause of this inactivity may probably be traced to the existence of a plan of no inconsiderable magnitude, which, or the first part of it at least, was carrying on in another quarter, and the result whereof it was necessary for the Brest fleet to await. Whether the invasion of England by France, to be attempted some time in the year 1798, was really meditated, or was solely meant to divert the attention of England from the Egyptian campaign, the French historians themselves seem unable to decide. At all events, the greatest and most expensive preparations were made, ostensibly to carry into effect the first part of the plan. Before, however, we enter into any of the details, we will introduce a document tending to show that General Buonaparte endeavoured to persuade the directory to convert the sham into a real attack; and surely none but a mind like his could have conceived a plan so vast and multifarious, and yet with such a unity of purpose, as the following letter discloses. It bears date on the 13th of April, 1798; and we here present such a translation, as we are enabled to give to it:

"In our situation we ought to wage a sure war against England, and we can do so. Whether in peace or war, we should expend from forty to fifty millions (francs) in reorganizing our navy. Our army need not be of greater or of less strength, so long as the war obliges England to make immense preparations, that will ruin her finances, and destroy the commercial spirit, and absolutely change the habits and manners of her people. We should employ the whole summer in getting the Brest fleet ready for sea, in exercising the sailors in the road, and in completing the ships that are building at Rochefort, Lorient, and Brest. With a little activity in these operations, we may hope to have, by the month of September, 35 sail of the line in Brest, including the four or five which may then be ready at Lorient and Rochefort.

"We shall have by the end of the month, in the different ports of the Channel, nearly 200 gun-boats. These must be stationed at Cherbourg, Hâvre, Boulogne, Dunkerque, and Ostende, and the whole summer employed in inuring the soldiers to the sea. In continuing to allow to the commission for the coasts of the Channel 300,000 francs per décade, 'a period of 10 days,' we shall be enabled to build 200 gun-boats of larger dimensions, capable of carrying cavalry. We shall then have, in the month of September, 400 gun-boats at Boulogne, and 35 sail of the line at Brest. The Dutch can also have ready, in this interval, 12 sail of the line in the Texel.

"We have in the Mediterranean two descriptions of line-of-battle ships: 12 of French construction, which, between this and the month of September, may be augmented by two new ships; and nine of Venetian construction. We may perhaps be able, when the expedition which the government projects in the Mediterranean is over, to send the 14 ships to Brest, and to retain in the Mediterranean only the nine Venetian ships; which will give us, in the month of October or November, 50 ships of the line at Brest, and almost an equal number of frigates.

"We may perhaps then be able to transport 40,000 men to any spot of England we wish, by avoiding, however, a naval action, if the enemy should be too strong: in the mean while, 40,000 men threaten to put off in the 400 gun-boats, and about as many fishing-vessels of Boulogne, and the Dutch fleet and 10,000 men threaten a descent upon Scotland. The invasion of England, put in practice in this manner in the months of November and December, would be almost certain. England would waste herself by immense efforts, but these would not secure her from our invasion.

"In fact, the expedition to the East will oblige England to send six additional ships of the line to India, and perhaps twice as many frigates to the entrance of the Red Sea: she would be obliged to have from 22 to 25 ships of the line at the entrance of the Mediterranean, 60 before Brest, and 12 before the Texel, forming a total of 300 line-of-battle ships, without reckoning those she now has in America and the Indies, and the ten or twelve 50-gun ships, with 20 frigates, which she would be obliged to have ready to oppose the invasion from Boulogne. We should always remain masters of the Mediterranean, since we should there have the nine Venetian ships of the line.

"There would yet be another way to augment our force in this sea: to oblige Spain to cede three ships of the line and three frigates to the Ligurian republic. This republic cannot be considered otherwise than as a department of France: it possesses more than 10,000 excellent seamen. It is politic in France to encourage the Ligurian republic, and to take care also that it has a few ships of the line. If any difficulties arise about Spain's ceding to us or to the Ligurian republic three ships of the line, I should think it would be proper for us to sell to the Ligurian republic three of the nine ships we took from the Venetians; and we should require of them to build three others: it would be a good squadron, manned with excellent sailors, which we should thus obtain. With the money received from the Ligurians we ought to build at Toulon three good ships upon our own models; for ships built after the Venetian plan require as many sailors as a good 74; and seamen – there is our weak point. As future events may turn out, it would be extremely advantageous to us that the three republics of Italy, which ought to be equal in force to the King of Naples and

Grand Duke of Tuscany, should have a stronger navy than that belonging to the King of Naples."*

We leave this extraordinary letter without comment or remark, except just to point out the singular circumstance that the navy of Spain, the ally of France, and which more than trebled that of Holland, should not have been called in aid of Buonaparte's grand scheme.

While the Brest fleet is remaining quiet in port, awaiting the issue of the Egyptian campaign, we will recount some adventures between the British cruisers stationed off the French coast and the gun-boats that were to be instrumental in effecting the overthrow of England. It will be necessary first to give a brief account of the origin and composition of a description of force, which we may name, in reference to its avowed, if not its real object, the invasion-flotilla.

Soon after his triumphant return from Italy, Buonaparte was appointed by the directory the commander-in-chief of an army called, in rather a more public manner than would, we should suppose, have been the case, had there been any thing but a diversion intended, "armée d'Angleterre." On the subsequent departure of the conqueror of Italy for Toulon, to superintend what, at his suggestion probably, was the main plan in agitation, General Kilmaine succeeded him in the command of an army, whose very name, coupled with the extravagant tales of its amount, was calculated, if not to create alarm, to cause many expensive preparations in the defensive way on the opposite side of the Channel.

The flat-bottomed boats which, during the latter months of the year 1797, were building in most of the French ports along the Channel frontier, were, it appears, constructed from a plan of the celebrated Swedish architect, Chapman, brought to France by an inhabitant of Antwerp, or Anvers, named Muskein; and whom the directory, besides appointing him to superintend the construction of these boats (usually called by the French sailors "bateaux à la Muskein"), made a capitaine de vaisseau. The business of providing the means of transport, including the flat and all other descriptions of vessels, was intrusted to a commission of three persons: General Andréossi, with the title of director-general; the engineer Forfait, with the title of director (ordonnateur); and Rear-admiral la Crosse, with that of inspector-general of the coasts between Cherbourg and Antwerp. A sum of eight millions of francs, drawn from the funds in the hands of the minister of marine, was placed at the disposal of the abovenamed commissioners, to be accounted for to Buonaparte, or to whomever else was the commanding officer of the expedition. To Rear-admiral la Crosse, owing to the great

* As this letter of General Buonaparte's is a very important one, we have given a transcript of the original; for which see Appendix, No. 13.

extent of his command, were associated the chefs de division, or commodores, Genteaume, Decrès, Casa-Bianca, and Dumanoir-le-Pelley.

In order that the expense, thus incurring in the ports of Normandy, might not be entirely lost, or perhaps to fix the attention of the British upon the Channel ports, while preparations were going on at Toulon, the French government ordered an attack to be made upon the small islands of Saint-Marcouf; of which, in July, 1795, Sir Sidney Smith, with the Diamond frigate, had taken unobstructed possession, and which were considered to give to the English great facility in intercepting the communication between the ports of Hâvre and Cherbourg. The islands of St.-Marcouf are two in number, lying close together; one named east and the other west, and each not more than 200 yards in length, by about 120 in breadth, exclusive of two large banks, which, at low-water, are seen stretching to a considerable extent from the shore. The islands are situated off the river Isigny on the coast of Normandy, and about four miles distant from the French shore. After being garrisoned with about 500 seamen and marines, including a great proportion of invalids, these small islands were placed under the command of Lieutenant Charles Papps Price, of the Badger, a cruiser-converted Dutch hoy, mounting four, or at most six guns.* To be prepared for an attempt at recapture, several pieces of cannon were also mounted, both on the principal or western, and on the eastern island; and, as an additional security, some small vessels of war were appointed to cruise near the spot.

Thirty-three flat-bottomed boats upon Chapman's construction having been launched at Hâvre, a body of troops, under General Point, was embarked on board of them, and Captain Muskein was ordered, with them and a few gun-brigs, to make a combined attack upon the isles of Saint-Marcouf. On the night of the 7th this little expedition set sail from Hâvre; but, the next afternoon, when near the entrance of Caen river, Captain Muskein found his progress obstructed by two British frigates, the Diamond, Captain Sir Richard John Strachan, and the Hydra, Captain Sir Francis Laforey. At 4 P.M. the gun-brigs and flats anchored in a line close to the shore; at 5h. 30 m. the Diamond and Hydra, having worked up to them, opened their broadsides, receiving in return a pretty sharp fire from the heavy long guns of the flotilla. Before the Diamond had discharged above two or three broadsides, she grounded in wearing, and lay fast; still, however, the frigate kept up a fire from such of her guns as would bear. At 8 h. 30 m. the flotilla ceased firing, not being able, owing to the darkness, to see the position of their opponents. The latter did the same; and the Hydra, to assist in getting her consort afloat, anchored close to

* See note w*, to Annual Abstract, No. 3.

her. Soon after midnight, by the united exertions of the two ships, the Diamond again got afloat, without any material damage, either from grounding or from several shells, which the enemy on shore, to interrupt their operations, had continued to throw at both frigates, but which, fortunately for the latter, fell short. The Diamond, however, had previously received some slight injury in her sails and rigging from the fire of the gunboats. At 6 A.M. on the 9th the flotilla weighed, and, standing along shore to the westward, reanchored at 9 A.M., under the town of Bernie. While the Diamond and Hydra were standing off and to watch the motions of the enemy, the 50-gun ship Adamant, Captain William Hotham, hove in sight in the offing. On observing this, Captain Muskein again got under way, and ran back to the eastward, pursued by the two frigates; who exchanged several broadsides with the flotilla, as well as with some batteries on shore. At 3 P.M., the French vessels having stood into Caen river, the Diamond and Hydra ceased firing and hauled off from the shore.

While Captain Muskein lay at anchor in the small port of Sallenelle, repairing the damages done to his vessels, seven heavy gun-brigs, and about 40 flat-boats and armed fishing vessels, joined him from Cherbourg, the head-quarters of Rear-admiral La Crosse. These vessels also brought an additional body of troops. After a three weeks' blockade in Caen river, Captain Muskein found an opportunity to put to sea with his now doubly-formidable flotilla, and was, this time, so fortunate as to reach unobserved the road of La Hougue, situated about half way between Cape Barfleur, and the isles that were to be attacked. Here it was necessary to await the concurrence of two circumstances; a stark calm, in order to prevent the British cruisers from approaching the scene of action, and neap-tides, when the currents, being at their minimum of violence, would offer less opposition to the progress of the flotilla.

Owing to the absence of these indispensable contingencies, matters remained quiet at the isles of Saint-Marcouf until the 6th of May, when Lieutenant Price received information that an attack was meditated in the course of that night. A boat was instantly despatched to reconnoitre the enemy, and every preparation made to receive him. By 10 P.M., owing to the prevailing calm, the small naval force on the station, consisting of the 50-gun ship Adamant, Captain William Hotham, 24-gun ship Eurydice, Captain John Talbot, and 18-gun brig-sloop Orestes, Captain William Haggitt, had not been able to approach nearer to the islands than six miles; consequently, the defence of the post was likely to rest upon the sole exertions of the garrison; precisely what the assailants wanted, in order to ensure success to their plan of attack.

At midnight the reconnoitring boat signalled the approach of the enemy, and the garrison, at the same time, heard the French officers giving orders to the men; but the darkness was so great that none of the boats were visible. The attacking force consisted of 52-gun brigs and flat-bottomed boats, having on board as was reported, about 6000 men (a number, we think, somewhat overrated), composed chiefly of a detachment from the Boulogne marine-battalion. At daybreak on the 7th the flotilla was seen drawn up in a line opposite to the south-west front of the western redoubt; and instantly was opened, upon the brigs and flats composing it, a fire from 17 pieces of cannon consisting of four 4, two 6, and six 24 pounder long guns, and three 24, and two 32 pounder carronades, being all the guns that would bear. The brigs remained at a distance of from 300 to 400 yards, in order to batter the redoubt with their heavy long guns while the boats, with great resolution rowed up until within musket-shot of the battery. But the guns of the latter, loaded with round, grape, and canister, soon poured destruction amongst these, cutting several of the boats "into chips," and compelling all that could keep afloat to seek their safety in flight. Six or seven boats were seen to go down, and one small flat, No. 13, was afterwards towed in, bottom upwards. She appeared, by some pieces of paper found in her, to have had 144 persons on board, including 129 of the second company of the Boulogne battalion.

The loss sustained by the British garrison in this highly creditable affair amounted to one private-marine killed, and two private-marines and two seamen wounded; a loss much less in amount than was to be expected from upwards of 80 bow-guns, many of which were long 36, and none of them, it is believed below long 18 pounders. Lieutenant Richard Bourne, of the Sandfly gun-vessel, who commanded the fort on the eastern island, was unable, at the commencement of the attack, to effect much; but when, towards the close of it, several of the French boats got within shell-range, two 68-pounder carronades, which were part of his guns, must, from their heavy and destructive discharges, have been of great service in repelling the assailants. Fortunately, no one of Lieutenant Bourne's party was hurt. According to one French account, the invaders lost about 900 in killed or drowned, and between 300 and 400 wounded. According to another, their loss was very trifling. The three British ships got up just as the remnant of the flotilla was retreating; but, owing to the calm state of the weather, were unable to intercept any of the boats in the way back to La Hougue. As a reward for their conduct on this occasion, Lieutenants Price and Bourne were each promoted to the rank of commander.

Shortly after this unsuccessful début of the famous flotilla, Rear-admiral Bruix, succeeding M. Pléville as minister of marine, directed Rear-admiral La Crosse to take the command, and to make a second attack upon the islands which had been the scene of their defeat. The French government, however, having good reason, from experience, to doubt the success of the measure, renounced the attempt; and Rear-admiral La Crosse, selecting an opportunity, conveyed back the principal part of his flotilla to Cherbourg, between which port, Granville, and Saint-Malo, the vessels were divided; while Captain Muskein, with his division, was ordered to Hâvre.

Intelligence having reached the British government, that a great number of transport-schuyts were fitting at Flushing, or Flessingue, preparatory to their being convoyed by the Bruges canal to Dunkerque and Ostende, in order to be employed in the long-threatened invasion of England, a squadron, consisting of one 44-gun ship flûte (mounting 26 guns), two 28-gun frigates, two 20-gun ships, three frigate flûtes (mounting about 14 guns each), and 17 sloops, bombs, and gun-vessels, under the orders of Captain Home Riggs Popham, in the Expedition flûte-44, assembled at Margate, and there received on board a body of troops, commanded by Major-general Eyre Coote.

On the 14th of May the squadron set sail for the opposite coast, but owing to an unfavourable change in the weather, did not, until the 19th, at 1 A.M., reach their intended anchorage in front of the town of Ostende. Soon afterwards the wind, shifting to west and blowing hard, raised a heavy surf on the shore. Still, as information had just been received, by a captured vessel, that the force in Ostende, Nieuport, and Bruges, was very small, it was resolved to land the troops immediately, and trust to the weather's moderating for their safe re-embarkation. One of the transports, the frigate-flûte Minerva, Captain John Mackellar, having on board the four light-infantry companies of the first regiment of guards, under Lieutenant-colonel Ward, had recently parted company. The remainder of the troops, with Major-general Coote at their head, consisting of two light-infantry companies of the Coldstream guards, two similar companies belonging to the third guards, the 11th regiment of foot, and the flank companies of the 23d and 49th regiments, numbering, including a small party of miners, about 1140 officers and men, with six pieces of ordnance, also wooden petards, tools, and the necessary quantity of gunpowder for effecting the intended explosion, disembarked, and at about 3 A.M., without opposition or even discovery, effected their landing at a short distance to the eastward of the town.

At about 4 h. 15 m. A.M. the batteries at Ostende opened their fire upon the three nearest British vessels, which were the brig-sloop Wolverine, Captain Lewis Mortlock, and gun-brigs Asp and Biter, Lieutenants Joseph Edmonds and John Dennis De Vitré; and, for upwards of four hours, a mutual cannonade was maintained. At the end of that time, however, the Wolverine and Asp had sustained considerable damage in their hulls and rigging; with, to the latter the loss of one seaman killed, and her commander wounded, and, to the former, of one seaman and one private of the 23d regiment killed, and 10 seamen and five privates of the same regiment wounded. The bombs Hecla and Tartarus, Captains Thomas Hand and James Oughton, had, in the mean time, been throwing their shells into the town and basin, with great quickness and some effect; much damage having, as alleged, been done to the shipping in the latter, and the former having been seen several times on fire.

Owing to the damaged state of the Wolverine and Asp, the commodore signalled them to weigh and move further off; and the ship-sloop Dart (carrying twenty-eight 32-pounder carronades), Captain Richard Raggett, and the 18-gun brig-sloops Kite and Harpy, Captains William Brown and Henry Bazely, forthwith proceeded to occupy the stations which the Wolverine and Asp had quitted; but, owing to its being low-water, the Dart and her companions were compelled to anchor at a greater distance from the shore than their commanders wished, or their short-gun batteries suited. Consequently, the subsequent cannonade between the shore and the shipping was neither animated nor effective.

At 9 h. 30 m. A.M. the Minerva came in and anchored; and Captain Mackellar, by the orders of the commodore, immediately went on shore in his boat to report the ship's arrival to the general. In the mean time, Lieutenant-colonel Ward, with a becoming zeal, had filled two flat-bottomed boats with the troops, and was on his way to disembark them, when, as the boats pulled near to the 20-gun ship Ariadne, her commander, Captain James Bradley, succeeded in persuading the colonel to return immediately on board the Minerva; and thus the four fine companies, commanded by Colonel Ward, to his and their present regret, but subsequent joy, were not allowed to land.

The troops that had landed appear to have fully succeeded in blowing up the locks and sluice-gates of the Bruges canal, and in destroying several gun-boats lying in the basin, with the trifling loss of one private soldier killed, and one seaman wounded. The explosion, as seen from the shipping, took place at 10 h. 20 m. A.M., and by noon the troops were ready to re-embark; but such was the state of the weather, that the measure was wholly impracticable. The British then took up a position on some sand-hills near the beach, and there remained under arms but unmolested, during the remainder of that day and the whole of the ensuing night. By daybreak on the 20th, however, the French had collected in considerable force; and, after a smart action in which the British sustained a loss of about 65 in killed and wounded, including, among the former, one lieutenant-colonel, and among the latter, the major-general and several distinguished officers, the whole, with Captain Mackellar and the survivors of his boat's crew, were compelled to surrender on terms of capitulation. Thus ended an expedition, of which both the object and the success appear to have been overrated; but of which the final result was, beyond all doubt, disastrous to one party, and proportionately triumphant to the other.

A week or two after the occurrence of this unlucky event, an exploit of a very different character was performed by some British cruisers off the French coast, and in sight of a part of the army destined, as was then supposed, for the invasion of England. On the 30th of May, at daybreak, the British 38-gun frigate Hydra, Captain Sir Francis Laforey, bomb-vessel Vesuvius (eight long 6-pounders, one 10 and one 13 inch mortar, with 67 men and boys), Captain Robert Lewis Fitzgerald, and 12-gun cutter Trial (eight long 3-pounders and four 12-pounder carronades, with 45 men and boys), Lieutenant Henry Garrett, standing in towards the port of Hâvre, close hauled on the larboard tack, with the wind at east-north-east, discovered about a point upon the weather bow, standing on the contrary tack, three sail, which eventually proved to be the French 36-gun frigate Confiante, Captain (de vais.) Etienne Pevrieux, 20-gun ship-corvette Vésuve, Lieutenant Jean-Baptiste-Louis Lecolier, and an armed cutter or gun-vessel; all of which, on the preceding night, had quitted Hâvre, bound to Cherbourg.

On approaching near enough to ascertain the character of the Hydra and her companions, the French vessels wore round on the larboard tack, and stood towards the shore, under a press of sail, chased by the former: especially by the Hydra, who was far ahead and to windward of her two consorts. When close in-shore, the Confiante and Vésuve tacked and hoisted their colours; and the latter, being at some distance on the lee beam of her consort, fired at the Hydra in passing.

Having fired in return, the Hydra quickly put about: as, shortly afterwards did the French frigate and corvette. At 6 A.M., just as the Hydra, while stretching on upon the starboard tack, had arrived abreast of and between the Confiante and Vésuve, then on the opposite or in-shore tack, the French frigate opened a passing but ineffectual fire; and, in a minute or two afterwards, the corvette from to-leeward also discharged her guns at the Hydra. The latter now opened upon the Vésuve so well-directed a fire, that the latter, crowding all sail, bore up before the wind towards the shore.

At 6 h. 30 m., leaving the Vesuvius and Trial to pursue the Vésuve, the Hydra tacked after the Confiante; who thereupon bore up, with the apparent intention of reaching the road of Hâvre. Bearing up in pursuit, the Hydra soon commenced pouring her broadsides into the French frigate; and the two continued a running fight until 7 h. 15 m., about the time of high-water; when the Confiante, then under a press of sail, ran on shore upon the sand opposite to Beuzeval, a village a little to the eastward of the mouth of the river Dive, and about three leagues to leeward of the port she wished to make.

In the mean while the Vésuve had run herself on shore near to a small battery off the entrance of the river Dive; but, floating again at the rising of the tide, the corvette attempted to run down to the mouth of the river Orne, or Caen. The near approach of the Vesuvius and Trial, however, compelled her again to run on shore at a short distance only from the spot on which she had first grounded. Here the bomb-vessel and cutter commenced cannonading the Vésuve; in which occupation we will leave them, while we attend to the two frigates.

The moment the Confiante struck the sand, the Hydra laid all her sails back, and kept up, with scarcely any return, an incessant fire, within musket-shot distance, until 9 h. 30 m. A.M.; when the falling of the tide obliged the British frigate, after having been near enough to read the name upon the stern of the French frigate (whose mizenmast had just fallen), to haul off into deeper water. The Hydra, as she stood to the offing, made the signal for her two consorts to leave off firing and do the same. Sir Francis, soon afterwards, sent the Trial to reconnoitre the French frigate; which at this time bore from the Hydra south by east, and the corvette south-south-west, distant five miles.

On the Trial's approach, the Confiante, whose crew had hauled her further in-shore, fired several shot at her, and a number of troops had assembled on the beach and adjoining heights, ready to protect the grounded frigate from an attack upon her by boats. Under these circumstances, Sir Francis thought it best to defer any attempt to board and destroy the Confiante, until a more favourable opportunity should present itself. In the mean while the Hydra continued, during the night, as close to the shore as a regard for her safety would permit.

On the 31st at 10 A.M., finding that a great part of the crew had quitted the Confiante, Sir Francis despatched the boats of the Hydra, under the orders of Lieutenants George Acklom and William J. Simonds, and Lieutenant Blanch of the marines, covered by the Trial, to haul down the colours of and burn the French frigate. At about 45 m. past noon the boats got alongside of and boarded the Confiante, whom the remainder of her crew had now abandoned, leaving her colours flying. These were presently hauled down by the British, and at 1 h. 30 m. P.M. the French frigate was on fire fore and aft; a service executed in the face of a party of cavalry drawn up on the beach, and of a small though ineffectual fire of musketry from some infantry on the adjoining heights. Having completely destroyed the Confiante, and ascertained that she carried 36 long guns, 12 and 6 pounders, besides a pair or two of carronades on her quarterdeck, with a crew, according to her rôle d'équipage, of 300 men, Lieutenant Acklom, with the boats, at about 2 h. 30 m. P.M. returned to the Hydra in the offing.

This dashing service was performed without injury to a single man on board of, or belonging to, any one of the three British vessels; and the only damage which the latter sustained was a slight wound by shot in the Hydra's mainmast, and some injury to her rigging. "From the number of slain left on board and the state of her decks," the Confiante appeared to have sustained a severe loss; but, as the wounded were carried off, and the killed are not enumerated in either the English or French accounts, we are unable to state its amount.

As soon as, on the ebbing of the tide on the morning of the 30th, the Vesuvius and Trial had hauled off from the Vésuve, the French crew began shoring up the corvette, to prevent her falling over: they next got down her yards and topmasts, and laid out an anchor in the north-west, ready to heave her afloat on the rising of the tide. This was effected while the Hydra's boats were boarding the Confiante; and, in the course of the afternoon, the Vésuve got safe into the river Dive. Here, at the little port of Sallenelle, was lying Captain Muskein's division of gun-boats on its return to Hâvre.

In order to protect the corvette from a second attack, Captain Muskein landed a portion of his guns, and erected batteries at Cabourg and other suitable spots at the entrance of the river. These batteries were worked by the seamen from the gun-boats, assisted by the 200 troops of the Boulogne battalion that had embarked in them. This prompt measure saved the Vésuve from sharing the fate of the Confiante; and, even when on the 1st of June the 38-gun frigate Diamond, Captain Sir Richard John Strachan, joined the little squadron before Hâvre, the British were obliged to retire without effecting any thing further. As soon as their departure was ascertained, and the Vésuve had rigged herself afresh, the corvette and gun-boats got under way, and reached Hâvre in safety.

A French writer complains, that Lieutenant Lecolier did very little to support his commodore; and it certainly would appear, as well that Captain Pevrieux, when he permitted the Vésuve, instead of running on shore, or making off as the cutter had just done, to follow the Confiante in tacking from the coast, did expect to derive some benefit from the co-operation of his consort, as that the latter bore up out of gun-shot the instant she felt the effects of the Hydra's heavy broadside. Nor, considering the disparity of force between the Hydra and Vésuve, and the apparent neglect of the Confiante, who was to windward, to close for his support, could Lieutenant Lecolier be blamed for the step he took.

As the Vesuvius and Trial had gone in pursuit of the corvette, then was the time for Captain Pevrieux to have emulated the conduct of many other French officers of his rank, and, instead of running from, to have at least "shown fight" with, the Hydra. Having, however, previously declined to engage a

British 18-pounder frigate, when commanding a French frigate of the same maindeck force,* Captain Pevrieux would hardly be the assailant now that the ship he commanded carried no heavier metal than twelves.

The same French writer, who blames Lieutenant Lecolier for his early abandonment of the action, would, in all probability, have been less lavish in his encomiums upon Captain Pevrieux for his intrepidity in conducting it, but for two mistakes, so happily coinciding as to double the intended effect. He calls the Confiante "une corvette," with as much reason as he calls the Hydra "un vaisseau rasé, portant du 24 en batterie et des caronades de 64 sur les gaillards."† Where can this French writer produce a corvette with a "capitaine de vaisseau" and a crew of 300 men? The Vésuve mounted 20 long 8-pounders, and yet was commanded, as the writer acknowledges, by a "lieutenant de vaisseau." Of the fact, that the Confiante was a frigate, similar in size and force to the Néréide and a great many others, we entertain not the slightest doubt; and, indeed, if our memory is not treacherous, we have seen the Confiante designated as a frigate in the columns of the Moniteur.

Since the failure of their attempt in December, 1796, to make a descent upon Ireland, the French had endeavoured, by means of spies and emissaries, to gain over the catholics to their cause. In this they at length succeeded, and unhappy Ireland became the theatre of open and bloody rebellion. The object of the French directory now was, at every risk, to aid the rebels with a few disciplined troops, and a great quantity of arms, ammunition, and clothing. This, indeed, the directory had pledged themselves to do, but they had let the summer nearly pass away before they made any attempt to fulfil their promise. At length two expeditions were set on foot, and were to have sailed simultaneously, one from Brest, the other from Rochefort.

Owing to some delay in paying the seamen and troops of the Brest expedition, that from Rochefort was the first to sail. It consisted of the following ships:

Gun-frig.		
40	Concorde	Commodore Daniel Savary. Captain André Papin.
36	Franchise	Captain Jean-Louis Guillotin.
36	Médée	Captain Jean-Daniel Coudin.
28	Vénus	Captain André Senez.

On board this squadron were 1150 troops, with four fieldpieces, under the command of General Humbert, having under him the Adjutant-generals Fontaine and Sarrazin. Each ship carried also a considerable quantity of powder, and the same of arms and accoutrements.

* See vol. i., p. 332.

† Victoires et Conquêtes, tome viii., p. 290.

On the 6th of August Commodore Savary got under way with his squadron from the road of the Isle of Aix, and escaped to sea unobserved. On the 21st the squadron made the westernmost end of Ireland, and the general intended to disembark the troops at Killembach; but contrary winds drove the ships towards the bay of Killala. The French squadron made its approach under English colours, and on the evening of the 22d cast anchor near Killcumin head, the western point of Killala bay. In the course of the evening the troops disembarked, taking on shore with them four field-pieces, four loaded ammunition waggons, 30,000 pounds of powder, and uniforms and equipments complete for 3000 rebel Irishmen.

The only British force at the post consisted of a small detachment of the Prince of Wales's fencible regiment, and a few yeomanry, attended by some clergymen of the neighbourhood, in number altogether about 200. These, or the loyal portion of them at least, offered what resistance they could, but were at length compelled to give way, after having lost a few in killed and wounded, and a great many willing and unwilling prisoners. An officer and 25 privates of the fencible regiment, being the whole of the prisoners who preferred captivity to freedom under the terms on which alone it was offered, were sent on board the French squadron. Commodore Savary soon afterwards weighed and set sail from the coast; and these four French frigates were fortunate enough to reach in safety the port whence they had departed.

The subsequent operations being wholly of a military nature, it may suffice to state, that General Humbert was soon joined by several bands of United Irishmen, but not in such numbers as he had been led to expect; that he had skirmishes with the loyal part of the inhabitants and the troops sent against him; and that finally, on the 8th of September, at Ballinamuck, the French general, with 843 of his followers, including officers, surrendered, at discretion, to a superior British force under Lieutenant-general Lake.

About a week after the surrender of General Humbert and his "Armée d'Irlande,"* the French privateer-brig Anacréon, from Dunkerque, having on board the Irish rebel Napper-Tandy, and the French General Rey, besides some other officers and a detachment of light artillery, together with a quantity of arms, ammunition, and clothing, appeared off the Irish coast, near a small island which lies to the westward of the county of Donegal. A communication from the shore soon acquainted General Rey with the fate of General Humbert, and the Anacréon immediately made sail on her return. Going north-about, the French brig fell in with and captured two British

* Victoires et Conquêtes, tome x., p. 390.

letters of marque from the Baltic; with which in her company, the Anacréon re-entered Dunkerque.

The expedition to which we alluded, as being appointed to sail from Brest at the same time as that under Commodore Savary, from Rochefort, consisted of one ship of the line, eight frigates, and an aviso, under the orders of Commodore Bompart, the captain of the Embuscade in her action with the Boston at the beginning of the war, and now on board the 74-gun ship Hoche.* This squadron contained about 3000 troops commanded by Generals Hardy and Ménage, a large train of artillery, and some battering cannon, with a detachment of men belonging to these two armies, under Colonel Pernetly and Captain Kirgenery, also a great quantity of military stores of every description. The French government having at length given the order for departure and a favourable wind occurring, Commodore Bompart, on the evening of the 16th of September, hoping to escape through the passage du Raz before daylight the next morning, put to sea with the

Gun-ship		
74	Hoche	Commodore Jean-Bapt.-Fr. Bompart. Captain Desiré-Marie Maistral.
Gun-frig.		
40	Immortalité	Captain Jean-François Legrand.
	Romaine	Captain Mathieu-Charles Bergevin.
	Loire	Captain Adrien-Joseph Segond.
36	Bellone	Captain Louis-Léon Jacob.
	Coquille	Captain Léonore Deperonne.
	Embuscade	Captain Nicolas Clement de la Roncière.
	Résolue	Captain Jean-Pierre Bargeau.
	Sémillante	Captain Martin-Antoine Lacouture.
Sch.	Biche	Lieut. Jean-Marie-Pierre Labastard.

On the 17th, at daybreak, the bec du Raz bearing east-half-north distant four or five leagues, and the weather nearly calm, the British 38-gun frigates Boadicea, Captain Richard Goodwin Keats, and Ethalion, Captain George Countess, and 18-gun brig-sloop Sylph, Captain John Chambers White, discovered the above French squadron about five leagues off in the east-south-east, steering west-north-west. At 8 A.M., a light breeze sprang up from the north-east; on which the French ships hauled their wind to south-south-west, and made sail. Now that the French squadron had fairly put to sea, Captain Keats made all sail to the northward, to communicate the intelligence to Lord Bridport; leaving Captain Countess, with the Ethalion and Sylph, to keep company with the enemy and watch his future motions.

On the 18th, at 2 A.M., Captain Countess was joined by the 38-

* Late Pégase, but newly named after the celebrated general; who had died at the head-quarters at Wetzlar on the 18th of September, 1797, of a disease in the chest, and was buried, with the highest military honours, by the side of General Marceau, in the redoubt of Petersberg, near Coblentz.

gun frigate Amelia, Captain the Honourable Charles Herbert, who the night previous had passed unobstructed, if not unobserved, through the French squadron. At daylight the French began working towards Isle Groix, as if intending to enter Lorient. At 8 A.M., however, they bore up, five of the frigates, of which the more advanced ones were the Loire and Immortalité, chasing the two British frigates, but without effect. At 10 h. 30 m. A.M., the Hoche and her nine companions hauled to the wind on the larboard tack, steering about south-west by south, the French commodore wishing to make it appear to his watchful and persevering pursuers, that he was bound to the Antilles. On the 19th it was nearly a calm all day. On the 20th, at 6 A.M., the 44-gun frigate Anson, Captain Philip Charles Durham, joined company. At noon the British were in latitude 46° 27' north, longitude 5° 3' west, and the French nearly hull-down in the south-west by south. On the 22d at noon, the British frigates again got within eight or nine miles of the French squadron, which was at this time steering west-north-west. On the 23d, in the afternoon, having now little doubt of M. Bompart's destination, Captain Countess despatched the Sylph to the commander-in-chief on the Irish station.

On the 25th, in the forenoon, latitude 44° 53' north, longitude 8° 57' west, a fleet, that proved to be an English convoy of more than 100 sail, among which were some East India ships, was descried to leeward of the French squadron, then about four miles off in the west-south-west. Whether deceived by the warlike appearance of the Indiamen, or apprehensive that some of his frigates, which were then rather scattered, would be exposed to an attack by the British frigates in company, or whether he was so tied up by his orders that he dared not take advantage of the chance thus thrown in his way, and which, by the by, would have been more beneficial to his country than the safe debarkation in Ireland of 3000 Frenchmen, and even the safe return to Brest of the squadron that had carried them out; whatever it was that influenced M. Bompart, he suffered the convoy to proceed unmolested. On the 26th, in the morning, the French ships tacked, and gave chase to the Ethalion and her two companions, but left off about noon. The latter immediately shortened sail, and again stood to the south-west after the French squadron. On the 27th the wind increased, and the sea became so rough, that all the ships were under their topsails and courses; but the British still maintained their position about four miles on the enemy's lee quarter. On the 29th, at 7 A.M., by which time the weather had moderated, the French squadron again went in chase. Three of the French frigates, of which the Loire was first, and the Immortalité second, came up fast with the three British frigates, and the latter got ready to fire their stern chasers; but about 9 A.M. the Hoche sprang her main topmast, and one of the French frigates carried away a topsail yard. On this the chasing ships shortened sail; as did also the three British frigates. Finding it in vain to hope to shake off the latter, who appeared as if they would really follow him to the Antilles, Commodore Bompart determined to steer for his destination. The French ships accordingly wore on the larboard tack, with their heads to the north-west, and were quickly followed in the manœuvre by Captain Countess's squadron. In the forenoon's chase the Anson had sprung her main topmast; and in the evening the Hoche was seen to lower hers down either to shift or fish it: at daylight on the 30th, however, the topmast of the French ship, to the credit of her officers and crew, was again in its place. At noon this day the ships were in latitude 44° north, longitude 14° 23' west. On the 1st of October the French began steering a more northerly course, and rather increased their distance from the British. On the 4th, in the evening, the weather continuing thick and coming on to blow very hard from the south-south-east, the Ethalion and her consorts hauled up and soon lost sight of M. Bompart's squadron. On the 7th, in the evening, the Amelia parted company. On the 8th, and a part of the 9th, it was calm; during which the Anson rolled away her main topmast and mizen top-gallantmast.

On the 11th, at daylight, the Ethalion and Anson, standing on the larboard tack, with the wind at north-north-west, saw and chased two sail on the lee bow; one of which proved to be the Amelia, and the other a ship (either the Robust or Magnanime) belonging to the squadron of Commodore Sir John Borlase Warren; who, with the 74-gun ship Canada, 80-gun ship Foudroyant, Captain Sir Thomas Byard, 74-gun ship Robust, Captain Edward Thornborough, and 44-gun frigate Magnanime, Captain the Hon. Michael De Courcy, had been despatched from Cawsand bay since the evening of the 23d of September, which was about as soon as intelligence arrived of the escape of the French squadron from Brest. The commodore then proceeded straight to Achil head, and on the 10th, the high land of Donegal being distant about 12 leagues, was joined by the 36-gun frigates Melampus, Captain Graham Moore, and Doris, Captain Lord Ranelagh; which frigates had sailed from Lough-Swilly a few days before, in consequence of the intelligence brought to the north-west coast by the Sylph brig detached by Captain Countess. Shortly after the junction of the Melampus and Doris, Sir John detached the latter to cruise off Tory island and the Rosses, and the former to give the alarm along the Irish coast. A gale of wind from the north-west rendering it unsafe to approach the land without a pilot, the Melampus kept company with the squadron; which was joined the same evening by the Amelia. So that, on the following day, the 11th, when, at about 10 h. 30 m. A.M., Captain Countess joined company, Sir John Warren had under his command the Canada, Robust,

Foudroyant, Magnanime, Ethalion, Anson, Melampus, and Amelia.

Relieved at length from the plagues that had stuck to him so closely, Commodore Bompart proceeded to fulfil his instructions, which were to land the troops in the harbour of Lough-Swilly. The first intention had been to effect the disembarkation in the bay of Killala; and the plan was only changed because the delay in the departure of the expedition rendered it probable that General Humbert, for whom of course the reinforcement was meant, would be found further to the northward. On the 10th, in the evening, the French squadron discovered the loom of the land. With the hope now of getting quite clear of the British frigates, M. Bompart bore away in the direction of Killala bay, and then, at midnight, hauled sharp up to the northward, with the wind, as already mentioned, at north-north-west, blowing strong. On the 11th, at daybreak, the French commodore, thinking all was safe, bore up for Tory island, but soon found cause to regret that he had not kept his wind a few hours longer; for, at noon, the Immortalité, the leading frigate, signalled the appearance of the British squadron. The French ships, by signal, now hauled close to the wind; but, owing greatly to an accident which we shall relate presently, that manœuvre proved of no avail.

At about the same time that the Immortalité signalled the enemy to her commodore, the Amelia did the same to hers, and pointed out the bearing to be north by west, which was about half a point before her weather beam. At this time the Robust and Magnanime were on the Amelia's weather quarter, standing on the same tack as herself, and the Canada and the rest of the squadron were on the opposite or starboard tack, at a considerable distance on her lee beam. Sir John Warren immediately made the signal for a general chase, and for the ships to "form in succession as they arrived up with the enemy." At about 2 h. 30 m. P.M. the Canada and ships near her wore on the larboard tack, and made all sail to the east-north-east, which was as high as they could lie. At 6 P.M. the body of the French squadron bore from the Canada north-east, distant 10 or 12 miles. As night approached, the weather became very boisterous, attended with a hollow sea; and at 9 h. 30 m. P.M. the Anson carried away her mizenmast, main yard, and maintopsail yard.

Some hours previous, owing to the violence of the same gale, a much greater misfortune than this was to Commodore Sir John Warren, had befallen Commodore Bompart. The Hoche carried away her main topmast, the latter, in its fall, bringing down the fore and mizen topgallantmasts, and tearing the mainsail nearly to pieces. This accident, of course, retarded considerably the progress of the French squadron; and at a few minutes before 8 P.M. the Résolue signalled that she had sprung a leak which she could not stop. The Biche was immediately despatched with orders to Captain Bargeau to run his ship on the coast, and, by burning blue-lights and sending up rockets, endeavour to draw the British squadron after him; while the Hoche and the remaining frigates should bear away to the south-west, the commodore intending to land the troops at any practicable point of the coast in that direction. This plan of sacrificing one ship for the safety of seven, or, taking the value of the Hoche into the account, of 10 or 12 ships, was well devised, and might have succeeded; but either the Biche never reached the Résolue with Commodore Bompart's orders, or Captain Bargeau now discovered that the danger was not so imminent as he had at first been induced to believe. At all events, no rockets or blue-lights were observed by the British squadron.

On the 12th, at daybreak, the French commodore, from having, an account of a sudden fall in the wind, run to leeward less fast than he expected, found himself and his squadron nearly surrounded by the ships of his enemies. We will endeavour to show the relative position of the two squadrons soon after 5 h. 30 m. A.M., which was about the time that the light permitted them to get a glimpse of each other. The French squadron, loosely formed in two rather distant lines, with the Hoche, who had bent herself a new mainsail, in the centre of the second line, was standing to the south-west, the wind, as before, from the north-north-west, but now very moderate. Right astern, at the distance of about four miles, were the Robust and Magnanime; about a point on the lee quarter, at a somewhat greater distance, the Amelia; a little further forward in that direction, and at about the same distance, the Melampus; a little before the lee beam, at the distance of seven or eight miles, the Foudroyant; and on the lee bow, about a mile nearer, the Canada. The Anson, at this time, was not in sight of either squadron. Consequently M. Bompart, in his crippled state the wind being in the north-west, found every avenue of escape shut against him except in the south-west, the direction in which he was steering.

Both squadrons now anxiously awaited, but with very different feelings, the signal to engage from the Canada; but Sir John, because, as he states in his letter, "it was impossible to close," did not make it until 7 A.M. The Robust was then directed to lead "and the rest of the ships to form in succession in the rear of the van;" a piece of formality that might have answered well enough, had three or four of the Hoche's companions been line-of-battle ships like herself. In the mean time, Commodore Bompart had formed his squadron in an irregular single line ahead, thus: Sémillante, Romaine, Bellone, Immortalité, Loire, Hoche, Coquille, and Embuscade. At 7 h. 10 m. A.M., by her time, the Robust, in obedience to the signal just made by the Canada, edged down towards the rear of the French line, followed closely by the Magnanime, and, on arriving within gun-shot, received a fire from the stern-chasers and quarter-guns of the Embuscade and Coquille. At 7 h. 23 m. A.M., the Rosses then bearing from the Canada south-south-west distant five leagues, the Robust returned the fire of the two French frigates, and at 7 h. 45 m., hauling up her mainsail and taking in her spanker, bore down to leeward of them, for the purpose of closing with the Hoche. This object Captain Thornborough accomplished at 8 h. 50 m., after having engaged the two French frigates in passing, and thus commenced a furious action, side by side, between the two 74s.

In a very few minutes after the Robust had closed with the Hoche, the Magnanime, following close upon her leader, opened her starboard broadside; and the Embuscade and Coquille, particularly the latter, very soon felt its effects. About this time, owing to the Robust checking her way to keep alongside of the Hoche, the Magnanime put her helm hard a-starboard, to avoid running foul of the former, and, ranging past the Robust to leeward, became exposed with the latter to a raking fire from the Loire, Immortalité, and Bellone, which ships had bore up out of the line for that purpose. After a few well-directed broadsides from the Magnanime and a few distant shots from the Foudroyant, the three French frigates ceased their annoyance and made sail to the south-west; while the Magnanime, putting her helm hard a-port, obtained a raking ahead of the Hoche. About this time, or soon afterwards, the latter was assailed on her stern and larboard quarter by the Amelia; who, as well as the Ethalion, had been prevented from getting earlier into action, by having to shorten sail in compliance with Sir John Warren's signal to form the line. Not minding, or perhaps "not seeing" this signal, the Melampus, although far to leeward when the action commenced, got near enough to fire in passing, as declared by Commodore Bompart himself, a few very destructive shot at the Hoche, just as the headmost French frigates were making sail to escape. The Canada, too, having, on tacking to the north-east been favoured by a shift of wind to nearly west, was enabled to fire a few distant shot from her bow-guns at the larboard quarter of the Hoche, already a mere wreck from the close and well-directed fire of the Robust. In this state, with her standing and running rigging all cut to pieces, her masts left tottering, her hull riddled with shot, five feet water in the hold, 25 of her guns dismounted, and a great portion of her crew killed and wounded, the Hoche, at 10 h. 50 m. A.M., struck her colours, and was taken possession of by the boats of the Robust and Magnanime; the first lieutenant of which latter ship, Mr. Charles Dashwood, had the honour of receiving Commodore Bompart's sword.

At about 11 h. 30 m. A.M. the Embuscade, after having, in addition to the injuries she had sustained by the fire of the Magnanime, received a fire from the bow-guns of the Foudroyant, as that ship was working up, surrendered also; and, dropping astern, was taken possession of by the Magnanime. The Coquille then made sail after her companions in the west-south-west-quarter; all of whom were immediately pursued by the Foudroyant, Ethalion, Amelia, and Melampus, and also by the Canada, as soon as Sir John Warren, with a very different feeling from that evinced by Captain Alms at the capture of the Alliance,* had sent his first lieutenant to take charge of the Hoche. The Magnanime on account of the shattered state of her rigging and sails, and detained, with the prize-frigate Embuscade, in the rear; and the Robust, whose condition was even much worse than the Magnanime's, remained to attend the Hoche. The Anson was away in the south-east, just heaving in sight, and vainly striving, without a mizenmast, to approach the scene of action.

The Loire, Immortalité, Bellone, and Coquille were now the nearest of the seven remaining French frigates; and the principal object of all was to cross the bows of the Foudroyant, then standing directly across their path. The Loire and Immortalité succeeded; but the Bellone, being an indifferent sailer, was obliged to haul up, to endeavour to escape to windward. This brought her upon the weather bow of the Foudroyant who opened upon her a heavy fire, and received one in return, which did some damage to her sails and rigging. A shot from the Foudroyant, however, struck the frigate's mizen top and ignited some hand grenades which had been placed there for use. These presently set on fire the rigging and sails; but, by the prompt exertions of Enseigne de Vaisseau François-Auguste Cotelle, and a few others of the crew, the flames were extinguished.

The Bellone, notwithstanding, weathered upon the Foudroyant, and would have got clear of her, but found a British frigate, the Melampus, coming up in her wake. Hoping to shorten the chase by bringing down some of the Bellone's spars, the Melampus, at about half-past noon, yawed and fired her broadside. A repetition of this two or three times, coupled with some slight injury done to her sails and rigging by the French frigate's stern-chasers, caused the Melampus to drop astern. About this time, after an hour's chase and a brave resistance, the Coquille hauled down her colours, and, by signal from the Canada, was taken possession of by the Magnanime. In the mean time the Ethalion had overtaken the Melampus in the chase of the Bellone, and was ordered by signal to continue the pursuit of the latter; while the Melampus, accompanied by the Foudroyant, Amelia, and Canada, bore up after the other French frigates, which now appeared to be meditating a serious attack upon the crippled Anson.

The Ethalion continued in pursuit of the Bellone, under a constant fire, during an hour and a half, of the stern chase-guns of the latter. The chief of the Bellone's shot, however, passed over the masts of the British frigate. Nor did the latter, to

* See vol. i., p. 292.

Captain Jacob's regret, yaw to fire. The Ethalion, on the contrary, kept a steady course, and thus gradually gained in the chase. At about 2 P.M. the Ethalion got abreast of the Bellone, but it was to leeward, and at a greater distance than Captain Countess wished. A smart action now ensued; yet, not until she had sustained the Ethalion's heavy fire for one hour and 54 minutes, had the principal part of her masts, rigging, and sails shot away, with five feet water in her hold, did the Bellone haul down the republican ensign.

The damages of the Ethalion were comparatively slight: she had her main topmast shot through, spritsail yard knocked away, sails and rigging much cut, and the boat on her starboard quarter shot to pieces; and one of the Bellone's shot had also entered between wind and water. The loss sustained by the Ethalion, however, was only one seaman killed and four wounded; while that on board the Bellone is represented to have been 20 killed and 45 wounded; an amount, if correctly stated, partly attributable to the crowded state of the Bellone's decks, her crew and soldier-passengers amounting, according to the disposition of her officers, to 519. It seems probable, that a proportion of the loss accrued in the general action; but it is not so stated in the gazette letter. The French accounts, indeed, represent the loss of the Bellone, in killed and badly wounded together, at no more than 35.

Of Commodore Bompart's squadron, we have already given an account of the capture of one line-of-battle ship and three frigates. Of the remaining five frigates, all standing to the west-south-west, the Loire was the headmost by nearly a mile and a half. On approaching the Anson, then about seven miles from the nearest ship of her squadron, the Loire shortened sail, in the expectation that her companions would unite with her in the attack upon the former. Finding that, while they apparently hung back, the Anson kept getting nearer, Captain Segond, by way of a ruse, hoisted the British flag over the French. It appears that Captain Durham, deceived by this appearance, hailed the Loire. Finding, however, that she did not shorten sail, the Anson, at about 4 P.M., opened a destructive fire. Shifting her colours to French, the Loire returned the fire, and, hauling up athwart the hawse of her disabled opponent, effected her escape. Three other French frigates followed in close order, and, at about 4 h. 30 m. P.M., exchanged broadsides with the Anson, in passing her to leeward. Shortly afterwards the fifth and last frigate bore down upon the Anson's weather quarter, and, like her companions, gave and received a passing fire. The effect of all this upon the Anson was tolerably severe: she had her fore and main masts, fore yard, fore topmast, and bowsprit shot through in several places, besides two seamen killed, and two petty-officers, eight seamen, and three marines wounded.

The loss on board the other British ships from the fire of their opponents in this action was comparatively trifling. The Canada had one seaman mortally wounded, by, we believe, the recoil of a gun when firing at the Hoche and frigates just before the French 74 surrendered. The Foudroyant had nine seamen wounded by the fire of the Bellone and other frigates passing near her. The Robust, in her close conflict with the Hoche and the frigates ahead of her, had ten seamen killed, her first lieutenant of marines (William Cottle) mortally, and 38 seamen and marines wounded; the Melampus one, and the Magnanime seven seamen wounded: making, with the loss of the Ethalion and Anson already enumerated, a total of 13 killed and 75 wounded. On board the French ships the loss was excessively severe. The Hoche, out of the 1237 men and boys that, according to the depositions of her officers, were on board of her, is represented to have lost, in killed and wounded together, 270. The Embuscade, out of a crew, including soldiers, of 486 men and boys, lost 15 killed and 26 wounded; and the Coquille, out of her 507 sailors and soldiers, 18 killed and 31 wounded. The loss on board the six remaining French frigates cannot with accuracy be stated. The Résolue appears to have had five, and the Romaine three men wounded; and the Loire, chiefly by the fire of the Anson, five seamen and soldiers killed, and 10 seamen and 14 soldiers wounded: making, with the loss of the Bellone already stated, the serious total of 462 in killed and wounded.

Having done with the action between the two squadrons, before we attend to the scattered remains of that of M. Bompart, we will briefly advert to the relative force of the parties. On the one side were an 80-gun ship, two 74-gun ships, five frigates, two of the latter (one with her mizenmast gone) carrying long 24, and the remainder, long 18 pounders; and on the other side, one 74-gun ship, without a main topmast, and eight frigates, two of the latter (the Romaine and Immortalité) carrying long 24, one of them (the Loire) long 18, and the remainder long 12 pounders. The brunt of the action, as has already been shown, was borne by the Robust and Magnanime, they having been, at the onset, the nearest ships to the enemy. The rest of the affair was of too detached and skirmishing a character, to be at all illustrated by confronting, in our usual manner, the aggregate force of the rival squadrons. We may here remark, that rather more consequence was attached to this action than it really merited, on account, chiefly, of some slight mistatements in the accounts given of the French squadron. The eight frigates, for instance, were all styled "heavy," although five of them mounted 12-pounders, a less caliber than was carried by any of the British frigates; and the Hoche was designated as an 85-gun ship, which was assigning her eight guns more than she had ports to fit them to.

As every publication, in which an account of this action appears, except one, has relied upon the statement at the foot of

Sir John Warren's letter, that the Hoche was a ship of "84 guns," we deem it necessary to show how many ports she was really pierced for on each deck of the ship. On her lower deck, the Hoche had 30 ports, but the French, acting more wisely than the English, had left the two foremost ones vacant: consequently, the ship mounted 28 guns, which, as usual, were 36-pounders. On the second deck her ports were also 30, and all fitted with guns, 18-pounders. On the quarterdeck the Hoche, leaving, as is customary in French line-of-battle ships, room for two ports of a side in the cabin, had ten ports, in which were as many 8-pounders. On the forecastle she had six ports, in four of which (two being chase-ports) were four more 8-pounders, making just 74 guns. But the Hoche also mounted four brass 36-pounder carronades on her poop, total 78 guns. Of Sir John Warren's account of the force of the Hoche, the French, however, must not complain, until they have made some connection in the following account of the force of the Ethalion: "Cette frégate, l'une des plus forte de la marine anglaise, portait cinquante bouches à feu, savoir: vingt-huit canons de 18 (so far right), douze de 12, et dix caronades de 42."*

There is not an action recorded in these pages, which has given us more trouble to comprehend in its details, than the one of which we have nearly disposed. The official letter contains no particulars, and the entries in the different ships' logs are confused, and, in some instances, contradictory. One fact, however, appears certain, that the action commenced when the Hoche and frigates were, as stated in Sir John Warren's letter, "on the starboard tack." Yet the following appears in the work of a contemporary: "In which (the admiral's letter) we are told, that the enemy bore down and formed a line on the *starboard* tack, &c.; but this is certainly incorrect. By a sketch from the hand of one of the best witnesses now living (Nov. 1822), Plate XXIII. has been formed; by which it appears that, although the enemy's squadron was considerably to windward of the *flagship*, it was very little so of the Robust, Magnanime, and Amelia, which ships, on the morning of the 12th October, discovered the enemy as given in the figure, on the *larboard* tack. The Robust and frigates brought the Hoche and others to action on the larboard side and to windward of them; and the action was nearly over before the Canada and Foudroyant, from being so far to leeward, could render any assistance."†

In answer to this, there is, besides the statement in the official letter, a pair of large engravings, dedicated to the Duke of Clarence, and purporting to be taken from drawings by a marine officer present in the battle, in which the French ships are placed on the starboard tack; but in which (proh pudor!) the officer's own ship, the Canada, is brought where she never was able to get, into the thick of the fire. Another officer who participated in the action, in

* Victoires et Conquêtes, tome x., p. 411.

† Ekins's Naval Battles, p. 251.

answer to our inquiries on the subject, has expressly stated, that the ships were on the starboard tack. But what will Admiral Ekins's "best witnesses now living," say to the following extracts from a respectable French account of the action? "Le vent était au N.-O., et la division française le recevait à tribord. L'escadre ennemie, en se plaçant sous le vent, coupait la terre aux bâtimens français," &c. "Bientôt le Robust, le Magnanime, et l'Amelia l'engagèrent, le premier vaisseau ayant pris poste par son travers à babord, et le Magnanime le canonnant en hanche et en poupe."*

On taking the Hoche in tow, as she had been ordered by the Canada, the Robust steered for Lough-Swilly. On the 13th, at 11 A.M. the latter ship's fore topmast, owing to injuries it had received in the action, fell over the side. At 1 h. 30 m. P.M., a squall carried away the wounded fore and mainmasts of the prize; and at 9 P.M., the tow-rope breaking, the Hoche went adrift. A stormy night ensued, and the latter was with difficulty kept afloat. In this emergency all national prejudices were laid aside, and the French united their exertions with the English in pumping, and performing the other duties of the ship; and, considering how numerous the former were to the latter, there cannot be a doubt that the French crew and soldiers were principally instrumental in saving the prize. To us it certainly appears unaccountable, that one crippled ship should have been sent to conduct home another; and that too, at so stormy a season of the year. On the 15th the Doris frigate fortunately joined the Robust, and took the Hoche in tow. We will now leave the three ships directing their course for Lough-Swilly, while we see what is become of the other ships of the two squadrons.

The Magnanime and Amelia were staying by the Coquille and Embuscade, and the Ethalion by the Bellone. The Anson, especially since her action with the retreating frigates, had enough to do to take care of herself. The Canada, Foudroyant, and Melampus, meanwhile, were chasing the five frigates making off to leeward. At 9 P.M. the Canada got sight of one of the frigates, the Romaine, standing into Donegal bay, and at 10 h. 30 m. P.M. was only one mile to the northward of her. Soon after this the breeze fell, and the Canada lost ground in the chase. At 11 P.M., getting very near to the land, the British 74 shortened sail and hauled to the wind. About this time the Melampus saw two other of the French frigates, the Immortalité and Résolue, bear up towards the land, and got a glimpse also of the Loire and Sémillante, hauling their wind to the westward.

On the 13th, at daybreak, the wind then about west-south-west, the Canada and Foudroyant were close together, the Melampus to leeward, the Anson about nine miles off in the north-north-east, and the Loire and Sémillante (the former

* Victoires et Conquêtes, tome x., p. 406.

somewhat disabled) nearly hull-down to the westward. Having made the signal that she had intelligence to communicate, the Melampus was ordered within hail of the Canada. At 8 h. 30 m. A.M. the two ships having approached each other, Captain Moore acquainted Sir John Warren with the course steered by two of the French frigates: whereupon the Melampus was directed to proceed to Donegal bay, in search of the frigate which the Canada had herself seen standing in towards that part of the land.

The Melampus, accordingly, made all sail to the south-east; but, the wind coming off the land, and blowing fresh, it was not until 11 h. 30 m. P.M., that she got well in with St.-John's point. At this moment, while the Melampus, on account of the gale then beginning to blow, was shortening sail, two large ships made their appearance at no great distance from her, one on the weather bow, the other on the weather quarter. These were neither of them the Romaine of which she had been sent in chase, but the Immortalité and Résolue, running before the wind out of St.-John's bay, where they had been lying at an anchor under English colours. By the time the Melampus had made sail in chase, the two French frigates had passed to leeward of her, and, owing to the excessive darkness of the night, had at that moment lost sight of each other. The nearest frigate to the Melampus was the Résolue; and it would not be doing justice to Captain Bargeau, his officers, and crew, were we to omit to mention some facts that have recently come to our knowledge. The Résolue was one of the old class of French 36-gun frigates, fitted with hanging ports to her main deck; and at the commencement of the gale, her 12-pounders were run in and double breeched, and the ports shut and barred, to meet the coming storm. That done, the frigate weighed, as already stated, in company with her consort.

In this comparatively defenceless state was the Résolue, when she descried the Melampus coming up astern. The French officer of the watch told Captain Bargeau, that the Immortalité wanted to speak him. The Résolue accordingly shortened sail, and, at 1 A.M. on the 14th, was hailed by the Melampus, then running at the rate of about ten knots an hour, and ordered to bring to. As, instead of that, the Résolue, who had now discovered her mistake, attempted to haul athwart the hawse of the Melampus, the latter opened her fire; and, at the same moment, the British officers and crew heard the drum on board the French frigate beat to quarters. To the last two or three broadsides of five that were discharged into her, the Résolue returned a feeble fire from her quarterdeck guns, and then surrendered.

That the guns of the Melampus, during the nine or ten minutes they had been at work, had been most ably handled, is clear from the following account of her opponent's damage and loss: The Résolue had her main yard shot away, and her main topmast and mizenmast shot through, and was so badly struck in the hull, that she made four feet of water an hour, until the Melampus, ten days afterwards got her into the Clyde. This leak, however, appears, from what has elsewhere been stated, to have existed before. Her loss, out of a crew, including troops, of 500 men and boys, amounted to ten killed and several wounded. Having had scarcely a rope cut and not a man hurt, as soon as Captain Moore had sent Lieutenant John Price and 21 seamen on board the prize, and had removed a portion of the numerous French prisoners, the Melampus was ready for the Résolue's consort, had Captain Legrand been disposed, or rather, from the distance and position of the Immortalité, been enabled, to try his luck in the chances of war. However, as the latter, being a new frigate, possessed none of the inconveniences of the old manner of construction, and was, moreover, of double the Résolue's force, it was better perhaps for the Melampus, excellently manned and appointed as she was, that the Immortalité did not molest her.

Deceived by the English accounts, deceived by the French accounts, we formerly joined in censuring both Captain Bargeau and Captain Legrand; the one for not having defended his ship, the other for not having made an effort to save his consort from capture. Had Captain Moore's letter been, as a contemporary calls it, "a clear and compact narrative,"* we should have had no excuse to offer for having spoken so slightingly of two brave officers. We have not obtained our information from either of the French captains, or from any of their countrymen, but from a British eyewitness of the transaction, an officer of the Melampus herself. Indeed we have generally found the officers of the British navy more ready to do justice to their enemies, than those gentlemen on shore who undertake to blazon their exploits; and yet all the mistatements and boastings of the latter, by the opposite nation at least (and there it is where the principal mischief lies), are usually laid to the charge of the former. A French writer, who, for lack of information, omits to tell his readers why the Résolue made no defence, or why the Immortalité was unable to render her any assistance, hopes to gratify them by the sneering remark, that the Melampus closed with the Résolue because she was the weaker ship, "s'attacha à la première, comme la plus faible."† We have no doubt that both Captains Bargeau and Legrand, if questioned, would have expressed it as their opinion, that Captain Moore, had he been permitted a choice, would not have hesitated an instant in selecting for his opponent the Immortalité.

Of Commodore Bompart's eight frigates, we have already disposed of four, the Embuscade, Coquille, Bellone, and

* Brenton, vol. ii., p. 366.

† Victoires et Conquêtes, tome x., p. 413.

Résolue. A fifth, the Loire, had her career first partially, then conclusively, interrupted by the keen vigilance of British cruisers. On the 15th of October, at 8 A.M., the British 38-gun frigate Révolutionnaire, Captain Thomas Twysden, and 12-pounder 32-gun frigate Mermaid, Captain James Newman Newman (senior officer), accompanied by the 18-gun brig-sloop Kangaroo, Captain Edward Brace, being near Black-Sod bay on the north-west coast of Ireland, discovered two large sail bearing north. The latter were soon made out to be enemy's frigates, and the British frigates proceeded in chase. At its commencement the two strangers, which were, as may be conjectured, the Loire and Sémillante, kept their wind, but, shortly afterwards, edged away gradually; so that, by evening, both the pursued and the pursuers were going right before the wind, with all sail set. The two French frigates then signalled and apparently spoke each other, and immediately afterwards steered separate courses. The Révolutionnaire now chased one; and the Mermaid, followed by the Kangaroo, far astern, the other. At 7 P.M., owing to the thick and squally weather, the two British frigates lost sight of each other, and soon afterwards of their respective chases. Captain Twysden saw his game no more. Captain Newman, as we shall presently see, was more fortunate. The Mermaid, on her enemy disappearing, hauled to the wind, on the larboard tack (the wind north by east), and was soon rejoined by the Kangaroo.

On the following morning, the 16th, at daylight, the French frigate was again seen and pursued by the Mermaid and Kangaroo. At 3 P.M. the Kangaroo, whose force was sixteen 32-pounder carronades and two long sixes, came up with and engaged the Loire, for such she was, in a most gallant manner; until, indeed, the brig had her fore topmast shot away, and foremast wounded, by the frigate's stern-chasers. The Kangaroo was then compelled to drop astern.

The Mermaid continued the pursuit, and kept the enemy in view during the night. At daybreak on the 17th the Loire, observing the Mermaid to be alone, evinced, by shortened sail, an inclination to engage; nor was the latter disposed to balk Captain Segond's wishes. Accordingly, at about 6 h. 45 m. A.M., both ships steering north-east, which was nearly before the wind, the action commenced, and soon became very animated on both sides. An early attempt, on the part of the Loire, to board the Mermaid, was frustrated by Lieutenant Michael Halliday's judicious management of the latter's helm. Shortly afterwards the Mermaid, who had stationed herself on the Loire's starboard bow, taking advantage of a sudden shift of wind from west-south-west to south-south-west, was enabled to gall the latter considerably, without receiving much damage.

In a little while, from repeatedly bearing away and luffing up, the Mermaid closed with her opponent to within pistol-shot;

when, the fall of the Loire's fore topmast and cross-jack yard gave proofs of the Mermaid's deliberate and well-directed fire. The fire from the great guns of the Loire had now evidently slackened, but that from her musketry, conspicuous at every part of the ship, was unremittingly kept up. At 9 h. 15 m. A.M. the Loire's maintopsail yard came down, and Captain Newman gave instant orders to run athwart her hawse and rake her. Just as she was about to execute this manœuvre, the Mermaid lost her mizenmast by the board, its wreck totally disabling the cabin and quarterdeck guns. Scarcely was the wreck of the mizenmast cleared, and the stern blown out, in order, now that the ship was unavoidably fallen off, to fire the stern-chasers, when the main topmast came down. By this time the Mermaid's stays, back-stays, shrouds, tacks, sheets, halyards, sails, spars, and boats were all cut to pieces or shot away; and, from the number of dangerous shot received in the hull, the ship made a deal of water. The main yard hung only by a part of the chain with which it was slung, the mainmast had received nine shots in its head, and both that and the foremast appeared likely every instant to fall. Two of the guns, likewise, were completely disabled. In this crippled condition, the Mermaid could do no otherwise than discontinue the action. The Loire, apparently not much less disabled than the Mermaid, nor seemingly more inclined to renew the engagement, put before the wind, and was soon out of sight.

Although her established complement was 212, the Mermaid had on board, when this long and spirited action commenced, only 208 men and boys. Of these she lost, exclusive of the carpenter, who, while busy in stopping a shot-hole outside, was swept away by the wreck of the main topmast and drowned, three killed, and thirteen wounded, three of the latter dangerously. The loss sustained by the Loire, out of a complement, including soldiers, of 624 men, is of course left to conjecture; but, from the excellent position maintained so long by the Mermaid, the crowded state of the Loire's decks, and her finally abandoning the field to an adversary of little more than half her size and strength (the Mermaid's guns were 32 twelves and sixes and eight 24-pounder carronades, the Loire's the same as No. 5 in the table at p. 54 of vol. i., with two additional 36-pounder carronades), the amount of both killed and wounded must have been considerable. Indeed it was represented that, towards the close of the action, the Loire's people were seen from the Mermaid to throw the killed overboard in great numbers.

Those who are of opinion that, in a statement of comparative force, the French troops ought to be included, can add them, their number having already been stated; but, when the equivocal aid to be derived from their musketry (see what slight effect it produced on the Mermaid's crew), is contrasted with the certain disadvantage accruing from the room which they and their baggage occupy, it is considered the fairer mode to confine the estimate to that number of men, the regular complement, which was originally fixed for and put on board the ship, as well to manage her sails, as to fight her guns, great and small. It is a fact, too, worth noticing, that the increased slaughter, which invariably attends increased numbers stowed in a small compass, has often a very discouraging effect upon the survivors of the crew. The panic may linger a while among the landmen and passengers, but its proverbially infectious nature will soon set it spreading. Where ships get foul, and boarding attempts are made, then it is that increased numbers carry their weight; and a case of that sort may merit to be an exception. With this remark, we present the following as the

COMPARATIVE FORCE OF THE COMBATANTS.

		MERMAID.	LOIRE.
Broadside-guns	No.	20	23
	lbs.	252	442
Crew	No.	208	330
Size	tons	693	1100

This would, indeed, have been a victory for the little Mermaid; but her inferiority of force, not a want of courage in her crew (of that they had given proofs in a previous contest with the French frigate of the Loire's class*), forbad such a consummation. It was not merely for her gallantry in attacking such an antagonist as the Loire, that the Mermaid deserved credit, but for the skilfulness of her crew in pointing their guns. For, although the French work to which we are referring, contains no enumeration of the French frigate's loss of men, the following account of her damages will show to what a state the shot of the Mermaid, described, in part palliation, as "une frégate de sa force," had reduced the Loire.

"Ce beau combat était le quatrième que la Loire avait eu à soutenir depuis cinq jours, et quoiqu'elle fût sortie avec gloire de toutes ces affaires, elle était réduite à l'état le plus déplorable. Elle ne possédait plus que ses deux basses voiles en lambeaux, et il était impossible d'en établir d'autres. Il n'y avait plus à bord ni bois, ni cordages, pour essayer d'installer des mâts supérieurs; les bas mâts eux-mêmes, criblés de boulets, menaçient de tomber. Tout ce que le capitaine put faire pour réparer sa frégate, fut de boucher le mieux possible les trous des boulets reçus à la flottaison, de jumeller ses bas mâts, et de bosser les ralingues des basses voiles, qui étaient coupées en plusieurs endroits. Dans cette triste situation, c'eût été un miracle que la Loire pût atteindre un port de France."†

We were at first a little puzzled to make out the four combats, which the Loire had so "gloriously" sustained. They were,

* See vol. i., p. 340.

† Victoires et Conquêtes, tome x., p. 420.

however, as follows: that fought in line with the Hoche, that between the Loire and four other frigates with the disabled Anson, that between the Loire and Kangaroo (we suppose this must be meant), and that with the Mermaid alone. That the heavy fire, which the Loire opened upon the latter, did not sink her appears, by the following remark, to have surprised the French themselves. "L'avantage n'était pas pour les canonniers de la Loire, qui, faute d'adresse, ou, ce qui est plus croyable, par trop de précipitation, n'ajustaient pas aussi bien leurs coups que les Anglais."* Yet, why the Loire, with her decided superiority of force and the subsequent fall of her opponent's mizenmast, did not push the contest to an issue, is nowhere explained; not even in an account which, by its minuteness in other respects, as clearly proves that it was drawn up on board the Loire, as that, from among the troops in his ship, or from somewhere else, "l'excellent manœuvrier le capitaine Segond" had provided himself with a still more excellent trumpeter.

Scarcely had the Mermaid's crew time to knot the remaining shrouds, and get their ship a little into order, before there came on a violent gale of wind. The men had just furled the fore topsail, when the remains of the mainsail blew away; and, in the act of hauling up the foresail, the foremast, fore topmast, fore yard, and foretopsail yard, all fell in-board on the forecastle. Constant fatigue was now endured by the crew, in refitting, pumping, and clearing the wreck; and the ship, under a bare pole, the mainmast, scudded before the wind in a dreadful sea, rendered ten times more alarming by the open state of the cabin, from the cause already explained. At length, on the 19th, the Mermaid was fortunate enough to get into Lough-Swilly. Fortunate, indeed, it was, as the bread had all been destroyed by a shot-hole leak in the bread-room, and the ship, having been eight weeks at sea, had only 12 tuns of water left.

The Loire had only escaped from one antagonist to fall into the hands of another. At daylight on the 18th, the very day succeeding that on which she had been so roughly handled by the Mermaid, the Loire unexpectedly found herself to leeward of a ship of more than double the size of her former antagonist. The Loire, at this time, lay without her fore and main topmasts; the one having been shot away by the Mermaid, and the other, as Captain Newman had conceived would be the case, having fallen over the top in the course of the ensuing night. The ship to windward, which was the 44-gun frigate Anson, Captain Philip Charles Durham, had lost her mizenmast, main yard, and main cross-trees; and, in her previous action, with the Loire and her four companions, had had her bowsprit and fore yard shot

* Victoires et Conquêtes, tome x., p. 418

through in several places. The Anson had also received considerable injury in her fore and main masts. Thus were the two ships about equally balanced in point of disabilities: if there was a difference in this respect, it was in favour of the Anson; but there was a third party present, who, although apparently very insignificant, was not to be overlooked or despised. On the preceding night the Anson had fallen in with the Kangaroo, and Captain Durham, thinking the latter's services might be useful in the Anson's disabled state, ordered Captain Brace to keep company. The Kangaroo, since her disaster of the morning of the 16th, had, with creditable alacrity, refitted herself with a new fore topmast; and at 8 h. 30 m. A.M. on this day, which was as soon as the strange sail was discovered by her, then far to windward of the Anson, got up her topgallantmasts, and made sail in chase.

The Anson, from her leeward position, in reference to the Kangaroo, was of course first up with the Loire; and at about 10 h. 30 m. A.M. the cannonading commenced between the two ships. At 11 h. 45 m. A.M. while the Loire and Anson lay mutually disabled, the latter with her head in a line with the former's stern, the Kangaroo bore down, and received a shot from the Loire, accompanied by several volleys of musketry. To this the brig immediately replied by a broadside. Shortly afterwards the Loire's mizenmast came down, and with it her colours. These the French ship, having six feet water in the hold, and being reduced to an utterly defenceless state by the Mermaid and Anson's shot, did not attempt to rehoist. As soon, therefore, as she was hailed for that purpose, the Loire surrendered, and was taken possession of by a boat from the Kangaroo.

Out of her complement of 327 men and boys, the Anson had one quartermaster and one seaman killed, her first lieutenant of marines (William Abell), two midshipmen (William Robilliard and Francis R. Payler), eight seamen, and two marines wounded; total, two killed and 13 wounded. The Kangaroo, whose complement was 120 men and boys, escaped without any loss. The Loire's loss, according to the French account, amount to 46 men killed and 71 wounded. Her total number of sailors and soldiers, at the commencement of the action, is stated in Captain Durham's letter at 664; but her officers, when examined in the prize-court, deposed to 624. A great part of the difference is probably to be accounted for by the Loire's loss in her two previous actions. If so, as only five men are admitted to have been killed on board the Loire in her first action, a great many more must have been killed in her action with the Mermaid.

The Anson and Loire, in point of relative force, had they each met in a perfect state, would have been similarly matched to the

Indefatigable and Virginie.* Whatever chance of success, therefore, the Loire may have had with the Mermaid, she had very little with the Anson, and none whatever with the Anson and Kangaroo united. The undoubted bravery, which Captain Segond, his officers, and crew displayed in this contest affords a tolerable proof, that the Loire would not have quitted her former antagonist, had not her injuries by the Mermaid's shot been of the most serious kind.

The Loire had on board a brass field-piece, with the necessary apparatus and stores, clothing complete for 3000 men, 1020 muskets, 200 sabres, 350 pouches, and 25 cases of musket-ball cartridges, evidently to serve for equipping the recruits expected among the Irish malecontents. Leaving the prize in tow of the Kangaroo, and attended by the Anson, we shall proceed to show which was the next of Commodore Bompart's frigates, that was successfully intercepted on her return to a French port.

On the 20th of October, at 8 A.M., in latitude 48° 23' north, and longitude 7° west, the British 38-gun frigate Fisgard, Captain Thomas Byam Martin, while standing on the larboard tack with the wind at west-south-west, saw a strange sail due west, on the opposite tack, steering free. At 8 h. 45 m. A.M. the Fisgard tacked in chase, and gained on the stranger; who was no other than the Immortalité, pursuing her course to Brest, and which port, but for this to her unlucky encounter, she would very soon have reached. At 11 A.M. the Immortalité hoisted French colours, and commenced firing her stern-chasers. At 11 h. 30 m. A.M. the Fisgard hoisted English colours, and opened a fire in return with her bow-guns, still, with a fine moderate breeze on the quarter, coming up with the object of her pursuit.

At half-past noon the Fisgard got close alongside her opponent, and a spirited action commenced. So effectual, however, was the Immortalité's fire, that, in 25 minutes, the Fisgard was rendered quite ungovernable, having her bowlines, braces, topsail-ties, back-stays, and the whole of her running rigging, cut to pieces. The Fisgard, in consequence, dropped astern; and the Immortalité, profiting by the occasion, crowded sail to escape. At 1 h. 30 m. P.M., by the active exertions of her crew, the Fisgard was again alongside her opponent; and a cannonade now commenced, more furious than the first. At the end of half an hour the Fisgard had received some shots so low in the hull, as to have six feet water in the hold. Still her resolute crew persevered; and at 3 P.M., after nearly an hour and a half's close engagement, the Immortalité, then nearly in a sinking state from the Fisgard's shot, and having her mizenmast gone close to the deck, and her fore and main masts, and all her other spars, as well as rigging and sails, much cut; and having,

* See vol. i., p. 325.

besides, lost her captain and first lieutenant, hauled down her colours.

The Fisgard had her masts, rigging, and sails a good deal injured, and was struck so low in the hull by some of the Immortalité's 24-pound shot, as to oblige her to keep one pump constantly going. Her loss out of a crew of 281 men and boys, and who, the more to their credit, were quite a young ship's company, amounted to 10 seamen killed, one lieutenant of marines (Mark A. Gerrard), 23 seamen and two marines wounded. The Immortalité, out of a crew, including soldier-passengers, of 580 (in which number both Captain Martin and the French officers agree), lost, including her brave commander and first lieutenant, also a general of the army (Monge), and seven other naval and military officers, 54 officers, seamen, and soldiers killed, and 61 wounded.

The Fisgard mounted 46 guns, the same as those of the Révolutionnaire, described at vol. i., p. 322. The Immortalité, as a French frigate, was of a class by herself. It is probable that she was intended, while building, to carry 26 long 18-pounders; but the Immortalité was afterwards constructed with one port less of a side, and fitted with 24 long French 24-pounders, making, with 14 long 8-pounders and four brass 36-pounder carronades on her quarterdeck and forecastle, a total of 42 guns. In comparing the force of these ships, we shall, for the reason given at a former page, not reckon the troops that were on board the French frigate.

COMPARATIVE FORCE OF THE COMBATANTS.

		FISGARD.	IMMORTALITE.
Broadside-guns	No.	23	21
	lbs.	425	450
Crew	No.	284	330
Size	tons.	1182	1010

Here we come again, after a long interval, to a well-matched pair of combatants; an action ably contested on both sides, doing credit to the vanquished as well as to the victor. No obtrusive vessel became a spectator of, much less a participator in, the long and arduous struggle. Considering the numerous cruisers, British in particular, that are usually roaming about the chops of the Channel, a fair single combat, from first to last, is rare, and therefore deserves to be prized.

This is the proper place to notice a paragraph that appeared in the Moniteur of the 27th of November, 1798: "Lorsque le capitaine Legrand a abandonné la frégate anglaise, après l'avoir mise hors d'état de le poursuivre, il était chassé par trois vaisseaux, tous à sa vue." There is always a ready way of confuting assertions like these. Had any British ship of war, much less "three ships of the line," hove in sight during the chase or at the capture of the Immortalité, she would have been entitled to a share of the prize-money; whereas it stands recorded, that no other ship than the Fisgard received, or claimed to receive, a doit of it. Moreover, as placing the matter beyond all doubt, the French officers, in the customary certificate to enable the captors to get their head-money, made not the slightest allusion to any other ship than the Fisgard.

The whole of the seven prizes, after the most shattered of them had put into port by the way, reached Plymouth. The Hoche was newly named the Donegal, after the bay near to which she had been captured. She was a fine ship of 1901 tons, and long proved a serviceable cruiser. The Embuscade was also a fine little frigate of 916 tons, and under the name of Seine (the Ambuscade being a name that, after the middle of December, excited in England no very pleasant recollections), was long attached to the 12-pounder 36-gun class. The Coquille, a similar frigate to the Embuscade, on the 14th of December, while lying at anchor in Hamoaze, and just after she had been surveyed preparatory to her purchase by the government, caught fire and blew up: by which accident, three midshipmen, seven seamen, and three women unfortunately perished. The Bellone and Résolue were frigates of a small class than either of the preceding; the one measuring 888, and the other 877 tons: both were purchased into the navy, but, being old and worn out, never afterwards went to sea. The Loire, on the other hand, was a fine new frigate, and had recently been presented to the French government by the city of Nantes. The Immortalité was also a fine frigate, but less than the Loire, by about 90 tons; and therefore very far from being, as a contemporary represents her, "one of the largest frigates that had fallen into our hands."* Not being considered capable of carrying to advantage a battery of 24-pounders (of which heavy guns, however, that same writer had assigned her "twenty-eight," instead of twenty-four), the Immortalité was fitted with twenty-six 18-pounders; and that was giving her one gun more of a side than she could fairly use upon her broadside.

We must not forget to mention, that the thanks of both houses of parliament were subsequently voted to commodore Sir John Borlase Warren, and the captains, officers, and men under his command, for the successful issue of the action, or actions rather, with the Hoche and her squadron; not, certainly for any extraordinary exertions that were either required or made use of, in achieving the victory, but because of the evil consequences which it in all probability averted from the sister-kingdom. Lieutenants William James Turquand, first of the Canada, and, after a while, David Colby, first of the Robust, were made commanders; as was also, for her capture of the Immortalité, the Fisgard's first lieutenant, John Surman Carden.

The dashing manner, in which the Robust went into action

* Brenton, vol. ii., p. 367.

was precisely what might have been expected from the captain of the Latona, in November, 1793; and we should have been better pleased with Sir John Warren's letter, imperfect as it is in many respects, had it contained a more particular notice of the (considering the *hors-de-combat* distance of the Canada and Foudroyant, some have thought *all*) important services of Captain Thornborough.

Very great credit was also due to Captain Countess, for his zeal and perseverance in keeping sight of the French squadron; which, had it not been so well watched by the Ethalion and her consorts, would have been on the coast of Ireland nearly a fortnight earlier than it was. In that case M. Bompart would probably have disembarked his troops without molestation, and might, with his squadron have got safe back to a French port. In his official account of the capture of the Bellone, Captain Countess speaks in the highest terms of the first lieutenant of the Ethalion, Mr. George Sayer; and the latter, upon whom the greater part of the active duty of keeping sight of the French squadron must necessarily have devolved, was, in consequence, made a commander.

We must be permitted to make one more remark before we quit this action. The noble behaviour of the French prisoners on board the Hoche and Coquille (for she, also, was mainly preserved by their exertions) ought to have obtained for them, after they were landed in England, some abatement of the hardships usually imposed upon prisoners of war. This would be holding out encouragement to men so circumstanced; particularly in cases where their numbers, as in the instances of both the 74 and the frigate, might otherwise be too formidable to be coerced into subjection. Upon national considerations, even this ought never to be overlooked.

It still remains to be shown, what became of the three uncaptured vessels of Commodore Bompart's squadron. The Romaine having anchored, under English colours, six or seven miles from the spot at which the Immortalité and Résolue had brought up, made preparations for disembarking her troops. A communication with the shore, however, soon cooled the zeal of the latter; and the soldiers were not so tired of the sea, or so alarmed at the perils both of weather and capture to be encountered in crossing it, but that they preferred even that risk to the certain fate that awaited them if they attempted to land. The Romaine, accordingly, weighed and stood off from the Irish coast, and, overtaking the Biche on the passage, anchored on the 23d of October in the road of Brest. About the same time, also, the Sémillante managed to get into Lorient.

The very day that sealed the fate of the Hoche, saw another expedition quit a port of France for the same destination. Commodore Savary, with the same four frigates with which he had made the former trip, namely, the Concorde, Médée, Franchise, and Vénus, having on board a small quantity of troops, sailed from Rochefort, in order to see what had become both of Commodore Bompart's squadron, which had now been out 26 days, and of General Humbart's army, which had been landed in Ireland since more than two months. On the 27th Commodore Savary had the good fortune to arrive in the neighbourhood of Killala bay, the scene of his former success. Here the commodore soon learnt the fate of both the French army and the French squadron; and, fearing it might be his turn next, put to sea again the same afternoon, and steered straight for France with the melancholy news.

On the 28th, at about 7 A.M., the weather nearly calm, these four French frigates were discovered in the south-east quarter, not far from the Stags of Broadhaven, by the British 80-gun ship Caesar, Captain James Saumarez, 74-gun ship Terrible, Captain Sir Richard Bickerton, Bart., and 38-gun frigate Melpomène, Captain Sir Charles Hamilton; and, as soon as the breeze would permit, were chased under all sail. At 3 P.M. the wind veered to the south-west. At 6 P.M. the four French frigates, then on a line in the larboard tack, were passed to windward by the Terrible, and between her and them several shots were exchanged, one of which struck the 74's mizenmast, and obliged her instantly to fish it. The Terrible then wore after the rearmost of the frigates, and bore away in pursuit to the north-north-west. Shortly afterwards the French frigates opened, in passing, a raking fire upon the Caesar, but at too great a distance to produce any effect; and, for that reason, the latter did not return it. At 11 P.M., just as she was fast coming up with the sternmost French frigate, the wind, having considerably freshened, carried away the Caesar's fore topmast and main topgallantmast; and this was not all, for the wreck demolished the foresail. At 11 h. 15 m. P.M., in consequence of this accident, the Terrible and Melpomène passed the Caesar in the chase.

On the 29th, at 1 A.M., the Caesar was entirely lost sight of by her two consorts; and at 8 A.M. the enemy's squadron was distant from these about two leagues in the north-west. At noon, owing chiefly, as it would appear, to the bad sailing of the Vénus, the Melpomène, who was at some distance ahead of the 74, got within two or three miles of the former. As the only means of averting the consequences likely to result from this retardation of the squadron, Commodore Savary made the signal for his frigates to separate. On this the Commodore hauled close to the wind (still at south-west) on the larboard tack, the Médée and Franchise kept, as before, about four points free on the same tack, and the Vénus put directly before it. The Melpomène immediately hauled up for the Concorde, and the Terrible pursued the two frigates in the north-west by west; upon whom the 74 gained so much, that at 4 P.M. she was only two miles astern of them. At 7 P.M. the Terrible and Melpomène lost sight of each other. On the 30th, at daybreak, the 74 found herself still only two miles distant from one of the frigates in the north-west, and soon afterwards passed several gun-carriages, also two horses, which had been thrown overboard by the French frigate. It is doubtful whether or not this would have saved her, if at 5 P.M. a violent and unexpected squall of wind from the south-east had not carried away the Terrible's fore and main topsailyards, and the topgallant ones also. There was now no alternative; and the Terrible, accordingly, left off chase and hauled her wind to the southward and westward. M. Savary was afterwards so fortunate as to reassemble all four of his frigates, and with them to re-enter Rochefort on the 22d day of his departure from it.

This was the last of four expeditions, which the French sent from their ports to assist the malecontents of Ireland. The first, or that of December, 1796, was scattered and discomfited by the weather. The second, under the same Commodore Savary whose fortunate escape we have just done detailing, succeeded, in August of the present year, in disembarking a body of men, but it was only for the survivors of them to yield up their arms in September. The third ended in the capture of the Hoche and her companions; and the fourth, rendered unavailable for the failure of the second and third, returned to port as it went.

During the last two months of the year, the Brest fleet remained as stationary as it had done during the first ten. In the attention we are about to bestow upon the fleet of Toulon, we may perhaps develop the principal cause for this forced inactivity of a fleet, which, with a proper application of its numbers and strength, might have done incalculable mischief to an enemy.

We must not, however, quit the Channel without mentioning, that, among the fruits of four years' hard fighting, was the assembling, in France, of 2800 English, and in England of upwards of 30,000 French prisoners. Since the month of January the two nations had agreed that each should maintain their own prisoners; that, for that purpose, an agent should reside in each country, and have the benefit of its market; and that the prisoners, instead of being scattered over the country, should be confined in three or four places of general rendezvous. Agreeably to this arrangement, the French prisoners were to be confined nowhere but at Portsmouth, Plymouth, Norman-Cross, Liverpool, Edinburgh, Chatham, and Stapleton. This was followed, towards the end of the year, by a second agreement, authorizing the reciprocal transmission of cartels, and settling the terms by which an exchange of prisoners was to be regulated.

In the course of the year the French directory issued a decree declaring that all persons, natives of, or originally belonging to, neutral countries, or countries in alliance with France, who might form a part of the crew of any of his Britannic majesty's ships of war, or of any British vessels, should be considered and treated as pirates. This savage order was met by a counter-declaration from the king of England, dated November 20, directing it to be signified to the commissary for French prisoners in Great Britain, that, if that decree should, in any substance, be carried into effect against any such persons, taken in any vessel or vessels the property of his majesty, or of his subjects, and navigated under the British flag, it was the king's determination to exercise the most rigorous retaliation against those subjects of the French republic, whom the chance of war had then placed, or might thereafter place, at his majesty's disposal. This had, in a great degree, the desired effect.

With the view of ascertaining the precise object of the rumoured preparations making at Toulon, the British admiralty had directed Earl St.-Vincent to detach from the Mediterranean fleet a few ships under Rear-admiral Sir Horatio Nelson; who, having been allowed, after the Santa-Cruz affair, to go to England for his health, had, on the 29th of April, returned to the fleet off Cadiz. On the 2d of May, Sir Horatio quitted the fleet in the Vanguard, and steered for the Mediterranean. The rear-admiral was to take with him two 74s lying at Gibraltar, and four frigates and a sloop cruising on that station. On the 4th the Vanguard arrived at Gibraltar; and on the 9th, having completed her water and provisions, sailed again, accompanied by the Alexander and Orion 74s, Emerald and Terpsichore frigates, and Bonne-Citoyenne sloop.

On the 17th, when off Cape Sicie, the rear-admiral received information, through a captured privateer, that there were, including the ex-Venetian ships, 19 sail of the line in Toulon harbour; that 15 of them were ready for sea; and that Buonaparte, at the head of an immense body of troops, was expected soon to embark, but for what destination could not be ascertained. On the 19th the wind blew strong from the north-west. On the next day, the 20th, it moderated, but, after dark, again blew strong; so strong, that on the 21st, at 1 h. 30 m. A.M., when about 25 leagues south of the Hyères islands, the Vanguard's main and mizen topmasts, in succession, went over the side. In two hours afterwards the increased violence of the gale carried away the foremast, in three pieces, and sprung the bowsprit in as many places. At daylight, by means of the remnant of her spritsail, the Vanguard was enabled to wear. The two other 74s and the Emerald wore also; and the four ships scudded before the wind. The Terpsichore, Bonne-Citoyenne, and a prize-ship, continued lying-to, under bare poles, and therefore parted company; as, during the night, did the Emerald.

The rear-admiral intended to steer for Oristan bay, island of

Sardinia: but, in the crippled state of the Vanguard, that was found impracticable. The latter, therefore, being taken in tow by the Alexander, who, with the Orion, had received very little damage in the gale, the rear-admiral proceeded to the Sardinian harbour of St.-Pietro; where, at noon on the 22d, the three ships safely cast anchor. Here we will leave them awhile, to attend to what is going on in Toulon.

During the negotiations at Campo-Formio, in the summer of 1797, General Buonaparte took away from the Ambrosian library at Milan, all the books he could find on subjects connected with the East; and, on their being brought to Paris, marginal notes were discovered in every page that treated specially on Egypt: hence it has been inferred, that Buonaparte was, even at this time, ruminating upon the plan, in the attempted execution of which his military fame subsequently received so serious a check, and his moral character so fatal a stab. At all events, in the early months of the year 1798, he submitted the plan of a campaign in Egypt to the directory, and on the 5th March, was appointed its commander-in-chief. "Les ministres de la guerre, de la marine, at des finances," proceeds the letter of appointment, "sont prévenus de se conformer aux instructions que vous leur transmettrez sur ce point important dont votre patriotisme a le secret, et dont le directoire ne pouvait pas mieux confier le succès qu'à votre génie et à votre amour pour la vraie gloire." This flattering letter was signed by "Lareveillère-Lépaux, Merlin, et Barras."*

In the mean time the most active preparations were making at Toulon, Marseille, Civita-Vecchia, Genoa, and Bastia; particularly at the first-named port, where an immense fleet of men-of-war and transports was getting ready, and whither troops were marching from all quarters of the republic. Buonaparte was to have quitted Paris on the night of the 21st of April; but the last despatches from General Bernadotte, the republican ambassador at the court of Vienna, having excited in the French government some dread of a rupture with Austria, the conqueror of Italy was detained, to try the effect of his influence with the Comte de Cobentzel, the emperor's ambassador at Paris. By this, or some other means, the matter was made up; and on the 3d of May Buonaparte quitted Paris, and on the 8th arrived at Toulon.

The expedition, now that it was complete, consisted of 13 sail of the line, eight frigates, two Venetian 64s and six frigates, armed en flûte, two brigs, with cutters, avisos, and gun-boats, in all 72 vessels of war; exclusive, when those from the outports joined, of 400 sail of transports. Of this immense fleet the crews alone were computed at 10,000 men; besides which there was a body of troops amounting to about 36,000 men. The commander-

* Victoires et Conquêtes, tome ix., p. 4.

in-chief of this formidable armament was Buonaparte, having under him, as his generals of division, Kléber, Desaix, Regnier, Bon, Duqua, Menou, Vaubois, Dumuy, and Dumas, besides 11 generals of brigade. The fleet was commanded by Vice-admiral Brueys, having under him Rear-admirals, Villeneuve, Blanquet, and Decrès, and, for his captain of fleet, Commodore Ganteaume. The admiral had his flag on board the 120-gun ship Orient, as the ci-devant Sans-Culotte was now, in reference to the object of the expedition appropriately named, and in her General Buonaparte embarked, accompanied by the principal part of his suite.

On the 19th of May, in the morning, the whole of this numerous fleet, except a portion of the transports, that were to join on the passage, got under way from Toulon road with a strong wind from the north-west, and running along the coast of Provence, stopped off Genoa, to be joined by the division of transports in that port; then stood straight across to Cape Corse, which was signalled on the 23d, at daybreak. The fleet remained in sight of the eastern coast of Corsica until the 30th and then stood leisurely along the island of Sardinia, in the expectation of being joined by the convoy from Civita-Vecchia; which convoy, it was known, had left that port on the 28th.

On the 3d of June, Buonaparte received intelligence, that three English ships of the line and two frigates had been seen off Cagliari. A division of French ships proceeded in that direction, but saw nothing and returned. Having waited in vain for the junction of the expected convoy from Civita-Vecchia, the fleet proceeded without it, and on the 7th passed within gun-shot of the port of Mazara in Sicily, having in view on the opposite side the small island of Pantellaria. On the 8th an English brig, captured by one of the look-out frigates, gave intelligence that Admiral Nelson's squadron, sent in pursuit of the French fleet, was not very far astern. This news, erroneous as it was, gave great uneasiness to the commander-in-chief.* On the same night the expedition quitted the coast of Sicily, and, steering to the south-east, gained, at 5 h. 30 m. A.M. on the 9th, a sight of the islands of Goza and Malta; off which the admiral was joined by the Civita-Vecchia division of transports numbering 70 sail.

The fate, which soon befel this, as a Mediterranean possession, important island, will be in some degree elucidated by a short account of the measures France had previously taken to undermine its independence. Since the month of January in the present year, M. Poussielgue, secretary to the French legation at Genoa, had been sent to sound the knights and grand-master of the order of St.-John of Jerusalem, as to their inclination to permit a French squadron to approach the shores of their island;

* Victoires et Conquêtes, tome ix., p. 10.

or, in other words, by all the insidious and corrupt arts so familiar to the agents of the French government at this epoch, to endeavour to excite an insurrection among the inhabitants. As a further step in the contemplated plan, Rear-admiral Brueys, when in March he was returning to Toulon with his six sail of the line from the Adriatic, sent one of his ships in the port to be repaired; where she remained eight days. The French squadron, meanwhile, sounded all round the island, and ascertained precisely every spot where it was possible to effect a debarkation.

Considering, therefore, the capture of the island of Malta, with its two dependencies, the small islands of Goza and Comino, as the work of treachery, we feel no inclination to give a recital of the few mock-fights that preceded its surrender; but shall merely state, that on the 10th a landing was effected in seven places, and that on the 12th the islands of Malta, Goza, and Comino, surrendered by capitulation. Among the spoils taken, were two 64-gun ships, one frigate, three galleys, and some vessels, 30,000 muskets, 12,000 barrels of powder, provisions for six months, and the plate and other treasure in the church of St.-John, valued at three millions of francs. Leaving Buonaparte and his army and fleet to rejoice over their good fortune, we will return to Rear-admiral Nelson and his three weather-beaten ships in the harbour of St.-Pietro.

By the indefatigable exertions of the officers and crews of the three British ships, or rather, as respects the men, of the Alexander and Orion only, for the Vanguard's was a very indifferent ship's company, the latter ship, in less than four days, got up a jury foremast and jury main and mizen topmasts, fished her bowsprit, and performed other necessary repairs; and on the next morning, the 27th, the squadron again put to sea. The three ships now steered for the rendezvous off Toulon, which they reached on the 31st. The rear-admiral, by this time, was fully acquainted with the sailing of the French armament, reported to consist of 15 sail of the line, 10 or 12 frigates, and 200 transports, with upwards of 40,000 troops on board, commanded by General Buonaparte; but nothing was known of its destination.

On the 5th of June the 16-gun brig-sloop Mutine, Captain Thomas Masterman Hardy, joined, with the highly gratifying intelligence that she had, on the 30th, parted from a squadron of 10 sail of the line and a 50-gun ship, that was on its way to join the rear-admiral. The brig also brought Sir Horatio full directions, when that junction was effected, to do what he so ardently desired to do – proceed in quest of the Toulon fleet. Immediately the three 74s and brig, spreading themselves, kept a sharp look-out; and, in so doing, fell in with the 15 sail of richly-laden Spanish merchantmen. The Alexander and Orion each captured one; but the rear-admiral, having his mind bent on nobler game, would not permit any more of the vessels to be molested. On the 7th, at noon, the two squadrons that were so desirous to join, gained a mast-head sight of each other, and by sunset were united.

About three weeks after Rear-admiral Nelson had been detached by Earl St.-Vincent, a reinforcement from England, consisting of eight sail of the line, under Rear-admiral Sir Roger Curtis, in the Prince-of-Wales 98, joined the fleet off Cadiz; and on the same evening (May 24) the in-shore squadron of nine sail of the line, commanded by that active officer, Captain Troubridge, having been relieved by an equal number of ships, sailed, in compliance with orders from home, to strengthen the force under Rear-admiral Nelson. The exchange between the two squadrons had been so admirably conducted, that the Spaniards, the next morning, were not aware that it had taken place; nor, of course, that the British admiral off the port had either detached, or been joined by, any ships.

Since his departure from Earl St.-Vincent's fleet, Captain Troubridge had been joined by the Audacious 74 and Leander 50; making the force under Rear-admiral Nelson, now consisting of the

Gun-ship		
74	Vanguard	Rear-admiral (b.) Sir Horatio Nelson, K.B., Captain Edward Berry,
	Orion	Captain Sir James Saumarez,
	Culloden	Captain Thomas Troubridge,
	Bellerophon	Captain Henry d'Esterre Darby,
	Minotaur	Captain Thomas Louis,
	Defence	Captain John Peyton,
	Alexander	Captain Alexander John Ball,
	Zealous	Captain Samuel Hood,
	Audacious	Captain Davidge Gould,
	Goliath	Captain Thomas Foley,
	Majestic	Captain George Blagden Westcott,
	Swiftsure	Captain Benjamin Hallowell,
	Theseus	Captain Ralph Willett Miller,
50	Leander	Captain Thomas Boulden Thompson,

amount to thirteen 74-gun ships, and one 50, with, instead of four or five frigates, one brig-sloop only; and yet the service intrusted to the rear-admiral, as we shall presently see, was one, the very success of which might depend on the facility of reconnoitring, and gaining intelligence of, the enemy's movements.

Nelson's instructions from his commander-in-chief were dated on the 21st of May. In these he was ordered "to proceed in quest of the armament preparing by the enemy at Toulon and Genoa; the object whereof appears to be either an attack upon Naples or Sicily, the conveyance of an army to some part of the coast of Spain for the purpose of marching towards Portugal, or to pass through the Straits, with a view of proceeding to Ireland." In some additional instructions of the same date, the rear-admiral is told, that he may pursue the French squadron to "any part of the Mediterranean, Adriatic, Morea, Archipelago, or even into the Black Sea."

It is clear, from the tenour of these instructions, that the British government were quite in the dark as to the real, or, at all events, the primary destination of the Toulon fleet. But, that their surmise that the fleet would pass the Straits was not wholly without foundation, will appear from the following extract of a letter addressed, under date of the 18th of April, 1798, by Buonaparte to the French directory: "Il serait possible, après l'expédition que le gouvernement projette dans la Méditerranée, de faire passer les quatorze vaisseaux* à Brest."† At all events, Rear-admiral Nelson was left entirely to his own discretion, as to the course to be steered in pursuit of the fleet, which he had been ordered by his instructions to use his utmost endeavour to "take, sink, burn, or destroy." The circumstance of the French having quitted port with a north-west wind rendered it likely, in his opinion, that their course was up the Mediterranean. Accordingly the British fleet, as soon as a provoking calm would allow it to make sail, steered towards the island of Corsica. On the 12th the fleet arrived off Cape Corse, and in the evening lay to off the isle of Elba; whence the Mutine was despatched for intelligence to Civita-Vecchia. It was the rear-admiral's intention, we are told, in case he overtook the French fleet, to make three divisions of his own, thus:

Vanguard,	Zealous,	Culloden,
Minotaur,	Orion,	Theseus,
Leander,	Goliath,	Alexander,
Audacious,	Majestic,	Swiftsure.
Defence,	Bellerophon,	

Two of these divisions, according to the plan laid down, were to attack the ships of war; and the third, to pursue and run down, or otherwise destroy, the transports. A contest between nine small 74s and a 50, on one side, and one three-decker and twelve 80s and 74s, four or five of them the largest two-decked ships in the world, on the other, however much desired by, could scarcely have ended to the advantage of, the admiral in command of the former.

Pursuing their course along the shore of Tuscany, the British passed the small island of Gianuti, with a fine breeze at north-north-west. Here the Leander spoke a Moorish vessel, that gave information (which, by the by, was incorrect) that the French fleet was at Syracuse, in Sicily. About this time the Mutine joined, without having gained any intelligence. On the morning

* It was calculated, we believe, that the late British ship Berwick might be got ready.

† Victoires et Conquêtes, tome ix., p. 75.

of the 17th the British stood in the bay of Naples; and Captain Troubridge was sent, with Captain Hardy in the Mutine, to obtain what information could be collected from the British ambassador. All Sir William Hamilton could tell was, that the French had not entered that port, but had coasted the island of Sardinia and proceeded to the southward, probably to Malta.

With this guide for a course, the British fleet set sail; but light airs, during the two succeeding days, retarded its progress, making it the morning of the 20th ere the celebrated Straits of Messina were entered. From the British consul at the latter port intelligence was received, that the French had possessed themselves of Malta and Goza, and that their fleet was lying at anchor off the last-named island. A fresh breeze at north-west and a rapid current soon carried the British clear of the Straits, and the island of Malta was now their destination. At daybreak on the 22d, however, when the fleet was about 12 leagues south-east of Cape Passero, in Sicily, the Mutine learnt from a Genoese, or rather, we believe, a Ragusian brig, which had the day before passed through the fleet unmolested, that the French had quitted Malta on the 18th, with the same wind that was then blowing. Alexandria now seemed the next probable destination of the enemy; and immediately the British fleet bore up and steered south-east, under all sail.

From the 22d to the 28th three vessels only were spoken, one from the Archipelago, and two from Alexandria; but no French fleet had they heard of, much less seen. Days like these would have been insufferably tedious, had not the seamen, by the excellent regulations adopted in the fleet, a daily employment that, while it heightened their spirits, augmented their powers. The exercise of great guns and small arms, if properly persevered in, excites among the crew an emulation, that makes them doubly anxious to give practical proofs of their skill: they look forward to the day of battle, as the knights of old did to the day of tournament; and, when it comes, their well-grounded confidence displays itself in the shattered sides and deserted decks of their opponents.

On the 18th the British came in sight of the city of Alexandria; and the empty state of the two harbours, except as to a Turkish ship of the line, four frigates and some merchant vessels, confirmed the account they had last received. On arriving off the Pharos, or castle that guards the entrance of the eastern harbour, the Mutine was sent in for intelligence. After some delay, Captain Hardy was allowed to land, and was conducted, under a guard, to the governor. The latter expressed his surprise, as well as uneasiness, at the appearance of so formidable a British force; and, on the object's being explained to him, was yet more alarmed, declaring his determination to resist the attempt of either power to land.

The British were now somewhat at a stand. At length a retrograde movement was resulted on, taking a more northerly course. On the 29th the fleet steered to the north-east, with a fresh breeze from north-north-west. In consequence of the continuance of north-westerly weather, it took the ships, under all the sail they could carry on a wind, until the 4th of July, ere they made the coast of Natolia. On the 5th the ships got scattered; and, on the night of the 6th, the Orion parted company. This occasioned the fleet, on the following morning, to wear and stand to the northward; a delay that was repaid by the junction, towards evening, of the missing ship. The fleet continued beating to windward till the 16th, when the weather turned favourable; and at 8 A.M. on the 18th, Cape Passero made its appearance. On the 19th the fleet, being much in want of water and provisions, stood towards Syracuse. The entrance to the harbour is intricate, and no person in the fleet had hitherto passed through it. Such, however, was the skill and attention of the officers, and the adroitness and discipline of the men, that at 30 h. 3 m. P.M. every ship had anchored in safety. Here we will leave the indefatigable British admiral and the congenial spirits around him, while we see what is become of the object of his and their solicitude.

After a stay of four days, Buonaparte, on the morning of the 19th of June, quitted Malta, having left General Vaubois as the governor, and 4000 troops as the garrison, of the island. Favoured by a fresh breeze at north-west, the expedition steered a direct course to the east, the advanced frigates detaining and destroying every vessel they fell in with, as the most effectual, if not the most legal, means of preventing the circulation of intelligence respecting the probable destination of the fleet. On the 30th the French came in view of Cape Durazzo in the island of Candia, and, crossing the gulf of that name, descried at daybreak on the 1st of July the Arab tower upon the African coast, and, in a few hours afterwards, the minarets of Alexandria.

A small vessel was immediately sent into the port to gain intelligence, and, in particular, to bring off the French consul, Citizen Magallon. On reaching the flag-ship, the latter acquainted the commander-in-chief with Nelson's appearance off the coast three days before, the hostile disposition of the inhabitants, and the necessity he would be under, if he persisted in making himself master of the city, of employing force. That was General Buonaparte's intention; and the dread that Nelson might arrive, before the disembarkation could be affected, caused the utmost expedition to be used in getting the troops on shore. In her haste to get near to the creek of Mirabou, opposite to the castle of which name situated at the distance of about two leagues from the city the fleet cast anchor, the Orient ran foul of the Dubois and one of the frigates, and carried away her bowsprit: both the latter ships also sustained some damage. The wind now got up, and the sea along with it, and the coast was lined with reefs; but the English were hourly expected, and Buonaparte knew full well how his plans would be foiled if the fleets met before his army was landed. On the 1st of July a portion of the troops disembarked, and Buonaparte had just stepped into the boat that was to land him, when the look-out ships signalled an enemy's sail to the westward. The uneasiness which the sight of this vessel caused in the breast of the commander-in-chief elicited from him the following exclamation: "Fortune! wilt thou abandon me? What! only five days!"* A minute or two more and Buonaparte's placidity was restored, for the vessel approaching announced herself as the French frigate Justice, from the island of Malta.

On the 2d, after an action in which the French had about 40 officers and men killed, and perhaps thrice the number, including General Kléber, wounded, Buonaparte gained possession of Alexandria. In the course of that and the succeeding day all the troops were disembarked. General Kléber, being disabled from immediate service by his wound, was appointed governor of the city, and Commodore Dumanoir-le-Pelley captain of the port. The port consists of two harbours, the old and the new; one to the south-west, the other to the north-east, with the city on a strip of land between them. Another strip of land, called the isle of Pharos, at nearly right angles from that on which the city stands, forms the north-west, as the main land of Egypt does the south-east, side of both harbours.

The channel leading to the old harbour, the only one at this time supposed capable of receiving the ships, being found shoal, narrow, and intricate, Buonaparte, on the 3d of July, ordered Vice-admiral Brueys to anchor the men-of-war in the road or bay of Aboukir, about 20 miles to the east-north-east of Alexandria. But, if the admiral found his position not a defensive one against an enemy's fleet, he was to direct his course for Corfu; leaving behind him the Causse and Dubois, with the guns for arming them complete, the frigates Diane, Junon, Alceste, and Artémise, the whole of the light flotilla, of which Commodore Perrée had been appointed the commander, and all the frigates armed en flûte, with their guns and stores. Admiral Brueys, accordingly, with his ships of the line and full-armed frigates, proceeded to the bay of Aboukir, and there cast anchor. In the mean time an active and intelligent French officer, Captain Jean-Baptiste Barré, was ordered to survey the old harbour of Alexandria, and report upon its capacity and facility of entrance. On the 15th Captain Barré made a report, in which he showed that, out of the three channels, there was one which, when a rock or two were blown up, would have

* "Fortune, m'abandonnerais-tu? Quoi! Seulement cinq jours!" – *Victoires et Conquêtes*, tome ix., p. 26.

25 feet (French) water; but Admiral Brueys, considering the risk too great to attempt entering the port with his line-of-battle ships, the smallest of which drew 22 feet, preferred remaining at Aboukir; where we will leave him awhile in the enjoyment of his apparent security, and revert to the proceedings of one who soon put that security to the test.

Notwithstanding the inconvenient situations of the watering-places in the port of Syracuse, the indefatigable exertions of the officers and men of the British fleet procured, by the fifth day, an ample supply; to which was added, owing solely to the influence of Lady Hamilton, the British ambassador's wife, with the court of "neutral" Naples, a sufficient quantity of fresh beef and vegetables. Thus victualled and refreshed, the ships of the fleet, on the 24th and 25th, again put to sea. All the accounts, received while at Syracuse, agreed in representing that the French fleet had not been seen, either in the Archipelago or the Adriatic, and yet that it had not gone down the Mediterranean: hence no other conclusion remained, than that it still lay to the eastward, and that Egypt, after all, was, or had been, its destination. To be certain it was so, the rear-admiral bent his course for the Morea; and on the 28th, being off Cape Gallo, despatched the Culloden to Coron. The Turkish governor behaved very graciously to Captain Troubridge, permitting him to take out as a prize a French wine-vessel at anchor in the port; and he dismissed him with a yet more valuable present, in the communication, that the French fleet had been seen about four weeks since on the coast of Candia, steering south-east. South-east, then, was steered by the British; and a fresh breeze astern, with a heavy following sea, drove them rapidly towards the goal of their hopes.

On the 1st of August, at 10 A.M., the towers or minarets of Alexandria, the Pharos, and Pompey's pillar, made their welcome appearance; and soon the two ports, which, when last seen, had been unopened and solitary, displayed to the view a wood of masts: as an unerring sign, too, of who were now the occupants of the city, the French flag waved upon its walls. The two British look-out ships, the Alexander and Swiftsure, as they drew nearer, caused a general disappointment to their friends in the offing, by the signal that their duty obliged them to make, that the enemy's fleet did not form part of the vessels at anchor; that there appeared to be but eight ships of war, of various sizes (the Causse, Dubois, and six ex-Venetian frigates), and that the remainder were transports and merchantmen. The disappointment to the fleet was, however, of short duration; as the Zealous, a little before 1 P.M., just as the Pharos tower bore from her south-south-west, distant four or five leagues, signalled, that 17 ships of war, 13 or 14 of them formed in line of battle, lay at anchor in a bay upon her larboard bow. Instantly the British fleet hauled up, steering to the eastward under topgallantsails, with a fine breeze from north by west to north-north-west.

Let us pause here, while we endeavour to explain how it happened that, in a sea so comparatively small as the Mediterranean, two hostile fleets, one of which was so strenuously seeking the other, that other, too, from its immense numbers, spread over so wide a surface, did not come in mutual contact. On the 24th of May, when the reinforcement for Rear-admiral Nelson quitted Earl St.-Vincent off Cadiz, the French fleet was running down the eastern coast of Corsica; and on the 8th of June, when Rear-admiral Nelson made sail from off Toulon, with a fleet which had only been formed the night before, vice-admiral Brueys was standing across from Sicily to Malta. It has already been stated, that the French fleet (part of it the day before) quitted the last-named island on the morning of the 19th. Singularly enough, on the night of the 22d, the two fleets crossed each other's track unperceived. That this should have happened, in a case in which one of the fleets numbered, as that of the French did, nearly 400 sail, must appear strange; but the surprise will diminish, when it is known that the spot of intersection was about midway between Cape Mesurata and the mouth of the Adriatic, the widest part of the Mediterranean; that the British fleet sailed in close order, and had no frigates to spread as look-outs; and that a constant haze pervaded the atmosphere. Subsequently to the 22d the French steered east, to make the Goza di Candia; while the British stood south-east, or straight along the African coast. Hence the latter reached its port of destination just two days before the former; and the British fleet, as it quitted the shore on its departure, was actually seen from the Pharos tower on the morning of the same day, the 30th, towards the evening of which the French fleet made its appearance off the coast of Egypt.

We have already mentioned that the French fleet anchored in the bay of Aboukir. That fleet consisted of the

Gun-ship		
120	Orient	Vice-adm.——— Brueys. Rear-adm.* Honoré Ganteaume. Commodore ——— Casa-Bianca.
80	Franklin	Rear-adm. Armand-Sim.-Mar. Blanquet.† Captain Maurice Gillet.
	Guillaume-Tell ...	Rear-adm. P.-C.-J.-Bap.-Silv. Villeneuve. Captain ——— Saulnier.
	Tonnant	Commodore Arist.-Aub. du Petit-Thouars.

* As captain of the fleet, but M. Ganteaume was not appointed a rear-admiral until the 7th of November following.

† According to the official list, but called Blanquet-Duchayla in most of the French accounts.

Gun	Ship	
74	Aquilon	Commodore Henri-Alexandre Thévenard.
	Généreux	Captain ——— Le Joille.
	Conquérant	Captain Etienne Dalbarade.
	Heureux	Captain Jean-Pierre Etienne.
	Guerrier	Captain Jean-F.-Timothée Trullet, *sen.*
	Mercure	Captain ——— Cambon, *acting.**
	Peuple-Souverain	Captain Pierre-Paul Raccord.
	Spartiate	Captain Maurice-Julien Emeriau.
	Timoléon	Captain Jean-Fr.-Timothée Trullet, *jun.*

Gun	Frigate	
40	Diane	Rear-adm. Denis Decrès. Captain Eléonore-Jean-Nic. Soleil.
	Justice	Captain ——— Villeneuve.
36	Artémise	Captain Pierre-Jean Standelet.
	Sérieuse	Captain Claude-Jean Martin.

Brigs, Alerte and Railleur; *Bomb-vessels,* Hercule, Salamine, and another, and several gun-boats.

Previously to our entering into the details of the famous battle that ensued, it will be useful to give a slight description of the spot in which it was fought. The bay of Aboukir commences, as already mentioned, about 20 miles to the east-north-east of Alexandria, and extends from the castle of Aboukir, in a semicircular direction, to the westernmost or Rosetta mouth of the Nile, distant from the castle about six miles. Aboukir bay has no depth for line-of-battle ships nearer than three miles from the shore, a sand-bank, on which there is not any where more than four fathoms, running out to that distance. Owing also to the width of its opening, the bay affords very little shelter, except on its west-north-west side (that from which the wind on this coast commonly blows) by a small island, situated about two miles from the point whereon the castle stands, and connected with it by a chain of sand-banks and rocks, between which, however, there is a passage for small-craft. Aboukir island is surrounded by a continuation of the shoal that runs along the bottom of the bay; and which extends from the island about 1650 yards, or nearly a mile, in a north-east direction.

It appears that, on first taking up this anchorage, Vice-admiral Brueys held a council of flag-officers and captains to determine whether, in case of attack, the fleet should engage at anchor or under sail. All the officers, except Rear-admiral Blanquet, approved of the fleet's remaining at anchor: he maintained, that it was only when a fleet could be supported by strong forts crossing each other in their fire, that any advantage was gained by anchoring. However, finding the majority against him, M. Blanquet requested that the Franklin might be placed as one of the seconds to the commander-in-chief. His request was granted, and the ships were formed in line ahead in

* For Commodore Perrée, appointed to command the gun-boats on the Nile.

the following order: Guerrier, Conquérant, Spartiate, Aquilon, Peuple-Souverain, Franklin, Orient, Tonnant, Heureux, Mercure, Guillaume-Tell, Généreux, Timoléon; with, in an inner line, about 350 yards from the first, and about midway between that and the shoal, the Sérieuse frigate, nearly abreast of the opening between the Conquérant and Spartiate, the Artémise abreast of the Heureux, and the Diane, of the Guillaume-Tell.

The van-ship bore from Aboukir island south-east, distant about 2420 yards, or a mile and seven-eighths; which is rather more than double the extent of the shoal in the same direction. Between the Guerrier and her second astern, and between all the other line-of-battle ships successively, the distance was about 160 yards: so that, reckoning each of the 13 ships to occupy upon an average, a space of 70 yards, the length of the line was rather under a mile and five-eighths. But this line was not a straight one. From the centre ship, the Orient, the van-ship bore north-east, the rear-ship south-east by south, and the Guerrier and Timoléon, from each other, about north-west half-north and south-east half-south. Hence the line was a curve, or, rather, a very obtuse angle, having its projecting centre towards the sea. The edge of the shoal at the back of the line, on the contrary, was concave; so much so, that the Orient was nearly twice the distance from it that either the van or the rear ship was, particularly the latter. To protect his flanks, the French admiral, besides giving suitable stations to his bomb-vessels and gun-boats, erected a battery on Aboukir island, and mounted with two brass and two iron 12-pounders, a few pieces of a lighter caliber, and two 13-inch brass mortars.*

Having thus moored his fleet in, what he considered, a strong position, the French admiral awaited the issue of General Buonaparte's plans on shore. In the mean while vessels frequently arrived at Alexandria, with information that the British were on their return to the Egyptian coast; and, on the 21st of July the two British frigates Seahorse and Terpsichore brought to, for a few minutes, off the bay, as if they had been sent to reconnoitre. Besides hoisting French colours, Captain Foot made some of the private signals, obtained out of the French frigate Sensible, which the Seahorse had recently captured; and Captain Gage hoisted French colours over English, to make it appear that his frigate had been captured by the one in company. It is probable that this had the effect of masking the national character of the two British frigates, otherwise, doubtless, two or three of the fine French frigates (including the Junon) then at anchor would have slipped and given chase.

The short interval that had elapsed between the departure of one fleet and the arrival of the other had encouraged the belief, that the British were aware of the proximity of the French fleet,

* The French accounts say, only two 12s and two mortars; but the guns stated in the text were subsequently brought off by the British.

but, for the want of sufficient strength, or for some other reason, declined attacking it. So that, when the Heureux, at 2 P.M. on the 1st of August, made the signal for a fleet of 12 sail of the line (Alexander and Swiftsure not then seen), in the north-north-west, the French ships were still lying at single anchor, without springs on their cables, and with a great proportion of their crews on shore getting water. In an instant the men were recalled on board; and the frigates, by the direction of the commander-in-chief, sent some of their men to augment the crews of the ships of the line. At 3 P.M. the French admiral made the signal to prepare for battle, and detached the Alerte and Railleur brigs to endeavour to decoy the advanced British ships upon the shoal off Aboukir island.

As yet but 12 two-deckers and a brig had made their appearance, and one of the former, from her comparative smallness, might be a hospital or store ship. At 4 P.M., however, two large ships, coming up under a press of sail, hove in sight over Aboukir point near the castle; thus convincing the French, if they had doubted it before, that the British were at least equal to them in force. The course of the British fleet and the rapidity of its approach indicating an immediate attack, Admiral Brueys ordered his ships to cross topgallant yards, as if intending to get under way; but shortly afterwards, observing some of the advanced British ships bring to, he appears to have adopted an idea, that the British would defer the attack until the next morning, when the shoals might be more easily avoided: he thereupon signalled, that he should remain at anchor. This change of plan was afterwards attributed, by some of the French writers, to a belief on the part of Vice-admiral Brueys, that his ships were not sufficiently manned, to fight with advantage when under sail. But the admiral's expressed opinion of the impracticability of the attack on that night was notorious; and it was equally well understood, that he only waited for darkness, to weigh and put to sea, with the intention, in compliance with the orders he had received from Buonaparte, of endeavouring to effect his escape.

If Admiral Brueys, as we have no doubt was the case, did come to the conclusion, that the British would wait till morning before they attacked him, he was soon undeceived, and then ordered each ship to lay out an anchor in the south-south-east, and to send a stream-cable to the ship next astern of her, making a hawser fast to it, in such a manner as to spring her broadside towards the enemy.* This measure was rendered the more necessary by the state of the wind, which blew from north-north-west, instead of north-west, the direction of the line formed by the six van-ships. Let us now see what preparatory arrangements

* Victoires et Conquêtes, tome ix., p. 89.

had been made, and were making, by the fleet under Rear-admiral Nelson.

At about 2 h. 15 m. P.M. the Alexander and Swiftsure, having been recalled by signal, stood under all sail, towards the body of their fleet then distant about four leagues, urging its course to the eastward. It was while they were standing out from the land to effect their junction, that the former, as already mentioned, were descried by the French over Aboukir point. At 3 P.M. the signal was made to prepare for battle; and at 4 P.M., when the body of the French fleet bore south-east by south distant nine or ten miles, the British ships were ordered to prepare to anchor by the stern. Each ship, accordingly, made fast a stream-cable to her mizenmast, and, passing it out of one of her gunroom ports, carried it along her side just below the first-deck ports, to several of which it was slung by a slight rope-yarn lashing, and then bent in to an anchor at her bow: so that, when the anchor was let go, the ship ran over her main cable, or that out of the hawse-hole, and brought up by the cable from her stern. This was to avoid the risk of being raked while swinging head to wind, as well as to enable the ship, by slackening one cable and hauling upon the other, to spring her broadside in any direction she pleased.

Shortly after the signal to prepare to anchor, another was made, to signify that the admiral meant to attack the enemy's van and centre. As far as can be gathered from the vague accounts on the subject, Sir Horatio intended, with his fourteen 74s, to pass the French line on its outer side, down to the seventh ship, the Orient; so that every French ship of the seven might have a British ship on her bow and quarter. With respect to the 50-gun ship, admitting that Captain Thompson could succeed in persuading the admiral to overlook her comparatively weak powers in such a conflict, it is probable that the Leander would have been ordered to assist two of the 74s in overpowering the three-decker.

As the British ships approached the bay, the two French brigs, already named, stood out to reconnoitre; and one of them, the Alerte, on arriving nearly within gun-shot of the leading ships, bore away directly across the rocky shoal off Aboukir island, in the hope that one or more of the 74s would have chased her and got on shore. But the ruse did not take, and the British van continued to steer a safe course. At 5h. 30 m., the fleet being nearly abreast of the extremity of the shoal, the signal was made to form in line of battle ahead and astern of the admiral, as most convenient from the then accidental position of the ships; and Rear-admiral Nelson, about this time, hailed the Zealous, to know if Captain Hood thought the ships were far enough to the eastward to bear up. Captain Hood replied, that the Zealous was then in 11 fathoms, and that he had no chart of the bay; but that he would bear up, and, by sounding carefully, carry the admiral as close to the shoal as could be done with safety.* This was agreed to; and the Zealous, then with the wind on the larboard quarter, bore away, and, rounding the shoal, brought the wind on her starboard beam. At this time the Goliath was a little advanced on her larboard bow. Shortly afterwards the Vanguard, who was next astern of the Zealous, hove to to speak a boat. This occasioned some of the other ships to shorten sail; and it was now that the Theseus was hailed by Captain Berry, and directed to be the admiral's second ahead. The Theseus accordingly ran past the Vanguard, and brought to in her station.

At about 6 P.M. the admiral made the signal for the fleet to fill and stand on. The ships did so, and were then ranged in the following order: Goliath, Zealous, Orion, Audacious, Theseus, Vanguard, Minotaur, Bellerophon, Majestic, Leander; with, away at some distance to the northward, the Culloden, and, at a still greater distance to the westward, the Alexander and Swiftsure, using every exertion to get up. The wind still continued to blow from the north-north-west: hence the 11 ships standing in line had it on the starboard beam, the Culloden nearly astern, and the Alexander and Swiftsure, until it changed and headed them, nearly on the larboard beam. The rapidity and precision with which the above 11 ships formed the line, elicited the admiration of the French; the more so on account of the "pêle-mêle" state in which the ships had previously bore down. Soon after the British ships had thus formed, they hoisted their colours, and subsequently union jacks in several parts of the rigging.

At about 6 h. 20 m. P.M. the French ships hoisted their colours; and the Conquérant, followed by the Guerrier, opened her fire upon the Goliath and Zealous, then in line close to each other, and at some distance ahead of their companions. The mortars on the island also began throwing shells, but without effect. At about 5 h. 30 m. P.M. the Goliath, who, in order to keep ahead of the Zealous, had been obliged, after taking in her topgallantsails, to set them again, crossed the head of the French line, and, pouring a raking broadside into the Guerrier, bore up for that ship's inner bow, where Captain Foley intended to take his station; but, the anchor not dropping in time, the Goliath ran past the Guerrier, and did not bring up until abreast of the inner or larboard quarter of the second ship, the Conquérant. The Goliath then commenced a warm action with

* Williams's Voyage, a book often quoted by Mr. James; the author of which was present at the battle of the Nile, gives the following version of this anecdote. "Nelson hailed Hood, and asked him if he thought there was sufficient depth of water for our ships between the enemy and the shore?" "I don't know, sir," replied Hood, "but with your permission, *I will stand in and try.*"

the latter, and occasionally fired a few distant shot from her foremost starboard guns at the Sérieuse frigate and Hercule mortar-brig, lying within her.

The Zealous, following the Goliath in her manœuvre, and dropping her anchor in five fathoms, brought up abreast of the inner or larboard bow of the Guerrier; which was precisely the position Captain Foley had intended to take. A prompt and well-directed broadside, at musket-shot distance, from the larboard guns of the Zealous, brought down by the board, in less than five minutes, the Guerrier's foremast. The sun was at this moment sinking into the horizon, and not a British ship, except the Goliath and Zealous, had yet fired a shot. So auspicious a commencement of the attack was greeted with three cheers by the whole British fleet.

This is the period we have selected, for showing the positions of the van-ships of the two fleets, as well as the courses by which those of the British fleet steered into their places.

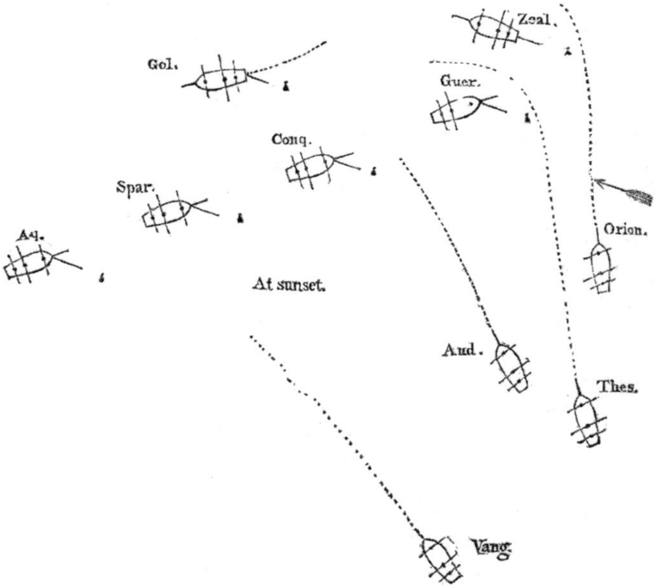

The Orion followed next; and, after firing in passing at the Guerrier, rounded the stern or starboard quarter of the Zealous, and ran along the same side of the latter and of the Goliath successively. The Audacious and Theseus, in the mean while, by taking rather a shorter course than the Orion, arrived at their stations before her. The first, steering for the opening between Guerrier and Conquérant, dropped her small bower and brought up within about 70 yards of the latter ship's bows;

into which the Audacious poured a well-directed discharge from her larboard guns. The Audacious, soon afterwards, swang round, head to wind, and came to again within about 50 yards of the Conquérant's larboard side, and rather upon the French ship's inner bow.

Steering close ahead of the Guerrier, and within the Zealous and Goliath successively, into whose respective opponents she fired in passing, the Theseus anchored by the stern in a line ahead of the Goliath, and abreast of, and at the distance of about 300 yards from, the Spartiate. Almost immediately after the Theseus had thus placed herself, the Orion, retarded by the circuit she had made, passed the latter ship's starboard, or, in reference to the French line, outer side, with the intention, we suppose, of bringing up abreast of the Aquilon, the fourth ship from the French van; but, the Sérieuse frigate, at anchor considerably beyond the track of the Orion, opening her fire, the 74's starboard guns were brought to bear upon this unworthy antagonist, and discharged with so good an effect, as besides dismasting her so to shatter her hull, that, after cutting her cables and drifting further upon the shoal, the frigate sank. Fortunately for Captain Martin and his men, a part of the upper works of the Sérieuse remained above water. Having done this, the Orion dropped her anchor, and, veering away, brought up head to wind nearly in a line with the Theseus, and abreast, or a little abaft the beam, of the Peuple-Souverain; but unavoidably, on account of her deviation to follow up the Sérieuse, at so great a distance, that her aftermost guns occasionally played upon the larboard bow of the Franklin.

The rear-admiral had judiciously resolved, as already in part stated, to complete the capture or destruction of the French van-ships, ere he made any serious attempt upon the ships in the rear; being well aware that these, from their leeward position, would be unable to afford any immediate support to the former. As the first ship in the execution of this plan, the Vanguard edged away towards the outer side of the French line, exposed, in passing, to a raking fire from the van; and at 6 h. 40 m., a few minutes after the Theseus had taken up her position, anchored within about 80 yards of the Spartiate's starboard beam. The Minotaur, anchoring five minutes afterwards next ahead of the Vanguard, found herself opposed to the Aquilon; and the Defence, still preserving the outer line, brought up, at about 7 P.M., abreast of the Peuple-Souverain. The Bellerophon and Majestic, following next in succession, passed on, with the intention of attacking the enemy's centre and rear.

In order to lessen the confusion of a night-attack, and prevent the British vessels from firing into each other, every ship had been directed to hoist at her mizen peak four lights horizontally; and the fleet also went into action with the white or St.-George's ensign, the red cross in the centre of which rendered it easily distinguishable, in the darkest night, from the tri-coloured flag of the enemy. At about 7 P.M., or soon afterwards, the lights made their appearance throughout the fleet; and it was nearly at the same time that the Bellerophon dropped her stern-anchor so as to bring up abreast, instead of on the bow, of the French three-decker. In a very few minutes the Majestic brought up abreast of the Tonnant, and soon lost her captain by that ship's heavy fire. Having thus placed at anchor and in hot action 10 British and seven French ships, we will now recommence with the head of the French line, and detail, as far as we are able, the operations that led to the victory which hath since given so much celebrity to the shores of an unknown bay.

The Guerrier, receiving a raking broadside in passing from the Orion and Theseus, and a succession of raking broadsides from the Zealous, who had stationed herself so judiciously, lost, within 10 minutes after the fall of her foremasts, her two remaining masts; and this without being able to bring guns enough to bear, to fall even a topgallantmast of the ship that was so annoying her. The safe position of the Zealous was partly the cause of this; and another cause existed in the unprepared state of the French ships on the supposed unassailable side, even admitted that, by the use of her springs, the Guerrier could have brought her larboard guns to bear. After pouring several more unrequited broadsides into his dismasted antagonist, Captain Hood hailed again and again to know if the Guerrier would surrender. No answer being returned, the work of slaughter went on, the canister and musketry from the Zealous driving the Frenchmen from the upper part of their ship; but the Guerrier continued to fire her stern-chasers occasionally at the Goliath and Audacious, who were assailing her in that direction. At a few minutes past 9 P.M., tired of killing men in this way, Captain Hood sent his first lieutenant on board the French ship, to ask leave to hoist a light and haul it down, as a signal of submission. This was gone, and the Guerrier became the prize of the Zealous.

The Guerrier's bowsprit and the whole of her head were shot away, and the two anchors on her bows each cut in two. Both bows, particularly the larboard one, were much shattered; and, from the latter to the gangway, her maindeck ports were nearly in one, and her gunwale in that part totally cut away. This had caused two of her maindeck beams to fall upon her guns; and most of the masts, having fallen in-board, lay with the rigging, over the dead and wounded of the crew. Yet the Guerrier's cable remained uncut, and still held her fast. Her loss, in killed and wounded together, was estimated at more than half her complement, or from 350 to 400 men; whereas the loss on board the Zealous amounted to no more than seven men wounded, and the ship was quite as perfect as her masts, and nearly so in her rigging, as when, three hours before, she had commenced the engagement.

The Conquérant, besides receiving a portion of the fire from the ships that ran by her, and a very warm fire from the quarter-guns of the Theseus, found two steady opponents in the Goliath and Audacious, the latter, for a while, in a raking position. At the end of 10 or 12 minutes, after having, by the united fire of two ships, upon whom, from the positions they had taken, she was unable to bestow a suitable return, had her fore and mizen masts shot away, and her mainmast left in the act of falling, the Conquérant hauled down her flag. This ship appears to have been the first that struck; but still, being entirely disabled, she could have resisted no longer. Her loss in killed and wounded we are unable to enumerate; but it is stated to have been nearly as severe as that of the Guerrier, including among the wounded her commander, M. Dalbarade. Of the Conquérant's two principal opponents, the Goliath had suffered the most; having had nearly the whole of her main and mizen rigging shot away, and all her masts badly wounded. The loss on board the Goliath was also severe, amounting to 21 killed and 41 wounded. The fore and main masts and main topmast of the Audacious were considerably injured; but her loss, owing to her secure position on the larboard bow of her principal opponent, was only one killed and 35 (an unusually large proportion) wounded.

The Spartiate, after sustaining the direct fire of the Theseus, until the Vanguard's position obliged that ship to drop a little further down the line, found herself assailed, on the starboard side, by the whole broadside force of the Vanguard, and by an occasional fire on the quarter, from the aftermost guns of the Minotaur. Subsequently, too, on the Conquérant's surrender, the Spartiate became exposed, on her larboard bow, to a fire from the quarter guns of the Audacious. Thus surrounded by foes, the Spartiate's masts did not long remain standing, and her colours came down nearly at the same time as the Guerrier's light. At the onset of the attack upon her, the Spartiate had found an able second astern in the Aquilon; who, from the slanting position she had obtained by springing her broadside, (having no opponent to occupy her attention on the larboard side), had succeeded in raking the Vanguard with destructive effect, until the Minotaur crippled the Aquilon's means of annoyance. With two such opponents as the Spartiate and Aquilon upon her, the Vanguard's damages might well be serious; and, although none of her masts fell over the side, they were all badly wounded. The loss on board the Vanguard was proportionately severe, amounting to 30 killed and 76 wounded, and that of the Spartiate, the Vanguard's principal opponent, although we are unable to state the amount, was still more severe, including among the badly wounded Captain Emeriuil.

The Aquilon, assailed from without the line by the powerful broadsides of the Minotaur (the only ship in the two fleets that, for an upper battery, had a tier of 32-pounder carronades), and from within by the occasional fire of the Theseus, was soon reduced to the dismasted state of her three companions ahead; and was compelled, at about 9 h. 25 m. P.M., to follow their example, with a loss nearly, if not quite as severe, including among the killed her commander, M. Thévenard. The Minotaur, the Aquilon's principal opponent, had 23 killed and 64 wounded; and the Theseus, with whom she was only partially engaged, had five killed and 30 wounded.

The Peuple-Souverain, by the close and animated fire of the Defence, also by a succession of raking broadsides from the Orion, as the latter lay on the Peuple-Souverain's inner quarter, having lost her fore and main masts, and become in other respects greatly disabled, parted her cable and dropped out of the line, reanchoring abreast of, and at about 400 yards distant from, the Orient, with, including her captain among the wounded, a severe loss, but which, as in most of the other cases, we are unable to enumerate.

The loss sustained by the Peuple-Souverain's outside opponent, the Defence, was only four killed and 11 wounded; while that of the Orion, the former's opponent within the line, amounted to 13 killed and 29 wounded. The Orion had her fore and mizen masts shot through in several places, and her yards and rigging greatly disabled. The ship had also a narrow escape from a more imminent danger. In the heat of the action a fire-raft, represented as the Guerrier's launch filled with combustibles, came drifting down with the tide, which runs here at a great rate. The Orion's stern-boat having been shot away, and no means existing to get another boat out for the purpose of towing the raft clear of the ship, preparations were made to boom off the unwelcome visitor and sink it by pigs of ballast; but, unfortunately, the raft passed clear of the larboard bow by about 25 yards. Just as the Peuple-Souverain had driven from the line and ceased firing, the fore topmast of the Defence fell over her side; and her three lower masts, as well as bowsprit, were much injured.

The Bellerophon soon found her station a hotter one than she could bear. At about 7 h. 50 m. her mizenmast was shot away; and, in a few minutes afterwards, the mainmast fell on the starboard side of the forecastle. Some combustible materials discharged from the Orient had also set the ship on fire in several places, but the crew succeeded in extinguishing the flames. At about 8 h. 20 m. P.M., being entirely disabled, the Bellerophon cut her stern cable, and, setting her spritsail, wore clear of the powerful three-decker to whose fire she had so long been exposed. Scarcely had the Bellerophon filled her fore topsail and dropped her foresail, than her shattered foremast, unable to bear the weight, fell over her larboard bow. In drifting along the rear of the French line, the Bellerophon received a broadside from the Tonnant, and a few distant shots from the Heureux. The Bellerophon's loss, therefore, might well amount to 49 killed and 148 wounded.

The Majestic had brought up under the guns of an opponent that, although nominally a two-decker, was more than a match for a British 98. In less than half an hour after she had commenced action with the Tonnant, the Majestic lost her captain by a musket-ball, a proof that this pair of combatants were not far asunder. The command of the Majestic, on the death of her captain, devolved upon her first lieutenant, Robert Cuthbert; who continued to fight the ship in the most gallant manner. At about 8 h. 30 m., finding she was drifting athwart the hawse of the Heureux, the Majestic slipped her stern cable, and, letting go her best bower, brought up head to wind; having the Heureux on her starboard quarter, and shortly afterwards, when in consequence of the accident that befel the Orient the Tonnant cut or slipped her cable, having also the latter ship on her larboard bow. Here we will leave the Majestic, while we attend to the three fresh ships, which, a few minutes previous, had reached the scene of action.

Just as the Alexander and Swiftsure had got nearly abreast of Aboukir island, and expected soon to be round the reef that lies off its north-eastern extremity, the wind shifted from north-north-west to north. The Alexander, being on the lee bow of her consort, was obliged to tack. This gave the Swiftsure the lead, and no time was lost in taking advantage of it. Fortunately for these two ships, but unfortunately for the Culloden, the latter, just a quarter of an hour after the action had commenced, had stuck fast on the reef off the island. The signals of the Culloden were now a warning to her two friends; and these, as they successively came up, rounded the shoal in safety.

At a few minutes past 8 P.M., having found, amidst the prevailing darkness, a sure beacon in the flashes of the guns of the combatants, the Swiftsure came up with a dismasted ship, without light or colours, quitting the scene of slaughter. On the supposition that she was an enemy, the Swiftsure was just about to pour in a broadside, when Captain Hallowell hailed, and was repaid for his considerateness by the immediate reply, "Bellerophon, going out of action disabled." Instantly the stern-anchor was let go, and the Swiftsure, without at the time, from the smoke and darkness, exactly knowing where, brought up about half a ship's length astern of the spot which the Bellerophon had just quitted. As soon as she had clewed up (but not, we should suppose, for the sake of her men's lives, "furled"*) her sails, the Swiftsure opened a heavy fire, with her foremost guns, at the distance of about 200 yards, upon the

* Brenton, vol. ii, p. 311.

starboard bow of the Orion, and her aftermost ones, at a somewhat greater distance, upon the same quarter of the Franklin; upon whose larboard bow, the Leander, keeping under way in the vacant space left by the Peuple-Souverain when she quitted the line (and to which the Leander had but recently arrived, on account of her detention by the Culloden), was pouring in a fire with scarcely the possibility of a return. As a proof that the Leander, in the position she had thus taken, was most effectually co-operating with her more powerful friends in bringing the business of the day to a conclusion, we quote from a French account of the battle the following passage: "De cette manière tous les boulets du Leander qui n'atteignaient pas le Franklin allaient à bord de l'Orient, du Tonnant, ou d'un des vaisseaux plus en arrière."* Shortly afterward the Alexander, coming rapidly up, passed through the wide opening which the driving of the Tonnant had left, and dropped her bow-anchor so as to open her starboard broadside directly on the French three-decker's larboard quarter.

Until the Leander took up a position to mask the fire of the Orion, the latter had been cannonading the Franklin; and the Minotaur had also found opportunities to bestow a few shots upon that noble two-decker. But, since the Peuple-Souverain had quitted the line, the Franklin had found a more unengaged opponent in the Defence; when, suddenly, an event happened, which struck both sides with awe, and suspended, for a while, the hostile operations of the two fleets. It was at 9 P.M., or a few minutes after, that the Swiftsure's people perceived a fire on board of the Orient; and which, as it increased, presently bore the appearance of being in the ship's mizen chains. It was, in fact, on the poop deck and in the admiral's cabin; and its cause we shall hereafter endeavour to explain. As many of the Swiftsure's guns as could be brought to bear were quickly directed to the inflamed spot, with, as was soon evident, dreadful precision.

After spreading along the decks, and ascending the rigging, with terrific and uncontrollable rapidity, the flames reached the fatal spot; and, at about 10 P.M., the Orient blew up, with a most tremendous explosion. Any description of the awful scene would fall short: we shall therefore confine ourselves to the effect it produced upon the adjacent ships. The Alexander, Swiftsure, and Orion, as the three nearest, had made every preparation for the event; such as closing their ports and hatchways, removing from the decks all combustible materials, and having ready with buckets a numerous body of firemen. The vibration shook the ships to their kelsons, opened their seams, and, in other respects, did them considerable injury. The flaming mass, except two large pieces of the wreck which

* Victoires et Conquêtes, tome ix, p. 92.

dropped, but without any evil consequences, into her fore and main tops, flew over the Swiftsure, as was wisely conjectured by her commander, when urged to attempt moving further off. A part also fell on board of the Alexander, who lay at a somewhat greater distance from the Orient, and upon her lee quarter; a port-fire setting her main-royal in flames, and some splinters, her jib. In both cases the crew extinguished the flames, but not without cutting away the jib-boom and spritsail-yard. With the little air of wind which the cannonade, and the more mighty concussion that interrupted it, had left, the Alexander then dropped to a safer distance. Among the French ships, the Franklin received the greater share of the Orient's wreck: her decks were covered with red-hot seams, pieces of timber, and burning ropes; she caught fire, but succeeded in extinguishing it. The Tonnant had, just before the explosion, cut or slipped her cable, and dropped clear of the burning wreck. The Heureux and Mercure, although too far off to be injured, had done the same.

Either amazement at what had happened, or a strong feeling towards self-preservation, or both causes united, made it full ten minutes ere a gun was again fired on either side. By this time, too, the wind, as if just recovering from the trance into which all nature had been hushed by the catastrophe, freshened up; and, as it ruffled the surface of the water, and rattled among the rigging of the ships, reanimated the half-benumbed faculties of the combatants. The French ship Franklin, although disabled in most of her guns, was the first to recommence hostilities: she opened a fire from her lower battery upon the Defence and Swiftsure; who, as they lay close on her starboard bow and quarter, returned it, particularly the Defence, with full effect. Being without a second either ahead or astern, and having, besides these two determined opponents, one or two other ships in commanding positions on her opposite bow and quarter, the Franklin waited until her main and mizen masts came down by the board; and then, having scarcely a gun to cannonade with, and being reduced by loss in the action to less than half of her complement, struck her colours.

It was now midnight, and the Tonnant was the only French ship whose guns continued in active play. Her shot gave great annoyance to the Swiftsure, particularly as the latter, owing to the position of the Alexander, could make little or no return; but the Majestic had been the principal opponent of that formidable French ship. At about 3 A.M. on the 2d, the heavy and unremitting fire of the Tonnant brought down, by the board, the Majestic's main and mizen masts; but, shortly afterwards, the Tonnant herself had her three masts shot away, equally close to the deck. The wreck of these compelled her to cease firing, but failed in inducing her to strike: the Tonnant had, indeed, by veering her cable, driven so far to leeward of her second position, as to have now no opponent near enough to put her resolution to a trial. The Heureux and Mercure, also, having, as already stated, withdrawn from the line, had left ample room for the Tonnant to take up a station ahead of the Guillaume-Tell and the two French ships in her rear. This the Tonnant did; and a second interval of silence ensued.

At 4 A.M., which was just as the day broke, the firing recommenced between the Tonnant, Guillaume-Tell, Généreux, and Timoléon, on the one side, and the Alexander and crippled Majestic on the other. This soon brought to the spot the Theseus and Goliath. Shortly after these ships had dropped their anchors the French frigate Artémise fired a broadside at the Theseus, and then struck her colours. A boat from the latter immediately proceeded to take possession; but the frigate was discovered to be on fire, and soon afterwards blew up. In the mean time the four French line-of-battle ships, and the two remaining frigates inside of them, kept dropping to leeward; so as, presently, to be almost out of gun-shot of the few British ships that had anchored to attack them.

At about 6 A.M. the Zealous, Goliath, and Theseus, got under way by signal; and soon afterwards the Zealous, in running down from the head of the bay, was directed by signal to chase the Justice French frigate; which, in compliance with the orders of Rear-admiral Villeneuve, was on her way to the Bellerophon, at anchor at the bottom of the bay, and supposed to be on shore, for the purpose of summoning the 74 to surrender. In the mean time the Goliath and Theseus, accompanied by the Alexander and Leander, stood towards the Heureux and Mercure; who, on quitting the line, had first anchored considerably within it, and had then run themselves on shore to the southward of the bay. These ships, after the interchange of a few distant shot, struck their colours; the Heureux first, then the Mercure. The latter was afterwards taken possession of by the Alexander, and the former by one of the other ships. On discovering the object of the Zealous, the Justice gave up her design on the Bellerophon (who was getting ready to give her a suitable reception), and returned to the cluster of ships from among which she had made sail. The Zealous thereupon by signal from the admiral, bore away to join the Bellerophon, and protect her from further molestation.

At about 11 A.M. the absence of the Goliath, Theseus, and Alexander, afforded to the Généreux and Guillaume-Tell, and the two frigates Justice and Diane, an opportunity to get under way and make sail to the north-east. The Timoléon, being too far to leeward to fetch clear, had run herself on shore, losing her foremast by the shock. The four other ships now hauled close on the larboard tack; and immediately the Zealous, who from the course she was steering happened to be the nearest British ship, hauled close on the same tack, with the bold intention of bringing this French 80 and 74 and two heavy frigates to action, and, if possible, of retarding their progress until some of her friends should come to her assistance; or, at all events, in the hope of so crippling one of the French ships, as to disable her at least from working out of the bay. The Zealous weathered the four fugitives within musket-shot, and obliged them to bear away to avoid being raked; but received in return a very destructive fire to her rigging and sails. Through her mainsail alone upwards of 40 round shot had passed; and yet no other loss was sustained by her, than one man, who had been slightly wounded by the Guerrier, killed, and one wounded. While the Zealous was endeavouring to get about in time to cut off the rearmost frigate, the former's signal of recal was made; and the French ships stretching on, effected their escape. For his gallantry upon this occasion, Captain Hood received the warm acknowledgements of the commander-in-chief.

Of the 13 French ships of the line, one had perished in the flames, eight had surrendered, and two had escaped; and of the remaining two, one, the Timoléon, was on shore with her colours flying, the other, the Tonnant, having had her second cable cut by the fire of the Alexander, lay about two miles from the Timoléon, a mere wreck, but also with her colours up, which were flying on the stump of her mainmast. Things remained in this state until the morning of the following day, the 3d; when the Theseus and Leander approached, and stationed themselves near the Tonnant. All further resistance being utterly hopeless, the latter hauled down her ensign: and, on replacing it with a flag of truce, was taken possession of by a boat from the Theseus. The principal part of the crew of the Timoléon had, during the preceding night, escaped on shore. The remainder, at about noon on the 3d, set fire to their ship; which, exploding soon afterwards, made the eleventh line-of-battle ship lost to the French by, in their nomenclature, the battle of Aboukir, "le combat d'Aboukir," but as the conquerors have named it, the battle of the Nile.

The damages sustained by the British ships were chiefly confined to their masts and rigging. The Bellerophon was the only ship entirely dismasted, and the Majestic the only one, besides her, that had lost any lower mast. The Defence had lost her fore topmast, and the Alexander her mizen topmast, and her fore and main topgallantmasts; and on the 3d, at 6 P.M., the latter's main topmast, from the wounds it had received, fell over the top, as on the same morning, had the main topmast of the Goliath. The lower masts, yards, and bowsprits of all the ships that had been engaged, were more or less damaged by shot. The Vanguard, it will be recollected, went into action with a jury foremast. The Bellerophon's hull was in a very shattered state. One of the carronades on her poop was broken to pieces. Seven of the quarterdeck guns were entirely disabled; as were six of the second, and two of the first or lowerdeck guns; and the greater part of her hammocks were more or less cut. The Vanguard had been struck very heavily by shot on her starboard bow; and the Swiftsure, as she was bearing down to engage, received in her larboard bow, several feet below the water-mark, a shot from the Tonnant, which, in spite of the constant use of the chain-pumps, kept four feet water in the hold from the commencement to the end of the action. The Theseus was also hulled, in more than 70 places; and the Majestic was nearly in as shattered a state as the Bellerophon.

The loss of the British was, in the aggregate, tolerably severe. We have enumerated the loss on board most of the ships. We will now, taking the ships in the order in which they advanced to the attack, give a more detailed account. The Goliath had one master's mate (William David), one midshipman (Andrew Brown), 12 seamen, and seven marines killed, one lieutenant (William Wilkinson), two midshipmen (Lawrence Graves and James Payne), her schoolmaster, 28 seamen, and nine marines wounded; the Zealous, one seaman killed, and seven wounded; the Orion, one captain's clerk, 11 seamen, and one marine killed, her captain, the boatswain (Peter Sadler), three midshipmen (Philip Richardson, Charles Miell, and — Lanfesty), nine seamen, and two marines wounded; the Audacious, one seaman killed, one lieutenant (John Jeans), her gunner, 31 seamen, and two marines wounded; the Theseus, five seamen killed, one lieutenant (Richard Hawkins), 24 seamen, and five marines wounded; the Vanguard, her captain of marines (William Faddy), two midshipmen (Thomas Seymour and John George Taylor), 20 seamen, and seven marines killed, the rear-admiral, by a contusion in the head, but not reported), two lieutenants (Nathaniel Vassall and John Miller Adye), the admiral's secretary (John Campbell), the boatswain (Mr. Austin), two midshipmen (James Weatherstone and George Antrim), 60 seamen, and eight marines wounded; the Minotaur, one lieutenant (John G. Kirchner), one master's mate (Peter Walters), 18 seamen, and three marines killed, one lieutenant (Thomas Irwin), one lieutenant of marines (John Jewell), her second master (Thomas Forster), one midshipman (Martin Wells), 54 seamen, and six marines wounded; the Defence, three seamen and one marine killed, nine seamen and two marines wounded; the Bellerophon, three lieutenants (Robert Savage Daniel, Philip William Launder, and George Joliffe), one master's mate (Thomas Ellison), 32 seamen, and 13 marines killed, her captain, master (Edward Kirby), captain of marines (John Hopkins), boatswain (Mr. Chapman), one midshipman (Nicholas Bettson), 126 seamen, and 17 marines wounded; the Majestic, her captain, one midshipman (Zebedee Ford), boatswain (Andrew Gilmore), 33 seamen, and 14 marines killed, two midshipmen (Charles Seward and Charles Royle), her captain's clerk (Robert Overton), 124 seamen, and 16 marines wounded; the Swiftsure, seven seamen killed, one midshipman

(William Smith), 19 seamen, and two marines wounded; the Alexander, one lieutenant (John Collins), and 13 seamen killed, her captain, captain of marines (John Creswell), master (William Lawson), two midshipmen (George Bully and Luke Anderson), 48 seamen, and five marines wounded; the Leander, 14 seamen wounded; making a total of 218 killed, and 678 wounded.*

Of the damages sustained by the captured French ships, more details, scanty as they are, have already been given, than are contained in any published account. They may now be summed up by stating, that the Guerrier, Conquérant, Spartiate, Aquilon, and Tonnant, were entirely dismasted, and, in the present state of their hulls (the two first especially), not seaworthy; and the Peuple-Souverain retained but her mizenmast, and the Franklin, her foremast, with their hulls in not much better plight than those of their captive companions. As to the Mercure and Heureux, their principal damages were not from shot, but from running on shore. These ships still lay with topgallant yards across, and, to all appearance, were as perfect as when the action commenced.

It was owing, probably, to the severe wound which Rear-admiral Nelson had received at the onset of the battle (a splinter struck him a little above his right or darkened eye, causing a piece of flesh to hang over the lid, which was afterwards replaced and sewed up), that no account was taken of the loss sustained by the different captured ships. This is perhaps the only general action, besides that of Valentine's day, in which so important an omission is to be complained of in the official despatch. The London newspapers, although they sometimes

* One more in the wounded than appears in the official account, owing to the exclusion of the rear-admiral's name. The following table shows at one view each ship's tonnage, complement, loss, and, to the best of our power in so difficult a research, first lieutenant present in the action.

Ships.	Tons.	Men and Boys.	Loss.		First Lieutenants.
			K.	W.	
Goliath	1604	584	21	41	George Jardine.
Zealous	1627	584	1	7	William Henry Webley.
Orion	1646	584	13	29	James Barker.
Audacious ..	1624	584	1	35	Thomas White.
Theseus	1680	584	5	30	Richard Hawkins.
Vanguard ...	1609	589	30	76	Edward Galwey.
Minotaur ...	1718	634	23	64	Charles Marsh Schomberg.
Defence	1603	584	4	11	Richard Jones.
Bellerophon .	1613	584	49	148	Robert Cathcart; *sen.surviving.*
Majestic	1642	584	50	143	Robert Cuthbert.
Swiftsure ...	1621	584	7	22	John Lev. Waters.
Alexander ..	1621	584	14	58	John Yule.
Leander	1052	338	0	14	William Richardson.
Total	20660	7401	218	678	

clear up points of this nature, afforded in the present instance, but little information, merely stating that, according to one account, the loss amounted to 2000, and, according to another, to 5000 men. The latter number, being within 225 of a sweeping balance, of "taken, drowned, burnt, and missing," at the foot of a loose statement of the complements of 19 French ships, including the 13 engaged, subjoined to the official letter, may be traced to that as its probable source. The origin of the former number is uncertain; but 2000 appears no unreasonable amount for the killed and wounded on board nine ships, eight of which were so dreadfully shattered as those in question.

Within the first hour of the action, the French commander-in-chief, Vice-admiral Brueys, while standing on the Orient's poop, received two wounds, one in the face, and the other in the hand. Towards 8 P.M., as he was descending to the quarterdeck, a shot cut him almost in two. This brave officer then desired not to be carried below, but to be left to die upon deck, exclaiming in a firm voice, "Un amiral français doit mourir sur son banc de quart." He survived only a quarter of an hour. Commodore Casa-Bianca fell, badly wounded, soon after the admiral had breathed his last. What other loss the Orient sustained by the shot of her opponents we are unable to enumerate, but it is represented to have been tolerably severe in both officers and men. By the melancholy event of the ship's explosion, nearly the whole of the survivors of her crew perished. How the accident happened has not been clearly explained. The French say, that the men, having just done painting the ship's sides, had placed the empty and unused oil-jars and paint-buckets on the poop, preparatory to taking them below; and that the wadding from the English guns fell among and set fire to these jars and buckets. Another account states, that the fire was communicated by some of the combustible missiles, used on board of all or most of the French ships; the chief of which was a sort of port-fire or carcass, that burnt fiercely under, as well as above water. In support of this statement, the French themselves declared that, although they threw bucket after bucket of water upon the spot, they could not extinguish the flames.

The lamentable effects of the accident, however, were but too certain. The French say, that about 70 were saved by the boats of the British ships. Of these, one lieutenant, one commissary, or purser, and nine men, appear to have got on board the Swiftsure, two men on board the Bellerophon, and 16 on board the Orion. The Alexander saved some, including Adjutant-general Motard, who, although badly wounded in the leg, managed to swim on board of her. Rear-admiral Ganteaume found means to throw himself into a boat, which carried him on board the Salamine brig. From her he reached the fort of Aboukir, and subsequently Alexandria. The Salamine afterwards stood out of the bay, and joined the squadron of Rear-admiral Villeneuve. Commodore

Casa-Bianca was not so fortunate. Among the two or three accounts given of this officer's death, that to which the French attach most credit is, that at the time of the explosion he was below having his wound dressed, attended by his son, a boy of 10 years of age.

Of the 10 French ships that were at all engaged, the admiral of one, and the captains of two, were killed, and six of the remaining seven captains, besides Rear-admiral Blanquet, wounded. That the captains of the Heureux and Mercure, who participated so slightly in the action, should have been wounded at all is extraordinary; but it is still more extraordinary that Captain Trullet, whose ship, the Guerrier, was the most shattered of any of the two fleets, should have escaped unhurt. This, on consideration, may be attributed to the position of the Guerrier's principal antagonist, the Zealous, whose shot, on that account did the most execution in the forepart of the ship. Of the two French captains that were killed, one underwent dreadful suffering, and exhibited a correspondent share of heroism, before life finally quitted him. Captain Du Petit-Thouars, of the Tonnant, had first both his arms, and then one of his legs shot away; and his dying commands to his crew were, not to surrender the ship. As a memento to this officer's patriotism and bravery, Buonaparte ordered one of the principal streets of Cairo to be named Petit-Thouars, and an armed brig at anchor in the port, Tonnant.

Before we proceed further, it may be necessary that we should show, how completely *hors de combat* the Culloden was placed by the accident that had befallen her. At 6 h. 40 m. P.M., according to her time, the Culloden, having just before hauled up to clear the Leander, and sounded in 11 fathoms, struck on the ridge of rocks off the island of Aboukir. At that very moment the three masts of the Guerrier were discovered to be down. This is so far of consequence as completely to falsify a statement made and insisted on by the French writers, that the Culloden took the ground at 5 h. 15 m. P.M., while leading the British fleet into action. One writer, after stating this, adds the following in a note: "Tous les rapports anglais s'accordent à ne faire échouer le Culloden qu'après la nuit close, et à attribuer cet accident à l'obscurité, tandis qu'il n'est pas un seul Français présent au combat d'Aboukir qui n'affirme que ce vaisseau était le premier de l'esacdre ennemie, et toucha, comme nous le disons, à cinq heures un quart. Cette circonstance est de peu d'importance; mais elle pourrait donner la mesure de la croyance à accorder aux bulletins des Anglais, et fournir un échantillon du caractère de ce peuple, qui pousse la vanité jusqu'à ne pas vouloir avouer qu'un vaisseau britannique puisse, comme un autre, s'échouer de jour en entrant dans une baie inconnue."*

* Victoires et Conquêtes, tome ix., p. 90.

Bestowing no more than a smile upon the writer's clever deductions about "the character of the people," we shall endeavour to explain how this nautical illusion may have happened. It will be recollected that, soon after 5 h. 30 m. P.M. (and which might easily be 5 h. 15 m. by the French time), and just as they had arrived abreast of the shoal, the leading British ships hove to, and many of them changed stations. The ships thus grouped together, as may have been seen by any good chart of the spot, conceal the point of the shoal from the French fleet. The British fleet stands on in a line; and, as the shoal opens in the rear of that line, a ship is discovered sticking on it. To us the mistake appears a very natural one; but how are we to convince the French writers that we are right, and that they are wrong, when they can cast in our teeth, from a respectable English publication, written too by an admiral, the following sentence: "The wind was perfectly fair, but unfortunately, in rounding the reef, the Culloden, the leading ship, ran aground, and could not be got at all into action?"*

Let us return to the Culloden. As quickly as possible after she struck, a stream anchor and cable were placed in the launch, and dropped at about a cable's length from the stern, in 11 fathoms' water. The Mutine now came and anchored within 500 yards of the Culloden, in six fathoms, in order to afford every assistance in her power. To do this more effectually Captain Hardy ran out two cables, firmly clinched together; and, joining a third, veered away until the brig was near the Culloden. The Mutine then let go another anchor, and, slipping the third cable, passed the end of it on board the 74. The swell, which had greatly increased, made the Culloden strike so hard, that her cable parted, her rudder was knocked off and sank alongside, and the ship made three feet of water an hour. However, on the 2d, before 2 A.M., after striking several times very heavily, the Culloden hauled herself off the rocks by the Mutine's cable, and then made seven feet water, or 120 tons, an hour. A sail was afterwards thrummed, and put under the ship's bottom; and on the morning of the 3d a spare topmast was converted into, and hung as, a temporary rudder.

Having thus made it clear that, for any part she took in the battle of the 1st and 2d of August, the Culloden might as well have been at anchor in Naples bay, as on shore at one extremity of Aboukir bay, we shall now present a general view of the force of the contending parties. Of the 13 ships that remain, after excluding the Culloden, one was not only no line-of-battle ship, but a ship decidedly unable to lay alongside of any ship in the opposite line; yet, as it would be paying a very poor compliment

* Ekins's Naval Battles, p. 237.

to the Leander's meritorious exertions, to consider that they were wholly without effect, we shall readily include her as one of the contending ships. Hence the British had twelve 74-gun ships and one 50; the French one 120, three 80, and nine 74-gun ships: the latter had, also, four frigates, two brigs, and some bomb-vessels and gun-boats; the former, but one solitary brig. The armaments of French and English ships of the line have been so often adverted to in these pages, that there will be no occasion to analyze the force of every ship of the two fleets. It may suffice to state, that a French 120-gun ship is fully equal to two British 74s, three French 80s to five of them, especially of the 18-pounder class, of which all that were present in this battle consisted, and nine French 74s to at least ten of the English 74s last described. With respect to the crews of the French ships, it has been stated, that each ship, when the action commenced, had a water-party on shore; but the same accounts that furnish this fact, supply us with another, namely, that a part of the absent men got back to their ships, and that the four frigates, whose united crews were at least 1300 men, had received orders to send a portion of their people to the line-of-battle ships. Moreover the head-money certificates, authenticated in the usual way, give the French ships their established complements; and among the prisoners were actually found several masters, pilots, and others, belonging to the numerous fleet of transports at anchor near Rosetta and in the harbour of Alexandria. On the other hand, none of the British ships were over manned; and some, we believe, had not their complements on board; what is extraordinary, too, the worst manned ship in the British fleet was that commanded by the admiral. The Vanguard had only been commissioned in the preceding December; and her ship's company, although instinctively brave, were new and inexperienced.

Even the presence of the Culloden in the action would still have left a preponderance, if not in number of ships, in number of men and in broadside weight of metal. With the Culloden excluded, the superiority of force was more than requisite to rank the victory of the Nile among the most brilliant of those achievements so familiar to the British navy. If any allowance is called for, because the French ships were conquered in detail, and that by a decided superiority of force, we may answer, that the same occurs in most general actions; that, in the present instance, the danger of a cross-fire, from which several of the British ships undoubtedly suffered, as well as that of grounding on the inner shoal, not an officer or man in the British fleet having ever before been in the bay and the only chart in the fleet being a roughly sketched one which the Swiftsure had recently taken out of a prize, were nearly equivalent to the advantage of doubling the van of the line. Moreover, had the six French rear-ships, the moment they saw the manœuvre that was about to be practised on their friends in the van, got under way and stood out, they would have found full employment for the five or six British ships that had not yet got into action: they would, undoubtedly, have captured the Culloden, and prevented the Alexander and Swiftsure from entering the bay. Had those six French ships weighed at any time before 7 P.M., they might, with the wind as it then was, have made a good stretch out of the bay, and, by tacking when the wind, as it soon afterwards did, shifted to north, might have stood for the van of their line with their yards nearly square.

Undoubtedly the sad accident which befel the three-decker gave a decided turn to the action; but it should be recollected that the Orient, before she exploded, had, according to the French accounts, sustained a very serious loss in officers and men; that five French ships had already struck; and that two others, the Franklin and Tonnant, were nearly in a defenceless state. It has been stated, we are aware, that the Orient herself hauled down her colours, before she blew up;* but no such occurrence happened. The Orient's flag at the main was, by several of the British ships, seen in its place when the masts were thrown into the air; and, until that flag was struck, there could have been no surrender. Moreover the men fired from the ship's lowerdeck battery, until they were driven from their quarters by the flames, and until some time after the Swiftsure and Alexander had ceased firing, to prepare for the explosion that ensued.

With respect to the behaviour of the French, nothing could be more gallant than the defence made by each of the six van-ships, by the Orient in the centre, and by the Tonnant in the rear. The Heureux and Mercure appear to have been rather precipitate in running themselves on shore; but the flaming body, that lay ready to explode ahead and to windward of them, justified them in quitting the line. Nor was it the least happy circumstance attending the battle of the Nile, that there was no complaint of individual misconduct to diminish the lustre of the victory. The French writers, as usual, multiplied the English ships in number and force; but the sober-minded part of the community knew well the near equality of the two fleets, and appreciated the unfortunate result of the battle as fairly as could be expected, where so many fine ships, and so much national glory, had been lost.

We will now hasten to acquit ourselves of the unpleasant task of noticing a few inaccuracies, that have crept into some English and foreign accounts of this celebrated action. One writer, after

* Clarke and McArthur's Life of Nelson, p. 81, and at p. 93, is the following paragraph: "He (Sir Horatio) also informed Mr. Wyndham, that l'Orient certainly struck her colours, and had not fired a shot for a quarter of an hour before she took fire."

stating that the French fleet "was moored in a compact line,"* tells his readers, that the line occupied "an extent of about two miles and a half, leaving a space of two hundred and fifty or three hundred yards from one ship to the other. This distance," proceeds the writer, "was too great." Assuredly it was too great, and so was the real distance, 160 yards: for that very reason, too, the French fleet was not "moored in a compact line." The word "moored" does not seem to be appropriately used. "At single anchor, with springs on their cables," is an expression that accords more with the fact. Unfortunately, the writer who uses this expression is the same that committed the mistake about the Culloden; the same, in whose work appears the following piece of extraordinary information: "Lord Nelson remarked, at a subsequent period, that he had committed one great error; namely, by not having directed the ships to heave *close* to their anchors, and then have *cut* (the cables) instead of weighing them; as in stowing their anchors, the navigation being so intricate and shallow, two of his ships grounded."† This, to be sure, is contained in a "note," but that note actually forms a part of the text: indeed, the work is almost wholly made up of "NOTES," "REMARKS," and "OBSERVATIONS." Had the attack upon Copenhagen by Lord Nelson in the year 1801 been one of the naval battles noticed by the writer, it is probable he would have found where it was that the rear-admiral had to complain, that two of his ships grounded, for the want of the precaution of cutting, instead of weighing, their anchors.

A French writer, because he is displeased with a highly exaggerated comparison between the force of the Bellerophon and that of the Orient, contained in "Clarke and McArthur's Life of Nelson," begins his refutation of the nonsense in this very liberal manner: "Les Anglais, celui peut-être de tous les peuples de l'Europe qui altère le plus le vérité dans ses bulletins, affirmèrent," &c.‡ It is unfair, in any case, to consider individual opinion as the sentiments of a nation; but with respect to the work, in which the angry Frenchman has discovered the proofs of this national propensity to lying (for that is what his charge amounts to), we can assure him that, in this country, where its merits are of course best known, "Clarke and M'Arthur's Life of Nelson" is not of the slightest authority. The same French writer, who is so severe in his strictures upon the English, admits that Captain Standelet of the Artémise, in setting fire to his frigate after having hauled down his colours to the Theseus, acted "au mèpris des lois de la guerre," but adds, "Les Anglais se sont vivement récriés contre la conduite du capitaine de l'Artémise, oubliant que le capitaine du Bellerophon en avait tenu une à peu

* Brenton, vol. ii., p. 305.

† Ekins, p. 243.

‡ Victoires et Conquêtes, tome ix., p. 94.

près semblabale."* Looking back to discover the nature of this charge against Captain Darby, we find that the Bellerophon "struck to the Tonnant;" that is, the cries and noise of the Bellerophon's people, when her masts were falling on deck and crushing them by scores, were mistaken for the cry of surrender. Nay, so delicate were the ears of the Frenchmen, that they could distinguish the cries of the officers from those of the men. "Son équipage," says the account, "et principalement les officiers, jetèrent de grands cris, pour faire connaître qu'il était rendu."† From our inquiries we believe we can assert (and, if we knew the fact to be otherwise, we should be the last to conceal it), that no surrender took place, or was even contemplated. The crew of the Bellerophon were neither the least brave, nor, as was pretty notorious, the least noisy, of any in the British fleet: it is not unlikely, therefore, that when the masts were tumbling about their heads, the men hallooed, and roared, and uttered "de grands cris," but not any cries, we can vouch, that were meant to signify that they surrendered.

Leaving the heads better versed in state affairs to discuss the political consequences, far and near, that attended the decisive victory which Rear-admiral Nelson and his fleet had gained, we shall merely transcribe from Mr. Williams's book a translated passage, purporting to be part of a letter from a very intelligent French officer, of some celebrity, M. E. Poussielgue, comptroller of the expenses of the army, and administrator-general of the finances, in Egypt; and which letter, among many others, was intercepted by the British fleet in the Mediterranean. M. Poussielgue says: "But the fatal engagement of Aboukir ruined all our hopes; it prevented us from receiving the remainder of the forces which were destined for us; it left the field free for the English to persuade the Porte to declare war against us; it rekindled that which was hardly extinguished with the Emperor of Germany; it opened the Mediterranean to the Russians, and planted them on our frontiers; it occasioned the loss of Italy, and the invaluable possessions in the Adriatic, which we owed to the successful campaigns of Buonaparte; and, finally, it at once rendered abortive all our projects, since it was no longer possible for us to dream of giving the English any uneasiness in India: add to this, that the people of Egypt, whom we wished to consider as friends and allies, instantaneously became our enemies; and, entirely surrounded as we were by the Turks, we found ourselves engaged in a most difficult defensive war, without a glimpse of the slightest future advantage to be derived from it."

On the 5th the Leander, having on board Captain Berry of the Vanguard, with despatches for Earl St.-Vincent off Cadiz, quitted the squadron; but, about 12 days afterwards, was fallen

* Victoires et Conquêtes, tome ix., p. 101.

† Ibid., p. 95.

in with and captured by the French 74-gun ship, Généreux, after an action highly honourable to the British 50-gun ship, and the full details of which will appear under the next head of the work.

The ships of the British squadron at anchor in Aboukir bay now set about repairing their damages, with all possible speed. Every exertion was also used to place the captured ships in a state to undertake the voyage to England with safety. The prisoners taken in them were sent on shore in a cartel, upon the usual terms; but Buonaparte, to show how he respected treaties, formed the men, soon after they landed, into a battalion, which he named the nautic legion, and gave the command of it to the late second captain of the Franklin, Jules-François Martinencq. On the 8th the island of Aboukir was taken possession of, and the two mortars, with the two brass 12-pounders, were brought off. The remainder of the guns, with the carriages of the whole, and the platform on which they had been mounted, were destroyed. The island was also newly, and far from inappropriately named, Nelson's island.

On the 10th Sir Horatio, aware of the designs of the French, in case of succeeding at Egypt, to attack the British East India possessions, despatched, over land to Bombay, with the intelligence of the victory, Lieutenant Thomas Duval, of the Zealous, an officer selected by Captain Hood.* On the 12th, in the evening, the British 36-gun frigate Emerald, Captain Thomas Moutray Waller, and 32-gun frigate Alemène, Captain George Hope, with the Bonne-Citoyenne sloop of war, hove in sight in the offing; but, on being chased by the Swiftsure, stood off. On the next day, however, the frigates got over their alarm, and joined the squadron. On the 13th the 16-gun brig-sloop Mutine, Captain the Honourable Thomas Bladen Capel, who had succeeded Captain Hardy, on the latter's promotion to the Vanguard, and was now the bearer of the rear-admiral's duplicate despatches, sailed for Naples.

On the morning of the 14th, after an incredible deal of labour in refitting the ships, the Orion, Bellerophon, Minotaur, Defence, Audacious, Theseus, and Majestic, accompanied by the Franklin, Tonnant, Aquilon, Conquérant, Peuple-Souverain (the two latter scarcely in a seaworthy state), and Spartiate, under the orders of Captain Sir James Saumarez, got under way and stood out of the road. The prizes, being rigged with jury-masts and very weakly manned, could hardly work out of the bay. At length they reached the mouth of it; and, by lying at single anchor for the night, again weighed, and proceeded on their voyage. On the 16th the Heureux, and on the 18th the Mercure and Guerrier, being all, particularly the last, in too bad a state to be refitted, were burnt, as they lay, the first two aground

* For a brief account of this officer's journey, see Appendix, No. 14.

on the beach, and the last at anchor in the road, of Aboukir bay, the scene of their discomfiture. On the 19th Rear-admiral Nelson, in the Vanguard, accompanied by the Culloden and Alexander, sailed for Naples; leaving Captain Hood with the Zealous, Goliath, Swiftsure (who had joined on the 17th), Emerald, Alemène, and Bonne-Citoyenne, to cruise off the port of Alexandria.

The news of the loss of his fleet reached Buonaparte on the 14th of August, when on his way from Salahieh to Cairo, in a despatch from Rear-admiral Ganteaume, delivered by an aide-de-camp of General Kléber's. While reading the despatch, Buonaparte did not betray in his countenance the least trait of the extraordinary sensations which the account must necessarily have caused in his mind. He called the messenger to him, and demanded, in a loud voice, to hear the details. As soon as they were related, Buonaparte said to the aide-de-camp with the utmost sang-froid, "We have no longer a fleet: well, we must either remain in this country, or quit it as great as the Ancients."* The power which this extraordinary man possessed of disguising his feelings was as remarkable, as the facility with which he could turn a disastrous event to his advantage. Great as he was in some matters, Buonaparte could also be mean, where, by being mean, an object was to be attained. Wishing, for some inexplicable reason, to inculpate the brave admiral who was second in command at Aboukir, Buonaparte, on the 24th of August, issued a general order, in which were these words: "The Franklin struck her flag without being dismasted or having sustained any damage."† Rear-admiral Ganteaume, as soon as he discovered this, hastened to defend the character of his brother officer, and pleaded his cause with so much effect, that Buonaparte, yielding a little, issued a second order, stating that Rear-admiral Blanquet had been wounded in the action; but which still left uncontradicted the false assertion, that the Franklin surrendered when in a perfect state. At the instance of Vice-admiral Bruix, the minister of marine, justice was at length done by the directory to the character of that brave officer; but we cannot discover that Rear-admiral Blanquet was ever afterwards employed.

The crippled state of the Nile prizes made it the middle of September, ere they and their escort arrived at Gibraltar. The Peuple-Souverain was in too bad a state to proceed further, and was therefore, under the name of Guerrier, converted into a guard-ship, the only service in which she could be useful. The five remaining prizes, after obtaining a tolerable repair, set sail for England, and arrived in safety at Plymouth. The British

* "Nous n'avrons plus de flotte: eh bien, il faut rester en ces contrées, ou en sortir grands comme les Anciens." – *Victoires et Conquêtes*, tome ix., p. 73.

† "Le Franklin a amené son pavillon sans être démâté et sans avoir reçu aucune avarie." – *Victoires et Conquêtes*, tome ix., p. 107.

government, in order that the captors might not suffer for the prowess they had displayed in riddling the hulls of the captured ships, paid for each of the three destroyed 74s, the Guerrier, Heureux, and Mercure, the sum of 20,000*l.*; which was as much as the least serviceable of the remaining three 74s had been valued at. Of these, the Conquérant was about 50 years old, and of no greater tonnage than the Theseus, the largest ship, except the Minotaur, in the fleet that took her. The Aquilon, or, as newly named, Aboukir, was built at Lorient in the year 1793, measured 1869 tons, and, but for her shattered state, would have been a useful ship; as it was, both of these ships remained in port until they were broken up. Not so with the remaining 74, the Spartiate, nor with the 80-gun ships Tonnant and Franklin. All three of these ships were built at Toulon; owing to which on account of the superior durability of the Adriatic oak,* their value became greatly enhanced. The Tonnant was launched in 1791-2, the Franklin, in the spring of 1797, and the Spartiate, as recently as the commencement of the year in which she was captured. The following are the principal dimensions of the three ships:

	Length of lower deck.	Breadth extreme.	Depth of hold.	Tons.
	ft. in.	ft. in.	ft. in.	
Tonnant	194 2	51 9¼	23 3	2281
Franklin	193 10	51 6¾	23 4½	2257
Spartiate	182 7	49 4½	21 7	1949

The two 80s were of about the same dimensions as the Sans-Pareil, taken by Lord Howe; but the Franklin, in point of materials, workmanship, and qualifications, was considered to be the finest two-decked ship in the world. In order to show what an immensely powerful ship a French 80 is, we here couple, with the force of the Franklin, that of a British three-decker of the 98-gun class:

	British 98.		French 80.		Weight of each of Franklin's guns.		
	No.	Pdrs.	No.	Pdrs.	Cwt.	qrs.	lbs.
First or lower deck	28 long	32	30 long	36 iron	73	2	18
First or lower deck	...	...	2 long	36 brass			
Second deck	30 long	18	32 long	24 iron	51	0	14
Second deck	...	...	2 long	24 brass			
Third deck	30 long	12					
Quarterdeck	8 long	12	12 long	12 iron	33	1	16
Quarterdeck	...	...	2 long	12 brass			
Forecastle	2 long	12	6 long	12 brass			
Poop	6 carrs.	18	6 carrs	36 brass			
	104		92				
Broadside-guns No.	52		46				
Broadside-guns lbs.	1012		1287				

* A very intelligent writer, when remarking on the properties and qualities

The Franklin had ports for, and subsequently mounted, four more guns on her quarterdeck. Without these even, is it not clear that a French 80-gun ship is superior in force to a British 98? This only shows, how necessary it is not to be led away by nominal distinctions.

The name of the Franklin was changed by her new masters to Canopus, that being the ancient name of Eboukhor, or Aboukir, a small town of Lower Egypt, near to the bay in which the battle had been fought. This fine ship still graces the lists of the British navy, not only in her proper self, but in nine noble counterparts, ships that will never be out of vogue while a navy is worth preserving.

We will now give a brief account of the principal honours that were awarded to the conquerors in the battle of the Nile, both by their own country, and by such foreign nations as derived, or considered that they derived, a benefit from the victory. Owing to the capture of the Leander, it was not until the arrival of Captain Capel, on the morning of the 2d of October that the British admiralty became acquainted with the result of the action of the 1st of August. Until that same 2d of October, the whole country rang with complaints against Nelson for his "tardiness;" but, the moment the news was promulgated, the English nation thought they could not do enough to make amends for the wrongs they had inflicted on so bright a gem of their favourite service.

On the 6th of October Sir Horatio was created a peer of Great Britain, by the title of Baron Nelson of the Nile, and of Burnham Thorpe in the county of Norfolk; and, on the 20th of November, when the Parliament met, the king thus expressed himself on the subject of the battle: "The unexampled series of our naval triumphs has received fresh splendour from the memorable and decisive action, in which a detachment of my fleet, under the command of Rear-admiral Lord Nelson, attacked, and almost totally destroyed a superior force of the enemy, strengthened by every advantage of situation. By this great and brilliant victory, an enterprise, of which the injustice, perfidy, and extravagance had fixed the attention of the world, and which was peculiarly directed against some of the most valuable interests of the British empire, has, in the first instance, been turned to the confusion of its authors: and the blow, thus given to the power and influence of France, has afforded an opening, which, if improved by suitable exertions on the part of other powers, may lead to the general deliverance of Europe."

of timber, says, "The oaks of the southern parts of Europe are preferable to any others; those of Provence, the Italian and Turkish sides of the Adriatic sea, have long been esteemed for their superior quality: with these, aided by supplies from Corsica, the ships at Toulon have been built, which are considered to exceed in durability all others constructed of oak." *Knowles on preserving the Navy*, p. 2.

This was followed by a pension of 2000*l.* per annum upon the rear-admiral and his two next heirs male, from the parliament of England, and of 1000*l.* from that of Ireland; also by a unanimous vote of thanks from both those parliaments. Gold medals were presented to Lord Nelson and his captains; and the first lieutenants of all the ships engaged were promoted to commanders. The word "engaged" striking Lord Nelson as likely to lead to a piece of injustice towards the first lieutenant of the Culloden, the rear-admiral, in a letter to Earl St.-Vincent, expresses himself on the subject thus: "I sincerely hope this is not intended to exclude the first lieutenant of the Culloden; for heaven's sake, for my part, if it be so, get it altered." The word was, however, retained, if only to prevent any unengaged ship, under different circumstances, from making a precedent of the case; but Lord Spencer directed Earl St.-Vincent to promote the Culloden's lieutenant: which, we believe, was forthwith done; but we cannot speak with certainty, not having been able to procure the officer's name.

Strictly speaking, too, only the captains that had been "engaged" were to have medals; but the king himself expressly authorized Lord Spencer to present one to Captain Troubridge, "for his services both before and since, and for the great and wonderful exertions he made at the time of the action, in saving and getting off his ship." Lord Nelson's opinion of this officer may be summed up in his own energetic words, when writing to Earl St.-Vincent: "The eminent services of our friend deserve the very highest rewards. I have experienced the ability and activity of his mind and body. It was Troubridge who equipped the squadron so soon at Syracuse: it was Troubridge who exerted himself for me after the action: it was Troubridge who saved the Culloden, when none that I know in the service would have attempted it: it is Troubridge whom I have left as myself at Naples; he is, as a friend and as an officer, a *nonpareil*."*

The East India company, with a proper sense of the benefit they derived from the Nile victory, made a present to Lord Nelson of 10,000*l.*; and the cities of London and Liverpool, and other cities and corporate bodies, took the opportunity of testifying their approbation of the rear-admiral's conduct. Foreign countries, also, were not slow in paying their tribute of respect to the conqueror. The grand signior presented Lord Nelson with a diamond aigrette (*chelengh*), and a sable fur with broad sleeves; also with 2000 sequins, to be distributed among the wounded of his crew. The Ottoman Porte instituted a new order, that of the Crescent; and made the English rear-admiral the first knight-companion of it. The mother of the grand signior sent Lord Nelson a rose, set with diamonds of great value; and many other were the presents and compliments which the rear-

* Clarke and McArthur's Life of Nelson, vol. ii., p. 119.

admiral received from foreign potentates, as tokens of the respect for his talents and bravery.

Our attention is again called to the Mediterranean. While passing Malta, on his way to Gibraltar with the Nile prizes, Sir James Saumarez fell in with the following Portuguese squadron, under the Marquess de Niza:

Gun-ship		
74	Principe-Réal	Rear-admiral the Marquess de Niza. Captain Puysigur.
	Rainha-de-Portugal ...	Captain Stone.
	San-Sebastian	Captain Mitchell.
	Alphonso-Albuquerque	Captain Campbell.
64	Lion (English)	Captain Manley Dixon.
Firesh.	Incendiary (ditto)	Captain George Barker.
Brig.	Falcao (Portuguese) ...	Captain Duncan.

This squadron, since the early part of July, had been detached by Earl St.-Vincent from off Cadiz, as a reinforcement to Rear-admiral Nelson, but, fortunately for the fame of the latter and his companions in arms, was unable to effect its junction in time to participate in the Nile victory.

Being detained off the island of Malta by light airs and calms, Sir James was waited upon by a deputation of the principal inhabitants, to solicit for a supply of arms and ammunition. The Maltese, at the same time, informed the British commodore that the French garrison at Valetta were driven to great distress, and that there was good reason for believing that the appearance of the English squadron would induce the French to surrender, if they were formally summoned. Accordingly, having obtained the concurrence of the Marquess de Niza, Sir James Saumarez, on the 25th of September, sent in a flag of truce, with a proposal couched in the usual terms. After three hours' deliberation, the French general, Vaubois, returned the following answer: "Vous avez, sans doute, oublié que des Français sont dans la place. Le sort des habitans ne vous regarde point. Quant à votre sommation, les soldats français ne sont point habitués à ce style."

The nature of the service upon which he had been ordered, left Sir James no alternative but to take advantage of the breeze which had just sprung up, and proceed on to his destination. Previously, however, to his final departure, Sir James furnished the islanders with about 1200 muskets, and a suitable quantity of ammunition, taken out of the captured ships; and to this seasonable supply the success that afterwards attended the Maltese, in the efforts they made to recover their liberty, was mainly attributable.

Lord Nelson, soon after his arrival at Naples, detached Captain Alexander John Ball, with his own ship the Alexander, and the Culloden and Colossus 74s, the latter commanded by Captain George Murray, for the purpose of co-operating with the

Marquess de Niza in the blockade of Malta. The effective commencement of this service may be dated from the 12th of October; on which day the French force in the island, and the whole of which had been obliged to retire within the walls of the new city of Valetta, consisted of about 3000 soldiers and sailors, the latter under the command of Rear-admiral Decrès, and of 100 Maltese, the only portion of the inhabitants who would take up arms for their invaders. In the harbour of Valetta, lay the French 80-gun ship Guillaume-Tell, and 40-gun frigates Diane and Justice; also the two ex-Maltese 64s, Athénien and Dégo, and 36-gun frigate Carthagénaise, the whole under the command of Rear-admiral Villeneuve. The Généreux, the other French line-of-battle ship which had escaped with the Guillaume-Tell from the battle of the Nile, was at Corfu, in company with her prize, the 50-gun ship Leander.

About 10,000 of the Maltese were in arms against the French, and occupied, as their head-quarters, the old city of Valetta, on the walls of which the Neapolitan colours were flying. The Maltese patriots possessed 23 pieces of cannon, of which 12 were mounted; they had, also, two armed galleys and four gun-boats. Several skirmishes had taken place between the French and the inhabitants, but the former were too strongly posted to be subdued.

On the 24th of October Lord Nelson, with the Vanguard and Minotaur, joined Captain Bull and the Marquess de Niza; and, on the 28th, the commandant of the French troops, 217 in number, in the castle of Goza, the neighbouring island to Malta, signed a capitulation, which Captain Ball had previously negotiated, and Lord Nelson now approved. Captain Creswell, of the Alexander's marines, immediately took possession of the castle, and the British colours were hoisted upon the walls. On the following day, the 29th, the place was delivered up in form to the deputies of the island; the colours of the Sicilian king were substituted for the British, and his majesty acknowledged as the lawful sovereign. The island of Goza contained about 16,000 inhabitants. In the castle were found 24 pieces of ordnance, consisting of four 6, two 12, and eighteen 18 pounders, all good; also 50 barrels of powder, shot in abundance, and 3200 sacks of corn, an article of great value in the then distressed state of the inhabitants.

Although it comports as little with our taste, as with our talents, to follow the French armies in their overthrow of states and countries, we must dip a little into the military occurrences of the latter part of the present year, in order to render the more intelligible some details of coast operations, necessary to be given before we take our final leave of the Mediterranean sea.

Encouraged by the success of Lord Nelson at the battle of The

Nile, the two weak monarchs, Charles-Emanuel of Sardinia, and Ferdinand IV. of Naples, began bestirring themselves to chase away republicanism from the vicinity of their respective kingdoms. The first hostile movement on the part of Charles Emanuel was the signal for the French to enter Turin. This they did on the 9th of December, and in three days made themselves masters of the whole of Piedmont. In a day or two afterwards the dethroned king, by the permission of the French General Jonbert, retired with his family from his late Piedmontaise dominions, and on the 20th of December arrived at Florence on his way to Sardinia.

King Ferdinand began his hostile demonstrations by sending General Mack with a large army to drive the French General Championnet out of Rome. This was accomplished, and on the 29th of November Ferdinand entered Rome in triumph. His Majesty's stay in the far-famed city was, however, of short duration. On the 15th of December the French repossessed themselves of Rome, and, after destroying the fortifications in and around the city, marched for Naples. In a few days afterwards General Championnet possessed himself of the strong fortresses of Pescara. Aware that the city of Naples would soon share the same fate, King Ferdinand, with the whole of the royal family, and their attendants and valuables, embarked, on the 21st of December, on board Lord Nelson's ship, the Vanguard, and, in five days afterwards, arrived at Palermo in Sicily.

It has already been stated that General Buonaparte, when in the summer of 1797 he dissolved the Venetian Republic, possessed himself, on behalf of the French Republic, of several of the islands belonging to Venice in the Adriatic. These were Corfu, Paxu, Ste.-Maura, Theaki, Cephalonia, Zante, and Cerigo. To these islands were attached, as dependencies on the neighbouring continent, the fortresses of Butrinto, Parga, Preveza, and Vonizza. Early in the month of September intelligence reached General Chabot, who had succeeded General Gentili in the chief command of these islands, that a combined Turkish and Russian fleet was waiting in the Dardanelles for a fair wind, to enter the Mediterranean, and commence hostilities against the French.

By the early part of October a powerful army of Turks and Albanians, under Ali-Pacha and his son Mouktar, had swept away the French from all the Ionian dependencies in Albania; and on the 6th of the month the Turco-Russian fleet, composed of 10 Russian sail of the line, four frigates, and several corvettes and brigs, under Vice-admiral Ouchakow, and of about 30 Turkish vessels, ships of the line, caravellas, corvettes, and brigs, under the orders of Cadir-Bey, appeared off the island of Cerigo. The Turkish division had on board about 8000 troops, but the Russian division very few. By the 10th of October the combined Turks and Russians had possessed themselves, with very little difficulty, the garrisons being weak and the principal inhabitants in their favour, of all the islands except Corfu. The number of killed, wounded, and prisoners of the French, at these islands and on the main land, was computed at 1500.

The time occupied by the enemy's fleet in reducing the other islands had enabled General Chabot to make the best dispositions in his power for defending Corfu. His garrison amounted to only 1500 infantry, and about 300 artillerymen. The naval force in the port consisted of the 74-gun ship Généreux, Captain Le Joille, the 50-gun ship Leander (but not in a state to be very useful), 28-gun frigate Brune, Captain Gabriel Denieport, a bomb-vessel, a brig, and four armed galleys. On the 20th the whole of the combined fleet came to an anchor in the Channel of Corfu, and in the course of a few days disembarked their troops. These commenced erecting batteries, and, when at length they were completed, began a cannonade upon the fortifications around the city. The tardy manner in which the besiegers proceeded in their operations, coupled with the skilful manner in which the French general conducted his defence, left the island still unsubdued at the close of the year. In the mean while the Généreux had sailed for Ancona, and the three ex-Venetian 64s, Stengel, La Harpe, and Beyrard, accompanied by some transports, had arrived off the small island of Faro, with a reinforcement of 3000 men from Ancona, intended for Corfu; but, finding how affairs in that island were likely to terminate, the commodore of the squadron steered in another direction.

The French naval force in Alexandria, off which port Captain Samuel Hood, with the three 74-gun ships the Zealous, Goliath, and Swiftsure, and frigates Seahorse, Emerald, and Alemène, was stationed, consisted of the ex-Venetian 64-gun ships Causse and Dupois, French 38-gun frigate Junon, and 36-gun frigates Alceste and Courageuse, and ex-Venetian 38-gun frigates Carrère and Muiron, and 32-gun frigates Leoben, Mantone, and Montenotte, four brig-corvettes, and nine gun-boats, manned on the 26th of August, as officially reported in one of Rear-admiral Ganteaume's intercepted despatches, with 4948 officers and seamen; the whole under the command of Rear-admiral Ganteaume, and subsequently of Commodore Dumanoir-le-Pelley.

It will be recollected, that the above-mentioned ships, although they were armed en flûte on leaving Toulon with the expedition, brought out, and were expressly directed to equip themselves with, their full number of guns. This accounts for their crews being so numerous. The Causse, for instance, appears by her muster-roll to have had 608 men, the Junon 368, and the Courageuse 334. Even the transports could muster among them as many as 3017 officers and men. Exclusive of the force stationed at Alexandria, there were 15 heavy gun-vessels, under commodore Perrée, upon the river Nile, following the motions of the army.

On the 22d of August the 32-gun frigate Alemène, Captain George Hope, cruising off Alexandria, captured the French gun-boat Légère, charged with despatches for General Buonaparte, but which the commanding officer of the vessel threw overboard just as the Alemène was approaching her. This act was not unperceived by two seamen of the frigate, John Taylor and James Harding; who, at the risk of their lives, the ship then going between five and six knots through the water, dashed overboard and saved the whole of them. Each of these brave fellows was afterwards rewarded by the city of London, with a pension of twenty pounds per annum.

On the 25th of August, at 1 A.M., Captain Foley, of the Goliath, despatched the boats of that ship, under the orders of Lieutenant William Debusk, to attack a French armed ketch, which was moored under the guns of the castle of Aboukir. The boats were soon alongside, and a spirited scuffle ensued. Lieutenant Debusk, for some time, fought hand to hand with the French commanding officer. At length after an obstinate resistance of 15 minutes, the French national armed ketch Torride, mounting three long 18-pounders and four swivels, with a complement of 70 men, surrendered. Her commander. Lieutenant de vaisseau Martin Bedar, and 10 of his men were badly wounded. The loss on the part of the British amounted to two wounded, including Lieutenant Debusk. The Torride may serve for a specimen of the description of gun-boat attached to the French fleet at the battle of the Nile. Ten or 12 such vessels, in a calm, would give very serious annoyance to a line-of-battle ship.

On the 2d of September, while Captain Hood with his squadron was cruising off Alexandria, a cutter made her appearance, standing towards the land. The Swiftsure and Emerald fired several shot at her, but the cutter persisted in not bringing to, and at length ran aground a little to the westward of the tower of Marabou. The boats were instantly despatched to bring her off; but, in the mean time, the crew of the cutter had made good their landing, and the cutter herself was shortly afterwards beaten to pieces by the high surf. The shore at this time presented, as far as the eye could reach, nothing but barren, uncultivated sands: very shortly, however, several Arabs were seen advancing, some on horseback, others on foot. The French, who had quitted the cutter, now perceived their mistake; but for the fate of nearly the whole of them, the discovery came too late. The British in the boats pulled lustily towards the shore in the hope of saving their unfortunate enemy, but, on account of the breakers, could not effect a landing in safety. A mishipman of the Emerald, Francis William Fane, with a noble spirit of humanity, threw himself into the water, and swam through a high surf to the shore; pushing before him an empty barrel or keg, to which a rope had been affixed. By this means the cutter's commanding officer, Enseigne de vaisseau Blaise Gaudran, and four of his seamen were saved. It now appeared that the cutter was the Anémone, of four guns and 60 men, from Malta in six days, and Toulon since the 17th of July; having on board Adjutant-general Camin, and Captain Valette, aide-de-camp to General Buonaparte, also a courier with despatches, and a small detachment of soldiers.

The general, perceiving no possibility of escape from the British boats, had ordered M. Gaudran to run the cutter on shore; but the latter represented the danger to his vessel and those on board, from the high surf, and particularly to all who landed, from the numerous hordes of wild Arabs that infested the coast. The general said he would cut his way through them to Alexandria, which was not more than two or three leagues off. No sooner, however, did the French land, than they perceived the Bedouins, who, till this time, had concealed themselves behind the numerous sand-hills near the spot. Terror and dismay now seized on the general and the unfortunate victims of his rash resolve; nor could the British behold their distress without commiseration, although the French had not only by refusing to surrender, brought it on themselves, but had actually fired on the British boats long after all hopes of escape were at an end.

A melancholy spectacle soon forced itself upon the British in the boats. The French officers and men were unresistingly stripped, and many of them murdered in cold blood, without any apparent cause. An Arab, on horseback, unslung his carbine, and presenting it at the general, who, with the aide-de-camp, was on his knees entreating for mercy, drew the trigger, but the piece did not go off. The Arab immediately renewed the priming, and, again, presenting his carbine at the general, shot the aide-de-camp who was kneeling a short distance in the general's rear: the murderer, then, with a pistol, fired at the latter, who instantly fell. The courier endeavoured to escape, but was pursued and killed. The Arab, who got possession of his despatches, instantly rode away with them, but, as was afterwards understood, restored them to the French for a sum of money. On the appearance of a troop of French horse from Alexandria, the Arabs retired to the desert with their surviving prisoners.

In the early part of October Captain Hallowell was detached to Rhodes, to look after an expected reinforcement of Turkish ships. On the 14th the Swiftsure reanchored off Alexandria. During her absence the Portuguese squadron, already named, under the Marquess de Niza, had joined Captain Hood, but, except the Lion 64, Captain Dixon, which remained, had since sailed to co-operate with Captain Ball in the blockade of Malta.

On the 19th two Turkish corvettes joined the British squadron off Alexandria, and on the 20th two Russian frigates, and 16 Turkish vessels, chiefly gun-boats. On the next day, or the day after, Captain Hallowell was detached, with these gun-boats, to the bay of Aboukir, for the purpose of making an attack upon the castle of that name, as well as upon the entrenched camp of the French a little to the southward of it, near lake Maadie.

On the 25th the Swiftsure's launch, pinnace, and yawl, in company with the Turkish gun-boats, on board of which were six British seamen, commenced an attack upon the castle; and in the evening they returned to the ship with one wounded Turk. On the next morning, the 25th, finding that his Turkish allies were very careful of their persons and would not, in consequence, approach near enough to the enemy to produce any effect, Captain Hallowell sent 15 of the Swiftsure's men on board each boat. Thus reinforced, the gun-boats continued daily, until the 28th, to cannonade both the castle and the French camp, but with little effect, and with no greater loss to the allies than one marine killed and one seaman wounded.

The principal part of the mischief done to the French camp arose from its having been set on fire by some shells thrown from the gun-boats. Owing to this, a complaint was made by one or more French officers, admitted to a conference on board the Swiftsure, that the British had "unfairly" used such missiles in the battle in Aboukir bay. "Captain Hallowell," proceeds Mr. Williams, "instantly ordered the gunner to bring up some of those balls, and asked him from whence he had them. To the confusion of the accusers, he related that they were found on board the Spartiate, one of the ships captured on the 1st of August. As these balls were distinguishable by particular marks, though in other respects alike, the captain ordered an experiment to be made, in order to ascertain the nature of them. The next morning I accompanied Mr. Parr, the gunner, to the island of Aboukir: the first we tried proved to be a fire-ball, but of what materials composed, we could not ascertain. As it did not explode, which at first we apprehended, we rolled it into the sea, where it continued to burn under water; a black pitchy substance exuding from it till only an iron skeleton of a shell remained. The whole had been crusted over with a substance that gave it the appearance of a perfect shell. On setting fire to the fusee of the other, which was differently marked, it burst into many pieces: though somewhat alarmed, fortunately none of us were hurt."*

No further use seems to have been made of the Turkish gun-boats; and in the month of December the whole Turkish squadron took its departure from the coast of Egypt. The two

*Williams's Voyage up the Mediterranean, p. 145.

Russian frigates did the same: and so did the Lion, to join Lord Nelson: consequently at the end of the year, Captain Hood had with him only the Zealous and Swiftsure 74s, and one or two frigates. We will now see what naval warfare the year has produced between Great Britain and Spain.

Between the fleet of Earl St. Vincent without, and the fleet of Don Joseph Massaredo within, the harbour of Cadiz, those privileged spies, flags of truce, were frequently passing: and the two admirals, and indeed the two nations, behaved to each other with all that courtesy which distinguishes polished from barbarian belligerents. As it was not an inferiority of force, it must have been either an excess of good breeding, or a deficiency of enterprise, that prevented the Spanish fleet from attempting to sail out, while the British fleet cruised off the port. On the 12th of April, however, when a strong off-shore gale presented a favourable opportunity, the Monarca 74 and two frigates, with a small merchant convoy in charge, allowed themselves to be driven before it, and got fairly to sea.

On the 24th of May the arrival from England of a reinforcement of eight sail of the line, commanded by Rear-admiral Sir Roger Curtis in the Prince 98, allowed the in-shore squadron of the same numerical force, under the orders of Captain Troubridge, to pass into the Mediterranean, as has already been stated. The judicious manner in which the exchange of the two squadrons was effected, so as to deceive the Spaniards, has also been related.* The continued inactive state of the Cadiz fleet leaves us now at liberty to attend to a small expedition, which Earl St.-Vincent, in the latter end of October, detached against the island of Minorca.

On the 7th of November Commodore John Thomas Duckworth appeared off Minorca with his own ship, the Leviathan 74, Captain Henry Digby, Centaur 74, Captain Thomas Markham, 44-gun ships Argo, Captain James Bowen, and Dolphin, Captain Josiah Nisbet, 28-gun frigate Aurora, Captain Thomas Gordon Caulfield, 20-gun ship Cormorant, Captain Lord Mark Robert Kerr, and 16-gun ship-sloop Peterel, Captain Charles Long; also the armed transports Ulysses, Captain Thomas Pressland, Calcutta, Captain Richard Poulden, and Coromandel, Lieutenant Robert Simmonds, hired armed cutter Constitution, Lieutenant John Whiston, and several merchant transports, having on board a detachment of troops commanded by General the Honourable Charles Stuart, destined for the reduction of the island.

The squadron brought to within five miles of the port of Fournella; but, in consequence of the wind blowing directly out of this harbour, the transports proceeded to Addaya creek, not far distant, accompanied by the Argo, Aurora, and Cormorant.

*See p. 152

In the mean time the two line-of-battle ships, for whom there was neither space nor depth of water in the creek, kept plying on and off the harbour of Fournella, in order to create a diversion in that quarter. As the smaller vessels rounded the northern point of Addaya creek, a battery of eight 12-pounders fired one gun at them; but, as soon as the Argo and her two consorts presented their broadsides to view, the people stationed at the battery spiked their guns, blew up their magazine, and fled. The transports, after this, got in without damage, and by 11 A.M. landed one battalion of troops, without the slightest opposition. The men immediately took possession of a neighbouring height; and, with the assistance of a cannonade from the three covering ships, drove off two divisions of Spanish troops that were advancing to regain possession of the battery at the point. By 6 P.M. the whole of the troops, along with eight 6-pounder field-pieces, two howitzers, and eight days' provisions, were safe on shore.

On the same evening the Leviathan and Centaur, who to facilitate the disembarkation had anchored just off the entrance of the creek, weighed, and, with the Argo, turned up to Fournella; while the Aurora and Cormorant, with seven transports, proceeded, by way of a division, off Port-Mahon. On arriving off the harbour of Fournella, the commodore found that the garrison had abandoned the forts: he then, after directing the Centaur and Leviathan to cruise off Fournella and Addaya, to prevent succours from being thrown in, shifted his broad-pendant to the Argo, and, with the able assistance of Captain Bowen, landed the supplies for the army.

After driving off the enemy at Addaya, the troops proceeded on their march to Mercadal; which they entered without resistance, the Spaniards having retired to Ciudadella, and thence to Mahon. On the 9th a detachment of 300 men, under Colonel Paget, marched to Mahon, and compelled Fort-Charles to surrender; whereby the colonel was enabled to remove the boom across the entrance of the harbour, and afford a free passage from without to the Aurora and Cormorant. The transports that had been in company with these ships, as well as those left in Addaya creek, had in the mean time been removed to Fournella, as a more safe and commodious harbour.

Late on the evening of the 11th Commodore Duckworth, who had shifted his broad-pendant back to the Leviathan, and then lay at anchor in Fournella, received information that four ships "supposed to be of the line," were seen between the islands of Minorca and Majorca. The commodore instantly put to sea with the Leviathan, Centaur, and Argo, and the men-of-war transports, Calcutta, Coromandel, and Ulysses, (each ship with a fifth of her crew on shore), and steered towards Ciudadella. At daybreak on the 13th, Ciudadella bearing east by south distant eight or nine miles, five ships were seen from the mast-head standing for that port. Chase was instantly given; where-upon the strange squadron, which consisted of the Spanish 40-gun frigates Flora and Proserpine, and 34-gun frigates Santa-Cazilda and Pomona, with their prize, the late British sloop Peterel, captured at noon on the preceding day, hauled to the wind for Majorca. The Peterel, hauling more up than the rest, was pursued and recaptured by the Argo; while the remainder of the British ships continued in chase of the four Spanish frigates. At 11 P.M. the Leviathan, taking with her the Calcutta and Ulysses, returned to Ciudadella; as, in the course of the next day, the 14th, did the Centaur and Coromandel, the Spanish frigates having completely outsailed their pursuers. It appears that the Spaniards had behaved extremely ill to the officers and crew of the Peterel, having plundered them of almost every thing. The chief part of the clothes belonging to Captain Long and his officers, however, are represented to have been subsequently recovered. This charge of ill-usage was officially contradicted in the Madrid Gazette of the 12th of the following April, but was, nevertheless, essentially true.

Upon his return, on the morning of the 16th, off Ciudadella, Commodore Duckworth found that, owing to the active measures pursued by General Stuart, the town had been summoned on the 14th, and that on the 15th the whole island had surrendered on terms of capitulation, without the loss of a single British subject. The Spanish troops, composing the different garrisons on the island, amounted to between 3000 and 4000 men. A great quantity of ordnance and ordnance-stores was taken in the forts; and in the arsenal at Mahon was found abundance of naval stores. No Spanish ship of war was afloat in any of the harbours; but the keel and stern-frame of a man-of-war brig was found on the stocks at Port-Mahon, with the whole of her timbers and rigging, and a part of her clothing. The vessel was afterwards completed, and launched as the Port-Mahon. She measured 277 tons, and is now the police-depôt moored off Somerset-house. Several gun-boats were also taken, but none of any value. Of merchant vessels there were three; a ship of 540 tons, partly laden with cotton, gum, and drugs, a ship of 200 tons, in ballast, a xebec of 60 tons, laden with horn, and four small tartans.

The conduct of the British seamen and marines, that had been detached from their respective ships to serve on shore, was on this, as we have shown it to have been on many other occasions, of the most exemplary description; so much so, as to call forth from General Stuart the following written testimonial, addressed to Lieutenant William Buchanan, second of the Leviathan, under whose orders the men had been placed: "I have the honour to return you, and the gentlemen employed on shore under your command, my sincere thanks for your activity, zeal, and assistance, in forwarding the light artillery of the army;

neither can too much praise be given to the seamen, for their friendly and cheerful exertions under very hard labour, exertions which were accompanied with a propriety of behaviour which I greatly attribute to your management, and which will ever merit my acknowledgments."

For his services on this occasion, General Stuart was made a knight of the bath; but Commodore Duckworth, who, according to a letter from Earl St.-Vincent to Earl Spencer, expected to be created a baronet, received no mark of royal favour. Without waiting to discuss the merits of the commodore's claims, we shall merely state, that he found a false friend in him whom he requested to urge them. Let Earl St.-Vincent be judged by his own words: "Commodore Duckworth will, I am sure, represent me as lukewarm to the profession if I do not at least state his expectations, which, I understand from Captain Digby, are, to be created a baronet. It is certainly very unusual for a person, detached as he was, under a plan and instruction from his commander-in-chief, from which the circumstances attending the enterprise did not require the smallest deviation, to be distinguished in the manner he looks for. Very different was the case of General Stuart, who received his instructions from the secretary of the war department, and was himself a commander-in-chief."* Had Captain Brenton, whom no one can accuse of being "lukewarm" in Earl St.-Vincent's cause, instead of publishing this letter, thrown it into the fire, he would have escaped the charge so expressively conveyed in the poet's deprecation, "Save me from my friends!"

So much had the Camperdown defeat damped the energies and crippled the resources of the Dutch, that no fleet which they could assemble dared to show itself outside of the Texel. Nor, even were every one of the 16 ships that had met Admiral Duncan restored to her station in the Batavian line, would the aggregate force have been able to contend against the united fleets, which now cruised between Holland and England. The command of the British North-sea fleet still remained with Admiral Lord Duncan; who had under his orders 16 sail of the line (four 74s and twelve 64s), besides more than double that number of 50-gun ships, frigates, and sloops. The Russian vice-admiral Mackaroff cruised also on the same station, with 10 sail of the line, of which number seven were 74-gun ships.

LIGHT SQUADRONS AND SINGLE SHIPS.

On the 3rd of January, at 6 A.M., the British armed sloop or tender George, of six guns (3 or 4 pounders) and 40 men, commanded by Lieutenant Michael Mackey, being on her passage

*Brenton, vol. ii., p. 348.

from Demerara to Martinique, discovered on her lee bow, and at once bore down upon, two sail, which proved to be Spanish privateers; one, a cutter, of 12 guns and 109 men, the other a schooner, of six guns and 68 men. An action immediately commenced between the George, then on the starboard, and the two privateers on the larboard tack. At the expiration of 40 minutes, the two latter evinced an intention to board. The helm of the George was instantly put a-lee, in order to preserve the weather-gage; but the sloop unfortunately missed stays, and, in the act of wearing, fell on board the cutter. The schooner having now gained a position on the George's weather quarter, both vessels immediately grappled the sloop, and made two vigorous but unsuccessful attempts to board. Having, in these assaults, killed the George's sailing-master and seven men, and wounded her commander and 16 men, the two privateers, at the third attempt, carried the British vessel; but not without having paid dearly for their victory, their united loss amounting to 32 men killed, and many more wounded.

A more heroic defence than this little affair exhibits has seldom been witnessed. The George, at the moment her colours were struck, had lost more than half of her crew; that crew having been originally less by three-fourths than the number of her opponents.

On the 5th of January, at 11 P.M., Ushant bearing east-north-east distant 94 leagues, the British 18-pounder* 40-gun frigate Pomone, Captain Robert Carthew Reynolds, steering to the eastward with a fresh breeze at west-south-west, crossed a ship standing under easy sail to the north-west. Chase was instantly given; and, as the stranger, deceived probably by the thickness of the weather as to the Pomone's strength, made no effort to escape, the two ships were presently alongside. An action now commenced; nor was it until the strange ship, whose force was only 26 guns, had lost her mizenmast, and received eight shots between wind and water, that her crew called out for quarter.

Possession was forthwith taken of the Cheri privateer, from Nantes, Captain Chassin, mounting, on her main or single deck, 26 long 12, 18, and 24 pounders, mixed, with a complement of 230 men; of whom 15, including her gallant commander, were killed, and 19 wounded. The privateer's fire had done some injury to the Pomone, having killed one, and wounded four of her men; and, besides cutting away much of her standing rigging, had so damaged the fore and main masts, that it became necessary for their immediate preservation to fish them.

As soon as the prisoners had been shifted, and the Pomone's carpenters had plugged the principal shot-holes in the prize, the Pomone prepared to take her in tow; when the officer in

*See p. 106.

command hailed, that she was sinking. All the boats of the frigate went immediately to the Cheri's assistance; but no efforts could save her. Scarcely had the Pomone's people and the wounded been taken from her, than the Cheri sank alongside; affording an indubitable proof that her unfortunate crew had not called for quarter until every hope of success had fled.

On the 8th of January, at daylight, the Burlings bearing east distant 50 leagues, the British 18-gun brig-sloop Kingfisher (6-pounders), Captain Charles Herbert Pierrepont, discovered on her weather quarter a strange ship, which soon afterwards bore up and stood towards her. At 9 A.M. the Kingfisher tacked; and at 9 h. 30 m. A.M. the stranger, which was the French privateer Betsey, of 16 French 6-pounders, hoisted her colours and began fire. The Kingfisher, then on the opposite tack, opened her fire in passing; the Betsey did the same; but the cannonade was too distant to be very effective. The Betsey then wore round; and the Kingfisher, being unable to gain the weathergage, shortened sail, in order that her opponent might get abreast of her. The Betsey was presently alongside to windward, and a smart action ensued. After it had continued for an hour and a quarter, the Kingfisher's jib-boom was shot away, and the Betsey, taking advantage of that, and of the prevailing light wind, ran ahead under all sail, firing her stern-chasers as soon as she could bring them to bear. Another jib-boom having been got out, and the wind freshening, the Kingfisher was enabled, by 1 P.M. to overtake her opponent, and renew the action. The latter held out for half an hour longer, and then surrendered.

In this well contested and mutually creditable action, the Kingfisher sustained but very trifling damage in hull, rigging, or sails; and, out of a complement of 120 men and boys, had only one man slightly wounded. The Betsey, out of a complement of 118, lost one seaman killed, her first and second captains, and six seamen wounded, three of them mortally, and the remainder badly.

On the 16th of January, early in the morning, as the British 20-gun ship Babet, Captain Jammett Mainwaring, was cruising about midway between the islands of Martinique and Dominique, an armed schooner was observed standing towards her. Soon afterwards the wind died away; and the schooner, having made out the Babet to be a man of war, took to her sweeps and rowed off. This afforded to Mr. Samuel Pym, first lieutenant of the ship, an opportunity of volunteering an attempt to capture the schooner by the boats. Accordingly Lieutenant Pym, with the pinnace and launch, containing between them 24 men, proceeded on the service.

After rowing four hours, and reaching a distance of three leagues from the ship, the boats arrived within gun-shot of the schooner; who immediately opened her fire upon them. The pinnace, having out-pulled the launch, was the first boat alongside. Lieutenant Pym and his 12 men at once boarded, and in spite of a very strenuous opposition, carried the schooner. She proved to be the Désirée, of six carriage-guns (4-pounders, probably) and 46 men; of whom she had three killed, eight drowned, and 15 badly wounded. The pinnace sustained a loss of one seaman killed, one marine drowned, a midshipman, Mr. Aslinhurst, and four seamen badly wounded, and Lieutenant Pym and the remainder of his boat's crew slightly wounded. The launch, much to the regret of those on board of her, did not reach the schooner till her colours were in the act of being struck. Few enterprises of this description, bold as they commmonly are, exhibit so much gallantry as the capture of the Désirée schooner.

On the 23rd of January, in latitude 50° north, longitude 12 west, the British 36-gun frigate Melampus, Captain Graham Moore, came up with and engaged the French corvette Volage, of 22 guns (20 long 8s and two long 18s) and 195 men; which, after a short but close action, struck her colours. The Melampus had two men mortally, and three dangerously wounded; The Volage, four killed and eight wounded.

The prize, although a national ship, had been lent to certain merchants of Nantes, and by them been fitted out as a cruiser. Her commander M. Desageneaux, according to his own account, was a capitaine de frégate, and his officers also appear to have belonged to the national marine; but, in the present instance, they all had a *congé*, or furlough for three months, to enable them to serve on board a ship, then in the temporary employ of private individuals. The Volage was a fine corvette measuring 523 tons, and was added to the British navy as a 20-gun ship.

On the 3d of February, at daylight, Vigo bearing east distant about 17 leagues, the British 14-gun brig-sloop, Speedy, (4-pounders), Captain Hugh Downman, discovered a strange brig, with all sail set, bearing down on her. This was the French privateer Papillon, a large brig of 360 tons, mounting 14 guns (but pierced for 18), four of them described as long 12s, and the remainder long 8-pounders, with a crew of 160 men. At 3 P.M. the Papillon, being about half a mile from the Speedy, hauled to the wind, and opened her fire. Whereupon the Speedy made sail to close, engaging her adversary until 5 h. 30 m. P.M.; when the latter tacked and stood off. The Speedy also went about and continued to engage until 7 h. 30 m. P.M.; when the Papillon, profiting by her superiority of sailing and the lightness of the wind, got out of gun-shot. Owing to the great swell that prevailed, the Speedy received no other injury than a shot through her fore topmast, and some damage to her rigging. It now fell calm, and the two vessels, in spite of every effort at the Speedy's sweeps, separated.

At midnight the privateer fired several guns at, and ultimately recaptured, a brig which the Speedy had the day before taken from the Spaniards; and on board of which the master, Mr. Marshall, with 12 seamen had been placed. No sooner, however, did these discover what fate was awaiting them, than first battening below the 12 Spaniards that were on board, Mr. Marshall and his men took to their boat, and fortunately reached their vessel although she was four leagues to windward.

On the 4th, at daylight, came a breeze of wind, that enabled the Speedy to fetch up to her antagonist. At 8 A.M. the latter, being within gun-shot, tacked and made sail, rowing at the same time with her sweeps. The chase was continued without effect until noon; when the Papillon, finding that she had the heels of the British vessel, shortened sail, wore, and stood towards her, with a red flag flying at the main topgallantmast head. At half an hour after noon, having again got within gun-shot, the Speedy recommenced the engagement with the wind upon the larboard quarter. At 2 P.M. just as the privateer's fire began to slacken, and the Speedy was about to lay her on board, the former wore, and came to the wind on the starboard tack; but, finding the Speedy close upon her starboard quarter, the Papillon took the advantage of the Speedy's braces and bow-lines being shot away, and put before the wind under all sail. The Speedy immediately wore after her; the two vessels firing musketry at each other for 20 minutes. The chase was continued, with every sail the Speedy could set, until 7 P.M.; by which time the Papillon had run herself completely out of sight. The Speedy then hauled to the wind, making short tacks all night, in the hope to fall in with her prize. Fortunately daylight on the 5th showed the latter to windward; and, at 10 A.M. the brig was retaken with 10 Frenchmen on board, part of the crew of the Papillon.

The Speedy lost one lieutenant (Richard Dutton), her boatswain, and three seamen killed, and four badly wounded. The loss on board the Papillon, although from her discontinuing the engagement in all likelihood severe, could not of course be ascertained; especially as the captured portion of her crew had quitted her on the previous night. From the decided disparity of force in this action, the result, although a trophiless one to the British brig, was highly creditable to the bravery and discipline of her officers and crew. The Speedy had received so much damage in her masts, bowsprit, main boom, and spars generally, as well as in her rigging, both standing and running, that she was compelled to put into Lisbon to refit.

On the 25th of February, at 7 A.M. Cromer, bearing west-south-west, distant 16 leagues, the British hired armed cutter Marquis-Cobourg, of twelve 4-pounders and 66 men and boys, Lieutenant Charles Webb, after a nine hours' chase and a run of 100 miles during half the time before a hard gale of wind at west-north-west, came up with the French lugger-privateer Revanche, of

16-guns and 62 men; and to a smart fire from whose musketry and stern-chasers, the Cobourg had been exposed for the last two hours of the nine. A spirited action now ensued, during which the lugger made two attempts to board the cutter, but was repulsed. After a two hours' running fight, close alongside, a well-directed broadside from the Cobourg shot away the Revanche's main and mizen masts by the board, and also her fore yard; whereupon the privateer's men called for quarter.

No sooner was the Revanche taken possession of, than she was found to be sinking, the effects of more than 40 shots which the lugger had received between wind and water. The utmost promptitude was used in shifting the prisoners, and getting back the Cobourg's people, who had been placed in possession; nor was it without the utmost difficulty that the whole were saved from going to the bottom in the prize. The Cobourg had sustained considerable damage in her spars, sails, and rigging; but was fortunate enough to escape with only two men wounded. Her fire, on the other hand, had killed seven, and wounded eight men belonging to the lugger, described as the largest that sailed out of Calais.

On the 22d of March, at 7 A.M., as the British 74-gun ship Canada, Captain Sir John Borlase Warren, 44-gun frigate Anson, Captain Philip Charles Durham, and 38-gun frigate Phaëton, Captain the Honourable Robert Stopford, were cruising about eight leagues to the westward of Pointe-Rousonirez, coast of France, with a moderate breeze at north-north-east, the Anson discovered a strange ship in the east quarter, standing to the southward. This was the French 36-gun frigate Charente, Captain Alain-Adélaïde-Marie Bruilhac, a few days from Rochefort, bound to Cayenne, with 193 unfortunate people, banished for their political sins to that unhealthy climate.

The chase continued throughout the day, with light and variable breezes; and at 1 h. 30 m. A.M. on the 23d, the Phaëton got near enough to open a fire upon the Charente; who, after returning the fire with her stern-chasers, hauled up for the channel des Graves, or southern passage into the river Gironde. This change of course brought the Charente within the range of the Canada's guns; and several broadsides were interchanged until about 4 A.M., when the Canada struck on a sand-bank, and remained fast.

The 74's signal for assistance occasioned a discontinuance of the chase by the Phaëton and Anson; and the Charente, after grounding on the Olives, and being obliged, in consequence, to throw the greater part if not the whole of her guns overboard, reached the river of Bordeaux. What loss, if any, the Charente sustained by the fire of the Phaëton and Canada, we are unable to state; but we believe the ship was greatly damaged by getting on shore: not, however, to the extent, as Sir John Warren in his public letter states, of "being bilged," or the French frigate would have remained where she had struck, instead of sailing again on a cruise as the Charente subsequently did. The Canada remained on the sand-bank about two hours and a half: when, having started 20 tons of water and being favoured by the rise of the tide, the ship floated off, making 14 inches of water per hour.

Great credit was undoubtedly due to Captain Bruilhac, for his persevering and, as we have seen, successful efforts to save his ship from capture by a force so superior; and we are a little surprised that no account of the escape of the Charente should have found its way into any French naval work, especially as the French minister of marine made a public boast of the Charente's performance.

On the 17th of April, the British king's schooner Recovery, of ten 3-pounders, and from 40 to 50 men and boys, commanded by Lieutenant William Ross, being on a cruise in the West Indies, fell in with the French privateer-schooner Revanche, of 10, believed to have been 4 pounders, and 54 men, commanded by Citizen Antoine Martin. The latter hove to for the Recovery, who was to windward, and reserved her fire until she got within pistol-shot. At the end of a 45 minutes' mutual cannonade, the Revanche, having had all her sails but the standing-jib cut to pieces, attempted to escape by the aid of her sweeps; but the Recovery, having her sails perfect, easily kept way with her antagonist, and at length compelled the Revanche to surrender.

The French privateer had three men killed and nine wounded, four of them dangerously. The Recovery did not have a man hurt, and suffered no greater damage than one gun dismounted and a few small shot in her masts. Lieutenant Ross describes his crew as consisting chiefly of young and inexperienced boys and lads, and yet declares that their conduct would have done honour to the most experienced seamen.

On the 7th of May, as the British 14-gun brig-sloop Victorieuse, Captain Edward Stirling Dickson, was passing to leeward of Guadeloupe, having in charge the trade from Trinidad to St.-Kitt's, two French privateers, a schooner of 12 guns and 80 men, and a sloop of six guns and 50 men, bore down for the purpose of carrying the brig by boarding. The Victorieuse soon compelled the sloop, which was the Brutus, Captain Rousel, to strike her colours; with a loss of four killed, and four wounded. Owing to Captain Dickson's not being able to chase far from his convoy, the schooner effected her escape; but evidently with considerable damage, and no doubt a proportionate loss. The Victorieuse sustained no loss whatever.

We do not know the calibers of the guns of these privateers, but, taking the number of men on board each as a guide, we should consider that the guns were 4, or, at most, 6 pounders. With respect to the Victorieuse, she was an anomaly as a 14-gun brig. Her establishment of guns and men, as ordered for her on the 6th of October, soon after her capture from the French, were 12 long 12-pounders, and two 36-pounder carronades, with a crew of 130 men and boys: and the size of the Victorieuse perhaps justified the armament, as she measured 349 tons. A contemporary describes the Victorieuse as mounting in this action "fourteen 6-pounders;"* against this statement we have nothing to offer, but the admiralty-order fixing the brig's establishment.

Although somewhat out of chronological order, we will here narrate another creditable performance by Captain Dixon, and those under his command.

On the 3d of December, at 2 A.M., the Victorieuse and 14-gun brig-sloop Zephyr, Captain William Champain, having received on board, by order of Colonel Picton, commanding at Trinidad, a major and 40 men of the York Rangers, landed the troops, along with a party of seamen near the river Caribe, in the island of Margarita, in order to attack the forts (how many, or of what force, does not appear in the official letter) in the rear, while the two brigs cannonading them in front; but, at daylight, the Spanish commandant sent to beg the British not to fire, as he would give them immediate possession. This he did; and the guns were brought off, and the troops re-embarked. The two brigs then made sail for the port of Gurupano, on the same island, and at 4 P.M. arrived there. Observing a French privateer in the harbour, Captain Dickson sent in a flag of truce, to say to the commandant of the fort, that the British were determined to take out the privateer, and warning him not to fire at them. The commandant replied that he would protect the vessel, which was the Couleuvre, of six guns and 80 men, and that the British should give him up the guns they had taken at Rio-Caribe.

No time was now to be lost; and having landed Major Laureil with the troops, also 30 seamen detached from the two brigs, and commanded by Lieutenants William Case and —— M'Rensey, Captain Dickson anchored with the Victorieuse and Zephyr, and opened a smart fire on both forts, one of which mounted four, the other two guns. In 10 minutes the troops and seamen, amounting together to no more than 70 men, carried the lower fort; and immediately the Spanish flag at the upper fort was hauled down and replaced by a French one. At the end of five minutes more, this fort also surrendered. The number of men that garrisoned the two forts, was estimated at 300; and who, as well as the crew of the privateer effected their escape. The Couleuvre and the guns on shore were carried off, and the forts destroyed. The casualties to the British were two men killed and two wounded, and some slight damage to the masts and rigging of the Victorieuse.

*Brenton, vol. ii., p. 441.

On the 4th of May, at 4 A.M. as a small British squadron, composed of the 38-gun frigate Arethusa, Captain Thomas Wolley, 12-pounder 32-gun frigate Niger, Captain Edward Griffith, and 44-gun ship Argo, Captain James Bowen, was cruising off the mouth of the river Seine, a fishing-boat pulled alongside the Argo, and was found to have on board Captain Sir Sidney Smith, Lieutenant John Westley Wright, and two French gentlemen, one of whom was Sir Sidney's particular friend, Mr. Phelipeaux. This party had effected their escape from the temple at Paris by means, as it would appear, of a forged order of removal to another prison, planned and executed by Mr. Phelipeaux. Sir Sidney and his companions proceeded straight to Rouen; and, embarking there in a boat, reached the British squadron as already related. The moment he learnt who were the persons received out of the French fishing-boat, Captain Wolley directed Captain Bowen to part company for England; and on the 6th, in the evening, the Argo came to at Spithead.

On the 16th of June the British 12-pounder 32-gun frigate Aurora, Captain Henry Digby, cruising off the bay of Curmes on the north-west coast of Spain, sent two of her boats, under the orders of Lieutenant Henry Lloyd, to destroy some vessels which had just run in there for shelter. The boats, covered in their approach by the frigate, succeeded in burning a brigantine laden with hemp and iron, and in scuttling a schooner laden with various merchandise, and got back to the Aurora with three men wounded, two of them slightly, by musketry from the village or town at the bottom of the bay, and by a wall-piece mounted to an adjacent height.

On the 19th, while standing in for Cape Prior, in thick hazy weather, with the wind from the westward, the Aurora discovered an enemy's ship, carrying 18 or 20 guns, and five merchant brigs, standing along the land to the eastward, in the direction of the harbour of Cedeira; which, at about 4 P.M., the armed ship and convoy all entered. The Aurora immediately stood in after the vessels, and at 4 h. 30 m. opened a fort on the north-east side of the town; which, as well as the ship, now with French colours flying, commenced a fire upon the Aurora. This the frigate promptly returned, but, soon losing the wind and being nearly land-locked, found it necessary, with the way she still possessed, to tack, and stand out. At about 6 P.M. the Aurora, by towing and sweeping, got out of the harbour without damage or loss; having left two of the brigs on shore, the corvette or privateer at the extremity of the harbour, and the fort damaged, and, it was thought, silenced.

On the 22d the Aurora, being then on the south shore of the bay of Biscay, off Cape Machichicao, chased a ship, apparently a corvette or privateer of 20 guns, scudding before a north-west wind. At about 3 h. 30 m. P.M., on discovering the Aurora to be a frigate, the ship hauled in for the land, and, hoisting

French colours, anchored with three cables ahead in an opening under a fort at or near to a place called Baquio. At 4 P.M. the Aurora brought to within half gun-shot of the ship, and opened upon her so well-directed and effectual a fire, that by the fourth broadside her cables and masts were shot away, and she soon afterwards drifted on shore, the sea making a fair breach over her. The British frigate now made sail, to weather the eastern land, and at length succeeded, carrying out from 13 to 19 fathoms' water, the fort firing at her all the while, but without effect.

On the 21st of June, at daybreak, his Britannic majesty's packet Princess-Royal, Captain John Skinner, of six guns (two 6s and four 4s) and 32 men and boys, exclusive of 17 passengers, nine days from Falmouth, on her way to New-York with a mail, fell in with the French brig-privateer Aventurier, of 16 guns (14 long 4-pounders, and two 12-pounder carronades) and 85 men and boys. At 5 A.M. the privateer made sail after the packet; who, on her part, crowded all sail to get away, but without much effect, the prevailing light air and smooth sea giving an advantage to the former in the use of her numerous sweeps. At 7 P.M. the Aventurier, hoisting English colours, fired a shot, which the Princess-Royal returned. The privateer fired another shot, and then dropped in the wake of the packet, as if intending to defer the attack until daylight.

On the 22d, at 3 h. 30 m A.M., the Aventurier came suddenly up with in pistol-shot, and fired a broadside, accompanied by musketry. This the Princess-Royal, having brought five of her six guns, including the two 6-pounders, to bear on one side, returned with spirit. One of the 6-pounders was commanded by a lieutenant, who was going out to join the 64-gun ship St. Albans; and the male passengers kept 14 muskets in constant use. Captain Skinner was unable to use one, having lost his right arm on board a frigate in the former war. After a two hours' engagement, the French privateer took to her sweeps and rowed off. One of the packet's 6-pounders was now brought to bear as a stern-chaser, and struck the privateer twice in the counter, to the evident confusion of the people on board. At 6 A.M. the privateer being entirely out of gun-shot, the packet ceased firing, and commenced repairing her damages, which were rather serious. Her sails and rigging were much cut, also her spare spars and boats: several round shot had struck the hull, and one large one had entered the counter; but yet the Princess-Royal had not a man hurt. On board the privateer, were 30 English and American prisoners. From some of these it was afterwards ascertained, that the Aventurier had all her masts shot through and her sails and rigging much cut, had received 19 shot in her hull below the wales, and sustained a loss of two men killed and four wounded. Her injuries, indeed, were so great, that the privateer was compelled to break up her cruise and return to Bordeaux to refit. Such a result did great credit to the skill, as well as gallantry, of the packet's crew; nor must we omit to state that, when all the 4-pound cartridges were consumed, Captain Skinner's sister and her maid employed themselves in the bread-room in making new ones.

On the 26th of June, at 4 P.M., the British 38-gun frigate Seahorse, Captain Edward James Foote, cruising off the coast of Sicily, fell in with the French 36-gun frigate Sensible, Captain Bourdé. Being charged with despatches, and having the general of division Baraguay-d'Hilliers and his suite, with a quantity of valuables on board, which she had brought from Malta and was carrying to Toulon, the Sensible crowded sail to escape. The chase, the latter part of it a running fight, continued until 4 A.M. on the 27th; when, the island of Pantellaria bearing west-north-west distant 12 leagues, the Seahorse came up with the Sensible. A close action now commenced, and continued for eight minutes; when the Sensible, having, besides much damage in her masts and rigging, received several shot in her hull, 36 of them between wind and water, and sustained a severe loss in killed and wounded, hauled down her colours.

The Seahorse, out of a complement, including some seamen belonging to the Culloden, of 292 men and boys, had one seaman and one drummer killed, her first lieutenant (David Wilmot, slightly), 13 seamen, one corporal, and one private of marines wounded. According to the British official account, the Sensible, out of a crew, including a few passengers, of 300, had 18 men killed, her first and second captains, and 35 men wounded; but, according to the French accounts, the Sensible's loss amounted to 25 killed, and 55 wounded.

The fact, that the Seahorse mounted 46 guns, consisting of long 18 and 9 pounders, and (14 it appears) 32-pounder carronades, and the Sensible, 36 guns, consisting of long 12 and 6 pounders, and (four, we believe) brass 36-pounder carronades, renders it tolerably certain that, even had the French frigate been quite free to act on the offensive, the superiority of her opponent's force would have led to a defeat. The Sensible's heavy loss, too, proves that she did not surrender until she had felt the effects of that superiority; and yet the French minister of marine thus publicly notices the capture of the Sensible: "It is time that the navy should know, that it is not enough to justify the loss of a ship, that it surrenders only to superior force; it is necessary that a long, an obstinate, and a terrible resistance should alleviate the sorrow of a defeat, and soften the regret of the republic. The executive directory will not suffer themselves to be seduced by any consideration repugnant to this determination, which I now communicate to you. It will give its confidence only to officers who shall deserve it by their talents and courage." We think we could point out some instances of French captures, to which this spirited denunciation more suitably applies than to the case of the Seahorse and Sensible.

A better feeling, however, appears afterwards to have prevailed. General Baraguay-d'Hilliers succeeded in convincing the directory that the French frigate had been bravely defended against a very superior force, and had been surrendered only when no other alternative remained. In consequence of this, a court-martial was ordered upon Captain Bourdé. It sat at Toulon, and honourably acquitted him. In this instance a clear exposition of the relative force of the ships, and a compliment to the behaviour of the weaker combatant, in the British official account, might have prevented the French directory from passing so unmerited a censure upon a brave officer.

According to some extracts from the French journals of November, 1797, the Sensible, with the 38-gun frigate Junon, 24-gun "corvette" (or which may be Anglicised 28-gun frigate) Brune, 20-gun corvette Fauvette, and 14-gun brig Railleur, had been hired by Messieurs Petit and company, merchants of Toulon. As this may elucidate what we had occasion to say on this subject at a former page, we shall give a translated abstract of the charter-party. "These five vessels, well known for their superior sailing, belong to the navy of the republic, and at present are at Toulon: they form *part* of those which the government has lent for the purpose of cruising, upon conditions, of which the principal are these: the vessels to be completely fitted out by the government; the freighters being only obliged to provide for and pay the crew. The cost of revictualling and touching at any place to be also at the charge of the freighters; but the costs for repairs of masts, for cordage, ordnance, and ordnance-stores, to be defrayed by the republic. The freighters to propose the commanders, who must be approved by the minister of marine. The freighters to choose the station for cruising, and the places at which the vessels are to stop. The net produce of the prizes to be divided as follows: one-third to the crew, and a third of the remaining two-thirds to the republic. The sale of the prizes to be confided to the freighters. If, during the existence of any such contract, or hiring, peace should be concluded between the belligerent powers, and the freighters should not have covered their advance, the vessels in use shall continue at their disposal for any commercial expedition. Any dispute that may arise to be referred to arbitration." The Egyptian expedition had seemingly restored all the hired ships to the owners, the French republic.

Earl St.-Vincent, when the Seahorse joined the fleet with her prize, manned the Sensible with six sailors from each ship, and had her completely equipped for sea in 12 hours. The admiral, also, made a commander of Lieutenant Wilmot, and appointed him to the Alliance frigate-flûte. Among the effects found on board the Sensible at her capture, was a brass cannon formerly taken from the Turks, and which Louis XIV. had presented to the knights of Malta; also a gilt silver model of a galley. After her arrival at Spithead in the following February, the Sensible, on account probably of her age and weakness, was not fitted out as a cruising frigate: as a troop-ship, however, she became useful for some years.

When Rear-admiral Sercey arrived at the Isle of France in June, 1796,* and during his subsequent stay there, the 36-gun frigate Preneuse and ship-corvette Brûle-Gueule were absent on a cruise in the Mosambique channel. Hence it was only on his return to Port-Louis from Batavia in February, 1797, that he was joined by those two ships. With his force thus augmented to seven frigates and a large corvette, the rear-admiral sailed from the Isle of France in the latter end of the summer, having on board the troops, in number, including the artillery, very few short of 1000, that had accompanied the two agents from France; and which troops the French squadron was now carrying to Batavia, ostensibly to succour the Dutch, but in reality to rid the colony of their presence, they having already attempted to excite an insurrection among the blacks. Rear-admiral Sercey carried the troops to their destination, disembarked them there, and returned to the Isle of France, without any occurrence of consequence.

On the 19th of January, 1978, two ambassadors from Tippoo-Saib arrived at the Isle of France, to solicit succours. They were accompanied by a Frenchman named Debay, as an interpreter, and by another Frenchman named Ribaud; who having, in the latter end of 1796, with the privateer he commanded, been forced by stress of weather into Mangalore, was arrested and thrown into prison. Questioned soon afterwards by Tippoo, as to the inclination and means possessed by France to second him in the war which he meditated against the British, Ribaud, in order to obtain his liberty, exaggerated the resources of the republic, and assured the sultan, not only that he might, on the part of France, reckon upon a powerful co-operation, but that there were already at the Isle of France an immense body of troops, which only waited his orders. These reports of the wily Frenchman determined Tippoo to commence hostilities, and led, as we shall hereafter see, to his ruin.

The principal part of the troops on the island had already been transported to Batavia. All therefore that the governor could now do, was to forward to France, with the utmost expedition, the letters from Tippoo-Saib. Accordingly the frigates Vertue and Régénérée were ordered upon this service; the latter commanded, as before, by Captain Willaumez, the former by Commodore Magon, late of the Preneuse; and who, at the

*See vol. i., p. 354.

particular desire of Rear-admiral Sercey, had exchanged with Captain l'Hermite. These two frigates set sail from the Isle of France on the 23d of January, but, unfortunately for an object that required despatch, not by themselves. Early in the month two ships belonging to the Philippine company, laden with silk, indigo, spices, and other precious merchandise, to the estimated value of four millions of piastres, had arrived at Port-Louis from Manilla. For 60,000 piastres, the colonial government agreed to convoy these galleons to Spain; and, with the two heavy-sailing hulks in company, the Vertu and Régénérée proceeded on their voyage.

We will now relate an exploit performed in the quarter whence these two richly-laden ships had recently arrived; an exploit in some degree connected with the proceedings of Rear-admiral Sercey's squadron, inasmuch as it owed its success to a simulation of two of his ships. On the 5th of January the British 38-gun frigate Sibylle, Captain Edward Cooke, and 12-pounder 32-gun frigate Fox, Captain Pulteney Malcolm, sailed from the road of Macao, for the purpose of reconnoitring the Spanish force in the Philippines, and, in particular, to endeavour to possess themselves of two richly-laden ships supposed to be nearly ready to sail from Manilla, the capital of the island of Luconia. On the 11th the two frigates made the island, and on the 12th, while coasting down it with French colours flying, captured a small vessel from the port off which they were bound. After taking out of her 3900 dollars, and ascertaining from her master that, of the Spanish squadron, reported by him to consist of four sail of the line and four frigates, in Cavita, the port belonging to the city of Manilla, one ship only of each class was in a state to put to sea, Captain Cooke allowed the vessel to proceed on her voyage. It being intended to pass for two frigates of M. Sercey's squadron, the Sibylle, we presume, for the Seine, and the Fox for the Prudente or Régénérée, the two captains began taking measures to disguise their ships.

On the 13th, at about 8 P.M., every thing being ready, the Sibylle and Fox entered the bay of Manilla, and, passing the small island of Corrigidore, whereon the signal-house stands, without detection, came to an anchor at about 11 P.M. in 14 fathoms, each ship keeping the topsails at her mast-heads, to be ready for a sudden start. On the 14th, at 5 h. 30 m. A.M., the two frigates weighed, and, hoisting French colours, began working up the bay. At sunrise three gun-boats made their appearance to leeward, also bound up the bay. At 9 A.M. the Fox opened the ships in Cavita road, which were seen to consist of three sail of the line and three frigates: of the six ships, four were without masts, and the remaining two, with only their lower masts in. The road of Cavita was about three miles distant from the leading frigate, the Fox; and, at 11 A.M., when the latter was about the same distance from the town of Manilla, lying nearly becalmed, a Spanish guard-boat, rowing 12 oars, and having a crew of 15 officers and men, including the second captain of the 34-gun frigate Maria-de-la-Cabeya, at anchor in Cavita, came on board, to inquire what ships the strangers were, and whence they came. Mr. Bernard, the pilot of the Fox, and who spoke French and Spanish, informed the visiting officer that the two frigates belonged to M. Sercey's squadron; that they had been cruising on the coast of China, and that, the crews being sickly, they were come to Manilla for refreshment, as well as to form a junction with the Spanish squadron, a part of which, a hope was expressed, would accompany them to sea. The Spanish captain said, in reply, that he had been directed by the governor to acquaint them that their wants should be supplied; but that he believed none of the ships in the port could be got ready in less than two months, as they were in want of every species of stores, and their crews were sickly.

At this moment Captain Cooke came on board, and Captain Malcolm introduced him as Commodore Latour; a name that, as the Spanish captain was doubtless as ignorant of that officer's death as the two British captains, answered as well as any other. To the new commodore many questions were put; and, having in full recollection the ability he had about four years before displayed at Toulon, we can have no doubt that Captain Cooke acted his part to the life. A very interesting, and, to one of the parties at least, very instructive conversation ensued, and lasted nearly an hour, during which the ceremony of drinking success to the united exertions of the Spaniards and French against the British, was not forgotten. Having pumped every thing they wanted out of their unsuspecting guest, and observing other boats approaching from the shore, Captains Cooke and Malcolm made known who they really were. The Spanish captain nearly fainted with astonishment; but a bumper of Madeira, coupled with an assurance that he should not be detained as a prisoner, recovered him.

Meantime the two boats had pulled alongside. One was Admiral Don Martin Alaba's barge, rowing 20 oars, with 23 officers and men, including the governor's nephew; the other a felucca, rowing 20 oars, with 23 officers and men, and among them one of Admiral Alaba's aides-de-camp, bringing compliments of congratulation on the safe arrival of their friends the French, with information, that all the latter could want or wish would be supplied; and that launches, with anchors and cables to assist the frigates into the harbour, were getting ready.

As soon as these new visitors had joined their friends in the Fox's cabin, no other point being now to be gained by deception, they also were made acquainted with the *rusé* that had been played off upon them. If they were surprised and mortified at first, the rear-admiral and his suite were still more so on witnessing, as they soon did, the success of another part of the plan, so happily conceived and executed by their enterprising enemies. While, for instance, this farce was enacting in the cabin, the Spanish boats' crews had been handed to the deck below. A party of British seamen then exchanged clothes with them, and, stepping into the Spanish boat, pushed off, in company with some of the boats belonging to the two frigates, towards three Spanish gun-boats, that lay just without the river leading to the town. The people in the gun-boats, being taken by surprise, were unable to resist the impetuosity of the British boarders, and actually surrendered, without a trigger's being pulled. One boat was No. 31, of 30 oars, carrying one long brass 36-pounder and four swivels, with a complement of 52 men; and the two others were Nos. 33 and 34, one of the 28, the other of 30 oars, each mounting one long 24-pounder and four swivels, with a complement of 50 men. A part of the crews, however, were either not on board, or succeeded in reaching the shore, as only 118 officers and men were brought away.

The capture of the gun-boats being perceived from the shore, and thought rather unaccountable, another felucca-rigged boat, rowing 18 oars, with 21 officers and men, including among them the captain of the port, came off, to know why the boats were detained, and to say that, if they were not immediately restored, the authorities in the town would consider the two frigates as enemies, and act accordingly. Previously to any serious reply to this message, the last-mentioned Spanish officer and his men were handed below. Up to this time the weather had remained perfectly calm, and might account for the frigates not entering the road to anchor; but now a breeze sprang up that facilitated discovery, and put a stop to all further stratagem.

From the different Spanish officers that had been brought on board, much information was obtained respecting the naval force in the port; which consisted, by their account, of the 74-gun ships Europa, Magnanime, and San-Pedro-Apostol, and the 34-gun frigate Maria-de-la-Cabeya, all under equipment at the arsenal, but not, for the reasons already mentioned, in a state to put to sea. There were also several gun-boats, all new, coppered, and, to judge from those captured, very well appointed. It appeared, likewise, that the merchant ships Rey-Carlos and Marquesetta, whose reputed rich cargoes had brought the two English frigates to the Philippines, were then lying in the Cavita. The former was supposed to be aground; and the latter was represented to have relanded her treasure on the appearance, some days back, of a suspicious vessel, ascertained to have been the 44-gun ship Resistance, Captain Edward Pakenham.

At 4 P.M. Captain Malcolm gave the Spanish officers a good dinner; and their men were at the same time regaled below with fresh China beef and grog in abundance. The discovery, that the two frigates were enemies, had now extended itself all round the bay. The kind usage to the prisoners while on board, and the circumstances of now permitting them to go on shore in the captured guard-boat, barge, and two feluccas, without parole or restriction of any sort, could not fail to impress, as well upon the prisoners themselves, who were in number 200, as upon the natives in general of these remote islands, very favourable ideas of the British character. The particular season of the year, in which this successful ruse was practised, being that wherein the Spaniards, from the prevalence of the monsoons, considered themselves in comparative security, a few additional ships and men might have captured the town and vessels of war, and destroyed the arsenal. As it was, the Sibylle and Fox had made a good morning's work: they had taken seven boats, about 200 men, three great guns, 12 swivels, 27 muskets, 32 cutlasses, 18 half-pikes, 13 pistols, 153 round shot, 137 grape shot, and 100 shells, with, of course, a proportion of powder and of musket-cartridges; all without the slightest casualty.

On the same evening, the two British frigates, accompanied by the three prize gun-boats, in charge of the three lieutenants, Thomas Fortescue Kennedy, Charles Elphinstone, and George Rutherford, anchored off the island of Corrigidore; and on the next morning, the 15th, they quitted the bay, and, the Sibylle with one, and the Fox, with two gun-boats in tow, stood to the southward, in the hope to precede, if possible, any information that they were among the islands. On the night of the 19th, one of the two gun-boats towed by the Fox, in a heavy squall, broke adrift. The fox immediately brought to and continued to fire guns and show lights during the whole night; but all in vain, the gun-boat having foundered with the loss of all her crew, consisting of Lieutenant Rutherford, one midshipman (Mr. Nicholson), nine seamen, and one boy. At day-light, on the 20th, the frigates made sail and coasted Mindora, Pany, Negros, and Magindano, without any occurrence worth notice.

On the 22nd, at day-light, being within a few miles of Samboangon, on the island of Majindinao, a settlement which they purposed to lay under contribution for water, wood, and refreshments, the frigates hoisted Spanish colours; but, while steering towards it, the Sibylle grounded on the north-west point of the small island of Santa-Cruz. The Fox and the two gun-boats then stood on; but, at 6 h. 20 m. A.M., being becalmed, were obliged to anchor just abreast of, and at the distance of about a mile and a half from, the fort of Samboangon. At about this time the Sibylle got off; but the state of the tide, coupled with the want of wind, prevented her from joining. A boat now approached the Fox from the shore, and, when, within hail, inquired the name and other particulars of the frigate. Receiving no satisfactory answer, the Spaniards pulled back to the shore, which, although several muskets were fired at them, they reached in safety. At 6 h. 30 m. A.M. the British vessels hoisted their proper colours, and the Fox and the two-gun-boats opened a fire upon the fort, which was returned as well by the latter as by a two-gun battery to the westward, but, owing to the distance, with very little effect. At 8 A.M. a fresh breeze sprang up from the land, and, aided by the tide, then running at the rate of three knots to the westward, drove the Fox off the bank on which she had anchored.

At noon, a fresh breeze springing up from the westward, the Sibylle and Fox, accompanied by the two gun-boats, made all sail towards the fort. At about 2 h. 5 m. P.M. the Sibylle fired an 18-pounder at the western battery to try the distance, and in five minutes more, being abreast of the fort of Samboangon, brought to and commenced the action. Shortly afterwards the Fox began firing at the western battery; and, at 3 P.M., being abreast of, and about half a mile distant from it, and about three quarters of a mile from the fort, dropped her anchor astern, but rather inside, of her consort. The Fox and the western battery, which mounted 12 or 14 guns, were soon as hotly engaged as the fort itself and the Sibylle. The fire from the battery abreast of the Fox being both heavy and well-directed, while the shot from the latter seemed to produce little or no effect, Captain Malcolm, at 3 h. 20 m. P.M., accompanied by the first lieutenant of the Fox, in conformity to directions previously received from Captain Cooke, proceeded, in three of the Fox's boats (and which were soon followed by three from the Sibylle), to endeavour to effect a landing to the westward of the battery.

As the boats approached, a shot from the battery struck and went though the Fox's cutter, killing two seamen, and wounding a master's mate (Mr. Davis), two seamen, and one marine. Fortunately, the cutter, when she swamped, was in shoal water and close to a sand-bank; upon which, Captain Malcolm and the remainder of the crew presently landed. Here the captain found, as well the surviving men of the cutter, as the crew of the launch, that had grounded on the same bank, and intended pushing for the shore; but, deep water being found inside the bank, and a strong party of men observed posted on the beach, the attempt was abandoned, and the party, at about 3 h. 30 m. P.M., returned to the ships. At 3 h. 40 m. a shot from the battery cut away two strands of the Fox's cable. Having received other considerable damage on board, the Fox now cut the remaining strand of her cable, and stood out of gun-shot to the southward. The Sibylle about the same time cut her cable, and removed further from the fort.

Of this fort and the adjoining batteries, the strength had evidently been much underrated by the commanding officer of the two frigates; one of which, the Sibylle, had her master (Richard Stanning) and one marine killed, and one wounded. It was the other frigate, however, which, owing to her nearness to the western battery, bore the brunt of the attack. One shot, as already stated, cut the Fox's cable: another passed through the mizenmast, about 12 feet from the head; another carried away the supporters of the wheel, and another the bits on the quarterdeck; about 28 others struck the ship's side. Her main stay and six of her lower shrouds, were also cut away, and her running rigging and sails much injured. With respect to the loss sustained on board, the Fox had two seamen killed, the captain's clerk and 10 seamen wounded; making, with the loss in the cutter, a total of four killed and 15 wounded.

At 9 P.M. the two frigates anchored about six miles to the eastward of Samboangon town. On the 23rd, in the morning, by which time the Fox had fished her mizenmast and repaired the most material to her damages the two frigates got under way and stood to the northward. On the same evening, the two gun-boats after all the stores had been taken out of them, were destroyed, as being unfit to proceed on the voyage to Canton. On the 27th, the frigates being much in want of water which they had been compelled to relinquish taking by force at Samboangon, put into the harbour of Pullock, situated to the northward of Majindinao. On the 31st, at daybreak, three boats from each frigate were sent to bring away the last load. At 9 A.M. some of the men belonging to the Sibylle's boats (those of the Fox had come on board) were perceived running to the beach and making signals. Instantly all the boats, manned and armed, of both frigates, led by their respective captains, pulled towards the shore. Here two seamen were found killed by the natives, one mortally wounded, and nine missing, supposed to have been carried into the woods. The remainder of the party, including Lieutenant Majeur, who commanded it, were fortunately rescued. Every effort to recover the men having failed, Captain Cooke ordered the village of the natives to be set on fire, and their corn cut down and then weighed and set sail for Mindanao. On arriving here, Captain Cooke was promised by the sultan that he would use his influence to recover, if they were alive, the missing men. The sultan eventually fulfilled his promise, and the men were restored, but not in time for the Fox and Sibylle to bring them away, Captain Cooke being obliged to hasten on to Canton, to be ready to convoy the homeward-bound trade.

On the 8th of March Tippoo-Saib's two ambassadors, with about 150 colonial volunteers (here was a reinforcement for a sultan who could bring into the field 70,000 horse and foot)! sailed in the Preneuse for Mangalore. On the 20th of April, having two days before received intelligence that two Indiamen were at Tellicherry, taking in a cargo of pepper, Captain L'Hermite looked into the port, but, finding only one ship there, doubted the accuracy of his information, and cruised off the coast for a day or two under English colours.

A periague, which the Preneuse captured on the morning of

the 21st, having assured the French captain that the ship in sight, however formidable in appearance, was nothing but an Indiaman, the Preneuse, disguised still as an English frigate, stood for the road of Tellicherry. In his way thither Captain L'Hermite fell in with another Indiaman steering for the same anchorage. The Preneuse now reduced her sails and yawed about, so as to let this ship enter the road first. At about 2 h. 30 m. P.M., while this manœuvre was practising, a thunderstorm came on; and at 3 P.M. the Preneuse was struck with lightning. The electric fluid entered at the frigate's main truck and, running down the mast into the hold, reascended to the main deck, killed one man, and wounded 15 or 16, and then passed out at one of the ports. Towards 4 P.M., just as the Indiaman had cast anchor, within about 100 fathoms of the one already in the road, the Preneuse steered between the two, and changing her colours to French, fired a broadside into each. The ship that had just anchored fired a broadside in return, cut her cable, and loosed her sails, with the intention of running on shore. The other ship, owing to her position, could only return one or two guns: in short, the two vessels were captured. One proved to be the Woodcot of 802 tons, Captain Andrew Hannay, the other the Raymond, of 793 tons, Captain Henry Smedley; both armed, and the latter, with a detachment of company's troops on board.

Having taken of the commandant of Tellicherry a receipt for his prisoners, 600 in number, and the half described as Europeans, Captain L'Hermite manned his two prizes and despatched them to the Isle of France, and then proceeded on his mission to Mangalore. Here the frigate arrived on the 24th of April, and, quitting the road on the 26th, steered for Java. At Batavia Captain L'Hermite arrived in the middle of June, and found there Rear-admiral Sercey; who had recently arrived in the Brûle-Gueule, with the intention of making the Dutch island his temporary head-quarters.* We will now see how far the Vertu and Régénérée, with their valuable charge, have got on their voyage home.

Before we quit the eastern hemisphere to accompany the French frigates Vertu and Régénérée on their voyage to Europe, we will give some account of a very melancholy ship-loss, with which the Straits of Banca were this year visited. On the evening of the 23rd of July the Resistance, which ship we mentioned as making her appearance off Manilla, anchored in the Straits, to await the approach of a Malay sloop, which Captain Pakenham had detained, on a suspicion that she was Dutch property, and which he was now about to restore to the Malay captain. On the 24th, at 1 A.M., the sloop joined, and dropped anchor under the stern of the ship. It appears from the

*Victoires et Conquêtes, tome viii., p. 304.

narrative of a seaman of the Resistance named Thomas Scott, one of the few survivors of the awful catastrophe which ensued, that, as he was sleeping on the larboard side of the quarterdeck, he was suddenly awakened by a fierce blaze that seized his clothes and hair, and which was succeeded, in an instant, by a tremendous explosion, from the shock of which, as he afterwards conjectured, he became utterly senseless for several minutes. From the appearance of daylight about an hour after he had been blown up, Scott supposed the accident to have happened at about four o'clock in the morning. The whole number of survivors, including Scott, appears to have been 13, of whom the highest in rank was a quartermaster. The number that had perished amounted to about 314 officers, seamen, and marines, three English women married on board, one Malay woman of Amboyna, and 14 Spanish prisoners taken in a prize; total 332 souls.

The subsequent sufferings of Scott and his companions, as related by himself, were very great. On recovering a little from the stupor into which the shock had thrown him, he found himself half-suffocated with water, floating and struggling for his existence, in company with several other persons. He made shift, as did 12 of those near him, to reach the hammock-netting of the ship on the starboard side, which was just above the water. At the dawn of day the people belonging to the sloop, then not out of hail astern, and who must have heard the shouts of the wretched beings that were clinging to the wreck, weighed anchor, and, callous to every impulse of humanity, stood over to the island of Borea. It would appear from this, either that no prize-crew had been placed on board the sloop, but merely the master taken out of her, or that the British, notwithstanding it was one o'clock in the morning when the sloop joined, had been withdrawn from her, and her own people put in possession.

The mild state of the weather enabled the 13 survivors, most of whom were badly scorched, to construct a raft to convey them to the low land of Sumatra, distant about three leagues from the spot, and about six from the Dutch settlement of Palambang. In the afternoon they committed themselves to the raft, with only a single pumpkin for food for the whole of them. A gale soon afterwards got up, and dashed the raft to pieces. Four of the seamen, including Scott, took to an anchor-stock which had formed part of the raft, and which they now steadied by means of two spars lashed across. These men, after first being nearly famished, and then nearly massacred, reached the Sumatra coast. There they all became prisoners to a party of Malays. Scott appears to have been the only one that subsequently became released from captivity. The eight poor wretches (or rather seven, for one had died), who remained on the shattered raft, were never heard of afterwards.

On the 24th of April, at 3 P.M., the British 12-pounder 32-gun frigate Pearl, Captain Samuel James Ballard, while running in for the Isles of Loss with a moderate breeze from the west-south-west, discovered a large ship at anchor under Factory island, four others at anchor between the islands, and an armed brig under sail. What the armed brig and one of the ships were we are unable to say; but the ship under Factory island we take to have been the Régénérée, and the "frigate, with yards and topmasts down," described in the Pearl's log as one of those at anchor between the islands, her consort the Vertu. At 5 h. 30 m. P.M. the latter, having hoisted her colours, opened a heavy fire upon the Pearl; who, at 6 P.M., while running, as she was compelled to do, between the two frigates, fired at both, and then hauled up in three fathoms through the eastern passage. At 7 P.M. the Pearl ceased firing, but found herself chased by the Régénérée; who continued the pursuit all that night, and until the next evening at dark, when she disappeared. On the afternoon of the next day, the 27th, the Pearl anchored in St.-George's bay, Sierra-Leone. The fire to which she had been exposed, in running past the French frigates, had shot away her foretopgallant yard, and several lower shrouds and other rigging, cut through her fore yard, hulled her in several places, some between wind and water, dismounted two of her carronades, and mortally wounded one man.

We must leave these two French frigates and their sluggish convoy at the Isles of Loss, while we attend to another frigate of Rear-admiral Sercey's squadron. On the 24th of April, the 40-gun frigate Seine, still commanded by Lieutenant Julien-Gabriel Bigot, with about 280 refractory troops on board, set sail from Port-Louis, for the same destination as the Vertu and Régénérée. On the 29th of June, at 7 A.M., the Penmarcks in sight to leeward, the British 38-gun frigate Jason, Captain Charles Stirling, 12-pounder 36-gun frigate Pique, Captain David Milne, and 12-pounder 32-gun frigate Mermaid, Captain James Newman Newman, cruising in company, descried and chased a French frigate in the south-south-west, or windward quarter. The Mermaid immediately stood to the northward, to cut off the stranger from the land. The latter, however, which was the Seine, after a fortunate passage of three months, just about to enter, as her people flattered themselves, a port of France, tacked soon afterwards, and steered to the southward; whereby the Mermaid, at best but an indifferent sailor, was completely thrown out. The Pique kept her wind; and the Jason steered about two points free, in order to prevent the enemy from entering Lorient.

The chase continued throughout the day; and at 9 P.M. the Pique got within gun-shot of the enemy, and kept up a constant fire with her bow-guns. At about 11 P.M., the Pique ranged up alongside the French frigate, and gave and received a broadside. A running fight now ensued, and the Pique and

Seine, keeping abreast of each other, continued an unremitting interchange of broadsides, for two hours and 35 minutes; when the British frigate, having had her main topmast shot away, dropped astern.

The Jason now coming up, Captain Stirling hailed the Pique, and desired her commander to anchor; but Captain Milne, not hearing what was said, and anxious to see the last of an opponent whom he had so long singly engaged, pushed up, under all the sail he could carry, on the larboard side of the Jason. There the Pique unfortunately grounded. Almost at the same instant, the land near Pointe de la Trenche was seen close upon the Jason's larboard bow; and, before the ship would answer her helm, she also took the ground near to the Seine, who, it was perceived, had likewise grounded, and was entirely dismasted. As the tide rose, the Jason hung only forward, and therefore swang with her stern fairly exposed to the enemy's broadside. Of this the Seine took proper advantage, and poured into the Jason several raking broadsides; which, besides inflicting nearly the whole loss she sustained, wounded her masts, and cut and tore to pieces her rigging and sails. In a little while, however, the Jason got some guns run out abaft; and the Pique, having by squaring her yards, forged a little ahead of the Jason, was enabled to point four of her foremost 12-pounders clear of the latter. On receiving a few shot from the guns of both opponents thus brought to bear, and seeing the Mermaid fast approaching, the Seine struck her colours.

The Pique, besides having lost her fore topmast, was exceedingly shattered in her masts, rigging, and sails, and had unfortunately lain near enough to receive some of the Seine's shots as they passed over the Jason; but, until towards the close of the combat, as already mentioned, the former could not return a shot without firing into or through her companion. Every attempt to get the Pique afloat was exerted in vain, and she bilged. The Jason was more successful, being heaved off into deep water by the Mermaid; who, notwithstanding every effort to get up, did not arrive in time to participate in the action.

The Jason lost her second lieutenant (Anthony Richard Robotier), one corporal of marines, and five seamen killed, her commander, two midshipmen (Frederick Bedford and Samuel Luscombe), and nine seamen wounded. The Pique had one seaman killed, and one missing, her boatswain, boatswain's mate, one seaman, and three marines wounded; total in the two ships, nine (including the one missing) killed, and 18 wounded. The loss on board the Seine, out of a complement including soldiers, of 610 men, is represented to have been as many as 170 killed (including, we believe, several that were drowned), and about 100 wounded.

The Pique, a very inferior antagonist to the Seine, bore the brunt of the action; but the Jason, no doubt, contributed her powerful aid in bringing it to a consummation. The Mermaid, on the other hand, was unable to take any share in the engagement. The heavy loss sustained by the French ship, places Lieutenant Bigot's defence in a highly creditable light; and it must be admitted, that the troops on board the Seine, with their women, children, and baggage, were rather an encumbrance than a benefit.

On the 30th, at daylight, the British 38-gun frigate Phaëton, Captain the Honourable Robert Stopford, 36-gun frigate, San-Fiorenzo, Captain Sir Harry Neale, and 12-pounder 32-gun frigate, Triton, Captain John Gore, hove in sight, and were called in by signal from the Jason, it appearing that two large frigates, a brig, and several gun-boats were coming out from Rochelle, with the view of driving away or capturing the British frigates. The French were induced, however, to put back, on witnessing the junction of Captain Stopford's squadron. Had the latter not been present, the state of the British frigates, with only the Mermaid in a condition to give battle, would have been extremely critical.

In the course of this day, by throwing overboard her guns, and by the San-Fiorenzo's assistance, the Seine was hove off, and, being a very strong ship, escaped without any material damage, beyond what she had sustained by shot. The Pique could not be got off. She was therefore destroyed, and her crew turned over to the prize; which, on her arrival in port, Captain Milne, his officers, and ship's company, were allowed, very justly, to commission as the British 38-gun frigate Seine.

We are pleased to see it stated in a respectable French work, that Lieutenant Bigot, on being carried to England, was treated with all the respect and attention due to his bravery and good conduct. He was also sent back to this country by the first exchange; and the directory, to evince their opinion of his merits, promoted Lieutenant Bigot to be a capitaine de vaisseau without passing through the intermediate rank of a capitaine de frégate.

On the 13th of May, the British 18-pounder 36-gun frigate, Flora, Captain Robert Gambier Middleton, chased the French Venetian-built brig-corvette, Mondovi, of 18 guns (12 brass 6, and four iron 12-pounders), and 68 men, commanded by Lieutenant Jean-Baptiste Bonavie, into the port of Cerigo in the island of that name, in the Archipelago.

Being resolved to attempt the capture or destruction of the corvette, and yet finding it impracticable, owing to the narrow entrance to the harbour and the commanding situation of the forts, to follow her with the frigate, Captain Middleton intrusted the service to the Flora's boats under the orders of the first Lieutenant William Russel, assisted by Lieutenant William Hepenstall, Lieutenant Richard Parry of the marines, Mr. Morton, master's mate. Mr. Tancock, the gunner, and Messieurs Petley and Hawkins, midshipmen.

On the same evening the boats quitted the Flora; and, in the face of a severe fire from the forts, the Mondovi herself, and several vessels in the harbour, the British gallantly boarded and cut out the corvette, with no greater loss on their part than one private marine killed, the lieutenant of marines (Mr. Richard Parry), master's mate, gunner, and five seamen wounded. The loss sustained by the Mondovi amounted to one seaman killed, four seamen drowned, from having jumped overboard as supposed, and eight seamen and soldiers dangerously wounded.

On the 26th of July, at 10 h. 30 m. A.M., the British 28-gun frigate Brilliant, Captain Henry Blackwood, standing close into the bay of Santa-Cruz, with the wind a fresh breeze at east by north, in order to discover if a strange sail, which she had chased on the preceding evening, had arrived there, saw two French frigates lying at an anchor. The latter, which were the Vertu and Régénérée, still on their way to France,* immediately slipped their cables and gave chase. The Brilliant stood off under all sail, cutting away her anchors and boats to facilitate her escape; but, in the mean time, got ready for action. At half-past noon, finding her pursuers were gaining upon her, she cut down the stern to make room for two 9-pounders as chasers, and got two 6-pounders aft on the quarterdeck for the same purpose. At 2 h. 30 m. the south point of the Grand Canary bore east-south-east six or seven leagues. At five P.M. the Brilliant began firing her stern-chasers, but, finding they did not reach, ceased until 6 h. 15 m. P.M.; when she recommenced her fire, and continued it with spirit. The Régénérée, who was ahead and to leeward of her consort, now opened her bow-chasers; and both ships were evidently coming up fast with the Brilliant.

It was now that the latter resolved, by a bold manœuvre, to attempt to extricate herself. At 7 h. 30 m. P.M., being then on the larboard tack, the Brilliant bore up athwart the bows of the Régénérée, and gave her a broadside, which shot away her maintopsail halyards, and badly wounded her bowsprit and foremast. After the exchange of a few broadsides, the Brilliant hauled to the wind on the starboard tack; leaving the Régénérée, with her main topsail down, and incapable, for the present of renewing the pursuit. The Vertu, having tacked, was now on the Brilliant's weather quarter, and soon opened upon her a heavy but ineffectual fire, which the latter answered by her stern-chasers. By midnight the wind had subsided to a perfect calm; and the Régénérée, who had again made sail in chase, now joined her consort in the distant cannonade. At

*See p. 211.

three quarters of an hour after midnight, a breeze sprang up from the north-east; and soon afterwards the Brilliant, losing sight of her pursuers in the dark, bore away south by east. An interchange of signals between the two French frigates, by rockets, and false fires, followed this alternation in the British frigate's course, but no further attempt at pursuit that the latter could discover.

The Brilliant suffered very little damage, and no loss, by the enemy's shot; but, in the chase, she sprang her foremast and spanker-boom. On the 3d of August Captain Blackwood fell in with the 36-gun frigate Flora, Captain Robert Gambier Middleton; and the two frigates, one of them having prisoners to exchange, proceeded off Santa-Cruz. Arriving there on the 10th, Captain Middleton sent in a flag of truce; which brought out nine men who had been prisoners on board the Vertu. These gave an account of the names and some other particulars of the ships which the Brilliant had engaged. Part of the information was, that the Régénérée's bowsprit, foremast, and main topmast, owing chiefly to their wounded state, had fallen overboard, while the ship was in the act of tacking after the Brilliant, a short time before the latter bore away to the southward.

Had the Flora joined company during the chase, the combat would most probably have been brought to a decisive issue; and, as an additional reward to the British, should the day have been theirs, intelligence might have been obtained of the two rich Spanish galleons, which the two French frigates had taken under their convoy; and which they escorted safe to their destination.

On the 4th of July, at 9 h. 45 m. P.M., the French ex-Venetian brig-corvette Lodi, of 18 long 6-pounders and at least 130 men, commanded by Lieutenant Sennequier, while running through the Piombino channel, on her way from Leghorn, which she had quitted that morning, to Alexandria, with despatches for General Buonaparte, was hailed and attacked by an armed brig. As soon as she had ascertained that the vessel approaching her so fearlessly was an enemy, the Lodi endeavoured to obtain a raking position ahead of her; but the British brig frustrated the attempt by running her own bowsprit through the Lodi's boom-mainsail.

A furious action now commenced; on the part of the Lodi by vivid and constant discharges of musketry, in which the officers and troops on board as passengers greatly assisted, and on the part of the British brig, who probably in the arm of musketry felt sensibly her deficiency, by discharges of grape and canister shot from such of her great guns as would bear. Twice the British attempted to put an end to the combat by boarding; but a part of the assailants, each time, fell dead into the sea, and the remainder were driven back to their brig, covered with wounds.

The French, now, as if taught by the ill success of their opponents, where their own chief strength lay, made a vigorous attempt to board the British brig, but were repulsed with slaughter.

Before the French were prepared or perhaps inclined to repeat the attempt, the two brigs separated, and each, we presume, soon found the means of bringing her cannon exclusively into play. At 2 A.M. on the 5th the fire of the British brig, having gradually slackened, ceased, and Captain Sennequier took this opportunity of hailing to know if she would surrender. The only reply he obtained was a discharge of musketry, accompanied by a few cannon-shot. Soon after this the British brig endeavoured to get off, and had scarcely made sail for that purpose, when a broadside from the Lodi brought down her foremast and main topmast.

This, one might suppose, left the Lodi nothing to do but to take possession of her prize. Far from it; the British brig, with only the stump of her mainmast standing, got away, and the Lodi, with rigging and sails cut, no doubt, but with both her masts standing in their places, in vain "fit tous les efforts pour le poursuivre," and could not overtake her until she had sheltered herself under the neutral coast of Tuscany. The Lodi, thereupon with the loss of two seamen killed, her commander, two other naval officers, some military officers, and 25 soldiers and sailors wounded, made the best of her way to Alexandria; where, in due time, she arrived safe. Here such a representation was made of the combat, which the Lodi had sustained with the British sloop of war "Aigle, of a force much superior to hers," "d'une force bien supérieure à la sienne," that Lieutenant de vaisseau Sennequier was immediately promoted by the directory to the rank of capitaine de frégate.*

Being well aware that there was no "Aigle" belonging to the British navy but a frigate, and no "Eagle," except an old 64 at Chatham, and a 4-gun "Dutch hoy," lying in Poole harbour, and having been taught by experience that French writers are very apt to mistake English proper names, we searched the log of every British brig-sloop cruising in the Mediterranean in the year 1798, but could discover no traces of an action fought by her at the time and place above-mentioned. A search through the London journals proved equally fruitless. At length a Paris newspaper, under the head of Leghorn, informed us that on the 28th of July, 1798, the English privateer-brig "Aquila, Captain Colonna," of 14 guns and 57 men, entered the port in distress, having on the 4th, in the Piombino channel, fought with a French brig, from eleven at night till half-past three in the morning, and that the former had lost a great many killed and wounded.

*Victoires et Conquêtes, tome x., p. 383.

Owing to the late period at which this information reached us, it has not been in our power to discover who were the owners of the Eagle privateer: a subject of regret, as, in all probability, we should then have been enabled to give more full and satisfactory details of an action so highly creditable to the British captain and his crew. At all events, sufficient has appeared to show clearly, that Lieutenant Sennequier, instead of being rewarded for having escaped from, ought to have been cashiered for not having captured the British privateer, which, after so long and well fought an action on her part, his most decided superiority of force had reduced to so crippled and defenceless a state.

On the 11th of July, the British 44-gun ship, Regulus, Captain George Eyre, cruising off the north-west end of the island of Porto-Rico, discovered five vessels at anchor in Aguada bay, under the protection of some batteries. Being resolved to attempt their capture or destruction, Captain Eyre manned a prize-schooner in company, and sent her with the boats of the Regulus under the orders of Lieutenant John Good, assisted by Lieutenant William Holman and master's mate, Thomas Finch, to execute the service; the Regulus herself standing in to cover and protect her boats in their advance.

Owing to the failure of wind, neither the ship nor the schooner were able to get near enough to afford any material assistance. Lieutenant Good, however, by his judicious arrangement and spirited conduct, executed the service with the boats alone; bringing out three of the largest vessels, a ship, a brig, and an armed schooner. Had there been the smallest breath of wind, the remaining two vessels having been boarded and in possession for a considerable time, would also have been carried off; but, it falling a dead calm at the moment the cables were cut, and there not being a sufficiency of boats to tow so many vessels, it became necessary to quit two of the vessels, in order to secure the three which appeared to be of the most importance.

Notwithstanding an incessant fire kept up by the batteries, close to which, for their security, the vessels had been moored, the British had only one man hurt, but that was the master's mate already named, and who was killed by a grape-shot.

On the 15th of July, at 9 A.M., Carthagena bearing about west by north, distant 29 leagues, the British 64-gun ship, Lion, Captain Manley Dixon, steering east, with a crowd of sail, the wind moderate at west-south-west, descried, in the south-east quarter, standing towards her, four strange ships, which we may at once introduce as the

Gun-frig.		
34	Pomona	Commodore don Felix O'Neil. Captain don F. Villamil.
	Proserpine	Captain don Quaj. Bial.
	Santa-Cazilda	Captain don D. Errara.
	Santa-Dorotea	Captain don M. Gerraro.

The Lion immediately shortened sail, and hauled up, so as to secure the weathergage; then bore down upon the four Spanish frigates, formed in close order of battle on the larboard line of bearing, the third frigate from the van, the Dorotea, with her fore topmast gone. In order to secure a general action, Captain Dixon meditated his first attack on this ship; which, being left astern by her comrades, the Lion was not long in cutting off. The three remaining frigates tacked in succession, and passed the Lion very gallantly within musket-shot; but, as their line, after tacking, was by no means a close one, they each received a well-directed broadside, the effect of which was evident by their standing a long time on the same tack. Captain Dixon still kept in chase of the Dorotea; who, notwithstanding the loss of her fore topmast, sailed nearly as well as the Lion, and galled her considerably in the rigging by her stern-chasers.

The three frigates, having at last tacked, made a second attempt, but not so close as the former, to succour their friend, and were each repaid by a broadside in return. At length the Lion closed with the Dorotea, and poured in a destructive fire, the yard-arms of the two ships passing just clear of each other. Sill the latter held out. Her consorts made a third, but a distant and feeble effort to cover; and then hauled close by the wind and stood to the north-west. The Lion, whose rigging and sails were much cut, succeeded, with difficulty, in wearing round on the same tack as the Dorotea; who, having, in addition to the loss of her fore topmast, had her mizenmast shot away, her mainmast and rudder damaged, and her rigging and sails cut to pieces, and being, besides, abandoned by her three comrades, very wisely substituted the British for the Spanish ensign.

As an additional proof that Captain Gerraro had maintained the action with becoming bravery, the loss on board his ship, out of a crew, supernumeraries included, of 371 men and boys, amounted to 20 men killed and 32 wounded. The loss sustained by the Lion was very trifling, amounting to no more than one young midshipman (Joseph Patey), wounded slightly in the shoulder, and who would not quit his quarters, and one seaman wounded dangerously.

It took Captain Dixon during the remainder of the day to repair the rigging and sails of the Lion, and to place the prize in a state to be conducted to her new destination. The Santa Dorotea measured 958 tons, and was afterwards added to the British navy, under the same name, as a 12-pounder 36-gun frigate.

On the 3d of August while the British 38-gun frigate Melpomène, Captain Sir Charles Hamilton, and 14-gun brig-sloop, Childers, Captain James O'Bryen, were cruising off Isle Bas, on the coast of France, the former determined, with the boats of the two ships, to attempt cutting out from the port of

Corigiou, a national armed brig, and several merchant vessels at anchor with her. At 10 P.M., five boats, manned with about 70 men, and placed under the orders of Lieutenant Thomas George Shortland, of the Melpomène, quitted the ships; and, amidst heavy rain, vivid lightning, and frequent squalls, all highly favourable to the enterprise, pulled for the French harbour. At 3 A.M. on the 4th, the boats were alongside of, and, after more resistance than had been anticipated, carried, the French 14-gun brig (4-pounders), Aventurier, commanded by Lieutenant René-Gillaume Raffi, and manned with a crew of 79 men. The gallant defence made by the brig cost the French 16 men wounded, several of them mortally; while the loss on the part of the British amounted to no more than one seaman killed, and one missing, and one midshipman (Mr. Frost) and three seamen wounded.

A difficult part of the enterprise still remained to be executed. The forts that commanded the Corigiou inlet, alarmed at what had taken place, now opened their fire; and the wind, having veered round to north-north-west, blew a fresh gale directly into the passage, the narrowness and intricacy of which rendered any attempt to beat out doubly hazardous. The brig, however, was presently under sail; and leaving the merchant vessels to some more favourable opportunity, Lieutenant Shortland, after being exposed, during two hours, to a heavy fire from the French batteries, brought out his prize without incurring any additional loss. The Childers had stood in to cover the boats, but, owing to the badness of the night and the dangers of the coast, with considerable risk. Viewed in every point, this boat-attack was a highly creditable affair to all who were engaged in it, not excepting the officers and crew of the French brig. Soon after his return into port, Lieutenant Shortland, for the gallantry he had displayed on the occasion, was most deservedly promoted to the rank of commander.

On the 7th of August, at 5 P.M., Cape Windmill, near Gibraltar, bearing north-east by north distant four or five leagues, the British brig-sloop Espoir, of fourteen 6-pounders and 80 men and boys, Captain Loftus Otway Bland, having in charge a part of the Oran convoy, discovered a large ship seemingly steering to cut off some of the vessels. The Espoir immediately hauled out from the convoy, and made all sail to meet the stranger, evidently a man of war; and who, at a little before 7 P.M., hove to for the former. The Espoir, as soon as she arrived within musket-shot, hoisted her colours; but the Liguria, instead of displaying hers, waited till the Espoir reached her weather quarter, and then hailed.

On the hail's being answered, an officer on board the Liguria desired the commander of the Espoir, in very good English, to go to leeward and strike, or he would sink him, enforcing his threat by one shot, and instantly afterwards by the Liguria's whole broadside; a salute, which, in well practised hands, might have rendered all further hailing unnecessary, unless on the part of the Espoir to save her drowning crew. As a proof, the Liguria mounted 26 carriage-guns, of various calibers, namely, 12 long "18-pounders," four long "12-pounders," and 10 long 6-pounders; also 12 long wall-pieces, and four swivels; and her crew consisted of 120 men of all nations.

The Espoir, notwithstanding her decided inferiority of force, was not slow in returning her adversary's broadside; and the two vessels continued a very heavy fire of great guns and musketry, until 10 h. 45 m. P.M., when the captain of the Liguria, Don Francisco de Orso, hailed the Espoir, begging her not to fire any more, as he was a Genoese. Captain Bland replied, that the Espoir was a British man of war, and ordered him to lower all his sails, and come on board. No attention being paid to his mandate, and the Liguria shooting ahead, as if to gain a raking position, the Espoir again brought her broadside to bear; and Captain Bland, judging very properly that his opponent's force was not to be trifled with, gave it to her with full effect. The Liguria again returned the fire; but, on the Espoir's shooting ahead and tacking to fire her opposite broadside, the Liguria's captain once more hailed, begging the Espoir not to fire again, and saying that he was badly wounded, but would obey Captain Bland's orders immediately. This was about 11 P.M., and instantly the Liguria lowered down her sails, and all firing ceased.

In this action of her own seeking, the pirate (for such the Liguria was) lost her boatswain and six men killed, her commander (dangerously) and 13 men wounded. The Espoir lost her master, Mr. Solsby, killed, and six men wounded, two of them badly.

It was fortunate for the Espoir that the Genoese were not, as we noticed before, practised men-of-war's men; or the brig's temerity, in risking a combat with an enemy of so formidable a force, might have ended in her discomfiture. The promptitude, bravery, and seamanship displayed throughout this long and harassing engagement, reflected great honour on Captain Bland, his officers, and brig's company. On the other hand, some allowance must be made for the indifferent crew, as well as for the inconvenient variety of calibers among the guns, of the Genoese ship. Few actions have been made more of by the painter than the action of the Espoir and Liguria. An engraving from the pencil of Pocock, representing "L'Espoir sloop of 14 guns, and her prize, the Liguria of 44 guns," appears in the Naval Chronicle, vol. vi., p. 277. The latter ship is there represented with 22 guns on the main deck, 18 on the quarterdeck, and two or four on the forecastle. One can hardly suppose that so respectable a man as Mr. Pocock would have put his name to a drawing, unless it was founded on reality.

But the matter might have been placed beyond a doubt, had Captain Bland, in his official letter, described the situation of the different guns of his prize; particularly, how many of them she mounted on the main deck. Were it not for Mr. Pocock's drawing, the inference would be, that the Liguria mounted 16 guns (12 and 8 pounders, rather than 18 and 12) on the main deck, and 10 sixes on the quarterdeck and forecastle, with the wall-pieces and swivels, for which there was ample room, arranged in the usual manner. The ship then might have been measured about 450 or 500 tons, and would still have been more than a match for the Espoir, whose size was only 215 tons.

On his return home, Captain Bland, very deservedly, was made a post-captain. His commission as such bears date on the 25th of September, 1798, and his commission as a commander, on the 1st of October, 1797; yet a contemporary says that, for his action with the Liguria, "Lieutenant" Bland was promoted to the rank of "commander and post-captain,"* two steps which, now at least, require a twelvemonth to intervene.

On the 7th of August, at daybreak, the British 44-gun frigate Indefatigable, Captain Sir Edward Pellew, cruising between the river Gironde and the Isle of Ré, fell in with, and, after a 24 hours' chase and the discharge of a few guns, captured, the French ship-corvette Vaillante, of 20 long 8-pounders and 175 men, commanded by Lieutenant la Porte, and bound to Cayenne; to which she was carrying 25 banished priests, 27 convicts, and Madame Rovère and family.

Being a fine new coppered and copper-fastened ship of 508 tons, the Vaillante became an acquisition to the British navy; to which, under the name of Danaë, and established with 20 carronades, 32-pounders, and two long sixes on the main deck, and 12 carronades 12-pounders, on the quarterdeck and forecastle, total 34 guns, with a net complement of 153 men and boys, she was forthwith transferred.

Here is a forcible illustration of the way in which the British usually equip French ships of war, particularly corvettes: they give them more guns, and fewer men, than they were ever intended to carry. If, when thus burdened with top-hamper,† the ship sails badly or upsets, the fault is laid to the manner of her construction, and a general anathema is pronounced upon "French corvettes." A contemporary, indeed, declares that "hundreds" of valuable British seamen perished in them, and that they were "totally unfit for his majesty's service."‡ He cites as examples, the Cheri, Dorade, Trompeuse, Railleur, and Gentille. The Cheri was a privateer, and went down, as has

*Brenton, vol. ii., p. 331

†The Danaë's twelve 12-pounder carronades, with their carriages and slides, would weigh 90 cwt.

‡Brenton, vol ii., p. 277.

already appeared, from shot-holes received in action. Of the Dorade, as a British cruiser, we never heard. The Trompeuse and Railleur were privateers; and the Gentille was a frigate, captured in 1795 and broken up in 1802. What can be alleged against such "flush-decked corvettes" in the British service as the Arab, Cormorant, Gaieté, Constance, and, above all, Bonne-Citoyenne?

On the 12th of August, at noon, latitude 46° 12' north, longitude 18° 23' west, the British 18-gun ship-sloop Hazard, mounting 24 or 26 guns, long sixes and 12-pounder carronades, Captain William Butterfield, gave chase to, and at 4 P.M. came within gun-shot of, the French armed ship, Neptune, mounting 10, but pierced for 20 guns; those 10 guns believed to have been 6-pounders, and which, Captain Butterfield in his letter says, were all fought on one side. The Neptune hauled up her courses, hoisted French colours, and fired a shot at the Hazard. Immediately an action ensued, during which the Neptune, having on board, exclusive of 53 seamen, 270 troops, made several attempts under cover of a heavy fire of musketry, to board the Hazard; but the crew of the latter repulsed the assailants with considerable loss, and, at the end of one hour and 50 minutes, compelled the French ship to strike her colours.

The Hazard received a few shot in her hull, and had her rigging slightly injured. Her loss amounted to only six men wounded. The Neptune, on the other hand, was a good deal cut up in hull, masts, and rigging, and lost, according to the representation of her officers, between 20 and 30 in killed and wounded together. A privateer, with French colours flying, was in sight to leeward during the whole of the action. Captain Butterfield's situation, even after he had made the French ship his prize, could not have been the most comfortable; as he had nearly 300 prisoners to keep in subjection, with a crew, owing to a prize which the Hazard had manned and sent away, of scarcely 100 men and boys.

At the close of our account of the battle of the Nile, it was stated that the British 50-gun ship Leander, Captain Thomas Boulden Thompson, had sailed on the 6th of August, from before Alexandria, with Rear-admiral Sir Horatio Nelson's despatches, addressed to the commander-in-chief on the Mediterranean station.

On the 18th, at daybreak, being within five or six miles of the west end of Goza di Candia, the Leander discovered in the south-east quarter, standing directly for her, a large sail, evidently a ship of the line: and which, although the Leander lay becalmed, was bringing up a fine breeze from the southward. The Leander being upwards of 80 men short of complement, and having on board several that were wounded in the Nile action, Captain Thompson did not feel himself justified in seeking a contest with a ship so superior in point of size and force; and therefore took every practicable means to avoid it. The Leander's inferiority of sailing, however, rendered an action inevitable; and it was only left to steer such a course, as would enable her to receive her powerful adversary to the best advantage.

That adversary was the French 74-gun ship Généreux, chef de division Lejoille, bound to Corfu, and armed, with the addition of two brass 36-pounder carronades on the forecastle, making 80 guns in all, the same as No. 4 in the table at vol. i. p. 54; while the Leander's force consisted of only 22 long 24-pounders on the lower deck, the same number of 12-pounders on the second deck, six long 6-pounders, on the quarterdeck and forecastle, and two, or rather one, for the other had been dismounted at the battle of the Nile, 12-pounder carronade on the poop, total 51 guns.*

At 8 A.M. the Généreux, still retaining exclusive possession of the breeze, and having by way of deception hoisted Neapolitan colours, approached within random-shot of the Leander, then steering, under every stitch of canvass she could spread, with the wind on the larboard beam. The French 74 now changed her colours to Turkish; but, from the first, her national character had been known. At 9 A.M. the Généreux ranged up, within half gun-shot, on the Leander's larboard and weather quarter. Finding that an action was inevitable, the Leander shortened sail, and hauled up until her broadside could be brought to bear. The Généreux now fired a shot ahead of the Leander and the latter immediately replied to it by a broadside.

A vigorous cannonade thus commenced on both sides; and the two ships continued nearing each other, keeping up a constant and heavy fire, until 10 h. 30 m. A.M., when the Généreux evinced a disposition to run her opponent on board. Such was the shattered state of the latter's rigging, sails, and yards, and so light the breeze, that the latter could make no movement to evade the shock. The French 74, accordingly, struck the British 50 on the larboard bow, and, dropping alongside, with a crash that bent double several of the Leander's lowerdeck ports, continued there for some time.

A spirited and well-directed fire, however, from the Leander's remnant of marines, stationed on the poop, and commanded by the sergeant (no officer having arrived on board to succeed Lieutenant Robinson killed at Teneriffe), and from the small-arm men on the quarterdeck, prevented the crew of the Généreux, numerous as they were, from taking advantage of the juxtaposition of the ships; and the Frenchmen every time they attempted to board, were driven back with loss. Meanwhile such

*A contemporary mistates the force of both ships. He gives the Généreux two guns too many on each of her principal decks, and calls her 8-pounders 12s. For the Leander's six 6-pounders, he substitutes eight 9s. Brenton, vol. ii., p. 322.

of the great guns of both ships, as would bear, continued in full activity.

After an interval of calm, a light air sprang up, still from the southward; and the Généreux, being from her lofty sails the first to feel its effects, forged ahead, and disentangled herself from the Leander, now lying with her mizenmast over the starboard quarter, her fore topmast over the larboard bow, and both her lower yards on the booms. The Généreux, soon afterwards, coming up in the wind on the starboard tack, the Leander, who by the aid of her spritsail had succeeded in wearing, was enabled to luff under the stern of her antagonist. The opportunity was not lost, and the Leander deliberately discharged into the Généreux every gun upon her starboard broadside, which the wreck of her spars did not cover.

The breeze again died away, and the sea became as smooth as glass; but no intermission took place in the mutual cannonade; it continued with unabated fury, until 3 h. 30 m. P.M. By this time the Généreux having, by the aid of a light breeze, paid round off upon her heel, stood athwart the hawse of the Leander, and stationed herself on the latter's larboard bow.* Here, unfortunately, the greater part of the guns, the foremost ones in particular, lay disabled with the wreck of the fallen spars. This gave a check to the Leander's firing, and the Généreux took that opportunity of hailing, to know if the British ship surrendered.

The Leander was now totally ungovernable, having her lower yards on the booms, and no stick standing, save the bowsprit and the shattered remains of the fore and main masts: the ship's hull was also cut to pieces, and her decks were strewed on every side with killed and wounded. The Généreux, on the other hand, having lost only her mizen topmast, was gradually passing along the Leander's larboard beam, as if intending to take up a position across her stern. In the defenceless state of the British ship, what other reply to the question of surrender could be given, than an affirmative? It was given, by holding out a pike with a French jack at the end of it, and the Généreux took possession of her comparatively insignificant, but far from easily won prize: not, however, by a boat, for the Leander had left the Généreux no boat in a situation to take the water, but by the French ship's boatswain, and one of her enseignes, or midshipmen, after they had swum on board.

An action so celebrated, and so truly creditable to the weaker party, we are happy to be able to illustrate with a diagram.

* "Starboard" in the Gazette, but we believe a misprint.

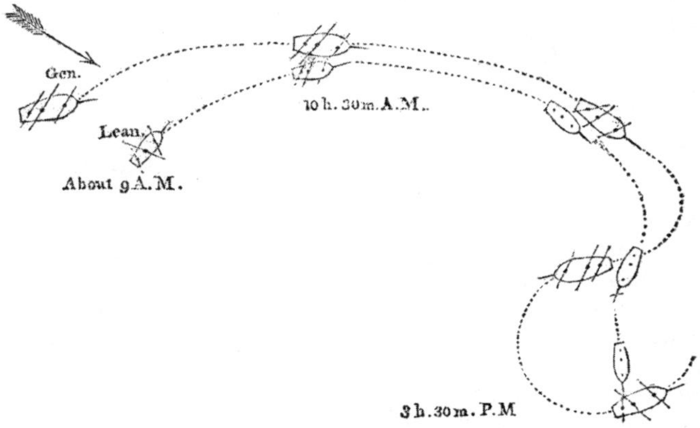

In this six hours' close and bloody conflict, the Leander lost three midshipmen (Peter Downs, —— Gibson, and Edward Haddon), 24 seamen, one sergeant (Dair), and seven private marines killed, her commander (badly, in three places), Captain Berry (slightly*), two lieutenants (Watkinson Bridges Taylor and William Swiney), her master (Michael Lee), boatswain (Mr. Mathias, badly), one master's mate (John Leckey), one midshipman (Mr. Nailor), 41 seamen, and nine private marines wounded – total, 35, killed and 57 wounded. This was a full third of her gallant crew; for, having left one lieutenant, one midshipman, and fifty men on board the prizes of Aboukir bay, and been originally short of her complement, the Leander had commenced the action with only 282 men and boys, including her 14 wounded in the Nile battle, and, we believe, her two passengers, Captain Edward Berry and a Mr. William Hill.

The Généreux, having received on board a portion of the Timoléon's crew,† as well as, on the day previous, when she parted company with the Guillaume-Tell, a number of men from her, had commenced the action with 936 men and boys. Of these, according to the information given by some of her officers to the late officers of the Leander, the Généreux sustained a loss of about 100, including her first lieutenant, killed, and 188 wounded; sufficient in amount, even admitting it to be slightly overrated, to prove that the 74's thick sides were not impenetrable to the 50-gun ship's comparatively light, but liberally bestowed, and well-directed shot. Some of the crew of the Généreux were even killed upon her orlop deck; and nothing but the smoothness of the water saved the French ship's foremast, which had been struck by 23 of the Leander's

*By "part of a man's skull, which was driven through his arm." – *Naval Chronicle*, vol. xv., p. 180.

† See p. 173.

shot, and was left at last with only one shroud of a side to support it.

COMPARATIVE FORCE OF THE COMBATANTS.

		LEANDER.	GENEREUX.
Broadside-guns	No.	26	40
	lbs.	432	1024
Crew	No.	282	936
Size	tons.	1052	1926

Where is there a single-ship action which has conferred greater honour upon the conqueror than in this instance lights upon the conquered? Such a defence is unparalleled, even in the British navy, where to be brave is scarcely a merit. Nothing, however, is without its alloy. Captain Thompson had the misfortune to be compelled to yield up his brave crew and himself to, we are sorry to say, a man who, by his subsequent treatment of his prisoners, disgraced both the profession he served in, and the country that employed him.

No sooner had the French midshipman and boatswain got on board the prize, than they began laying their hands upon every thing within their reach. The chief matter of surprise here is, that the Leander's people should have permitted such spoliations, when, in the twinkling of an eye, they might have thrown the plunderers back into the element out of which they had just before raised them. Never was there a finer illustration of the opinion entertained by honourable minds, of the duties which a state of surrender imposes, than the non-resistance of the Leander's crew under treatment so oppressive; the lions were now changed to lambs; and all the British crew did was, to hasten in patching up a boat, as well to convey Captain Thompson and his principal officers on board of the Généreux, as to bring back from the latter some officer of high rank, and, it was hoped, of more honourable feelings, than the one they had been forced to receive.

Captain Thompson and his officers soon found, to their cost, how fallaciously they had judged of the French captain and his lieutenants. By these the British were plundered of every thing, save very little more than the clothes on their backs. Captain Thompson owned a very large stock of shirts; but Captain Lejoille would allow him to retain three only, tied up in a handkerchief; and, in exchange for all the remainder of his clothes, gave him an old great-coat; the wretch refused to the gallant officer even his cot, although badly wounded.

In vain did Captain Thompson and his officers expostulate with the captain on this harsh treatment: in vain they reminded him of the very opposite treatment experienced by the French officers taken prisoners at the battle of the Nile. Captain Lejoille, with perfect nonchalance, answered, "J'en suis fâché, mais le fait est, que les Français sont bons au pillage." Captain Berry expressed a wish to have returned to him a pair of pistols, of which he had been plundered. They were produced by the man who had taken them, and were immediately secured by the conscientious Lejoille, who told Captain Berry that he would give him a pair of French pistols to protect him on his journey home; that promise, it need scarcely be added, was never fulfilled.*

In short, Captain Thompson and his people experienced, while on board this French ship of the line, acts of cruelty that would have disgraced a Barbary corsair. The French carried their inhumanity to such a pitch, that, just as the surgeon of the Leander had commenced performing the necessary operations upon the wounded, they robbed him of his instruments; and the severe wounds of Captain Thompson had nearly proved fatal, by a refusal to allow his surgeon to visit him! It was actually not until after the Généreux and her prize had arrived at Corfu, which was on the 1st of September, that Captain Thompson could get the attendance of Mr. Mulberry to extract the musket-ball which had entered his arm; nor was that even then accomplished, until the latter gentleman had been smuggled on board the French ship unknown to her barbarian of a captain.

A sailor's wardrobe being scarcely worth plundering, Captain Lejoille found other means of turning to his advantage the resources of the poor fellows who had been in that capacity on board the Leander. Those who had been allowed to remain in the prize, were obliged to rig her with jury-masts, and refit her for the voyage to Corfu; and those who had been transhipped to the Généreux, were compelled to splice the whole of that ship's damaged rigging, before any other food was served out to them than bread and water.

On the 28th of August, while the Généreux, having the Leander in tow, was proceeding with her to Corfu, the 16-gun brig-sloop Mutine, Captain the Honourable Thomas Bladen Capel, bound as we have already stated, to Naples, with duplicates of the despatches with which the Leander had been charged, hove in sight; and such was the alarm on board the Généreux, at even this puny force, that the Frenchmen were preparing to secure the prisoners below, cast off the prize, and make the best of her way into port without her. Had the Mutine been rigged with three masts instead of two, and approached somewhat nearer than she did, the Généreux, in all probability, would have fled, and the Leander been recaptured. Captain Capel, however, as appears by the subjoined letter to Rear-admiral Nelson, written on the arrival of the Mutine at Naples, mistook the two vessels for ships of greater force; and that under circumstances of rather an extraordinary nature. "On the 28th of August," says Captain Capel, "in latitude 37° 45',

*Naval Chronicle, vol. xiv., p. 10.

longitude 16° 50', I fell in with two line-of-battle ships, one under three jury topmasts, the second had a jury mizen topmast, having the other ship in tow. I passed so close as to make their hulls out distinctly. I also showed them French colours, which they answered by the same; and I have not the smallest doubt, from those circumstances, and the perfect recollection I have of the Guillaume-Tell and the Généreux, that it was those ships: they were steering to the north-east, apparently for Corfu."*

The sufferings of the Leander's men did not cease with the arrival of the two ships at Corfu. The republican authorities there seem to have considered the example of Captain Lejoille and his officers worthy of imitation to the very letter; and, with all their characteristic hardihood, the seamen, more especially the wounded portion of them, nearly perished under the load of ill-treatment which was continued to be heaped upon them.†

At length the principal part of the officers, late belonging to the Leander, were allowed to return home on their parole; but Captain Lejoille actually detained the carpenter, Thomas Jarrat, because he refused to furnish him with the dimensions of the Leander's masts and yards. Several of the seamen also were compelled to remain at Corfu; and when, at a subsequent day, a Turco-Russian squadron was blockading the Généreux in the port, Captain Lejoille tried to persuade some of the Leander's men, of whose prowess he had received so indubitable a proof, to assist him in forcing his way out to sea. But the noble fellows lent a deaf ear to all the French captain's promises of reward; and, in particular, a maintopman, named George Bannister, replied, "No, you d—d French r——l, give us back our little ship, and we'll fight you again till we sink."

Had Captain Thompson found an enemy in such a man as Captain Bergeret,‡ or in any one of those by whom Captain Bligh of the Alexander had been captured,§ or, in short, any among 50 other French officers that might be named, his persevering defence of his ship, his noble support of the flag under which he served, would have gained him the esteem of his conqueror. Far from plundering , he would have protected him. Far from belying him, he would have told a plain tale of his own good fortune. Far from wishing to degrade his prisoner, that he

*Clarke and McArthur's Life of Nelson, vol. ii., p. 97

†See letter from Mr. Stanley, the British Consul at Trieste, in Naval Chronicle, vol. xiv., p. 11

‡While a prisoner in England, (see vol. i., p. 464,) Captain Bergeret was permitted to go to France on his parole, to endeavour to effect an exchange between himself and Sir Sidney Smith; but, failing in his object, he returned to England. Sir Sidney having in the mean time escaped, the British government, with a proper feeling, gave Captain Bergeret his liberty.

§See vol. i. p. 183.

might make him a stepping-stone to his own exaltation, he would have paid him the homage one brave man pays to another; he would even have endeavoured to heighten, rather than to diminish, the splendour of a resistance, which to overcome had cost him so dearly.

In the former edition of this work we gave an extract from, and commented rather severely upon, a letter, or rather the translation of a letter, bearing the signature of the captain of the Généreux, and transcribed at length in several English publications. We have since sought in vain among the French newspapers for the original of this letter, and begin to doubt whether it ever appeared at all in a French dress. The alleged writer, we now find, has long ceased to be among the living. We will not, therefore, make use of the contents of what has the appearance of being a spurious production, to heap additional disgrace upon the memory of Captain Lejoille.

In a respectable French historical work, from which we are in the habit of occasionally quoting, is a brief notice of the Leander's capture, as fairly stated in one part, as it is unfairly, or rather, to those who know the facts, ludicrously stated in another. The account represents the Leander to have mounted 50 guns, "cinquante canons," and to have fought the Généreux "four hours." Then follows in a note the following just remark; "Le poids des boulets d'une bordée du vaisseau français était double de celui des boulets d'une bordée du Leander, et la coque de ce vaisseau offrait infiniment moins de résistance. Notre impartialité nous fait un devoir de mentionner cette circonstance, qui devient honorable pour les défenseurs de vaisseau ennemi."

This is truly refreshing, after the highly exaggerated accounts of the Généreux's performance, which we recollect to have read in two or three numbers of the Moniteur. We wish the writer's "impartiality" had stimulated him to make further inquiry before he gave insertion to what follows, and which we shall first present in English: "Lejoille possessed yet further claims (alluding to his alleged valorous conduct at the battle of the Nile) to the esteem of his enemies, by the manner in which he treated the two English captains whom the chances of war had thrown into his power. After having paid them every imaginable attention, he sent them on their parole to England, the moment the captain of the Leander was sufficiently recovered of his wounds to support the journey." "Lejoille acquit encore de nouveaux droits à l'estime de ses ennemis par la manière dont il traita les deux capitaines anglais que le sort des armes avait fait tomber en son pouvoir. Après avoir eu pour eux toutes les attentions imaginables, il les renvoya sur parole en Angleterre, aussitôt que le commandant du Leander fut assez bien rétabli de ses blessures pour supporter le voyage."*

*Victoires et Conquêtes, tome x., p. 386.

At length Captains Thompson and Berry, with most of the Leander's officers, reached their native country. The court-martial, which sat on Captain Thompson, his officers and men, for the loss of their ship, was held on the 17th of December, 1798, at Sheerness, on board the America 64. The following was the sentence pronounced: "The court having heard the evidence brought forward in support of Captain Thompson's narrative of the capture of the Leander, and having very maturely and deliberately considered the whole, is of opinion, that the gallant and almost unprecedented defence of Captain Thompson, of his majesty's late ship Leander, against so superior a force as that of the Généreux, is deserving of every praise his country and this court can give; and that his conduct, with that of the officers and men under his command, reflects not only the highest honour on himself and them, but on their country at large, and the court does therefore most honourably acquit Captain Thompson, &c." The president, Captain George Tripp, then addressed the captain nearly as follows: "Captain Thompson, I feel the most lively pleasure in returning you the sword with which you have so bravely maintained the honour of your king and country; the more so, as I am convinced that when you are again called upon to draw it in their defence, you will add fresh laurels to the wreath you have already so nobly won." The thanks of the court were also given to Captain (knighted on the 12th) Sir Edward Berry; and Captain Thompson, upon his return to the shore, was saluted with three cheers by all the ships in the harbour.

Thus had Captain Thompson received from the sentence of a court-martial, as honourable an acquittal as his heart could desire; and he soon afterwards received, from the hand of his sovereign, a boon which the proudest victor usually, but not more rightfully claims, the honour of knighthood.

As every officer, who was on board the Leander in her action with the Généreux, is entitled to have his name included in the account, we are happy in having it in our power to record the names of the greater part, if not the whole, of those not already mentioned in the return of loss. Her first lieutenant was William Richardson; her second and third, and her master, appear among the wounded. Two master's mates were Jeremiah Russel and John Whitehead; a third is among the wounded. Her midshipmen were, Charles Hardy, William Reynolds, George Lemprière, John Coates, and Caesar William Richardson; exclusive of the three killed and the one wounded; clerk, Charles Bullman; surgeon, boatswain, and carpenter have been already named. The gunner was John Burns, and the purser, Daniel Hogg. Marine officer there was none on board but sergeant Dair, and he gallantly fell at his post.

It is not a little singular that, towards the close of the preceding war, this same Leander had an engagement with a

French 74. At midnight, on the 18th of January, 1783, while cruising in the West Indies, the Leander, Captain John Willet Payne (the same who commanded the Russel in Lord Howe's action), fell in with the French 74-gun ship Pluton, Captain d'Albert de Rioms, partially disabled, it appears, either by a gale or an action. The Leander herself commenced the attack, and soon obtained a capital raking position on the 74's starboard bow. After a smart contest of two hours, the Pluton sheered off, with the loss of one lieutenant and four seamen killed, and 11 seamen wounded. The loss on board the Leander amounted to 13 killed and wounded; the latter so badly, that two only of them survived.

On the 22d of August, at noon, the British 38-gun frigate, Naiad, Captain William Pierrepont, cruising off Cape Finisterre, discovered and chased a French frigate in the east-north-east, but at dark lost sight of her. Soon after midnight, however, the Naiad again saw the French frigate steering south-east, and continued the pursuit, with light breezes, during the remainder of the night, and until 2 P.M. the next day; when the British 44-gun frigate, Magnanime, Captain, the Honourable Michael De Courcy, hove in sight, and joined in the chase.

At about 5 P.M. the French 36-gun frigate, Décade, Captain Villeneuve, began firing her stern-chasers at her pursuers, particularly at the Naiad, the more advanced ship of the two; and who, at 6 h. 15 m. P.M., commenced a fire in return. After a running fight of about an hour from its commencement, but by which, as it appears, no damage or loss was inflicted on either side, the Décade hauled down her colours.

The frigate was last from Cayenne; whither she had carried the banished persons whom the Charente, on account of her accident, had been obliged to reland.* The Décade had on board a crew of 326 men, but had left at Cayenne ten of her guns: consequently she mounted but 30 at the most, while the Naiad alone mounted 46, and of a heavier caliber. The prize measured 915 tons, and was added to the British navy as a 12-pounder, 36-gun frigate.

On the 7th of September, at noon, the British 38-gun frigate, Phaëton, Captain, the Honourable Robert Stopford, and 44-gun frigate Anson, Captain Philip Charles Durham, cruising in company off the French coast in the neighbourhood of the river Gironde, fell in with, and after a chase of 24 hours, captured the French 32-gun frigate Flore, eight days from Bordeaux, on a cruise.

Although called a frigate in Captain Stopford's letter, the Flore, it would appear, was not, at the time of her capture, a national frigate, but a privateer, similar to the Citoyenne-Française, the ship which, the first year of the war, had the

*See p. 296.

action with the Iris.* The Flore, however, had been a national frigate, and a very remarkable one, as the following account of her will show.

In the year 1757, the French frigate, Vestale, measuring 698 tons English, and pierced to carry 32 long 12 and 6 pounders, was launched at the port of Hâvre. In the spring of 1761, the Vestale was captured, off the Penmarcks, by the 28-gun frigate, Unicorn, the look-out ship of a British squadron cruising off Brest, and was added to the British navy by the name of Flora. In the year 1778, the Flora was sunk by the British, at the evacuation of Rhode-Island, in order that she might not fall into the hands of the Americans. The latter, however, with their accustomed ingenuity, weighed the frigate, and then sold her to her original masters, the French government; from whose service on account probably of her age and comparatively small dimensions, she appears to have been finally dismissed at the conclusion of the peace in 1783.

On the 24th of October, at 8 A.M., the Texel bearing south by east, distant 10 leagues, the British 18-pounder, 36-gun frigate, Sirius, Captain Richard King, while reconnoitring that port, fell in with two Dutch ships of war, one the 36-gun frigate, Furie, Captain Pletz, the other, the 24-gun corvette, Waakzaamheid, Captain Neirop; but the ships were not in a situation for mutual support, being about two miles part. Passing within gun-shot of the former, which was the leewardmost, the Sirius stood on until she could nearly fetch the Waakzaamheid. At about 9 A.M., Captain King, having thus, as was his object, prevented the junction of the two ships, fired at and brought to the Waakzaamheid, who immediately discharged a lee gun, and hauled down her colours.

As soon as possession was taken of the Waakzaamheid, the prisoners removed, and a prize-crew put on board, the Sirius made sail after the Furie; who, the instant she had witnessed the bloodless surrender of her commodore (for Captain Neirop was the senior officer), bore up, and, by the time the Sirius was ready for pursuit, had nearly escaped out of sight. By 5 P.M., however, the Sirius had the good fortune to overtake the escaping ship. A running action now ensued, at times within musket-shot distance, the Furie returning the heavy fire of the Sirius, with a smart but ill-directed discharge of cannon and musketry. This continued for about half an hour; when the Furie, having her hull, masts, rigging, and sails much cut up, surrendered. The damage done to the Sirius was but trifling, she having only received a shot through her bowsprit, had her rigging and sails a little injured, and one man wounded by a musket-ball.

The guns of the Sirius, a frigate of 1049 tons, were 44 in

* See vol. i., p. 91.

number, similar to those of the Phœbe at a preceding page. The 36 guns of the Furie, a frigate of 827 tons, were long Dutch twelves and sixes; and the 26 guns of the Waakzaamheid, a ship of 504 tons, were all, except two brass sixes, long Dutch eights: two of these also brass and, we believe, mounted in the bridleports. Even then, 24 ports, calculated for 8 or 9 pounder guns, appear to be a great many for a ship of 504 tons. It is true, that the Waakzaamheid had two ports of a side on a lower or birth-deck; but the official letter expressly states, that she mounted 24 guns on her main deck.

The Furie, out of a complement, including 165 soldiers, of 328 men and boys, suffered a loss of eight men killed and 14 wounded. The Waakzaamheid, as we have seen, made no defence; therefore her crew, including 122 French soldiers, of 222 men and boys, escaped unhurt. This renders it unnecessary to exhibit any formal statement of the comparative force of the combatants: suffice it that, could the two Dutch ships have united their strength in defence of their flag, they would still have been hardly a match for the Sirius.

The two prizes contained on board, between them, 6000 stands of arms, besides other ordnance stores; which, along with the troops, they were carrying to Ireland. Both ships were purchased for the use of the British navy. One, under the name of Wilhelmina (a Fury being already in the service), became a 12-pounder 32-gun frigate; the other, under her own hard name, was, for the short time she reigned as a cruiser, attached to the 20-gun class. As a proof, too, that we had reason to doubt her having mounted, when captured, 24 guns on the main deck, 20 only were established there when the Waakzaamheid was fitted out in the British service.

In the latter part of November, as the British privateer-schooner Herald, of Jersey, Captain Thomas Pistock, was cruising off the Neapolitan coast, three French privateers commenced a furious attack upon her. Captain Pistock, by an animated address, so inspirited the Herald's crew, that, after an action of three hours' duration, the Herald beat off all three of her opponents, leaving them with shattered hulls, and a loss, between them, as reported to have been afterwards ascertained, of 30 in killed and wounded; while the British vessel had the good fortune not to lose a man.

The Herald was only of 80 tons, and mounted 10 guns, 3, 4, and 6 pounders, with a complement of 28 men; whereas the largest of the French privateers mounted, it is said, five long 18-pounders (one on a traversing carriage), and the other two, four 8-pounders each: consequently the united crews of the three must have amounted to at least 180 men. It is related also that, on the night of the action, a felucca, with 22 men, suddenly appeared alongside the Herald, with the view of carrying her by boarding; but that a well-directed broadside from the Herald sent the felucca and all that were in her to the bottom.

On his arrival at Naples shortly afterwards, Captain Pistock received from all ranks, for his spirited behaviour, the highest marks of attention and respect. The Duke of Sussex, who was then at Naples, is said to have twice honoured Captain Pistock with an invitation to breakfast, and to have presented him with a hanger of considerable value, marked with the initials of his royal highness's name; and one of the prince's suite, a Mr. Veers, gave a pair of pistols to the gallant privateer's-man. The latter was also received with great attention by Sir William Hamilton, the British envoy. The brave crew of the Herald did not pass unnoticed; as the British merchants at Naples raised by subscription and distributed between them, the sum of 200 dollars.

On the 7th of December, as the British 22-gun ship Perdrix, Captain William Charles Fahie, mounting 20 French 6-pounders and two English 12-pounder carronades, was cruising to leeward of the island of St.-Thomas, an American master gave information that his vessel, the preceding evening, had been boarded by a French ship of war, seven leagues to the eastward of Virgin-Gorda. Captain Fahie used every exertion to get to windward of the last-named island; but, owing to the prevailing strong gales, accompanied at times by heavy squalls, the Perdrix did not, until the 10th, effect that object. On the 11th, at daylight, a ship was discovered from the mast-head in the south-east quarter, and soon ascertained to be a cruiser. Not a moment was lost in pursuing her; and, after a 16 hours' chase, the Perdrix brought to close action the French privateer-ship Armée-d'Italie, Captain Colachy, mounting 18 guns, four of them long 12, and the remainder long 8 pounders. An animated fire was kept up for 42 minutes; when the latter, being reduced to an unmanageable wreck, struck her colours.

The damages of the Perdrix were confined to her rigging and sails, and, out of a crew of 153 men and boys, she escaped with only one man wounded; while the loss on board the Armée-d'Italie, whose crew numbered 117, amounted to six men killed and five wounded. Captain Fahie, in his official letter, highly commends the conduct of the two lieutenants of the Perdrix, Edward Ottley and James Smith; also of Mr. Moses Crawford, the master, and Mr. Samuel Piguenet, the purser, the latter of whom volunteered to serve on deck.

On the 5th of December the British 12-pounder 32-gun frigate Ambuscade, mounting eight 24-pounder carronades beyond her 32 long guns, or 40 guns in all, Captain Henry Jenkins, leaving some of her men in charge of a prize with which she had just arrived at Portsmouth, again set sail on a cruise off the French coast. In a few days afterwards the

Ambuscade captured a brig and a chasse-marée, and placed in charge of the former her second lieutenant and a party of her best men, receiving on board, from the two vessels, about 30 French prisoners. At this time her third lieutenant, Joseph Briggs, was confined to his cabin with a dangerous illness, and, of her complement of 212, including a large proportion of boys, no more than 190 remained.

Thus circumstanced, the Ambuscade, on the 14th, at 7 A.M., while lying to off the port of Bordeaux, in momentary expectation of being joined by the 32-gun frigate Stag, Captain Joseph Sydney Yorke, discovered a sail coming down from the seaward. None seemed to doubt that this was the Stag; and, as the ship approached end-on, no opportunity was afforded of judging from the appearance of her hull. Accordingly, at the usual hour the officers and men went unconcerned to breakfast. At a little before 9 A.M. the stranger had approached nearly within gun-shot; when, suddenly, she hauled close to the wind, and made all sail to get away. The mistake was now discovered: the hands were turned up; and, in a little while, the Ambuscade was under a press of sail in chase. In order to quicken her progress to windward, the hammocks were piped down. After this the Ambuscade gained upon the chase; and at length, between 11 and 12 in the forenoon, got near enough to fire a shot. This was immediately returned by the stranger, whom we may now introduce as the French 28-gun frigate, or, in the old nomenclature, when the quarterdecks of this class were not armed, "24-gun corvette," Baïonnaise, mounting 24 long French eights upon the main deck, and six long sixes, with two brass 36-pounder carronades, upon the quarterdeck, total 32 carriage-guns, besides eight large swivels mounted upon her barricade. The Baïonnaise was commanded by Lieutenant de vaisseau Jean-Baptiste-Edmond Richer, and had on board, including an officer and 30 troops which she had brought from Cayenne, a crew of at least 250 men and boys. Indeed, according to the "rôle de'équipage," found on board this same ship when destroyed by a British ship of war at a subsequent day, her established crew alone amounted to 280.

Each ship, as soon as she had fired a shot in the manner related, hoisted her colours. Soon afterwards the Baïonnaise shortened sail, and the action commenced. After it had continued about an hour, to the evident disadvantage of the French ship, one of the Ambuscade's maindeck 12-pounders, abreast of the gangway, burst. By this unfortunate accident the gangway was knocked to pieces, the boats on the boom stove, the lower sill of the port blown away even with the deck, and 11 men badly wounded. An accident of the kind never fails to damp the ardour of the bravest and best disciplined ship's company: what then must have been its effect upon a set of men so utterly worthless, with a few exceptions, as those of Ambuscade?

In the midst of the confusion consequent upon this disaster, the Baïonnaise made sail. The Ambuscade followed presently, and recommenced the action to leeward; but, coming up with a crowd of canvass, shot far ahead. The Baïonnaise, by this time, had sustained considerable damage in her hull, rigging, and spars, as well as a heavy loss in officers and men, including among the wounded her captain and first lieutenant; when, according to the French accounts, the commandant of the troops suggested to the only sea-officer remaining on deck, the probable success of an attempt to board.

The plan being concurred in, the helm of the French ship was put up, and the Baïonnaise ran foul of her opponent, carrying away, with her bowsprit, the Ambuscade's starboard quarter-deck bulwark, mizen shrouds and mizen mast, and unshipped the wheel. We are left to conjecture in what state the Ambuscade was, to have permitted this: at all events, the ship could not have been under command. The Baïonnaise then dropped under the Ambuscade's stern; but still remained foul, having, by the fluke of her anchor or a grappling-iron, caught the latter's rudder-chain. The French troops, from the bowsprit, the head of which had fallen with the jib-boom and spritsail yard, now commanded, with their powerful musketry, the whole range of the Ambuscade's quarterdeck.

A smart fire, in return, was kept up by the remnant of the British marines. So much, however, to the disadvantage of the Ambuscade, that, in a very short time, her first lieutenant, Dawson Main, received a musket-shot in his groin, and was handed below, where he almost immediately expired. Directly afterwards Captain Jenkins received a shot that carried away the top of his thigh-bone. He also was necessarily taken below. Almost at the same instant Lieutenant Sinclair, of the marines, received a wound in his thigh, and then another in the shoulder: he, too, was compelled to quit his quarters. Scarcely had he been handed below, when the master, Mr. Brown, was shot through the head, and fell on the deck amidst a heap of killed and wounded. The only surviving lieutenant, Joseph Briggs, had come out of his sick cot to take a part in the action: he was wounded in the head. After this, the command devolved upon Mr. William Bowman Murray, the purser.

The gunner now came on deck, and reported that the ship was on fire abaft; whereupon the majority of the surviving crew, apprehensive of the magazine, quitted their quarters and went below; where they remained, in spite of every endeavour of Mr. Murray to rally them. The alarm was occasioned by the explosion of some cartridges, carelessly left upon the rudder-head during the discharge of a gun through the cabin windows into the bow of the Baïonnaise; an accident which, besides the fatal panic it caused, badly wounded every man at the gun, and blew out a part of the Ambuscade's stern, and shattered the jollyboat that had been hanging there. In the height of all this confusion, the French soldiers, followed by the crew of the Baïonnaise, of whose bowsprit they made a bridge, rushed upon the now nearly abandoned quarterdeck of the Ambuscade; and, after a very short struggle, possessed themselves of the British frigate.

The loss sustained by the Ambuscade amounted to 10 killed, and 36 wounded; including, among the former, her first lieutenant and master, and, among the latter, her captain very dangerously, third and only surviving lieutenant, and a lieutenant of marines. The loss on the part of the Baïonnaise appears, by the French accounts, to have amounted to 30 killed, and 30 badly wounded; including, among the former, the officer in command of the troops, and, among the latter, Captain Richer and his first lieutenant. The number of slightly wounded is not stated; but the whole wounded, if they bore something less even than in the usual proportion to the killed, could not have amounted to fewer than from 60 to 70 men.

Few actions in the accounts of them, have been worse handled than that of the Ambuscade and Baïonnaise. The English historians have been either too sensitive to touch upon it, or more than usually negligent in supplying themselves with details. Captain Schomberg, who in vol. iii., comprises his account in about 30 lines, calls the Baïonnaise a French "privateer" of 32 guns. It was, however, some excuse, that even the sentence of the court-martial upon Captain Jenkins, as published, avoided naming the ship by which the Ambuscade had been captured. In the dreadfully wounded state of Captain Jenkins and his few surviving officers, it was as much as he and they could do, merely to enumerate the guns mounted by the Baïonnaise. This they did, stating them at 32, but of what calibers, or whether a part of them were not swivels, they left unexplained. Next came a paragraph in the Moniteur, stating in an official manner, that the English frigate Ambuscade, of 40 guns, had been captured by the French corvette Baïonnaise, of 20 guns. Thus was the British public left to decide to which account they would give credit; one of them not very flattering, the other quite humiliating, to the national pride.

We have now before us a French engraving of this action, underneath which is inscribed, "La Baïonnaise, corvette française, de vingt-quatre canons de huit, prenant à l'abordage l'Embuscade, frégate anglaise, de vingt-six canons de seize, le vingt-neuf Décembre, 1798. Dessinée et gravée par les ordres de Monsieur L'Amiral Bruix, ministre de la marine et des colonies." The statement, that one ship mounted "24 guns," waits but to be explained until we read that the other mounted "26 guns." The fact is, much to the credit of Admiral Bruix, where a different mode of stating the guns would have cast a greater slur upon the British vessel, the maindeck guns of each ship are all that are enumerated. The print represents a full broadside view of the Baïonnaise, without a single port obscured by smoke. She has 12 guns run out on her main deck, with a bow or bridle port, making 13 ports in all. Her forecastle is without a bulwark, and, of course without guns; but the exposed side of her quarterdeck shows four ports, with guns in them, the aftermost one apparently a carronade: four swivels also appear, mounted in their usual place along the top of the barricade. Here, then, we have, as admitted by the French themselves, 30 long guns and two carronades; comprising the number stated, not only by the officers of the Ambuscade, but by those of the Ardent, which ship, at a subsequent day, drove on shore and destroyed this same Baïonnaise.

We may here remark, that the drawing is executed in a masterly manner, and is minute even to a block. The stern of the English ship, of which there is a full view, agrees, in all the carved work, and in every other particular, with the stern of the Ambuscade, according to the sheer-draught of the ship at the navy-office, which we have inspected. This commendable accuracy affords a lesson to English naval painters. The Baïonnaise, at each of whose lower yard-arms a grappling-iron is suspended, perfectly resembles in her general appearance, as far as our information extends, the several captured ships of her class. These were the Bienvenue, Mignonne, Belette, Blonde, Tourterelle, Unité, Républicaine, and a few others; all of which ships mounted, like the Baïonnaise, 24 long eights on the main deck. Besides these guns, the Tourterelle had six, and the Républicaine eight, brass 36-pounder carronades on the quarter-deck; the others, long 6-pounders , with or without carronades. The established complement of the class appears to have been at this time, however it may afterwards have been increased in the case of the Baïonnaise, 220 men and boys; and the size of the captured ships, except in the cases of the Bienvenue and Mignonne, whose measurements, having been taken in foreign dock-yards, are, as we shall hereafter show, not to be relied upon, varied only between 579 and 581 tons. The Ambuscade measured 684 tons; and, believing the picture, from which this engraving was taken, to have been that "displayed in the Louvre, and shown in the Luxembourg in 1821," we cannot concur with a contemporary in the statement, that "the size of the British ship was as much magnified beyond, as that of her opponent was diminished below, the real fact."* On the contrary, we think that here, as in the minutiae of detail already noticed, English naval artists have something to learn.

*Brenton, vol. ii., p. 372.

We wish we could speak as favourably of an account in a recently published French work of general respectability, as we have been induced to do of Vice-admiral Bruix's picture. The gist of that account is, that the Baïonnaise "de vingt canons de 8" captured the Ambuscade, "portant quarante-deux bouches à feu de 18, 24,et 6."* We have known cases wherein a French minister of marine's account, on a point of pure naval concern especially, might even exceed the bounds of moral probability, and yet be maintained as true by a French historical writer. We now find, that it is only when no other French account exceeds it in exaggeration, that such implicit reliance is placed.

The disparity of force, in guns at all events, which did really exist between the Ambuscade and Baïonnaise, should, and, but for a succession of untoward accidents, doubtless would, have led to a very different result. The bursting of a gun on board a ship is irremediable. Who knows but that the next gun, and every gun in succession along the side, may prove equally treacherous. They are all of the same caliber, were put on board at the same time, and cast at the same foundry. If the man who had loaded the gun survived the explosion, he would naturally insist, whatever was the fact, that no more than the proper charge had been used. Hence, the ship's company would attribute the misfortune to some flaw in the gun; whether the effect of original construction, or of age or negligence, no matter. After the occurrence of such an accident, the remaining guns are seldom well loaded, or well pointed. Many shots would have been thrown away, and much injury from the enemy's unabated fire be sustained, ere that confidence, which is so necessary towards success, would again reign throughout the ship.

The gun-force of the Ambuscade, even while the cannonade lasted, was of little comparative effect; and as soon as the Baïonnaise got on board her adversary, it gave place to musketry. Here a new species of contest commenced; a contest in which the French ship from superior numbers had some, and, from superior tactics and other circumstances, many advantages. Thirty veterans of the famous regiment of Alsace, headed by an enterprising officer, and assisted by a French crew of more than seven times their number, stood opposed to about 20 young marines, and 170 seamen (officers, men, and boys), of whom three fourths, we mean of the men, were the scum of the British navy. Nor had the sailors been improved in discipline, or in love for the service, by the partial and ill-judged conduct of Captain Jenkins; who, it seems, had brought with him from the 74-gun ship Carnatic a party of seamen, whom he styled the "Gentlemen Carnatics;" distinguishing those he found on board the frigate, by the opprobrious epithet of "Blackguard

*Victoires et Conquêtes, tome x., p. 427.

Ambuscades." Captain Jenkins thus raised two parties in his ship; and it may easily be conceived by which he was abandoned in the hour of trial. The early fall of the principal officers, the explosion in the cabin, and the reported fire in the neighbourhood of the magazine, were turned to advantage the cowardly and disaffected; and the Ambuscade was lost, under circumstances discreditable to the ship, and to every one belonging to her. There can be no doubt that Captain Jenkins, and his officers, and several of the Ambuscade's seamen and marines, were brave men: they proved themselves so in the blood they spilt at their quarters. But what excuse can be offered for not having ascertained, by the customary mode of signals, the true character of the strange ship when she first hove in sight? Had that been done, much confusion would have been avoided, and the Ambuscade might have obtained the weathergage, and thereby kept her adversary from boarding. Another ten minutes' cannonade from her 12-pounders would then, in all probability, owing to the loss which the fire of the first ten had already inflicted on the French ship, have totally reversed the issue of the battle. Why were the hammocks not brought on deck and restowed? Of what use were they, if not to shelter the men from the enemy's musketry?

After the action the two ships proceeded to Rochefort; where, on the 20th, they arrived in safety. The rejoicings of the French were loud and general; and who can say they were ill founded? It was literally, that an English frigate had been captured by a French corvette. The executive directory, to express their sense of the merits of the action, decreed that there should be paid to the officers and crew of the Baïonnaise, to be distributed according to the prize-law, 3500 francs (about 146*l.* sterling) for every long gun and carronade on aboard the Abuscade; and the government immediately promoted Captain Richer from "lieutenant," over the next step, to "capitaine de vaisseau." This, it will be admitted, was no more than he merited; and, had the officer in command of the troops survived the action, he too would undoubtedly have been promoted. The Ambuscade was added to the French navy under the same name translated into French (Embuscade), but she was not, as stated in the Moniteur, "une frégate neuve," having been built as long ago as the year 1773.

Captain Jenkins and his surviving officers and ship's company as soon as they returned to England, were, as a matter of course, brought to a court-martial for the loss of the Ambuscade. The court sat on the 26th, 27th, and 28th of August, on board the Gladiator, in Portsmouth harbour. At the expiration of three days of the most minute and patient investigation, a sentence of acquittal was pronounced upon the captain and his surviving officers, and the loss of the ship was attributed to many of the circumstances already detailed. Part of the ship's company were praised for their meritorious exertions, and the remainder animadverted upon for conduct of a quite opposite character. The court, however, not possessing the means of discrimination, and fearful of involving the innocent with the guilty, acquitted the whole ship's company. Captain Jenkins was still suffering under the effects of the dreadful wound he had received, and looked extremely ill. This probably operated in mitigating the sentence. Otherwise the captain no doubt would have been, if not more seriously dealt with, severely reprimanded, for the undisciplined state of his ship, and for the unseamanlike manner in which the action, from first to last, had been conducted.

COLONIAL EXPEDITIONS. – WEST INDIES.

It being found expedient for the British troops to evacuate Port-au-Prince, St.-Marc, and Arcahaye, in the island of St.-Domingo, Brigadier-general the Honourable Thomas Maitland, the British commanding officer on shore, sent a flag of truce on the 22d of April, to the Republican General Toussaint-Louverture, with a proposal for the suspension of arms, not to exceed five weeks, and for a guarantee in favour of the lives and properties of all those inhabitants who might choose to remain. These terms being agreed to, and properly ratified, the troops, stores, and such of the inhabitants as were desirous to quit, were embarked on board the Thunderer 74, Abergavenny, 54, and other British ships of war; and on the 9th of May, the republican French were put in possession of the ceded places. The ships then proceeded to Cape Nicolas-Mole, where the troops and French refugees were safely disembarked. Shortly after this the three French 36-gun frigates Bravoure, Cocarde, and Sirène, arrived at Cape François from Europe with supplies, and on the 4th of December got safe back to Lorient.

In the month of August the Spaniards evinced a disposition to attack the British settlement at the bay of Honduras. The regular force on shore at the post was composed of small detachments of the 63d and 6th West-India regiments and of the royal artillery, under the command of Lieutenant-colonel Thomas Barrow; and the naval force consisted of only one British vessel of war, the 16-gun ship-sloop Merlin, Captain John Ralph Moss, lying at anchor in the port of Belize. Besides the Merlin, however, the following colonial gun-boats had just been fitted up, the Towzer, Tickler, and Mermaid, sloop-rigged, the latter with one long 9, and each of the others with one long 18 pounder, and 25 men; the schooners Swinger and Teazer, the one with four 6 and two 4-pounders, and the other with six 6-pounders, and 25 men each; and eight gun-flats, with one 9-pounder in the prow and 16 men each: making, with one supernumerary, 254 men, including officers. The Towzer and Tickler were commanded by two masters of merchantmen, and partly manned with their sailors: the remainder of the officers and men belonging to the flotilla consisted of volunteers from the colonial troops.

The force with which the Spaniards were preparing to make the attack consisted of about 20 schooners and sloops, armed, the greater part of them with one long 24-pounder in the bow, and two long 18s in the stern, besides from eight to 22 swivels along the waist. There were, also, 10 or 11 transports or victuallers, schooner and sloop rigged, each armed with heavy bow and stern guns, and swivels on the sides. The seamen employed on board this flotilla numbered, as was understood, about 500, and were under the orders of Captain Bocca-Negra: the troops amounted to about 2000, and were commanded by Field-marshal Arthur O'Neil.

On the 3d of September the Spaniards endeavoured to force a passage over Montego-key shoal, with five vessels, two of which carried long 18 or 24 pounders, and the provison and stores of all of which, in order to lighten them, had been shifted to other vessels. The Tickler, Swinger, and Teazer, instantly proceeded to annoy these five Spanish vessels, and by dark, compelled them to retire. This afforded to the commanding officer of the British vessels the opportunity of drawing and destroying all the stakes and beacons which the Spaniards had placed in the narrow and intricate channel, and without the use of which none but vessels of a very light draught of water could pass. On the following day, the 4th, the attempt to pass the shoal was renewed, and defeated in a similar manner. On the 5th the same Spanish vessels, accompanied by two others, and by several launches filled with troops, endeavoured to get over the same shoal by another passage, but were repulsed, apparently with loss. On this, as well as on the two preceding days, the Spaniards expended an immense quantity of ammunition to no manner of purpose; while the British fired comparatively little, but with a steady precision that produced a sensible effect.

Having no doubt that the next effort of the Spaniards would be against St.-George's key, from which they might easily go down to the Belize, only nine miles distant, and there destroy the town and harass the inhabitants, Captain Moss, in the night of the 5th, weighed, and by noon on the following day, worked up to the key. Twelve of the heaviest among the Spanish vessels were then under way, for the purpose of making the attempt; but, on seeing the Merlin and the flotilla of gun-boats so near, the Spaniards hauled to the wind and returned to their former anchorage, between Long-key and Key-chapel.

The Spanish vessels continued working and anchoring among the shoals, at the distance of four or five miles from the Merlin and gun-boats, until the 10th; when, at 1 P.M., nine sail of armed sloops and schooners, each with a launch astern full of men, bore down through the channel that led to the Merlin. Five smaller vessels, also with troops on board, were at anchor to windward, at the distance of about a mile and a half; and the remainder of the Spanish flotilla lay at Long-key Spit, as if awaiting the issue of the contest. The Spanish vessels approached, in line abreast, using both sails and oars; and, on arriving within long gun-shot, dropped anchor. It seeming to be their intention to board the Towzer and Tickler, which vessels lay much nearer to them than the bulk of the flotilla, Captain Moss, at 1 h. 30 m. P.M., made the signal to engage. The British immediately opened an animated and apparently destructive fire, which was returned by the Spaniards, and the cannonade lasted two hours and a half. At the end of that time the Spaniards, in evident confusion, cut their cables, and sailed and rowed off, assisted by a number of launches, which took in tow the greater part of their vessels. No man was hurt on the part of the British; but the Spaniards, from the hasty manner of their retreat, appeared not to have been so fortunate. Owing to the shoal water, the Merlin was unable to follow the Spanish vessels; and the remainder of the British flotilla, without her support, would have been no match for them. The whole therefore effected their escape. The Spaniards remained under Key-chapel until the night of the 15th, when they moved off with a light southerly wind. Some of the vessels went to Baccalar, and others to Campeachy; nor did the Spaniards again venture to attack the British possessions in Honduras bay.

BRITISH AND FRENCH FLEETS.

WITH respect to the state of the British navy at the commencement of the present year, it will suffice to refer to the usual abstract of its numbers and strength.* We may notice, however, that two fine line-of-battle classes, L and M, have more than doubled themselves since the beginning of the preceding year. Indeed all the principal columns in the abstract exhibit an increase of numbers; arising, in part, from newly-built vessels, but chiefly from captures made at the expense of the French, Dutch, and Spanish navies respectively.† The number of British ships of war, wrecked and foundered during the year 1798, is still of considerable amount;‡ but fewer of the crews, it is gratifying to observe, perished, than amidst the similar mishaps of the preceding year. We may here remark, in passing, that, as respects the French, Dutch, and Spanish navies, the foundered, wrecked, and burnt cases do, in all probability, fall short of the real number, no nation but England publishing any list of the losses that her navy sustains.

The number of commissioned officers and masters, belonging to the British navy at the commencement of the year, was,

Admirals		21
Vice-admirals		36
Rear-admirals		42
Rear-admirals	superannuated	28
Captains		547
Captains	superannuated	19

*See Appendix, Annual Abstract No. 7.
†See Appendix, Nos. 15, 16.
‡See Appendix, No. 17.

Commanders, or sloop-captains		386
Lieutenants		2157
Lieutenants	superannuated	50*
Masters		535

and the number of seamen and marines voted for the service of the year 1799, was 120,000.†

The opening of the present year saw France with a second coalition formed against her. Naples and Sardinia had, as we have seen, recommenced hostilities with no great éclat; but Austria was preparing to lend them her powerful aid, and Russia had already united with Turkey in revenging Buonaparte's flagrant attack upon Egypt. France, on the other hand, was making great exertions to withstand the host of foes which, thus aroused, had again confederated against her; and, among other measures taken, orders had issued, since the 25th of the preceding November, for the construction of 16 ships of the line, 18 heavy frigates, and 12 corvettes.

Vice-admiral Eustache Bruix, the French minister of marine, also went down from Paris, with money to pay the seamen at Brest, and remained at that port superintending the equipment of the ships. In consequence of this, the utmost activity pervaded every department, and, towards the middle of April, 25 ships of the line and several frigates were ready for sea. The minister addressed a proclamation to the seamen, much in the same style as the "instructions" transmitted from the directory at the commencement of the year 1794. Vice-admiral Bruix adverted to the splendid actions of the Charente and of the Baïonnaise, as well as to the vigorous resistance made by the Seine, and by the squadron under Commodore Bompart. The address, or that part of it at least, which promised that the families of the seamen should be provided for in their absence, and that a third part in value of the prizes should be paid to them immediately after capture, drew the seamen from the privateers to the national ships, and thus answered the purpose intended.

In the first three or four months of the present year, the British force cruising off Brest consisted of a squadron of eight or nine sail of the line, under the successive command of Vice-admiral Sir Charles Thompson, baronet, in the Formidable 98, Vice-admiral Lord Hugh Seymour, in the Sans-Pareil 80, and Rear-admiral the Honourable George Cranfield Berkeley, in the Mars 74. On the 16th of April, at 6 P.M., a French convoy, consisting of the armed store-ships Dromadaire and Nécessité, and 50 other vessels, escorted by Captain Pierre-Marie Le Bozec, with the corvettes Etonnante, Société, Mignonne, and Cigogne, and lugger Vautour, were chased by Rear-admiral

*With the rank of commanders. †See Appendix, no. 18.

Berkeley's squadron, but effected their escape into Brest. On the 17th, early in the morning, Admiral Lord Bridport, who, with the Royal-George and five or six other ships, had sailed from St.-Helen's on the 13th, arrived off Ushant, and superseded Rear-admiral Berkeley in the command.

On the 25th, Lord Bridport looked into the port of Brest, and counted 13 French line-of-battle ships at anchor, and five under way, in the road of Bertheaume, as if preparing to put to sea with the fresh north-east wind then blowing. The British fleet was at this time right in the centre of the Iroise passage, and not above five or six miles to the south-west of the Black Rocks. At 2 P.M. Lord Bridport made sail to the west-north-west, and in two hours was about four leagues to the west-south-west of Ushant, with, including the Russel, which was then about joining, the following 16 sail of the line:

Gun-ship		
100	Royal-George	Admiral (w.) Lord Bridport, K.B. Rear-adm. (r.) Charles Morice Pole. Captain William Domett.
98	Prince	Rear-adm. (r.) Sir Charles Cotton, bart. Captain Thomas Larcom.
	St.-George	Captain Sampson Edwards.
	Neptune	Captain James Vashon.
	Glory	Captain Thomas Wells.
80	Caesar	Captain Sir James Saumarez,
74	Mars	Rear-adm. (b.) Hon. G. Cra. Berkeley. Captain John Monckton.
	Dragon	Captain George Campbell.
	Impétueux	Captain Sir Edward Pellew, bart.
	Terrible	Captain William Wolseley.
	Achille	Captain George Murray.
	Superb	Captain John Sutton.
	Ajax	Captain Hon. Alex. Inglis Cochrane.
	Pompée	Captain Charles Stirling.
	Magnificent	Captain Edward Bowater.
	Russel	Captain Herbert Sawyer.

Frigates, three or four, but their names are uncertain.

On the evening of the same 25th of April, on which Lord Bridport had thus left open the principal passage in and out of Brest, Vice-admiral Bruix put to sea with, except the Convention, which did not join until the next morning, the following well-appointed fleet:

Gun-ship		
120	Océan	Captain Alain-Adélaïde-Marie Bruilhac.
110	Invincible	Commod. Louis L'Héritier.
	Terrible	Commod. Yves.-Mar.-G.-P. Le Coat St. Haouen.
	Républicain	Captain Charles Berrenger.
80	Formidable	Commod. Pierre-Julien Thréouart.
	Indomptable	Captain —— Chambon.
74	Jemmappes	Commod. Julien-Marie Cosmao-Kerjulien.
	Mont-Blanc	Commod. Esprit-Tranquille Maistral.
	Tyrannicide	Commod. Zacharie-Jac.-Théodore Allemand.
	Batave	Commod. Franç-Hen.-Eugène Daugier.
	Constitution	Commod. Julien Le Ray.

Gun-ship		
74	Duquesne	Commod. Pierre-Maurice.-Julien Querangal.
	Fougueux	Commod. Pierre-marie Bescond.
	Censeur	Commod. Ant.-Jean-Baptiste Faye.
	Zélé	Commod. —— Dufoy.
	Redoutable	Commod. —— Moncousu.
	Wattigny	Captain Antoine-Louis Gourdon.
	Tourville	Captain Jean-Baptiste Henry.
	Cisalpin	Captain Mathieu-Charles Bergevin.
	Jean-Bart	Captain François-Jacques Meynne.
	Gaulois	Captain Gabriel Siméon.
	Convention	Captain Charles Lebozec.
	Révolution	Captain Pierre-Nicolas Rolland.
	J. J. Rousseau	Captain Julien-Gabriel Bigot.
	Dix-Août	Captain Jacques Bergeret.

Frigates, Romaine 44, Créole 40, Bravoure, Cocarde, and Fraternité 36. *Flûte*, Fidelle; *Corvettes*, Berceau and Tactique; *Avisos*, Biche and Découverte.

It being the custom among the French for their admirals to embark on board frigates, we are unable to particularize all the flag-ships in this fleet. We believe, however, that the Océan, Républicain, and Terrible, carried the flags of the three senior admirals; and find, by the French accounts, that the names of all the flag-officers attached to this formidable fleet were as follow:

Vice-admiral Eustache Bruix.
Rear-admiral Jean-Louis Delmotte.
Rear-admiral Jacques Bedout.
Rear-admiral Jean-François Courand.
Rear-admiral Alain-Joseph Dordelin.
Rear-admiral Chas.-Alex.-Léon Durand-Linois.

Of all the fleets that ever sailed from France, this appears to have been, as far as relates to the fighting complement of each ship, the most numerously manned. The four three-deckers alone had 4645 men. The two 80s averaged 874 men each; and the nineteen 74s, although one of them had as few as 660 men, averaged 780 each: making the total of men in the fleet 23,761. Of this number, about 1000 appear to have been soldiers; but even, with these deducted, the crews were immoderately large. Nor were the men, as was too commonly the case with the French crews, raw and inexperienced. They had, for the most part, been serving in the gun-boats all the preceding summer. What a fleet of 25 sail of the line, thus manned, might accomplish, may readily be conceived: what it did accomplish we shall presently proceed to show.

It was about 9 A.M. on the 26th, just as the last 10 or 11 ships of this immense fleet were rounding the Saintes, that the British 36-gun frigate, Nymphe, Captain Percy Fraser, discovered them. Making all sail to rejoin her fleet with the intelligence, the Nymphe, at noon, Ushant bearing east-north-east, distant five leagues, lost sight of the French ships; and at 1 P.M., with the signal for an enemy flying, fell in with the

Dragon, who quickly repeated the signal to Lord Bridport's fleet. The admiral immediately made sail towards Brest to ascertain the truth of the information, and on the 27th at noon found that the French fleet had really eluded his vigilance. Lord Bridport instantly sent despatch-vessels home, and ordered all reinforcements to join him off Cape Clear; whither, after sending two other small vessels, with the important information, to Lord Keith off Cadiz, and to Earl St.-Vincent at Gibraltar, the admiral himself departed with all possible speed.

On the 30th, Lord Bridport arrived off Cape Clear, and soon found his force augmented to 26 sail of the line. Among the small vessels that joined his lordship, was the hired armed lugger, Black-Joke; which, on the 27th, when 20 leagues west of Ushant, had fallen in with and captured the French chasse-marée Rebecca, of four swivels and seven men, just out of Brest, having on board a capitaine de frégate with despatches for Ireland. This was of course a *ruse*, and a successful one it proved; as it fixed the British admiral to the Irish coast, when, according to the concurrent testimony of several respectable merchant-masters, the Brest fleet had, on the 30th, reached the latitude of 46° and the longitude of 9°, and was left steering south-west with a fine wind at north.

But, then again, the Paris journals persisted in declaring, that the destination of the armament was Ireland; and some of them augmented the number of troops on board the fleet to 25,000. Perhaps, too, it was a part of the plan, for the malecontents in Ireland, to circulate reports now and then, that a strange fleet had made its appearance on the coast. The British admiralty, however, having a large disposable line-of-battle force, had sent, and continued to send, strong detachments to the coast of Spain and the Mediterranean; but the time for striking the blow had undoubtedly gone by.

The chief command of the British naval force along the coast of Spain and in the Mediterranean still remained with Admiral Earl St.-Vincent; but, owing to his lordship's indifferent state of health, the active part of the duty fell upon the second in command, Vice-admiral Lord Keith. During the first four months of the year, the vice-admiral, with a squadron sometimes of 11, but at no time exdeeding 15 sail of the line, and a single frigate or so, or perhaps none at all, lay at anchor about eight miles from Cadiz, blockading 19 Spanish sail of the line, 17 of which at least were sea-going ships, four frigates, and one or two corvettes. Even the occasional trips, that the British were obliged to make to Tetuan for water, failed to rouse the Spaniards from that state of inactivity which habit had seemingly rendered the chief enjoyment of their lives. Whenever the British came to the anchorage, the ships of war in Cadiz harbour exhibited the same quiescent appearance as when last seen.

The French line-of-battle force in the Mediterranean had been reduced by the victory of the Nile to a very insignificant amount. At Malta was the 80-gun ship Guillaume-Tell, also the ex-Maltese 64s Athénien and Dégon; at Corfu, the 74 Généreux; and, at the several ports named, the following nine ex-Venetian 64s: at Alexandria, the Causse and Dubois, at Ancona, the Beyrand, Hoche (the second), Laharpe, and Stengel, and at Toulon, recently returned from Corsica, the Banel, Fromintin, and Robert; all named after generals who had distinguished themselves under Buonaparte in Italy and Germany. Of these eleven 64-gun ships, not above seven, if so many, were fully armed and fit for service.

It was stated in the first edition of this work, that the French Venetian fleet consisted of "twelve 64-gun ships, and 32 frigates, corvettes, and galleys." A contemporary first misquotes the passage thus, "twelve line-of-battle ships and thirty frigates and corvettes,"* whereas the galleys alone were in number 18; and then adds: "But of their existence there is every reason to doubt, and certainly they were never seen or heard of by the commander-in-chief in the Mediterranean."† Strange this, when we shall soon have occasion to name several of the 64s, and most of the frigates, as connected with the operations of the belligerents in that very Mediterranean sea.

On the morning of the 3d of May, four days only after Lord Keith's fleet had returned off Cadiz from watering at Tetuan, the 12-pounder 32-gun frigate Success, Captain Shuldham Peard, and 14-gun brig-sloop Childers, Captain James Coutts Crawford, joined company; the brig with intelligence, that five Spanish sail of the line had escaped from Ferrol, and the frigate, that she had, at noon on the 1st, when about 35 leagues west of Oporto, fallen in with the Brest fleet, steering south-west by south, and had been chased by it until 4 P.M. on the 2d, when the two leading ships hove to for their companions astern, and the Success escaped. At this time the British fleet before Cadiz consisted of the

Gun-ship		
112	Ville-de-Paris	Captain Walter Bathurst.
98	Barfleur	Vice-admiral (r.) Lord Keith, K.B. Captain George Barker.
	Prince-George	Vice-adm. (w.) Sir William Parker, bart. Captain William Bowen.
	London	Captain John Child Purvis.
	Princess-Royal	Captain John William Taylor Dixon.
90	Namur	Captain William Luke.
80	Foudroyant	Captain William Brown.
	Gibraltar	Captain William Kelly.

*Brenton, vol. ii., p. 378
†Ibid.

Gun-ship		
74	Montagu	Captain John Knight.
	Northumberland	Captain George Martin.
	Marlborough	Captain Thomas Sotheby.
	Warrior	Captain Charles Tyler.
	Hector	Captain John Elphinstone.
	Defence	Captain Lord Henry Paulet.
	Majestic	Captain Robert Cuthbert.

Immediately on the receipt of this news the fleet, accompanied by one frigate only, the Success, got under way, and prepared for action. At 11 A.M. the Childers, with three transports under her protection, was despatched to Earl St. Vincent at Gibraltar. During the remainder of the day, and throughout the ensuing night, Lord Keith, with his 15 line-of-battle ships formed in line, continued to stand off and on the harbour, with the wind blowing fresh from the northward and westward.

On the 4th, at 8 h. 30 m. A.M., the French fleet was seen about five leagues off in the west-north-west. At 10 A.M. the Majestic signalled that the strange fleet numbered altogether 33 sail. The French ships then wore from the rear, and formed on the larboard tack, with their heads to the north-east; and the British ships immediately formed on the same tack. Soon afterwards the French fleet again wore, and stood away to the south-west, the wind then a perfect storm. At 5 P.M. the town of Cadiz bore from the Barfleur, south-east by south distant five or six leagues, and the French ships, in the hazy state of the weather, had all disappeared. The gale, blowing right into the harbour of Cadiz, rendered it impossible for the Spanish ships to come out to join their friends in the offing, even had they been ready or disposed. The same wind blew fair for the Straits, and drove the French ships before it.

On the 5th, at daybreak, the town of Cadiz then only eight miles distant from the British fleet, four French ships of the line, standing on the starboard tack, with the wind fresh at south-west, showed themselves in the north-west. At 8 A.M. these ships, which, on account of the bad weather probably, had dropped astern of their companions, passed about seven miles to windward of the British fleet, and by 10 A.M. were out of sight. On the same day, at 5 P.M., in thick hazy weather, 26 French ships, of which 19 at least were ascertained to be of the line, were seen from the rock of Gibraltar, passing through the Straits in the Mediterranean. These were known to be the Brest fleet, as, early on the preceding day, the Childers had arrived with despatches from Lord Keith.

On the 6th the ships of war in Cadiz were observed with their topgallantmasts struck, and their topsails loosed to dry; a proof that they were not then, however they may have been before the gale commenced, ready to proceed to sea. At noon

Lord Keith proceeded off Cape Spartel, and at noon on the 8th was cruising within five leagues of it. The fleet shortly afterwards stood back nearly to the entranc of Cadiz bay, and one or more of the ships were sent close in to reconnoitre the harbour. Finding the Spanish ships, now counted, as it appears, at 22 of the line, still in port; Lord Keith steered for the bay of Gibraltar, having received on the evening of the 9th an order to that effect from Earl St.-Vincent. Admitting the number of line-of-batle ships in Cadiz to have been correctly reported, of which we have some doubt, one of the three beyond the 19 known to have been in the port, was the French 74 Censeur; which ship had lost her fore topmast, and been otherwise disabled, in the gale of the 4th, and had since slipped in unperceived by the British fleet.

Notwithstanding the assertion of a contemporary, we confess our inability to discover, either that the French fleet of "twenty-six" sail of the line "wished to enter" the harbour of Cadiz, or that the British fleet of "sixteen" sail of the line "offered battle."* We believe it was not the intention of Admiral Bruix to enter Cadiz, but merely to show himself off each of the three Spanish ports, Ferrol, Cadiz, and Carthagena, in order that the ships within them might sail out and effect their junction. The Ferrol ships had actually quitted port with that object in view, and, by a mere accident, had missed the Brest fleet; and, if the weather had permitted them, the Cadiz ships, or 17 sail of them at least, would in all probability have put to sea. No doubt, in such a case, Lord Keith would have been bound to make a retreat; and there can be as little doubt that, should the British fleet have been forced to engage, all that a fleet so inferior in force could accomplish would have been effected. Beyond this it was idle to hope; and we can only suppose that Earl St.-Vincent, when in a letter to the secretary of the admiralty he used the expression, "the French squadron eluded the vigilance of Lord Keith by the darkness of the atmosphere,"† was unacquainted with the real strength of that French squadron.

The Childers brig, immediately upon her arrival at Gibraltar from Lord Keith, was despatched with orders to rejoin immediately the Edgar 74, Captain John M'Dougall, lying in Tetuan bay. Rear-admiral Frederick, who was residing on shore at Gibraltar on account of extreme ill health, took this opportunity of hoisting his flag on board an effective line-of-battle ship. Vessels were also despatched by the commander-in-chief to Rear-admirals Duckworth at Minorca, and Nelson at Palermo, and to Captains Ball off Malta, and Sir Sidney Smith off Alexandria. Several expresses had also been sent to Lord Keith; but, owing to the continuance of the south-west gale, the

*Brenton, vol. ii., p. 475.
†Ibid., p. 358.

vice-admiral did not receive his order of recal, we believe, until the evening of the 9th. On the 10th, at 9 A.M., Lord Keith anchored in Gibraltar; as, on the same afternoon, did the Edgar from Tetuan.

Every despatch was now used in victualling the ships; and on the 11th, at sunset, Earl St.-Vincent shifted his flag from the Souverain guardship to the Ville-de-Paris; as did also Rear-admiral Frederick, from the Edgar to the Princess-Royal. On the 12th, at 11 A.M., the British fleet, consisting of 16 sail of the line, weighed and bore up for the Mediterranean. On the 17th and 18th the ships encountered a severe gale of wind, but escaped without much damage. On the 20th, at noon, when off the island of Minorca, the fleet was joined by the

Gun-ship		
74	Leviathan	Rear-admiral (w.) John Thomas Duckworth. Captain Henry Digby.
	Centuar	Captain John Markham.
	Bellerophon	Captain Henry d'Esterre Darby.
	Powerful	Captain William O'Brien Drury.

On the same evening the fleet, with the exception of the Edgar, who had run aground to the south-east of Hospital island, anchored in Port-Mahon. The Edgar remained on shore until midnight on the 21st; when, having removed all her guns into some transports, and been assisted in heaving off by the Barfleur and Defence, she floated, and anchored in the harbour.

The departure of Lord Keith from before Cadiz, on the 6th, enabled the Spaniards, by the 14th, to put to sea with 17 sail of the line, of which six were three-deckers. On the 17th this fleet passed the Straits, and, not being in very good trim for withstanding foul weather, suffered considerably by the gale of that and the following day. Eleven of the ships were more or less dismasted by it; but, on the 20th, the whole, except one ship which arrived afterards, succeeded in gaining Carthagena. In order to show how differently the same gale could treat an English and a Spanish fleet, the names of the dismasted ships of the latter, as offically announced in the Madrid Gazette, are here subjoined:

Gun-ship		
112	Concepcion	lost her foremast, and very leaky.
	Mexicano	totally dismasted; four men killed, &c.
74	Conquistador	totally dismasted.
	Oriente	lost her main and mizen masts.
	Pelayo	ditto, and sprung her foremast.
	San-Francisco-de-Asis	lost her foremast.
	San-Joaquim	ditto mainmast, and sprung her foremast.
	San-Telmo	totally dismasted.
	Soberano	lost her mainmast.
Gun-frigate		
34	Matilda	totally dismasted.

It appears, also, that the Santa-Ana three-decker made 20 inches of water per hour, and that the San-Francisco-de-Paulo and San-Pablo 74s had sprung or carried away their tillers. One of the brigs, too, had lost her foremast and bowsprit. Just a week previous to the arrival of the Spanish fleet at Carthagena, the French fleet, consisting, according to the French accounts, of 25 sail of the line, five frigates, and four or five corvettes, entered Toulon. In passing the Straits, two of the ships had run on board each other, and received considerable damage.

On the 22d of May, at noon, Earl St.-Vincent got under way from Port-Mahon; and on the 23d, at 5 A.M., the Edgar, who, highly to the credit of her officers and crew, had since early on the preceding morning reshipped and remounted the whole of her guns, weighed also, and joined the admiral off the harbour. Having now under his command 20 sail of the line and a few smaller vessels, Earl St.-Vincent made sail in the direction of Toulon.

On the 26th, when in latitude 42° north, in consequence, we suppose, of information that the Spanish fleet had arrived at Carthagena, the British fleet steered to the westward, and at noon on the 27th was about 35 miles to the east-north-east of Cape San-Sebastian, waiting to intercept the Spanish fleet in case it should attempt to effect a junction with the French fleet in Toulon. On the 30th, while cruising off Cape San-Sebastian with this object in view, the admiral received intelligence of the sailing of the French fleet from Toulon three days before. On this, Earl St.-Vincent, at 2 P.M., detached Rear-admiral Duckworth with the Leviathan, Foudroyant, Northumberland, and Majestic, to reinforce Lord Nelson at Palermo, and at 6 P.M. was joind by the

Gun-ship		
100	Queen-Charlotte.........	Rear-admiral (w.) James Hawkins Whitshed. Captain John Irwin.
74	Captain	Captain Sir Richard John Stachan, Bart.
	Defiance....................	Captain Thomas Revell Shivers.
	Bellona	Captain Sir Thomas Boulden Thompson.
64	Repulse	Captain James Alms.

The British fleet, thus augmented to 21 sail of the line, steered along the Spanish coast, and at noon on the 1st of June was about 40 miles to the eastward of Barcelona. Seeing no enemy in this direction, the fleet put back to the northward and eastward, under all sail. On the 2d, when about 70 miles south-west of Toulon, Earl St.-Vincent, finding his health getting worse, parted company in the Ville-de-Paris; and Lord Keith took the command of the fleet, now deprived of the use of the heaviest ship in it, by her departure upon a service for which a frigate would have answered.

On the 3d, in the afternoon, having arrived close off Toulon, the two advanced ships of the fleet, the Centaur and Montagu, opened a fire upon a brig-corvette and several settees standing into the road, and took possession of four of the latter, which they dismantled and burnt. The French forts fired at the two British 74s, but without effect. From the prisoners intelligence was obtained, that the French fleet, on quitting Toulon, had steered to the eastward; and to the eastward the British fleet accordingly bent its course. On the 5th, in the afternoon, when the fleet had just crossed the gulf of Fréjus, the British hired armed brig Telegraph, Lieutenant James Alexander Worth, joined company, with intelligence of having, the preceding evening, seen the French fleet at anchor in Vado bay. The British fleet immediately made all sail in that direction. On the 6th the forts on the small islands of Sainte-Marguerète and La-Garoupe, near Antibes, fired at the fleet in passing, particuarly at the Espoir brig, who was nearest in shore. The French papers boasted of having dismasted an English ship of the line and frigate; but it does not appear that any vessel was injured.

On the 8th, Cape Delle-Melle at noon bearing north-north-east distant 31 leagues, Lord Keith received three despatch-vessels (all within seven or eight hours) from the commander-in-chief at Minorca, containing orders for him, after detaching two 74s as an additional reinforcement to Lord Nelson, to repair to the bay of Rosas, to be ready to intercept the French fleet on its way to join the Spanish fleet in Carthegena. Accordingly, after sending away the Bellerophon and Powerful to Palermo, Lord Keith, with 18 sail of the line, crowded sail to the south-west. It would appear, however, that, instead of steering straight to the bay of Rosas, Lord Keith proceeded towards the south end of Minorca, probably to facilitate a junction with the Ville-de-Paris. On the 12th the British fleet was lying becalmed close off the small island of Ayre. On the 13th, Cape Mola bearing north-east half-east distant five leagues, Lord Keith shifted his flag to the Queen-Charlotte, and Rear-admiral Whitshed to the Barfleur; and Captains Irwin and Barker followed their respective chiefs. On the 15th, when the fleet was within four miles of Cape Mola, the Ville-de-Paris rejoined, having left Earl St.-Vincent at Port-Mahon, preparing to take his departure for Gibraltar and England.

With his fleet again consisting of 19 sail of the line, Lord Keith, passing round the eastern side of the Minorca, steered to the northward. On the 19th, when about 20 leagues to the southward of Cape Sicie, the advanced division, consisting of the Centaur, Captain, and Bellona 74s, and the Emerald and Santa-Teresa frigates, captured the following French ships, 33 days from Jaffa, bound to Toulon:

Gun-frig.		
38	Junon	Rear-admiral —— Perrée. Captain Honoré Pourquier.
36	Alceste	Captain Jean-Baptiste Barré.
	Courageuse*	Captain —— Buille.
Brigs.	Salamine	Lieut. François-Timothée Landry.
	Alerte	Lieut. Pi.-Ant.-Toussaint Demai.

The whole of these five vessels were added to the British navy; but the first, a fine Toulon-built frigate of 1029 tons, was of greater value than all the others. There being a Juno already in the service, the Junon was named Princess Charlotte, and attached to the 18-pounder 36-gun class. Her name was subsequently altered to the Andromache, and the ci-devant Junon is even yet a serviceable frigate.

After capturing the squadron of M. Perrée, Lord Keith stood close into Toulon, and during the 20th, 21st, 22d, and 23d, cruised off that port, as if expecting that the French fleet would attempt to re-enter it. Finding this not to be the case, the vice-admiral made sail to the eastward, and on the 24th crossed Vado bay. On the 25th, some of the forts near Genoa, fired several shot at the British 16-gun brig-sloop, Vincejo, but ceased when the latter hoisted Spanish colours. On the 26th, the British fleet was within six or seven miles of Genoa mole. Hearing no tidings of the French fleet in this quarter, except perhaps, that it had anchored in the port nearly a month ago, Lord Keith stood away towards Minorca. While the British fleet is on its way thither, we will proceed to show, as well as we are able, what course the French fleet had actually been steering.

On the 27th of May, one of the three or four days during which the British fleet, of 20 sail of the line, five frigates, and smaller vessels, was cruising off Cape San-Sebastian, the French fleet of 22 sail of the line (the two damaged ships being still under repair, and the Censeur, as already mentioned, left at Cadiz), 11 frigates and corvettes, and, we believe, two of the three ex-Venetian 64s in the port armed en flûte, and laden with provisions and military stores, sailed from the road of Toulon.

Steering to the eastward, the French fleet on the 30th or 31st anchored in the bay of Vado, and there disembarked, for the relief of Savona, then attacked by an Austro-Russian army, the 1000 troops received on board at Brest. On the 3d of June the French fleet showed itself off Genoa, and on the 5th, when the British fleet was nearly abreast of Cape Roux, anchored in Genoa mole, with a wheat-laden convoy, which the French admiral had escorted from the westward. General Moreau, who had

*In the London Gazette, owing, we conceive, to a typographical error, this frigate is described as of "22," instead of 32 "guns, 12-pounders, and 300 men." A contemporary, overlooking this, has given the "Courageux," not only no more than "22 guns," but, what he considered an adequate complement, "160 men." – *Brenton*, vol. ii., p. 488.

arrived at Genoa two days before, took this opportunity of holding a conference with Vice-admiral Bruix on board the Océan. On the 6th, in the morning, the General quitted the flag-ship for the shore; and at noon, when the British fleet, having been recalled to the bay of Rosas, had put about for that destination, the French fleet weighed and made sail to the westward, the French accounts say, but we much doubt the fact, in consequence of information that the British fleet, of "22 sail of the line," had been seen off Toulon.

Thus was the seeking fleet unconsciously running before the sought fleet, and the latter as unconsciously pursuing the former. No doubt, had this fact been known in France, the Moniteur would have declared, and with some show of reason, that Vice-admiral Bruix had chased Lord Keith and could not bring him to action. On the 9th, the French fleet passed in sight of Toulon, and on the 22d appeared off Carthagena. On the 23d, Vice-admiral Bruix cast anchor in the road, and thus effected a junction with the Spanish fleet, now, with most surprising alacrity, after the damage it had received in the storm of the preceding month, nearly ready for sea.

As far as we can gather from the obscure accounts in the French and Spanish journals, this fleet, soon after its arrival from Cadiz, had transferred to a large body of transports, purposely assembled at Carthagena, about 5000 troops, for disembarkation at Majorca, and to be employed, as it would appear, more for defending that island, than for making any attempt to recapture Minorca. On the 24th, the day after their junction, and when the British fleet, having gone the round we have described, was increasing its distance in the direction, first of Toulon, and then of Genoa, the French and Spanish fleets, numbering together 40 sail of the line, with a suitable train of frigates and corvettes, sailed from Carthagena, bound out of the Mediterranean.

On the 6th, Lord Keith, whom we left steering for Minorca, arrived off the east end of the island; and on the 7th, close off Mount Toro, was joined by the following reinforcement from the Channel fleet:

Gun-ship		
98	Prince	Rear-admiral (r.) Sir Charles Cotton. Captain Samuel Sutton.
	Formidable	Captain Edward Thornborough.
	St.-George	Captain Sampson Edwards.
	Neptune	Captain James Vashon.
	Glory	Captain Thomas Wells.
74	Triumph	Rear-admiral (w.) Cuthbert Colllingwood. Captain Thomas Larcom.
	Dragon	Captain George Campbell.
	Impétueux	Captain Sir Edward Pellew, bart.
	Terrible	Captain Jonathan Faulknor.
	Superb	Captain John Sutton.
	Pompée	Captain Charles Stirling.
	Canada	Captain Hon. Michael de Courcy.

This reinforcement, when it quitted the Channel fleet, consisted of 16 sail of the line, under Admiral Sir Alan Gardner; but the latter, taking with him the Royal-Sovereign, Caesar, Magnificent, and Russel, had put into the Tagus, to escort home the Lisbon convoy, and the Nile prizes.

While a part of Lord Keith's fleet, now augmented to 31 sail of the line, four frigates, and two or three smaller vessels, lay off and on Port-Mahon, the remaining ships, including the Queen Charlotte, anchored in the harbour to get a supply of water. Scarcely had the vice-admiral been an hour at his anchorage, ere intelligence arrived of the junction of which he had been forewarned. All was now bustle in the port; and on the 10th Lord Keith weighed and set sail for the Straits, having previously sent an order to Rear-admiral Nelson, at Palermo, to detach a part of his force for the protection of Minorca. On the 26th, the British fleet anchored in Tetuan bay, to get, what the ships had only partially procured at Mahon, a supply of water, and on the 29th, reached Gibraltar; just three weeks after the French and Spanish fleets had passed the rock on their way to Cadiz. Even the two French 74s left repairing at Toulon, had since followed the combined fleets out of the Mediterranean.

With such limited means as we possess, it is not easy to say how it happened, first, that the Spanish fleet, scattered and discomfited by a gale, was suffered to enter Carthagena; and next, that the French fleet, although it spent nearly four weeks in twice traversing that small portion of the Mediterranean which divides Genoa from Carthagena, was missed by a British fleet cruising on the same sea. Not a jot of information on the subject appears in a work in which, from its title and the relation that subsisted between its author and Earl St.-Vincent, a solution of the difficulty might reasonably be expected.

To show that this writer's account of the proceedings of the British fleet after it had arrived at Gibraltar from Cadiz, brief as it is, contains many mistatements, we have only to subjoin an extract. "Here, with all the zeal and vigilance of Earl St.-Vincent and the anxiety of every officer to forward the work, it took five days," that is, from 9 A.M. on the 10th, to 11 A.M. on the 11th, "before the provision and water could be completed, and the ships sufficiently repaired to follow the enemy; when the Earl of St.-Vincent hoisted his flag on board the Ville de Paris, and taking Lord Keith under his orders, made all sail for Cape Dell Mell. At this place (see p. 262) he received intelligence, that the enemy had anchored in Vado bay; but his lordship, having every reason to think that the Spaniards meditated an attack on Minorca, went to Mahon, and ordered Lord Keith to cruise off the island, the Spaniards having collected a large body of troops at Majorca."*

*Brenton, vol. ii., p. 476.

Being desirous to attend the combined fleets in their further movement, we shall merely advert to two untoward circumstances, which may assist in explaining how the British and French fleets twice missed each other: one was when Lord Keith on the 8th of June, in compliance with Earl St.-Vincent's orders, put back, just when a 24 hours' run in the course he had been steering, would have brought him in front of M. Bruix; the next, when, instead of waiting off Cape San-Sebastian Lord Keith, of his own accord as it appears, steered for Minorca, and in the neighbourhood of that island wasted several days.

On the 7th of July, while the combined fleets were passing the Straits, some of the ships amused themselves with firing at two vessels belonging to the Algerines, and then steering close in with the Barbary shore. Earl St.-Vincent, who was on board the 44-gun ship Argo, at anchor in the bay, despatched the hired cutter Penelope, of 16 or 18 guns, Lieutenant Frederick Lewis Maitland, to ascertain the cause of the firing. Having stretched across the gut with very light winds during the night, Lieutenant Maitland, at daybreak on the 8th, found himself nearly within gun-shot of Admiral Massaredo's advanced ships, the boats of which, in the prevailing calm, were ordered to tow the 14-gun brig-corvette Vivo towards the Penelope. The latter, however, on approaching the British cutter, received so warm a salute, that she soon dropped astern.

A breeze now springing up, the Spanish 34-gun frigate Del Carmen ran down, and placing herself about a cable's length on the Penelope's weather beam, opened a heavy fire, by which the cutter was soon unrigged and compelled to surrender. An officer from the Vivo now boarded the Penelope, and demanded her commander's sword; but Lieutenant Maitland refused to deliver it, alleging that the British colours had been struck to the frigate. Shortly afterwards, one of the Carmen's boats boarded and took possession of the Penelope, and sent away the boat of the Vivo.

The Penelope, when thus suddenly ordered from Gibraltar, had on board a considerable sum in specie, intended for the island of Minorca, but which, rather neglectfully we think, was not removed. "When her crew found there was no chance of escape from the combined fleets, they made an attempt to plunder the treasure, which Lieutenant Maitland most honourably and successfully resisted, alleging that, as public property, it was the lawful prize of the captors."*

On the 10th, 11th, and 12th, the French and Spanish fleets entered the harbour of Cadiz. The Censeur being still not in a state to proceed on the voyage, the Spanish monarch presented to the French republic the 74 San-Sebastian; and into the latter, newly and appropriately named the Alliance, Captain

*Marshall, vol. ii., p. 383.

Faye and his officers and crew instantly removed. That done, on the 21st the combined fleets got under way, bound to Brest. Scarcely, however, had the two fleets made sail from the anchorage, than two of the Spanish three-deckers, the Mexicano and Santa-Ana, returned; the latter after having run on shore and been with difficulty got afloat again. This left Admiral Massaredo with the following 15 sail of the line:

Gun-ship		Gun-ship	
112	Concepcion,	74	Pelayo,
	Conde-de-Regla,		San-Francisco-de-Asis,
	Principe-de-Asturias,		San-Francisco-de-Paulo,
	Reyna-Louisa,		San-Joaquin,
80	Neptuno,		San-Pablo,
74	Bahama,		San-Telmo,
	Conquistador,		Soberano.
	Guerrero,		

Exclusive of four frigates and three brigs; making the aggregate number of the combined Spanish and French fleets 59 sail, of which 40 were of the line.

On the 30th, at 2 A.M., the wind coming to the eastward, Lord Keith, with his 31 sail of the line, got under way from Gibraltar, and stood towards the channel, but heard nothing of the object of his pursuit until the 8th of August; when, being off Cape Finisterre, he was informed by a Danish brig, that on the 6th, she had passed through the combined fleets, steering to the north-east. On the 9th, the British 36-gun frigate Stag, Captain Joseph Sydney Yorke, came into the fleet with information, that she had seen the French and Spaniards off Cape Ortegal, steering, as before, to the north-east. On the 12th, the British fleet arrived in soundings, and at noon on that day, was about 80 miles to the westward of Ushant. On the 14th, Lord Keith detached the Impétueux, Pompée, and Ethalion, to look into Brest; where Sir Edward Pellew found the French and Spanish fleets, which had arrived only on the preceeding day, safely moored in the road.

Whatever may have been the errors or mismanagement of Lord Keith while cruising in the Mediterranean, so soon as the British fleet was clear of the island of Minorca, the ships pushed, under all sail, in pursuit of the Franco-Spanish fleet, and actually gained upon it so much, that, had there been another degree of distance to pass over, the two fleets, in all probability, would have come in contact. Those who might dread the result of a meeting, under such a numerical disparity as 40 to 31, should recollect, that a fleet of 30 sail of the line, equipped, manned, and commanded like Lord Keith's, was a match for any fleet that could be sent to sea; especially one made up of the ships of two national navies, between which there was little or no concert, and the fleet of one of which had given so decided a proof that numbers were a disadvantage to it.

We may observe, in passing, that the alleged object of the voyage of M. Bruix to the Mediterranean appears to have been much overrated. He had landed a few soldiers at Savona, and convoyed a fleet of coasters to Genoa; services which his frigates alone could just as well have performed. Even when the two fleets had joined, they envinced no intention to act against Minorca and Sicily, or to overpower the British naval force in that sea. The French fleet when alone, and even the two fleets when united, rather shunned than sought an engagement; nor had a single hostile port been visited, nor even threatened. The result was, that the Brest and Cadiz fleets had united, and now lay moored together, to the ridicule of monarchial Spain, in the great naval depôt of republican France.

Among the ships that, just before the Brest fleet appeared off Cadiz, had ecaped out of port to effect a junction with it, were five ships of the line from Ferrol. It was on the 28th of April that these five sail, consisting of one 112-gun ship (the Real-Carlos) bearing an admiral's flag at the main, one 80 bearing a vice-admiral's flag at the fore, and three 74s, accompanied by one frigate, and one ship and one brig corvette, sailed from Ferrol; not unseen, however, by the British 44-gun frigate Indefatigable, Captain the Hon. Henry Curzon. The Spaniards, as if expecting to fall in with the Brest fleet, lay to, off Corunna, for the greater part of two days; during which time the Indefatigable kept them in sight. The latter then hastened homewards with the intelligence, and shortly afterwards spoke the Childers brig, on her way to Earl St.-Vincent with desptaches from Lord Bridport. On the 8th of May the Indefatigable arrived at Plymouth. In the mean time the Spanish squadron had made sail with the intention of entering Brest, but, finding or fearing some obstruction, had since put into Rochefort.

Towards the latter end of May, while, with 26 sail of the line at anchor in Bear Haven, waiting for the French fleet to come to Ireland, Lord Bridport received intelligence, as well of this Spanish squadron being in Rochefort, as of the Brest fleet having steered for the Straits. Accordingly, on the 1st of June, in pursuance of orders from home, Lord Bridport detached Admiral Sir Alan Gardner with 16 sail of the line as a reinforcement to Earl St.-Vincent, and, with his remaining 10 line-of-battle ships, sailed for Basque road.

On the 4th of June Lord Bridport arrived off the road, and got a sight of the Spanish squadron; but which immediately afterwards retired to the road of Aix, a small fortified island about 12 miles from Rochefort. On the 8th, taking with him the Royal-George, Atlas, Achille, and Agincourt, the admiral sailed for England, leaving, as a blockading force off the port, the

Gun-ship		
74	Mars	Rear-adm. (b.) Hon. G. Cran. Berkeley. Captain John Manley.
	Venerable	Captain Sir William George Fairfax.
	Renown	Captain Albemarle Bertie.
	Ajax	Captain Hon. Alex. Inglis Cochrane.
	Ramillies	Captain Richard Grindall.
	Robust	Captain Herbert Sawyer.

In a few days afterwards the 80-gun ship Sans-Pareil, Captain William Browell, joined this squadron; and on the 1st of July Rear-admiral Charles Morice Pole, arrived from Cawsand bay, in the Royal George, accompanied by the bomb-vessels Sulphur, Explosion, and Volcano, and their tenders, for the purpose of making an immediate attack upon the Spanish squadron. One admiral being deemed sufficient for this purpose, Rear-admiral Berkeley, with the Mars and Ramillies, parted company from the squadron; which now consisted, besides the five line-of-battle ships, Royal-George, Sans-Pareil, Venerable, Renown, Ajax, and Robust, and the three bomb-vessels, of the 38-gun frigates Boadicea, Captain Richard Goodwin Keats, and Uranie, Captain George Henry Towry, San-Fiorenzo 36, Captain Sir Harry Neale, Unicorn 32, Captain Philip Wilkinson, and 18-gun brig-sloop Sylph, Captain John Chambers White.

On the 2d of July, early in the morning, Rear-admiral Pole, with his squadron, bore up for the Pertuis-d'Antioche; and, while the five line-of-battle ships, at about 11 A.M., came to an anchor in Basque roads, the frigates, sloop, bomb-vessels, and some cutters, proceeded on towards the isle of Aix, near to which were the Spanish ships, moored in a line ahead, extending from the isle last named towards the Boyart shoal, which runs nearly parallel to the isle of Oleron. For the better protection of the Spanish ships, a floating mortar-battery had been stationed between this island and the Boyart. At nearly the same time that the line-of-battle ships came to in Basque roads, the frigates, sloop, and bomb-vessels were anchored by Captain Keats under the isle of Aix. At noon a fire was opened upon the British vessels at this anchorage from the isles of Oleron and of Aix, the floating battery, and the Spanish admiral's ship. The British bomb-vessels, having taken their stations, commenced throwing their shells. So superior, however, was the range of the French mortars, that, while the shells from these, as well as several of the shots from the floating battery, were flying over the British frigate and bomb-vessels, the shells from the latter all fell short. At 2 P.M. Captain Keats sent the Sylph to the admiral with this information. In the mean time the wind had fallen to nearly a calm; thus affording, at 3 P.M., an opportunity for several gun-boats, armed with long 36-pounders, (and one of which gun-boats every Spanish line-of-battle ship, by a paragaph in the Moniteur, appears at this time to have had on board), to advance and open a fire upon the bombarding squadron. At about 4 h. 30 m. P.M. the frigates and bomb-vessels weighed and stood out, followed and fired at by the gun-boats until 6 P.M.; which was at least an hour after any shot could possibly reach.

Thus ended an affair, which, on both sides, was perfectly harmless. A British squadron continued to cruise, for a while, off the Isle of Ré, to prevent the escape of the Spanish ships. The latter, nevertheless, found an opportunity, in the middle of September, to escape to sea. The Spaniards, at first, made an attempt to join their countrymen at Brest; but, finding the port too well watched, they afterwards stood away to the southward, and succeeded in re-entering Ferrol. Although increased by five French sail of the line fitted out since the departure of M. Bruix in April, including a fine new 80-gun ship, the Indivisible, the powerful Franco-Spanish fleet at anchor in Brest road, the whole of the pendants in which, according to the French accounts, exceeded 90, made no attempt to put to sea during the remainder of the present year.

Our attention is now called back to the Mediterranean, but to a more easterly part of it than was visited by the French and Spanish fleets, of whose separate, as well as conjoint cruises we have given some account. We left the French General Championnet, after having seized upon Rome and dethroned the Pope, on his full march towards Naples. On the 10th of January the republicans took Capua, and on the 24th, after a smart but ineffectual resistance on the part of the mob or lazaroni, possessed themselves of Naples; from which city, however, the king and royal family, as has already been stated, had retired to Palermo, in Sicily.*

The terrrories of the Grand Duke of Tuscany, into which Pope Pius VI., as well as the King of Sardinia, had sought a refuge, where the next to be invaded. A seasonable intimation of the republican General Gauthier's intentions enabled Charles Emmanuel and his family to quit Florence for Leghorn; whence, finding themselves not safe even there, they embarked for Cagliari, in Sardinia. On the 29th of March General Gauthier and his 3000 troops took quiet possession of Florence; and on the following day the Grand Duke and his family, escorted by a detachment of French, retired to Venice, on their way into the dominions of Austria. Two days after General Gauthier had entered Florence. General Miollis, at the head of 4000 republicans, made himself, with equal facility, master of Leghorn.

Among the prisoners that fell into the hands of the French, on taking possession of Tuscany, was the pope. By order of the French directory, the latter was conducted to Parma, then across the Alps, to Briançon, and subsequently to Valence;

*See p. 190.

where, overcome by his sufferings both of mind and body, the old man died.

At the close of the preceding year we left the Russians and Turks, beseiging the city and fortress of Corfu. On the 3d of March, and not before, the garrison capitulated; and the republican troops obtained permission to return to France, on their parole not to serve again within the period of 18 months. We formerly mentioned that the French 74-gun ship Généreux, Captain Lejoille, had quitted Corfu, and proceeded to Ancona in the gulf of Venice. The only vessels of war, therefore, except a few gun-boats, which the conquerors of Corfu found in the harbour, were the late British 50-gun ship Leander, and the French 28-gun frigate Brune. The first-named ship the Emperor of Russia afterwards restored to Great Britain.

A few days after the occupation of Corfu by the Turks and Russians, but before the event had become known at Ancona, the Généreux, accompanied by nine transports, having on board about 1000 troops under General Clément, with a considerable quantity of provisions and military stores, sailed for the relief of their countrymen. Previously, however, to his entering the channel of Corfu, Captain Lejoille wished to learn the fate of this finest of the Ionian islands. He accordingly steered, with his 74 and transports, towards Brindisi, a small port in the Neapolitan province of Otranto, and now occupied by a weak detachment of Cardinal Ruffo's troops. Owing to the carelessness of the pilot, the Généreux grounded, close under the guns of the castle of Brindisi; and upon which, from her position, she could only bring her aftermost guns to bear. Almost the first shot fired from the castle killed Captain Lejoille, and badly wounded General Clément.

After the cannonade had lasted in this partial manner for about two hours, and several of the French seamen and soldiers had been killed or wounded, the fortress surrendered. The transports immediatley anchored in the harbour; as did the Généreux, as soon as she could be got afloat. The news of the surrender of Corfu arriving a day or two afterwards, the Généreux, now under the command of Lieutenant Claude Touffet, accompanied by the nine transports, sailed back to Ancona.

Six or eight weeks after the surrender of Corfu, a Turco-Russian squadron of six or seven sail of the line, under the Russian Rear-admiral Woinowich, set sail to make an attack upon Ancona. About the middle of May the squadron arrived and anchored off the town. The French troops within it amounted to between 2000 and 3000, and were commanded by General Monnier. The three ex-Venetian 64s, Beyrand, Laharpe, and Stenge, lay at the entrance of the harbour with springs on their cables. Anoterh ex-Venetian 64, the Hoche, but without any guns on board, was inside of the harbour; as were two or three ex-Venetian corvettes. The Généreux had quitted Ancona, a week or two before, and had since arrived safe at Toulon.

On the 19th the Russian admiral commenced cannonading the town and adjoining fortresses; but, the guns of the ships being too much elevated, all the shot flew over the town and did little or no damage. Preferring a safe to an effective position, the Turks had stationed their ships outside of those of their allies, and began their part in the engagement by shooting away the colours and a great portion of the rigging of the Russian admiral's ship. In short the Turco-Russian squadron could produce little or no effect upon the place, although the inhabitants of the coast were ready to co-operate with them. The siege was at length turned into a blockade: nor was it until towards the end of the year that Ancona surrendered; and then, not to the Turco-Russian squadron, but to an Austrian army. The long and obstinate defence of the besieged obtained for them, as it always should do, the most honourable terms, and General Monnier and his troops were highly complimented for their bravery by the Austrian General Frœlich.

The first object of Lord Nelson's care when at Palermo, was to urge the Sicilian government to place the island in the best possible state of defence. A body of troops was immediately assembled; and preparations were made under the rear-admiral's auspices, to fit out gun-boats, and to mount the batteries with the sixty-five 24-pounders which had been brought from Naples.

On the 18th Captain Troubridge arrived at Palermo from off Alexandria, with the Culloden, Zealous, Swiftsure, Seahorse, and the Perseus and Bulldog bomb-vessels. On the 24th the Minotaur also arrived. Having received this reinforcement, Lord Nelson, on the 31st, detached Captain Troubridge, with these four 74s, frigate, and bomb-vessels, and also with the Portuguese 74 San-Sebastian, to blockade the port of Naples.

On the 2d of April Captain Troubridge, with the squadron, stood into the bay, and anchored off the island of Procida, the governor of which had previously gone on board the Culloden. There being no French troops at Procida, the island, which lies about 13 miles from Naples, was taken quiet possession of: and his Sicilian majesty's colours were cheerfully hoisted by the inhabitants. On the next day, the 3d, Ischia, Capria, and all the other of the Ponza islands followed the example of Procida.

On the 12th of May, while Rear-admiral Lord Nelson was lying at Palermo, with the Vanguard 74, Captain Thomas Masterman Hardy, a Portuguese 74 (Principe-Real) and frigate, and the armed en flûte 64-gun ship Haerlem, Captain George Burlton, the 14-gun brig Espoir, Captain James Sanders, arrived with intelligence that the French fleet had been seen off Oporto. On the 13th, at 9 P.M., an officer of the Peterel joined overland, with the additional intelligence, that on the evening of the 5th, 35 sail of French men of war had passed the Straits. On hearing this, the lion roused himself; and the idol of that focus of corruption, the Neapolitan court, again shone forth as Nelson of the Nile. Instantly he despatched orders to Captain Troubridge at Naples bay, to come to Palermo with the whole of his line-of-battle force, and if possible, a frigate. He also forwarded instructions to Captain Ball, at Malta, who, with the Alexander and Goliath 74s, and occasionally a Portuguese 74, was blockading the port of Valette; also to the Russian admiral wherever he could be found, and whose force, in alliance with that of the British in this quarter, consisted of four or five sail of the line and some frigates and smaller vessels. Much effective co-operation, however, was not expected from these.

On the 17th, in the morning, his lordship repeated the orders as to the ships of the line in and off Naples bay, but added that the frigates must remain to take care of the recently surrendered islands. On the same afternoon the rear-admiral was joined by the 74-gun ships Culloden, Commodore Troubridge, Swiftsure, Captain Benjamin Hallowell, and the San-Sebastian, a Portuguese 74.

On the 20th, having been reinfoced by the 74-gun ship Minotaur, Captain Thomas Louis, and a third Portuguese 74, the Alphonso, Lord Nelson got under way, and cruised for several days near the islands of Levanzo and Maritomo. On the 30th the squadron, having been further reinforced by the 74-gun ship Zealous, Captain Samuel Hood, and the Lion 64, Captain Manley Dixon, returned to Palermo, and anchored off the Mole, in a line opposite to the Marino. On the 1st of June the Audacious 74, Captain David Gould, joined; and on the 7th, Rear-admiral Duckworth, with the 80-gun ship Foudroyant, Captain William Brown, the 74-gun ships Leviathan, bearing the rear-admiral's flag, Captain Henry Digby, Northumberland, Captain George Martin, and Majestic, Captain George Hope. On the 8th Lord Nelson shifted his flag to the Foudroyant, and Captains Hardy and Brown exchanged ships.

On the 13th, having now under his command the Foudroyant, Leviathan, Culloden, Minotaur, Northumberland, Zealous, Audacious, Swiftsure, Vanguard, Majestic, Alphonso, Principe-Real, San-Sebastian, and Lion, also the reduced 64-gun ship Haerlem, but not, we believe, a single frigate, Lord Nelson again put to sea from Palermo, and was the next day joined by the Powerful and Bellerophon, forming a total of 16 sail of the line. With this fleet, Lord Nelson cruised off and on the coast of Sicily; but, as we have elsewhere shown, neither the French nor the Spanish fleets arrived there to seek a battle with one, who had already conviced both nations, that, whatever might be his inferiority of force, he was not to be attacked with impunity.

On the departure of Captain Troubridge with his three 74s

from the bay of Naples, to join Lord Nelson at Palermo, the blockade of the port devolved upon Captain Edward James Foote, of the 38-gun frigate Seahorse; who, on the 22d of May, anchored off Procida with, besides his own ship; the Perseus bomb-vessel, Captain James Oswald, and Mutine and San-Léon brigs, Captains William Hoste and John Harward. In the mean time, important operations were carrying on upon shore. An immense Austro-Russian army, under the famous general Soworow, had since the middle of April entered Italy, and was now bearing down all opposition.

On the 5th of June Cardinal Ruffo defeated the French near Naples. On the 14th the fortified rock of Rivigliano, and on the 15th the important fortress of Castel-à-Mare, capitulated to the Seahorse and squadron. The terms were, that the respective garrisons should march out with military honours, and such of them as chose be allowed to avail themselves of the protection of the British flag. On the 17th the Seahorse and Perseus quitted Castel-à-Mare, and proceeded to the bottom of Naples bay, in order, with the aid of the gun and mortar boats at the Piedi-Grotta, to attack Castel-del' Uovo, which, with Castel-Nuovo, constituted the principal sea-defence of the capital. The latter is in the heart of the city, and has a communication with the palace; but the former runs out into the bay, and is joined to the land by a narrow pass and drawbridge. These two forts, and that of St.-Elmo on the western side of the city, were the only strong holds at this time possessed by the French in the immediate neighbourhood of Naples.

On the 18th Captain Foote despatched Captain Oswald of the Perseus, with a letter to the commandant of the Castel-del' Uovo, offering him and his garrison an asylum under the British flag. To this a verbal and a very offensive negative was returned; such as, "Nous voulons la république une et indivisible: nous mourrerons pour elle. Voilà votre réponse. Eloignez-vous, citoyen; vite, vite." We should have premised that, among the orders which Captain Foote had received for his guidance, was one, that he should co-operate with Cardinal F. Ruffo, the chief of the royalist army on shore, and the vicar-general and confidential agent of his Sicilian majesty. Captain Foote had all along done so, and now acquainted the cardinal with the reply which he had received to his letter and his intention of immediately attacking the fort. In this the cardinal appeared heartily to concur; but, on the 19th, after the naval attack had commenced, Captain Foote, to his surprise, received a letter from the cardinal, requesting him to cease hostilities, and not to recommence them while the flag of truce was flying, as a negotiation had taken place. On the same night Captain Foote, sent an officer to the cardinal to acquaint him that the British were not accustomed to grant so long a suspension of arms; and that, as the King of England was a principal ally of the King of the two Sicilies, he, Captain Foote, claimed a right to be informed of all proceedings. The cardinal sent back word, that the Chevalier de Micheroux, the Russian minister, and a detachment of whose troops was then serving with the Neapolitan royalists, conducted the treaty, and that he, the chevalier, would furnish the particulars; but Captain Foote, knowing no other person than the cardinal as intrusted with the interests of his Sicilian majesty, refused to act with Micheroux. To this the cardinal replied, that he himself knew nothing of what was going on, that he stood in great need of the aid of the Russians; and repeated, that it was they who conducted the treaty.

On the 20th Captain Foote received from the cardinal a plan of a capitulation already signed by him and the chief of the Russians, with a request that he, Captain Foote, would affix his signature to it. The latter did so, to avoid throwing the least impediment in the way of the interests of his Sicilian majesty, but failed not to state, that he thought the terms rather favourable to the republicans. On the 22d the capitulation for the forts of Nuovo and del' Uovo was signed in form, by Cardinal Ruffo, by the Russian as well as Turkish commanders, and by Captain Foote as commanding officer of the British ships in the bay of Naples; the French commandant at Fort St.-Elmo, Colonel Méjan, having previously, as stipulated in the last article, approved the terms. Among these it was agreed, that the two garrisons, consisting of about 1500 individuals, chiefly Neapolitan revolutionists, should march out with the honours of war; that private property should be respected; that the individuals should have their choice of embarking on board cartels for Toulon, or of remaining at Naples; that, until the cartels were ready to sail, the garrisons should keep possession of their forts; and that four hostages should be detailed at Fort St.-Elmo, until the arrival of the individuals at Toulon should be ascertained.*

It of course required some days to assemble the necessary quantity of transports to convey the garrisons to their destination; and, in the mean time, the flags of truce remained hoisted, as well at the two forts as on board the British and Neapolitan ships of war at anchor in the bay. On the 24th, while matters were in this state, Lord Nelson, with his fleet, comprising as already stated, 16 sail of the line and a reduced 64-gun ship, appeared in sight, bearing at the mast-head of the Foudroyant a signal, annulling the flag of truce then flying on board Captain Foote's squadron. On the same afternoon, at a conference held on board the flag-ship, at which were present Cardinal Ruffo, and Sir William and Lady Hamilton, the cardinal maintained inflexibly, that the treaty ought to be kept sacred. Lord Nelson, on the other hand, was of opinion that the treaty, as one

*For a copy of the treaty both in French and English, see Captain Foote's *Vindication of his Conduct*, &c, 2d edition, p. 195.

"entered into with rebels," ought not to be carried into execution without the approbation of his Sicilian majesty.* Upon this, the cardinal retired from the conference in disgust. In the evening, when Captain Foote came on board the Foudroyant, Lord Nelson gave him full credit for his zeal, assiduity, and good intentions, but declared that he, Captain Foote, had been imposed upon by "that worthless fellow, Cardinal Ruffo, who was endeavouring to form a party hostile to the views of his sovereign." Captain Foote replied that, when he concluded the treaty, he had more reason to expect the French, than the British fleet in the bay of Naples, and that he could not be supposed to know, or even imagine, that the cardinal was acting contrary to his sovereign's interest, when he still retained so high and confidential a station.†

On the 26th, two days after the arrival of Lord Nelson in the bay, the garrisons of Castel-Nuovo and Castel-del' Uovo, in obedience to the ninth article of the treaty, set at liberty the state prisoners and the English prisoners of war. The garrison, then, as stipulated in the third article, marched out with the honours of war, and grounded their arms.‡ After this, such of them as chose, comprising nearly the whole present, embarked on board 14 transports, chiefly polacres and feluccas, in order, as they understood, to be conveyed to Toulon, conformably to the fifth article, but, in reality, to be held as prisoners on board their vessels, until the King of the two Sicilies, then at Palermo, should determine how he would dispose of them. Here, then, was a gross infraction of the treaty, and by whom? By Lord Nelson. Had he and his fleet, by any fortunate chance, been prevented from entering the bay until the 27th or 28th, the wretched garrisons, the unhappy victims of violated faith, would have been on their way to Toulon, and British honour have been preserved without a tarnish.

Prince Francesco Caraccioli, a younger branch of one of the most noble families in Naples, an officer once high in command, and not only of deserved distinction in the Neapolitan navy, but who had commanded a ship, with credit to himself, in a British line of battle, accompanied the king, when he and his court, in the preceding December, fled to Sicily. Shortly afterwards the Neapolitan revolutionary government, or Parthenopaean republic, as it was styled, issued an edict, ordering all absent Neapolitans to return, on pain of confiscation of their property. Caraccioli, having great estates in the country, obtained the king's permission to go to Naples to see after them. He departed from Palermo, and, in a short time, was found at the head of the republican naval forces, acting against the king and his allies.

*Harrison's Life of Lord Nelson, vol. ii., p. 101.

†Captain Foote's Vindication, p. 22.

‡Letters of the prisoners to Lord Nelson. See attested copies, in French and English, in the Appendix to Helen Maria Williams's *Sketches of the State of Manners and Opinions in the French Republic*, vol. ii., pp. 319–328; also Captain Foote's Vindication, p. 39.

"Perhaps he thought," says an intelligent writer, "as many others have thought, that the king's abdication of his throne, without making so strenuous an opposition as he might have done to the revolutionary system, and his quitting his capital several weeks before any enemy approached it, might plead his excuse for joining those who were now resolved to erect a new government, since they were abandoned by their old."*

When the recovery of Naples was evidently near, Caraccioli applied to Cardinal Ruffo, and to the Duke of Calvinrano, for protection, hoping that 40 years of faithful services would outweigh the few days during which, as he stated, he had been forced to obey the French. Not being successful in his application, and knowing the temper of the Sicilian court, he fled from one of the two forts which had last capitulated. Whether this occurred a day or two before or after the treaty had been concluded, is uncertain and perhaps immaterial. A price was set upon his head; and on the 29th of June, at about 9 A.M., Caraccioli, in the disguise of a peasant, was brought alongside of the Foudroyant. We shall give what immediately followed in the words of Lord Nelson's biographers, Messieurs Clarke and M'Arthur: "Captain Hardy, who was on deck at the time, had his attention suddenly attracted to a clamour that prevailed, and it was some time before he could gain information from the Italians who were on board, that the 'traitor Caraccioli was taken.' It was with the utmost difficulty that this humane officer could restrain the insults and violence of the Neapolitan royalists toward this unhappy victim of French perfidy; who, with his hands bound behind him, and wretchedly attired, displayed a painful instance of the uncertainty of all human grandeur. When last on board, this prince had been received with all the respect and deference that were then due to his rank and character. Captain Hardy immediately ordered his noble prisoner to be unbound, and to be treated with every attention that was in his power. Some refreshment was immediately offered, which he declined, and he was then given in charge as a prisoner to the first lieutenant, Mr. W. S. Parkinson, and shown into his cabin. Two additional sentinels were then placed at the outside of the wardroom."†

In acting thus, Captain Hady had but obeyed the impulses of an upright mind and a manly heart. Unhappily, the mind of another person, equally well-disposed when in health, was now possessed by a demon, who had the power to expel every generous feeling, and substitute in their stead the worst of those vindictive passions which degrade human nature. The sequel to Caraccioli's capture is too well known to need a full recital. At 10 A.M. he was put upon his trial, before a court-martial composed of Neapolitan naval officers, with Commodore Count

*Williams's Voyage up the Mediterranean, p. 210.
†Clarke and McArthur, vol. ii., p. 184.

Thurn, Caraccioli's bitterest enemy at their head, and assembled on board the British flag-ship, the Foudroyant, the very ship in which Captain Hardy could, "with the utmost difficulty restrain the insults and violence of the Neapolitan royalists" towards the prisoner. This was done, because "it would have been very dangerous to have ordered a court-martial to assemble on board a Neapolitan ship, from the love which the Sicilian seamen bore to Caraccioli; and moreover, because "the Foudroyant was considered as the seat of government of the King of Naples,"* although the latter was then at Palermo. In two hours the court passed sentence of death on this poor old man (he was upwards of 70 years of age), and Lord Nelson immediately issued an order for his execution on board the Neapolitan frigate Minerva, Count Thurn's ship. "During the awful interval that ensued, from the close of his trial to the execution of his sentence, Caraccioli twice requested Lieutenant Parkinson to go and intercede with Lord Nelson; at first, for a second trial, and afterwards that he might be shot. "I am an old man, sir,' said Caraccioli, 'I have no family to lament my death; I therefore cannot be supposed to be very anxious about prolonging my life, but the disgrace of being hanged is dreadful to me.' Lord Nelson replied, 'Caraccioli has been fairly tried by the officers of his own country; I cannot interfere.' On being urged a second time by Lieutenant Parkinson, he exclaimed with much agitation, 'Go, sir, and attend to your duty!' Caraccioli then, as a last hope, asked Lieutenant Parkinson, whether he thought an application to Lady Hamilton would prove beneficial. Upon which that officer went to the quarterdeck, but, not being able to meet with her,† he returned. At 5 P.M. Caraccioli was removed from the Foudroyant, and hanged at the fore yard-arm off the Neapolitan frigate La Minerva. His body was afterwards carried out to a considerable distance, and sunk in the bay of Naples."‡

On the day previous to Caraccioli's caption, trial (for so we must for form sake call it), and execution, Captain Foote had sailed for Palermo, to bring their Sicilian majesties to the spot. On the 8th of July the latter arrived, in their own frigate, the Sirena, accompanied by the Seahorse as an escort. Imbecility of mind, where not the associate, is often the tool of depravity of heart. Ferdinand IV., although not naturally a cruel, was undoubtedly a weak man. Lady Hamilton and his ministers did with him as they pleased; and, in consequence, such scenes were now acted on board the prison-ships (the cartels that had been!) as would scarcely be believed, even if those cartel-converted

*Clarke and McArthur, Vol. ii., p. 105.

†The partial biographers of Lord Nelson have softened this. She would not be seen. But even they admit (vol, ii., p. 188), that Lady Hamilton was present at Caraccioli's execution!

‡Clarke and McArthur, vol. ii. p. 186.

prison-ships had not been moored in the midst of a fleet of British men-of-war. "It is now," says a letter from one of the unhappy victims of (what we will not call British, but) Lord Nelson's breach of faith, "24 days that we are lying in this road, unprovided with every thing necessary to existence: we have nothing but bread to eat; we drink nothing but putrid water, or wine mingled with sea-water, and have nothing but the bare planks to sleep on. Our houses have been entirely pillaged, consequently we can receive no assistance from them, and the greater part of our relations have been either imprisoned or massacred. Our deplorable situation has already been productive of diseases: and on board this polacre there are five persons sick of an infectious fever, which threatens the lives of the whole."* Among the many who fell a sacrifice to this order of things, were some of the most eminent characters in Naples. Even a woman, that woman one of the capitulators and no other than the celebrated Madame de Fonséca, was doomed to end her days by the hangman's knot.

Comments are unnecessary. We shall only offer a remark or two on the character of the capitulation, from the rupture of which so much disgrace has emanated. One of Lord Nelson's apologists calls the treaty an armistice, or truce;† another calls it the *projet* of a capitulation:‡ whereas, in truth, it was as complete a capitulation as had ever been executed. Another writer styles Lord Nelson "commander-in-chief," and on that founds the assertion that, as representative of the King of England, he might annul treaties. But Lord Nelson was only third, or, admitting Earl St.-Vincent to have resigned, second in command; and even a king's power does not extend to the enemies of his country, without whom as parties a treaty could not exist. Some stress has also been laid upon the circumstance of Lord Nelson's arrival within 36 hours after Captain Foote had subscribed the treaty in question. Had his lordship arrived at the end of one hour, the signature of all the parties had already stamped upon the capitulation its sacred character. But, in fact, two of the articles, the 5th and 9th, had begun to be acted upon: the transports were gettng ready, and the prisoners in the forts either had already been, or were about to be, set at liberty. Even after Lord Nelson had arrived and by signal annulled the truce, the articles in the treaty were made use of to inveigle the garrisons out of the forts; and that, too, solely for their destruction. If Captain Foote, in signing the treaty, had exceeded his orders, he should have been tried and punished; but, even then, the faith of the nation, having been once solemnly pledged, ought not to have been compromised. Every tittle of the treaty should have been executed.

*Helen Maria Williams's Sketches, &c., p. 399.
†Harrison's Life of Lord Nelson, vol. ii., p. 101.
‡Clarke and McArthur, vol. ii., p. 184.

In answer to the question, why Captain Foote himself did not demand to be tried, that ill-used officer says thus: "I was inclined to request, that a public inquiry should take place, upon what concerned my signing the capitulatons. But, before taking this step, I understood from a naval member of the admiralty, and many other respectable friends, that, by urging a public investigation, I should act injuriously to my country, and in some measure attach myself to a party; for which there seemed to me to be good ground, in consequence of the speech which the late Honourable Charles James Fox made on the 3d of February, 1800, on the address thanking his majesty for refusing to negotiate." Respecting the policy of agreeing to a capitulation with the garrisons of Uovo and Nuovo, Captain Foote remarks, "These facts and reasonings may show, that there was nothing so very weak, or senseless, in agreeing to such measures as tended rather to reconcile men to each other, than to urge them to a savage fury, to which all were at this time so ferociously bent; and this may be further corroborated by the situation of the castle of St.-Elmo, which so completely overlooked and commanded the whole city of Naples, that the fire of that castle could have reduced the greatest part of it to a heap of rubbish. The French, at the time of the capitulations in question,were in possession of this castle, with no probability of being forced to surrender and the arrival of their fleet being expected, whilst I was in daily expectation of being compelled to make a precipitate retreat."* Let us now quit this painful subject, and hasten to narrate occurrences, more creditable to the character, and more congenial to the habits, of the officers and seamen of the British navy.

Since the surrender of the castles of Nuovo and Del'Uovo, the French troops had evacuated the city of Naples; but a detachment of them, amounting to about 800 officers and men, under Major-general Méjan, still garrisoned the fort of St.-Elmo. An immediate attack upon the latter was therfore resolved upon; and on the 29th Captain Troubridge, having two days before landed at the head of a detachment of British and Portuguese marines, with a part of which he had since garrisoned Nuovo and Del' Uovo, opened his trenches. A summons was then sent to the commandant of fort St.-Elmo; but the latter expressed his determination to stand siege. Captain Troubridge, on the other hand, was equally determined to storm the fort, as soon as two practicable breaches could be made. Accordingly, on the 3d of July, he opened a battery of three 36-pounders and four mortars within 700 yards of the walls, and, on the 5th, another battery of two 36-pounders. On the same day the Russians, under Captain Baillie, and Englishman, who had entered the Russian service at the conclusion of the first American war, and at this

*Vindication, pp. 8 and 83.

time commanded a ship of the line, opened against the angle opposite to that which the British were attacking, a battery of four 36-pounders and four mortars; to which four more mortars were subsequently added.

On the 11th, the three-gun battery having been entirely destroyed, the guns dismounted, and the breastwork knocked down, by the fire of the besieged, Captain Troubridge directed Captain Hallowell, in the absence of Captain Ball, the second in command, to construct another battery of six 36-pounders within 180 yards of the walls. Between this battery and the fort some trees intervened, which it was necessary to fell, before the fire of the former could be opened with effect. This was a service of such danger, that none of the labourers could be induced to perform it. Captains Troubridge and Hallowell, with Colonel Tehudy, a Swiss officer, whose regiment formed part of the besieging forces, and M. Monfrère, an emigrant of great merit and abilities, advanced before the works, to cheer the men by their example. While here, a gun, loaded with grape, was levelled at them with such precision, that the shot actually cut the boughs, and struck the ground beneath their feet, and yet not one of them was hurt. A second battery of one 18-pounder and two howitzers was also getting ready, at the same short distance. After a few hours' smart cannonade from the six-gun battery, an officer appeared on the walls of the fort with a flag of truce. At this time most of the guns in the fort were dismounted, and the works nearly destroyed. A capitulation being then agreed to, the garrison marched out with the honours of war, and, in this instance, were honourably conveyed to Toulon, the stipulated French port. The loss sustained by the British, Russian, and Neapolitan forces, amounted to five officers and 32 rank and file killed, and five officers and 79 rank and file wounded. Among the former were Lieutenant Milbanke, of the artillery, killed by a musket-shot while reconnoitring the castle, and two Neapolitan officers in one of the mortar-batteries, who fell by the same cannon-ball.

The fort at Capua, a small town situated on the river Volturno, and distant about 15 miles from Naples, became the next object of attack. On the 20th Captain Troubridge, with the English and Portuguese troops, the former consisting of about 1000 seamen and marines from the British fleet, marched from Naples; and, having rested a while at Caserta, encamped before Capua on the morning of the 22d. On the same day a bridge of pontoons was thrown across the Volturno, to facilitate the communication between the different detachments of the army; and the batteries of guns and mortars were immediately begun to be constructed within 500 yards of the works of Capua. On the 25th a battery of four 24-pounders, another of two howitzers, and a mortar-battery, commenced playing upon the fort and were answered by a fire from 11 guns with equal spirit. On the next day, the 26th, fresh trenches were opened, and new batteries begun, within a few yards of the glacis. This induced the besieged to propose terms of capitulation. These were rejected, and others sent back by Captain Troubridge; to which, at length, the French commandant agreed.

On the morning of the 29th the French garrison, numbering 2817 officers and men, under Brigadier-general Girardon, marched out as prisoners with the honours of war, and were afterwards conveyed to Toulon. The subjects of the Sicilian monarch, according to an article of the treaty, were delivered up to the allies. The fort was mounted with 108 pieces of ordnance, exclusively of 10 that were unserviceable; and contained 12,000 muskets, 414,000 filled musket-cartridges, and 67,848 lbs. of powder. The allied forces do not appear to have sustained any loss. It certainly would have been more creditable to the French general, if, with such a force at his disposal, he had insisted a little more strenuously, that the lives of the Neapolitan insurgents in the fort should not be sacrificed.

The surrender of Capua was followed, on the 31st, by that of the neighbouring fort of Gaeta, although the latter had not been regularly besieged, but only blockaded. On this account, chiefly, the French garrison, numbering 1498 officers and men, obtained leave to march out with their arms and personal effects, and, on being sent to a French port, were not to be considered as prisoners of war. Here, again, the poor Neapolitan insurgents were handed over, without an effort on their behalf, to those who, it was well known, would soon be their executioners. The same general, Girardon, who had signed the capitulation of Capua, negotiated and signed that of Gaeta; on the walls of which were mounted 72 pieces of cannon, including 58 brass 24 and 18 pounders, and 13 heavy mortars; the magazines contained an immense quantity of powder and other garrison stores.

About the 11th of August Captain Troubridge, by Lord Nelson's directions, sent the Minotaur, and one or two smaller vessels, with a summons to the republican commandant at Civita-Vecchia. Some delay occurring in the transmission of the reply, the Culloden herself went off the port; and on the 29th and 30th of September Captain Troubridge, with 200 seamen and marines from his two ships, landed at Civita-Vecchia, and, aided by a detachment of Neapolitan royalist troops under General Bouchard, took possesion of that town, Corneto, and Tolfa. The same treaty by which these places were surrendered, gave up Rome; which was taken possession of by General Bouchard, aided by a detachment of seamen under Captain Louis, of the Minotaur. The last-named officer rowed up the Tiber in his barge, and hoisted the English colours on the capitol. Thus were Naples, Rome, and Tuscany (Leghorn had been evacutaed since the 17th of July), freed from the dominion of the French, by, in a very great degree, the persevering exertions of the officers and seamen of the British navy. We will now proceed to give accounts of other Mediterranean coast-operations, by the final success of which the British navy did really (for many, with reason, have doubted it in the case of Naples) afford relief to a suffering people.

The junction, in the latter end of October, 1798, of a few Russian and Turkish frigates, corvettes, and gun-boats, with the three or four ships with which the British cruised off the coast of Egypt, and the threatening posture which the combined squadron occasionally assumed, induced Buonaparte to strengthen Damietta, Rosetta, and particularly Alexandria; to the command of which latter city, on General Kléber's rejoining the army in Cairo, Buonaparte had appointed General Marmont. Having made these dispositions, the general in chief busied himself in forming schemes that had for their object the junction of the Red and Mediterranean seas, by means of a canal through the isthmus of Suez. In order to have ocular demonstration of the practicability of such a plan, Buonaparte resolved to go himself to Suez; first sending, however, a detachment of troops to take possession of the town and neighbourhood.

On the 2d of November, General Bon departed from Cairo with a suitable body of troops; and on the 8th, the advanced division, commanded by Eugène Beauharnois, one of Buonaparte's aides-de-camp, entered the seaport of Suez, a small town, situated at the northern extremity of the western arm of the Red sea, and distant about 30 leagues from Cairo, and nearly the same from the Mediterranean. The inhabitants of Suez all fled on the approach of the French, and a few merchant vessels were all that were found in the port. Buonaparte would soon have followed General Bon to this interesting spot, but was retarded in his movements, by the breaking out of the plague among his troops, and by the knowledge which he had just acquired of the hostile intentions of Turkey.

Believing he could remove these by diplomatizing, Buonaparte, on or about the 12th of December, despatched the consul of Mascata, Citizen Beauchamp, on board a Turkish caravella in Alexandria, to the French ambassador at Constantinople, Taleyrand-Périgord, as Buonaparte supposed, but who had not yet quitted Paris on his mission. Early in the month of January, the Turkish vessel sailed from Alexandria, and was detained by the British commanding officer off the coast, Captain Troubridge; who took out M. Beauchamp, and, considering him to be a spy, sent him to Constantinople as a prisoner. Captain Troubridge, however, with characteristic generosity, restored to M. Beauchamp a sum nearly equal to 600*l.* sterling, found concealed among his clothes, and which, although ostensibly M. Beauchamp's private property, had no doubt been supplied to him by Buonaparte for purposes of bribery and corruption.

Having, chiefly by the excellent regulations of the physicians in his army, checked the ravages of the plague; and having sent one messenger to Constantinople, and another (the nature of whose mission we shall presently unfold) to Achmet-Djezzar, pacha of Acre in Syria, Buonaparte, on the 25th of December, quitted Cairo, and in two days afterwards arrived at Suez, attended, among others, by the members of the "institute of Egypt," Monge, Berthollet, Costaz, and Bourienne. Without losing a moment, Buonaparte proceeded to reconnoitre the town, the harbour, and the neighbouring coast. He afterwards crossed the arm of the Red sea, at the end of which Suez stands, by means of a ford only practicable at low water, in order to reach a spot which the Arabs still call the 'fountain of Moses,' and where, according to the traditions of the country, lie the rocks from the striking of one of which the water was produced. Here were seen the vestiges of a small modern aqueduct for conveying this water to some cisterns on the sea-shore, about three miles off, and by which vessels were, or rather had been supplied. In their way back to Suez, Buonaparte and his escort nearly suffered the fate of Pharaoh and his army. The ford, which the caravan had crossed with so much ease in the morning, being now covered with the tide, the travellers were obliged to descend to the bottom of the arm or gulf. Here, owing to some mistake about the depth of water, Buonaparte was obliged to be carried upon the shoulders of his guide, and both with difficulty escaped being drowned.*

On the 31st of December, Buonaparte again quitted Suez; and, while one part of his attendants took the route to Adjaroud, he coasted the Red sea to the northward, and, at the distance of about two leagues and a half from Suez, discovered some traces of the ancient canal. These he followed during four hours, and until, indeed, the traces disappeared in some lakes named Ammers. On his return to Suez, Buonaparte received advices which called for his active exertions in another quarter; but, on arriving at his head-quarters at Cairo, he did not neglect to despatch to Suez his principal engineer, Lepère, with directions, that he should take the geometrical level of the course of the supposed canal across the isthmus. Having made this digression, we now hasten to relate what it was, that, while Buonaparte appeared so intent upon pursuing his geological researches, thus gave a new impulse to his active mind.

About a month previous to his departure for Suez, Buonaparte had sent an officer of his staff to Achmet-Djezzar, for the purpose of engaging his vizier to preserve the relations of peace with him. The messenger was not permitted an audience, nor even to disembark from the vessel in which he had arrived in the bay of Acre. The vessel, with Colonel Beauvoisins on board, returned

*Victoires et Conquêtes, tome ix., p. 246.

to Egypt, and Buonaparte's rage knew no bounds. He, however, mastered it so far as to send to Djezzar, by two Arabs, the following letter: "I do not wish to go to war with you, if you are not my enemy; but it is time that you explain yourself. If you continue to afford refuge to Ibrahim-Bey, and allow him to remain on the frontiers of Egypt, I shall consider that as an act of hostility, and arch to Acre. If you are disposed to live in peace with me, you will remove Ibrahim-Bey 40 leagues from the frontiers of Egypt, and let there be a free commerce between Damietta and Syria. In that case, I promise to respect your sovereignty, and to allow a free commerce, by land or sea, between Egypt and Syria."*

The letter met no better fate than the message sent by Colonel Beauvoisins. Buonaparte now commenced prepartions for fulfilling his promise to Djezzar. This he felt the more inclined to do, conceiving it would gain him favour with the grand signior, to whom the pacha of Acre, as was well known, had long been a rebellious subject. Djezzar had anticipated Buonaparte, by throwing a body of troops into the castle of El-Arich, situated just within the frontiers of Egypt. The news of this quickened the movements of Buonaparte; and early in January, an army consisting, in effective strength, of 12,995 men, with 27 field-pieces, and 11 howitzers,† marched from the neighbourhood of Cairo to effect the conquest of Syria. The generals under Buonaparte in this army were Regnier, Kléber, Bon, Lannes, and Murat. The remainder of the army, which probably amounted to about 17,000 men, was scattered over the different provinces of Lower and Upper Egypt. On the 18th of February, the whole of the army destined to invade Syria, had assembled before El-Arich; where we will leave it awhile, until we have given some account of the proceedings of the British squadron cruising off the Egyptian coast.

On the 2d of February Captain Troubridge, in the Culloden 74, with the Theseus of the same force, Captain Ralph Willett Miller, bomb-vessels Bull-dog and Perseus, Captains Adam Drummond and James Oswald, and Alliance frigate armed en flûte, Captain David Wilmot, arrived off Alexandria, to relieve Captains Hood of the Zealous, and Hallowell of the Swiftsure 74s, from their long and unproductive cruise on that station. On the following day, the 3d, at 3 P.M., the Bull-dog and Perseus stood towards the town of Alexandria, throwing in their shells as they approached. At 6 P.M. they discontinued the bombardment; but resumed it for three or four hours at a time, on the 4th, 5th, 7th, 8th, 13th, and 22d. On the last-named day there were two bombardments, one at 4 h. 30 m. A.M, and the other at 8 P.M. The latter had not continued long, before the

*See Appendix, No. 19.
†Victoires et Conquêtes, tome x., p. 76.

13-inch mortar on board the Perseus burst, whereby one man was killed and three wounded, and the mainmast sprung. This, besides sinking two French transports in the harbour, and frightening the Turkish ships of war out of it (consisting of one or two frigates or corvettes), appears to have been all the mischief which the seven bombardments had occasioned.

On the 3d of March the British 74-gun ship Tigre, Commodore Sir William Sidney Smith, in company with the Marianne armed galliot, a French gun-vessel captured two days before, arrived off Alexandria, to supersede Captain Troubridge in the command of the squadron on that station. Sir Sidney had been invested with the rank of minister plenipotentiary to the Sublime Porte, jointly with his brother, Mr. John Spencer Smith, and had since been at Constantinople and at the island of Rhodes, arranging a plan of active co-operation on the part of the Turks against the French in Egypt.

Having obtained the concurrence of Captain Troubridge, Sir Sidney immediately despatched to Achmed-Djezzar at St.-Jean-d'Acre Lieutenant John Westley Wright of the Tigre, attended by an interpreter, in order to arrange with that personage the plan of future operations. In the mean time another bombardment was made upon Alexandria, but with as little effect as any of the preceding ones. On the 7th Captain Troubridge, with the Culloden and two bomb-vessels, sailed to join Lord Nelson; leaving Sir Sidney with the Tigre, Theseus, Alliance, and the two gun-vessels Torride and Marianne. On the same evening an express arrived from Djezzar with an account of the invasion of Syria by Buonaparte, and of his having, that very day, carried Jaffa by storm.

On the 8th, in consequence of this intelligence, the commodore despatched the Theseus to Acre, with Colonel Phelipeaux, of the engineers, a French royalist officer of distinction and a tried friend of Sir Sidney's. The Tigre, meanwhile, remained before Alexandria to observe the enemy's maritime movement; when, remarking that most of the vessels in the old or western port had removed to the eastern or new, Sir Sidney conjectured that an expedition by sea was on foot. Receiving a confirmation of this from a neutral vessel which had sailed from Alexandria on the night of the 9th, Sir Sidney, on the 10th, detached Mr. James Boxer, midshipman of the Tigre, in the prize galliot Marianne, with orders to examine minutely the coast to the eastward, and to rejoin the commodore in the road of Caïffa, a port about eight miles south-west of St.-Jean-d'Acre, and towards which the Tigre immediately made sail.

On the 15th, having been rejoined off Caïffa by the Marianne, the Tigre anchored in the bay of Acre, in company with the Theseus, who had arrived two days before. On the 16th Sir Sidney landed and paid a visit to Djezzar; and, assisted by Colonel Phelipeaux, Captain Miller, and some other officers, commenced putting the town of Acre, with its rotten and ruined walls, in the best possible state for resisting the attack of an European army. Encouraged by the presence of a British naval force, particularly so by the zeal and activity of Sir Sidney and his friends, the pacha and the garrison seemed determined to make a vigorous defence. On the 17th Sir Sidney detached the Theseus to reconnoitre the coast to the southward, while he himself, with the boats of the Tigre, proceeded to the anchorage of Caïffa near the promontory of Mount Carmel, in order to intercept the maritime portion of the French expedition, which the commodore was convinced would soon make its appearance. At 10 P.M. he discovered the French advanced guard, mounted on asses and dromedaries, marching by the seaside. Sir Sidney immediately returned to the Tigre, and sent the launch, with a 32-pounder carronade and 16 men under the orders of Lieutenant John Busby, to the mouth of the river Kerdanneh, to guard and defend the ford; a service most ably and effectually performed.

On the 18th, at daybreak, the launch opened a fire on the French troops, so unexpected and vigorous, as to oblige them to retire precipitately to the skirts of Mount Carmel. The main body finding the road between the sea and mount thus exposed, came in by the Nazareth road, but not without being much harassed by the Samaritan Arabs, who were more inimical to the French than even the Egyptians, and better armed. After being driven by the guns of the British ships, directed at the trenches, from making an attack along the coast to the northward, the French invested the town of Acre to the north-east, where the defences were much stronger.

The non-employment of cannon against the British boats convinced Sir Sidney, that the French expected their artillery by sea; and on the very next day, the 18th, at 5 A.M., a French flotilla, consisting of one corvette and nine sailing gun-vessels, hove in sight of the Tigre. Afer a three hours' chase, the following seven gun-vessels, including one, the Torride, which had been taken from the British that morning, were captured:

Foudre	8	guns, and	52	men.
Négresse	6	"	53	"
Dangereuse	6	"	23	"
Vierge-de-Grâces	4	"	35	"
Deux-Frères	4	"	23	"
Marie-Rose	4	"	22	"
Torride	2	"	30	"

These vessels were laden with battering cannon, ammunition, and every kind of siege-equipage, which they had brought from Damietta, under the escort of a corvette commanded by Captain Standelet; the same officer who, at the battle of the Nile, so treacherously set fire to the Artémise frigate after having struck her colours, and who had now the good fortune to effect his escape. Although intended for the attack, the French guns were presently landed for the defence of Acre; and the prizes themselves were manned, and sent to co-operate with the boats in harassing the enemy's posts, impeding his approaches, and cutting off his supplies of provisions by the coasters.

For five days and nights in succession, the gun-vessels and boats were occupied in this laborious duty, to the annoyance of the French and the encouragement of the Turks, but, on one occasion in particular, not without a serious loss to the British. That occasion was an unsuccessful attempt on the 21st, to cut out of the port of Caïffa four djerms, or sailing lighters, which had got in there on the 18th from Alexandria, with supplies for the French army. The attack was made at 10 A.M. by the boats of the two 74s (the Theseus having rejoined the preceding day), covered by some of the gun-vessels, in one of which was Colonel Phelipeaux.

In Sir Sidney's letter, the account of loss includes that incurred in capturing the gun-boats on the 18th, but which, we believe, was comparatively trifling. The total stands thus: four midshipment (Arthur Lambert, John Goodman, John Gell, and John Carra), and eight seamen killed, one midshipman (John Waters) and 26 seamen wounded; eight of whom, along with 12 others, had been taken prisoners. The officers, other than those mentioned, that are named by Sir Sidney as having distinguished themselves in this, as it appears to us, scarcely adequate service even had it been successful, are Lieutenants John Bushby, Samuel Hood Inglefield, William Knight, and James Stokes, and Lieutenant of marines Charles F. Burton.

Owing to a violent gale of wind and the unsheltered state of the anchorage, the Tigre and Theseus were compelled to weigh and stand off, until the weather moderated, which was not until the 6th of April. In the mean time the French had pushed their approaches to the counterscarp, and even into the ditch of the north-east angle of the town; and were employed in mining the tower, so as to increse the breach which, by their field-pieces, they had already made in it. Although the fire from the prize-guns, which had been admirably mounted under the direction of Colonel Phelipeaux and Captain Wilmot of the Alliance, appeared to slacken that of the French, yet much danger was to be apprehended from the mine. A sortie was therfore determined upon, in which a detachment of seamen and marines form the three British ships were to force their way into the mine, while the Turkish troops attacked the enemy's trenches on the right and left.

Just before daybraek on the 7th the sally took place. The impetuosity and noise of the Turks rendered abortive the attempt to surprise the besiegers, but, in other respects, the Turks performed their part well. Lietuenant John Westley Wright, of the Tigre, who commanded the seamen pioneers, notwithstanding he had received two balls in his right arm as he advanced, entered the mine with the pike-men, and proceeded to the bottom of it; where he verified its direction, and, by pulling down the supporters, destroyed all that could be destroyed in its present state. Major John 'Douglas, of the marines, ably supported the seamen in this despearte service, bringing off the wounded, and among them Lieutenant Wright, who had scarcely strength left to get out of the enemy's trench.

The loss sustained by the British was, one major of marines (Thomas Oldfield) and two private marines killed, one lieutenant (John Westley Wright), one lieutenant of marines (George Beatty), two midshipmen (Richard Janverin and James Morrison Bigges Forbes), one lieuteant of marines (George Beatty), two midshipmen (Richard Janverin and James Morrison Bigges Forbes), one sergeant and six privates of marines, and 12 seamen wounded. The return of the detachment to the garrison was well covered by the fire of the Theseus, who had taken an excellent position for that purpose. The Turks, as proofs of their prowess, brought in 60 Frenchmen's heads, a great number of muskets, and some intrenching tools, of which last the besieged were greatly in want.

When Buonaparte set out on his march to Syria, he sent orders to Alexandria for Rear-admiral Perrée to put to sea with the French frigates Junon, Alceste, and Courageuse, and brig-corvettes Salamine and Alerte, having on board a quantity of battering cannon and other heavy munitions of war for the Syrian army. These were in addition to those directed to sail from Damietta. The bloackade of Alexandria by Captain Troubridge prevented M. Perrée's departure; but, about a month after Sir Sidney Smith, Captain Troubridge's successor, had sailed for the bay of Acre, the French rear-admiral quitted Alexandria, and reached Jaffa with his valuable cargo: in addition to which, by Buonaparte's desire, he landed four of the Junon's 18-pounders.

In the mean while the garriosn of Acre continued to make occasional sorties, under the protection of field-pieces in the boats of the ships, until the evening of the 1st of May, when the French, after many hours' heavy cannonode from 23 pieces of artillery, including nine battering 24 and 18 pounders brought to Jaffa by Rear-admiral Perrée's squadron, and which, on the 27th of April, had arrived thence overland, made a fourth desperate attempt to mount the breach, now much widened. The Tigre by this time had moored herself on the one, and the Theseus on the other side of the town, so as to flank the walls of it; and the gun-vessels, launches, and other rowing boats, had stationed themselves in the best manner for flanking the enemy's trenches.

Opposed to so destructive a cross-fire, the French troops, in spite of their bravery, were repulsed with a heavy loss. Nor did the British escape with impunity, having had one captain (Wilmot, killed by a rifle-shot, as he was mounting a howitzer on the breach), one midshipman (Edward Morris), and four seamen killed, and one lieutenant (William Knight), one boatswain's mate, six seamen, and one marine wounded. In addition to their loss in the action, the British had to regret the death of Colonel Phelipeaux, an officer of great zeal and ability, in consequence of a fever brought on by want of rest and exposure to the sun.

The Turks, to their credit, brought the gabions, fascines, and all such materials as the garrison could not supply, from the face of the enemy's works, setting fire to what they could not carry away. The French, on the other hand, usually repaired in the night all the mischief that the combined forces had done to them in the day; and, in spite of the unremitting fire kept up by Lieutenant William Knight of the Tigre, from the ramparts, remained within half pistol-shot of the walls.

As well as we can gather from the published accounts, the gun-boats in the attack just detailed, were commanded by, among others, Lieutenant Stokes, and midshipmen George Nicholas Hardinge, James Boxer, and Samuel Simms; and the small boats by Lieutenant Thomas Charles Brodie, and Messieurs Thomas Atkinson and Edmund Ives, the masters of the Theseus and Tigre.

The French continued to batter in breach with progressive effect; and, up to the night of the 6th of May, had been repulsed, with great slaughter, in seven or eight attempts to storm. A similar succession of failures had attended their attacks on the two ravelins which the persevering Sir Sidney had caused to be erected, in order to flank the nearest approaches of the besiegers, from which the ravelins were only ten yards distant. The best mode of defence was found to be frequent sorties, which impeded the French in their covering works, and were only suspended during the short intervals caused by the excessive fatigue of every individual on both sides. At length, on the 7th of May, the 51st of the siege, the long-expected reinforcement from Rhodes, consisting of some Turkish corvettes, and between 20 and 30 transports with troops, and which at first had been mistaken in the French camp for a reinforcement to them, made its appearance in the offing.

The approach of this additional strength was the signal to Buonaparte for a most vigorous assault, in the hope to get possession of the town before the troops could disembark. Accordingly, the fire from the French suddenly increased tenfold; and the flanking fire from the British afloat was plied to the utmost, but with less than the usual effect, the besiegers having thrown up epaulments and traverses of a sufficient thickness to proect them from it. The guns that could be worked to the greatest advantage were a French brass 18-pounder in the Lighthouse castle, under the direction of Mr. Christopher Scroeder, master's mate, and the last mounted 24-pounder in the north ravelin, manned from the Tigre, under the direction of Mr. Jones, midshipman. These guns, being within grape-distance of the head of the attacking column, added to the Turkish musketry, did great execution. The Tigre's two 68-pounder carronades, mounted in two djerms lying in the mole, and worked under the able direction of Mr. James Bray, carpenter of the Tigre, threw shells into the centre of that column with evident effect, and checked it considerably.

Still, however, the besiegers gained ground, and made a lodgment in the second story of the north-east tower, the upper part being entirely battered down, and the ruins in the ditch forming the ascent by which they mounted. Daylight on the 8th discovered to the besieged the French standard, hoisted on the outer angle of the tower. The fire from the former had comparatively slackened, and even the flanking fire was become of less effect, the French having covered themselves in the lodgment, and the approach to it by two traverses across the ditch. These the French had constructed under the fire of the whole preceding night: they were composed of sand-bags, and the bodies of the dead built in with them, and were so high that their bayonets only were visible.

Hassan-Bey's troops were in the boats, although as yet only half way to the shore. This was a most critical point of the contest; and an effort was necessary to preserve the place for a short time until the newly arrived troops could take their stations at the walls. Accordingly, Sir Sidney himself landed with the ships' boats at the mole, and led the crews, armed with pikes, to the breach. Many fugitives accompanied the British; and the latter found the breach defended by a few Turks, whose most destructive missiles were heavy stones, which, striking the assailants on the head, overthrew the foremost down the slope, and impeded the progress of the rest. Fresh parties of French, however, ascended to the assault, the heap of ruins between the two parties serving as a breastwork for both: here the muzzles of their muskets touched, and the spear-heads of their standards locked.

Djezzar-Pacha, according to the ancient Turkish custom, had been sitting in his palace, rewarding such as brought him the heads of his enemies, and distributing musket-cartridges with his own hands. Hearing that Sir Sidney and his brave shipmates were on the breach, the old man hastily quitted his station, and, coming behind the British, pulled them down with violence, saying, that if any harm happened to his English friends, all would be lost. This amicable contest as to who should defend the breach, occasioned a rush of Turks to the spot; and thus time was gained for the arrival of the first body of Hassan-Bey's troops.

Sir Sidney's next difficulty was to overcome the pacha's repugnance to the admission of any troops but his Albanians into the gardens of the seraglio; which were now become a very important post, as occupying the terre-plein of the rampart. Of those Albanians, originally 1000, not above 200 were left alive. This was no time for debate, and Sir Sidney overruled the pacha's objections by introducing the Chifflic regiment, of 1000 men, armed with bayonets, disciplined after the European method under Sultan Selim's own eye, and placed by the commands of the latter at the disposal of the British commodore. The garrison, animated by the appearance of such a reinforcement, were now all on foot, and soon formed in sufficient numbers to defend the breach. This being the case, Sir Sidney proposed to the pacha, to let the Chifflic regiment make a sally, and take the assailants in flank. The gates were accordingly opened, and the Turks rushed out; but, not being equal to such a movement, they were driven back with loss. The Tigre's 68-pounders, however, protected the town-gate, as hitherto, most efficaciously.

The sortie produced this good effect; it obliged the besiegers to expose themselves above their parapets; so that the flanking fire of the British brought down numbers of them, and drew their force from the breach: the small number remaining on the lodgment were then killed or dispersed by some hand-grenades thrown by Mr. R. H. Savage, a midshipman of the Theseus. After this, the French began a new breach, by an incessant fire directed to the southward of the lodgment; every shot knocking down whole sheets of a wall, much less solid than that of the tower on which they had expended so much time and ammunition.

The group of French generals and aides-de-camp, which the shells from the two 68-pounders had so frequently dispersed, were now assembled on Richard Coeur de Lion's mount. Buonaparte was distinguishable in the centre of a semicircle. His gesticulations indicated a renewal of the attack, and his despatching an aide-de-camp to the camp showed that he waited only for a reinforcement. Sir Sidney immediately directed Hassan-Bey's ships to take their stations in the shoal water to the southward, and made the Tigre's signal to get under way, and join the Theseus to the northward.

A little before sunset a massive column appeared advancing to the breach, with a solemn step. The pacha's idea was, not to defend the breach this time, but rather to let a certain number of the besiegers enter, and then close with them according to the Turkish mode of war. The column thus mounted the breach unmolested, and descended from the rampart into the pacha's garden. Here, in a few minutes, the bravest and most advanced of the Frenchmen lay headless corpses; the sabre, with the addition of a dagger in the other hand, proving more than a match for the bayonet. The rest of the besiegers retreated precipitately;

and the French commanding officer, General Lannes, who was seen manfully encouraging his men to mount the breach, was carried off, wounded by a musket-shot. General Rambeaud was killed.

Much confusion had risen in the town from the actual entry of the French; it having been impossible, nay impolitic, to make fully known the mode of defence intended to be adopted, lest the besiegers, by means of their numerous emissaries, should come to a knowledge of it. The English uniform, which had hitherto, wherever it appeared, served as a rallying-point for the old garrison, became, in the dusk, mistaken for French, the newly-arrived Turks not distinguishing, in the crowd, between one hat and another. In consequence of this, many a severe sabre-blow was parried by the British officers; and Major Douglas, and Messieurs Ives and Jones, as they were forcing their way through a torrent of fugitives, nearly lost their lives. Calm was at length restored, chiefly by the pacha's exertions; and, both parties being so fatigued as to be unable to move, an end was put to the 25 hours' contest. In this very splendid affair the British had one seaman killed, seven seamen wounded, and one midshipman (Thomas Lamb) and three seamen drowned.

Conceiving now that the ideas of the Syrians, as to the alleged irresistible prowess of their invaders, must be changed since they had witnessed the checks which the besieging army daily experienced in their operations before the town of Acre, Sir Sidney wrote a circular to the princes and chiefs of the Christians of Mount Lebanon, and also to the sheiks of the Druses, recalling them to a sense of duty, and exhorting them to cut off the supplies from the French camp. The Syrians immediaely sent two ambassadors to Sir Sidney, and commenced active operations against Buonaparte's overland supplies. The latter's career further northward was thus effectually stopped by a war-like people inhabiting an impenetrable country. General Kléber's division, which had just been recalled from the fords of the Jordan, was intended to be the next to take its turn in the daily efforts to mount the breach at Acre. To frustrate this, if possible, another sortie was resolved on.

Accordingly, in the night of the 19th, the Turkish Chifflic regiment, led by its lieutenant-colonel, Soliman Aga, rushed out of the gates, and gained the third parallel of the besiegers; but the impetuosity of the men carried them to the second trench, where they lost some of their standards: previously to their retreat, however, they spiked four of the French guns. Kléber's division instead of mounting the breach, as had been General Buonaparte's intention, was thus obliged to spend its time and its strength in recovering these works; in which it did not succeed until after a three hours' conflict and a heavy loss.

The loss of the British in the action is, in Sir Sidney's letter, mixed up with the heavy loss sustained on board the Theseus by the bursting of some shells that had been placed on the deck for immediate use. The accident alluded to was a very serious one. On the 14th of May, at 9 h. 30 m. A.M., just as the Theseus, having on the preceding day been detached to chase, the squadron of M. Perrée, twenty 36-pounder, and fifty 18-pounder shells, which had been got up and prepared for service, in an instant, no one could tell how, caught fire and exploded. The ship was presently in flames, in the main rigging and mizen top, in the cockpit, in the tiers, in several places about the main deck, and in various other parts. Captain Miller had just run aft from the forecastle, to ascertain the cause of the unusual bustle, when a splinter struck him in the breast, and he fell dead on the deck. The same was the melancholy fate of the ship's schoolmaster (Thomas Segbourne), two midshipmen (James Morrison Bigges Forbes and Charles James Webb), 23 seamen, on boy, and three private marines, who were killed, and six seamen and three private marines, who were drowned, by jumping overboard; total 40 killed and drowned. The number wounded (the greater part of them shockingly burnt) amounted to 47, including two lieutenants (James Summers and —— Beatly), the master (Thomas Atkinson), surgeon (Robert Tainsh), chaplain (Frederick Morris), one midshipman (Charles Dobson), and the carpenter (mortally); making a total of 87 killed and wounded by the explosion.

The whole of the poop and afterpart of the quarterdeck were entirely blown to pieces, and all the booms destroyed. Eight of the maindeck beams were also broken; and, in their fall, they jammed the tiller. All the wardroom bulkheads and windows were blown to pieces, and the ship was left a perfect wreck; nothing, indeed, but the greatest exertions one the part of Lieutenants Thomas England and James Summers, Mr. Atkinson, the master, and the surviving officers and crew, subdued the fire and saved the Theseus.

The accident is thus accounted for. The carpenter of the ship and one of the midshipmen who perished, were endeavouring to get the fusees out of the shells; the one by an augur, the other by a mallet and spike-nail. It may readily be conceived, that the latter mode was that by which the shells became ignited: beyond this conjecture nothing is known respecting the origin of the lamentable accident. Nor were its sad effects on board the only misfortune. The chase of the French frigates was obliged to be discontinued; and, as the Tigre could not move without risking the safety of Acre, and Sir Sidney had no effective frigates to detach, Commodore Perrée escaped. The same cause, the want of frigates, enabled the French to receive at Jaffa from Alexandria some very important supplies, especially ammunition; of which the British ships had scarcely enough left to continue the cannonade.

The loss occasioned by the fire of the enemy appears to have amounted to only one seaman killed, and one sergeant and one private of marines wounded; all belonging to the Tigre. This makes the loss sustained by the three ships in the different attacks, as follows: Tigre, 17 killed, 48 wounded, four drowned, and 77 prisoners; Theseus, four killed, 15 wounded, and five prisoners; and Alliance, one killed and three wounded; total 22 killed, 66 wounded, four drowned, and 82 prisoners.

After their last failure, the French grenadiers refused to mount the breach any more over the putrid bodies of their unburied companions, sacrificed in former attacks by their general's impatience and precipitation, which led him to commit such palpable errors as even seamen could turn to advantage. Two attempts to assassinate Sir Sidney in the town having failed, a flag of truce was sent in by the hands of an Arab dervise, with a letter to the pacha, proposing a cessation of arms, for the purpose of burying the dead bodies; the stench of which had become intolerable, and threatened the existence of every person on both sides. Many, indeed, in the garrison had died delirious, within a few hours after having been seized with the first symptoms of infection. It was therefore natural that the besieged should listen to the proposal, and be off their guard during the conference. While the answer was under consideration, a volley of shot and shells (the latter taken out of some captured Turkish vessels) announced an assault; which, however, the garrison was ready to receive, and the assailants only contributed to increase the number of dead bodies. Sir Sidney rescued the Arab from the indignation of the Turks, by conveying him on board the Tigre; whence he was sent back to the French general, with a message, that must have made the army ashamed of having exposed itself to so well-merited a reproof.

All hopes of success having vanished, the French army, in the night between the 20th and 21st, raised the siege, and made a precipitate retreat, leaving 23 pieces of battering cannon (except the carriages, which had been burnt) in the hands of the besieged. According to Berthier's account, the army reached Cantoura on the afternoon of the 21st, the ruins of Caesarea on the 22d, and Jaffa on the 24th. Here it rested three days. It then moved forward, and reached Gaza on the 30th. On the 1st of June it entered the desert, and stopped on the 2d at El-Arich, where Buonaparte left a garrison. The main body then continued its march, arriving on the 4th at Cathich, and on the 14th at Cairo. Berthier omits to notice how the French had been harassed in their retreat by the Syrians: he, however, sums up the loss of the French army, during the last four months, at 700 men who had died by disease, 500 killed in the different actions, and about 1800 wounded. But, where the lives of men were so little valued, the probability is, that the returns were very deficient; and, therefore, that the loss which the French sustained, in their expedition into Syria, was much greater than they were willing, or even able, to make known.

After affording to the Turks such further assistance as was in his power, Sir Sidney, on the 12th of June, set sail from the bay of Acre; and proceeded, first to Beruta road on the same coast, and afterwards to Lamica road, Cyprus, in order to refit his little squadron. He then departed for Constantinople, to concert with the Porte measures for entirely extirpating the French from Egypt.

On the 3d of July Rear-admiral Ganteaume, who had been attending Buonaparte at his head-quarters at Cairo, arrived at Alexandria, after a narrow escape from the Arabs in his way down the Nile. In obedience to the orders he had received, the rear-admiral immediately began preparing for sea the Muiron and Carrère. By these, the two fastest sailing and best-conditioned of the ex-Venetian frigates in the port, Buonaparte intended, when the opportunity offered, to attempt to get back to France; in compliance, it would appear, with the wish of the directory in the present critical state of France, as expressed in a letter from them, dated on the 26th of May, and received by Buonaparte soon after his return to Cairo from the Syrian expedition. On the 11th, the signal-post at Alexandria unexpectedly announced the appearance of 76 vessels, of which number 12 were made out to be Turkish men of war. In the course of the day 15 other vessels hove in sight, and followed the first to the bay of Aboukir; where these two divisions, with a third not seen from Alexandria, came to an anchor; forming a total of 113 vessels, including thirteen 74s, nine frigates, and 17 gun-boats: the remainder were transports with troops. This numerous fleet was under the command of Hassan-Bey; and the troops, whose reputed number was 18,000, under that of Seid-Mustapha-Pacha.

General Marmont, the governor of Alexandria, as soon as he had despatched a messenger to the commander-in-chief, marched with 1200 men and five pieces of cannon towards Aboukir, to oppose the Turks on their landing. But, meeting an express from Captain Godard, who with 300 men commanded at Aboukir, announcing that the Turks had already disembarked, and were now investing the fort, the general returned to Alexandria, to await further reinforcements. For this, General Marmont was afterwards much blamed by Buonaparte. "Avec vos douze cents hommes," says the latter in his usual confident manner, "je serais allé jusqu'à Constantinople."*

The fort or castle of Aboukir was situated at the extremity of a narrow neck of land upon a rock of difficult access, and was protected on the land side by a redoubt thrown up at the entrance of the peninsula. Into this redoubt Captain Godard

*Victoires et Conquêtes, tome xi., p. 25.

retired with 265 men, leaving shut up in the fort the remaining 35, in command of an artillery-officer named Vinache. On the 15th, at daybreak, the Turks, assisted by their gun-boats, commenced a furious attack upon the redoubt; which, at night, they carried by assault, after having killed Captain Godard and the greater part of his men: the remainder of the little garrison was put to the sword. The Turks now bestowed their undivided attention upon the castle; which, after a two days' siege, surrendered by capitulation. Notwithstanding this, the Turks, it appears, would have massacred their 35 prisoners, but for the interference of Captain Sir Sidney Smith, who, with the Tigre and Theseus, had just returned to the coast.

Having removed the only obstacle to the disembarkation of their troops and artillery, the Turks landed the whole; but, instead of marching on Alexandria, where General Marmont was staying with only 1800 troops of the line (including a reinforcement of 600 just received), and 200 sailors of the nautic legion, the mussulmans began intrenching themselves on the peninsula. On the night of the 23d Buonaparte arrived at Alexandria, and on the 25th, having assembled his army, resolved to attack the Turks in their intrenchments: he did so, and, after a dreadful carnage, possessed himself of all the redoubts, as well as of Aboukir village. In the latter was made prisoner the Turkish commander-in-chief, Seid-Mustapha-Pacha.

The achievement of this victory cost the French 200 officers and men killed, and 750 wounded: among the latter were Generals Murat (slightly) and Fugières; and among the former, Gernals Crétin, Leturcq, and Duvivier. The Turkish prisoners, including the wounded, amounted to 2000. If, therefore, as alleged in the French accounts, the Turks had 12,000 men outside the Castle of Aboukir, 10,000 men must have been killed and drowned. "La déroute," says a French writer, "est complète; l'ennemi dans le plus grand désordre, est frappé de terreur, trouve par-tout les baïonnettes et la mort. Dix mille hommes se précipitant dans la mer; ils y sont fusilés et mitraillés. Cette glorieuse (!) journéé, &c."*

On the same day, the 25th, on which this battle was won, General Lannes, at the head of a division of troops, summoned the 5000 Turks shut up in the castle of Aboukir to surrender. The latter refused; and on the morning of the 27th the French opened their batteries upon the fort. The Turks had retired thither with such precipitation, that they were without either ammunition or provisions, but not, it appears, without their women and horses.† Famine at length effected what the battering cannon of the besiegers could not, and on the 2d of August the "band of horrid spectres" rushed out of the castle and surrendered. Their sufferings had been so great, that very

*Dictionnaire Historique, tome i., p. 10.

†Victoires et Conquêtes, tome xi., p. 34.

few, notwithstanding the care that appears to have been taken of them, survived.

On the 5th of August Buonaparte quitted Alexandria for Cairo, to make final prepartions for leaving the army. On the 18th, after a stay of 11 days, Buonaparte quitted the capital of Egypt, with Generals Berthier, Lannes, Murat, Marmont, and Andréossi, also the literary men (les savans) Monge, Berthollet, and Vivant-Denon, and on the 21st arrived at Alexandria.

With his usual utter disregard of truth where an object was to be attained, Buonaparte addressed to the divan of Egypt the following letter: "Being informed that my squadron is ready, and that a formidable army is embarked; being convinced, as I have often said, that, until I can strike a blow which shall crush at once all my enemies, I shall not enjoy in tranquillity and peace the possession of Egypt, the finest country in the world, I have resolved to put myself at the head of my ships, leaving the command, in my absence, with General Kléber, a man of distinguished merit, and whom I have directed to treat the alemas and scheicks with the same friendship which they have experienced from me. Do all in your power to induce the people of Egypt to repose on him the same confidence that they have had in me; and, upon my return, which will be in two or three months, I shall be pleased with the people of Egypt, and have nothing but praises and recompenses to bestow upon the scheicks."*

On the same day, Buonaparte writes confidentially to General Kléber: he expects to be in France in the beginning of October, and hopes that will be in time to save Italy; adding, with good reason, "L'arrivée de notre escadre à Toulon, venant de Brest, et de l'escadre espagnole à Carthagène, ne laisse aucune espèce de doute sur la possibilité de faire passer en Egypte les fusils, sabres, et fers coulés dont vous aurez besoin, et dont j'ai l'état le plus exact, avec une quantité de recrues suffisante pour réparer la perte des deux campagnes." Kléber is then told that, should no news or reinforcement reach him by the month of May, and his army lose, by sickness and skirmishes with the natives, more than 1500 men, he is to endeavour to conclude a treaty of peace with the Porte, of which treaty the principal article is to relate to the evacuation. If possible, however, the execution of the order to evacuate is to be deferred until a general peace takes place. Should the Porte be inclined to listen to the terms which he, Buonaparte, has already offered, General Kléber is to continue the negotiation, requiring the Porte to withdraw from the coalition, to grant the French a free commerce in the Black Sea, to set at liberty all French prisoners, and to allow a six months' suspension of hostilities, in order that, in the interval, the ratifications may be exchanged. Then follows this paragraph: "Supposant que les

*For the original, see Appendix, No. 20.

circonstances soient telles, que vous croyiez devoir conclure le traité avec la Porte, vous feriez sentir que vous ne pouvez pas le mettre à l'exécution qu'il ne soit ratifié, selon l'usage de toutes les nations. L'intervalle entre la signature d'un traité et la raitification doit toujours être une suspension d'hostilités." The fortifications of El-Arich and Alexandria are to be strengthened; and General Kléber is assured that there will arrive, in the course of the winter, at Alexandria, Burlos, or Damietta, some French ships of war; by which the General is to send to France a body of 600 mamelukes, in order that the latter may see "la grandeur de la nation," and on their return to Egypt, in a year or two afterwards, give a favourable account of the French manners and language. In case mamelukes cannot be obtained, Arab hostages, or even El-Beled scheicks, will suffice.*

On or about the 9th of August Commodore Sir Sidney Smith, with the Tigre, Theseus, and the two or three Turkish men of war that remained on the Egyptian coast, made sail from before the western harbour of Marabou, and on the 16th anchored in Baffa road, island of Cyprus. No time was now to be lost. Buonaparte had appointed to meet General Kléber on the 24th, at the town of Rosetta; but, dreading the reappearance of Sir Sidney Smith's two ships, he embarked, at 10 P.M. on the 22d, on board the Muiron, bearing the flag of Rear-admiral Ganteaume. The French accounts say, that at this moment a British frigate was signalled off the port; which we doubt; it might, however, have been a Turkish corvette.

On the 23d the two frigates made sail out of the harbour. On board the Muiron, besides General Buonaparte, were Generals Berthier and Andréossi; Messieurs Monge, Berthollet, and Vivant-Denon; Buonaparte's aide-de-camp M. Lavalette, and his secretary M. Bourrienne. On board the Carrère, commanded by Commodore Dumanoir-le-Pelley, were Generals Lannes, Murat, and Marmont, and the distinguished literary character, M. Parceval-Grandmaison. Three small vessels, the Revanche, Indépendant, and Foudre accompanied the two frigates. The Foudre, however, not sailing so well as had been expected, was ordered back to Alexandria.

Thus importantly freighted, the two French frigates, in company with their two remaining tenders, the better to avoid the British cruisers, kept close along the African shore. A constant wind from the north-west occasioned the little squadron to be 20 days traversing 100 leagues. At length the wind changed in their favour; and passing Cape Bona unseen, the Muiron and Carrère, made the island of Corsica. On the 1st of October the frigates cast anchor in the port of Ajaccio. Here Buonaparte heard of the capture of Mantua, the battle of Novi, the invasion

*Victoires et Conquêtes, tome xi., p. 220.

of Holland by an Anglo-Russian, and the entire conquest of Italy by an Austro-Russian army.

Contrary winds detained the frigates in port. Buonaparte took advantage of the delay in getting ready a felucca with a set of excellent rowers; and which, on the evening of the 7th, when the frigates were enabled to proceed on their voyage, was taken in tow by the Muiron. Buonaparte had done this, in order that, should an engagement suddenly ensue between the frigates and any enemy's ships, he might be enabled to reach the French coast. On the 8th, at sunset, the coast of France was signalled; but the joy this was calculated to inspire received a check in the signal which immediately followed, announcing that eight or ten large ships were in sight in the offing. Amidst the general consternation produced by this incident, Buonaparte alone, it appears, preserved his presence of mind. The danger appeared so imminent, that Rear-admiral Ganteaume was for tacking and returning to Corsica. "Non, non," replied Buonaparte, "cette manœuvre nous conduirait en Angleterre, et je veux arriver en France."* The two frigates immediately cleared for action and laid their heads to the north-north-west. The strangers whatever they were, disappeared; and at midnight land was seen close ahead. The frigates now lay to; and, at daylight on the 9th, Cape Taillat was in sight. On the same day Buonaparte and his suite disembarked at Fréjus. Leaving Buonaparte to make the most of his good fortune in having accomplished so perilous a voyage, we shall hasten back to the spot where he had left his army.

We formerly mentioned the visit of Buonaparte to Suez. On his return to Cairo, he left a small detachment of troops in possession of the town and environs of Suez; and Kosseïr, and a few other places along the coast of Upper Egypt, were similarly garrisoned. Much about the time that Buonaparte arrived at Suez, the British 50-gun ship Centurion, Captain John Sprat Rainier, and 18-gun brig-sloop Albatross, Captain Charles Adam, anchored in the road of Mocha, a seaport of Arabia, near the Straits of Babelmandel.

Early in the month of April Captain Rainier, with the Centurion and Albatross, made sail from Mocha, and on the 27th arrived in sight of the town of Suez. Here the boats of the British 50 and brig-sloop, covered by the latter, chased two French gun-boats into the harbour, but were unable to get at them owing to the shallowness and intricacy of the navigation. On the next day, the 29th, after the Albatross had sounded and discovered a safe anchorage, the two vessels brought up. We believe these were the first ships of war which had ever before been seen from the town of Suez, and their appearance created so much alarm to the French, that they began throwing up

*Victoires et Conquêtes, tome xi., p. 224.

breastworks on a hill that commanded the town and harbour. As, however, the troops, the principal part of whom were Maltese, pressed into the service, were constantly swimming off to the British ships, the probability is that a very small British military force would have relieved the inhabitants of Suez from their oppressors. After staying in the neighbourhood of Suez until the latter end of June, Captain Rainier sailed back to Mocha; at which anchorage he found Rear-admiral John Blankett, in the 50-gun ship Leopard, Captain Thomas Surridge, with two or three frigates and smaller vessels.

On the 14th of August, at daybreak, the 12-pounder 32-gun frigates Dædalus, Captain Henry Lidgbird Ball, and Fox, Captain Henry Stuart, part of the squadron above mentioned, while standing into Kossiër bay, boarded one of seven or eight dows or trading vessels, from the town of Kosseïr bound to Yambo. From this vessel information was obtained, that 100 Frenchmen were stationed at Kosseïr. Captain Ball being determined to attack the place, the two frigates at 9 A.M., made all sail, and at 10 A.M. discovered the town, with republican colours flying at the small 5-gun fort that defends the road. At 2 h. 30 m. P.M. the two frigates anchored about a quarter of a mile from the fort, and began a cannonade. At 3 h. 30 m. P.M., the Dædalus ceased firing and hoisted a flag of truce; but, no notice being taken of it, the two frigates resumed their fire. At 5 P.M. Captain Ball sent in the boats, which cut out a dow from under the fort.

Throughout the night the two frigates each fired a gun occasionally; and on the 15th, at 5 A.M., recommenced a heavy fire, and continued it until noon, still without any return. At this time several breaches were observed in the walls of the fort, and the lower town was nearly in ruins. At 4 P.M. the boats of the Dædalus, in the face of a heavy fire of musketry opened from the ruins of the town, cut out two dows. At 5 h. 30 m. P.M. the boats of both frigates, the launches of each with an 18-pounder carronade in them, led by Captain Stuart, landed to the southward of the town, for the purpose of destroying the wells from which the French troops obtained their water. The latter, however, had collected in such numbers, that the boats were obliged to return without effecting their object. The frigates continued the cannonade till night. On the 16th, at daylight, the boats again proceeded from the ships, with about 70 seamen and marines, commanded as before by Captain Stuart, and strengthened by two of the Fox's 6-pounders. Just as the party had landed, an unexpected flanking fire was opened upon them from a gun stationed in one of the breaches of the fort; which, coupled with a heavy fire of musketry, obliged the British to return to their ships, with the loss of one man killed in the Fox's launch, and one of the 6-pounders left in the surf. In the forenoon the Dædalus and Fox got under way, and were soon out of sight of Kosseïr, its battered fort, and ruined town.

The French, as may be supposed, made the most of this affair. They declared that Adjutant-general Donzelot, with two companies of the 21st regiment, had, without any loss on his part, defeated 400 British troops, although supported by two frigates. That the British retired with such precipitation, as to leave a 6-pounder and more than 60 of their killed and wounded upon the beach.* False as this account undoubtedly is, for even the one man killed was carried on board the Fox, and buried with Christian rites, there appears some truth in the statement that 6000 round shot, fired from the two frigates, were picked up in the fort and town. This amounts to about three-fourths of the quantity of shot to which two frigates of the class of the Dædalus and Fox are entitled; nor, at such a distance from home, was it very easy to supply the deficiency. Hence, it seems doubtful which side lost the most by an enterprise, the utility of which, taking all the circumstances into consideration, is not very apparent.

General Kléber was by no means pleased with the sudden, and to him quite unexpected, departure of the commander-in-chief from the shores of Egypt. From the following abstract of the state of the French resources in Egypt on the 26th of September, Buonaparte may have considered that, if he did not abandon the army, the army would, in all probability, abandon him. The effective strength of that army was about 20,000 men, or not much more than half what it amounted to 14 months before, when it disembarked at Marabou. These 20,000 men occupied all the principal posts of the triangle formed by the Cataracts of the Nile on the south, the fortress of El-Arich on the east, and the city of Alexandria on the west. The troops were in want not only of pay and clothing, but of arms and ammunition. Buonaparte had not left a sous in the chest, and the arrears of pay due to the army amounted to four millions of francs. All the siege artillery, except some sea-service guns, had been lost in the Syrian campaign; and the latter were used in arming the two frigates in which Buonaparte had taken his passage. The number of sick was greater than when the army was of nearly double the strength. Egypt had the appearance of being quiet; but the natives naturally looked upon the French as enemies, who had invaded their soil, and whom, at the first opportunity that presented itself, they would be justified in destroying. The mamelukes had been dispersed, but not destroyed. Mourad-Bey was harassing the French in Upper Egypt; and Ibrahim-Bey was at Gaza with about 2000 mamelukes. On the plains of Acre was the grand vizier's army, numbering, with that under Djezzar-Pacha, nearly 30,000 men. To add to all this a Turkish naval force of considerable amount was again assembling on the coast.

* Victoires et Conquêtes, tome xii., p. 28.

In the latter end of October Sir Sidney Smith arrived from the island of Rhodes, with a fleet of Turkish men-of-war and a considerable reinforcement of troops, from Constantinople. On the 29th the Turks disembarked, near the Bogaz or Damietta mouth of the Nile, under cover of the fire of their gun-boats. To this spot Sir Sidney proceeded in the hope, by an attack there, to draw the attention of the French from the side of the desert, towards which the grand Turkish army was then advancing. Accordingly the coast was sounded, and the pass to Damietta marked with buoys and Turkish gun-boats. The attack began by the boats of the Tigre taking possession of a ruined castle, situated on the eastern side of the Bogaz: which castle the inundation of the Nile had insulated from the main land, leaving a fordable passage.

The Turkish flag, displayed on the tower of this castle, was at once the signal for the Turkish gun-boats to advance, and for the French to open their fire, in order to dislodge the little garrison within it. This the French did from a redoubt on the main land, at point-blank-shot distance, mounted with two French 36-pounders and an 8-pounder field-piece. The fire was returned from the launch's carronade, an 18 or 24-pounder, mounted in a breach in the castle, and from field-pieces in the small boats; which soon obliged the French to discontinue working at an intrenchment they were making to oppose the landing.

Lieutenant Stokes, in the mean while, had been detached, with the boats, to check a body of cavalry advancing along a neck of land: in which he succeeded, but with a loss of one man killed and one wounded. This interchange of firing continued, with little intermission, during the 29th, 30th, and 31st; when, at length, owing chiefly to the shells from the carronade at the castle, the magazine at the redoubt blew up, and one of the 36-pounders was silenced. Orders were now given to disembark, but it was not until the morning of the 1st of November, that the landing could be effected.

The delay had given time to the French to collect a force more than double that of the first division landed, and to be ready to attack it before the return of the boats with the remainder. The French advanced to the charge with bayonets. The Turks, when the former were within ten yards of them, rushed on, sabre in hand, and, in an instant, routed the first line of the French infantry. Their impetuosity, however, carried them too far, and the fate of the day was suddenly changed. The flanking fire from the castle and boats, which had hitherto been plied with effect, was now necessarily suspended by the impossibility of pointing clear of the Turks in the confusion. The latter then turned a random fire on the boats, to make the latter take them off; and the sea was presently covered with turbans. The Turks sent up piteous moans for assistance, which with difficulty and risk was afforded to them; all being brought off, except 2000 killed, and about 800, whom the French took prisoners, by wading into the water after them.

The French declare, that they had not actually engaged in this affair, in which General Verdier was the commanding officer, more than 1000 men; and that their loss was so comparatively trifling, as 30 killed and 80 wounded.

About five weeks after the departure of General Buonoparte from Egypt, General Kléber wrote the directory a very full and by no means flattering account of affairs in that country. This important letter he intrusted to the Maltese Chevalier Barras, (cousin to the director of that name), who on the 4th of November sailed from Alexandria in a vessel named the Marianne, on board of which had also embarked General Vaux and several other wounded officers.

The Marianne, it appears, had a successful voyage until she gained a sight of the coast of France, when a British sloop of war fell in with and captured her. We have here so much dearth of information to complain of, that we cannot give the name of the ship, nor the date of the capture. Neither are we able to state whether the Marianne was a brig or a fore-and-aft rigged vessel; we conjecture, however, that she was the gun-vessel of that name, since (as, we presume, was also the case with the Foudre) recaptured by the French.

The despatches, as is customary on such occasions, were thrown overboard, but not with the customary carefulness. They were wrapped up in an old silk handkerchief, through which the cannon shot intended to sink them immediately pierced, and one of the British sailors picked them up as they were floating by the side of the vessel. The captain of the sloop of war carried the important papers to the commander-in-chief: and Vice-admiral Lord Keith, who had returned to Gibraltar from England on the 6th of December, after making himself acquainted with their contents, transmitted the despatches to his government.

Shortly after the defeat of the Turks at Damietta Sir Sidney Smith conveyed to General Kléber, as the commanding officer of the French army in Egypt, the reply of the Sublime Porte to Buonaparte's overtures to the Sultan formerly noticed; which reply was simply to the purport, that no negotiation could be entered into without the concurrence of England and Russia. Resting on the belief that England possessed the inclination, and Commodore Sir Sidney Smith the power, to conclude a treaty jointly with the grand vizier, General Kléber made proposals to that effect to the latter and Sir Sidney; and it was at length agreed, that General Desaix and the administrator of the finances Poussielgue should repair on board the Tigre, and there confer with the commissioners on the other side. Owing to the badness of the weather, the two French commissioners were unable to reach the Tigre, who had purposely anchored off

Alexandria, until on or about the 29th of December; and almost immediately afterwards a heavy gale of wind drove the ship and the negotiators out to sea.

In the mean while the French had been dispossessed of one of their Syrian fortresses, in a manner quite sudden and unexpected; nominally by the advanced body of the grand vizier's and a detachment of British marines under Major Douglas of that corps, but really by the treachery of the garrison. The army of the grand vizier, it appears, marched from Gaza to El-Arich on the 20th of December, and immediately summoned the fort to surrender. This being refused, Major Douglas and some other British officers reconnoitred the defences; and on the 25th the batteries opened upon El-Arich. The firing continued, without producing any sensible effect, until the morning of the 29th; at which time the French garrison, "presque toute entière,"* revolted, and let down a rope for Major Douglas to ascend into the fort.

When we read of a fortress, after a hard struggle, being carried by storm, and of the brave garrison, instead of being crowned with chaplets, put to the sword, we cannot withhold our pity, and feel a difficulty in suppressing our indignation; but the official announcement, that 300 of the garrison of El-Arich fell beneath the sabres of the mussulmans, move us not at all. We only regret that any British officer should have been present, to reap a benefit from the crimes of a traitor, and , "by means of a rope which was let down for him,"† to possess himself of that which can only be honourably acquired by fair fighting or fair cession. Operations carrying on in a more northern quarter now demand our attention.

An alleged change in the public mind in Holland, favourable to the views of the dethroned stadtholder, induced the British cabinet, early in the summer of the present year, to plan an expedition against that country, upon a much more enlarged scale than that which had failed in the second year of the war. On account of the unshackled state of her press, and the activity and intelligence of her journalists, England, of all countries in the world, is the least adapted for carrying into effect a secret expedition. In this instance, however, the British government had, in a most surprising manner, concealed its designs, until the expedition, which was upon an immense scale, was on the eve of departure.

The British North-Sea fleet was still under the command of Admiral Lord Duncan; and a suitable detachment from it had for a long time blocked up in the Texel the following Dutch squadron:

* Victoires et Conquêtes, tome xii., p. 43.

† See London Gazette.

Gun-ship		
74	Washington	Rear-admiral Story. Captain Van de Capelle.
64	Cerberus	Captain De-Younge.
	De-Ruyter	Captain Huijs.
	Guelderland	Captain Waldeck.
	Leyden	Captain Van-Braam.
	Utrecht	Captain Kolf.
50	Batavier	Captain Van-Senden.
	Beschermer	Captain Eilbracht.
Gun-frigate		
44	Mars	Captain De Bock.
40	Amphitrite	Captain Schutter.
32	Ambuscade	Captain Riverij.
Gun-brig		
16	Galathéa	Captain Droop.

Besides the above squadron ready for sea, there were a few old ships lying in ordinary in the Nieueve Diep. But the strongest portion of the Dutch navy lay at Amsterdam and in the Meuse. In the first-named port there were, in commission, if not in readiness for sea, four 74 and two 64 gun ships, and in the second, one 74 and seven 64 gun ships, besides several frigates and brigs.

For employment in this expedition to Holland troops, in large numbers, were assembled at Southampton under Lieutenant-general Sir Ralph Abercromby, and others had rendezvoused at Ramsgate, Margate, Barham-Downs, and Yarmouth; the whole, amounting to about 27,000 men, placed, as on the former occasion under the command of his Royal Highness the Duke of York. A treaty had also been entered into between Great Britain and Russia; wherein the latter stipulated to furnish 17,593 men, also six ships of the line and five frigates, all armed en flûte, and two transports, to carry a portion of the troops. The emperor was to receive for the hire of his troops, 88,000*l.* sterling; half of which was to be paid when the troops were ready to embark at Revel, and the remainder in three months afterwards. A subsidy of 44,000*l.* a month was also to be paid, from the day on which the troops were ready. For the ships Great Britain was to pay 58,976*l.* 10s. sterling, as a three months' subsidy for expenses of equipments, &c., to be computed from the day on which the ships should depart from Cronstadt; and, after the expiration of those three months, she was to continue to pay at the rate of 19,642*l.* 10s. sterling a month. All this was independently of subsistence. The emperor, therefore, made a tolerable market of his ships and troops.

On the 13th of August a fleet, composed of about 150 sail of ships of war, transports, and cutters, having on board the first division of the troops destined for Holland, put to sea from Margate roads and the Downs; the troops, numbering about 17,000, commanded by Lieutenant-general Abercromby, and the naval part of the expedition, by Vice-admiral Andrew Mitchell, the effective force of which consisted of the following ships:

Gun-ship			
74	Ratvison	Captain —— Greig.	Russian.
66	Mistisloff	Captain A. Moller.	
64	Monmouth	Captain George Hart.	
	Ardent	Captain Thomas Bertie.	
	Belliqueux	Captain Rowley Bulteel.	
	America	Captain John Smith.	
	Overyssel	Captain John Bazely.	
	Veteran	Captain Arch.-Collingwood Dickson.	
54	Glatton	Captain Charles Cobb.	
50	Isis	Vice-Adm. (b.) Andrew Mitchell. Captain James Oughton.	
	Romney	Captain John Lawford.	

Frigates, Melpomène, Latona, Shannon, Juno, and Lutine.

On the 15th, at 10 A.M., Admiral Lord Duncan, in the 74-gun ship Kent, Captain William Hope, joined and took the command of Vice-admiral Mitchell's squadron. At noon a gale from the south-west began to blow, and continued, with slight intermission, until the morning of the 20th; at which time the fleet, consisting of 200 sail of square-rigged vessels with troops on board, 11 luggers and cutters, and 50 flat-bottomed boats, lay about 16 leagues from the Texel. A calm succeeded the gale, and delayed the progress of the expedition until the next day, the 21st; when the outer ships of the Dutch in the Texel were seen to be moving further in. On that evening the whole British fleet anchored, within two miles of the shore, off a spot called Kirkdown. On the 22d, at 8 A.M., which was as soon as the tide served, the transports weighed, for the purpose of re-anchoring within half a mile of the shore; and shortly afterwards the Cobourg cutter, having on board Captain Robert Winthorp of the Circe frigate, and Colonel Frederick Maitland, departed from Lord Duncan's ship, with a flag of truce, to the Dutch Admiral Story.

While the transports were anchoring, and the gun-boats and smaller vessels getting ready to receive the troops, and just as the ships of war had made sail to stand into the Texel, the wind, from a fine easterly breeze, shifted to the south-west, with every appearance of a gale. Such of the transports as had anchored quickly weighed again, and the whole stood off from the land. By noon it began to blow very hard, and continued to do so during the remainder of that, and the whole of the two following days and nights; but, on the morning of the 25th, the weather cleared up, and the wind again blew a fine breeze from the north-west.

The British officers, who had been sent in with the flag of truce, took with them, first, an invitation from Admiral Duncan to Admiral Story, to deliver up his ships for the use of the Prince of Orange; next, a proclamation by Sir Ralph Abercromby, addressed in a similar strain to the Dutch troops; and lastly, a proclamation, signed by the Prince of Orange himself, and addressed to Dutchmen in general. To the first, Admiral

Story replied, under date of the 22nd August, that he should be unworthy of Lord Duncan, and forfeit the esteem of every honest man, were he to accept the proposal made to him; that he knew his duty to his flag and his country; and that, were Admiral Duncan's force double what it was, he should still retain the same sentiments. The Dutch admiral concluded with an assurance, that he should certainly defend his ships when attacked, but that he would immediately forward the summons to his government. He did so; and, at five o'clock on the morning of the 23rd, the executive directory formally expressed their approval of Admiral Story's reply. To the two proclamations no reply was returned.

Force being now the only alternative, the British fleet, on the morning of the 26th, again bore up; and by 3 P.M. the transports, with the bomb-vessels, sloops and gun-vessels, to cover the troops, had taken their appointed stations. Owing to the lateness of the day, the disembarkation was obliged to be delayed until 3 A.M. on the 27th; when a landing was effected, with no loss (except what arose from some boats oversetting in the surf), under a smart cannonade from the covering vessels. This, as we see, occurred on the 27th; and yet Admiral Duncan's summons, dated on the 20th, a week previous, began, "More than 20,000 men being, at this moment, disembarked at the Helder, &c." Such an oversight was well calculated to throw a ridicule upon the proposals sent in.

No sooner had the first division of troops begun to move forward, than they were attacked by a Gallo-Batavian force under General Daendels. The engagement lasted from 5 A.M. until evening, when the latter retired to Kéeten, a position two leagues in the rear. The British army lost on this occasion, one lieutenant-colonel, one subaltern, three sergeants, 51 rank and five killed; one colonel, one lieutenant-colonel, one major, nine captains, six subalterns, 18 sergeants, one drummer, 334 rank and file wounded; and 26 rank and file missing. The Gallo-Batavian army lost 1400 men killed, wounded, and missing, including 57 officers.

Having thus gained possession of the whole neck of land between Kirk-down and the road leading to Alkmaar, the British prepared to attack the Helder point, which contained a garrison of 2000 men. In the night, however, the garrison, first spiking the guns and destroying some of the carriages, evacuated the Helder, and retired across the marshes towards Medemblick. On the 28th, at daylight, the important post of the Helder, in which was a numerous train of artillery, both heavy and field, was taken quiet possession of by a detachment of British troops, under Major-general Moore; as were, at the same time, by Captain Winthrop, of the Circe, the following 13 Dutch ships of war, at anchor in the Nieueve Diep:

Gun-ship		Gun-ship		Gun-ship	
64	Vervachten,		Expeditie,		Alarm,
50	Broederchap,	44	Hector,	24	Pollock,
	Belle-Antoinette,		Unie,		Venus.
44	Constitutie,		Heldin,		
	Duifze,	28	Minerva,		

Also, three Indiamen, and a sheer-hulk; together with the naval magazine at Nieueve Werk, containing, among a great quantity of valuable ordnance stores, 97 pieces of cannon.

The possession of the Helder having now left the Texel open to the British, Vice-admiral Mitchell, on the 30th, at 5 A.M., got under way with his squadron, and stood for the Texel; in entering which, the Ratvison, America, and Latona took the ground. Passing the Helder point and Mars Diep, the British squadron, formed in line ahead thus: Glatton, Romney, Isis, Veteran, Ardent, Belliqueux, Monmouth, Overyssel, Mistisloff, and frigates, stood along the narrow and intricate channel of the Vlieter (the buoys of which, although purposely removed, the British, with surprising alacrity, had since replaced), towards the Dutch squadron, of eight two-deckers and frigates, at anchor in line ahead in the east-south-east channel, near the red buoy upon the Vogel sand.

While standing in, with his nine two-deckers and frigates (including the Latona who had since got off), along a channel, through which the Dutch themselves never venture to pass with more than two ships at a time, Vice-admiral Mitchell despatched the 18-gun ship-sloop Victor, Captain James Rennie, with a summons to the Dutch admiral. Captain Rennie, on his way, met a flag of truce, with Captains Van de Capelle and De Yong, coming from Admiral Story. These officers, Captain Rennie instantly conveyed on board the Isis. After some conversation, the British admiral consented to anchor at a short distance from the Dutch admiral, and to give the latter one hour to make up his mind. In less than the time specified, the two Dutch captains returned to Vice-admiral Mitchell, with a verbal message agreeing to surrender. Possession was immediately taken of the Dutch squadron already named; and, for the purpose of maintaining order among the different crews, a British officer was sent on board of each ship.

It remains to explain why those who, not many months before, had fought so valiantly off Camperdown, now surrendered, without a blow, at their moorings in the Texel. The fact is, the sailors had become politicians; and, differing in opinion from their officers, had adopted a course which, if not the most honourable, was, under present circumstances, undoubtedly the most safe. They mutinied, and refused to fight; and, as if fearful that the guns would go off by themselves, they, in many instances, drew the charges, and threw the shot overboard. Under such, we must add, discreditable circumstances, Admiral Story and his officers had no alternative but to surrender; and surely no one will think that, in so doing, they compromised, in the slightest degree, their professional character.

The British navy, on this occasion, had no opportunity of displaying its wonted prowess; but, nevertheless, great praise was due to Vice-admiral Mitchell for the whole of his arrangements, and to his officers and crews in general, for their skill in working the ships through channels so narrow, intricate, and shallow, as those through which they were obliged to pass. The loss of 16 two-deckers (one 74, six 64s, two 50s, and six 44s), five frigates, three corvettes, and one brig, out of a total of about 55 vessels, was a serious blow to the Dutch navy; and yet half a dozen first class French frigates would have been a greater acquisition to the British navy than the whole 25 vessels which had thus surrendered. The Dutch squadron had, it is true, been taken possession of in the name of the stadtholder, but the British government afterwards purchased such of the ships as appeared likely to be useful. Of the 17 ships and one brig so purchased, eight never went to sea as British cruisers; and the Washington 74, afterwards named Princess-of-Orange, measured only 1565 tons, which was smaller, by 37 tons, than any British 74, then in a serviceable state.

Although our business is not with military details, we will endeavour to present a summary of what occurred on shore. While the Dutch squadron was changing masters, the army under General Abercromby, now amounting to between 16,000 and 17,000 men, had advanced and taken post behind the Zype, a low and intersected piece of ground about eight miles in extent, that lies at the entrance of the peninsula, and has near it a dyke, behind which the troops intrenched themselves, defending their position by a numerous artillery. The advanced posts of their right extended from Pelten to Eenigenburg; those of the centre, a little behind and parallel to the Great Dyke, were at St.-Martin's, Volkoog, and Schagen; those of their left at Havinghuysen and Zydawind. In this position the Gallo-Batavian army, composed of, at the least 25,000 men,* and commanded by General Brune, having under him the Generals Vandamme, Dumonceau, and Daendels, on the 10th of September, at daybreak, attacked the British army, and after a most severe conflict, was repulsed and driven back to its former position in the neighbourhood of Alkmaar, with the loss, as represented, of nearly 1000 men, in killed, wounded, and prisoners. The loss of the British on the same occasion was, 37 rank and file killed; one major-general, one lieutenant-colonel, one major, four captains, five subalterns, two sergeants, 135 rank and file wounded; one sergeant, 18 rank and file missing. The French attributed their overthrow, in part, to a defection among their allies the Batavians.

On the 13th of September the Duke of York landed at the

* Dictionnaire Historique, tome i., p. 64.

Helder from on board the Amethyst frigate; and at the same time was disembarked the stipulated body of Russian troops, under General Hermann; making the combined British and Russian army amount to about 35,000 men. On the 10th, at daybreak, a part of the latter, amounting to about 20,000 men, attacked the whole line of the French and Batavians; but, towards the close of the day, were compelled to fall back to their intrenchments at the Zype, with the loss of the British army, of one lieutenant-colonel, two captains, two subalterns, one staff, two sergeants, 121 rank and file, killed; seven lieutenant-colonels, six majors, 15 captains, 15 subalterns, 20 sergeants, two drummers, 364 rank and file wounded; and 22 sergeants, five drummers, 479 rank and file missing; and to the Russians, of about 1500 killed, wounded, and prisoners, including, among the latter, General Hermann himself. General Brune, in his official letter, states his force to have been 20,000 men, and his loss only 50 killed, and 300 wounded. He declares also, that he made 2000 men prisoners, and took 25 pieces of cannon. On the other hand, the British account states, that 60 officers and upwards of 3000 French and Batavians fell into the hands of the allies, and that 16 pieces of their cannon were destroyed. Three gun-boats, each armed with a 12-pounder carronade, and placed under the orders of Captains Sir Home Popham and William Godfrey, of the navy, had acted with considerable effect on the Alkmaar canal, but not without sustaining a loss of four seamen killed, one lieutenant and seven seamen wounded.

On the 2d of October, at 6 A.M., the Duke of York made a general attack upon the Gallo-Batavian line. The conflict was long and bloody, continuing till six in the evening, when General Brune was compelled to retire, leaving the British and Russians masters of the field of battle. This was accomplished after a loss, to the British army, of one major, five captains, five subalterns, 11 sergeants, 215 rank and file, 44 horses, killed; two colonels, two lieutenant-colonels, three majors, 22 captains, 39 subalterns, one staff, 46 sergeants, seven drummers, 980 rank and file, 78 horses, wounded; one captain, four subalterns, seven sergeants, three drummers, 178 rank and file, three horses, missing; and to the Russians, of about 170 killed or taken prisoners, and 423 wounded.

On the 6th, in another general battle, the French and Batavians, having been considerably reinforced, defeated the British and Russians, with a loss, to the British, of two lieutenant-colonels, two subalterns, three sergeants, one drummer, 85 rank and file, nine horses, killed: one colonel, one lieutenant-colonel, three majors, seven captains, 23 subalterns, one staff, 23 sergeants, 673 rank and file, 13 horses, wounded; two lieutenant-colonels, one major, five captains, 11 subalterns, 13 sergeants, two drummers, 576 rank and file, missing; and to the Russians, of 382 killed or taken prisoners, and 735 wounded. Soon after this, a council of war decided that the allied British and Russian army should retire to the Zype. It did so, and the Duke of York took up his quarters at Schagenburg; where he entered into a negotiation with General Brune, for a suspension of arms, and the unmolested evacuation of Holland by the combined British and Russian forces. The retreat of the latter, in consequence of the convention, was followed by the evacuation of the Zuyder Zee and adjacent parts, on the part of Vice-admiral Mitchell; who, having shifted his flag from the Isis to the 20-gun ship Babet, had, with that ship and a flotilla of six smaller vessels, proceeded over the Enkhausen flat to the road of that name. The appearance of the British flotilla in the Zuyder Zee changed the politics, for a while, of several of the bordering towns and villages. Even Amsterdam had begun making defensive preparations. The batteries of Dugerdam and Deimerdam had been strengthened; and soon after Vice-admiral Mitchell got into the Zuyder Zee, 60 French gun-vessels arrived at Amsterdam, by the canal, from Dunkirk.

Thus terminated the expedition to Holland; an expedition in which the British, exclusively, lost three ships of war by being wrecked on the coast, and Nassau, a reduced en flûte 64, and the Blanche and Lutine frigates. The most serious part of the loss was that a full fourth of the crew of the first-named, and the whole of the crew except two of the last-named, ship perished. The Lutine had on board specie to the amount of 140,000*l.*, which she had shipped at Yarmouth, and was carrying to the Texel, to be applied in paying the troops. That went also; and the loss of it was no slight augmentation to the disasters of the expedition. In the different actions on shore, as enumerated in the official accounts, the British alone lost about 556 men killed, 2791 wounded, and 1455 missing. Their gain in ships of war we have already shown to have been much overrated. Whatever else the British gained was, certainly, not that of which they had any reason to boast. However, as no blame was imputed to them, the thanks of parliament were unanimously voted to Lieutenant-general Sir Ralph Abercromby and Vice-admiral Mitchell, as well as to the officers and men under their respective commands. Shortly afterwards the vice-admiral received an additional honour in the order of the Bath.

Among the operations on shore in this quarter, the defence of Lemmer-town, West Friesland, which had been intrusted to a detachment of seamen and marines, 157 in number, under the command of Captain James Boorder, of the 16-gun brig-sloop Espiègle, must not be passed over. On the 11th of October, at 5 A.M., an advanced party of French and Batavians, consisting of one officer, one sergeant, one corporal, and 28 privates, attempted to storm the north battery. The British soon got their opponents between two fires; and the seamen, armed with their pikes, so effectually surrounded them, that they instantly laid down their arms, with the loss of two privates killed. Scarcely had the British secured their prisoners, when the enemy's main body, 670 in number, attacked them; but, after a sharp contest of four hours and a half, in which the French and Batavians sustained a loss of five men killed and nine wounded, the latter gave way in every direction. The marines went in pursuit, and certainly, if the allied forces had not broken down a bridge in their retreat, would have taken their stand of colours and two field-pieces. While the fugitives were in the act of destroying the bridge, the fire from the marines is represented to have killed 18, and wounded 20 of their number; making their total loss on this occasion, 25 men killed and 29 wounded, while the British had not a man hurt.

LIGHT SQUADRONS AND SINGLE SHIPS.

On the 4th of January the British bark-rigged sloop Wolverine, of 12 guns and 70 men, Captain Lewis Mortlock, being on a cruise off Boulogne, in very foggy weather, discovered two large French luggers, close to her to windward. These luggers were privateers; one, the Rusé, of eight 4-pounders and about 70 men, commanded by Citizen Pierre Audibert, the other, the Furet of fourteen 4-pounders and about 80 men, commanded by Citizen Denis Fourmentin. Captain Mortlock, judging that, if the privateersmen suspected the Wolverine to be a ship of war, they would make off, approached them under Danish colours. On being hailed by the Furet, Captain Mortlock replied, that he was from Plymouth bound to Copenhagen. This lugger was now close upon the starboard quarter of the Wolverine, with her bowsprit between the latter's mizen chains and side. The Wolverine instantly hoisted English colours, and opened a fire of great guns and musketry, Captain Mortlock, with his own hands, lashing the Furet's bowsprit to one of the iron stanchions of the Wolverine's mizen chains.

Boarding was now the only resource left to the Furet; and her people made a vigorous assault on the British vessel, but were driven back with loss. In the mean time the Rusé had shot ahead, and run foul of the Wolverine on the larboard bow. Here, also, a desperate attempt was made to board; and, at one time, it required almost every man in the Wolverine to repulse the Rusé's crew. Three of the boldest of the Furet's men, taking advantage of the exposed state in which the scuffle on the Wolverine's forecastle had left the afterpart of the vessel, sprang on the roundhouse; and one man gave three cheers, as if to encourage those in the lugger to come on board to his support. Captain Mortlock instantly ran from forward, to dispute with this daring Frenchman the possession of his post. The latter as the former approached, presented a pistol to his face. It missed fire; and, as the Frenchman was again cocking it, Captain Mortlock plunged a half-pike into his body, and the man fell overboard.

The French on board the Furet now threw into the Wolverine's cabin windows some leather bags filled with combustibles. These immediately set the vessel on fire, and a blaze burst forth directly over the magazine. While the Wolverine's people were occupied in extinguishing the flames, the two luggers took the opportunity to effect their escape. As one of them (the Furet, it is believed) was retiring, she fired a shot which mortally wounded Captain Mortlock, who had previously, although he kept on deck, been wounded in the hand, in the breast, and in the loins. Giving the necessary orders to his lieutenant, this brave young officer went below, saying, "Luff, luff, keep close to them." He soon afterwards fainted from loss of blood. The Wolverine, finding she had no chance with the luggers in sailing, on a wind especially, bore up for Portsmouth.

The Wolverine had two men killed, and eight, including her gallant commander, wounded. Captain Mortlock died at Portsmouth on the 10th of the month. The loss of the privateers, as acknowledged by themselves, was rather severe. The Furet had five men killed, her captain and five men mortally, and 100 men badly wounded; the Rusé had her first and second lieutenants, another officer, and two seamen killed, and five mortally, and several badly wounded.

In this affair, which was almost entirely a hand-to-hand struggle, 70 British were opposed to at least 150 Frenchmen; and yet the latter were compelled to retire without effecting their object. Had the two luggers kept off at long-shot, the Wolverine, from the nature of her armament, must have cut them to pieces. She was originally the merchant vessel Rattler, of London, measuring 286 tons, and was purchased, in order to be fitted with guns upon Captain Schank's principle. Accordingly, on the 22d of February, 1798, the Wolverine, as she had then been named, was established with two long 18-pounders and six 24-pounder carronades on her main deck, four 12-pounder carronades on the quarterdeck, and one of the same caliber on the forecastle, total 13 guns. In order that the eight maindeck guns might be fought on one side, eight ports, exclusive of the bow-port, were cut, and grooves were made in the deck running across from side to side. To these grooves the trucks of the gun-carriages were attached, by a pivot fore-locked, in order to shift the guns from one side to the other as occasion required. Thus armed, the Wolverine was a much more formidable vessel than her appearance indicated.

On the 28th of January, at noon, the British 28-gun frigate Proserpine, Captain James Wallis, having on board the Honourable Thomas Grenville and suite on a mission to Berlin, sailed from Yarmouth road, bound to Cuxhaven. Early on the morning of the 30th the frigate arrived off Heligoland, and took on board a pilot for the Elbe. Having a fair wind at north-north-east and a fine clear day, the Proserpine, by evening, reached and anchored at the Red buoy. Here it was found that the other buoys had been removed; but the three pilots on board, including two that belonged to the ship, concurred in stating the practicability of ascending the river to Cuxhaven without the buoys, provided Captain Wallis would proceed between half-ebb and half-flood, as they should then see the sands, the marks of which were perfectly well known to them.

Accordingly, on the morning of the 31st, the Proserpine weighed, and stood up the river, with the same favourable wind and weather as on the preceding day; having ahead of her the Prince-of-Wales packet, which had kept company from Yarmouth. At about 4 P.M., then within four miles of Cuxhaven, it began to snow, and soon came on so thick, that the Proserpine was compelled to anchor. At this time very little ice was seen in the river; but at 9 P.M. the wind shifted to east by south, and blew a most dreadful snow-storm; causing such heavy masses of ice to press on the frigate, that it was only by having all hands on deck, and using every precaution to save the cables from being cut, that she preserved her station till morning.

On the 1st of February, at 8 A.M., the flood-tide, having carried back the ice, and left an opening below; while the river above was completely blocked up. No possibility now existing of proceeding higher up, the Proserpine weighed and stood out, to endeavour to make a landing on some part of the coast of Jutland, Mr. Grenville urging to Captain Wallis the necessity of his being put on shore as early as possible. Scarcely had the pilots declared that the Proserpine was clear of all the sands, when, at about 9 h. 30m. P.M., the ship struck on nearly the extremity of the Scaron, or the sand that stretches out from Newark island. As it blew a heavy gale of wind, the Proserpine, although with no other sail set than the foretopmast staysail, had struck with great force. On sounding, no more than 10 feet of water was found under the forepart of her keel.

Immediately the boats were got ready to carry out an anchor: but, it being high water, the ice pressed so upon the ship as to render the attempt impracticable, and the boats were hoisted in again. All hands were now employed in shoring the ship, in order that she might heel towards the bank. The first run of the tide, however, brought down such heavy masses of ice, that the shores were carried away, the copper torn off from the starboard side of the ship, and the rudder cut in two, the lower part lying on the ice under the counter. Hopes were still entertained of getting the ship off at the next high water; and, in order to lighten her for that purpose, her guns and stores were thrown overboard, all of which were borne up by the ice.

At 10 P.M., which was the time for high water, the south-east gale had so kept back the tide, that there was less water by three feet than when the ship had struck. All hopes of saving the Proserpine were thus at an end; and, on the return of the ebb-tide, the ship was expected every moment to be torn to pieces by the ice. This sad expectation, the darkness of the night, the extreme coldness of the weather, and the heavy snowstorm that raged, rendered the situation of the people on board the frigate truly deplorable. On the next morning, the 2d, the gale increased, and the ice rose to the cabin windows; the stern-post also broke in two, and the ship received other important damage. It was then proposed, that the officers and crew should attempt to reach the shore over the ice. This, considering the severity and thickness of the weather, the ignorance of the way, and the numberless dangers attendant on such a journey, struck every one as hazardous in the extreme. But, to stay any longer on board was useless, and might be attended with the most dreadful consequences.

Accordingly, at 1 h. 30m. P.M., the ship's company, in subdivisions, attended by their respective officers, commenced their march on the ice; and, at 3 P.M., Captain Wallis, and Lieutenant Ridley of the marines, the two last persons on board, quitted the Proserpine. After a journey of six miles, in the severest of weather, over high flakes of ice, and sometimes up to their middles in snow and water, the ship's company, whose subordination and perseverance were highly praiseworthy, reached the island of Newark; but not without the melancholy loss of seven seamen, one boy, four marines, and one woman and her child, frozen to death. Others had had their legs and fingers frozen, but were fortunate enough not to lose the use of them. The whole number of males, mustered on landing, were 173.

The storm lasted, without intermission, until the night of the 5th. On the following morning, the 6th, owing to the scarcity of provisions, half the officers and ship's company, accompanied by Mr. Grenville and his suite, proceeded to Cuxhaven; travelling, as before, over the ice, and encountering a similar succession of difficulties. At length, however, the party arrived in safety. The captain, with the remainder of his officers and men, remained at Newark, in hopes to be able to save some of the stores from the ship. On the 8th, the master, Mr. Anthony, volunteered, with a party of seamen, to go on board for that purpose. He did so, and found the frigate lying on her beam-ends, with seven and a half feet of water in her hold; having her quarterdeck separated from the gangway six feet, and to all appearance, only kept from entirely parting by the ice that surrounded her. From this account, it was agreed not to visit her again; but, on the 10th, the clearness of the day induced Mr. Anthony, taking with him the surgeon, one midshipman, the boatswain, and two seamen, to go off a second time. These bold adventurers got safe on board, but neglected to return when the tide suited. At about 10 P.M., a violent storm came on from the south-south-east; and the tide rose, in consequence to an uncommon height. This, as it raised the ice that stuck to the ship, floated her and that together; and the wreck, after beating about for some time, was at length cast on shore at the island of Baltrum. From this spot Mr. Anthony and his little party providentially escaped, and soon afterwards joined their friends at Cuxhaven; whither the whole of the officers and crew left at Newark, except the captain, had since arrived.

Ill-health, occasioned chiefly by anxiety of mind at the supposed loss of the master and the five persons with him, detained Captain Wallis at Newark island till towards the end of February. On the 26th of March the captain, his officers, and ship's company, having arrived home, were tried for the loss of their ship. It need hardly be stated, that they all received an honourable acquittal: in addition to which the highest encomiums were passed upon the late Proserpine's seamen for their unparalleled good conduct throughout the whole of the melancholy and trying occasion. To mark their sense of the hospitable treatment which they had experienced from Lorenti Wittké, of the island of Newark, the officers and men presented him with a piece of plate in the shape of a coffee-urn, bearing a suitable inscription.

Of Rear-admiral Sercey's Indian squadron of seven frigates, we have already shown that three had quitted him for Europe; and we rather think a fourth, the Cybèle, got back to Lorient. This frigate had arrived at the Isle of France a year or two before the war commenced, and therefore could not, towards the close of the year 1797, when her name last occurs, have been in a very good state. Without reckoning the Cybèle, the French frigates which, at the commencement of the present year, were still cruising in the Indian seas, were the Forte, Preneuse, and Prudente. In what manner the last of these was stopped in her career, we shall now proceed to relate.

On the 9th of February, soon after daybreak, in latitude 31° 30' south, and longitude 33° 20' east, the British 12-pounder 32-gun frigate Dædalus, Captain Henry Lidgbird Ball, steering to the southward and westward, with the wind right aft, or north-east, discovered two sail on her starboard bow. These were the French 36-gun frigate Prudente, Captain Emanuel-Hippolite Le Joliff, and an American ship from China, her prize; and on board of which, it would appear, the frigate had placed, with a crew of 17 officers and men, all her quarterdeck 6-pounders but two; thus leaving herself with 26 long 12 and two long 6-pounders, and two brass 36-pounder carronades, total 30 guns. The force of the Dædalus consisted of 32 long 12 and 6 pounders, and six 24-pounder carronades.

At 7 A.M., the Dædalus hauled to the northward in chase; and the two strangers now seen to be ships, separated, the smaller one standing to the southward, and the larger, which was distant from the Dædalus about six miles, bearing away north-west. The Dædalus immediately bore up after the large ship; which, at about 10 A.M., put right before the wind, and was followed by the Dædalus under all sail. At 3 P.M., the Prudente hoisted her colours, and opened a fire from her stern chasers. At 10 minutes past noon the Prudente shortened sail, hauled to the wind on the larboard tack, and fired a broadside at the Dædalus; who, by this time, had shortened sail to her topsails. At 25 minutes past noon the British frigate bore up across the stern of the French frigate, within half pistol-shot, and, after pouring in a raking broadside, luffed up under her lee. The two ships, thus side by side, commenced an animated interchange of broadsides; and, in a quarter of an hour, the mizenmast of the Prudente fell over her quarter. The latter, nevertheless, continued the cannonade until 1 h. 21 m. P.M.; when, being much cut in masts, rigging, and sails, and considerably shattered in hull, the Prudente struck her colours.

The damages done to the Dædalus were of comparatively trifling amount. Her main stay was cut through, and her running rigging and many of her lower shrouds injured; but her hull was scarcely touched. Out of a crew of 212 men and boys, she had one seaman and one marine killed, and 11 seamen and one marine wounded. The Prudente was much shattered in both hull and masts, and, out of a crew, as deposed by her officers, of 301 men and boys (four less than the number stated in Captain Ball's letter), lost 27 officers and men killed and 22 wounded.

COMPARATIVE FORCE OF THE COMBATANTS.

		DÆDALUS	PRUDENTE
Broad-side guns	No.	19	15
	lbs.	246	214
Crew	No.	212	301
Size	tons	703	920

The slight disparity in the broadside weight of metal by no means equals the disparity in execution. Not a doubt therefore remains that, had the Prudente mounted the few 6-pounders which she wanted of her establishment, the result of the action would have been precisely the same; a result, especially when the difference in number of men is considered, highly creditable to Captain Ball, his officers, and ship's company. On the other hand, let us in justice remark, that the reason the Prudente made sail, when first descried by the Dædalus, does not appear to have been to avoid an engagement, but to allow her prize an opportunity of effecting her escape. As soon as the latter was considered to be out of danger, and the prize did, we believe reach the Isle of France in safety, the Prudente shortened sail for her adversary to come up; and that Captain Le Joliff did not surrender at an earlier moment than was consistent with his duty, the damage and loss which his ship sustained in the action abundantly proves.

Taking her prize in tow, the Dædalus proceeded to Table bay;

where, on the 15th, the two ships came to an anchor. The cost of repairing the prize in that country being deemed by the naval commanding officer at the Cape, Captain George Losack of the 50-gun ship Jupiter, more than the ship, although a very fine frigate of her class, was worth, the Prudente was not purchased for the use of the British navy. It would gratify us to be able to state, that the first lieutenant of the Dædalus, who brought in the prize, and whom Captain Ball recommends "in the strongest terms," received the reward usually conferred on first lieutenants, after actions of far less merit than that of the Dædalus and Prudente; but an admiralty-list before us, of July, 1823, still contains among the lieutenants the name of Nicholas Tucker.

On the 6th of February, at 4 P.M., while the British 44-gun ship Argo, Captain James Bowen, accompanied by the 74-gun ship, Leviathan, Captain John Buchanan, was drawing round the east end of Majorca, under storm staysails, with a violent westerly gale, two Spanish frigates were discovered at anchor, near a fortified tower on the south point of the Bahia de Acude. The latter, which were the 34-gun frigates Santa-Teresa and Proserpine, immediately cut their cables and made sail to the north-north-east. The two British ships, as quickly as possible, were under all the canvas they could bear; under more, indeed, than the Leviathan could, for she presently split her main topsail and dropped astern.

This accident to the largest of their pursuers the two Spanish frigates saw, and, shortly after the close of day, having previously spoken each other, took advantage of, by separating. The Proserpine hauled sharp up to the northward, and the Santa-Teresa, setting her topgallantsails, kept right before the wind. The Argo, selecting the point of sailing in which she excelled, followed the latter, and signalled her consort to alter her course to port in pursuit of the former. But the Leviathan, neither seeing the Proserpine's change of course nor the Argo's signal, continued to follow the latter. At midnight, after having fired her bow-guns for some time previous, the Argo got alongside of the Santa-Teresa; who, notwithstanding that her small sails had all been cut by shot, or carried away in the chase, and that the Leviathan was at no great distance from her, persevered in her endeavours to get off, not surrendering until she had received, without returning it, the Argo's whole broadside: which wounded two of her men, and did much damage to her rigging.

The Santa-Teresa mounted 34 long Spanish 12 and 6 pounders, and, we believe, eight 24-pounder carronades, total 42 guns, besides swivels and cohorns. She was commanded by Captain don Pablo Perez, with a crew of 280 seamen and marines, besides 250 soldiers, and was stored and victualled for four months. Being a fine ship of 949 tons, and just out of dock, the Santa-Teresa became an acquisition to the class of

British 12-pounder 36-gun frigates. Her consort, the Proserpine, of the same force but rather smaller, effected her escape.

In the course of the month of May the Argo was detached by Earl St.-Vincent to Algiers, to negotiate with the dey for a supply of fresh provisions for the British army and navy at Minorca. Captain Bowen not only succeeded in his mission, but, prompted by his own feelings, exerted himself so strenuously with the dey for the enlargement of six British prisoners, who had been 14 years in slavery, that the despot ordered them to be set free. The poor fellows, grateful and happy, embarked on board the Argo, once more to enjoy the blessings of life and liberty.

The rupture which, towards the end of the year 1798, occurred between France and the United States of America, gave to Great Britain a maritime ally, who, though not able to afford a very powerful, nor willing perhaps to bestow a very cordial co-operation, might yet be of some service in desultory warfare; particularly among the Antilles, and along the western shores of the Atlantic, where the number and audacity of the French cruisers oftentimes did serious mischief to British commerce. Previously to our entering upon the details of the first action that was fought between the French and the Americans, we may be allowed to present a slight sketch of the formation and growth of the United States' navy.

At the commencement of the disturbances between Great Britain and her American colonies, the latter formed themselves into a confederated body-politic. A congress, representative of this confederacy, and of the states, was organized. Its members were elected by the state-legislatures; and it was invested with the powers of national defence, the superintendence of the welfare of the confederacy, and the accomplishment of the great object of the union, redress of grievances. Both legislative and executive functions were united in this body. The greater part of the year 1775, that in which the revolutionary war commenced, was occupied in the more immediate business of organizing an army, to resist the aggressions of one already in the country. It was not, therefore, until the 5th of October in the same year, that the attention of congress was directed to any kind of operations on the ocean; and then only because information had been received that two English unarmed merchant brigs, laden with arms, powder, and other warlike stores, had on the 11th of the preceding August, quitted England for Quebec, without convoy.

A committee of three members of congress was appointed to prepare a plan for intercepting these vessels; and, upon the report of the committee, the congress directed General Washington to apply to the council of Massachusetts-bay, for their two armed vessels, and then to despatch the same, properly armed, stored, and appointed, with instructions to intercept and capture the two brigs in question, or any other transports laden with warlike stores, for the use of the ministerial army or navy in America. On the 13th of October two small vessels, one of 10, the other of 14 carriage-guns; and on the 30th, a ship to mount 20, and another to mount as many as 36 carriage-guns, were ordered to be got ready and equipped as cruisers. On the 2d of November the committee, to which four members had been added, were authorized to draw upon the continental treasury for funds, and to engage officers and seamen to serve on board the four vessels that had been ordered to be fitted out. By way of encouragement to the latter, they were to have half in value of all prizes, being ships of war, and a third of such as were transports. On the 2d of November two battalions of marines were ordered to be raised. On the 11th of December congress ordered to be built 13 ships; five of 32, five of 28, and three of 24 guns; all the stores of which, except canvass and powder, could, it was declared, be furnished in the colonies.

On the 14th of June, 1777, congress decreed, that the flag of the United States should be 13 stripes, alternate red and white; and that the union should be 13 stars, white in a blue field, representing a new constellation. On the 28th of October, 1779, congress established a board of admiralty, to consist of five commissioners; of whom three were to form a board for despatch of business, and were each to have a salary of 14,000 dollars per annum; the secretary's salary was to be 10,000. On the 29th of August, 1781, both this board and the naval committee were abolished, and an agent of marine, at a salary of 1500 dollars, with a clerk at 500 dollars, was appointed in lieu of them.

It appears that the Americans, at a very early day, meditated the construction of 74-gun ships. According to a document in the journals of congress, they, in May, 1778, had one upon the stocks at Portsmouth, in New-Hampshire. The plan, on being submitted to a M. Landais, a French naval officer of great experience in the construction of ships, was found fault with; and, at his suggestion, congress, on the 29th of that month, ordered the ship to be converted into a flush two-decker, to carry twenty-eight 24-pounders on the lower, and twenty-eight 18-pounders on the second deck. This order appears afterwards to have been revoked; for, according to another entry, the agent of marine was directed, on the 3d of September, 1782, to present that 74-gun ship, then launched and named the America, to the Chevalier de la Luzerne, for the service of his most christian majesty, in lieu of the Magnifique, of similar force, which had recently been lost on the American coast.

The published accounts are not explicit in reference to the identity of these ships. It is simply from not finding a 56-gun ship in any American navy-list of the time, nor that any second 74 was ordered to be built, and that it is concluded there was but one. At the reduction of Charlestown, in April, 1780, an American ship named the Bricole, alleged to have been pierced for 60 guns (as, with four bridle-ports, a ship of 56 guns would have been), and to have mounted 44, consisting of 24 and 18 pounders, was certainly destroyed, among other ships, by the British forces. But, turning to a French navy-list of 1778, we find the Bricole *flûte*, of 24 guns, which may have been a reduced 60-gun ship. The non-appearance of that ship's name in a French list of January, 1783, added to the certainty that several French ships of war had been purchased by the Americans, and were actually among those destroyed at Charlestown, strengthens the supposition, that the 74 on the stocks at Portsmouth, New-Hampshire, in May, 1778, and that presented to the King of France in September, 1782, were one and the same vessel. The peace that took place, about five months after this present had been made by America to France, readily enabled the new ship to cross the Atlantic to a French port; but, owing to her comparatively small size and light armament, and perhaps, in part, to the perishable materials of her frame, the America does not appear to have lived long enough to be of service in the war by which that peace was succeeded.

The low ebb of the treasury and the tranquil state of the republic occasioned the navy to dwindle, until the conduct of the Algerines in 1794 stimulated congress, on the 27th of March in that year, to order the construction and equipment of four ships of 44, and two of 36 guns, to be ready to protect American commerce in the Mediterranean.

We have reason to think that the armament originally intended for each of these classes was as follows:

	The 44.			The 36.		
	No.		Pdrs.	No.		Pdrs.
Main deck	30	long	24	28	long	18
Quarter deck and forecastle	14	long	18	8	long	12
	44			36		
Carronades	12			12		
	56			48		

Subsequently the carronades (42 and 32 pounders) were increased, and the long-guns in battery with them reduced in number to the same extent, but changed to a higher caliber. Into this, however, we shall hereafter have occasion more fully to enter.

On the 30th of April, 1798, an act of congress passed, authorizing the establishment of a navy-department, the chief officer of which was to be styled, "Secretary of the navy." He was to execute all orders that he might receive from the President of the United States, relative to the construction, armament, equipment, and employment of vessels of war, and other matters connected therewith; and was to have a competent number of clerks, to assist him in performing the duties of his office.

Towards the middle of the year 1798, some interruption

occurred in the commercial relations of the United States and France; and the former, conceiving themselves the aggrieved party, commenced hostilities against the ships and vessels of the French republic. At this time the navy of the United States, by the spirited exertions of the general government, consisted, besides several smaller vessels, of 15 frigates, four of them the largest and heaviest that had ever been constructed. Six 74-gun ships were also ordered to be built; but, as the differences between the two countries were soon adjusted, they were not laid down. We shall now proceed to give an account, as well as our scanty materials will enable us, of the first naval action fought between France and the United States of America.

On the 9th of February, at noon, the island of Nevis bearing west-south-west distant five leagues, the United States' 36-gun frigate Constellation, Commodore Thomas Truxton, sailing with the wind at north-east, discovered a strange ship to the southward, with, if the French accounts are correct, her main topmast gone. The Constellation, hoisting American colours, bore down; and the stranger, which was the French 36-gun frigate Insurgente, Captain Michel-Pierre Barreaut, hoisted her national colours, and fired a gun to windward. At 3h. 15m. P.M., the Insurgente hailed the Constellation; for what purpose, the American accounts are as silent as about the previous loss of the French frigate's main topmast; but if, as the French insist, Captain Barreaut was ignorant of the war, it might be for an explanation of the hostile manner in which the American frigate was approaching. At all events, very soon after the hail, the Constellation, ranging alongside the Insurgente, opened her broadside, and a spirited action ensued, which lasted one hour and 15 minutes; when the French ship, having, as already stated, lost her main topmast, and been in other respects greatly damaged, struck her colours.

The Constellation, out of a complement of about 440 men and boys, had the good fortune, besides receiving little or no injury in hull or spars, to escape with so slight a loss as one man killed and two wounded; while the Insurgente, out of a complement of 340 men and boys, is represented to have lost 29 men killed and 44 wounded.

As this victory, like many we have recorded, was gained by a "36," over a "40," or as most of the English journals had it, "44-gun frigate," there was no end to the panegyrics upon the American Commodore Truxton. Nor was it empty praise alone that the commodore received; for in addition to the substantial testimonials which his transatlantic friends showered upon him, he was presented by the merchants of London with a handsome piece of plate, expressly for having captured a French frigate of "superior force."

Commodore Truxton carried his prize to the island of St.-Kitt's. The Insurgente cruised for a few years in the American service, and was then intended to be restored to France, but, in the mean time, she became lost at sea. Captain Barreaut, towards the end of the present year, was tried by a court-martial at Lorient for the loss of his ship, and, after an investigation which lasted nine days, honourably acquitted, chiefly because of the enormous disparity of force between the two vessels.

Of the relative force in the above case it will be sufficient to state that the Constellation at this time mounted, although she afterwards exchanged them for eighteens, 28 long 24-pounders on the main deck, and 10 long 12-pounders, with ten 32-pounder carronades, on the quarterdeck and forecastle; total 48 guns: the French say 50. The Insurgente was armed, according to the French accounts, with "trente-six canons," meaning without her four carronades; making her guns in all 40; as enumerated in Commodore Truxton's letter, and particularized at No. 7 of the little table at p. 54 of the first volume.

On the 22d of February, at a quarter past 12 at noon, the town of Marbella in Spain bearing north-north-west distant three leagues, the British brig-sloop Espoir, of fourteen 6-pounders and 80 men and boys, Captain James Sanders, discovered in the south-east and windward quarter two brigs and two xebecs. Both of the latter and one of the former appearing to be cruisers, the Espoir hoisted her colours; whereupon one of the brigs and one of the xebecs hoisted Spanish colours, and, with the other xebec, formed in line ahead, to receive the Espoir. The second brig was a Moorish vessel, which had been towed by one of the others, and was now cast off. The Espoir immediately hauled to the wind in chase, but was unable to weather her two opponents; with whom, however, the Espoir exchanged broadsides in passing, on opposite tacks. The Espoir then put about, and soon brought to close action the leewardmost of the vessels, which was his catholic majesty's xebec Africa, Captain Josef Subjado, mounting 14 long Spanish 4-pounders and four brass 4-pounder swivels, with a crew of 75 seamen and 38 soldiers. The firing continued with spirit for an hour and a half; when, a favourable opportunity presenting itself, the Africa was boarded, and after a sharp struggle of 20 minutes carried, by the British crew. The Africa's two consorts, in the mean time, had continued standing on towards the shore, which, when the action ended, was only three miles distant; and they eventually effected their escape.

The Espoir's loss on this occasion amounted to two seamen killed, and two wounded. That of the Africa amounted to one officer and eight seamen killed, her commander, two other officers, and 25 seamen wounded.

The British 74-gun ship Majestic, Captain Robert Cuthbert, was in sight during the action, but, being between five and six miles to leeward, had of course no share in it. Captain Subjado, while he lay wounded in the Espoir's cabin, told Captain Sanders, that he fully expected to have carried the Espoir into

Malaga. Upon the whole, the result of the action was highly creditable to the officers and crew of the British brig.

In the month of June, 1798, we left Rear-admiral Sercey at Batavia, whither he had just arrived from the Isle of France in the Brûle-Gueule corvette.* Of the subsequent cruises and performances of several of his frigates, we have since given some account. The Forte herself now demands our attention. Sometime in the latter end of the year 1798, this formidable French frigate, commanded by Captain Beaulieu-le-Long, sailed from the Isle of France on a cruise in the bay of Bengal. The depredations committed by the Forte on eastern commerce soon attracted attention; and on the 19th of February, the British 38-gun frigate, Sibylle, Captain Edward Cooke, sailed from Madras road in quest of her. On the 23d the Sibylle fell in with a cartel, bound to Madras, having on board some English prisoners taken out of one of the Forte's prizes, and on the 26th, anchored in Balasore road. While lying there, Captain Cooke despatched his boats for information to some country ships also in the road, but without success. The Sibylle then weighed, and bent her course towards the Sand-heads off the river of Bengal.

Although no information had been gained respecting the present movements of the Forte, enough had been learned of her formidable force to alarm a man of less intrepidity, or of less zeal in the duties of his profession, than the captain of the Sibylle. When the officer, in charge of the Forte's cartel fallen in with on the 23d, was brought on board the Sibylle, and informed of the special object of her cruise, he at once candidly pronounced her to be no match for the Forte; and, anticipating the glory that, in the event of a contest, would accrue to his countrymen, naturally expressed a wish that he had not quitted his ship. A Captain Johnstone, also, whose ship, the Chance, had been taken by the Forte, on coming on board and viewing the force of the Sibylle, trembled for the consequences of a meeting; but, like a brave man, he volunteered to serve in the action.

Let us then, before we proceed further in the account of what ensued, see how this British and French frigate really stood in point of relative force. The Sibylle had been a French 40-gun frigate, until captured by the Romney 50, in June, 1794. On being fitted out in the British service, the Sibylle, a fine Toulon-built frigate of 1091 tons, was armed with 44 long 18 and 9 pounders; but, subsequently, 10 of her 16 nines were exchanged for fourteen 32-pounder carronades. This gave her 28 long 18-pounders on the main deck, and six long nines and fourteen 32-pounder carronades on the quarterdeck and forecastle, total 48 guns; which was the precise force of the Sibylle on the present

* See p. 217.

occasion. Her net complement, as originally established, was 297 men and boys; but the ship, at this time, accidentally had on board a greater number, as we shall presently show.

Frigates, mounting 24-pounders on the main deck, have always been rare. The British possessed none until the three 64s, Indefatigable, Anson, and Magnanime, were reduced; nor the French until the Pomone was launched. The capture of the latter by the British gave birth to the Endymion; and, about the time that the Endymion was launched, the Americans set afloat three of the largest and heaviest frigates that the world had ever seen. The second 24-pounder frigate built by the French was, we believe, launched at Rochefort, in the summer of 1795, and she was very appropriately named La Forte. The Pomone was about 1270 tons, and mounted twenty-six 24 pounders on her main deck. The Forte measured 1400 tons, and carried, for which she had ample room, one gun more of a side on her main deck than the Pomone; making, with 14 long eights and four brass 36-pounder carronades on her quarter-deck and forecastle, a total of 46 guns.

These, we have no doubt, were all the guns which, with a complement of 480 or 500 men, the Forte originally carried. But subsequently, when perhaps Rear-admiral Sercey hoisted his flag on board of her in the beginning of the year 1796, four additional brass 36-pounder carronades were added to her armament; and, subsequently again, two long English 24-pounders, taken out of some prize probably, were placed in her two maindeck bow-ports; thus making her guns amount to 52, exclusive of eight 1-pounder swivels mounted along the top of her waist hammock-nettings. After this, it is hoped, not profitless digression, we return to the Sibylle, whom we left hastening towards the Sand-heads, which lie off the mouth of Bengal river, in the hope there to meet this same truly formidable French frigate.

On the 28th, at 8 h. 30 m. P.M., the outer edge of the western sea-reef bearing by account about north-east, the wind a light breeze from the south-south-west, and the night dark, the Sibylle, then standing to the south-east, observed several flashes in the north-west; which at first were supposed to be vivid lightning, very common in this quarter. A repetition of the flashes, however, until a few minutes before 9 P.M., when they ceased altogether, raised a suspicion that they proceeded from guns. At 9 P.M. the Sibylle, having extinguished all lights to prevent discovery, tacked to the westward, and at 9 h. 30 m P.M., saw three ships in a cluster in the south-east quarter. These were the Forte, and two rich prizes which she had just made, the Endeavour and Lord Mornington country ships from China. The flashes had proceeded from the Forte's guns, and she and her prizes had gained their present bearing by standing to the eastward.

Rightly conjecturing that one of these ships would prove to be the object of his search, Captain Cooke continued to stand to the westward, in order to get the weathergage; and soon afterwards the Sibylle passed about two miles to leeward of them. At 10 P.M., having brought the three ships sufficiently on her quarter to enable her to weather them by going on the other tack, the Sibylle put about, and, taking in her topgallantsails and courses, kept the centre ship, which, from her superior size and the lights in her stern, marked her out as the Forte, on her lee or larboard bow. The water was at this time quite smooth, with a light and steady breeze still blowing from the south-south-west, and the Sibylle, under her topsails, jib, and spanker, was going about two knots an hour. At 11 h. 30 m. P.M. the Sibylle saw that the three ships were lying to on the starboard tack, or that on which she was standing.

At midnight, when the Sibylle had approached within a mile of the Forte, the latter's two rows of ports (having two guns of a side in her gangways, a small blank space only was observable in the centre of the upper row), lighted up as they were, gave the ship a very formidable appearance. The Forte then filled, hove in stays under the Sibylle's lee bow, and, as her larboard guns began to bear, fired six or seven of them, the instant and principal effect of which was to bring down her opponent's jib. The Forte, as she passed on, fired also her after guns, and one of the prizes opened her fire; but still the Sibylle, as a proof of the judgment of her commander and the steadiness of her crew, reserved her fire for a shorter and more effective distance.

The patience of the latter, however, was put to no longer a trial than until the Forte passed abaft the beam of their ship; when, at three quarters past midnight, the Sibylle put her helm up, and fired the whole of her larboard broadside into the Forte's stern, at less than pistol-shot distance; so close, indeed, that the French ship's spanker-boom was scarcely cleared. Luffing quickly up, the Sibylle was presently close alongside her antagonist to leeward, and poured in a second broadside as well directed as the previous raking one. The bearing up of the Sibylle had been so sudden and unexpected, that several of the Forte's larboard or weather guns went off after the former had passed to leeward.

Thus this furious night-action commenced. For nearly the first hour, during which the two ships lay broadside to broadside at a distance that never exceeded point-blank musket-range and was sometimes much nearer, the Forte returned a spirited, but far too elevated and consequently an almost harmless fire. At 1 h. 30 m. A.M. on the 1st of March, Captain Cooke was mortally wounded by a grape-shot, and the command devolved upon Lieutenant Lucius Hardyman. About ten minutes after Captain Cooke had been carried below, Captain Davies of the army, an aide-de-camp of Lord Mornington's and a volunteer on this occasion, while encouraging the men at the quarterdeck guns, of some of which he had charge, was killed by a cannon-shot that nearly severed his body. At this time the fire from the Forte began to slacken, and at 2 h. 30 m. A.M. entirely ceased.

On this the Sibylle discontinued her fire, and hailed to know if her antagonist had struck. Receiving no reply, although the ships were still so close that the voices of the Forte's people were distinctly heard, the Sibylle recommenced firing with renewed vigour. Finding no return, the British frigate a second time ceased, and a second time hailed, but again without effect. At this moment, perceiving the Forte's rigging filled with men, and her topgallantsails loose, as if with the intention of endeavouring to escape, the Sibylle recommenced her firing for the third time, and set her own foresail and topgallantsails. In five minutes after this the Forte's mizenmast came down, and in another minute or two her fore and main masts and bowsprit. The Sibylle ceased firing; her crew gave three cheers; and thus, at 2 h. 28 m. A.M., being about two hours and a half from its commencement, the action ended.

The Sibylle immediately dropped her anchor in 17 fathoms, and all hands began repairing the rigging and bending new sails. At about three P.M. one of the English prisoners on board the Forte, finding that the ship was drifting upon the Sibylle, hailed the latter to request that a boat might be sent on board, as all theirs had been shot to pieces. Although no doubt existed on board the Sibylle, as to the name of the ship of which she had made such a wreck, the question was put, and "The French frigate Forte," was the answer returned. While possession is taking of the prize, we will give some account of the damage and loss of the ship that had so gallantly captured her.

The Sibylle had most of her standing, and all her running rigging and sails shot to pieces, all her masts and yards, particularly the main and mizen masts, and the yards on them, badly wounded; but, with all this the Sibylle had only received in the hull and upperworks six shot: one of which, however, had dismounted a gun, and another, a 24-pounder, having entered one of the officer's cabins, had shivered to atoms a large trunk and a smaller one near it, carried away two legs of a sofa, and passed out through the ship's side.

Before stating the Sibylle's loss of men, it will be necessary for us to show what number were on board at the commencement of the action. Owing to sickness, the Sibylle's original crew, according to a muster taken four days before the action, had been reduced to 221 officers and seamen, 10 boys and nine marines; and many of these were scarcely well enough to go to quarters. To make the deficiency, the governor-general of India sent on board the Sibylle a detachment of the Scotch brigade; and some officers and men belonging to the Fox, including Lieutenant James Hingston Tuckey, also joined the Sibylle out of a prize which they had brought to Madras; thus making the supernumeraries amount to 131, and the total of men and boys on board to 371. Of these the Sibylle had Captain Davies (already described as one of the Earl of Mornington's aides-de-camp), one seaman, one marine, and two soldiers killed, and Captain Cooke (mortally), 15 seamen, and one soldier wounded; total, five killed, and 17 wounded.

When Lieutenant Nicholas Manger, third of the Sibylle, with his boat's crew, went on board the Forte, the scene of wreck and carnage that presented itself to their view was such, by all account, as no other persons than the actual spectators could form an adequate idea. A summary on our part must suffice. The bowsprit had gone close to the figure-head, the foremast one foot above the forecastle, the mainmast 18 feet above the quarterdeck, and the mizenmast 10 feet above the poop. As the masts had fallen with all the sails set, it was remarked that the three topsails were very slightly injured; the Sibylle's shot had taken a lower and more fatal direction. All the boats, booms, the wheel, capstan, binnacle, and other articles on deck were cut to pieces. A most extraordinary circumstance, too, the forecastle bell was pierced by a grape shot and yet not cracked: it is still, we believe, to be seen at Fort-William, Calcutta.

The Forte's upperworks were lined with cork to prevent splinters; and, for the same purpose, nettings were fixed fore and aft, as well on the main deck as on the quarterdeck, forecastle and gangways. Another stout netting was spread, like an awning, over the quarterdeck. This is common on board French ships; and, being put up to prevent blocks and other heavy articles falling from aloft on the heads of the officers, is appropriately named "la sauve-tête." The starboard, quarter-deck and forecastle bulwarks were completely destroyed; and the same side of the Forte, from the bends upwards, was nearly beat in. Upwards of 300 round-shot were counted in her hull; several of her guns were dismounted; and, as already mentioned, her very cables in the tiers were rendered unserviceable.

The loss on board the Forte may well have been severe. Let us first ascertain what number of men she had on board. It appears that her original crew, including a portion of Malays taken on board at Batavia, amounted to 513 men and boys. Of this number she had sent away in various prizes, according to the account given by her officers, 143: leaving 370 as the number present in the action. Of these she lost, as appears, 65 killed, including her captain, first lieutenant, and some other officers, and 80 wounded, including also several of her officers; of these 80 wounded, many died after suffering amputation.

The number of prisoners, including the wounded, amounted to 305; which, with the 65 represented as killed, makes the 370. This, we must observe, is more by 10 than the number sworn to by the French officers, to entitle the captors to head-money; and which number, if correct, would reduce the killed to 55. In the present case, however, we are diposed to rely more upon the account that gives 370 as the number on board; because we believe that the officers deposing, if officers at all, were not of a rank to be entitled to implicit credit, or even to be well informed, in a matter of this nature; especially, where so many draughts had been made from the crew into prizes, including two a few hours only before the action commenced.

We are not quite certain as to the propriety of considering the Forte's two English 24-pounders as part of her broadside-guns. We doubt, unless they were of a much shorter pattern than common, whether they could be used otherwise than as chase-guns. It appears, however, that the Forte was subsequently established with 30 guns for her main deck; hence we must conclude that she had broadside ports to fit them to.

COMPARATIVE FORCE OF THE COMBATANTS.

		SIBYLLE.	FORTE.
Broadside-guns	No.	24	26
	lbs.	503	604
Crew	No.	371	370
Size	tons.	1091	1401

Here in point of guns, is a slight superiority on the part of the French frigate; but still the issue of the combat is far less surprising than that, after a close engagement of two hours, the British frigate should have escaped with so trifling a loss. Several causes, we believe, combined to produce this disparity in execution. We must consider, in spite of some assertions to the contrary, that the Forte was in an unprepared state when she wore to attack the Sibylle. Either her people mistook the latter, in the dark, for an Indiaman, and were only undeceived when the Sibylle's raking broadside laid so many of them low; or, as some of the English prisoners on board afterwards stated, the Frenchmen knew the ship advancing to be the Sibylle, but, on account of their superiority of force, expected to make of her an easy conquest.

An officer present in the action, and whose name, were we permitted to use it, would give to his remarks tenfold the weight of any thing we could offer, has thus accounted for the bad gunnery exhibited by the Forte's men: "The only good reason that can be given for their ill-directed fire (for they had trained artillerymen stationed at every gun), is that, from being always used to elevate their guns for point-blank range, or about a mile, on a level, they never considered that their shot would naturally pass over a low object so much nearer to them." To this may undoubtedly be added, the destructive and appalling effects of the Sibylle's first two broadsides, and the early fall of the Forte's brave captain and his first lieutenant; a loss the more sensibly felt by her men on account of the absence in prizes of several of her officers.

For their most excellent gunnery, the greatest credit is due to the crew of the Sibylle; not forgetting their officers, by whose practical instructions, constantly applied, they had become such proficients. We must not pass over without notice (especially as none is taken of them in the gazette-letter) the officers and men of the Scotch brigade. These, during the action, were stationed on the gangways, quarterdeck, and forecastle; and the effects of their unremitting fire were seen in innumerable bullet-holes all along the Forte's topsides, and were felt, we doubt not, by many a poor fellow who, as is customary with the French, was employed in loading his gun on the outside of the ship.

It is singular that the Forte, as far as was observed, used no musketry in the action; and although she had on board a variety of destructive missiles, such as hand-grenades, langridge, and rockets with barbs intended to fix upon and set fire to the sails and rigging, they remained unused. In conclusion, we will say, that the action of the Sibylle and Forte was gallantly fought on both sides, but skilfully fought on one side only; the weaker side, and, by the due exercise of that very skill, the one which was ultimately successful.

The Forte's stream-anchor (all her bower-cables had been cut through by shot), after it had been let go, fell foul of the wreck of the foremast and bowsprit; and Lieutenant Manger was obliged, for the safety of the ship, to clear the stream-anchor from the wreck, which could only be done by slipping the cable. The Sibylle now sent the end of her bower-cable to the prize; and the Forte, in the course of a few minutes rode by the Sibylle's anchor.

During the action the Sibylle had been too much occupied to pay any attention to the Forte's two prizes. At daylight these were seen lying to, hull-down to windward. By way of decoying them down, French colours over English were hoisted on board the Sibylle, and, upon the stumps of the Forte's mizenmast, French colours only. Presently the Mornington bore down. On observing this the Sibylle, who had already repaired her rigging forward where it had been most damaged, and bent new sails, began getting under way; but the few hands remaining on board after having manned the Forte being greatly fatigued, as well with their last night's hard work in making the latter their prize as with the loss of rest from having slept nowhere but at their quarters since their departure from Madras, were a longer time than usual in performing their task. In the mean time the Mornington, having arrived within long gun-shot, discovered her mistake, she immediately tacked and stood away, under a heavy press of sail, to rejoin the Endeavour, to whom she made signals apprizing her of the danger. Lying directly on the weather bow of the Forte, the Sibylle was delayed some minutes in making sail. At length she cleared her prize, and set all sail on her fore and mizen masts, but very little upon her mainmast on account of its wounds. No sooner was the mizen topsail full, than the cross-jack yard went. Hence, after about an hour's chase, and the discharge of a few shots from her bow-guns, the Sibylle was obliged to return without success to her anchorage near the Forte.

The two frigates remained at anchor off the Sandheads, until the Sibylle had finished and secured her masts, and the Forte rigged herself jury-ones. This occupied two or three days: at the end of which time the Sibylle, taking the Forte in tow, steered towards Calcutta. On arriving there, the Forte was added to the British navy as a 44-gun frigate, established with thirty long 24-pounders on the main deck, and twenty 32-pounder carronades and two long 12-pounders on the quarterdeck and forecastle, total 52 guns; and the command of her was given, pro tempore, to Lieutenant Hardyman (promoted to commander on the occasion), who had so gallantly fought the action after his captain had been carried below. It being in our power to give the names of the other commissioned officers present in this very gallant action, we gladly state that James G. Vashon was the second lieutenant, and James Douglas, the master. The names of the first and third lieutenants, and also of the volunteer lieutenant from the Fox, have already appeared. No marine officer was on board.

Some of the published accounts having represented the Forte's quarterdeck and forecastle guns as "12-pounders," we here subjoin the weight, in French and English pounds, of every nature of gun which the ship had on board.

			Fr. wt. lbs.		Eng. wt. Cwt.	qrs.	lbs.
Long	24-pounder,	iron	6240	==	51	1	0
Long	8-pounder,	iron	3150	==	25	3	14
Car.	36-pounder,	brass	802	==	6	2	10

The loss of the Forte by shipwreck, before she was brought to a port of England, and properly surveyed and measured, prevents us from giving a very accurate account of her principal dimensions, as well as of establishing some other doubtful facts concerning her. With such materials as we have, we present the following as the relative length and breadth of the two frigates:

	Length of 'tween decks:		Extreme breadth.	
	ft.	in.	ft.	in.
Sibylle	154	3	40	1½
Forte	170	0	43	3

Before we take our final leave of this action, we must offer a remark or two upon the account given of it by a contemporary. That account, to be sure, is contained in a very few lines; but still, upon one who has read the preceding accounts in the work, and who may not be otherwise informed as to the merits of this particular action, it is calculated to produce very erroneous impressions. "La Forte, a French frigate of the largest class, was captured on the 28th of February, by his majesty's ship La Sibylle, of forty-four guns, commanded by Captain Edward Cooke."*

Now, nearly all of the French 18-pounder frigates, whose capture is noticed in the same work, are represented as frigates "of the largest class," or "of the first class," which amounts to the same; while the two captured French 24-pounder frigates, the Pomone and Immortalité, have the calibers of their guns carefully expressed. Hence, why may not the reader infer, that the Forte was an 18-pounder frigate, similar, for instance, to the Virginie, "one of the finest frigates in the French navy."† On the other hand, as all British frigates, agreeing in their real force with the Sibylle, are described as "of thirty-eight guns," who but would imagine, that the Sibylle, declared to be "of forty-four guns," was a frigate of a higher class, and consequently of a greater force, than they were?

Captain Cooke's principal wound was not merely a mortal, but a most painful one. It was occasioned by a large-sized grape-shot, which, after passing through the flesh on the inside of the arm, had entered the side and came out near the spine. His other arm and his breast were also wounded. After lingering at Calcutta until the 25th of the ensuing May, this active and enterprising officer (see his proceedings at Toulon and Manilla) died, how generally lamented it would be superfluous to add. He was buried with the highest military honours, and a monument was erected to his memory by the honourable court of East India directors. After Captain Cooke's death, Captain Hardyman continued in command of the Forte, and was made post on the 27th of January, 1800.

On the 18th of March, at daylight, the Isle of Bas, bearing south-east distant nine leagues, the British hired the armed brig Telegraph, of 14 carronades, 18-pounders, and two long sixes, with sixty men and boys, commanded by Lieutenant James Andrew Worth, discovered about two miles on her lee bow, the French privateer-brig Hirondelle, of 16 guns (8 and 6 pounders) and 72 men on board, out of a complement of 89. The Hirondelle immediately tacked, and stood towards the Telegraph. At 7 h. 30 m. A.M., the two brigs, having got close alongside each other, commenced a spirited cannonade. During the progress of the action, each vessel vainly tried, several times, to board the other. At length, after the struggle had continued three hours and a half; and when, having had all her rigging shot away, she was in an unmanageable state, the Hirondelle struck her colours.

* Brenton, vol. ii., p. 175.

† Ibid., vol. i., p. 397.

The Telegraph had five men wounded; the Hirondelle five killed, and 14 wounded. In this close engagement the carronades of the Telegraph produced their full effect, and Lieutenant Worth, who was promoted to the rank of commander on the occasion, Mr. George Gibbs, the master, and the remainder of the British officers and crew, conducted themselves in a very creditable manner; nor, considering the obstinate defence they made, can much less be said of the officers and men of the Hirondelle.

On the 30th of March the British 36-gun frigate Trent, Captain Robert Waller Otway, while cruising, in company with the 12-gun cutter Sparrow, Lieutenant John Wiley, off the west end of the island of Porto-Rico, discovered, in a small bay about seven leagues to the northward of Cape Roxo, a Spanish merchant ship and three schooners at anchor in shoal water, close to the shore, and under the protection of a 5-gun battery. Captain Otway immediately despatched the boats of the ship, commanded by Lieutenants Nathaniel Belchier and George Balderston, and Lieutenant George M'Gie of the marines, and covered by the Sparrow, to attempt cutting them out. A party of marines under Lieutenant M'Gie, and of seamen under Lieutenant Belchier, landed and stormed the battery; which, after killing five and wounding several of the Spaniards stationed at it, they carried. While the British on shore were engaged in spiking the guns and destroying the battery, those in the boats, led by Lieutenant Balderston, and greatly assisted by the fire from the Sparrow, boarded and brought off the ship and one out of three schooners, two of which had been scuttled by the Spaniards. This creditable exploit was effected with no greater loss to the British than two seamen and one corporal of marines wounded.

On the 9th of April, early in the morning, the British 18-pounder 36-gun frigate San-Fiorenzo, Captain Sir Harry Neale, and 38-gun frigate Amelia, Captain the Honourable Charles Herbert, having reconnoitred two French frigates at anchor in the port of Lorient, stood towards Belle-Isle. As the British approached, some vessels were seen at anchor in the great road, but, being under the land, were not distinguishable until the frigates had run the whole length of the island; when the strangers were at once seen to be three French frigates and a large cutter gun-vessel, having their topsail yards hoisted ready for a start. At this instant, which was just at 9 A.M., a sudden and heavy squall of wind from the north-west carried away the Amelia's main topmast, and fore and mizen topgallantmasts; the topmast, in its fall, tearing a great part of the mainsail from the yard.

So fine an opportunity was not lost upon the French commodore; whose three frigates, the Cornélie, Vengeance, and Sémillante, dropping their topsails, got under way, and, accompanied by the gun-vessel, made sail in line ahead towards the two British frigates. The San-Fiorenzo immediately made the signal to prepare for battle; and, followed by the Amelia, stood on to meet the French. After the San-Fiorenzo had shortened sail to keep company with her disabled consort, the two frigates bore up in close order, preserving the weathergage. The Cornélie, Vengeance, Sémillante, and gun-vessel now tacked to engage, and at 10 h. 10 m. A.M. opened their broadsides upon the San-Fiorenzo and Amelia; who promptly returned the fire.

In this manner the action commenced, a battery on Hædic rocks occasionally joining in the cannonade. So disinclined were the French to a close combat, that the British had to bear up three times in order to be within gun-shot. At length, at about 1 h. 5 m. P.M., the three French frigates, two of which appeared to be much crippled, wore, and, followed by the gun-vessel, effected their escape; the frigates bearing up for the river Loire and the gun-vessel returning to Belle-Isle.

In this one hour and 55 minutes' engagement, the San-Fiorenzo had all her lower masts wounded, and her spanker-boom, and most of her starboard shrouds and running rigging, shot away. The Amelia's damages by the enemy's shot were nearly to the same extent; but she was in a more disabled state than the San-Fiorenzo, in consequence of the previous loss of her main topmast and fore and mizen topgallantmasts. The San-Fiorenzo, out of a complement of 271 men and boys, had one seaman killed and 18 seamen wounded, two of them dangerously; the Amelia, out of her net complement of 281 men and boys, one midshipman (Mr. Bayley) and one seaman killed, and 17 seamen wounded, one of them dangerously.

A French brig, which the San-Fiorenzo captured on the evening of the action, and which had just quitted the Loire, represented the loss on board the French frigates as particularly severe; and that the commodore's ship alone, the Cornélie, had upwards of 100 men killed and wounded, including among the latter, the commodore himself. According to a paragraph in the Moniteur, Captain Caro of the Vengeance was mortally wounded, and the loss of the Sémillante included 15 men killed.

Without reckoning the gun-vessel, or the battery on Hædic rocks, there was, in this action between two British 18-pounder frigates and two French 18-pounder and one 12-pounder frigate, and whose aggregate crews alone must have amounted to very few short of 1000 men, a sufficient disparity of force to excite surprise at the abandonment of the contest by the French ships. The latter were met by the English ships almost within the jaws of their own port: the French commodore, therefore, had no interference to dread, and in the event of success, might have harboured his prizes before the sun had ever set upon his victory.

The comparatively heavy metal of the three British rasés, Anson, Indefatigable, and Magnanime, invested them with such powers of ubiquity, that every British single-decked ship larger than a sloop, seen or encountered along the French coast, was pronounced "un vaisseau rasé." As the difference in size between the Amelia and San-Fiorenzo (two French frigates originally, one the Proserpine, the other the Minerve) was only 27 tons, we are at a loss to conceive to which of the two the Moniteur meant to apply the wonder-working designation. At all events, whatever may be thought of the conduct of the French commodore, there can be but one opinion, among those acquainted with the facts, as to the gallant behaviour, and the (let the French themselves speak to that) well-directed fire, of Captains Neale and Herbert, and their respective officers and ships' companies.

On the 13th of April, the east end of Jamaica bearing south-south-west distant 25 leagues, the British 14-gun brig-sloop Amaranthe (12 carronades, 24-pounders, and two light long guns), Captain Francis Vesey, after a long chase came up with and engaged, nearly within pistol-shot, the French schooner letter-of-marque Vengeur, of six 4-pounders; and the latter, notwithstanding her great inferiority of force, fought for one hour and eight minutes.

The Amaranthe, out of a crew of 86 men and boys, had one quartermaster killed, and three seamen slightly wounded; and the Vengeur, out of a crew of 36, including passengers, 14 men killed and five wounded, one of them mortally. The schooner was from San-Jago de Cuba bound to Jérémie, with a cargo of flour. The noble defence, made by her officers, crew, and passengers, was worthy of every praise, and to the credit of Captain Vesey, did not pass unnoticed by him.

On the 4th of May the British 10-gun polacre Fortune, commanded by Lieutenant Lewis Davis, in company with the Dame-de-Grâce, a prize gun-boat, sailed from the bay of Acre, having been ordered by Sir Sidney Smith, of the Tigre, to cruise for three weeks on the coast of Syria, in order to cut off any supplies that might arrive from Alexandria for the use of the French army before Acre. On the 8th, at 3 A.M., when about four miles from the shore near Jaffa, the Fortune and gun-boat fell in with Rear-admiral Perrée's squadron, of three frigates and two brigs. At daybreak one of the latter, the Salamine, displaying a British red ensign, ran alongside of the Fortune. Lieutenant Davis hailed her, and was answered with a broadside and a volley of musketry; after which the Salamine hauled down the British, and hoisted French colours. The Fortune promptly returned the salute, and a smart conflict ensued.

At 6 A.M. all the cartridges, and the greater part of the shots, of the Fortune were expended, three of her guns dismounted, and her masts, yards, and rigging cut to pieces. While she was in this utterly defenceless state, the Salamine came close upon her larboard quarter with intent to board; whereupon the Fortune, seeing the three frigates also approaching, struck her pendant; her colours, having just been shot away the third time, were already down.

The Fortune's guns were French 4 and 3 pounders, all in bad condition, and her crew amounted to 28; of whom she had two seamen killed, and her commander and three seamen wounded. The Salamine mounted 16 long French 6-pounders, with a crew of 126 men. What loss or damage, if any, the Salamine sustained does not appear. The gun-boat also fell into the hands of M. Perrée, who immediately scuttled and sank both his prizes.

The Fortune had been captured on the 11th of the preceding August by the Swiftsure 74. She was then called, by mistake, a corvette of 18 guns. The Fortune, in fact, was a mere shell of a vessel, and measured only 150 tons; while the Salamine, which was afterwards in the British service, was a regular man-of-war brig, and measured 240 tons. Considering the very great disparity of force, the defence of the Fortune was highly creditable to her commander and crew.

On the 12th of May, in the morning, the British hired armed cutter Courier, of twelve 4-pounders and 40 men, commanded by Lieutenant Thomas Searle, while on her way from Yarmouth roads, to join the Latona frigate off the Texel, discovered an armed brig about eight or nine leagues off Winterton, in the act of capturing a merchant sloop. The Courier immediately made sail, and at 1 h. 30 m. P.M., brought to close action a French privateer of 16 guns. The two vessels continued engaged at close quarters for an hour and 40 minutes; when the brig, being the better sailer, and having the advantage of the wind, effected her escape. The Courier continued in chase until midnight; at which time, the weather becoming thick, she lost sight of her adversary. The Courier had five men wounded. The obvious damages received by the brig, whose guns were afterwards ascertained to have been 6 and 8 pounders, indicated that her loss was far more severe than the cutter's. A French lugger-privateer lay to leeward during the whole of the action, but evinced no inclination to interfere.

On the 13th, at daylight, Lieutenant Searle saw a sail in the north-east, which he at first judged to be his old opponent; but, the vessel, as the Courier neared her in chase, proved to be schooner-rigged. At 8 A.M. the cutter arrived up with, and without any resistance captured, the French privateer-schooner Ribotteur, of four (originally six) 3-pounders and 26 men; a consort, as it turned out, of the brig which Lieutenant Searle, with so much gallantry and effect, had engaged the day before.

On the 9th of June, the British 12-pounder, 32-gun frigate, Success, Captain Shuldham Peard, chased a Spanish polacre into the harbour of La Selva, a small port about two leagues to the northward of Cape Creux. There being no appearance of batteries to defend the harbour, and the weather being favourable, Captain Peard detached 42 officers and men in three of the frigate's boats, under the command of Lieutenant Philip Facey in the barge, assisted by Lieutenant Gustavus Stupart in the launch, and Lieutenant John Davison, of the marines, in the cutter, to endeavour to bring out the polacre; with instructions, however, to Lieutenant Facey to return, should he find any opposition of consequence.

Notwithstanding that the polacre, which was the Bella-Aurora, from Genoa bound to Barcelona, laden with cotton, silk, and rice, mounted 10 carriage-guns, 8 and 6 pounders, had on board a crew of 113 men, and was surrounded with a boarding-netting, and supported by a small battery, and by a large body of men at small-arms on the shore, Lieutenant Facey (himself the first on the enemy's deck), and the 41 officers and men under his command, gallantly carried and brought out the vessel.

This bold and well-conducted enterprise was not, however, performed without so serious a loss to the British, as four seamen killed and mortally wounded, and Lieutenant Stupart and eight seamen badly wounded. For the firmness and bright example he had shown on this trying occasion, Lieutenant Facey, a few months afterwards, was deservedly promoted to the rank of commander.

On the 22d of June, latitude 38° 50' north, longitude 31° west, the British 18-pounder 32-gun frigate Alcmène, Captain Henry Digby, discovered a strange ship boarding an American vessel, and was soon afterwards informed by the latter that the ship, then about two leagues distant was a French privateer. The Alcmène immediately proceeded in chase, and by great exertions, succeeded during the night, in spite of calms and light winds, in getting round the island of Corvo.

On the 23d, at daybreak, the privateer again made her appearance, towing and sweeping to the westward with all her strength. The chase continued, in this slow manner, during the whole of that and the two succeeding days, on one of which the Alcmène passed an English convoy of 40 vessels, in charge of two brig-sloops, bound to Lisbon. At length a breeze sprang up from the northward, which, by 6 A.M. on the 26th, brought the Alcmène within gunshot of the privateer.

A running fight now commenced, and continued, but without, as it appears, any loss or important damage on either side, until about 7 A.M.; when, in latitude 39° 23' north, longitude 33° west, the French privateer Courageux, of Bordeaux, mounting 28 guns, described as 12 and 9 pounders, but more likely 8 and 6 pounders, with a complement of 253 men, commanded by Captain Jean Barnard, struck her colours.

On the 18th of the succeeding month, having received

information from the British lugger-privateer Phoenix, Captain Hammond, belonging to Jersey, of several vessels being in the port of Vivero, on the north-west coast of Spain, the Alcmène, at sunset, stood into the harbour, and, running between two Spanish vessels distant from each other about 500 yards, sent Lieutenants Charles Gayton Warren and William Sandford Oliver, with armed parties to board them; a service which these officers executed in a spirited and becoming manner.

One of the prizes was the Felicidad, a ship between 700 and 800 tons, "pierced for 22 guns," but, we believe, mounting none, and laden with a cargo of hemp, lower masts, and ship-timber, bound to the arsenal at Ferrol: the other prize was the Bisano, a brig of "400 tons," also unarmed, and laden with ship-timber and iron, for the same destination.

As soon as the prizes began to get under sail, two forts and a detached gun opened upon them and the frigate; but the smoke from the guns of the Alcmène, and the gathering shades of night, prevented the enemy from directing his guns with effect. Thus favoured, and assisted, also, by the Phoenix lugger, whose commander had gallantly followed the Alcmène into the harbour, the two prizes were brought safe off without, as far as the accounts go, the slightest casualty to any of the parties concerned.

On the 9th of August the British 14-gun brig-sloop Speedy (4-pounders, with 80 men and boys), Captain Jahleel Brenton, and 14-gun brig-privateer Defender, of Gibraltar, gave chase to three Spanish armed vessels, one of four 6-pounders, another of six, and the third of ten, 8 and 6 pounders; all of which ran for shelter into a small sandy bay, about five leagues to the eastward of Cape de Gata. There they moored themselves in a close line, within a boat's length of the beach. The two brigs soon opened their fire, and engaged the Spaniards for an hour and three quarters, under sail, being unable to get soundings although not more than a cable's length distant from the rocks.

Finding that to keep under sail and in motion was giving an advantage to the enemy, the Speedy pushed for and obtained an anchorage, within pistol-shot of the centre vessel. The Defender meanwhile, having but 22 men of her crew on board, had stood out to meet one of her boats in the offing. After three quarters of an hour's cannonade by the Speedy, the Spanish crews took to their boats, having first cut the cables of two of their vessels, which, in consequence, drove on shore. These and the vessel still afloat were, however, brought off by the Speedy's boats, and that under a constant fire of musketry from the hills. In this well-conducted little enterprise, the Speedy had two seamen wounded, and the Defender one, but neither dangerously. On board the Spanish vessels two dead men were found. The wounded, if any, must have been carried on shore.

On the 11th of August the British 16-gun ship-sloop Pylades,

Captain Adam McKenzie, 16-gun brig-sloop Espiègle, Captain James Boorder, and 10-gun hired cutter Courier, Lieutenant Thomas Searle, part of a light squadron under Captain Frank Sotheron, of the 38-gun frigate Latona, cruising off the coast of Holland, proceeded to attack the late British gun-brig Crash, which lay moored in a narrow passage between the island of Schiermonikoog on the main land of Groningen. The Courier, working fastest to windward, was sent ahead, and, in a very gallant manner, commenced engaging the Crash, whose force was 12 carronades, consisting of eight 18, two 24, and two 32 pounders, with a crew of 60 men.

Having frequently not two feet of water more than they drew, with the wind right down the channel, and only room for either, in tacking, to go twice her length, the Pylades and Espiègle found a very difficult navigation. At length they arrived within pistol-shot of the Crash, and, in conjunction with the Courier, opened a heavy fire upon her. It was not, however, until she had sustained that fire for nearly 50 minutes, that the Crash struck her colours.

The Pylades and Espiègle were greatly damaged in their rigging and yards. The latter, as well as the Courier, escaped without any loss; but the Pylades had one seamen killed and two wounded. Although Captains McKenzie and Boorder each wrote an official letter on the subject of this action, and concur in representing the long and obstinate defence made by the Crash, they neither mention her loss, which must have been severe, nor the name of the officer who had fought so bravely against a force so decidedly superior.

Previously to the attack of the Crash, the boats of Captain Sotheron's two frigates, and of the Pylades and Espiègle, had been sent to cut out an armed schooner that lay to the eastward of a sand, and could not be otherwise approached. The schooner ran herself on shore, and opened a heavy fire on the boats, by which one man was killed. The boats then returned to their ships.

On the 12th, at 3 P.M., having fitted out the Crash, and armed a schuyt, which the boats had recently cut out, with two 12-pounder carronades, also the launches of the Latona and Pylades each with one, Captain McKenzie despatched them, accompanied by all the other boats of the ships, some armed with swivels, others only with small-arms, under the orders of Lieutenant James Slade, first of the Latona, assisted by Lieutenant Salusbury Pryce Humphreys, who commanded the schuyt, to attack the Dutch schooner Vengeance, of six guns, two of them long 24-pounders, and a large row-boat, both moored under a battery of four long 12 and two brass 4 pounders, on the island of Schiermonikoog. The Courier was to have covered the boats in their advance, but grounded, and was with difficulty saved. The Crash, Undaunted (the schuyt's new name), and the boats, then went on, until the latter grounded within half pistol-shot of, and under a heavy fire from, the schooner and battery.

Having placed their small-craft as advantageously as they could, the British immediately opened a smart fire in return. This soon drove the people from the battery; and the crew of the schooner, just as some of the boats were about to board her, ran on shore, having previously set fire to their vessel so effectually that it could not be extinguished. Some of the British then landed; and, of the six guns on the battery, spiked the four iron 12-pounders, and brought off the two brass 4-pounder field-pieces. They afterwards took possession of the row-boat, and of the 12 schuyts that were lying near her. The whole service was executed without the loss of a man on the British side; nor could it be discovered that any loss of lives had been sustained by the Dutchmen.

The Crash, it appears, drawing too much water, had, as well as the Courier, grounded so far from the shore as to be of little service in co-operating with the boats; but the Undaunted succeeded in getting alongside of the Dutch schooner soon after, as already related, the crew had abandoned and set fire to her. The tide, however, was so rapid, that the Undaunted could not hold on, and the roundness of the sides of the two vessels prevented Lieutenant Humphreys from springing on board. "He therefore seized a rope, and, leaping into the sea, attempted to reach the schooner for the purpose of attaching it to her, but soon found he had no chance against the tide, and was consequently obliged to be hauled back to the Undaunted. Fortunate for him was this failure; for, scarcely had he obtained a footing on his own deck, when an explosion took place on board the Vengeance, by which she was blown to atoms."*

On the 20th of August, at 8 h. 30 m. A.M., Cordovan lighthouse bearing east by south distant six or seven leagues, the British 38-gun frigate Clyde, Captain Charles Cunningham, having with the wind to the northward just worked off from reconnoitring the port of Rocheforte, descried two sail in the south-west. The Clyde immediately gave chase, and at 11 A.M. made them out to be enemy's cruisers standing towards her. At half an hour after noon the strangers, having then approached within two miles of the Clyde, bore up and made sail, each going away large on a different tack. The Clyde, selecting the one that appeared the more formidable of the two, crowded sail in pursuit. At 1 h. 30 m. P.M., having arrived within gun-shot, the Clyde hoisted her colours and fired a gun; whereupon the French 36-gun frigate Vestale (the Terpsichore's old opponent), Captain Mayor-Michel-Pierre Gaspard, hoisted her colours, and answered with a broadside the gun which had been fired by the Clyde.

* Marshall, vol. ii., p. 235.

A warm engagement, during which the Vestale made several skilful manœuvres, now ensued, and continued, without intermission, for one hour and fifty minutes; when the French frigate, having had all three masts badly wounded, her rigging and sails cut to pieces, and her hull, both above and below her water-line, pierced with shot in several places, hauled down her flag to the Clyde; whose principal damages were confined to her rigging and sails. The Vestale's consort, which was the French 20-gun corvette Sagesse, was in sight in-shore during the whole of the action.

The Clyde, out of her net complement of 281 men and boys, had a quartermaster and one private marine killed, and three seamen wounded. The Vestale, although her established complement was at least 275, had on board, when the action commenced, no more than 230 men. Of these the French frigate lost 10 seamen and marines killed, and two officers and 20 seamen and marines wounded; one officer and several seamen afterwards died of their wounds.

If the Sagesse withdrew owing, not to the defection of her own, but to the command of the Vestale's captain, the latter must have formed a very erroneous judgment of the relative strength of himself and his opponent. The Clyde would not have been overmatched, nor would Captain Cunningham have declined fighting, had the two French ships united their strength against him.

The comparative force of the two combatants has already appeared in that of the Révolutionnaire and Unité.* The Seahorse and Sensible were also similarly matched. Circumstanced therefore as he was, Captain Gaspard behaved with commendable gallantry, and, as well as his officers and crew, merited the most honourable acquittal for the loss of the Vestale. Nor could the French captain have a better witness in his favour than Captain Cunningham; who, in his modestly-written official letter, passes a very high encomium on the behaviour of his antagonist.

Having secured his prize, Captain Cunningham directed his attention towards her late consort; but, availing herself of the vicinity of the Gironde, the Sagesse had already effected her escape. Although a fine frigate of 946 tons, the Vestale, in her two rough encounters, first with the Terpsichore, and now with the Clyde, had received too much injury to be repaired with advantage. The captured frigate, therefore, was not purchased for the use of the British navy. Since the capture of the Réunion by the Crescent, and of the Unité by the Révolutionnaire, it had not been customary to knight the captains of 18-pounder frigates for their success over the 12-pounder frigates of the enemy. Hence Captain Cunningham was not so rewarded; but the

* See vol. i., p. 322.

Clyde's first lieutenant, Alexander Robert Kerr, and who, it will be recollected, lost an eye when second lieutenant of the Boston in her action with the Embuscade, was made a commander.

There is a proverb as old as the hills, which tells us, in meaning if not in words, that an indiscreet friend is often more injurious than an avowed enemy. This is completely exemplified in the notice taken by Vice-admiral Lord Keith of Captain Cunningham's exploit in capturing the Vestale. His lordship wrote thus to the admiralty on the occasion: "I have the honour to enclose for their lordships' information, a letter from Captain Cunningham, of H. M. S. Clyde, containing an account of one of the most brilliant transactions which have occurred during the course of the war; he having with great gallantry pursued two French frigates; one of which he has captured, and driven the other into port."

The lords of the admiralty, acting wisely, refrained from publishing this letter; but a biographical writer has since obtained a copy of it, and has, he must excuse us for saying, with less than his usual discrimination, inserted it in his work, with the following additional information: "His late majesty was at one of the theatres, when an account of the above event was brought to him. He immediately stood up in his box, and commanded the news to be communicated to the audience: "when '*Rule Britannia*' was loudly called for from every part of the house, and performed with reiterated applause."*

Before taking our final leave of this action, we deem it but just to set right another contemporary, in his account of the force of the Sagesse. "When the Vestale was first discovered," says Captain Brenton, "her consort of equal force was with her."† Let us first make it clear, that Captain Cunningham was no party to this exaggeration. His words are, "Her consort, the Sagesse, of 30 guns." It so happened, that the British afterward captured this very Sagesse; and she was then found to mount 20 French 8-pounders on the main deck, and eight 4-pounders on the quarterdeck and forecastle. Even this was a greater force than the ship, from her size, could conveniently carry; for she measured only 481 tons, or about half as much as the Vestale.

Our contemporary will be further obliged to us for correcting him in a mistake respecting the tonnage of the Clyde. He says, vol. i., p. 44, "This class (that of the Arethusa) was soon after succeeded by a larger, such as the Artois, Diamond, Diana, Seahorse, and Apollo; these were thirty-eight gun frigates of eleven hundred tons." Now, not one of these five frigates (a sixth, the Jason, has been omitted) measured more than 998 tons. The Clyde and Tamar, built of fir in the year 1796, were

* Marshall, vol. ii., p. 80.

† Brenton, vol. ii., p. 381.

from the same draught: the first measured 1002, and the second 999 tons.

On the 25th of August, in the evening, the British 38-gun frigate Tamar, Captain Thomas Western, being off the island of Surinam, discovered and gave chase to the French 28-gun frigate ("corvette de 24 canons") Républicaine, Captain Pierre-Marie Le Bosec; but the latter, getting into shoal water, where the former, in the darkness of the night, could not follow her, effected her escape. Soon after daylight, however, when about four leagues to the westward of "Orange," the Tamar descried her preceding night's acquaintance in the west-north-west. Chase was instantly given; but, owing to the excellent sailing of the French ship, it took the British frigate until 5 h. 30 m. P.M. before she could get fairly alongside of her opponent. An animated fire then commenced; and, after a close action of about ten minutes' duration, in which the Républicaine was reduced to a mere wreck, the latter struck her colours to the Tamar, whose damages were confined to her rigging and sails.

The Tamar, out of a complement of 281 men and boys, came off with the trifling loss of two seamen wounded; but the loss of the Républicaine, who, having manned two American prizes, had on board only 175 men and boys out of a complement of 220, amounted to nine killed and 12 wounded.

Of the Tamar it is sufficient to say that she was a sister frigate to the Clyde, and armed like her, with 46 guns. The Républicaine, a ship of 580 tons, was precisely of the same class as the Tourterelle, Baïonnaise, and several others named in this work. Her guns were 24 long 8-pounders on the main deck, and eight brass 36-pounder carronades on the quarterdeck and forecastle.

A most decided disparity of force, therefore, existed between these combatants; and it was rendered still more so by the circumstance that the Républicaine's eight brass carronades, from their ill-construction and awkward mode of mounting, could not be used with any effect. A similar complaint, it is true, has been urged against all the French carronades employed during the war of 1793; but, in no other case than the present, did they form so large a portion of the armament. Captain De Bosec, consequently, made quite as creditable a defence as his very inferior force would permit. The Républicaine, owing probably to her age and the cost it would take to repair her damages, was not added to the British navy: indeed, there already belonged to it too many "frigates" of her insignificant class.

On the 9th of September the British ship-sloops Arrow, of twenty-eight 32-pounder carronades, 24 of them on a flush deck,* Captain Nathaniel Portlock, and Wolverine, of 13 guns, already

* For some account of this extraordinary sloop and her sister-vessel, the Dart, see note 2* to Annual Abstract, No. 4.

particularized,* Captain William Bolton, parted company from Vice-admiral Mitchell's squadron, stationed near the Vlieter, in quest of a Batavian republican ship and brig, of which intelligence had just been received. On the same evening, as soon as the ebb tide commenced, the two sloops anchored abreast of the Texel. At the return of flood they got under way; and, in the afternoon of the following day, the 10th, when the tide again ebbed, they anchored on the edge of the flack or flat, abreast of Wieringen. Here it became necessary to lighten the Arrow from 12 feet eight inches to 12 feet. That done, the two sloops, on the 11th, stood over the flack, carrying shoal water from one side to the other.

On the morning of the 12th they again weighed, and as they approached the Vlie-island, saw a ship and brig at anchor in the narrow passage leading from that island to Harlingen. These, as the British ships advanced, displayed Batavian republican colours, and were evidently vessels of some force. The Arrow and Wolverine, having the British and the ancient Dutch colours flying together, stood direct for the enemy; and, when within half gun-shot of the brig, which was the nearest vessel, the Dutch colours were hauled down, and Captain Portlock made the signal to engage, intending the Wolverine to close with the brig, while the Arrow passed on towards the ship.

The Wolverine anchored, in a very masterly manner, at the distance of about 70 yards on the weather quarter of the brig. Having hove on the spring until her broadside could be brought to bear, the Wolverine fired one shot, to try the disposition of her opponent; whereupon the Batavian republican brig Gier, of 14 long 12-pounders and 80 men, fired three guns to leeward and then hauled down her colours. Captain Bolton immediately took possession of his prize, and, agreeably to his orders, sent her pilot to conduct the Arrow to the ship, Captain Portlock's Dutch pilots having declined to take further charge of the vessel.

The Arrow now pushed on towards her opponent, and had to work to windward against a strong tide, which retarded her progress. Meanwhile the enemy's ship, which was the Draak, Captain Lieutenant Van-Esch, mounting two long 32, and 16 long 18 pounders, with six "50-pound" brass howitzers, lay with springs on her cables, so that her broadside was directly opposed to the Arrow; who, from the moment the Draak opened her fire, had to sustain it for 20 minutes, before she could bring a gun to bear in return, and became, in consequence, much cut up in hull, rigging, and sails. At length the Arrow got within 70 or 80 yards of her opponent, and, after taking a proper position, opened her broadside. The contest was maintained, with mutual spirit, for about 15 minutes; when, the Wolverine being

* See p. 314.

nearly up to co-operate with the Arrow, the Draak struck her colours.

The Arrow, out of her 120 men and boys, had one seaman killed, her commander (slightly), one master's mate (William Wilson), and seven seamen wounded. From the Draak's howitzers langridge had probably been fired; as, after the action had ceased, several pieces of iron were picked up on the Arrow's decks. The Draak's loss could not be ascertained with any certainty. Two men killed, and three badly wounded, were found on board; but great quantities of blood, attempted to be concealed from view by tarpaulins, were discovered by Captain Bolton. Some of the prisoners also acknowledged that, immediately as the ship struck, several of her killed and wounded were put into a boat, and sent on shore at Harlingen; close off which place the action had been fought. Moreover the number of prisoners, added to the five killed and wounded by no means agreed with the established complement, 180, as testified by the papers. There were, also, ready to join the two Batavian vessels in the attack, two schooners, and four schuyts, mounting, between them, 16 long 8-pounders, and manned, altogether, by 120 men. But it does not appear that the latter vessels, any more than the Gier brig, offered any resistance.

Having been built for a sheer-hulk, and being extremely old, the Draak was set on fire and destroyed; but the Gier, being a fine new brig, of 324 tons, was carried to England and fitted out as a cruiser.

On the 20th of September, at 4 P.M., as the British armed store-ship, or 44 en flûte, Camel, Captain John Lee, and 16-gun ship-sloop Rattlesnake, Captain Samuel Gooch, with yards and topmasts down and topgallantmasts on deck, were lying at anchor in Algoa bay, near the Cape of Good Hope, the Camel with stores for the use of the army under General Dundas then marching against the Caffres in the interior, a large sail, steering south-west, with the wind fresh from the east-south-east, made her appearance in the east quarter. At this time the two captains were serving on shore with the army; Captain Lee with his first lieutenant, and 30 of the Camel's men, out of her complement of 116 men and boys. The pinnace of the Rattlesnake also, with her second lieutenant, and 15, out of a total of 106 men and boys, was detained on shore by the violence of the surf.

The stranger, which was the French 36-gun frigate Preneuse, Captain L'Hermite, whom, in June of the preceding year we left at Batavia,* continued on her course until 5 P.M.; when she wore, and, hoisting a Danish jack at her mizen peak, stood in for the bay. At 6 P.M., now nearly dark, the Preneuse handed her sails; and, having dropped down till within about 800 yards of the

* See p. 217.

Rattlesnake, brought up, with her broadside bearing upon the latter's larboard beam and bow. At this time the Camel's boat, which was rowing guard, pulled towards the Preneuse, with the intention of boarding her; but, when the boat had got nearly alongside, two men with cutlasses in their hands were observed getting out of the ship's ports. On this, and the additional discovery that the ship was a large frigate, the boat hastened back to the Camel with the intelligence.

In the mean while an English prize-schooner, the Surprise, which, while working out of the bay, had passed close to and been hailed by the Preneuse, had since put back and informed the Rattlesnake, that the stranger was a French frigate. Lieutenant William Fothergill, first of the Rattlesnake, and upon whom, in the absence of both captains and the Camel's first lieutenant, the command of the two vessels had devolved, made the private signal for an enemy to the Camel, and fired a shot under the stern of the Preneuse, as did also the Camel; but of which shots the French frigate took not the slightest notice. Shortly after the firing of these two shots, which took place at about 6 h. 30 m. P.M., the Camel's boat reached the Rattlesnake with the intelligence previously communicated to her by the Surprise; and it was settled that the Camel, when ready to engage, should hoist a light at her mizen peak. Both British ships cleared for action and got springs on their cables.

At 8 h. 30 m. P.M., although the signal of being ready had not been made by the Camel, Lieutenant Fothergill, suspecting by the manœuvres of the Preneuse, in veering away until within about 500 yards of the two British ships, that she intended to board the Rattlesnake, got the broadside of the latter to bear on the French frigate, and immediately opened it upon her. The Camel quickly did the same; and, towards 9 P.M., the Preneuse, substituting a French ensign for the Danish jack, returned the fire of her two opponents, but directed nearly the whole of her guns at the Camel.

In this way the action continued until midnight; when the wind suddenly shifting to north-west, the three ships canted, whereby the Camel, in order to bring her broadside again to bear, was obliged to slip her small-bower cable and veer to two cables on the best bower. Scarcely had this been done, when the carpenter reported that, from a shot received under the magazine, the ship had six feet water in the hold and was making more. In consequence of this the Camel's crew broke off from the guns and manned the pumps.

Fancying, from this suspension of firing on the part of the Camel, that he had effectually silenced her, Captain L'Hermite now devoted his principal attention to the Rattlesnake; upon whom the Preneuse continued a heavy cannonade until 3 h. 30 m. A.M. on the 21st. The French frigate, then, to the surprise of the British both afloat and on shore, ceased firing, cut or slipped her cable, and ran off before the wind to a distant part of the bay. Here the Preneuse again anchored, and continued there until a few minutes before 10 A.M.; when the French frigate got under way, and leaving her anchor and cable, from which she had, in the first instance, cut or slipped, as a trophy to her two opponents, stood to the south-west on the starboard tack, under her courses and main topsail only, as if damaged in her masts.

The Camel's fore and mizen masts, main yard, and maintopsail yard, were wounded, her rigging a good deal cut, and her hull struck in several places. Her loss, notwithstanding, amounted to no more, out of the 101 men and boys she had on board, than six men wounded. The Rattlesnake had her main and mizen masts, main topmast, and bowsprit wounded, some immaterial injury to her rigging, and eight shot-holes between wind and water; with the loss, out of 92 men and boys on board, of her carpenter and one seaman killed, another mortally, and six or seven slightly wounded.

The disparity of force in this case will be evident when we state, that the Preneuse was a frigate mounting 40 guns, 12 and 6 pounders, with a crew of about 300 men; and that the Camel, mounted 20 long 9 and four long 6 pounders, and the Rattlesnake, 16 long 6-pounders and a few 12-pounder carronades, with on board the two ships, a total of only 193 men. Great credit was therefore due to Lieutenants Fothergill and Charles Shaw, which latter commanded the Camel, and to their respective officers and crews for their persevering defence. Nor must we omit to state, that Captains Lee and Gooch made several attempts to get from the shore to their ships in time to participate in the action; but the surf was so high, that no boat could be got off the beach. In almost every effort that was made, the boat, with the two captains on board, upset, and the crew with difficulty escaped drowning.

To specify the damage or loss sustained by the Preneuse, in this to her somewhat discreditable encounter, is not in our power, the historian, who has hitherto assisted us in recording the exploits of Captain L'Hermite in the Indian seas, having stopped short of the latter's adventure in Algoa bay: and that although "Désastres et revers" form a part of the promised matter of his book. This is the more extraordinary, as with the Camel's two rows of ports, if not of guns, and the Rattlesnake's three masts, and detached quarterdeck, a case might have been made out, such as a French writer need not have been afraid to publish, nor a French reader of the most sensitive kind displeased to peruse.

The apparently crippled state of the Preneuse as she stood out of Algoa bay, and the south-westerly course steered by her when last seen, affording a reasonable hope of her being overtaken by any ship, that, not being in the unprepared state of either the

Camel or Rattlesnake, could be speedily despatched after her, Captain Lee sent an express overland to Captain George Losack, the senior British officer in Table bay. On what day the messenger arrived, or whether he arrived at all, we cannot say; but on the 1st of October the British 50-gun ship Jupiter, Captain William Granger, acting in the absence (through sickness, we presume) of Captain Losack, sailed from Table bay, and on the 8th joined the Camel and Rattlesnake at Algoa bay.

On the next day, the 9th, the Jupiter weighed and made sail in quest of the Preneuse. On the 10th, in the afternoon, latitude 34° 41' south, longitude 27° 54' east, while running before a strong gale from the north-west by west, the Jupiter descried, and immediately stood towards, a ship in the north-east. As the Jupiter approached her, the ship, which was no other than the Preneuse herself, bore away to north-east, and made all sail to escape, followed by the British 50.

At 9 P.M. the Jupiter fired a shot at the Preneuse, which the latter, hoisting French colours, returned by a fire from her sternchasers. As it could not be owing to the Jupiter's good sailing, it was, in all probability, owing to the crippled state of the Preneuse, that the Jupiter soon got near enough to discharge her maindeck guns at the French frigate: her lowerdeck guns, although of double the caliber, it was found impossible to use, the turbulent state of the sea, and the little height allowable to such small-sized two-deckers, not admitting the opening of the ports. A running fight was thus kept up between the British 50 and French frigate during the whole of the night, and until 2 P.M. on the next day; when the Jupiter succeeded in bringing the Preneuse to close action.

Although the weather was now moderate, the sea was still so high that, on opening the lowerdeck ports to get the 24-pounders into play, the water rushed in in such quantity, that the ports were obliged to be shut again; and the Jupiter had to continue the action with her 12-pounders only. The consequence was, that, before the British 50 could produce any serious effect upon the French frigate, the latter had shot away the greater part of the former's running rigging, and badly wounded her fore and main masts: some loss, we believe, had also been inflicted, but its amount we are unable to state. In short, the Jupiter found it necessary to bear away to repair her damages; and the Preneuse, satisfied with having beaten off an antagonist whom it would perhaps have been dangerous to press too closely, hauled to the wind on the starboard tack under all the sail she could carry, and effected her escape. The Preneuse's opponent, as soon as she had spliced her ropes and secured her masts, made sail also, but it was only to return to the port she had quitted on this unfortunate mission; and on or about the 16th the discomfited Jupiter reanchored in Table bay.

This was a bad business certainly; and, as no court of inquiry, to our knowledge, was held, we are unable to give a satisfactory explanation of the cause that may have led to it. Were the facts all made known, perhaps they would exonerate the Jupiter's officers and crew from every particle of blame. Undoubtedly it was a cause of just triumph to Captain l'Hermite, and well calculated to wipe away the disgrace incurred by the Preneuse at Algoa bay; yet not a French writer, that we can discover, has touched upon the subject.

The Preneuse continued her cruise, but it proved her last. On the 11th of December, in the forenoon, the British 74-gun ship Tremendous, Captain John Osborn, and 50-gun ship Adamant, Captain William Hotham, cruising off Port-Louis in the Isle of France, discovered and chased the Preneuse; who, finding it impossible to escape from the Adamant, ran herself on shore on the west side of the river Tombeau, about three miles from Port-Louis, and near to some batteries. At 3 P.M. the frigate cut away all her masts, and at 3 h. 30 m. P.M., in conjunction with the batteries, opened a fire upon the Adamant, who was using every exertion to work up to her. At 5 h. 30 m. P.M. the latter opened a fire in return; and, in about 15 minutes afterwards, the Preneuse hauled in her ensign from the quarter as a signal of submission: whereupon the Adamant discontinued the action.

After a communication between the two British captains, Captain Osborn consented that two boats of the Adamant and one of the Tremendous should be sent in to attempt to destroy the French frigate. Accordingly at 7 P.M., one 12, and two six-oared cutters, containing about 35 men, and placed under the orders of Lieutenant Edward Grey, first of the Adamant, assisted by Lieutenant John Walker, and Lieutenant of marines, John Owen, of the same ship, and Lieutenant Benjamin Symes of the Tremendous, put off from the Adamant, to execute the service intrusted to them.

At about 8 P.M., the French batteries began firing shots and shells at the boats and at the Adamant, who was still working up towards the object of attack. At about 9 P.M., just as the boats were getting alongside of the Preneuse, two of her launches filled with men, pulled from her towards the shore. Shortly afterwards Lieutenant Grey and his party, under a heavy fire still kept up from the batteries, gallantly boarded the French frigate. Having removed Captain L'Hermite, 14 or 15 other officers, and a few men, all that remained in her, and, greatly to Lieutenant Grey's credit, saved as much as possible of the private property belonging to them, Lieutenant Grey set fire to and destroyed the Preneuse, and returned to the Adamant without the loss of a man.

That the commanding officer in this gallant and well-executed boat-attack should not have been rewarded with promotion savours of injustice; but we shall by and by come to a case, in which Lieutenant Grey's claims were still stronger, and yet, we regret to say, were overlooked.

On the 3d of October, the 14-gun brig-sloop Speedy, still commanded by Captain Jahleel Brenton, while running through the gut of Gibraltar, observed several small vessels coming out of Algesiras, apparently to molest a British convoy then in sight. Determined to defeat their plans, the Speedy stood towards them, and soon discovered that they were not, as at first supposed, Spanish gun-boats but Spanish coasters, eight in number, under the protection of an armed cutter and schooner.

In a short time, two of the coasters, finding themselves nearly overtaken by the Speedy, ran under the guns of a castle; a prompt fire from which prevented Captain Brenton from bringing them off. The Speedy, accordingly, stood on in chase, and at 4 P.M., having passed under the shot of Tariffa castle, came up with four others, just entering a bay to the eastward of Cape Trafalgar. One of the vessels immediately anchored under a fort, and the three others under an old ruinous castle that appeared only to have one gun mounted.

As it blew very heavy from the eastward, and the Speedy in consequence was upon a lee shore, the brig could not with safety approach nearer than 900 yards. Having here come to an anchor, the Speedy opened her fire upon the castle and the vessels; and in a short time, as the castle made no return, compelled the Spaniards to abandon their vessels, after cutting their cables that they might drift on shore. Captain Brenton immediately sent Lieutenant Richard William Parker, with the boats, to endeavour to bring off or destroy the vessels. Owing to the heavy surf that broke over them, it was found impracticable either to get them afloat or set them on fire. At a considerable risk, however, the British succeeded in boarding the vessels and brought away or destroyed their fire-arms; leaving the vessels themselves, two of which were valuably laden, full of water and complete wrecks.

It was not long ere Captain Brenton, in his little 4-pounder brig, met with a fleet of more worthy antagonists; such as would undoubtedly have overpowered the Speedy, had they possessed a tithe of the spirit which animated her officers and crew. On the 6th of November, at 3 P.M., while the Speedy was lying to off Europa point, to await the coming up of her convoy from the Tagus, consisting of the transport ship Unity, George Robinson, master, with wine for the British fleet, and a merchant brig bound to Trieste, 12 Spanish gun-boats, two of which were schooners carrying two long 24-pounders and 50 men each, and the remainder lateen-rigged vessels with one 24 and 40 men each, bore down from Algesiras to attack the Speedy and get possession of her convoy.

Having sent his despatches on shore, Captain Brenton, at 3 h. 30 m. P.M., commenced firing on the gun-boats as they advanced towards the merchant brig; but the latter, covered by the Speedy's fire, bore up to the eastward and effected her escape. At 5 P.M., finding themselves foiled in their attempts upon the brig, the gun-boats bore up to capture the ship. The Speedy bore up also; and, passing through the midst of the gun-boats, near enough to carry away a part of their oars, poured in from both sides so well directed a fire of cannon and musketry, that the Spaniards fled in confusion. At 6 P.M. the Unity, who, notwithstanding that she had been exposed to a galling fire, had manœuvred with skill and steadiness, was out of danger; and at 6 h. 30 m P.M. the gun-boats ran for shelter under the guns of Fort Barbary.

In this very gallant exploit on the part of Captain Brenton, who in his official letter bestows much praise upon Lieutenant Parker, Mr. Marshall the master, and the remainder of his officers and brig's company, the Speedy had most of her running rigging shot away, her maintopsail yard shot through, and her fore rigging much cut: she had also received so many shot in her hull below the water-line, that the water was up to her lower deck. With this serious damage, the loss on board the Speedy amounted to no more than two seamen killed and one wounded.

Being, on account of the shot-holes in her larboard side, and the direction of the wind, which blew strong from the westward, unable to enter Gibraltar, the Speedy ran for Tetuan bay; where on the 7th, at 2 A.M., she came to an anchor, and commenced stopping her numerous leaks. The Spanish gun-boats are represented to have lost 11 men killed, besides several wounded; and four of the gun-boats, it appears, were seen from the rock of Gibraltar to strike to the Speedy.

Having rendered herself seaworthy, the Speedy stood across the Strait, and anchored at Gibraltar. The following account of what followed we extract from a contemporary work, but must preface it by stating, that the account of the Speedy's action with the gun-boats is the most confused and imperfect of any that has been published. Indeed, according to Captain Brenton, his brother sustained two separate attacks, on different days; but, upon the authority of the Speedy's log, one only occurred. "The captain and crew," says our contemporary, "were much out of humour with General O'Hara, the governor; but when Captain Brenton waited on him, his excellency thus addressed him: 'I conclude, sir, you think I have treated you very ill in not affording you assistance, but I have made arrangements with the governor of Algesiras, to prevent this town being kept in a constant alarm and annoyance by the Spanish gun-boats, which in consequence are never to be fired on from the rock. There is the copy of a letter which I have written to the admiralty, and I most sincerely wish you may obtain your promotion.' The letter was so handsomely worded, that the captain could say nothing about the transaction of the preceding night, and shortly afterwards he was promoted to the rank of post-captain."*

The Speedy's vigorous attack had created such a panic on board the gun-boats, that they remained three days under Fort Barbary, and then bore up for Malaga, instead of standing across to Algesiras; thus leaving the trade through the Straits unmolested for two months, at the end of which, the Spaniards, having recovered from their alarm, managed to get back to their port.

Among the many weary hours to which a naval life is subject, none surely can equal those passed on board a stationary flagship; especially in a port where there is a constant egress and regress of cruisers, some sailing forth to seek prizes, others returning with prizes already in their possession. During the whole of the year 1797, and the greater part of 1798, the 54-gun ship, Abergavenny, as she lay moored in Port-Royal harbour, Jamaica, daily exposed her officers and men to these tantalizing torments. At length it was suggested, that a small tender, sent off the east end of the island, or even into Cow bay, scarcely out of sight of the harbour, might acquire for the parent-ship some share of the honours that were reaping by the cruisers around her. A 38-gun frigate's launch having been obtained, and armed with a swivel in the bow, the next difficulty was, to find an officer who, to a willingness, could add the other requisites, for so perilous and uncomfortable a service. It was not every man who would like to be cramped up night and day in an open boat, exposed to all kinds of weather, as well as to the risk of being captured by some of the many picaroons that infested the coast.

An acting lieutenant of the Abergavenny, one, on whom nature had conferred an ardent mind, habit, an indifference about personal comfort, and 18 or 20 years of active service, an experience in all the duties of his profession, cheerfully consented to take charge of the cruiser-boat. Mr. Michael Fitton soon gave proofs of his fitness for the task he had undertaken; and the crew of the Abergavenny could now and then greet a prize of their own, among the many that dropped anchor near them. With a part of the funds that a succession of prizes had brought to the ship, a decked vessel was at length purchased: with the fruits of her gains, another; and so on, until the schooner, whose little exploit we are now about to record, came, in her turn, to be the Abergavenny's tender.

On the 5th of October, the schooner Ferret, mounting six 3-pounders, with a crew of 45 men and boys, and commanded by acting Lieutenant Michael Fitton, while cruising off the north-east end of Jamaica, discovered a larger schooner, with eight

* Brenton, vol. ii., p. 490.

ports of a side, and an English ensign and pendant, bearing down upon her. Judging from the immense size of the ensign and length of the pendant (one large enough for a line-of-battle ship, and the other longer than was worn by any British man of war), that she was an enemy's cruiser, Lieutenant Fitton tacked to speak her. Resolved, at the same time, with such apparent odds against him, to try for the weathergage, he trimmed his sails as if close hauled, and yet edged a little off the wind, to induce the schooner, who had now substituted Spanish for English colours, to come into the tender's wake. Having at length got her there, the latter hauled up, and soon weathered the Spaniard.

A brisk action now commenced, and lasted for half an hour; when the privateer sheered off, and made sail. Lieutenant Fitton immediately proceeded in chase, and at 11 P.M., with the help of her sweeps, the Ferret again got alongside of the privateer. The action was now renewed, and continued as long as before; when the tender, having had her rigging and sails much cut, and being close in with San-Jago de Cuba, gave over the chase. On account of the privateer's firing high, the Ferret incurred no loss; but it was afterwards ascertained, by the capture of some of the men belonging to the same privateer, that the latter had 11 men killed and 20 wounded, out of a crew of 100, and that she mounted fourteen 6-pounders. The inhabitants of the east end of Jamaica were spectators of the contest; and, seeing the disparity of force between the two vessels, and that the British vessel followed the privateer towards the Cuba shore, sent information to Port-Royal, that the Abergavenny's tender had been captured.

It is not the sole misfortune under which the commanding officer of a tender labours, that, while he incurs all the risk, and all the responsibility, he only shares prize-money as one of the lieutenants of the flag-ship: the case is harder where that flagship remains idle in port, otherwise the prizes she might make by cruising would perhaps afford to the tender's commander a counterbalancing advantage. Another misfortune, and one more sensibly felt by an enterprising officer, is, that his little skirmishes with enemy's privateers, unless he takes a vessel which the admiral or the captain of the flag-ship wishes to have purchased into the service, or that some relative or protégé of the admiral or captain is on board the tender, are seldom noticed. Desirous as we have been to get at all these cases, we are satisfied that there are many, highly creditable to the parties concerned, of which the public are yet in ignorance.

On the 11th of October, at 7 h. 30 m. A.M., the British 38-gun frigate Révolutionnaire, Captain Thomas Twysden, cruising off the coast of Ireland in a heavy gale from the south-south-west, discovered to leeward and immediately chased a strange ship; which, at 5 P.M., after a run of 114 miles in the nine hours and a half, hauled down her colours without, as it appears, making any resistance, and proved to be the French privateer Bordelais, of Bordeaux, an extraordinary fine ship, mounting 24 guns on a flush deck, 16 of them long brass 12-pounders, and the remainder brass 36-pounder carronades, with a complement of 202 men.

The Bordelais was of very large dimensions, measuring 625 tons, and was esteemed one of the fastest sailing privateers out of France. This was only her second cruise: in her former one she had taken 29 valuable prizes. It was a singular coincidence, not merely that the Bordelais was constructed by the same builder who had constructed the Révolutionnaire, but that the builder, at a splendid dinner given by the owners of the Bordelais to her officers soon after the termination of her first trip, should have said, "England has not a cruiser that will ever touch her except the Révolutionnaire; and, should she ever fall in with that frigate in blowing weather, and be under her lee, she will be taken."* The Bordelais was added to the British navy by the same name, and established with 22 carronades, 32-pounders, and two long nines, and a complement of 195 men and boys.

On the 12th of October, at 10 P.M., the British ship-sloop Trincomalé, of 16 guns, probably 6-pounders, and about 100 men and boys, Captain John Rowe, cruising in the Straits of Babelmandel, fell in with the French ship privateer Iphigénie, of 22 guns (16 long 8 and 6 pounders, and four 36-pounder brass carronades), Captain Mabroux. A smart engagement immediately ensued, and was warmly maintained for two hours, when the combatants fell on board each other. Captain Mabroux, placing great confidence in the number of his crew, had had the Iphigénie's studdingsail-booms rigged out, and grappling irons placed at their extremities, ready to board; when, suddenly, the Trincomalé, by some accident, blew up, leaving alive of her officers and crew only one seaman and one lascar.

As the ships at the time of the explosion, touched each other, the shock stove in the side of the privateer, and forced the main and mizen masts clear out of her. In a very few minutes the Iphigénie went down, and with her, about 115 officers and men. The remainder of the French crew, consisting of about 30 or 35, saved themselves on pieces of the wreck. Several of the crew of the Pearl Indiaman, which the Iphigénie had taken on the 7th of the month, and was in company and being engaged by the Comet Company's cruiser, perished in her. Owing to some unexplained cause, the Pearl escaped from the Comet, and reached the Isle of France in safety.

On the 14th of October the British 18-gun ship-sloop Echo,

* Marshall, vol. ii., p. 205.

Captain Robert Philpot, cruising off Porto-Rico, chased into Lagnadille bay, at the north-west end of the island, the French letter-of-marque brig Buonoparte, carrying twelve 4-pounders and 30 men, commanded by citizen Pierre Martin, enseigne de vaisseau. Seeing several vessels at anchor in the bay, Captain Philpot, on the 15th, sent the pinnace and jollyboat, under the command of Lieutenants Charles Frederick Napier and John James Rorie, to attempt to cut some of them out. The boats arrived too late to effect their purpose, but were fortunate enough to capture a Spanish brig, from Canana, in South America, to Old Spain, laden with cocoa and indigo, and mounting two 4-pounders, with 20 men.

On the 16th, in the evening, the same two boats, now commanded by Lieutenant Napier and Mr. Wood the boatswain, and containing between them 16 men, officers included, pulled into the bay to cut out what they could. On the 17th, at about 2 A.M., the boats arrived at the anchorage; where they found the brig which they had chased in on the 14th, moored within half a cable's length of the shore, with her broadside presented to the sea, and protected by two field-pieces, and by one 18-pounder and some smaller carriage-guns, placed on the beach.

In spite of this formidable preparation, the British in the boats did not hesitate an instant, but boarded the Buonaparte on the bow, the French and Spaniards, who were all upon deck with matches lighted and guns primed, making the best of their way down the hatchways. By the time the boats' crews had cut the cables of their prize, the guns on the beach opened a fire on them. The third shot sank the pinnace, while she was ahead towing the jollyboat, but not a man in her was hurt. The Buonaparte was several times hulled; but, a light breeze springing up from the land, her captors soon escaped with her out of gun-shot.

The prize was a fine copper-bottomed American-built brig, and had on board a valuable cargo, which she was carrying to Curaçoa. When the disparity of force is considered, the successful issue of the attack must be pronounced highly creditable to Lieutenant Napier and Mr. Wood, and the few seamen they commanded; fewer than would have been sent, had Captain Philpot been aware of the force and preparation of the enemy. It is due to justice to state, that M. Martin, at the time his vessel surrendered, was not on board of her: he was on shore, lending his aid at the battery.

On the 15th of October, at 8 P.M., in latitude 44° 1' north, longitude 12° 35' west, the British 38-gun frigate Naiad, Captain William Pierrepont, discovered and chased two frigates; which at midnight were ascertained to be enemies, and which were, in fact, the Spanish 34-gun frigates Santa-Brigida, Captain Don Antonio Pillon, and Thetis, Captain Don Juan de Mendoza, from

Vera-Cruz, with a cargo of specie, bound to any port in Spain which they could fetch, and now steering to the south-east with the wind right aft.

Regardless of the apparent odds against her, the Naiad continued the pursuit under all sail, and, at 3 h. 30 m. A.M.,* on the 16th, discovered a third large ship in the south-west; which soon made herself known as the 38-gun frigate Ethalion, Captain James Young, and who, bearing up, joined in the chase. Just as the day broke the British 12-pounder 32-gun frigate Alcmène, Captain Henry Digby, joined from the westward; and shortly afterwards the 12-pounder 32-gun frigate Triton, Captain John Gore, made her appearance astern.

At 7 A.M. the two Spanish frigates, for their safety, took different routes: on which Captain Pierrepont, who was the senior officer, directed the leading British frigate, the Ethalion, to pass the sternmost frigate, and stand on for the headmost, which was the Thetis. At 9 A.M. the Ethalion, being within random-shot of the Santa-Brigida, fired a few guns at her in passing, and compelled her to steer a course still further from her consort. The Ethalion then, as she had been ordered, continued in chase of the Thetis, and owing to her good sailing gained upon her so, that at 11 h. 30 m. A.M. the Thetis, having no other alternative, bore up athwart the bows of the Ethalion, at the distance of only half musket-shot. The British frigate quickly wore, and bestowed upon her opponent two well-directed broadsides. At length, after a running fight of one hour, in which the Ethalion had not a man hurt, and the Thetis no more than one killed and nine wounded, the latter hauled down her colours.

The Thetis had on board specie to the following amount: 333 boxes containing each 3000 dollars, four boxes containing each 2385 dollars, 93 boxes containing each 4000 dollars, one box containing, besides 4000 dollars, two doubloons and 90 half-doubloons, of gold; making, altogether, 1,385,292 dollars, equal, at 4*s.* 6*d.* the dollar, to 311,690l. sterling.

The Santa-Brigida, when she altered her course, as related above, bore up to the southward, and, early on the morning of the 17th,† succeeded by her fast sailing in rounding Cape Finisterre. To accomplish this, the Santa-Brigida had run so close to the rocks off Monte Lora, that at 5 A.M. the Triton, who was the first in pursuit, and then going at the rate of seven knots, struck upon them. The Triton, however, soon got off; and at 7 A.M. commenced an animated fire at the Spanish frigate; the Alcmène doing the same, and steering so as to cut

* The gazette-account is rendered somewhat obscure by this being made "P.M."

† In the Naiad's log, but 18th in Captain Pierrepont's letter; in which, also, the first appearance of the two Spanish frigates is stated to have been "on the evening of the 16th," as was the case *by log*, the 16th, by this silly and perplexing custom (long since abolished), commencing at noon on the 15th.

off the Santa-Brigida, who had just before thrown overboard her anchors and boats, from Port de Vidre. At 8 A.M. the three British frigates closed with the Spanish frigate amidst the rocks of Commarurto at the entrance of Muros; whereupon the Santa-Brigida, after a brave resistance, preceded by the most skilful efforts to escape, hauled down her colours.

The Triton had one seaman wounded, and received considerable damage from striking on the rocks. The Alcmène had one seaman killed, and one petty officer and eight seamen wounded. The Naiad did not get near enough to sustain any loss; nor had the Santa-Brigida herself any more than two seamen killed and eight wounded.

All four ships were over foul ground; but, a breeze springing up from the shore, they were enabled to put their heads to the sea. While the prisoners were exchanging, four large ships, one with a broad pendant, came out of Vigo, as if with the intention of attacking the British frigates. The latter immediately got ready to receive them; but the Spaniards, owing to some unexplained cause, suddenly put back to their port.

On the 21st the Thetis, and on the following day the Santa-Brigida, in company with the frigates which had captured them, arrived at Plymouth. The cargo of the Santa-Brigida consisted of two bales or serons of indigo, 26 of cochineal, 23 of cocoa, and 16 of sugar, of the estimated value, altogether, of about 5000*l*. This frigate had also 446 boxes, containing each 3000 dollars, 59 bags of dollars, and many others of uncertain number, and three kegs likewise uncertain. Neither the Santa-Brigida nor the Thetis were considered eligible for the British navy: their chief and almost only value was in the cargoes they carried.

As some readers may feel an interest in these matters, we will show how the treasure was subsequently disposed of. On the 28th and 29th, the days on which the two cargoes were landed, 63 artillery wagons, escorted by horse and foot soldiers and armed seamen and marines, and accompanied by bands of music and an immense concourse of people, conveyed the treasures to the dungeons of the citadel of Plymouth. Thence, towards the latter end of November, it was removed to London, with all the pomp and ceremony usual on such occasions, and was finally deposited in the bank of England. The share of prize-money which each class received for the Spanish frigates, exclusive of the value of their hulls, stores, masts, &c., appears to have been as follows:

	£	*s.*	*d.*
Captains .... each,	40,730	18	0
Lieutenants .... each,	5091	7	3
Warrant-officers .... each,	2468	10	9½
Midshipmen, &c. .... each,	791	17	0¼
Seamen and marines .... each,	182	4	9¼

One could wish that, in cases of this kind, it were the practice to give the officers of the captured ships a portion, at least, of the freight that they probably would have received from their own government, had they carried home the treasure with which their ships were laden. Its comparatively small amount would scarcely be felt by one party, and yet might contribute greatly to the relief of the other.

On the 20th of October, at 5 P.M., Cape Ortugal bearing south-west, distant eight or nine leagues, the British 18-pounder 32-gun frigate Cerberus, Captain James Macnamara, discovered a fleet to windward, which proved to be a Spanish convoy of 80 vessels, in charge of the 40-gun frigate Ceres (18-pounders), and 34-gun frigates Diana, Esmeralda, Mercedas, and another, and two brig-corvettes, bound to the north-east coast of Spain. Undismayed at their formidable appearance, the Cerberus immediately stood towards them, and at 8 P.M., having approached to windward of and hailed a frigate who was ahead and somewhat detached from her convoy, commenced the action; and that at such close quarters, that the two ships almost touched each other.

Not dreaming of an enemy so near, the Spanish frigate seemed more desirous to join her consorts to leeward than to engage the Cerberus, and consequently returned but feebly the latter's fire. The instant the Spanish frigate made sail, the Cerberus, to frustrate her intention of joining her consorts, wore round, and engaged her to leeward. By 8 h. 30 m. P.M., the Cerberus had silenced the fire of her opponent, but was prevented from taking possession of her, by the near approach of the four other frigates. At 9 P.M., on hauling up to avoid being raked, the Cerberus fell on board the leading frigate of those advancing, and carried away the latter's maintopsail yard. This fresh frigate, replacing the one which had been so beaten, now opened her fire on the Cerberus, and a smart cannonade ensued between them. Soon afterwards a third frigate took part in the action, and the Cerberus had frequently to fire both broadsides at once.

At 9 h. 30 m., P.M. Captain Macnamara deeming it time to consult the safety of his ship, the Cerberus wore, and endeavoured to get clear of her numerous foes; by whom, at 10 h. 30 m. P.M., she was nearly surrounded. The Cerberus very soon afterwards hauled to the wind, and effected her escape. At 11 P.M. she captured a brig, one of the convoy; but, as the Spanish frigates were within a mile of her, the Cerberus was obliged to be contented with setting the brig on fire; a service which Lieutenant Hassard Stackpoole, in spite of a strong wind and heavy sea, promptly executed.

The damages of the Cerberus were confined to her sails and rigging, and her loss amounted to only four men wounded. This was attributed to the state of confusion in which the Spanish frigates were; some of whom are represented to have fired, towards the latter part of the engagement, whole broadsides without shot. Had the 38-gun frigate Arethusa, Captain Thomas Wolley, who had parted company from the Cerberus only the preceding day, been present, the obviously unprepared state of the five Spanish frigates renders it probable, that two of them, at least, would have been carried off by the British.

We have already given an account of the horrid manner in which the British 12-pounder 32 gun frigate Hermione came into the hands of the Spaniards at La Guayra, a fortified seaport of Terra-Firma.* The Spaniards afterwards repaired and fitted for sea their shamefully acquired prize. In the British service the Hermione, a ship of 715 tons, had mounted, with her carronades, 38 guns; but the Spaniards, it appears, gave her 44; to do which, they must have cut at least four additional ports. Her complement had been 220. That was increased to 321, exclusive of a detachment of soldiers and artillery-men numbering 72; and the command of the frigate, thus strongly armed and manned, was given to Don Raimond de Chalas.

In the month of September, 1799, intelligence reached Admiral Sir Hyde Parker, the British commander-in-chief at the island of Jamaica, that the Hermione was about to sail from Puerto-Cabello, whence she had recently arrived from Aux-Cayes in the island of St.-Domingo, bound, through the channel between the island of Aruba and Cape San-Roman, to Havana. For the purpose of intercepting the Spanish frigate in this her voyage, the admiral detached from Port-Royal, on the 20th of the month, the 28-gun frigate Surprise, Captain Edward Hamilton. This ship had been the French "24-gun corvette" Unité, and mounted, when captured by the Inconstant frigate, in April, 1796, 32 guns. On being fitted out in the British service, the Surprise was made a 28-gun frigate, and armed with 24 carronades, 32-pounders, on her main deck, and eight carronades, 18-pounders, with two, if not four long fours or sixes, on the quarterdeck and forecastle: total, at the least, 34 guns. Her net complement, like that of her class, was 197 men and boys. Although a ship of only 579 tons, the Surprise was fitted with a 36-gun frigate's mainmast, but with the fore and mizen masts of a 28. This was a plan of Captain Hamilton's; and, thus rigged, the Surprise appears not to have been complained of as a sailer.

It appears that Captain Hamilton proposed to Sir Hyde Parker at Jamaica, to attempt the cutting out of the Hermione if the commander-in-chief would add a barge and 20 men to the crew of the Surprise; but Sir Hyde thought the service too desperate and refused the request. The next morning Captain Hamilton sailed under sealed orders to be opened off the east end of Jamaica. Arriving there, Captain Hamilton found directions to proceed off Cape Della-Vella, on the Spanish main,

* See p. 103.

a point of land about 60 or 80 leagues to leeward of Puerto-Cabello, in which port the Hermione was anchored. The orders further instructed Captain Hamilton to remain off the Cape as long as his provisions, wood, and water would allow, and to endeavour to intercept he Hermione, supposed to be bound to the Havana. Accordingly Captain Hamilton proceeded to his station, and there remained several weeks. When finding his provisions growing short, and not certain but that the Hermione might have eluded his vigilance during the night, he resolved before he returned to Jamaica, to ascertain if the frigate was still in Puerto Cabello, and accordingly he worked to windward for that purpose.

On the 21st of October, in the evening, the Surprise arrived off the harbour of Puerto-Cabello, and discovered the Hermione moored head and stern between two strong batteries situated at the entrance of the harbour, said to mount nearly 200 guns, with her sails bent and ready for sea.

Captain Hamilton having stood within gun-shot of the enemy on the 21st of October, continued off and until the evening of the 24th, he never having mentioned one word of his intentions to any officer onboard the ship until that evening after his dinner, when he detailed his plans to the officers present, and desired them to second his wishes when he addressed the ship's company. After quarters, the hands were sent aft, and Captain Hamilton reminded his crew of the frequent successful enterprises they had undertaken, concluded a stirring address, nearly thus: "I find it useless to wait any longer; we shall soon be obliged to leave the station, and that frigate will become the prize of some more fortunate ship than the Surprise; our only prospect of success is by cutting her out this night." (Three tremendous cheers convinced Captain Hamilton that his men would follow him and were eager for the service.) "I shall lead you myself," he continued, "and here are the orders for the six boats to be employed, with the names of the officers and men to be engaged in this service."

The crews were instantly mustered, and every thing placed in readiness for the service. Every man was to be dressed in blue, and no white of any kind to be seen. The pass-word was Britannia; the answer, Ireland. At half-past seven the boats were hoisted out, the crews mustered, and all prepared. The boarders were to take the first spell at the oars, to be relieved as they neared the Hermione by the regular crews, proceeding in two divisions; the first consisting of the pinnace launch and jolly-boat, to board on the starboard (or inside) bow, gangway and quarter; the second division, consisting of the gig, black and red cutters, to board on the outside or larboard bow, gangway and quarter. The captain to command in the pinnace, having with him the gunner, Mr. John Maxwell, one midshipman, and sixteen men. The launch, under the orders of Lieutenant Wilson, contained one midshipman and twenty-four men: the jolly-boat to contain one midshipman, the carpenter, and eight men; these boats composed the first division. The pinnace was to board on the starboard gangway, the launch on the starboard bow; to retain three men who were to cut the bower cable, for which purpose a platform was erected over her quarter, and sharp axes provided. The jollyboat to board on the starboard quarter, to cut the stern cable, and to send two men aloft to loose the mizen topsail. The gig, with sixteen men, to board on the larboard bow, under the directions of Mr. John M'Mullen the surgeon, to send four men aloft to loose the fore topsail, and to take good care to cut the bunt-lines and clew-lines, and to foot the sail well clear of the top rim. The black cutter, under the command of Lieutenant Hamilton (no relation whatever to the captain), with the acting marine officer, M. de la Tour du Pin, and with 16 men in all, to board on the larboard gangway. The red cutter under the command of the boatswain, and containing likewise 16 men, to board on the larboard quarter. Each division to be in tow. The concluding orders to the whole six being, that in the event of reaching the ship undiscovered, only the boarders were to board; the crews to remain in the boats, and take the ship in tow directly the cables were cut, hook ropes being provided for such emergency. If, however, the enemy, always watchful when an adversary was near, should be prepared, and see the advancing boats, and thus destroy any favourable approach, then the crews of each boat were to board, and each man lend his best aid in the perilous enterprise. The rendezvous to be on the Hermione's quarterdeck. Such were the orders of Captain Hamilton – clear, impossible to be mistaken, and yet not so conclusive as to have rendered a failure improbable; nay, a circumstance did arise which nearly frustrated the whole.

From the moment of quitting the Surprise, till the Hermione was boarded, Captain Hamilton never lost sight of her for a moment – he stood up in the pinnace with his night-glass, by the aid of which he steered a direct course towards the frigate. When within a mile of the Hermione the advancing boats were discovered by two gun-boats armed with a long gun each. The instant the English were discovered, the alarm was given, and the firing commenced. Captain Hamilton instantly cut off the tow, gave three cheers, and pushed for the frigate, concluding that all would do the same, and that the concentrated force might reach the Hermione at one moment, leaving the Spanish gun-boats, as too trifling an opposition when so much was at stake; but in this idea Captain Hamilton was deceived, for some of the boats immediately engaged the gun-boats, and by this disobedience of orders nearly caused the failure of the gallant enterprise.

The alarm created by the firing, soon awakened the crew of the Hermione to the meditated attack. Lights were seen at every port, and the ship's company were at quarters, ready for immediate service. On the pinnace crossing the frigate's bows in order to reach her station, a shot was fired from the forecastle, which passed over her, whilst a rope which ran from the bows of the Hermione, to the buoy over her anchor, caught the rudder of the pinnace, and stopped her. The coxswain reported the boat *aground*; but Captain Hamilton knew that to be impossible, as the frigate was evidently afloat; he desired the coxswain therefore to unship the rudder, but as the starboard oars of the pinnace touched the bends of the Hermione, Captain Hamilton gave the orders to lay in the oars and board, the boat being then under the starboard cat-head and fore chains, laying head and stern with the frigate. The crew obeyed the word instantly, and the captain would have been the first on board, but from some mud on the anchor, which was hanging from the cat and shank painter, and which had been weighed that day, his foot slipped, but he retained his hold on the foremost lanyard of the fore-shrouds, by which he recovered himself, his pistol going off in the struggle. Having succeeded in gaining a footing on the forecastle, the English freed the foresail ready for bending and hauling out to the yardarms, laying over the forestay, and this served for an excellent screen to these few daring men now aboard. On advancing to the break of the forecastle, the English were much astonished to find the crew of the Hermione at quarters on the main deck, and firing at some object which their fears had magnified into two frigates coming to attack them, and still unconscious that the enemy was actually on board. Not so those on the quarterdeck, who, when Captain Hamilton, the gunner, and fourteen men pushed on the starboard gangway, having cleared the forecastle, prepared to give a warm reception, they formed themselves in a compact body, and advanced to dispute the possession of the gangway, with the gunner and his party leaving the quarterdeck unoccupied; but the surgeon's party forgetting the order to rendezvous on the quarterdeck, followed the Spaniards as they advanced on the starboard gangway, thus placing them between two fires from which they suffered severely; still, however, the Spaniards advanced and succeeded in beating back the gunner's party, and of gaining possession of the forecastle. In the mean time Captain Hamilton was alone on the quarterdeck, waiting the arrival of those who as yet had not boarded, when he was attacked by four Spaniards, one of whom felled him to the deck by a blow from the butt of his musket. He fell on the combing of the after hatchway stunned by the blow, which even broke the weapon which inflicted the wound. The timely arrival of two or three of the Surprise's men, saved their captain who recovering from the blow, had soon sufficient occupation in resisting the attempts of the Spaniards to gain the quarterdeck by means of the after-hatchway, and at this critical moment Monsr. de la Tour du Pin boarded with the marines from the black cutter over the larboard gangway, and gave a favourable turn to the then not over-promising affair.

It appears from Mr. Hamilton's account, that when he first attempted to board, his men mounted the gangway steps, following their officer, who, as he advanced up the side was knocked down, his fall occasioned that of the men on the steps, and some were much injured by this retrograde movement. They instantly shoved off and tried the other side, and this not succeeding, they returned again to the larboard gangway, and at last accomplished their desires. The marines were instantly formed; a volley was fired down the after-hatchway, and the gallant English rushed down with bayonets fixed on the main deck. About 60 Spaniards retreated to the cabin and surrendered; they were instantly secured, and the doors closed. The fighting still continued on the main deck and under the forecastle. By this time the carpenter had cut the stern cable, and the ship was canting head to wind, when the bower cable which ought to have been cut before, had the launch instead of idling with the gun-boats been at her proper station, was cut, the foretopsail was loose, the boats had the frigate in tow, and the gunner and two men, all three severely wounded, stood at the wheel and steered the ship; and those can best comprehend the feelings of Captain Hamilton, and his few brave companions, when the foretopsail filled, the mizentopsail became useful, and the Hermione was standing out of Puerto-Cabello, who have been engaged in enterprises of this sort, and who have had their exertions crowned by success.

The batteries now opened upon the frigate, the main and spring stays were shot away, the gaff came down, several shot took effect below the water-line, and Antonio, the Portuguese coxswain of the gig, who spoke Spanish, reported that he overheard the Spaniards making preparations and resolutions to blow up the frigate. A few muskets fired down the hatchway restored quiet; and by one o'clock, nearly one hour after the pinnace had boarded, all opposition ceased, and the Hermione was a prize. At 2 A.M., the ship being out of gun-shot from the batteries and in complete possession of the captors, the towing boats were called alongside. It was now, for the first time, that the people from them set their feet on board the frigate.

In effecting this surprising capture, the British sustained so comparatively slight a loss as 12 wounded,* including Captain Hamilton, by several contusions but not dangerously, and Mr. Maxwell, the gunner, dangerously and in several places. Of their 365 in crew, the Spaniards had 119 killed and 97 wounded, most

* Mr. Marshall, by mistake (vol. i., p. 826), has included in the loss on this occasion acting Lieutenant John Busey, who had been killed nine days before in cutting out some vessels at the island of Aruba.

of them dangerously. The survivors were afterwards put on board a captured schooner, and landed at Puerto-Cabello.

It is impossible to do justice to Captain Hamilton, the gunner Mr Maxwell, and the first boarders from the pinnace; they were unsupported for more than ten minutes, and this gallant handful of men succeeded in possessing themselves of the quarterdeck. The history of naval warfare, from the earliest time to this date, affords no parallel to this dashing affair: it was no surprise, no creeping upon the sleepy unawares; the crew of the frigate were at quarters, standing to their guns, aware of the attack, armed, prepared, in readiness; and that frigate was captured by the crews of *three* boats, the first success being gained by sixteen men. It is useless to waste words in endeavouring to do justice to Captain Hamilton, Mr. Maxwell, and Mr. McMullen: the first received an adequate reward in the honour of knighthood, the second received a sword from the lieutenants, and the third shared prize money with that class; but the best record of this well-planned, well-executed, daring, gallant enterprise, is to be found in the Painted Hall at Greenwich Hospital – there it remains to gratify the eyes of all who are willing to do justice to English seamen and their gallant commander.

Captain Hamilton, with his prize in company, made sail for Jamaica, and on the 1st of November anchored in Port-Royal. Having while in the Spanish service undergone a thorough repair, the Hermione was immediately restored to her former rank in the British navy; at first under the new name, as given to her by Admiral Sir Hyde Parker, of Retaliation, but subsequently, on her return to England, under the more appropriate name of Retribution.

The recovery of a frigate, so infamously acquired by the Spaniards as the Hermione, could not fail to be gratifying to the re-captors: how much more so must it have been, when the achievement was effected under circumstances so transcendently glorious to the British name and character. Undoubtedly, the cutting out of the Hermione, by Captain Hamilton and his brave shipmates, stands at the head of that desperate class of services; and on no occasion was the honour of knighthood more deservedly bestowed, than upon him who had planned, conducted, and bled in the attack.

Captain Hamilton's wounds, indeed, although not vitally dangerous, were of a very serious nature, and merit a more particular account than we have given of them. He first received a tremendous blow from the butt-end of a musket, which broke over his head and knocked him senseless on the deck; he next received a severe sabre-wound on the left thigh, another wound by a pike on the right thigh, and a contusion on the right shinbone by a grape-shot. One of his fingers was much cut, and his loins and kidneys were so much bruised, that he still at times requires the best medical advice and assistance.

Owing probably to the severity of his wounds, Captain Hamilton, in his official letter, has not given a very explicit account of an achievement that has done him so much honour. He does not name an officer as present in the attack, except the surgeon and gunner; and yet he disclaims any intention of making an exception by saying, "Every officer and man on this expedition behaved with an uncommon degree of valour and exertion."

"In the month of April, 1800," says Mr. Marshall, "Sir Edward Hamilton, returning home in the Jamaica packet for the cure of his wounds, was captured by a privateer and carried into a French port; from whence he was sent to Paris, where he was taken particular notice of by Buonaparte, who at length agreed to his being exchanged for six midshipmen."* Previously to his departure from Jamaica, the house of assembly of that island, with its accustomed liberality, voted Captain Hamilton a sword of 300 guineas value; and, on his arrival in England after his exchange, the common council of London voted him the freedom of their city.

On the 24th of October, at 1 P.M., the British 12-pounder 32-gun frigate Orpheus, Captain William Hills, being on her passage from the island of Ternate, one of the Moluccas, to the Straits of Banca, discovered and chased two sail off Togolanda; which eventually proved to be the Dutch India-company's ships Zeelast and Zeevraght, each mounting 22 guns of different calibers, and laden with rice, powder, shot, gun-carriages, and other stores; the first having a crew of 42 men, commanded by Captain Pieter Janson, and the other a crew of 33 men, commanded by Captain Pieter Meuse.

At 3 P.M. it fell calm, and the Orpheus had to hoist out all her boats to tow. At 5 P.M., on a breeze springing up, the frigate cast off the boats, and made all sail, but did not arrive up with the ships until 8 h. 45 m. P.M.; when, having one on each bow, the Orpheus opened her fire upon the two, and in a quarter of an hour compelled them to surrender; the Zeelast with the loss of one man killed, and the Zeevraght of six men wounded. The Orpheus herself had also one of her best seamen killed while employed in the main top, and five seamen wounded.

On the 15th of November, at daybreak, the south-west end of Porto-Rico bearing north-east distant 10 or 12 leagues, the British 18-pounder 36-gun frigate Crescent, Captain William Grenville Lobb, and 16-gun ship-sloop Calypso, Captain Joseph Baker, having in charge a convoy from England and Cork bound to Jamaica, fell in with a Spanish squadron, consisting of the 64-gun ship Asia, Commodore Don Francesco Montes, 40-gun frigate (18-pounder) Anfitrite, Captain Don Diego Villo-gomez, and 16-gun ship-corvette Galgo, Captain Don Josef de Arias, from Santo-Domingo bound to Havana.

The two former of these ships being directly in the course of

* Marshall, vol. i., p. 827.

the convoy to leeward standing on the larboard tack, Captain Lobb made the signal for his charge to haul to the wind on the starboard tack. Meanwhile the Calypso, followed by the Crescent, stood on ahead to reconnoitre the strangers; and, on discovering them to be enemies, made the signal to that effect to the convoy. Ordering the Calypso by signal to chase north-west, the direction in which lay the body of the convoy, the Crescent bore up to within random-shot of the Spanish 64 and frigate in the hope to draw them from the merchantmen. At 9 A.M. the Asia and Anfitrite tacked towards the convoy: immediately on which the signal was made for the vessels to disperse.

About this time the Spanish corvette was observed standing for the ships of the convoy which had hauled their wind. To relieve these, the Crescent hauled her wind: a manœuvre which was every way successful; as she not only captured and carried off the Galgo, but induced the Asia and Anfitrite to discontinue the chase of the leewardmost vessels, and haul up also, in the vain hope to save their companion. Moreover, while the Calypso ran off to leeward with one part of the convoy, the Crescent and her prize led the other part to windward; and in less than a week afterwards the whole convoy, except one ship, the General-Goddard, were at anchor in Port-Royal, Jamaica. In this case, whatever we may think of the indeterminate behaviour and gross mismanagement of Commodore Don Francisco Montes, we cannot but admire the prompt decision and skilful manœuvres of Captain Lobb.

On the 22d of November, at 5 P.M., the British hired cutter Courier, of 12 long 4-pounders and 40 men, Lieutenant Thomas Searle, cruising off Flushing, observed a suspicious sail bring to a bark. The cutter immediately hauled her wind in chase, and, as she passed the bark, learnt from her that the other vessel was a French privateer. The Courier thereupon crowded sail in pursuit; and on the 23d, at 9 A.M. Lowestoffe bearing north-west by west distant 10 or 12 leagues, succeeded in overtaking the French cutter-privateer Guerrier, of 14 long 4-pounders and 44 men, commanded by Citizen Felix L. Lallemand. A warm and close action ensued, and lasted 50 minutes, when the Guerrier struck her colours.

The Courier had her master, Mr. Stephen Marsh, killed at the commencement of the action, and two seamen wounded, the Guerrier, four killed and six wounded. These as is evident without the aid of a tabular statement, were a well-matched pair of combatants; and the action was manfully sustained on both sides. Shortly after his capture of this privateer, Lieutenant Searle obtained that promotion, to which, by his previous gallantry on more than one occasion, he had fully entitled himself.

On the 24th of November, at daybreak, the British 12-pounder

32-gun frigate Solebay, Captain Stephen Poyntz, cruising off the island of St.-Domingo, discovered four vessels under easy sail in the north-west or windward quarter. Although rather scattered, owing to a strong gale which had blown during the night, the strangers were a French squadron, composed of the Egyptien, an armed store-ship having a broad pendant and two rows of ports, out of the upper of which she carried 18 long brass 12-pounders and two brass 36-pounder carronades, with a complement of 137 men; the ship-corvette Eole, of 16 long brass 8-pounders and two brass 36-pounder carronades, and a crew of 107 men, the brig-corvette Levrier, of 12 long brass 8-pounders and 96 men, and the schooner Vengeur (late Charlotte, British), of eight long brass 6-pounders and 91 men. This squadron had recently arrived at Cape-François from Rochefort, and was now bound on a particular service to Jacmel.

At 6 A.M., after making some signals which convinced Captain Poyntz that the squadron was French, the Egyptien set all sail, and, accompanied by her consorts, steered towards Cape Tiburon. The Solebay, crowding sail also, followed in pursuit, and kept watching for an opportunity to separate a force which, while it remained united, was too formidable to be attacked. By 2 P.M. the wind had very much decreased; but the Solebay, being the weathermost ship, continued to feel its influence in a considerable degree, while the Egyptien and her consorts lay nearly becalmed, and were still much disunited, the commodore and the brig being to windward, and the second ship and the schooner at some distance to leeward. Thus favoured, the frigate ran between the two divisions; and, closing with the two weathermost vessels, captured them in succession after a slight resistance. Observing the fate of their commodore, the ship and schooner to leeward now endeavoured, by a light air of wind which then sprang up, to effect their escape; but they were soon overtaken by the Solebay, and, after receiving a few of her shot, hauled down their colours.

Thus were taken, at one time, four French vessels, mounting between them 58 guns and manned with 431 men, by a British frigate mounting at the most 38 guns, with a crew of about 212 men; and all without a casualty on either side. In this affair, so highly creditable to the officers and crew of the Solebay, no gazette-letter was published: we therefore suppose that none was transmitted to Admiral Sir Hyde Parker, the commander-in-chief on the station. If an omission of this kind affected only the individual who was the cause of it, no one would have a right to complain; but, on board a frigate especially, there are several commissioned officers whose main hope of advancement in their profession may be for ever blighted by such an apparent neglect in their captain. In this very instance, Lieutenant Robert Scott, first of the Solebay, was not made a commander until three years after the capture of the Egyptien and her three consorts; and yet there can be little doubt that he would have been promoted immediately, had the usual letter been transmitted to the admiralty. We presume, however, that the board did, at a subsequent day, become acquainted with the particulars of the Soleabay's performance, as Admiral Parker was directed to signify to Captain Poyntz their lordship's high approval of his conduct.

One only of the four vessels captured by the Solebay, was found calculated to serve in the British navy. The Eole, or Eolan, as named in Steel, a fine fast-sailing corvette of 395 tons, became afterwards the 18-gun ship-sloop Nimrod, and continued for several years to be an active cruiser.

On the 3d of December, in the morning, the British 18-gun brig-sloop Racoon (16 carronades, 32-pounders, and two long sixes), Captain Robert Lloyd, being about five miles from Dover, observed an enemy's lugger board a merchant brig. Instantly the Racoon made sail, and, after a running fire of about 40 minutes, laid the lugger alongside. A smart fire was then maintained by both vessels, until the lugger, which was the Intrépide, of Calais, mounting 16 guns (probably 4-pounders), with a crew of 60 men, having had her foremast and bowsprit shot away, and being otherwise much damaged, struck her colours.

The Racoon had all her fore shrouds on the starboard side shot away, and her foremast badly wounded: her loss, however, was trifling, amounting, out of her crew of 120 men and boys, to only two wounded, the captain (slightly) and one seaman. The loss of the Intrépide amounted to 13 killed and wounded; a loss which, coupled with the privateer's disabled state, proves how resolutely her commander, Citizen Saillard, his officers and crew, had defended their vessel, and that, too, against an opponent of a most decided superiority of force. The injured state of the Racoon's foremast prevented her from pursuing the brig; which was the Melcombe, from London to Plymouth, with malt. The Intrépide was quite a new vessel, and, for a lugger, of very large dimensions, measuring nearly 200 tons. The Racoon measured 317 tons.

On the 17th of December, at 9 A.M., while the British 18-pounder 36-gun frigate Glenmore, Captain George Duff, and 12-pounder 32-gun frigate Aimable, Captain Henry Raper, having in charge an outward-bound West India convoy of between 40 and 50 sail, were off the island of Porto-Santo, steering to the south-west with a fresh breeze from north-west by north, one of the convoy made the signal for a strange sail in the south by west. At 9 h. 30 m. the Aimable discovered three sail; two of which appeared to be ships of war, and the third a large merchant ship without topgallantmasts. They were, in fact, the

French 36-gun frigate Sirène, Commodore Jean-Marie Renaud, and 18-gun ship-corvette (long 12-pounders) Bergère, with the Calcutta extra-Indiaman, of 819 tons, which they had that morning captured. The frigate and corvette had sailed from Rochelle, and were bound to Cayenne; the latter with 150 troops, and the former with 300, besides Victor Hugues, of West India notoriety, and his family.

At 10 A.M. the Aimable spoke the Glenmore; and shortly afterwards the two frigates, the latter preceding, made sail in chase. At a few minutes past 11 A.M. the merchant prize hauled up to about east-south-east, while the French frigate and corvette continued their course to the south-west. This manœuvre, in all probability, was meant to operate as a decoy to the two British frigates; and it partially succeeded, for at about 11 h. 30 m. A.M. the Glenmore, in consequence of the merchant ship without topgallantmasts "having the appearance of a rasé," hauled up in chase of her, making the signal to the Aimable "to prepare for battle." After about an hour's chase, and the discharge of one or two shot by the Glenmore, the Calcutta showed an English ensign, hove to, and was recaptured; the Glenmore herself lying to and sending her boat on board, although, as it would appear, an armed merchant ship was close at hand ready to perform the office, and quite able to have secured the prize, had the latter made the slightest attempt to escape.

The Aimable meanwhile, having clearly, from the first, made out the peaceable character of the ship to windward, had stood away south-south-west after the two ships to leeward; and which, as evidently, to her at least, were an enemy's frigate and corvette. So fast did the Aimable leave her consort, who still continued lying by the recapture, that at 1 P.M. the lower masts of the Glenmore were half immerged in the horizon, and at 1 h. 30 m. no part of her was to be seen. As the Aimable neared the enemy, the Bergère appeared to be making increased efforts, by setting every stitch of canvass, to keep way with the Sirène, then about 500 yards ahead, with her sails proportioned to those of her comparatively slow-moving consort.

At 2 h. 40 m. P.M., having arrived within random-shot of the Bergère, the Aimable hoisted her colours, and fired at the latter one of her forecastle guns; whereupon the Sirène discharged a gun to leeward, and hoisted a French ensign and commodore's pendant. The corvette also hoisted her colours, and commenced firing at the Aimable; who returned the fire, hoping to disable the Bergère, but still kept up a little, to engage the Sirène to advantage. With the view of frustrating the apparent design of the Aimable upon the corvette, the French frigate wore round and came astern of her. In consequence of this the Aimable was obliged to shorten sail and keep away at the same time, in order to follow the motions of the Sirène, along whose gangways were now seen, planted three deep, a numerous body of troops.

Although the wind was fresh and the sea high, the Sirène, a ship of about 920 tons, appeared by her stability and steadiness to feel little of its effects; while the Aimable, a ship of 782 tons, and very deep with stores and provisions, kept rolling her maindeck guns in the water. Under these circumstances, and perceiving no chance of separating the two ships, the Aimable remained within gun-shot on the frigate's weather-quarter, in the hope that the Glenmore, a ship of 926 tons, and, as carrying a tier of 18-pounders, a match for the Sirène and Bergère together, would come to her assistance. At one time, indeed, a ship was seen to windward; but, having no studding-sails set, she did not promise a speedy reinforcement. Nor was this ship the Glenmore, but one of the armed vessels of the convoy, the Bellona, who had followed the Aimable in her chase, in order, as the master of her, with a feeling that, had he been otherwise circumstanced, might have prompted him to do more, said, "to look on." Had the Bellona gone yet further beyond the strict line of her duty, and set her studding-sails, the Sirène, in all probability, would have mistaken the bold merchant ship for a vessel of war, and, abandoning the Bergère to the Aimable, have sought her own safety in flight.

Having maintained his station within gun-shot of the French frigate and corvette until dark, and being, by the ship's reckoning, 15 miles at least from the convoy intrusted to his joint-charge, and at an equal distance, as then appeared and really was the case, from those alone to whom he could look for support, Captain Raper considered that he was not justified in a further pursuit of the Sirène and Bergère, now especially that they had bore up. The Aimable accordingly, after making signals with rockets and blue-lights, none of which were answered, stood away to the north-west in search of her consort and convoy. On the 18th, at 1 h. 30 m. A.M., the Aimable rejoined them, fortunately without any loss of men, and with only a slight damage to her rigging and sails.

This affair excites a mixed feeling of regret, that Captain Duff should first have mistaken a merchant ship for a rasé, and, then have felt himself bound to keep in the midst of his convoy, even after his consort, by his permission, had gone in chase of a superior force; and of the highest admiration at the gallantry of Captain Raper, who, had fortune placed him in the command of an 18, instead of 12 pounder frigate, would, most likely, unless flight saved them, have captured both the Sirène and Bergère.

According to the brief notice of this affair in the Moniteur, no damage or loss worth mentioning was sustained by either French ship, or rather by the Sirène, for no other French ship is allowed to have been present. The "sang-froid" of Victor Hugues is much praised, and so is the gallantry of the French, and the shyness of the British commodore; in which, however, is meant, not Captain Duff of the Glenmore, but Captain Raper of the Aimable, as appears by the following passage in the account: "Un combat s'engagea entre la Sirène et une frégate anglaise, qui, après quelques volées de canons et de mitraille, et *quoique soutenue par plusieurs autres frégates* qui étaient en vue, quitta la partie," &c. We need only to remind the reader, that it was a Commodore Jean-Marie Renaud who, about five years before, when commanding the French 36-gun frigate Prudente, behaved in so discreditable a manner off the Isle of France.* There, too, the French account contained several mistatements, and bestowed very great praise upon monsieur the commodore.

On the 21st of December, in the evening, the British hired 10-gun cutter Lady-Nelson, while off Cabrita point, was surrounded and engaged by two or three French privateers and some gun-vessels, in sight of the 100-gun ship Queen Charlotte and 36-gun frigate Emerald, lying in Gibraltar bay. Vice-admiral Lord Keith, whose flag was flying on board the former ship, immediately ordered the boats of the two to hasten towards the combatants, in the hope that it might encourage the Lady-Nelson to resist, until she could approach near enough to be covered by the guns of the ships.

Before the boats could get up, however, the Lady-Nelson had been captured, and was in tow by two of the privateers. Notwithstanding this, Lieutenant William Bainbridge, in the Queen-Charlotte's barge, with 16 men, ran alongside of, boarded with the greatest impetuosity, and after a sharp conflict carried, the Lady-Nelson; taking as prisoners seven French officers and 27 men: six or seven others had been killed or knocked overboard in the scuffle.

In the mean time the two privateers, having cut the tow-ropes and made off towards Algesiras, were pursued by Lord Cochrane in the Queen-Charlotte's cutter. The darkness of the night prevented the boats from acting in concert, otherwise both privateers would probably have been taken. Lieutenant Bainbridge was severely wounded in the head by the stroke of a sabre, and slightly in other places. Some of his men were also wounded. These boat-attacks are desperate affairs, and few have exhibited more gallantry than that which ended in the recapture of the British cutter Lady-Nelson.

On the 26th of December, at 10 h. 15 m. A.M., the Dodman bearing north distant seven or eight leagues, the British cutter Viper, of fourteen 4-pounders and 48 men and boys, Lieutenant John Pengelly, perceiving a suspicious-looking vessel to windward, tacked and stood after her. At 10 h. 45 m. A.M. the Viper brought the stranger to close action, which continued for

* See vol. i., p. 213.

three quarters of an hour, when the latter sheered off. The Viper immediately gave chase; and, after a running fight of an hour and a half, had the good fortune to lay her opponent on board. Two well-directed broadsides then compelled the French lugger-privateer Furet, of fourteen 4-pounders, and 57 out of a complement of 64 men (seven having been sent away in a prize on that morning), commanded by Citizen Louis Bouvet, to strike her colours.

The Viper had her mainmast rendered unserviceable by the privateer's shot, and her rigging and sails very much cut; but the cutter escaped with only her commander (slightly) and one seaman wounded. The Furet's rigging and sails were in as bad a condition as the Viper's, and her loss much greater; amounting to four seamen killed, her first and second captains, and six seamen wounded, four of them dangerously.

This was a very spirited little affair, and ranks with the Courier and Guerrier as to the near equality of the match. Moreover it was, as will be recollected, the second occasion where the Viper cutter, under the same commander, had captured a French privateer of equal force.*

COLONIAL EXPEDITIONS. – WEST INDIES.

On the 31st of July an expedition intended to act against the Dutch island of Surinam, composed of the 98-gun ship Prince-of-Wales, Captain Adrian Renou, bearing the flag of Vice-admiral Lord Hugh Seymour, 74-gun ship Invincible, Captain William Cayley, four frigates, one 20-gun ship, and one gun-brig, having on board a body of troops commanded by Lieutenant-general Trigge, sailed from Port-Royal bay, Martinique.

On the 11th of August the expedition made the coast of Surinam to windward of the river that name, and on the 16th, in the afternoon, stood in and came to an anchor off the mouth of the river. A summons was immediately sent in to the governor of the colony, who requested and received 48 hours to consider of the proposals. On the 18th the Dutch governor consented to treat; and on the 19th, on account of the shallowness of the water, the troops were removed from the two line-of-battle ships to the frigates. This done, the latter, with the admiral and general on board of one of them, weighed and proceeded to a fresh anchorage about two miles up the river.

In this situation the British squadron continued until the night of the 20th, when the capitulation was returned finally ratified and confirmed by the governor; and on the following day, the 21st, Fort New-Amsterdam was taken possession of, and the garrison, numbering 750 men, of whom 250 only were regulars, marched out with the honours of war. On the 22d several other forts and posts, including the town of Paramaribo,

* See p. 82.

the capital of the colony, were taken quiet possession of, and the whole of Surinam surrendered to the arms of Great Britain.

The only vessels of war, found lying in Surinam river, were the French ship-corvette, Hussar, of 20 long 8-pounders,* and the Dutch brig corvette, Camphaan, of 16 long 6-pounders. Both vessels were added to the British navy; the latter by her own name, and the former by the name of the colony in whose waters she had been captured.

EAST INDIES

Although, from its situation, not a place at the reduction of which the British navy could co-operate, yet, as the capital of an immense territory, and the residence of a powerful and enterprising chief already named in these pages, the fortress of Seringapatam claims to have its surrender noticed.

The British and native troops assembled for the reduction of this important fortress were commanded by Lieutenant-general Harris; and on the 30th of April, the batteries of the former began to batter in breach. On the 3d of May, a breach was reported practicable; and on the 4th, the capital of Mysore was carried by assault, with a loss to the British and native troops of 83 killed (13 only of the latter), 297 wounded, and six missing. Among the killed in defending Seringapatam, was the Sultan Tippoo-Saib, whose body after a long search, was found under a heap of slain in one of the gateways. Several of the gallant Tippoo's chiefs and head men fell on the same occasion.

Among the numerous prisoners taken in the fortress were a few French officers; and, among Tippoo's papers, was found the clearest evidence of the good understanding that had subsisted between the deceased Sultan and the French government; and this even while Tippoo was negotiating, in seeming heartiness and good faith, with the Earl of Mornington. Of the origin and ill success of a previous application on the part of the sultan for a supply of French troops, we have already given some account.† By the documents found at Tippoo-Saib's death, it appears that the French government was also to supply him with naval officers, who were to receive a large pay; that Mangalore was to be Tippoo's principal seaport, and that Goa and even Bombay were to have been attacked: the first of which settlements, on their anticipated easy reduction, was to be retained by Tippoo, and the latter to be given up to the French.

* So, with the usual substitution of 9 for 8 pounders, represented in Lord Hugh's letter; but as the ship was only 413 tons, we consider that the guns were either fewer in number, or of a lighter caliber, probably 6-pounders.

† See p. 213.

APPENDIX.

No. 1. See p. 1.

A list of ships of the line and frigates, late belonging to the French navy, captured, destroyed, wrecked, foundered, or accidentally burnt, during the year 1796.

Gun-ship		Name.	How, when, and where lost.
74	...	Séduisant	Wrecked, December, 16, on the Grand Stevenet, in going out of Brest. About 686 of her 1300 seamen and troops perished.
Gun-frig.			
44	...	Scévola	Foundered, December 30, off the coast of Ireland. Crew saved by the French 74 Révolution.
	...	Impatiente	Wrecked, at same time, on the Mizen-head; crew, except seven, perished.
40	(Z)	Proserpine	Captured, June 13, by the Dryad, 36, off Cape-Clear.
	"	Virginie	Captured, April 22, by the Indefatigable and squadron, off the Lizard.
36		Andromaque	Destroyed, August 22, after being run on shore, on the coast of France, by Sir J. B. Warren's squadron.
	(D)	Renommée	Captured, July 12, by the Alfred 74, off St.-Domingo.
	"	Tribune	Captured, same day, by the Unicorn 32, off Ireland.
	"	Unité	Captured, April 13, by the Révolutionnaire 38 (other frigates in company), off the coast of France.
		Vestale	Captured, December 13, by the Terpsichore 32, near Cadiz, but recaptured next day.
32	(H)	*Tamise*	Captured, June 7, by the Santa-Margarita 36, off Ireland.
28	(I)	*Nemesis*	Captured, March 9, by a British squadron, near Tunis.
	"	Unité	Captured, April 20, by the Inconstant 36, in the Mediterranean.

No. 2. See p. 1.

A list of ships of the line and frigates, late belonging to the Dutch navy, captured, destroyed, wrecked, foundered, or accidentally burnt, during the year 1796.

Gun-ship		Name.	How, when, and where lost.
64	(P)	Dordrecht	Captured, August 17, by Vice-admiral Elphinstone's squadron at the Cape of Good Hope.
	"	Revolutie	
54	"	Zealand	Captured, March 4, by Vice-admiral Richard Onslow, commanding the ships of war at Plymouth, having been detained in port, by the orders of the British government, since the commencement of the preceding year.
	(T)	Brakel	
	"	Van-Tromp	Captured, August 17, as Dordrecht, &c.
Gun-frigate			
40	(Z)	Casthor	Captured, August 17, as Dordrecht, &c.
	(B)	Tholen	Captured, March 4, as Zealand, &c.
	(D)	Braave	Captured, August 17, as Dordrecht, &c.
36	(G)	Jason	Captured, June 8, by her crew mutinying and carrying her into Greenock; where the 18-gun brig-sloop Pelican took possession of her.
	(H)	Argo	Captured, May 12, by the Phoenix 36, and other ships, in the North Sea.
	"	Zephyr	Captured, in March, by the Andromeda 32, and two sloops, in the Firth of Forth; where she was lying, unapprized of hostilities.
26	(I)	Sirène	Captured, August 17, as Dordrecht, &c.
	(K)	Bellona	
	...	Thetis	Captured, April 23, by the British, at the surrender of Demerara.

No. 3. See p. 1.

A list of ships of line and frigates, late belonging to the Spanish navy, captured, destroyed, wrecked, foundered, or accidentally burnt, during the year 1796.

Gun-frig.	Name.	How, when, and where lost.
40	.... Sabina	Captured, December 20, by the Minerve 38, off Carthagena, but recaptured on the following day.
34	(D) Mahonesa	Captured, October 13, by the Terpsichore 32, near Cape de Gata, Mediterranean.

An abstract of French, Dutch, and Spanish ships of the line and frigates, captured, &c., during the year 1796.

		Lost through the enemy.		Lost through accident.			Total lost to the F.D.&S. navies.	Total added to the British navy.
		Capt.	Dest.	Wrecked	Found'd	Burnt		
Ships of the line	Fr.	...	...	1	...	...	1	...
	Du.	3	...	...	...	...	3	3
Frigates	Fr.	9	1	1	1	...	12	8
	Du.	11	...	...	...	...	11	10
	Sp.	2	...	...	...	...	2	1
Total		25	1	2	1	...	29	22

No. 4. See p. 1.

A list of ships and vessels, late belonging to the British navy, captured, destroyed, wrecked, foundered, or accidentally burnt, during the year 1796.

Gun		Name.	Commander.	How, when, and where lost.
Gun-ship.				
80	(K)	*Ca-Ira*	Chas. D. Pater	Burnt by accident and blown up, April 11, in San-Fiorenzo bay: crew, except four, saved.
74	(N)	*Courageux*	B. Hallowell	Wrecked, December 18, near the foot of Ape's Hill, Straits of Gibraltar: crew, except 124, perished.
74	(O)	Bombay-Castle	Tho. Sotheby	Wrecked, December 21, in the river Tagus: crew saved.
54	(S)	Malabar	Thomas Parr	Foundered, October 10, in coming from the West Indies: crew saved.
50	(T)	Salisbury	Wm. Mitchell	Wrecked, May 13, on the Isle of Avache, St. Domingo: crew saved.
Gun-frig.				
38	(Z)	*Undaunted*	R. Winthrop	Wrecked, August 27, on the Morant Keys, West Indies: crew saved. Had been *Aréthuse* c. 1793.
36	(C)	Leda	John Woodley	Foundered, January 11, by unpsetting in a heavy squall, in lat. 38° 8', long. 17° 40': crew, except seven, perished.
36	(D)	*Réunion*	H.W. Bayntun	Wrecked, December 7, in the Swin: crew saved.
32	(H)	Active	Ed. Lev. Gower	Wrecked, in July, in the river St. Lawrence: crew saved.
32	"	Amphion	Israel Pellew	Burnt by accident and blown up, September 22, in Hamoaze, Plymouth; and most of the crew perished.
28	(I)	Hussar	James Colnett	Wrecked, December 27, on the cost of France: crew saved.
Gun p. ship				
20	(O)	Narcissus	Percy Fraser	Wrecked, Oct. 3, on Sandy key, New Providence; crew saved.
G. sh. slp.				
18	(R)	Cormorant	Thomas Gott	Burnt by accident and blown up, Dec. 24, at Port-au-Prince, St.-Domingo: crew, except 20, perished.
16	(T)	*Arab*	Step. Seymour	Wrecked, June 10, on the Penmarcks near Brest: crew saved.
G. bg. Slp.				
18	(Y)	Curlew	F. Ventris Field	Foundered, December 31, in the North Sea: crew perished.

No. 4—*continued*

Guns		Name.	Commander	How, when, and where lost.
G. bg. slp.				
16	(a)	Scourge	William Stap	Foundered, date unknown, off the coast of Holland: crew saved.
16	"	*Sirène*	Daniel Guerin	Wrecked, date unknown, in the Bay of Honduras: crew perished.
16	(a)	*Trompeuse*	James R. Watson	Wrecked, date unknown, on the Farmer-rock, Kinsale: crew saved.
14	(b)	*Bermuda*	Thomas Maxtone	Foundered, date unknown, in the Florida gulf: crew perished.
14	"	Helena	Jeremh. J. Symons	Foundered, Nov. 3, on the coast of Holland: crew perished.
Gun-brig				
10	(1)	Experiment	George Hayes	Captured, October 2, by a Spanish squadron in the Mediterranean.
8	(m)	*Berbice*	John Trefahar	Wrecked, in Nov., on the coast of Dominica: crew saved.
8	"	*Vanneau*	John Gourly	Wrecked, in Nov., at Porto-Ferrajo, Mediterranean: crew saved.

ABSTRACT.

	Lost through the enemy.		Lost through accident.			
	Capt.	Dest.	Wrecked	Found'd	Burnt	Total
Ships of the line	...	...	2	...	1	3
Ships under the line	1	...	11	6	2	20
Total	1	...	13	6	3	23

No. 5. See p. 2.

	£	s.	d.
For the pay and maintenance of 100,000 seamen and 20,000 marines; also the expense of sea-ordnance	6,240,000	0	0
" the ordinary expenses of the navy, including the half-pay to sea and marine officers	653,573	1	7
" the extraordinaries; including the building and repairing of ships, and other extra work	768,100	0	0
Towards defraying the expenses, and preventing the increase of the debt of the navy	5,000,000	0	0
To defray the expense to be incurred by increase to the pay of the seamen and marines, and by the proposed issue of full allowance of provisions	472,000	0	0
Total supplies granted for the sea-service	£13,133,673	1	7

No. 6. See p. 72.

The following statement will show the intended order of battle of the British fleet in the Camperdown battle, the tonnages and complements of the respective ships, together with the damages, as far as they can be ascertained, and the loss officially reported to have been sustained in the action.

	SHIPS	Tons.	Principal Damages.	Complement.	LOSS.	
					K.	W.
Larboard or lee division.	Russel	1642	No damage of any consequence	584	0	7
	Director	1377	Foreyard shot away, bowsprit shot through; also boats, booms, &c.	485	0	7
	Montagu	1631	No damage of any consequence	584	3	5
	Veteran	1397	Three guns disabled, but nothing further of consequence	485	4	21
	Monarch	1612	Hull greatly damaged. Very leaky. Spars and rigging unhurt	593	36	100
	Powerful	1627	A good deal hit in hull; and masts, &c. much wounded	584	10	78
	Monmouth	1439	No damage of any consequence	485	5	22
	Agincourt	1434	One shot through wind and water. Nothing else material	485	0	0
Starboard or weather division.	Triumph	1825	Very leaky from shot-holes. Three guns and seven carriages disabled. Masts, &c. much cut	634	29	55
	Venerable	1669	Much cut up in hull, and very leaky. Some light spars, but no lower masts, shot away	587	15	62
	Ardent	1422	Hull pierced in all directions: all masts, &c. cut, but none of any consequence shot away	485	41	107
	Bedford	1606	Hull hit in many places and very low. Ship leaky in consequence. No principal spars shot away, but most of them wounded	584	30	41
	Lancaster	1430	No damage of any consequence	485	3	18
	Belliqueux	1379	Hull and spars, particularly the former, much shattered	485	25	78
	Adamant	1060	No damage of any consequence	338	0	0
	Isis	1051	Ditto	338	2	21
		23602		8221	203	622

The order of the battle was reversed: hence, the starboard division led. But several of the ships were out of their places.

No. 7. See p. 72.

The following statement contains the names of the Dutch ships in the order in which they were drawn up in line, together with their respective tonnages and complements, and, as far as they can be ascertained, the principal damages and loss sustained by the ships.

SHIPS	Tons.	Principal Damages.	Complement.	LOSS.	
				K.	W.
Beschermer	1052	Probably not much damaged in hull or spars	350		
Gelykheid*	1305	Believed not to have been dismasted; but uncertain	450	40	‡
Hercules*	1266	Hull torn to pieces, and much burnt near the stern. Mizenmast shot away, and all spars, &c. much cut	450		
Devries*	1360	In the same state of uncertainty as Gelykheid	450		
Vryheid	1562	Hull riddled, so as to be scarcely seaworthy; and all three masts shot away by the board	550	‡	‡
States-General	1560	Hull a good deal hit: wheel shot away: spars, &c. wounded	550	20	40
Wassenaer*	1269	Uncertain	450		
Batavier	1048	Very trifling, it is believed	350		
Brutus	1560	Ditto	550	10	50
Leyden	1307	Ditto	450		
Mars	1357	Mizenmast shot away	400	1	14
Cerberus	1317	No damage of any consequence	450	5	9
Jupiter*	1559	Hull greatly shattered. Main and mizen masts shot away. Other masts, &c. cut to pieces	550	‡	‡
Haerlem	1324	Ditto: also main topmast and mizen mast shot away	450	‡	‡
Alkmaar*	1041	Hull much cut up: mizen mast and main topmast shot away, fore and main masts fell afterwards	350	26	62
Delft*	1050	Hull torn to pieces	375	43	76
	20937		7175	490	580
		Monnikendam frigate*		50	40
Total, as published, in gross, in a French newspaper				540	620

The ships marked *, were captured; the mark ‡ in the loss denotes that the amount was great, but, as well as where a blank appears, is unascertainable.

No. 8. See p. 105.

A list of ships of the line and frigates, late belonging to the French navy, captured, destroyed, wrecked, foundered, or accidentally burnt, during the year 1797.

Gun-ship		Name.	How, when, and where lost.
74	...	Droits-de-l'Homme	Wrecked, January 13, during an action with Indefatigable and Amazon frigates, near the Penmarcks.
Gun-frig.			
40	...	Méduse	Foundered, in November, on her passage from Amercia: crew saved by Insurgente.
	(Z)	Résistance	Captured, March 9, along with the 22-gun corvette Constance, by the San Fiorenzo and Nymphe frigates, off Brest.
	...	Tortue	Captured, January 5, with troops, by the Polyphemus 64, off Ireland.
36	...	Calliope	Destroyed, July 17, by Sir J.B. Warren's squadron, on the coast of France.
	...	Hermione	Destroyed, April 17, after being run on shore, by the Thunderer and Valiant 74s, off St.-Domingo. Misnamed Harmonie in the official account and in Steel.
	(D)	Néréide	Captured, December 22, by the Phœbe frigate, off Sicily.
	...	Surveillante	Wrecked, in January, in Bantry bay.

No. 9. See p. 105.

A list of ships of the line and frigates, lately belonging to the Dutch navy, captured, destroyed, wrecked, foundered, or accidentally burnt, during the year 1797.

Gun-ship		Name.	How, when, and where lost.
74	(O)	Jupiter	Captured, October 11, by Admiral Duncan, off Camperdown. The Delft foundered on her way into port.
	"	Vryheid	
64	(P)	Devries	
	"	Gelykheid	
	"	Haerlem	
	"	Hercules	
	"	Wassenaer	
50	(T)	Akmaar	
	"	Delft	

No. 10. See p. 105.

A list of ships of the line and frigates, late belonging to the Spanish navy captured, destroyed, wrecked, foundered, or accidentally burnt, during the year 1797.

Gun-ship.	Name.	How, when, and where lost.
112	(B) Salvador-del-Mundo	Captured, February 14, by Admiral Sir John Jervis, off Cape San-Vincent.
	" San Josef	
80	(K) San-Nicolas	
	... San-Vincente ...	Destroyed, Feb. 17, in Shaggaramus bay, island of Trinidad, to prevent capture by Rear-admiral Harvey.
74	... Arrogante	
	... Gallardo	
	(M) San-Damaso ...	Captured, on the same occasion.
	" San-Ysidro	Captured, with Salvador-del-Mundo, &c.
Gun-frig.		
34	(D) Ninfa	Captured, April 26, by the Irresistible 74, in Conil bay, near Cadiz.
	... Santa-Elena	Destroyed, on the same occasion, after having been run on shore.
	... Santa-Cecilia ..	Destroyed, at the same time as San-Vincente, &c.

An abstract of French, Dutch, and Spanish ships of the line and frigates, captured, &c. during the year 1797.

		Lost through the enemy.		Lost through accident.			Total Lost to the F.D.&S. navies.	Total added to the British navy.
		Capt.	Dest.	Wrecked	Found'd	Burnt		
Ships of the line ..	Fr.	...	...	1	...	...	1	...
	Du.	7	...	...	...	...	7	7
	Sp.	5	3	...	...	...	8	5
Frigates	Fr.	3	2	1	1	...	7	3
	Du.	2	...	...	...	...	2	1
	Sp.	1	2	...	...	...	3	1
Total		18	7	2	1	...	28	17

No. 11. See p. 105.

A list of ships and vessels, late belonging to the British navy, captured, destroyed, wrecked, foundered, or accidentally burnt, during the year 1797.

Gun-		Name.	Commander.	How, when, and where lost.
Gun-frig. 38	(A)	Artois	Sir Edmund Nagle	Wrecked, July 31, on the coast of France: crew saved.
36	(C)	Amazon	Rt. Carth. Reynolds	Wrecked, Jan. 14, on the French coast, near Isle Bas: crew saved, but made prisoners.
	(D)	*Tribune*	Scory Barker	Wrecked, Nov. 16, off Halifax, Nova-Scotia: crew, except seven, perished.
32	(H)	Hermione	Hugh Pigot	Captured, Sept. 22, by her crew mutinying and carrying her into La Guira, South America.
28	(I)	Tartar	Hon. C. Elphinstone	Wrecked, in April, at the island of St.-Domingo: crew saved.
G. sh. slp. 18	(U)	Swift	Thomas Hayward	Foundered, date unknown, in the China seas: crew perished.
	(V)	Hunter	Tudor Tucker	Wrecked, Dec. 27, on Hog-island, off Virginia: crew, except five, saved.
G. bg. slp. 16	(a)	Fortune	Valentine Collard	Wrecked, date unknown, near Oporto: crew perished.
		Vipére	Hen. Harding Parker	Foundered, January 2, off the Shannon: crew perished.
14	(b)	*Hermes*	William Mulso	Foundered in January, at sea: crew perished.
Gun-brig 14	(f)	*Pandora*	Samuel Mason	Foundered, date unknown, in the North Sea: crew perished.
		Resolution	William Hugget	Foundered, date unknown, at sea: crew perished.
12	(g)	Growler	John Hollingsworth	Captured, in December, off Dungeness, by two French row-boats.
		Lacedemonian	Matthew Wrench	Captured, in May, in the West Indies, by the French.
Gun-cut. 10	(1)	*Fox*	John Gibson	Destroyed, July 24, in front of Santa-Cruz: 96 of crew and passengers perished.
		M.-Antoinette	John McInerheny	Captured, date unknown, by her crew mutinying and carrying her into a French port in the West Indies.

No. 11—*continued.*

F.B.	(u)	Albion	....Henry Savage	Wrecked, April 27, on the Middle sand, in the Swin: crew saved.
D.S.	(y)	Providence	W. Hen. Broughton	Wrecked, May 16, in the Pacific ocean: crew saved.

ABSTRACT.

	Lost through the enemy.		Lost through accident.			
	Capt.	Dest.	Wrecked	Found'd	Burnt	Total
Ships of the line	...	...	...	...	...	...
Ships under the line	4	1	8	5	...	18
Total	4	1	8	5	...	18

No. 12. See p. 107.

	£	s.	d.
For the pay and maintenance of 100,000 seamen .... and 20,000 marines; also the expense of sea-ordnance	6,630,000	0	0
" the wear and tear of ships in which they are to serve	4,290,000	0	0
" the ordinary expenses of the navy, including the half-pay to sea and marine officers	689,858	19	7
" the expense of the transport service, and for maintenance of prisoners of war in health	1,200,000	0	0
" the extraordinaries; including the building and repairing of ships, and other extra work	639,530	0	0
Total supplies granted for the sea-service	£13,449,388	19	7

No. 13. See p. 113.

Dans notre position, nous devons faire à l'Angleterre une guerre sûre, et nous le pouvons. Que nous soyons en paix ou en guerre, il nous faut quarante ou cinquante millions pour reorganiser notre marine. Notre armée de terre n'en sera ni plus ni moins forte, au lieu que la guerre oblige l'Angleterre à faire des préparatifs immenses qui ruinent ses finances, détruisent l'esprit du commerce, et changent absolument la constitution et les moeurs de ce peuple. Nous devons employer tout l'été à armer notre escadre de Brest, à faire exercer nos matelots dans la rade, à achever les vaisseaux qui sont en construction à Rochefort, à Lorient et à Brest. Si l'on met quelque activité dans ces travaux, nous pouvons espérer d'avoir, au mois de Septembre, trente-cinq vaisseaux à Brest, y compris les quatre ou cinq nouveaux que l'on peut construire à Lorient et à Rochefort.

Nous aurons vers la fin du mois, dans les differens ports de la Manche, près de deux cents chaloupes canonnières: il faut les placer à Cherbourg, au Hâvre, à Boulogne, à Dunkerque et à Ostende, et employer tout l'été à amariner nos soldats. En continuant à donner à la commission des côtes de la Manche trois cent mille francs par décade, nous pouvons faire construire deux cent autres chaloupes d'une dimension plus forte et propres à transporter des chevaux. Nous aurions donc au mois de Septembre quatre cents chaloupes canonnières à Boulogne, at vingt-cinq vaisseaux de guerre à Brest. Les Hollandais peuvent avoir également dans cet intervalle douze vaisseaux de guerre au Texel.

Nous avons dans la Méditerranée deux espèces de vaisseaux: Douze vaisseaux de construction française, qui peuvent, d'ici au mois de Septembre, être augmentés de deux nouveaux; neuf de construction vénitienne. Il serait possible, après l'expédition que le gouvernement projette dans la Méditerranée de faire passer les quatorze vaisseaux à Brest, et de garder dans la Mediterranée simplement les neuf vaisseaux vénitiens, ce qui nous ferait, dans le courant du mois d'Octobre ou de Novembre, cinquante vaisseaux de guerre français à Brest, et presque autant de frégates.

Il serait possible alors de transporter quarante mille hommes sur le point de l'Angleterre que l'on voudrait, en évitant même un combat naval, si l'ennemi était plus fort, dans le temps que quarante mille hommes menaceraient de patir sur les quatre cents chaloupes canonnières et autant de bateaux-pêcheurs de Boulogne, et que l'escadre Hollandaise et dix mille hommes de transport menaceraient de se porter en Ecosse. L'invasion en Angleterre, exécutée de cette manière, et dans les mois de Novembre et de Décembre, serait presque certaine. L'Angleterre s'épuiserait par un effort immense, et qui ne la garantirait pas de notre invasion.

En effect, l'expédition dans l'Orient obligera l'ennemi d'envoyer six vaisseaux de guerre, de plus dans l'Inde, et peut-être le double de frégates à l'embouchure de la Mer Rouge: elle serait obligée d'avoir de vingt-deux à vingt-cinq vaisseaux l'embouchure de la Méditerranée; soixante vaisseaux devant Brest et douze devant le Texel; ce qui formerait un total de cent trois vaisseaux de guerre, sans compter ceux qu'elle a aujourd'hui en Amérique et aux Indes, sans compter le dix ou douze vaisseaux de 50 canons avec une vingtaine de frégates, qu'elle serait obligée d'avoir pour s'opposer, à l'invasion de Boulogne. Nous nous conserverions toujours maîtres de la Méditerranée, puisque nous y aurions neuf vaisseaux de construction vénitienne.

Il y aurait encore un moyen d'augmenter nos forces dans cette mer: ce serait de faire ceder par l'Espagne trois vaisseaux de guerre et trois frégates à la république ligurienne. Cette république ne peut plus être aujourd'hui qu'un departement de la France:* elle a plus de vingt mille excellens marins. Il est d'une très-bonne politique de la part de la France de favoriser la république ligurienne, et d'exiger même qu'elle ait quelques vaisseaux de guerre. Si l'on prévoit des difficultés à ce que l'Espagne cède à nous ou à la république ligurienne trois vaisseaux de guerre, je croirais utile que nous-mêmes vous vendissions à la république ligurienne trois des neuf vaisseaux que nous avons pris aux Vénitiens, et que nous exigeassions qu'ils en construisissent trois autres: c'est une bonne escadre, montée par de bons marins, que nous trouverons avoir gagnée. Avec l'argent que nous aurons des Liguriens, nous ferons faire à Toulon trois bon vaisseaux de notre construction: car les vaisseaux de construction vénitienne exigent autant de matelots qu'un bon vaisseau de 74; et des matelots, voilà notre partie faible. Dans les événemens futurs qui peuvent arriver, il nous est extrêmement avantageux que les trois républiques d'Italie, qui doivent balancer les forces du roi de Naples et du grand-duc de Toscane, aient une marine plus forte que celle du roi de Naples. – *Victoires et Conquêtes*, tome x., p. 375.

* Tel fut en effet son sort six au sept ans plus tard.

No. 14. See p. 183.

On the 10th, at 9 A.M., Lieutenant Duval embarked on board a three-masted, lateen-rigged Scanderoon boat, laden with beans, and armed with two swivels. On the 11th, at 4 P.M., he lost sight of the fleet, and steered north-east, passing within a mile and a half of the Swiftsure and her prize, the Fortune corvette. On the 16th, at 5 P.M., the boat anchored within three-quarters of a mile of Scanderoon; and saluted the town (a little paltry place, in the midst of a swamp) with five swivels, but was not answered. This, and the non-appearance of any colours, raised a suspicion that the French party prevailed in the town. At length a boat came off, having on board a Turk, who called himself captain of the port. At Lieutenant Duval's request the colours were hoisted: he then went on shore, saw the governor in his mud-house, delighted him with the account of the action, and obtained his promise to furnish guards for the journey to Aleppo. On the 18th, at 5 A.M., Lieutenant Duval, having, the preceding day, sent his eight men to Cyprus, for the English consul to forward them to Naples, and having procured for himself an Arab dress and a servant, and been furnished by the governor with the two promised guards, set off on his journey. At 4 P.M. the party arrived at Aleppo. It took until the 27th, to make the necessary preparations for crossing the desert. At noon on that day the cavalcade, consisting of 24 Arabs, 19 camels, and a horse for Mr. Duval, quitted Aleppo. At noon on the 4th of September, after undergoing the usual fatigue of a journey across the desert, Lieutenant Duval and his escort arrived at Juba, a small town situated on the Euphrates. On the 7th, at 2 P.M., he reached Bagdad. On the next day, the bashaw, who was highly pleased with the news of the defeat sustained by the French, requested Lieutenant Duval to wait upon him, dressed in his uniform. He did so; and, passing an ante-room filled with guards and attendants, found the bashaw seated in state, on a very rich cushion, with a minister on each side of him. The floor of the apartment was covered with a rich carpet, and the walls and pillars hung with mirrors of various hues, the reflection from which gave to the room a very splendid appearance. The bashaw then ordered two attendants to clothe Lieutenant Duval with a handsome pelisse; and, pointing to a boat riding in the Tigris, asked him if she would answer his purpose. The lieutenant made a suitable reply, and departed. On passing through the streets, he was greeted with "God save and prosper the English." On the 9th Lieutenant Duval, with a proper escort of servants and guards, embarked in the governor's boat; and, on the 19th, landed on the west side of the river, within four miles of Bassorah. Shortly afterwards the lieutenant got on board the Fly packet, and on the 21st of October arrived in safety at Bombay.

No. 15. See p. 252.

A list of ships of the line and frigates, late belonging to the French navy, captured, destroyed, wrecked, foundered, or accidentally burnt, during the year 1798.

Gun-ship		Name.	How, when, and where lost.
120		Orient	Destroyed by fire, August 1, in the action with Rear-admiral Nelson's fleet, in Aboukir bay.
80	(K)	Franklin	Captured on the same occasion.
80	"	Tonnant	Captured on the same occasion.
74	(M)	Aquilon	Captured on the same occasion.
74	"	Spartiate	Captured on the same occasion.
74	(O)	Conquérant	Captured on the same occasion.
74	"	Peuple-Souverain	Captured on the same occasion.
74		Guerrier	Captured on the same occasion.
74		Heureux	Captured on the same occasion.
74		Mercure	Captured on the same occasion.
74	...	Timoléon	Destroyed on the same occasion by her own crew, after having been run on shore.
74	(M)	Hercule	Captured, April 21, by the Mars 74, near the Bec du Raz, coast of France.
74	"	Hoche	Captured, October 12, by Sir John Borlase Warren's squadron, off the north-west coast of Ireland.
74	...	Quatorze-Juillet	Accidentally burnt, May 1, at Lorient.
Gun-frigate			
40	(Z)	Loire	Captured, October 18, by the Anson 44, off coast of Ireland.
40	"	Seine	Captured, June 30, by the Jason and Pique frigates, in the Passage Breton, coast of France.
40	*(B)*	Immortalité	Captured, October 20, by the Fisgard 38, near Brest.

No. 15—*continued*

Gun-frig.	Name.	How, when, and where lost.
36	... Artémise	Destroyed by fire, at the capture of Franklin, Tonnant, &c.
	... Sérieuse	Destroyed by being sunk on same occasion.
	... Confiante	Destroyed, May 31, after being run on shore by the Hydra frigate, a cutter, and bomb, near Hâvre.
	... Coquille (D) Embuscade	Captured at the same time as the Hoche.
	... Bellona	Captured, October 12, by the Ethalion frigate, off Ireland.
	... Décade	Captured, August 24, by the frigates Magnanime and Naiad, off Cape Finisterre.
	... Résolue	Captured, October 13, by the Melampus frigate, off Ireland.
	... Sensible	Captured, June 27, by the Sea-horse frigate, Mediterranean.

No. 16. See p. 252.

A list of ships of the line and frigates, late belonging to the Dutch navy, captured, destroyed, wrecked, foundered, or accidentally burnt, during the year 1798.

Gun-frig.	Name.	How, when, and where lost.
36	(*G*) Furie	Captured, October 24, by the Sirius frigate, in the North Sea.
24	(*O*) Waakzaamheid .	

A list of ships of the line and frigates, late belonging to the Spanish navy, captured, destroyed, wrecked, foundered, or accidentally burnt, during the year 1798.

Gun-frig.	Name.	How, when, and where lost.
34	(*D*) Santa-Dorotea ..	Captured, July 15, by the Lion 64, off Carthagena.

An abstract of French, Dutch, and Spanish ships of the line and frigates, captured, &c. during the year 1798.

		Lost through the enemy.		Lost through accident.			Total Lost to the F.D.&S. navies.	Total added to the British navy.
		Capt.	Dest.	Wrecked	Found'd	Burnt		
Ships of the line ..	Fr.	11	2	...	...	1	14	8
Frigates	Fr.	10	3	...	...	...	13	8
	Du.	2	...	...	...	...	2	2
	Sp.	1	...	...	...	...	1	1
Total		24	5	...	...	1	30	19

No. 17. See p. 252.

A list of ships and vessels late belonging to the British navy, captured, destroyed, wrecked, foundered, or accidentally burnt, during the year 1798.

Gun	Class	Name.	Commander.	How, when, and where lost.
Gun-ship.				
74	(N)	Colossus	George Murray	Wrecked, December 10, off Sicily: crew saved;.
50	(T)	Leander	T. Bould. Thompson	Captured, August 18, by the French 74, Généreux, near Candia, Mediterranean.
44	(V)	Resistance	Edward Pakenham	Burnt and blown up, July 24, in the Straits of Banca: crew, except about five, perished.
Gun-frig.				
38	(*A*)	*Aigle*	Charles Tyler	Wrecked, July 18, off Cape Farina, coast of Spain: crew saved.
	"	Jason	Charles Stirling	Wrecked, October 13, near Brest: crew saved, but made prisoners.
36	(*D*)	*Hamadryad*	Thos. Elphinstone	Wrecked, date unknown, on the coast of Portugal.
	"	*Pique*	David Milne	Wrecked, June 29, on the coast of France: crew saved.
32	(*E*)	Lively	James Nic. Morris	Wrecked, April 12, on Rota point, near Cadiz: crew saved.
	"	Pallas	Hon. Henry Curzon	Wrecked, April 4, on Mount-Batten point, Plymouth Sound: crew saved.
32	(*H*)	Ambuscade	Henry Jenkins	Captured, December 14, by the French 28-gun frigate Bayonnaise.
28	(*I*)	Garland	James Athol Wood	Wrecked, July 26, off the coast of Madagascar: crew saved.
G. sh. sl.				
16	(*S*)	Peterel	Charles Long	Captured, December 14, by a Spanish frigate-squadron, off Majorca.
	(*V*)	Rover	George Irvine	Wrecked, date unknown, in the gulf of St. Lawrence: crew saved.
G. b. slp.				
18	(*Y*)	Kingfisher	Fred. L. Maitland	Wrecked, Dec. 3, on the bar of Lisbon: crew saved.
	"	Raven	J. W. Taylor Dixon	Wrecked, February 3, on the Middle ground, near Cuxhaven: crew saved.
16	(a)	*Braak*	James Drew	Foundered, May 23, by upsetting in the Delaware: captain and 34 of her crew perished.

No. 17—*continued*

		Name.	Commander.	How, when, and where lost.
Gun-brig 12	(g)	Crash	B. M. Praed	Captured, Aug. 26, on the coast of Holland.
Gun-slp. 6	(n)	*George*	Michael Mackey	Captured, January 3, by two Spanish privateers in the West Indies.
A.T.	(r)	Medusa	Alexander Becher	Wrecked, November 26, on the coast of Portugal: crew saved.
A.T.	(z)	*Etrusco*	George Reynolds	Foundered, Aug. 15, in coming from the West Indies: crew saved.

ABSTRACT

	Lost through the enemy.		Lost through accident.			
	Capt.	Dest.	Wrecked	Found'd	Burnt	Total
Ships of the line	...	...	1	...	...	1
Ships under the line	5	...	11	2	1	19
Total	5	...	12	2	1	20

No. 18. See p. 253.

	£	s.	d.
For the pay and maintenance of 100,000 seamen and 20,000 marines	5,850,000	0	0
" the wear and tear of ships, &c.	4,680,000	0	0
" the ordinary expenses of the navy, including the half-pay to sea and marine officers; also the expense of sea-ordnance	1,119,063	6	7
" the extraordinaries; including the building and repairing of ships, and other extra work	693,750	0	0
" the expense of the transport-service, and of maintaining the prisoners of war in health	1,311,200	0	0
Total supplies granted for the sea-service	£13,654,013	6	7

No. 19. See p. 285.

Je ne veux pas vous faire la guerre, si vous n'êtes pas mon ennemi; mais il est temps que vous vous expliquiez. Si vous continuez à donner refuge et à garder sur les frontières de l'Egypte Ibrahim-Bey, je regarderai cela comme une hostilité, et j'irai à Acre; si vous voulez vivre en paix avec moi, vous éloignerez Ibrahim-Bey à quarante lieues des frontières d'Egypte, et vous laisserez libre le commerce entre Damiette et la Syrie. Alors, je vous promets de respecter vos états, et de laisser la liberté entière au commerce entre l'Egypte et la Syrie, soit par terre, soit par mer. – *Victoires et Conquêtes*, tome ix., p. 243.

No. 20. See p. 298

Ayant été instruit que mon escadre était prête et qu'une armée formidable était embarquée dessus; convaincu, comme je l'ait dit plusieurs fois, que tant que je ne frapperai pas un coup qui écrase à la fois tous mes ennemis, je ne pourrai pas jouir tranquillement et paisiblement de la possession de l'Egypte, la plus belle contrée du monde, j'ai pris le parti d'aller me metrre moi-même à la tête de mes vaisseaux, en laissant pendant mon absence le commandement au Général Kléber, homme d'un mérite distingué, et auquel j'ai recommandé d'avoir pour les ulemas et les scheicks la même amitié que moi. Faites ce qu'il vous sera possible pour que le peuple d'Egypte ait en lui la même confiance qu'il avait en moi, et qu'à mon retour, qui sera dans deux ou trois mois, je sois content du peuple d'Egypte, et que je n'aie que des louanges et des récompenses à donner aux scheicks. – *Victoires et Conquêtes*, tome xi., p. 217.

NOTES

TO

ANNUAL ABSTRACTS

NOTES TO ABSTRACT NO. 5

H*. It will be here observed, that, although the columns of both the Increase and Decrease compartments are vacant, the grand total of this class differs, by 217 tons, from that of the same class in the preceding year's Abstract. This is because one of the ships, the Prince, was lengthened 11 feet, and thereby became enlarged from 1871 to 2088 tons.

P*. The four purchased vessels of this class had been laid down for Indiamen, and, together with a fifth not yet launched, were purchased of the company by the British government. They chiefly differed from the larger individuals of R, in being constructed with a detached quarterdeck and forecastle, and in having one port fewer of a side on each deck; so as, from the increased width of the ports, to carry 24 instead of 18 pounders on the first deck.

*A**, *C**, and *G**. The frigates in the launched columns were all built of fir.

*E**, Of 880 tons and upwards.

T*. The purchased ship was the Pylades, which had been driven on shore in Haraldswick bay, Isle of Nest, in the year 1794 (see the British casualty list for that year, vol. i., p. 391), but was afterwards got off, and being deemed irreparably damaged, sold at Leith. The new owners, however, contrived to repair the ship, and in 1796 sold her back to the British government.

* The hired vessels numbered about 74. Of course both the line and the general grand totals of this Abstract, exhibit, when compared with the corresponding totals in Abstract No. 4, the difference remarked upon and explained at note H*. Thus: 592 | $\overset{1}{530423}$ + 99 | $\overset{2}{63548}$ = 691 | 593971 —39 | $\overset{3}{32916}$ = 652 | 561055 – 19 | $\overset{4}{10724}$ = 633 | $\overset{5}{550331}$ + 217 tons = 633 | $\overset{6}{550548}$. Of these sets of figures, 1 is the grand total of Abstract No. 4; 2 is the Increase total, and 3 the Decrease total of the present Abstract: 4, such of the ships in the two launched columns as, having been ordered to be built in 1795, are already included in the totals of Abstract No. 4: they comprise all but the two cutters at i. The next set of figures, 5, would have been the grand total of Abstract No. 5, but for the Prince's 217 tons, the addition of which gives 6, the true grand total of the Abstract.

NOTES TO ABSTRACT NO. 6

P*. The purchased individual of this class, is the ship referred to in the corresponding note to the last Abstract.

X*. The newly-built individual is the Endymion, armed with twenty-six 24-pounders on the main deck. Her draught was copied from that of the Pomone, taken from the French in April, 1794, and she would have measured the same; but the merchant-builders, from some neglect, suffered her frame to fall out nearly eight inches, which increased her measurement by 38 tons: thus,

	Length of birth-deck.		Breadth Extreme.		Tons.
	ft.	in.	ft.	in.	
By draught	159	2¾	41	11¾	1239
When built	159	3⅜	42	7⅜	1277

It should have been so stated at p. 106, instead of that it was an error in the measurement of the Pomone. This oversight occasioned the Pomone's tonnage, at p. 326, to be stated at "about 1270" instead of "1240."

It may be here remarked, that the two ships of this class and the three *rasés* in the class next above, in mounting but 26 guns on the main deck, similar to the classes from *B* to *H* inclusive, are additional exceptions to those mentioned in note †, vol. i., p. 397. Both W and X may be considered, however, as temporary classes; and besides, they contain too few individuals to disturb the general rule.

Y*. One of these newly-built ships, the Cambrian, was first fitted with 24-pounders, but 18-pounders were found to suit her better. The other ship was the Acasta, armed with thirty 18-pounders on the main deck, by which her quarters were too much crowded.

N*. One of these captured ships was the late British 24-gun ship Hyaena. The French had cut away her quarterdeck and forecastle, and made her a flush ship. As such, the Hyaena, on being restored to the British service, was allowed to remain; and was armed with twenty 32-pounder carronades and two long 9-pounders.

S*. Two of the newly-built ships were the Dasher and Driver (averaging 400 tons), constructed at Bermuda, of the sweet or pencil cedar. They proved very durable vessels.

Y*. The new brig was the Cruiser, the first of the fine set of brigs of which this class is at present wholly composed. One of the two new ships of the class S left unnoticed, was the Osprey, built from the same draught as the Cruiser, but ship-rigged, by way of trying which mode of rigging would best answer.

a*. The reason of moving these ships, by the "Converted" columns, to a new class, in preference to simply transferring them to the "Stationary" compartment of their respective classes, E and P, is to avoid making an exception to the rule that no cruiser ever quits the "Stationary" columns, but to be sold or taken to pieces: whereas the Victory and Sampson, on being subsequently repaired, again went to sea full-armed. The rule, it may be observed, does not extend to the "&c., or non-cruising classes;" otherwise, these very ships could not be restored to their former rank.

* The hired vessels numbered about 78.

NOTE TO ABSTRACT NO. 7.

* The hired vessels numbered about 94.

No. 5.

An ABSTRACT of the ships and vessels belonging to the British navy at the commencement of the year, 1799.

Letters of reference.	RATE.	CLASS.	Cruisers. In commission. No.	Tons.	In ordinary, under or for repair. No.	Tons.	Total. No.	Tons.	No. Brit. built.	For. built.	Stationary Harbour-ships, &c. In commission. No.	Tons.	Not in commission. No.	Tons.	No. Brit. built.	For. built.
	Three-deckers.															
A	First.	120-gun ship,	...	...	...	...	...	...	...	...	...	...	1	2747	...	1
B	„	112 „	1	2351	...	...	1	2351	1	...	...	...	...	...	...	...
D	„	100 „ 18-pounder,	2	4572	...	...	2	4572	2	...	...	...	...	...	...	...
E	„	„ „ 12 „	3	6428	...	...	3	6428	3	...	...	...	...	...	...	...
F	Second.	98 „ 18 „ large,	...	...	...	...	...	...	...	...	...	...	...	...	...	...
G	„	„ „ „ „ small,	...	...	...	...	...	...	...	...	...	...	...	...	...	...
H*	„	„ „ 12 „	13	25197	2	3880	15	29077	15	...	1	1869	...	...	1	...
I	„	90 „	1	1814	...	...	1	1814	1	...	2	3699	...	...	2	...
	Two-deckers.															
K	Third.	80 „	4	8573	...	...	4	8573	1	3	...	...	...	...	...	...
L	„	74 „ 24-pounder,	2	3754	1	1889	3	5643	1	2	...	...	...	...	...	...
M	„	„ „ 18 „ large,	4	7344	1	1887	5	9231	3	2	1	1799	...	...	...	1
N	„	„ „ „ „ middl.	4	6862	...	...	4	6862	4	...	1	1778	...	...	...	1
O	„	„ „ „ „ small,	46	75227	2	3229	48	78456	48	...	3	4803	6	9725	9	...
P*	„	64 „	28	38880	2	2771	30	41651	28	2	6	8251	9	12537	9	6
Q	Fourth.	60 „	...	...	...	...	...	...	...	...	1	1226	3	3718	1	3
		Line,	108	181002	8	13656	116	194658	107	9	15	23425	19	28727	22	12
R	„	56 „ flush,	2	2682	...	...	2	2682	2	...	...	...	...	...	...	...
S	„	54 „ „	2	2431	...	...	2	2431	2	...	...	...	...	...	...	...
T	„	50 „ quarter-decked,	10	10551	2	2157	12	12708	10	2	2	2101	3	3192	4	1
V	Fifth.	44 „	5	4486	...	...	5	4486	5	...	1	882	2	1693	2	1
	One-deckers.															
W	„	44-gun frigate,	3	4129	...	...	3	4129	3	...	...	...	...	...	...	...
X	„	40 „ 24-pounder,	1	1239	...	...	1	1239	...	1	...	...	...	...	...	...
Y	„	„ „ 18 „	...	...	...	...	...	...	...	...	...	...	...	...	...	...
Z	„	38 „ large,	5	5472	2	2122	7	7594	...	7	...	...	...	...	...	...
*A**	„	„ „ small,	17	16790	...	...	17	16790	16	1	...	...	...	...	...	...
B	„	36 „ „ „ large,	1	1032	...	...	1	1032	...	1	...	...	1	1011	...	1
*C**	„	„ „ „ „ small,	15	13647	...	...	15	13647	15	...	...	...	1	882	1	...
D	„	„ „ 12 „	13	11979	2	1856	15	13835	...	15	2	1791	5	4512	...	7
*E**	„	32 „ 18 „ large,	...	...	...	...	...	...	...	...	...	...	...	...	...	...
F	„	„ „ „ „ small,	7	5608	...	...	7	5608	7	...	...	...	...	...	...	...
*G**	„	„ „ 12 „ large,	6	4772	...	...	6	4772	4	2	...	...	...	...	...	...
H	„	„ „ „ „ small,	31	21460	7	4808	38	26268	35	3	...	...	3	2114	2	1
I	Sixth.	28 „	20	11853	3	1801	23	13654	18	5	1	594	3	1826	4	...
K	„	24-gun post-ship,	6	3152	...	...	6	3152	4	2	...	...	2	1147	...	2
N	„	22 „ flush,	1	524	...	...	1	524	...	1	...	...	...	...	...	...
O	„	20 „ quarter-decked,	6	2788	1	432	7	3220	4	3	1	481	...	...	1	...
P	„	„ „ flush,	2	935	1	564	3	1499	...	3	...	...	...	...	...	...
Q	Sloops.	Arrow & Dart, mounting 28 carronades	2	772	...	...	2	772	2	...	...	...	...	...	...	...
R	„	18-gun ship-sloop, quarter-decked,	11	4697	1	453	12	5150	10	2	...	...	2	966	...	2
S	„	„ „ flush,	2	684	...	...	2	684	...	2	...	...	...	...	...	...
*T**	„	16 „ quarter-decked, large,	15	5600	1	367	16	5967	13	3	...	...	3	1037	3	...
U	„	„ „ „ small,	9	2912	...	...	9	2912	9	...	...	...	1	319	1	...
V	„	„ „ flush,	5	1592	...	...	5	1592	2	3	...	...	1	355	...	1
W	„	14 „ quarter-decked,	8	2386	...	...	8	2386	8	...	1	304	2	608	3	...
X	„	„ „ flush,	1	200	...	...	1	200	1	...	...	...	...	...	...	...
Y	„	18-gun brig-sloop, large,	9	3319	...	...	9	3319	8	1	...	...	...	...	...	...
Z	„	„ „ small,	7	2221	...	...	7	2221	7	...	...	...	...	...	...	...
a	„	16 „	8	2235	...	...	8	2235	1	7	...	...	1	275	1	...
b	„	14 „	9	2147	3	612	12	2759	9	3	...	...	1	202	1	...
d	Bombs, of	8 guns and 2 mortars,	2	609	...	...	2	609	2	...	...	...	...	...	...	...
e	Fire-ships,	14 guns,	3	1273	...	...	3	1273	3	...	...	...	1	423	1	...
f	Gun-brigs,	„ „	6	1264	...	...	6	1264	2	4	...	...	1	202	...	1
g	„	12 „	14	2121	3	442	17	2563	16	1	...	...	...	...	...	...
h	„	10 „	3	480	...	...	3	480	...	3	...	...	1	170	...	1
i	Cutters, &c.	14 „	4	772	...	...	4	772	3	1	...	...	1	181	1	...
k	„	12 „	8	1163	...	...	8	1163	7	1	...	...	2	275	2	...
l	„	10 „	4	537	...	...	4	537	...	4	...	...	...	...	...	...
m	„	8 „	2	220	...	...	2	220	...	2	...	...	...	...	...	...
n	„	6 „	4	361	...	...	4	361	...	4	...	...	...	...	...	...
o	„	4 „	4	274	...	...	4	274	1	3	...	...	1	88	1	...
p	First-rate,	50 „	...	...	...	...	...	...	...	...	...	...	...	...	...	...
r	Fourth „	26 „	...	...	...	...	...	...	...	...	5	6035	...	...	5	...
s	Fifth „	24 „	...	...	...	...	...	...	...	...	16	14323	...	...	16	...
t	„ „	18 „	...	...	...	...	...	...	...	...	...	...	1	697	...	1
u	Float. Batt.	58 and 46 guns,	...	...	...	...	...	...	...	...	2	3035	...	...	2	...
v	„	20 guns and under,	...	...	...	...	...	...	...	...	4	1489	...	...	4	...
w	Gun-vessels, from 1 to 4 guns,		...	...	...	...	...	...	...	...	15	1226	7	466	...	22
y	Sloops on Discovery,		...	...	...	...	...	...	...	...	1	406	1	337	2	...
z	Armed Transports,		...	...	...	...	...	...	...	...	8	2432	1	677	6	3
b	Yachts,	royal, or large,	...	...	...	...	...	...	...	...	3	515	3	568	6	...
c	„	small,	...	...	...	...	...	...	...	...	3	264	2	135	5	...
		*Grand Total,......	401	344371	34	29270	435	373641	336	99	80	59303	72	53085	96	56

Increase and Decrease in the classes since the date of the last year's Abstract.

Building, or ordered to be built.		Grand Total.		Launched. King's yards.		Launched. Merchants' yards.		Purchased.		Captured.		Converted from other classes.		Ordered to be built.		Total of Increase.		Loss by capture, &c.		Converted to other classes.		Sold or taken to pieces.		Total of Decrease.	
No.	Tons.	No.	Tons.	No	Tons.	No	Tons.	No	Tons.	No	Tons.	No	Tons.	No	Tons.	No	Tons.	No	Tons.	No	Tons.	No	Tons.	No	Tons.
2	5124	3	7871	...	...	...	...	...	...	...	...	1	2747	...	...	1	2747								
...	...	1	2351																						
...	...	2	4572																						
...	...	3	6428																						
1	2276	1	2276																						
3	6363	3	6363																						
...	...	16	30946																						
...	...	3	5513																						
1	2062	5	10635	...	...	...	...	...	...	...	...	...	...	...	...	...	...	1	2210	...	...	...	...	1	2210
9	17258	12	22901	...	...	...	...	...	...	...	...	...	...	1	1919	1	1919								
4	7538	10	18568	...	...	...	...	...	...	...	...	...	...	...	...	...	...	...	...	...	...	1	1801	1	1801
2	3549	7	12189	...	...	...	...	...	...	...	...	...	...	...	...	...	...	1	1721	...	...	...	...	1	1721
...	...	57	92984	...	...	...	...	...	...	...	...	...	...	...	...	...	...	1	1628	...	...	...	...	1	1628
...	...	45	62439	...	...	...	...	4	5738	3	4037	...	...	...	...	7	9775								
...	...	4	4944																						
22	44170	172	290980	...	...	...	...	4	5738	3	4037	1	2747	1	1919	9	14441	3	5559	...	...	1	1801	4	7360
...	...	2	2682	...	...	...	...	...	...	...	...	...	...	...	...	...	...	...	...	2	2774	...	...	2	2774
...	...	2	2431	...	...	...	...	...	...	...	...	...	...	...	...	...	...	1	1252	2	2341	...	...	3	3593
3	3344	20	21345	...	...	...	...	...	...	2	2150	...	...	...	...	2	2150	1	1051	1	920	...	...	2	1971
...	...	8	7061	...	...	...	...	...	...	...	...	...	...	...	...	...	...	...	...	4	3617	...	...	4	3617
...	...	3	4129																						
1	1277	2	2516																						
3	3474	3	3474	...	...	...	...	...	...	...	...	...	...	1	1172	1	1172								
3	3181	10	10775	...	...	...	...	...	...	3	3190	...	...	...	...	3	3190	1	1064	...	...	...	...	1	1064
4	4074	21	20864	2	2001	...	...	...	...	...	...	...	...	...	...	2	2001								
1	1049	3	3092	...	...	...	...	...	...	1	1011	...	...	...	...	1	1011								
...	...	16	14529	2	1852	...	...	...	...	...	...	...	...	...	...	2	1852	1	881	...	...	...	...	1	881
...	...	22	20138	...	...	...	...	...	...	5	4624	1	932	...	...	6	5556	1	951	...	...	...	...	1	951
1	914	1	914	...	...	...	...	...	...	...	...	...	...	1	914	1	914								
...	...	7	5608																						
...	...	6	4772	3	2463	...	...	...	...	1	748	...	...	...	...	4	3211								
...	...	41	28382	...	...	...	...	...	...	3	2063	...	...	...	...	3	2063	2	1376	...	...	...	...	2	1376
...	...	27	16074	...	...	...	...	...	...	3	1751	...	...	...	...	3	1751	1	594	...	...	2	1200	3	1794
...	...	8	4299	...	...	...	...	...	...	2	1028	...	...	...	...	2	1028								
...	...	1	524																						
...	...	8	3701	...	...	...	...	...	...	...	...	...	...	...	...	...	...	1	430	...	...	...	...	1	430
...	...	3	1499	...	...	...	...	...	...	2	1075	...	...	...	...	2	1075								
...	...	2	772	...	...	2	772	...	...	...	...	...	...	...	...	2	772								
1	422	15	6538	1	427	4	1695	...	...	1	453	...	...	...	...	6	2575	1	427	...	...	1	480	2	907
4	1528	6	2212	...	...	...	...	...	...	2	684	...	...	2	727	4	1411								
1	365	20	7369	...	...	2	781	1	367	1	365	...	...	...	...	4	1513								
...	...	10	3231																						
...	...	6	1947	...	...	...	...	2	692	1	300	...	...	...	...	3	992	1	315	...	...	...	...	1	315
...	...	11	3298																						
...	...	1	200																						
1	384	10	3703	...	...	...	...	...	...	...	...	...	...	1	384	1	384								
1	337	8	2558	...	...	2	631	...	...	...	...	...	...	1	337	3	968	1	316	...	...	...	...	1	316
...	...	9	2510	...	...	...	...	...	...	1	234	...	...	...	...	1	234	3	896	...	...	1	250	4	1146
...	...	13	2961	...	...	...	...	...	...	2	500	...	...	...	...	2	500	2	390	...	...	...	...	2	390
...	...	2	609																						
...	...	4	1696																						
...	...	7	1466	...	...	...	...	...	...	4	853	...	...	...	...	4	853								
...	...	17	2563	...	...	...	...	...	...	1	195	...	...	...	...	1	195								
...	...	4	650	...	...	...	...	...	...	2	350	...	...	...	...	2	350								
...	...	5	953																						
...	...	10	1438	...	...	2	297	1	123	...	...	...	...	...	...	3	420								
...	...	4	537	...	...	...	...	...	...	3	350	...	...	...	...	3	350	1	111	...	...	...	...	1	111
...	...	2	220	...	...	...	...	...	...	2	220	...	...	...	...	2	220	2	241	...	...	...	...	2	241
...	...	4	361	...	...	...	...	...	...	3	290	...	...	...	...	3	290								
...	...	5	362	...	...	...	...	...	...	3	227	...	...	...	...	3	227								
...	...	...	...	...	...	...	...	...	...	...	...	...	...	...	...	...	...	...	...	1	2747	...	...	1	2747
...	...	5	6035	...	...	...	...	...	...	...	...	5	6035	...	...	5	6035								
...	...	16	14323	...	...	...	...	...	...	...	...	4	3617	...	...	4	3617								
...	...	1	697	...	...	...	...	...	...	...	...	...	...	...	...	...	...	...	...	1	932	...	...	1	932
...	...	2	3035																						
...	...	4	1489																						
...	...	22	1692																						
...	...	2	743																						
...	...	9	3109	...	...	...	...	1	125	...	...	...	...	...	...	1	125								
...	...	6	1083																						
...	...	5	399	1	102	...	...	...	...	...	...	...	...	...	...	1	102								
46	64519	633	550548	9	6845	12	4176	9	7045	51	26698	11	13331	7	5453	99	63548	23	15854	11	13331	5	3731	39	32916

No.

An ABSTRACT of the ships and vessels belonging to the British Navy at the commencement of the year 1798.

Letters of reference.	RATE.	CLASS.	Cruisers. In commission. No.	Cruisers. In commission. Tons.	Cruisers. In ordinary, under or for repair. No	Cruisers. In ordinary, under or for repair. Tons.	Cruisers. Total. No.	Cruisers. Total. Tons.	Cruisers. No. Brit. built.	Cruisers. No. For. built.	Stationary Harbour-ships, &c. In commission. No	Stationary Harbour-ships, &c. In commission. Tons.	Stationary Harbour-ships, &c. Not in commission No	Stationary Harbour-ships, &c. Not in commission Tons.	Stationary Harbour-ships, &c. No. Brit. blt.	Stationary Harbour-ships, &c. No. For. blt.
	Three-deckers.															
A	First.	120-gun ship	...	...	...	...	...	...	...	...	...	...	1	2747	...	1
B	„	112 „ 18-pounder,	1	2351	...	...	1	2351	1	...	...	...	...	...	...	...
C	„	„ „ 12 „	...	...	1	2457	1	2457	...	1	...	...	1	2398	...	1
D	„	100 „ 18 „	2	4572	...	...	2	4572	2	...	...	...	...	...	...	...
E	„	„ „ 12 „	1	2175	1	2091	2	4266	2	...	...	...	...	...	...	...
F	Second.	98 „ 18 „ large,	...	...	...	...	...	...	...	...	...	...	...	...	...	...
G	„	„ „ „ „ small,	1	2119	...	...	1	2119	1	...	...	...	...	...	...	...
H	„	„ „ 12 „	13	25316	2	3761	15	29077	15	...	1	1869	...	...	1	...
I	„	90 „	1	1814	...	...	1	1814	1	...	2	3699	...	...	2	...
	Two-deckers.															
K	Third.	80 „	3	6430	1	2143	4	8573	1	3	...	...	1	1942	...	1
L	„	74 „ 24-pounder,	3	5596	1	1889	4	7485	2	2	...	...	...	...	...	...
M	„	„ „ 18 „ large,	4	7344	1	1887	5	9231	3	2	1	1799	2	3648	...	3
N	„	„ „ „ „ middl.	4	6862	...	...	4	6862	4	...	1	1778	...	...	...	1
O	„	„ „ „ „ small,	45	73662	2	3229	47	76891	47	...	5	7974	6	9623	11	...
P*	„	64 „	26	36126	7	9392	33	45518	27	6	10	13887	7	9608	10	7
Q	Fourth.	60 „	..	...	...	...	...	...	...	...	1	1226	3	3718	1	3
		Line,	104	174367	16	26849	120	201216	106	14	21	32232	21	33684	25	17
R	„	56 „ flush,	2	2682	...	...	2	2682	2	...	...	...	...	...	...	...
S	„	54 „ „	1	1182	...	...	1	1182	1	...	...	...	...	...	...	...
T	„	50 „ quarter-decked,	11	11661	2	2088	13	13749	10	3	2	2101	3	3192	4	1
V	Fifth.	44 „	5	4486	...	...	5	4486	5	...	1	882	2	1693	1	2
	One-deckers.															
W	„	44-gun frigate,	3	4129	...	...	3	4129	3	...	...	...	...	...	...	...
X*	„	40 „ 24-pounder,	2	2516	...	...	2	2516	1	1	...	...	...	...	...	...
Y*	„	„ „ 18 „	2	2302	...	...	2	2302	2	...	...	...	...	...	...	...
Z	„	38 „ large,	7	7583	3	3345	10	10928	1	9	...	...	...	...	...	...
A	„	„ „ small,	18	17889	1	941	19	18830	17	2	...	...	...	...	...	...
B	„	36 „ „ „ large,	3	3092	...	...	3	3092	2	1	...	...	...	...	...	...
C	„	„ „ „ „ small,	13	11823	1	890	14	12713	14	...	...	...	1	882	1	...
D	„	„ „ 12 „	14	12823	2	1878	16	14701	...	16	2	1791	5	4512	...	7
E	„	32 „ 18 „ large,	...	...	...	...	...	...	...	...	...	...	...	...	...	...
F	„	„ „ „ „ small,	7	5608	...	...	7	5608	7	...	...	...	...	...	...	...
G	„	„ „ 12 large,	6	4772	...	...	6	4772	4	2	...	...	...	...	...	...
H	„	„ „ „ small,	26	17950	10	6919	36	24869	34	2	...	...	1	704	1	...
I	Sixth.	28 „	17	10076	5	2991	22	13067	17	5	2	1220	2	1200	4	...
K	„	24-gun post-ship,	6	3152	...	...	6	3152	4	2	1	528	1	619	...	2
*N**	„	22 „ flush,	2	1046	1	532	3	1578	1	2	...	...	...	...	...	...
O	„	20 „ quarter-decked,	6	2745	1	432	7	3177	5	2	1	481	1	472	1	1
P	„	„ „ flush,	3	1589	...	...	3	1589	...	3	...	...	...	...	...	...
Q	Sloops.	Arrow and Dart, mounting 28 carronades,	2	772	...	...	2	772	2	...	...	...	...	...	...	...
R	„	18-gun ship-sloop, quarter-decked,	11	4706	...	...	11	4706	10	1	...	...	2	930	...	2
*S**	„	„ „ flush,	5	1900	...	...	5	1900	4	1	...	...	1	312	...	1
T	„	16 „ quarter-decked, large,	15	5627	...	...	15	5627	12	3	...	...	3	1034	2	1
U	„	„ „ „ small,	5	1621	3	960	8	2581	8	...	...	...	1	319	1	...
V	„	„ „ flush,	3	956	...	...	3	956	1	2	...	...	2	655	...	2
W	„	14 „ quarter-decked,	7	2086	...	...	7	2086	7	...	1	304	2	601	3	...
X	„	„ „ flush,	2	461	...	...	2	461	1	1	...	...	...	...	...	...
*Y**	„	18-gun brig-sloop, large,	9	3319	1	384	10	3703	9	1	...	...	...	...	...	...
Z	„	„ „ small,	10	3255	...	...	10	3255	8	2	...	...	...	...	...	...
a	„	16 „	6	1624	1	310	7	1934	...	7	...	...	1	275	1	...
b	„	14 „	11	2590	3	612	14	3202	9	5	...	...	1	202	1	...
d	Bombs, of	8 guns and 2 mortars,	11	3525	...	...	11	3525	10	1	...	...	...	...	...	...
e	Fire-ships,	14 guns,	3	1273	...	...	3	1273	3	...	...	...	1	423	1	...
f	Gun-brigs,	„ „	5	1033	...	...	5	1033	2	3	...	...	1	202	...	1
g	„	12 „	57	9030	1	147	58	9177	57	1	...	...	...	...	...	...
h	„	10 „	3	480	...	...	3	480	...	3	...	...	1	170	...	1
i	Cutters, &c.	14 „	5	960	...	...	5	960	3	2	...	...	1	181	1	...
k	„	12 „	9	1311	...	...	9	1311	7	2	...	...	2	275	2	...
l	„	10 „	3	350	...	...	3	350	...	3	...	...	...	...	...	...
m	„	8 „	2	220	...	...	2	220	...	2	...	...	...	...	...	...
n	„	6 „	4	361	...	...	4	361	...	4	...	...	...	...	...	...
o	„	4 „	5	360	...	...	5	360	2	3	...	...	1	88	1	...
r	Fourth-rates,	26 „	...	...	...	...	...	...	...	...	5	6035	1	1249	6	...
s	Fifth „	24 „	...	...	...	...	...	...	...	...	14	12524	2	1799	16	...
t	„ „	18 „	...	...	...	...	...	...	...	...	1	697	...	...	...	1
u	Float. Batt.	58 and 46 guns,	...	...	...	...	...	...	...	...	1	1373	...	...	1	...
v	„	20 guns and under,	...	...	...	...	...	...	...	...	4	1489	...	...	4	...
w	Gun-vessels,	from 1 to 4 guns,	...	...	...	...	...	...	...	...	12	950	8	527	...	20
y	Sloops on Discovery,		...	...	...	...	...	...	...	...	...	...	...	...	...	...
z	Armed Transports,		...	...	...	...	...	...	...	...	9	3109	...	...	6	3
*a**	Temporary Prison-ships,		...	...	...	...	...	...	...	...	2	3542	...	...	2	...
b	Yachts,	royal, or large,	...	...	...	...	...	...	...	...	3	513	3	570	6	...
c	„	small,	...	...	...	...	...	...	...	...	3	264	2	135	5	...
		*Grand Total,	451	351293	51	49278	502	400571	391	111	85	70035	73	56905	96	62

6.

Increase and Decrease in the classes since the date of the last year's Abstract.

Building, or ordered to be built.		Grand Total.		Launched. King's yards.		Launched. Merchant's yards.		Purchased.		Captured.		Converted from other classes.		Ordered to be built.		Total of Increase.		Loss by capture, &c.		Converted to other classes		Sold or taken to pieces.		Total of Decrease.	
No	Tons.	No.	Tons.	No	Tons.	No	Tons.	No	Tons.	No	Tons.	No	Tons.	No	Tons.	No.	Tons.	No	Tons.	No	Tons.	No	Tons.	No	Tons.
2	5124	3	7871																						
...	...	1	2351																						
...	...	2	4855																						
...	...	2	4572	...	...	...	...	...	...	2	4855	...	...	...	...	2	4855								
...	...	2	4266																						
1	2276	1	2276	...	...	...	...	...	...	...	...	...	...	...	...	...	...	...	...	1	2162	...	...	1	2162
2	4244	3	6363	1	2119	...	...	...	...	...	...	...	...	...	...	1	2119								
...	...	16	30946																						
...	...	8	5513																						
1	2062	6	12577	...	...	...	...	...	...	1	1942	...	...	...	...	1	1942								
8	15416	12	22901	1	1842	...	...	...	...	...	...	...	...	...	...	1	1842								
4	7538	12	22216	...	...	...	...	...	...	2	3648	...	...	...	...	2	3648								
2	3549	7	12189																						
...	...	58	94488	...	...	...	...	...	...	2	3121	...	...	...	...	2	3121	...	...	...	...	1	1617	1	1617
...	...	50	69013	...	...	...	...	1	1430	5	6524	...	...	...	...	6	7954	...	...	1	1380	...	...	1	1380
...	...	4	4944																						
20	40209	182	307341	2	3961	...	...	1	1430	12	20090	...	...	...	...	15	25481	...	...	2	3542	1	1617	3	5159
...	...	2	2682																						
...	...	1	1182	...	...	...	...	...	...	...	...	...	...	...	...	...	...	...	...	1	1249	...	...	1	1249
3	3344	21	22386	...	...	...	...	...	...	1	1041	...	...	...	...	1	1041								
...	...	8	7061																						
...	...	3	4129																						
...	...	2	2516	...	...	1	1277	...	...	...	...	...	...	...	...	1	1277								
1	1172	3	3474	...	...	2	2302	...	...	...	...	...	...	...	...	2	2302								
2	2129	12	13057	...	...	1	1052	...	...	2	2282	...	...	...	...	3	3334								
2	2081	21	20911	...	...	3	3036	...	...	...	...	...	...	1	1043	4	4079	1	996	...	...	...	...	1	996
2	2097	5	5189	...	...	1	1049	...	...	...	...	...	...	2	2097	3	3146								
...	...	15	13595	...	...	...	...	...	...	...	...	...	...	...	...	...	...	1	934	...	...	...	...	1	934
...	...	23	21004	...	...	...	...	...	...	2	1782	...	...	...	...	2	1782	1	916	...	...	...	...	1	916
1	914	1	914																						
...	...	7	5608																						
...	...	6	4772																						
...	...	37	25573	...	...	...	...	...	...	...	...	...	...	...	...	...	...	1	715	...	...	3	2094	4	2809
...	...	26	15487	...	...	...	...	...	...	...	...	...	...	...	...	...	...	1	587	...	...	...	...	1	587
...	...	8	4299																						
...	...	3	1578	...	...	...	...	...	...	2	1054	...	...	...	...	2	1054								
...	...	9	4130	...	...	...	...	...	...	1	429	...	...	...	...	1	429								
...	...	3	1589	...	...	...	...	...	...	1	514	...	...	...	...	1	514	...	...	...	...	1	424	1	424
...	...	2	772																						
1	422	14	6058	...	...	...	...	...	...	...	...	...	...	...	...	...	...	...	...	...	...	1	480	1	480
3	1214	9	3426	...	...	4	1528	...	...	...	...	...	...	3	1214	7	2742								
1	365	19	7026	...	...	...	...	...	...	...	...	...	...	...	...	...	...	...	...	...	...	1	343	1	343
...	...	9	2900	...	...	...	...	...	...	...	...	...	...	...	...	...	...	1	331	...	...	...	...	1	331
...	...	5	1611	...	...	...	...	...	...	...	...	...	...	...	...	...	...	1	336	...	...	...	...	1	336
...	...	10	2991	...	...	...	...	...	...	...	...	...	...	...	...	...	...	...	...	...	...	1	307	1	307
...	...	2	461	...	...	...	...	...	...	1	261	...	...	...	...	1	261								
...	...	10	3703	...	...	1	384	...	...	...	...	...	...	...	...	1	384								
...	...	10	3255	...	...	1	337	...	...	2	697	...	...	...	...	3	1034								
...	...	8	2209	...	...	...	...	...	...	2	551	...	...	...	...	2	551	2	562	...	...	1	290	3	852
...	...	15	3404	...	...	...	...	...	...	3	653	...	...	...	...	3	653	1	210	...	...	...	...	1	210
...	...	11	3525	...	...	...	...	8	2579	...	...	1	337	...	...	9	2916								
...	...	4	1696																						
...	...	6	1235	...	...	...	...	...	...	...	...	1	200	...	...	1	200	2	431	...	...	...	...	2	431
...	...	58	9177	...	...	31	5107	11	1690	1	181	...	...	...	...	43	6978	2	364	...	...	...	...	2	364
...	...	4	650																						
...	...	6	1141	...	...	...	...	1	193	1	195	...	...	...	...	2	388	...	...	1	200	...	...	1	200
...	...	11	1586	...	...	1	148	...	...	...	...	...	...	...	...	1	148								
...	...	3	350	...	...	...	...	...	...	1	104	...	...	...	...	1	104	2	291	...	...	...	...	2	291
...	...	2	220																						
...	...	4	361																						
...	...	6	448	...	...	...	...	1	86	...	...	...	...	...	...	1	86								
...	...	6	7284	...	...	...	...	...	...	...	...	1	1249	...	...	1	1249								
...	...	16	14323																						
...	...	1	697																						
...	...	1	1373	...	...	...	...	...	...	...	...	...	...	...	...	...	...	1	1662	...	...	...	...	1	1662
...	...	4	1489																						
...	...	20	1477	...	...	...	...	...	...	...	...	...	...	...	...	...	...	...	...	...	...	2	215	2	215
...	...	...	...	...	...	...	...	...	...	...	...	...	...	...	...	...	...	1	406	1	337	...	...	2	743
...	...	9	3109																						
...	...	2	3542	...	...	...	...	...	...	...	...	2	3542	...	...	2	3542								
...	...	6	1083																						
...		5	399																						
36	53947	696	581458	2	3961	46	16220	22	5978	32	29834	5	5328	6	4354	113	65675	18	8741	5	5328	11	5770	34	19839

No. 7.

An ABSTRACT of the ships and vessels belonging to the British navy at the commencement of the year, 1799.

Letters of reference.	RATE.	CLASS.	Cruisers.								Stationary Harbour-ships, &c.					
			In commission.		In ordinary, under or for repair.		Total.		No.		In commission.		Not in commission.		No.	
			No.	Tons.	No.	Tons.	No.	Tons.	Brit. built.	For. built.	No.	Tons.	No	Tons.	Brit. built.	For. built.
	Three-deckers.															
A	First.	120-gun ship	...	...	...	...	...	...	...	...	1	2747	...	...	...	1
B	„	112 „ 18-pounder,	1	2351	...	...	1	2351	1	...	...	...	...	...	...	...
C	„	„ „ 12 „	...	...	1	2457	1	2457	...	1	1	2398	...	...	...	1
D	„	100 „ 18 „	2	4572	...	...	2	4572	2	...	...	...	...	...	...	...
E	„	„ „ 12 „	1	2175	1	2091	2	4266	2	...	...	...	...	...	...	...
F	Second.	98 „ 18 „ large,	...	...	...	...	...	...	...	...	...	...	...	...	...	...
G	„	„ „ „ „ small,	2	4240	...	...	2	4240	2	...	...	...	...	...	...	...
H	„	„ „ 12 „	12	23433	2	3701	14	27134	14	...	1	1869	1	1943	2	...
I	„	90 „	1	1814	...	...	1	1814	1	...	2	3699	...	...	2	...
	Two-deckers.															
K	Third.	80 „	6	13030	1	2143	7	15173	2	5	1	1942	...	...	...	1
L	„	74 „ 24-pounder,	7	13370	1	1889	8	15259	6	2	...	...	...	...	...	...
M	„	„ „ 18 „ large,	10	18670	2	3777	12	22447	6	6	3	5447	...	...	...	3
N	„	„ „ „ „ middl.	3	5145	...	...	3	5145	3	...	1	1778	...	...	...	1
O	„	„ „ „ „ small,	38	62259	8	12989	46	75248	46	...	10	16106	4	6500	12	2
P	„	64 „	22	30610	4	5421	26	36031	23	3	12	16597	4	5496	9	7
Q	Fourth.	60 „	..	...	...	...	...	...	...	...	1	1226	3	3718	3	1
		Line,	105	181669	20	34468	125	216137	108	17	33	53809	12	17657	28	17
R	„	56 „ flush,	2	2682	...	...	2	2682	2	...	...	...	...	...	...	...
S	„	54 „ „	2	2431	...	...	2	2431	2	...	...	...	...	...	...	...
T	„	50 „ quarter-decked,	10	10692	...	...	10	10692	9	1	3	3145	2	2148	4	1
V	Fifth.	44 „	3	2687	1	904	4	3591	4	...	1	882	2	1693	2	1
	One-deckers.															
W	„	44-gun frigate,	3	4129	...	...	3	4129	3	...	...	...	...	...	...	...
X	„	40 „ 24-pounder,	2	2516	...	...	2	2516	1	1	...	...	...	...	...	...
Y	„	„ „ 18 „	2	2302	...	...	2	2302	2	...	...	...	...	...	...	...
Z	„	38 „ large,	9	9946	1	1100	10	11046	1	9	...	...	1	1065	...	1
A	„	„ „ small,	15	14935	1	954	16	15889	14	2	...	...	...	...	...	...
B	„	36 „ „ „ large,	3	3132	1	1010	4	4142	2	2	...	...	1	1011	...	1
C	„	„ „ „ „ small,	11	10056	1	888	12	10944	12	...	...	...	1	882	...	1
D	„	„ „ 12 „	12	11085	6	5595	18	16680	...	18	2	1791	6	5303	...	8
E	„	32 „ 18 „ large,	1	914	...	...	1	914	...	1	...	...	...	...	...	...
F	„	„ „ „ „ small,	5	4010	...	...	5	4010	5	...	...	...	...	...	...	...
G	„	„ „ 12 large,	6	4820	1	779	7	5599	4	3	...	...	...	...	...	...
H	„	„ „ „ small,	27	18626	6	4163	33	22789	32	1	...	...	1	704	1	...
I	Sixth.	28 „	15	8891	6	3577	21	12468	16	5	2	1220	2	1200	4	...
K	„	24-gun post-ship,	5	2646	...	...	5	2646	4	1	1	528	2	1125	...	3
N	„	22 „ flush,	3	1569	1	532	4	2101	1	3	...	...	...	...	...	...
O	„	20 „ quarter-decked,	7	3253	1	504	8	3757	4	4	1	481	1	472	1	1
P	„	„ „ flush,	4	2094	...	...	4	2094	...	4	...	...	...	...	...	...
Q	Sloops.	Arrow and Dart, mounting 28 carronades,	2	772	...	...	2	772	2	...	...	...	...	...	...	...
R	„	18-gun ship-sloop, quarter-decked,	11	4706	...	...	11	4706	10	1	...	...	2	930	...	2
S	„	„ „ flush,	17	6196	...	...	17	6196	12	5	...	...	1	312	...	1
T	„	16 „ quarter-decked, large,	16	5992	...	...	16	5992	13	3	...	...	3	1034	3	...
U	„	„ „ „ small,	5	1621	...	...	5	1621	5	...	...	...	1	319	1	...
V	„	„ „ flush,	2	554	...	...	2	554	...	2	...	...	2	655	...	2
W	„	14 „ quarter-decked,	6	1780	...	...	6	1780	6	...	1	304	3	907	4	...
X	„	„ „ flush,	2	461	...	...	2	461	1	1	...	...	...	...	...	...
Y	„	18-gun brig-sloop, large,	8	2965	...	...	8	2965	7	1	...	...	...	...	...	...
Z	„	„ „ small,	10	3255	...	...	10	3255	8	2	...	...	...	...	...	...
a	„	16 „	6	1679	...	...	6	1679	...	6	...	...	1	275	1	...
b	„	14 „	13	3121	...	...	13	3121	5	8	...	...	1	202	1	...
d	Bombs, of	8 guns and 2 mortars,	14	4610	1	307	15	4917	14	1	...	...	...	...	...	...
e	Fire-ships,	14 guns,	7	2094	...	...	7	2094	6	1	1	423	...	...	1	...
f	Gun-brigs,	„ „	8	1613	1	258	9	1871	3	6	...	...	1	202	...	1
g	„	12 „	57	9017	...	...	57	9017	56	1	...	...	...	...	...	...
h	„	10 „	5	797	...	...	5	797	...	5	...	...	1	170	...	1
i	Cutters, &c.	14 „	3	572	...	...	3	572	...	3	...	...	1	181	1	...
k	„	12 „	9	1311	...	...	9	1311	7	2	...	...	2	275	2	...
l	„	10 „	4	460	...	...	4	460	...	4	...	...	...	...	...	...
m	„	8 „	3	315	...	...	3	315	...	3	...	...	...	...	...	...
n	„	6 „	3	256	...	...	3	256	...	3	...	...	...	...	...	...
o	„	4 „	6	400	...	...	6	400	2	4	...	...	1	88	1	...
q	Third-rate,	36 „	...	...	...	...	...	...	...	...	7	9487	...	...	4	3
r	Fourth „	26 „	...	...	...	...	...	...	...	...	7	8243	...	...	5	2
s	Fifth „	24 „	...	...	...	...	...	...	...	...	19	17210	1	886	19	1
t	„ „	18 „	...	...	...	...	...	...	...	...	3	2093	...	...	2	1
u	Float. Batt.	46 „	...	...	...	...	...	...	...	...	1	1373	...	...	1	...
v	„	20 „ and under,	...	...	...	...	...	...	...	...	4	1489	...	...	4	...
v	Gun-vessels, from 1 to 4 guns,		...	...	...	...	...	...	...	...	11	896	6	402	...	17
:	Armed Transports,		...	...	...	...	...	...	...	...	9	2514	...	...	7	2
a	Temporary Prison-ships,		...	...	...	...	...	...	...	...	2	3542	...	...	2	...
b	Yachts,	royal, or large,	...	...	...	...	...	...	...	...	3	513	3	570	6	...
c	„	small,	...	...	...	...	...	...	...	...	4	357	1	42	5	...
		*Grand Total,	469	359632	48	55039	517	414671	383	134	115	110300	62	40710	110	67

Increase and Decrease in the classes since the date of the last year's Abstract.

Building, or ordered to be built.		Grand Total.		Launched. King's yards.		Launched. Merchants' yards.		Purchased.		Captured.		Converted from other classes.		Ordered to be built.		Total of Increase.		Loss by capture, &c.		Converted to other classes.		Sold or taken to pieces.		Total of Decrease.	
No.	Tons.	No.	Tons.	No	Tons.	No	Tons.	No	Tons.	No	Tons.	No	Tons.	No	Tons.	No	Tons.	No	Tons.	No	Tons.	No	Tons.	No	Tons.
2	5124	3	7871																						
...	...	1	2351																						
...	...	2	4855																						
...	...	2	4572																						
...	...	2	4266																						
2	4554	2	4554	...	...	...	...	...	...	...	...	...	...	1	2278	1	2278								
1	2123	3	6363	1	2121	...	...	...	...	...	...	...	...	...	...	1	2121								
...	...	16	30946																						
...	...	3	5513																						
...	...	8	17115	1	2062	...	...	...	...	2	4538	...	...	...	...	3	6600								
6	11413	14	26672	...	...	4	7774	...	...	...	...	...	...	2	3771	6	11545								
1	1917	16	29811	...	...	3	5621	...	...	4	7595	...	...	...	...	7	13216								
2	3549	6	10472	...	...	...	...	...	...	...	...	...	...	...	...	...	...	1	1717	...	...	...	...	1	1717
...	...	60	97854	...	...	...	...	...	...	2	3366	...	...	...	...	2	3366								
...	...	42	58124	...	...	...	...	...	...	...	...	...	...	...	...	...	...	...	...	7	9487	1	1402	8	10889
...	...	4	4944																						
14	28680	184	316283	2	4183	7	13395	...	...	8	15499	...	...	3	6049	20	39126	1	1717	7	9487	1	1402	9	12606
...	...	2	2682																						
...	...	2	2431	...	...	...	...	...	...	...	...	1	1249	...	...	1	1249								
2	2221	17	18206	1	1123	...	...	...	...	...	...	...	...	...	...	1	1123	1	1052	3	3128	...	...	4	4180
...	...	7	6166	...	...	...	...	...	...	...	...	...	...	...	...	...	...	1	895	...	...	...	...	1	895
...	...	3	4129																						
...	...	2	2516																						
1	1172	3	3474																						
2	2129	13	14240	...	...	...	...	...	...	2	2246	...	...	...	...	2	2246	...	...	1	1063	...	...	1	1063
2	2081	18	17970	...	...	...	...	...	...	...	...	...	...	...	...	...	...	2	2000	1	941	...	...	3	2941
2	2099	7	7252	...	...	1	1051	...	...	1	1010	...	...	1	1053	3	3114								
2	1927	15	13753	...	...	...	...	...	...	...	...	...	...	2	1927	2	1927	...	...	2	1769	...	...	2	1769
...	...	26	23774	...	...	...	...	...	...	6	5500	...	...	...	...	6	5500	2	1756	...	...	1	974	3	2730
1	894	2	1808	...	...	1	914	...	...	...	...	...	...	1	894	2	1808								
...	...	5	4010	...	...	...	...	...	...	...	...	...	...	...	...	...	...	2	1598	...	...	...	...	2	1598
...	...	7	5599	...	...	...	...	...	...	1	827	...	...	...	...	1	827								
...	...	34	23493	...	...	...	...	...	...	...	...	...	...	...	...	...	...	1	684	2	1396	...	...	3	2080
...	...	25	14888	...	...	...	...	...	...	...	...	...	...	...	...	...	...	1	599	...	...	...	...	1	599
...	...	8	4299																						
...	...	4	2101	...	...	...	...	...	...	1	523	...	...	...	...	1	523								
...	...	10	4710	...	...	...	...	...	...	2	1012	...	...	...	...	2	1012	...	...	1	432	...	...	1	432
...	...	4	2094	...	...	...	...	...	...	1	505	...	...	...	...	1	505								
...	...	2	772																						
1	422	14	6058																						
1	443	19	6951	...	...	2	771	6	2104	4	1421	...	...	...	...	12	4296								
...	...	19	7026	...	...	1	365	...	...	1	365	...	...	...	...	2	730	1	365	...	...	...	...	1	365
...	...	6	1940	...	...	...	...	...	...	...	...	...	...	...	...	...	...	...	...	3	960	...	...	3	960
...	...	4	1209	...	...	...	...	...	...	1	279	...	...	...	...	1	279	1	356	...	...	1	325	2	681
...	...	10	2991																						
...	...	2	461																						
...	...	8	2965	...	...	...	...	...	...	...	...	...	...	...	...	...	...	2	738	...	...	...	...	2	738
...	...	10	3255																						
...	...	7	1954	...	...	...	...	...	...	...	...	...	...	...	...	...	...	1	255	...	...	...	...	1	255
...	...	14	3323	...	...	...	...	...	...	3	740	...	...	...	...	3	740	...	...	4	821	...	...	4	821
...	...	15	4917	...	...	...	...	...	...	...	...	4	1392	...	...	4	1392								
...	...	8	2517	...	...	...	...	...	...	...	...	4	821	...	...	4	821								
...	...	10	2073	...	...	...	...	...	...	2	450	2	388	...	...	4	838								
...	...	57	9017	...	...	...	...	...	...	...	...	...	...	...	...	...	...	1	160	...	...	...	...	1	160
...	...	6	967	...	...	...	...	...	...	2	317	...	...	...	...	2	317								
...	...	4	753	...	...	...	...	...	...	...	...	...	...	...	...	...	...	...	...	2	388	...	...	2	388
...	...	11	1586																						
...	...	4	460	...	...	...	...	...	...	1	110	...	...	...	...	1	110								
...	...	3	315	...	...	...	...	...	...	1	95	...	...	...	...	1	95								
...	...	3	256	...	...	...	...	...	...	...	...	...	...	...	...	...	...	1	105	...	...	...	...	1	105
...	...	7	488	...	...	...	...	...	...	1	40	...	...	...	...	1	40								
...	...	7	9487	...	...	...	...	...	...	...	...	7	9487	...	...	7	9487								
...	...	7	8243	...	...	...	...	...	...	...	...	3	3128	...	...	3	3128	1	920	1	1249	...	...	2	2169
...	...	20	18096	...	...	...	...	...	...	...	...	4	3773	...	...	4	3773								
...	...	3	2093	...	...	...	...	...	...	...	...	2	1396	...	...	2	1396								
...	...	1	1373																						
...	...	4	1489																						
...	...	17	1298	...	...	...	...	...	...	...	...	...	...	...	...	...	...	...	...	...	...	3	179	3	179
...	...	9	2514	1	324	...	...	...	...	...	...	...	...	...	...	1	324	1	919	...	...	...	...	1	919
...	...	2	3542																						
...	...	6	1083																						
...	...	5	399																						
28	42068	722	607749	4	5630	12	16496	6	2104	38	30939	27	21634	7	9923	94	86726	20	14119	27	21634	6	2880	53	38633

List of Abbreviations

A	Admiral
act	acting
actn	action
Ad	Adjutant
AdG	Adjutant-General
Algrn	Algerine
Amb	Ambassador
App	Appendix
As	Assistant
B	Boatswain
bldg	building
blt	built
Br	British
Brg	Brigadier, Brigade
bts	boats
C	Captain
captd	captured
capts	captures
Car	Carpenter
Ck	Clerk
cl	class
Cmde	Commodore
Com	Commanding
Cox	Coxswain
Cr	Commander
Crsg	Cruising
d	died
Da	Danish
DAG	Deputy-Adjutant-General
des	destroys
destd	destroyed
drnd	drowned
Du	Dutch
E.I.C.	East India Company
E I ser	East India service
exped	expedition
F	French
Flt	Fleet
fndrd	foundered
fndrs	founders
FS	fire ship
G	General
gbts	gunboats
Gvr	Governor
hs	hospital ship
invas	invasion
Ital	Italian
k	killed
kntd	knighted
LCom	Lieutenant-Commander
MC	Captain Marines
ML	Lieutenant Marines
Mar	Marshal
Medn	Mediterranean
Mid	Midshipman
Mr	Master
Mt	Mate
Neap	Neapolitan
PC	Post-Captain
Por	Portuguese
Pr	Purser
priv	privateer
pro	promoted
RA	Rear-Admiral
Rds	Roads
recaptd	recaptured
recapts	recaptures
rprg	repairing
Rus	Russian
S	Surgeon
Sard	Sardinian
Sig	Signalman
Sp	Spanish
Sq	Squadron
SS	store ship
Swd	Swedish
TS	transport or troop-ship
Turk	Turkish
US	United States
VA	Vice-Admiral
Ven	Venetian
Vol	Volunteer
w	wounded
wrkd	wrecked

Foreign officers in *italics*
The name of a captured ship is not repeated, but a fresh line is used to indicate her career under a new flag